Thank You
Music Lovers

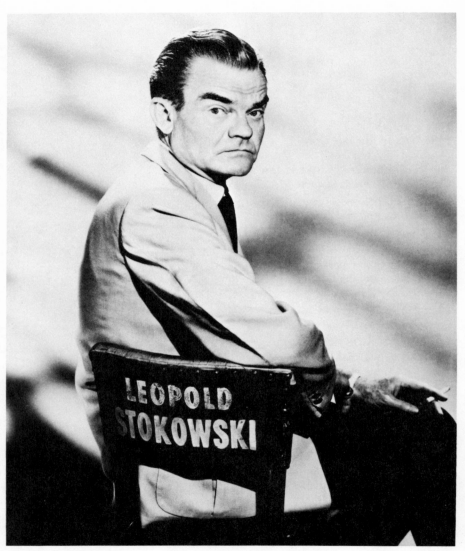

Spike Jones

Thank You
Music Lovers

A Bio-discography of Spike Jones
and His City Slickers, 1941 to 1965

compiled by JACK MIRTLE
with the assistance of TED HERING
Foreword by PETER SCHICKELE

DISCOGRAPHIES, NUMBER 20

Greenwood Press
New York • Westport, Connecticut • London

Library of Congress Cataloging-in-Publication Data

Mirtle, Jack, 1936-
  Thank you music lovers.

  (Discographies, ISSN 0192-334X ; no. 20)
  Bibliography: p.
  Includes index.
  1. Jones, Spike, 1911-1965. 2. Jones, Spike,
1911-1965—Discography. 3. City Slickers—Discography.
I. Hering, Ted. II. Title. III. Series.
ML156.7.J66M6 1986   016.7899'125   85-27128
ISBN 0-313-24814-1 (lib. bdg. : alk. paper)

Library of Congress Catalog Card Number: 85-27128
ISBN: 0-313-24814-1
ISSN: 0192-334X

First published in 1986

Greenwood Press, Inc.
88 Post Road West, Westport, Connecticut 06881

Printed in the United States of America

The paper used in this book complies with the
Permanent Paper Standard issued by the National
Information Standards Organization (Z39.48-1984).

10 9 8 7 6 5 4 3 2 1

Copyright Acknowledgments

The author and the publisher gratefully acknowledge permission to reprint materials from the
following sources:

"He Plays Louder than Anybody," reprinted from *The Saturday Evening Post,* © The Curtis
Publishing Company.

Lyrics from "War Bond Jingle" and Gilmore Oil commercial by Del Porter, properties of Tune
Towne Tunes, by permission of Spike Jones, Jr.

Inventory: Spike Jones' Musical Insanities, compiled by Ray Harrison, and lyrics from "Riders
in the Sky," Spike Jones estate, for Arena Stars, by permission of Spike Jones, Jr.

Unpublished material (Spike Jones itinerary, 1947-48), by permission of A. Purves Pullen ("Dr.
H. Q. Birdbath").

Unpublished material (working diaries of Don Anderson, 1941-43), by permission of Don
Anderson.

Unpublished material (Spike Jones Bibliography; interview with Del Porter), by permission of
Ted Hering.

        ...a drummer himself, a good one at that, surpassed only by
a razor-sharp acerbic wit perpetually coiled like a serpent ready to
strike with deadly accuracy. It was not prompted by any malice but
rather an exercise of will much like a sharp-shooter or whip snapper.
He shot from the hip as a natural spontaneous reflex and then would
enjoy the 'aftertaste' of the remark with a sly satisfaction as
though the remark was made by a homunculus within him. Spike was a
fascinating and utterly complex multi-faceted individual.

        I shall never forget him.

                        - S. Stevan Dweck, Ph.D., October 1983

Contents

Illustrations

Foreword

In the eyes, or should I say ears, of a nine-year-old boy, there is nothing more revolting than a sentimental love song. I couldn't really hear the words of the record that was being played in the store, but it certainly sounded sappy, and I paid very little attention to it as I browsed among the record bins. When the singer came to what should have been the last note of the song, however, something amazing happened: two pistol shots rang out instead of that last note, and the band took off on a jubilant dixielandish rendition of the song, this time sung by someone who sounded as if she had studied singing with a hog-caller. That was my introduction to Spike Jones--the record was "Serenade to a Jerk"--and though those two shots may not have been heard around the world, they certainly changed my life. Put me where I am today, you might say.

For the next few years, most of my allowance and paper-route money went to buying Spike Jones records, and much of my free time was spent acting them out with my brother and friends. As I remember it, we would usually take turns, but sometimes we would team up, each of us covering a character. In "Glow Worm," for instance, one of us would lip-sync the soprano, one the baritone, and another the sound effects. (Finding visual equivalents to the sound effects was probably the most challenging assignment, but it's hard to resist portraying a hammy opera singer.) About ten years ago I turned my own kids on to Spike Jones and discovered in the process that I could still, three decades later, get up and act those records out without dropping a syllable, note or noise.

Soon, of course, acting out the records wasn't enough: we wanted to do our own versions of songs. So we went into the recording studio, by which I mean a coin-operated booth that stood in the concessions building of the Washington, D.C. Zoo, conveniently located at the foot of the hill we lived on. You inserted your quarters, waited for the little light, and then you sang, yelled and rocked the booth, making various sound effects for as long as the little light stayed on (about a minute), and then you waited till the six-inch disc (plus mailing envelope and cardboard backing!) dropped out of the slot. Later one of the kids on the block got a home record-cutting machine, and I still have our mind-bogglingly silly versions of "The Anniversary Waltz," "Momma's Little Baby Loves Shortnin' Bread," and other classics. (Somebody also had a wire recorder, but that didn't last long, and tape was still, but just, around the corner.)

Eventually I got to see the master himself, when Spike Jones and his City Slickers came to town. It was a fine, feisty show in the old vaudeville tradition, and featured visual equivalents of those sound effects beyond anything my friends and I had ever dreamed up, or even of. During intermission I went around to the stage door, hoping for a chance to meet Mr. Jones. I saw him--he glanced in my direction and spit out what looked like a tooth--but he seemed so dour and forbidding that I didn't have the nerve to approach him.

Soon after my twelfth birthday we moved to Fargo, North Dakota, and within a year or two after that an exciting new comedy band burst upon the scene. Jerky Jems and his Balmy Brothers consisted of my brother David on violin, John Helgeson and myself on clarinet, and

George Tharleson on tom-tom and suspended cymbal. We made our music desks out of orange crates: each one was painted a different color and sported a three-dimentional J J on the front. We put on shows in the Schickele basement, d/b/a The Nitso Theatre (admission: 1¢). A party my parents gave in our backyard was the only non-theatrical gig I can remember.

The very first piece I ever composed, "The Sheik of Palamazoo," was written for Jerky Jems and his Balmy Brothers, and I ended up contributing most of the arrangements in the band's repertoire. But the original impetus was theatrical: in addition to the plays about cowboys, detectives and ape-men that constituted the bulk of Nitso Theatre fare, I simply wanted to be able to do an act like Spike Jones. One of our convulsingly hilarious routines featured a kid pulling a rope tied to a tiny "boat" (a five-inch piece of one-by-four with a pointed end) across the floor while the band played "The Song of the Volga Boatmen." We had a lot of other stuff just as funny.

Like Spike Jones and his Other Orchestra, however, we also had some serious numbers in the book, as well as a few about which it was hard to decide whether they were supposed to be funny or not. Gradually (or was it suddenly?) the musical part of it became more important than the theatrical part of it and by the time I got to college I was a composer, writing constantly and to the exclusion of any non-musical theatrical involvement.

Now, almost forty years after that first record store encounter, I spend about half my time perpetrating the irresponsible works of P.D.Q. Bach, and the other half writing and performing the (usually) more serious music of Peter Schickele. The debt of the former activity to Spike Jones is obvious: the unexpected musical twists, the decorum-deflating lyrics and the use of instruments such as the bicycle, left-handed sewer-flute and windbreaker have led more than one critic to label P.D.Q. Bach "the Spike Jones of classical music" (although the City Slickers' desecrations were not completely confined to popular music, the hit songs of the day were their most frequent victims). But in retrospect it seems clear that Spike Jones was for me not just a door to musical humor, but a door to music itself. The reason his band, and his arrangers, were so funny is that they were so good. (Most people know that precision is one of the essential ingredients of humor: the secret ingredient is seriousness.)

People like Jack Mirtle are the reason we know as much as we do about Bach, Mozart and Beethoven, not to mention Frederick the Great and Attila the Hun. Mirtle's a bulldog: once he bites into a subject, he won't let go. On the bandstand, Spike Jones liked to give the impression of not particularly caring what happened next, but the following pages demonstrate that he, like Bach, Mozart and Beethoven, was actually what we now call a workaholic. This virtual day-by-day log of the height of his career reminds us all that nothing comes easy.

Peter Schickele,
sole discoverer of the
music of P.D.Q. Bach

Preface

During the history of the City Slickers and since the death of Spike Jones in 1965, a mystique has clouded much of the fact behind their success. This was due, in part, to Spike's own PR which so often belittled himself, his music and his musicians, thus reducing the credibility of the organization, and the zany public image which belied their actual musical capabilities.

What began as idle curiosity in 1979 quickly developed into an interesting hobby, and this book is the result of taking the hobby seriously. Rather than allowing the project to continue indefinitly with little chance to share the research, a self-imposed time limit of 1985, the 20th anniversary of Spike's death, was set and has been realized.

In attempting to "dig" up facts - such as "who", "when", and "where" regarding Jones' recordings - it was staggering to find that there was no information on this artist whose records had sold in the millions and whose RCA titles are continuously re-issued both at home and internationally. The occasional magazine articles, vintage or recent, gave seemingly conflicting information. The task of piecing together the Jones saga has proven complex. Spike Jones recordings are just the tip, and a small one at that, of a fascinating musical career - virtually an unknown organizational empire. While this book is far from complete, there is more than enough material to separate fanciful fiction from "tongue-in-cheek" fact.

Three main sources form the broad basis of the book, with the substance of hundreds of letters and phone calls binding it all together.

Ted Hering, a friend of Spike Jones, Jr., was asked to catalog (or as we say in Canada, catalogue) the existing material in Jones' home at the time of Spike's death. Spike also had a warehouse full of props, PR material and old files on Clark Street in Los Angeles. Unfortunately, most of the useful files had been dispersed by the time Ted finished at the home. All of his information was compiled as a bibliography (basically a discography) in 1965, and a half-dozen copies were given to friends. These copies have been surreptitiously duplicated over the years and are a "must" for any serious Jones collector.

Despite the lack of continuity in the Jones estate files, Ted has kept his knowledge comprehensive through personal interviews with many ex-Slickers (such as Del Porter, Freddy Morgan and Billy Barty) and continual contact with collectors worldwide. Acutely attuned to the aural and visual idiosyncrasies of the Slickers over the years, he is virtually "the Oracle" of Jones knowledge - an honorary Slicker, so to speak. For the use of his files and his patience with the finer editing details, simple thanks seem inadequate. Ted is presently Program Director for radio station KVIP in Redding, CA.

Indirectly, through Ted, many details are the result of contributions by Skip Craig (particularly the V-Disc and AFRS basis), John Wood of England, Randy Morris, Warren Dexter and Larry Kiner, to name but a few. Thank you all.

Don Anderson, trumpet, now living near Puget Sound in the
Pacific North west, kept working diaries of his career in Los
Angeles. Thanks to these documents and his permission to use the
information for this project, an unprecedented view of the actual
work of a free-lance musician, including those important initial
years of the Slickers, is presented.

Meeting with Purves Pullen ("Dr. Horatio Q. Birdbath") is
always a treat. "Doc" is very approachable and affable about his
career and his years with Spike. Through his generosity, the daily PR
schedules as maintained by "Doc" and a few of the interesting travel
details covering the busy years 1947-48 are included. Constantly involved with PR, he lives on Lovers Lane in Vacaville, CA.

Many added bits of information unite these sources - from
the public libraries across Canada and many in the U.S. and England,
to scores of collectors who have shared their Jones holdings. All
newspaper and magazine articles excerpted for use are verbatim, including errors.

All domestic and international companies who handled Jones
material have been canvassed, with only RCA Schallplatten GmbH,
Hamburg, W. Germany, indicating my listing as complete. Foreign release info was supplied by: the British Institute of Recorded Sound,
London, England; Bibliotheque Nationale of France at Paris; National
Library of Australia at Canberra; personal stock and that of many
collectors.

Of immense value from RCA New York were copies of the recording sheets concerning Jones. Thanks to Amanda Armstrong, Berna-
dette Moore of the Listing Department, and to Ethel Gabriel. What
these sheets do in some cases is to provoke questions instead of
giving answers. These 8-1/2x11" sheets are really instrumentation
listings, label accreditations, titles, timings, matrix and original
release info. Session personnel who were to be paid directly by Spike
are seldom listed. This included the choir or chorus (usually a
studio group), effects personnel and more often than not, the soloists. Often too, names are given label credit but not listed for that
session. In such cases, it was Spike's and not RCA's responsibility
to pay these added personnel. Red Ingle and Dick Morgan, for example,
are continually listed as instrumentalists, yet they provided many
uncredited voices and effects. Every session also had guests, or
observers, in the control room.

It would be foolish to make the claim that all known issues
of records, transcriptions and shows, etc. are accounted for, as
there are always surprises. A safe estimate would be that 99% of all
known Spike Jones and his City Slickers output is herein included.
While most, if not all, live show dates are carefully documented,
there is no record of the hundreds of free benefit appearances to the
military, hospitals and charitable organizations that occurred over
the years.

Prior to tape, the take numbers were straight forward and
easily understood. With the advent of tape, RCA did not, in later
years particularly, list the various overdubbings used, with the
issued take simply designated -1, and the safety as -1A. Taping techniques improved throughout the '50s, with Jones' issued titles being
composites of many takes. The recording/instrumentation sheets will
be referred to in the text as "RCA inst".

All known special recordings, such as Slickers promotional
discs, are included in their approximate time slot. Recorded at RCA
Victor, Hollywood, and occasionally in Chicago, these recordings do
not show on any RCA listing and are identified and dated by their
mastering number only.

Thank you, music lovers, the title of this book, was taken
from Spike's acknowledgment to his audience following every Slickers
opener on the road and on radio for many years. The book is as complete as possible with regard to the work pattern, itinerary and
personnel up to 1950. Beyond 1950, the traveling statistics become
ponderous and from 1951 on, only radio/television appearances, recordings with personnel and pertinent newspaper articles will be
listed.

Although the various personnel indexes read like a musical "Who's Who", with many whose careers are deserving of biographical research, apologies are in order to those many unmentioned musicians and personalities whose unique talents added to the Slickers popularity over the years.

Without the suggestions, help and encouragement of my colleagues at CFB Esquimalt, my patient and enduring family, and from the following, this project would be considerably less than it is.

Dick Anderson, Don Anderson, Louis Adrian, Mary Jane Barton, Gil Bernal, Ralph Berton, Stanley Black, Mel Blanc, Hans Bodendorfer, Carl Brandt, Eddie Brandt, Red Callender, Frank Carlson, Milton Charles, Larry Collins, Joe Colvin, Herman Crone, Ralph Dadisman, John DeSoto, Chet Defty, Stevan Dweck, Virgil Evans, Ray Foster, Russell "Candy" Hall, Ralph Hansell, Walter Heebner, Wally Heider, Al Hendrickson, Ted Hering, Milton Holland, Luella Howard, Ernest Hughes, Bruce Hudson, Don Ingle, Bill Jacoby, Harry James, Bernie Jones, Linda Jones, Spike Jones, Jr., Thomas Clark Jones, Mickey Katz, Ted Klages, Wally Kline, Ed Kusby, Bea Lipschultz, Henry Mancini, Julian Matlock, Billy May, Edwin Metcalfe, Tommy Morgan, Randy Morris, Arthur Most.

Ted Nash, Leighton Noble, Dick Noel, Abe Nole, Theodore Norman, Helen Owens, Tommy Pederson, Bob Poland, E. Purves Pullen, Dorothy Rae, Arthur "Doc" Rando, Herschell Ratliff, Randy Rayburn, Henri Rene, Marshall "Tiny" Rips, Eddie Robertson, George Rock, Harry H. Rodgers, David Rose, Luther "Red" Roundtree, Brian Rust, Al Saparoff, Richard Sears, Red Skelton, James Thomasson, Charlotte Tinsley, Danny Van Allen, Rudy Vallee, Cindy Walker, Joe Wolverton, Rubin "Zeke" Zarchy.

British Broadcasting Corporation; USO/LA; National Archives, Washington, D.C., Motion Picture, Sound and Video Branch, Les Waffen; AFN Europe CDR ATC Charles Crescioni, Program Director Robert Harlan (for allowing access in 1982 to their transcription library, surely one of AFRTS' most complete); AFRTS/LA, Mrs. Dorothy McAdams; Defence Audiovisual Agency, Norton AFB, CA; Library of Congress, Recorded Sound Division, Reference Librarian Sam Brylawski, Head Curatorial Services Gerald Gibson (for the additional AFRS ET and NBC-TV listings); Dept. of the Navy, Recruiting, Naval Historical Center, Medical Command, Navy Internal Relations Activity; Department of the Army, Office of the Adjutant General; Radio Recorders, Los Angeles; AFofM Locals: 47, Los Angeles (Bob Manners, President, Max Herman, past President, and their office staff who allowed me to interrupt their heavy work schedule); 70-558 Omaha, Neb; 174-496 New Orleans, LA; 369 Las Vegas, Nev; 353 Long Beach; 148-462 Atlanta, GA; 2-197 St. Louis, MO; 161-710 Washington, DC; 75 Des Moines, IA; 10-208 Chicago, IL.

In 1982, the Association for Recorded Sound Collections (ARSC), in their wisdom, awarded a grant to aid in the expenses incurred during the research involved. Thanks go to their Grants Committee and Directors: Tom Owen, Les Waffen, J. Weber, Mike Biel, Tim Brooks and all responsible, for their patience and continuous encouragement.

How to Use This Book—
Format and Abbreviations

Titles, as performed fully by the City Slickers, the Other Orchestra and Big Band, excluding fill or chaser music, are <u>underlined</u>. Titles appearing in the later medleys and production numbers as used on television are not underlined.

Personnel names are <u>underlined</u> on their first known appearance with the City Slickers.

The original record release, or catalog number, is <u>underlined</u>. The original is assumed to be 78 RPM when the 45 RPM has an identical catalog number. Verve, Warner and Liberty original issues are assumed to be on LP, except where noted.

Dates are written out in full, i.e., April 1943 (or 8 Apr 43) as abbreviated.

Format for recording sessions:

Date   Studio, Location, studio time (where known)
                        A & R Rep. (where known)

                        Personnel (Slickers and additional studio
                            musicians and singers)

Matrix, take no.   <u>Release number</u> (applicable album no.); additional
(where known)   release numbers (incl. albums) in the order of:
                            78 RPM (although pressed in England, HMV issues
                            appeared in the catalogs of many countries)
                            followed by <u>45</u> RPM, including singles (albums)
                            and EP's; <u>LP</u> (Long Play 7", 10" and 12"
                            issues); <u>ET</u> (all radio transcriptions including
                            AFRS, Government, etc.)
            (Time) <u>Title</u> - from the rec/inst sheets with credits as
                        originally intended

Note: Here will be noted discrepancies between RCA inst and the actual label credits, plus other pertinent data. There are instances of the session titles at variance with the issue title; i.e., "A Goose to the Ballet Russe" was recorded, but issued as "Rhapsody from Hunger(y)"

Disc Jockey (DJ)/promotional copies for Victor had their own numbering system (e.g., DJ 613, etc.) to mid-1950, after which they were issued with the matrix number, e.g., D9-CB-1346. Liberty issued DJ copies with the actual catalog number. All promotional issues had different labels from the commercial releases and are plainly marked "NOT FOR SALE". Most of the couplings are identical to the commercial releases.

Format for radio and television broadcasts:

Date   SHOW TITLE*
                    Network, location, b'cast time (where known)

                    Master of ceremonies, personalities, orchestra
                        credits, announcer (as applicable and where
                        known)

ET number   Personality - "Song Title in Quotes"
(where known)   *<u>Slickers Titles</u> - with known credits

                    *after b'cast show title indicates incomplete
                        information, e.g., contents unknown or
                        partial; date or network unknown.
        * or #before Slickers titles will identify titles
                    issued on LP or ET, and the issuing company
                    or agency

        All locations are in California unless otherwise noted. If
any reader can supply further information to any show marked *, this
will be appreciated. Please address c/o Greenwood Press.

Abbreviations of domestic and foreign record companies, with release
prefixes as may be used. Monophonic, unless otherwise indicated.

7M	HMV 7" 45 RPM Popular series
20	RCA 10" 78 RPM Popular series
27	RCA 7" 45 RPM Collector's series
30	Bluebird 10" 78 RPM Popular series
42	RCA 10" 78 RPM Popular series
44	RCA 10" 78 RPM Coin Operators' special
	(both sides identical)
45	RCA 10" 78 RPM "Little Nipper"
47	RCA 7" 45 RPM Popular series
74	RCA 7" 45 RPM Popular series (condensed)
420	RCA 10" 78 RPM Gold Standard series
447	RCA 7" 45 RPM Gold Standard series
547	RCA 7" 45 RPM Extended play

ACL	Pickwick 12" LP
AFRS	Armed Forces Radio Service
AGL1	RCA 12" LP Red Seal
ANL1	RCA 12" LP Popular
AYL1	RCA 12" LP Popular
B	Bluebird 10" 78 RPM Popular release; or HMV, all issues,
	10" 78 RPM Popular; or Warner Bros. 12" LP,
	as applicable
B7	RCAIT 7" 45 RPM EP
BB	Bluebird (RCA budget issue 78 RPM)
BD	HMV, all issues, 10" 78 RPM Popular
BR	Brunswick 10" 78 RPM Popular
BS	Warner Bros. 12" LP, stereo
CAS	RCAAU (Camden release) 12" LP
CCL2	RCA (Camden release) 12" LP
CL	RCAIT 12" LP, Popular
CO	Columbia 10" 78 RPM Popular
Corno	Cornographic 12" LP
CP	RCA 10" 78 RPM album, Canadian issue
DJ	RCA 10" 78 RPM Disc Jockey release
DML1	RCA 12" LP Special Products
DPL1	RCA 12" LP Special Products
(e)	electronically induced stereo
EA	HMVAU 10" 78 RPM Popular

EP	7" 45 RPM extended play record or album
EPA	RCA, RCAG 7" 45 RPM EP
EPB	RCA 7" 45 RPM EP double album
EPV	Verve 7" 45 RPM EP
ET	Electrical transcription
EYA	RCA 7" 45 RPM EP, "Little Nipper" series
FONIT	Fonit-Cetra Italy 12" LP
GO	Goldberg & O'Reily 12" LP, mail order only
Gramaphone	RCAF 10" 78 RPM Popular
GS	Golden Spike 12" LP
HA	Liberty England 12" LP
HMV	His Master's Voice, England
HMVAU	HMV, Sydney, Australia; Wellington, New Zealand
HMVI	HMV, Dum Dum, India
HMVS	HMV, Sweden
HMVSK	HMV, Scandinavia (Skandinavisk Grammophon)
HSR	Hindsight 12" LP
HY	RCAE 12" LP Popular
INTS	RCAE 12" LP Popular
K	Kapp 7" 45 RPM
KL	Kapp 12" LP
LIB	Liberty Records
LIBE	Liberty Records, England
LP	Long Playing microgroove disc, 7", 10" & 12": 33-1/3 RPM
LPM	RCA 10"/12" LP Popular; or RCAG 12" LP Popular
LRP	Liberty 12" LP
LSA	RCAE 12" LP Popular
LSC	RCA Red Seal 12" LP
LSP	RCA, RCAG 12" LP Popular
LST	Liberty 12" LP, stereo
LST-4	Liberty 7" LP, stereo
(m)	monophonic
MBR	Mar Bren 12" LP
MF	Manheim Fox Distribution Co.(3-4 record sets, mail order)
MGM	Metro Goldwyn Mayer
MGV	Verve 12" LP
MM	Liberty 12" LP (radio & in-store demo)
Mode	Warner Bros. France 12" LP
NCS	IX Chains 12" LP
NE	HMVI 10" 78 RPM Popular
NL	RCAE 12" LP
NW	New World 12" LP
ODLP	RCAAU 10" LP Popular
OR	Cash 12" LP
P	RCA 10" 78 RPM album
PJM	RCAG 12" LP, double album
PK	Pickwick 12" LP
PL	RCAF 12" LP, double album
POP	HMV 10" 78 RPM Popular
R	Standard Transcription 16", 33-1/3 RPM
RCA	RCA Victor, domestic
RCAAU	RCA Australia
RCADJ	RCA Disc Jockey
RCAE	RCA England
RCAF	RCA France
RCAG	RCA Germany
RCAIT	RCA Italy
RCAJ	RCA Japan
RCS	RCAG 12" LP, double album; or RCAE 7" 45 RPM EP
RD	RCAE 12" LP Popular
RLP	Rori 12" LP (Santa and the Satellite)
RNLP	Rhino 12" re-issue (Santa and the Satellite)
RVP	RCAJ 12" LP
SAH	Liberty England 12" LP, stereo
SE	MGM 12" LP, electronic stereo
SP	Warner Bros. 12" LP, 2 record set
SPD	RCA 7" 45 RPM EP, 7 record set
SS	Liberty 12" LP, stereo (radio & in-store demo)
ST	Starlite 10" 78 RPM

ST45	Starlite 7" 45 RPM
TAS	RCA 10" LP, disc jockey issue
TMT	Tiara 12" LP
TST	Tiara 12" LP
UA	United Artists 12" LP, stereo
V	Verve 10" 78 RPM & 7" 45 RPM; or Viva 12" LP, as applicable
VAU	Verve Australia
V-Disc	12" 78 RPM Armed Forces Special Services issue
VEP	Verve Scandinavia 7" 45 RPM EP
VF	Verve France
VJ	Verve Japan
VK	Verve Scandinavia (Karusell)
VPM	RCA LPM re-issue, 2 record set
VSM	RCAF 10" 78 RPM (La Voix de son Maitre)
VV	Viva 12"LP, double album
WB	Warner Bros., or Warner Bros. 7" 45 RPM
WBE	WB England
WEP	WB England 7" 45 RPM EP (Decca issue)
WM	WB England 12" LP
WP	RCA 7" 45 RPM Popular album
WS	WB & WBE 12" LP (Decca issue)
WSEP	WB & WBE 7" 45 RPM EP, stereo (Decca issue)
WY	RCA 7" 45 RPM "Little Nipper" album
X	HMVSK 10" 78 RPM Popular
XS	WB 12" LP, stereo
Y	RCA 10" 78 RPM "Little Nipper" album
Z	Standard Transcription 16", 33-1/3 RPM

RCA inst   Commonly referred to as recording sheets, giving
            session data, instrumentation and original credits.

AFRTS/LA   American Forces Radio and Television Service, Los Angeles.

        The following table of abbreviations is inluded to
facilitate reference to personnel in their activity with Spike Jones
and his City Slickers.

acc	accordion	mand	mandolin
act	act, actor, actress	mel perc	melodic percussion
ann	announc(er)-(ment)	org	organ (electric)
arr	music arranger	perf	performance
aud	auditorium	pno	piano
bass	tuba, string bass	picc	piccolo
b'cast	broadcast	PR	Public Relations
b/clar	bass clarinet	prod	producer
bjo	banjo	PSA	Public Service Ann.
bsn	bassoon	reeds	sax, clar, oboe, bsn
cel	violoncello	sax	soprano, alto, tenor,
clar	clarinet		baritone, bass
comp	composer		saxophone
cond	conductor	st bass	string bass
drm	drums, trap set	tpb	trombone
effts	effects, audibles	tpt	trumpet
feat	feature, featuring	vib	vibraphone
fl	flute	vla	viola
fr hrn	French horn	vln	violin
guit	guitar	voc	vocal, vocalist
hrp	harp	whist	whistle(r)
int	interview	ww	woodwinds (reeds,
inst	instrument(al)-(ation)		incl. fl)
ltn perc	latin percussion	xyl	xylophone

*Thank You
Music Lovers*

Spike Jones Biographical Sketch, 1911–1941, with Selected Recordings and Radio Appearances

Lindley Armstrong Jones, known to the world as Spike Jones, was born 14 December, 1911, in the California community of Long Beach. The only child of a school-teacher mother, Ada Armstrong, and railway depot agent father, Lindley Murray Jones, the ten-week old Lindley Jr. moved with his parents to Calexico in the Imperial Valley, just north of Mexicali, Mexico, when the Southern Pacific Railroad transferred Mr. Jones.

Growing up in a mature (his father was 43 years old when Lindley was born) and musical home atmosphere (his Methodist parents loved the Quaker hymns – the religion of the father's parents, and the old songs), the blue-eyed, sandy-haired youngster found he was more often by himself than with children his own age and developed an independent trait early in life.

A piano career was cut short when, at age 10, the family moved to Niland, a depot north of Calexico, Calipatria and the Salton Sea, and found their piano would not fit into the depot accommodations.

A black chef, employed by the station restaurant, piqued the young Jones' interest with his rattling of knives, forks and other culinary utensils in interesting rhythms, as Spike has often mentioned in later biographies. After hearing Lindley trying to imitate these rhythms with the same household "instruments", a black Southern Pacific porter whittled two chair rungs into rudimentary drum sticks for him and, with the addition of the household washboard, Junior began to accompany tunes.

It was about the same time that young Lindley was nicknamed, by a telegrapher friend of his father, "Spike" – a vague reference to the railroad and its tracks. For Christmas, reportedly, Mr. Jones bought young Spike his first set of drums, and soon a creditable rhythm was accompanying the very few records in the home. Not holding back on the reins of progress, Lindley Sr. agreed to lessons for Spike from a local orchestra teacher.

In 1924, he and three other local musical youths, aged 15 to 18, formed the "Jazzbo Four", and planned on playing for dances and club events. Realizing in advance that his strict parents would object to this type of outlet for their only son, Spike and the three others in the band individually campaigned the senior Mr. Jones for the necessary permission for 12 year old Spike to play professionally – they would garner $3 per engagement.

The campaign worked, and the "Jazzbo Four", also referred to as the "Calipatria Melody Four", played in the area for about a year until Mr. Jones was transferred back to Long Beach in 1926.

Spike's talents as percussionist were futher developed at the Long Beach Polytechnic High School by the music teacher, Dwight Defty. A professional cellist, Defty worked hard, ran a tight ship, and the resultant band and orchestra were among the finest in the state. The very large orchestra played only from originals – Defty did not use the diluted high-school arrangements of classics with his students. His band played the Rose Bowl Parade and was especially noted for, at that time, a very fast march tempo.

In a letter of 13 Oct 1983, Chet Defty, Dwight's son, mentions his father's recounting of Spike: "As a music student, he was excellent...a talented and fine drummer. He was also a clown and... having him as a member of any class would have always been lively.... One time when he was sassed by Spike...Gramps (Dad) told him to pack up his drums and leave...doesn't sound like a class room of today, does it?? Spike left with his drums, but was back several days later with a box of fruit from his folks place."

"Another time Gramps made Spike drum major of the band... most bands have tall drum majors...the taller the better. As Spike was a little on the short side, they had a large drum major baton made just for Spike...what he lacked in size must have been made up by the baton."

An undated and unidentified newpaper clipping carries on: "though there will be only a short interval between halves at the Glendale-Poly High football game here Saturday, an unusual drill will be presented in front of the stands, Mr. Defty said today. Lindley ("Spike") Jones heads the aggregation as drum major. In selecting Jones for this position Mr. Defty departed from precedent and chose the shortest, rather than the tallest, man for the position. Jones barely passes the five-foot mark but makes up for his lack of height with a magnetic personality and considerable drum major flair.

"Striking uniforms distinguish the Poly High Band, which numbers sixty student musicians. White trousers, green and gold sweaters, and the well-known 'beanies', or skull caps, form the..." (balance of article missing).

Chet Defty continues, "One parade the band was in was quite special. With Spike out in front a signal was made and at the next intersection the band turned off a side street, but Spike just kept on his way not knowing that he was out there by himself. It seems that one was getting even with the other for something??? Gramps said that when he found himself out there all alone it didn't take him long to retreat much like a clown would, much to the laughter of the audience."

Many of Los Angeles's finest musicians owe their musical impetus to Dwight Defty's music program and similar school programs in the many satellite cities of Los Angeles. Some of the musicians who who were contemporary with Spike were Bill Schoeder, trumpet; Danny Van Allen, drums; Herschell Ratliff, bass; Ed Wade, trumpet; Seth Storm, piano; Eldon Sackett, violin; Bob Calloway, flute/clarinet; George Carl, sax; Maurice Wishon, drums; George Porter, violin.

Chet Defty's letter of 21 Dec 1983 mentions Schoeder telling him that "he and Spike and some of the boys were in Humphrey's Music Store in Long Beach...Now Humphreys had a basement and the fellas went in and Spike went down to the basement. When he returned he had a number of cymbals hidden in his (seat of) pants." The end result is unknown.

As there was no dance band in the Long Beach Poly music program, students serious about dance and jazz music formed their own groups, picking up valuable experience - and money. Shortly after enrolling in school, Spike joined Long Beach Local 353 AF of M and played drums for Al Rowland's "Varsity Six" with Jack Young, sax; Frank Birch, banjo; Burl Ubben, trombone and Dale Miller on piano. Al Rowland was the leader, with Spike on drums, while the trumpeter is unidentified. Another school dance band working at this time was the "California Tantalizers", which included Bud Beckley, leader/sax; Don Lazenby, sax/clar; Ed Wade, trumpet; Paul Tibbets, drums; Lawrence Marsh, banjo; Herschell Ratliff; sousaphone/violin; and Ron Oakley, piano. Most of this group, who copied the style and arrangements of Red Nichols and his Five Pennies, graduated in June, 1927.

The Varsity Six continued working after its older members graduated or moved (Dale Miller to Woodrow Wilson High, for example). Spike left Rowland after one season, his place taken by Paul Lawrence. Showing an enterprising nature, Spike took over the Nichols-inspired library of the "Tantalizers" and re-formed them as "Spike Jones and his Five Tacks". They played for various school dances and broadcast over KFOX from Beacon Street's Club Del Rio in Long Beach. Spike was 16 at the time, the youngest of the group.

According to some sources, Spike, because of his smallish size and obvious interest, was the mascot of the Red Nichols band when they played summer gigs in Long Beach. With the aid of some old

arrangements given to him by Nichols, Spike thus started his "Five
Tacks", the name influenced by Nichols' "Five Pennies" (which had
been suggested to Nichols by Vic Berton). Among the "Tacks" (the
almost official jazz band of Long Beach Poly) were Carl Vidana,
piano, and Bill Harris, trombone. On occasion, Herschell Ratliff also
played. Spike Jones and his Five Tacks (occasionally augmented to
six) also billed themselves as "The Patent Leather Kids" when playing
over KGER for Dobyn's shoe store. Spike was showing signs of a very
positive approach to personal P.R., managing and promotion.
    As time would allow, Spike journeyed to Balboa to catch the
current bands: Trombonist Arthur Most remembers diminutive Spike
hovering around the bandstand, helping turn the pages of Most's music
- when necessary. Many years later, when Spike required a special
trombonist for some titles he was cutting, Most was the 'bone he
asked for, and reminded him of those Balboa evenings.
    "Spike was a real character, even in those days, but a
really nice character" (Dale Miller, written communication, 10 Nov
1974), and continued to play drums at every opportunity. Danny Van
Allen, who was to leave for England's Orpheum circuit in 1934, remembers Spike taking tap dancing lessons to improve his sense of rhythm
and always practicing, spending his homework hours with pianist Carl
Vidana, working on repertoire and technique. Movies with sound had
now replaced the earlier silent movies with their accompanying
orchestras. Jazz and dance music was becoming increasingly common and
acceptable, being heard on record and radio. There was much for Spike
and his interested friends to listen to and learn from.
    However, he also studied diligently and graduated from Long
Beach Poly in 1929 with 15 credits, which, he explains in True Story
magazine of 1949, "means I got an A in everything except one subject,
chemistry. This made my folks very happy. For Dad, it was kind of
compensation for my being a bandsman." In a later biography (c.1960)
Spike cites his grade average as B-plus.
    Returning to school at Chaffey Junior College in Ontario,
while working virtually full-time at nights, Spike, recounted in his
1949 True Story biography, entered a speaking contest held in the
college and won the first three elimination rounds. But he was ruled
out of the contest finals when it was discovered he was a professional musician (He had joined Los Angeles Local 47, AF of M, upon graduating in June 1929). To Spike, who felt he needed the self-
confidence brought about by public speaking to overcome his self-
consciousness of actually having to act, with his associates and
friends, more mature and sophisticated than his physical age, this
was a bitter disappointment. He left Chaffey soon after, never to
return to college (as a student) and devoted himself to continually
practicing and playing and climbing up the pro music ladder.
    Spike would not have been different from other aspiring
young musicians in the Los Angeles/Hollywood area - or any area with
such a high level of musicianship and its associated activities.
While not playing, rehearsing or practicing and honing their own
abilities and connections, all would take it on themselves to know
who, when and where, and make themselves known. The professional
music scene anywhere is a highly competitive business where success
is more often than not a healthy blend of abilities and connections.
    Independent, mature in outlook and ability, he worked hard
at his craft and personal promotion. Spike played with a succession
of large and small local bands through these depression years (good
musicians never felt the devastating effects of the depression): Earl
Burtnett and the L.A. Biltmore Hotel Orchestra, (with Gene Conklin,
sax); the Ray West Orchestra at the Narconian Resort (with pianist
Randy Rayburn); Kearney Walton, then Al Lyons at the Biltmore Hotel
(a coveted job); Rube Wolf at the Paramount (with trumpeter Harry
Geller). It was here that Spike met Patricia Middleton, Lyons' vocalist and one of the Paramount chorus line.
    In the summer of 1934, the society band of George Hamilton
was playing the Casino Gardens. Along with Spike were Dick Murray,
sax; Harry Geller and Ray Foster on trumpets and Leighton Noble,
vocalist/pianist. Noble recalls the bored Spike, during rehearsal and
show breaks, frantically chain-smoking (he was already heavily ad-

3

dicted to tobacco, but always chewed gum on the job) and beating his
drum sticks throughout the area - on table tops, walls, railings,
etc. - to relieve his boredom and check out the percussive response
of these and other inert objects. Spike and Pat were dating by this
time and both knew Leighton quite well. Noble remembers Spike as very
out-spoken - his comments could be very cutting - and Pat as a wonderful influence on Spike, prompting him to study, study, study.

The Hamilton band, with changed personnel, played in Denver
for the season, and Spike went with Everett Hoagland, a fine society
band at Balboa's Rendezvous Ballroom (before it burned down). Others
in this big band included Vido Musso and Archie Rosate, sax; Ray
Foster, Wally Kline and Wayne Williams, trumpets; Slim Smith, trombone; Herschell Ratliff, bass; and Freddie Slack, piano. Changes
brought Hugh "Lumpy" Branum in on bass and Stan Kenton on piano. Don
Baird drummed in Spike's absence. (More recently, "Lumpy" was Mr.
Greenjeans on the Capt. Kangaroo television show).

Several months later, Noble started with the Hoagland band,
however, Jones had moved on. Shortly, Noble would go with the Orville
Knapp band, taking over the reins on Knapp's untimely death and going
on to lead one of the finer society bands on the East coast. He returned to the West coast 10 years later and recorded extensively for
the Vocalion and Coral labels.

It is now into 1935, and on September 7th, Patricia
Middleton became Mrs. Spike Jones.

New York, Chicago, Kansas City, New Orleans - all had a rich
history of music, particularly jazz, and were home base to many of
the nations top dance bands. Los Angeles, though not as deeply rooted
in these basics, was becoming a Mecca for enlightened musicians, due
in the main to the movies of Hollywood and its associated industries,
and to the agreeable climate. Although the Musicians' Union tried to
prevent an uncontrolled mass influx of the excellent Eastern musi-
ians, the pressure was constant and the mid-'30's saw many fine
musicians from New York, Chicago, etc. wait out the Union's residency
requirements and restart their careers in Los Angeles.

In general, members transferring into a local union's jurisdiction were required to play casual, non-contract gigs only, until a
specific length of time had passed, e.g., six months or a year, after
which they would be eligible for full membership status and its ben-
efits. Instituted for the protection of their current membership,
similar rulings are still in effect within the AF of M.

Wally Kline and others recall that Spike was not a good
reader of music at this time. Despite his natural ability, he had
difficulty correctly interpreting the "dots", a decided handicap to
any musician's progress, where reading of any style (through the
written notation and, more importantly, through what is not written)
must be fast, secure and virtually second nature. There are no specific instances to cite, but there would have been occasions where
Spike would have been embarrassed by this shortcoming. Interpretation
was but one technique he kept working on and improving.

Spike had been studying all the mallet percussion instruments, later mentioning that his teacher had been a retired tympanist
from Sousa's Band. This is quite likely in view of the fact that many
of Sousa's musicians had retired to the Long Beach Municipal Band
under the directorship of the eminent and renowned soloist and conductor, Herbert L. Clarke. Although a full union member and a good
percussionist, Spike was not yet working the studios of Los Angeles.
Local 47 AF of M was loaded with expert musicians - both the local
instrumentalists who had worked their way up and the "imports" who
waited their turn. It would soon be Spike's turn to enter the scene
and the break which brought Spike into this sphere of elite musicians
has been only occasionally mentioned in his own PR packages of later
years.

Illness or conflicting bookings were reasons for musicians
to hire a substitute to "stand in". Free-lance musicians were on call
by contractors and leaders for work calls anywhere and at anytime,
often in conflict with a gig already booked. As an example: while
working shows, there could be a work call for a recording, and to
decline could mean being struck off the bookers call list. The date

would be accepted - sometimes at a lower pay scale - and a "sub"
contacted to stand in on the show rehearsals (marking the music to be
played at sight on the actual job by the other), and sometimes the
actual b'cast. A "sub" was usually a colleague not on call at that
time, a younger musician or an "import" waiting to break into the big
time. Most, but not all, musical directors allowed "subs". Inherent
personal politics aside, "subs" had to perform competently to remain
on call, and also had to have a call list of their own in cases of
double booking.

Substituting for Vic Berton ("a driven man - driven to alcohol, driven to women, driven to chain-smoking!" - Ralph Berton,
Remembering Bix), one of the top studio percussionists of his time,
in the Victor Young Orchestra was the break for Spike. Berton, who
had worked for Young and Abe Lyman at New York's Paramount in 1931,
was well known to never have sent in a "sub" due to illness, virtually dying on the job many years later with the mallets in his hand
after playing a transcribed xylophone concerto with the L.A. Philharmonic. But he was often in the cross-booking situation where he
had to have a "sub". Victor Young's guitarist and contractor, Perry
Botkin, who had worked for many years in New York with most of the
name bands and musicians in the area, including Berton, had recently
played casuals with Spike and didn't hesitate to contact him. Spike
was competent and was now "in".

Vic Berton, pivotal at this time in Spike's career, and the
ephemeral Beiderbecke era, so influential to jazz and its disciples
(including Spike), are excellently covered in Remembering Bix by
Ralph Berton, brother of Vic.

Victor Young's current guitarist and contractor, Perry
Botkin, was an exceptional musician and business man who had moved
his family to Los Angeles in the early 30s. In New York, he had performed and recorded with such musicians as the Dorsey Brothers, Glenn
Miller, Benny Goodman, Gene Krupa, Red Nichols, Phil Napoleon, Mannie
Klein, Artie Bernstein, Larry Gomar, Hank Stern, Hoagy Carmichael and
Del Porter. On the West coast, he was virtually Bing Crosby's personal guitarist and was heard as such throughout the Kraft Music Hall
series.

The following Decca session may very well be the first for
Spike now "subbing" for Vic Berton.

9 August, 1936 (SUN) - Decca Studios, Hollywood
                Victor Young Orchestra (Spike Jones, drums)

DLA 546A   Decca 926
                   I Cried For You - voc Gene Austin

DLA 547A   Decca 926
                   If I Had My Way - voc Gene Austin

DLA 548A   Decca 904
                   When I'm With You - voc Gene Austin

DLA 549A   Decca 904
                   Until Today - voc Gene Austin

Russell "Candy" Hall worked extensively with Gene Austin
during these years and may very well have been present on this
recording date.

Spike's skills, not only as a rhythm man but also as a percussionist soon brought him to the attention of all the contractors,
conductors and producers for the movie and radio studios. A show
drummer is virtually a sound effects man, in that it is he who augments the illusory effects of the actual sound effects man that are
necessary in reinforcing stage action (important for shows, radio
work and the silent movie era). Most of these effects, such as swami
(or swanee) whistles, bird and duck calls, auto horns, temple blocks,

cowbells and sandpaper blocks are manufactured and are part of every respectable drummer's kit. Every show drummer had, and still has, devices of his own construction for effects.

It was physically impossible for any musician to work every radio show; moreover, the quota system spread the work around so that although Spike and his colleagues did play all the shows, it was on a slow rotation over the radio years. In an effort to keep the work as evenly distributed among its members as possible, Local 47 set up a quota system, restricting the number of shows and hours any individual musician could work and therefore monopolize. But there was a loophole: if specifically requested by a producer, a musician could then be contracted beyond his quota. All work was covered by contract.

"Frankly, I like money, I always did like it and I could see I wasn't getting anyplace. There were too many other drummers in town for anybody to look me up", Spike was quoted in the Saturday Evening Post, 10 Apr 1943, as saying. He was now starting to use his collection of assorted percussionist's effects, many of which he had started to accumulate from his Long Beach Poly days. Such treasures as doorbells, washboards, auto horns, pistols, large and small anvils with iron mallets, and tuned cowbells would soon pay off. Astute enough to know when to use such effects in excess of requirements, he was soon in demand in excess of his quota.

"The union couldn't kick because he was the one drummer in Hollywood whose services could not be duplicated outside a combined boiler works, three-alarm fire and running gun battle", was the Saturday Evening Post's view of Spike at work.

Not only was he excelling at personal promotion, but on every contracted job, Spike was liable to earn in excess of minimum through sanctioned doubling or tripling plus cartage. The increased rate applied only to certain instruments. Booked on sax, a musician would receive double and triple if he played clarinet and flute. Tuba was the double for string bass. With drums, playing the basic trap set would earn a minimum rate, while the addition of melodic instruments (glockenspiel, xylophone, etc.) for playing as little as one note increased the rate. The further addition of tympani (tripling) would increase the pay yet again. All larger instruments, such as harp, tuba, and all percussion were also allowed a cartage fee to compensate for the use of their own or special vehicles in transporting these bulky instruments to playdates. It was very lucrative to those prepared to work for it.

The 1936 movie Born To Dance, which featured songstress Frances Langford and the spectacular dancing talents of Eleanor Powell, also introduced to the movie audiences a new group from New York, The Foursome, which consisted of vocalists Del Porter, Ray Johnson, Marshall Smith and Dwight Snyder. The history of The Foursome and particularly that of Del Porter are important to the ultimate development of the City Slickers.

Delmar Smith Porter was born in Newberg, Oregon in 1902, where he studied the violin and later the xylophone, sax and clarinet. Other musical and entertaining youths in the area at that time were Mel Blanc, later a legendary character actor, and trombonist Arthur Most, who spent a good deal of his time in the 20's playing in the old Vancouver, B.C., Hotel. Moving to Spokane, Porter became well known in the area and a musical acquaintance of the young Bing Crosby.

Moving to Los Angeles in the early 20's, Del performed in a multitude of casuals, eventually recording on sax/clar with Glen Oswald's Serenaders in 1924. Having a naturally pleasing voice, it was not too long before he was singing as often as playing. He soon became involved with three other musicians and formed, by 1926, The Foursome. Working the rehearsal circuit, they ended up in New York after recording in Chicago with the Paul Ash Orchestra that year. Working in and out of New York, Porter, Smith, Snyder and Johnson must have been among the finest of male quartets as they attracted enough attention to be featured in the Gershwins' Broadway success, Girl Crazy. Their feature was "Bidin' My Time", recreated in 1953 for the Glenn Miller film biography. The Girl Crazy pit orchestra was led by Red Nichols, and included Gene Krupa, Glenn Miller, Benny Goodman, Jimmy Dorsey and Jack Teagarden. On stage were Ethel Merman and Ginger Rogers. They recorded "On Revival Day" in September of 1930 with the Red Nichols Band. Other shows followed, notably Anything Goes. Porter recorded solo with the Roger Kahn Orchestra in 1932; the guitarist at that session was Perry Botkin.

Later recordings of The Foursome prove them to be an exceedingly good vocal group, excellently in tune and using many devices of shading and blend for variety. Their recordings, few as they are, will be a pleasant surprise to anyone who wishes to become familiar with quality vocalization. In addition to first-class solo and group, or part singing, their added features included choreography and the instrumental diversion of playing a consort of ocarinas, or "Sweet Potatos". In addition to these unusual sounds, which at times resembled a family of recorders, Del would play, in a humorous fashion, on the "penny-whistle". It should be noted now that Porter was much more fluent on the sax, preferably the baritone, and played the clarinet as he did the penny-whistle, more for humor and "kicks".

The filming of Born To Dance took a month (the music soundtrack has recently been issued on Sandy Hook LP SH 2088) but the promise of future films proved hollow. The Foursome did record on the West coast, eventually to be featured with Bing Crosby on his Kraft Music Hall. Here are some Foursome recordings to look for:

20 September, 1937 (MON) - Decca Studios, Hollywood
 Perry Botkin Instrumental Quartet (Perry Botkin, leader/guit; Jack Mayhew, reeds; Slim Taft, bass; Spike Jones, drm)

DLA 935
 Decca 1529-B
 When the Midnight Choo Choo Leaves For Alabam - voc The Foursome

DLA 936
 Decca 1529-A
 There'll Be Some Changes Made - voc The Foursome

DLA 937
 Decca 1480-B
 Sweet Potato Swing - voc The Foursome

DLA 938
 Decca 1480-A
 Nobody's Sweetheart Now - voc The Foursome

15 November, 1937 (MON) - Decca Studios, Hollywood
 Perry Botkin Instrumental Quartet (as above)

DLA 1080
 Decca 1595-B
 Sweet Georgia Brown - voc The Foursome

DLA 1081
 Decca 1867-B
 My Honey's Lovin' Arms - voc The Foursome

DLA 1082
 Decca 1595-A
 Chinatown, My Chinatown - voc The Foursome

DLA 1083
 Decca 1867-A
 Blue (and Broken Hearted) - voc The Foursome

The above two dates are approximate. A comment would be appropriate about these versions: the brilliant clarinet of Jack Mayhew, one of the four Mayhew brothers in professional music, is a model of tasty musicianship. Spike's drumming is certainly secure but unobtrusive, showing excellent shading and sympathy with the vocal and instrumental solos. During "ride-out" choruses, Spike laid down a backbeat that meant business. All had a good feel for each others abilities. Considering the elite personnel on these sessions, it is not surprising that most of these titles flowed - actually swung, and swung with a lighter yet tighter rhythm than some of the swing groups of the day.

The following titles featuring The Foursome are also known. Persian Rug, unaccompanied, is dated c.1928.

    Lady Be Good - with Victor Young Orch
    Bidin' My Time - with Victor Young Orch
    Persian Rug (a cappella)

The Kraft Music Hall starred Bing Crosby at his relaxed and personable best and was probably one of radio's most popular variety shows! The orchestra conductor was John Trotter, former pianist/arranger for Hal Kemp, who had recently padded his name to John Scott Trotter. Spike may have worked the show from this year, 1937, and it was not long before he was percussionist with the orchestras of Billy Mills (Fibber McGee and Molly), Cookie Fairchild (Eddie Cantor), Oscar Bradley (Screen Guild Theatre), and Victor Young (probably earlier, during the Shell Chateau of Al Jolson).

To reinforce the above paragraphs regarding the varied work Spike encountered, a very few of the engagements he played, including several with the Foursome, are listed below. He was becoming well known as an unusual rhythm man, always having a few extra and unorthodox effects with him on every engagement - more than any previous drummer had accumulated or needed.

25 April, 1938 (MON) - Decca Studios, Hollywood
            Harry Sosnik Orchestra (incl. Mannie Klein, Andy
            Secrest, tpt; Abe Lincoln, trb; Jack Mayhew,
            clar; Claude Kennedy, pno; Perry Botkin, guit;
            Slim Taft, bass; Spike Jones, drm

DLA 1280-A   Decca 1821
                    The Old Oaken Bucket - voc Pinky Tomlin

DLA 1281-A   Decca 1821
                    Smiles - voc Pinky Tomlin

DLA 1282-A   Decca 2187-B
                    Red Wing - voc Pinky Tomlin

DLA 1283-A   Decca 2187-A
                    Red River Valley - voc Pinky Tomlin

25 June, 1938 (SAT)
            Jack Mayhew, reeds; Spike Jones, perc; Andy Secrest, cornet;
Tommy Dorsey, trb; Perry Botkin, guit; Ray Mayer, John Trotter, Bill
Pollard, pno; form the pit band (the "Split-Lip Four"), for "The
Westwood Marching and Chowder Club, North Hollywood Branch, 2nd
Breakaway Minstrel Show". Thirty-two skits, prepared and presented by
the top actors, entertainers and musicians in Hollywood for themselves and their spouses were the fare for the long evening's frivolities. Two of the "Split Lip Four" (or Six - or Eight) taking part in
the costumed skits were Two Ton Trotter and P. "Trains" Botkin!

1 July, 1938 (FRI) - Decca Studios, Hollywood
            Victor Young's Small Fryers (incl. Andy Secrest,
            tpt; Abe Lincoln, trb; Jack Mayhew, John
            Cascales, clar/sax; Perry Botkin, guit; Slim
            Taft, bass; Spike Jones, drm)

DLA 1297-A   Decca 1960
                    Small Fry - voc Bing Crosby

8

DLA 1298-A   Decca 1960
            Mr. Gallagher and Mr. Shean - voc "as sung by
                Mr. Crosby and Mr. Mercer"

17 July, 1938 (SUN) - Brunswick Studios, Hollywood
            Perry Botkin Orchestra (incl. Lou Bring, pno;
                Spike Jones, drm)

LA 1684-A   BR 8300
                Phil, the Fluter's Ball - voc Ella Logan

LA 1685-A   BR 8196
                My Bonnie Lies Over the Ocean - voc Ella Logan

LA 1686-A   BR 8196
                The Bluebells Of Scotland - voc Ella Logan

LA 1687-A   BR 8232
                Come To the Fair - voc Ella Logan

        The same orchestra may have accompanied Logan on 13 Sept 38,
on the titles "Adios Muchachos", "Cielito Lindo", "I'm Forever Blowing Bubbles", "Ragtime Cowboy Joe", and on 2 Apr 40 on "The Curse of
an Aching Heart", "Whiffenpoof Song", "I Wonder Where My Baby Is
Tonight" and "Oh! By Jingo".

15 August, 1938 (MON) - Decca Studios, Hollywood
            Harry Sosnik Orchestra - The Foursome, vocal
                assist

DLA 1404-A   Decca 2014
                In Ole Oklahoma - voc Pinky Tomlin

DLA 1405-A   Decca 2014
                Ragtime Cowboy Joe - voc Pinky Tomlin

14 October, 1938 (FRI) - Brunswick Studios, Hollywood
            Perry Botkin Orchestra (incl. Mannie Klein, tpt;
                Abe Lincoln, trb; Jack Mayhew, clar; Charlie
                LaVere, pno; Jim Taft, bass; Spike Jones, drm)

LA 1730-B   BR 8250
                Two Sleepy People - voc Hoagy Carmichael and
                    Ella Logan

LA 1731-A   BR 8255
                Hong Kong Blues - voc Hoagy Carmichael

        Four days later, the same orchestra accompanied Logan and
Carmichael, but the mastering numbers ran consecutively from 14 Oct.

18 October, 1938 (TUES) - Brunswick Studios, Hollywood
            Perry Botkin Orchestra (Spike Jones, drm)

LA 1732-A   BR 8255
                Riverboat Shuffle - voc Hoagy Carmichael

LA 1733-A   BR 8250
                New Orleans - voc Hoagy Carmichael and Ella
                    Logan

12 December, 1938 (MON) - Decca Studios, Hollywood
            John Scott Trotter's Frying Pan Five (Sam
                Freed, vln, with Crosby/Foursome)

DLA 1636-A   Decca 2237
                When the Bloom Is On the Sage - voc Bing Crosby
                    with The Foursome

9

19 December, 1938 (MON) - Decca Studios, Hollywood
                    John Scott Trotter Orchestra

DLA 1691-A   Decca 2237
                       It's a Lonely Trail - voc Bing Crosby with
                       The Foursome

        Alexander's Ragtime Band, an Academy Award nominee movie
which was more of a vehicle to present the songs of Irving Berlin
than a tangible story, was released in 1938, and among the small
combo of musicians visually active is Spike Jones.

15 March, 1939 (WED) - Decca Studios, Hollywood
                    John Scott Trotter's Frying Pan Five

DLA 1722-A   Decca 2494
                       Ida, Sweet As Apple Cider - voc Bing Crosby
                       with The Foursome

DLA 1723-A   Decca 2385-B
                       Poor Old Rover - voc Bing Crosby with The
                       Foursome

3 April, 1939 (MON) - Decca Studios, Hollywood
                    John Scott Trotter's Frying Pan Five

DLA 1752-A   Decca 2494
                       Alla En El Rancho Grande - voc Bing Crosby
                       with The Foursome

        It is interesting to note that these 78RPM versions of "El
Rancho Grande", "Ida" and "Bloom Is On the Sage" were having broadcast royalties paid as late as 1958.
        During the years bracketing 1939, Bing often recorded with
brother Bob's orchestra and "Bobcats". The personnel varied from time
to time but usually included, among many others, Zeke Zarchy or Max
Herman, tpt; Matty Matlock or Arthur "Doc" Rando, clar; Eddie Miller,
sax; Bob Haggart, bass; and Ray Bauduc, drm; with the arrangements of
Paul Wetstein (later, Weston).

5 July, 1939 (MON) - Decca Studios, Hollywood
                    Victor Young Orchestra

DLA 1808   Decca 2878
                       Mine - voc Shirley Ross, accompanied by The
                       Foursome

DLA 1809   Decca 2878
                       That Certain Feeling - voc Shirley Ross,
                       accompanied by The Foursome

29 July, 1939 (SAT) - Decca Studios, Hollywood
                    Victor Young Orchestra (incl. Perry Botkin,
                        guit; Spike Jones, drm)

DLA 1850-A   Decca 18543
                       Zing! Went the Strings Of My Heart - voc
                       Judy Garland

DLA 1851-A   BR 02969
                       I'm Just Wild About Harry - voc Judy Garland

DLA 1852-A   Unissued
                       Swanee - voc Judy Garland

DLA 1853-A   Decca 18543
                       Fascinating Rhythm - voc Judy Garland

Jones may have played the Victor Young, Judy Garland session of 16 Oct 39 (DLA 1868/71) as well as the many other Victor Young sessions for Judy Garland. While it is speculation, it is also a fair assumption to place Spike in the film orchestra for the many films scored at this time by Victor Young, including <u>Wizard of Oz</u>.

Linda Lee, daughter of Pat and Spike Jones, was born on October 23rd, 1939.

It was about this time that Spike put himself into the hands of an agent to aid in his promotion and a business manager who handled all his personal affairs. Spike and Pat were given an allowance, with the balance, after fees, saved or invested. With the quantity of work he was involved with, Spike soon paid off his first house mortgage!

Colleague Jimmy Thomasson, trombonist and special effects man, recalls "We were working with Oscar Bradley on the Screen Actors Guild radio show and each Sunday at rehearsal Spike would show up with his newly acquired cowbells and horns, purchased during the week. Of course the cowbells and horns were not used on the show and it puzzled us why he was gathering all those silly gadgets.

"Shortly after Spike was on this spree, Johnny Cascales, a tenor saxophone player and terrific arranger, put a band together, changed his name to Johnny Richards, and got a job at a night club in the Los Angeles area. Spike was in this band and it was at this time that he signed up with an agent. All of us were sure he was cracking-up because the agent was taking all of his income, doleing out a scant cost-of-living payment and retaining a 10% fee. It became quite evident that by retaining this agent Spike not only got the proper exposure, he also learned to budget himself." (Thomasson, written communication, 15 Aug 1982)

It is rumored but as yet unconfirmed that Spike has been identified in the Dead End Kids (or "Little Tough Guys") Universal movie <u>Give Us Wings</u>. There is no Leo Gorcey involvement, and Spike is on screen for approximately two minutes. Date: c.1939/40.

15 December, 1939 (FRI) - Decca Studios, Hollywood
John Scott Trotter's Frying Pan Five

DLA 1909-A/B   Decca 2999 and 11030
                      Sweet Potato Piper (film: "Road To Singapore")
                      voc Bing Crosby assisted by The Foursome

Although remembered in later years by Arthur Rando as "a complete musician and one of the finest legitimate drummers in the business - and the most sought after drummer during the 'Radio Days'" (Rando, written communication, 18 Mar 1984), Spike was thriving on the constant work and the money it brought in, but did not enjoy being an unknown beyond his colleagues. He wanted to be a leader, to have a band of his own.

Now handled by an agent and a business manager (who gave him an allowance which everyone recalls as not quite adequate - Spike always had to borrow a couple of dollars until his next payday), Jones tried several ventures which helped define his future. He became the A & R (Artist and Repertoire) Director for Cinematone Records. A very responsible position in any recording company, the A&R Rep was a musician/sound engineer/talent scout/politician and public relations man. Spike tried to institute "Penny Phono" (Phonograph). Second-rate bands were to cut sides for the small booth-sized juke boxes which were to play at a penny per selection. This was short-lived when it was realized that juke boxes were having a difficult time, in these post-depression, pre-war times, at a nickel a play, let alone a penny! Cinamatone Records were unusual in that it is reported they had a constant groove speed, i.e.: as the needle traveled nearer the center, the pitch (sound vibrations) increased. There is a known photograph of a "Penny Phono" group with Spike with an unknown band.

Del Porter's Foursome had just broken up, and each was working with other vocal/instrumental groups in Los Angeles. Porter, who

11

had a flair for lyric and song writing, had formed a music publishing company, finding a market for his light-hearted and often humorous songs. One of Porter's partners in the song publishing business, called "Tune Towne Tunes", was pianist Carl Hoefle. Hoefle moved his family from Chicago in 1938, living in the San Fernando Valley until 1940. He was not in the area very long before he and Porter combined business and song-writing talents. The Hoefles now lived near "composers row", the tunesmiths of Hollywood and close to Oliver Wallace, an old and, as it will turn out, very important friend.

One of Spike's next ventures was to manage a group, and while he could never lay claim to being successful at this time, it is fortunate that he started an association with this particular combo, "The Feathermerchants", so named because of the "Elfin" or Tyrolean style hats worn with a large feather. The Feathermerchants, started by Porter at Spike's urging, consisted of Del Porter, vocals, bari sax, clarinet and ocarina; Jack Winters, trumpet, personality; Randy Rayburn, piano; Al Glenn, vocals, guitar; Jack Cascales (Johnny Richards brother), bass; and Danny Van Allen, drums. The name lasted longer than their hats.

This group played for dancing, but included what could be called a spontaneous show during their performance. Before each night's show, they talked in general as to what the show would comprise, but invariably surprised themselves at what they could do and get away with. Danny Van Allen, who, after graduating from Long Beach Poly, "trod the boards" on England's Orpheum circuit, but more recently led a small band at the Steel Pier in Atlantic City, splitting the bill with the bands of Phil Harris and Mal Hallett, was the "live-wire", or instigator, of many of their skits. He recalled many of these as "off the top of his head", but also tried to pattern certain skits in the Mal Hallett style, a slow build-up of semi-comedic happenings to a grand flourish - quasi vaudeville. Randy Rayburn had been rehearsal pianist (for sidelining) at MGM, and carried on there for many years afterwards. (He was still in the studios in 1984).

As the Feathermerchants manager, Spike "broke the group in playing for market openings, which were very frequent then. We set up a truck at the curb, played for clowns & singers, etc., rushed into the store to buy food at specials every now and then, and generally tried to amuse whatever crowd assembled. At night there were huge search lights to help draw customers..;I don't believe we used any 'charts', maybe a few, but certainly not a regular book like the big bands had." (Randy Rayburn, written commuication, 13 Nov 1983)

Following this breaking in period, they were booked for the winter tourist season to Easter 1940 at the Santa Rita Hotel in Tucson, Arizona, (where Rayburn recalls being "knocked out" on his first hearing of "Perfidia") then back to Sunset and Vine in Los Angeles and Sardi's Restaurant. There they played three to four nights a week. Their loyal clientele - Dennis Day caught them almost every night - was not large enough to keep the club financially stable. Business was not good at that time for any group and the Feathermerchants, all family men, suffered, as did many other groups dependent upon clubs and casuals for survival. When Spike's checks started to bounce (Sardi's deposits to Spike's business account were insufficient), they reluctantly but quickly folded the Feathermerchants. But Spike learned valuable management lessons, and he was enthralled at the reception their music and shows had received. Some of the shows featured choreographed skits to Porter's "Pass the Biscuits, Mirandy", "Siam" and "Drip, Drip, Drip".

25 June, 1940 (TUES) - FIBBER McGEE AND MOLLY
              NBC Hollywood   Sponsor: Johnsons Wax

            Kiss Me Again - Billy Mills orchestra, with
             audible percussion by Spike Jones, eg:
             cowbell cadenza ala Hotcha Cornia of 1942

22 September, 1940 (SUN) - Columbia Studios, Hollywood
Perry Botkin Orchestra

        Leader, arranger, guitar - Perry Botkin
        Brass - Mannie Klein, Mickey Bloom, Clayton
          Nash, tpt; Ed Kusby, trb;
        Reeds - Joe Krechter, Jack Mayhew, Mort Friedman,
          Dick Clark, clar/sax
        Rhythm - Charlie LaVere, pno; Fred Whiting,
          bass; Spike Jones, drm

LA 2357-A   CO 35815
                Love Of My Life - voc Fred Astaire

LA 2358-A   CO 35852
                Poor Mr. Chisholm - voc Fred Astaire

LA 2359-A   CO 35815
                Me and the Ghost Upstairs - voc Fred Astaire

LA 2360-A   CO 35852
                (I Ain't Hep To That Step, But I'll) Dig It -
                voc Fred Astaire

      Musicians in such an active center had as much work as their
physical capacity would allow. A free-lance musician, not bound by
contract to, for example, a movie studio orchestra, was free to work
(should he be asked) all of the recording and transcription sessions,
casual dance engagements, local shows and club dates, shows and their
allied activites and the private parties which abounded in such a
center of universal entertainment production. But a shroud of
anonymity hovered over the many hundreds of musicians and singers
whose talents were known mainly to their peers and to the leaders who
became famous to the general populace. Most of these elite artists
were happy with the money brought in by the staggering number of work
calls, the constant variety of work (every session was different),
and the anonymity.
      Spike wanted a band - he knew what he wanted, but musically
speaking, didn't know how to go about it. Late in 1940, with the aid
of his Kraft Music Hall colleagues, namely Bruce Hudson, alumnus of
the Ben "The Maestro" Bernie band, on trumpet; King Jackson, trombone; Stan Wrightsman, "Boogie Woogie" specialist on piano; Perry
Botkin (who was playing guitar and acting in the filming at Paramount
of Birth of the Blues with Bing Crosby about this time), guitar/
banjo; and Hank Stern, from New York where he had worked with many
bands in the late 20's, including the original Dorsey Brothers, Joe
Venuti and McKinney's Cotton Pickers, on string bass/tuba. To these
instrumental specialists and personalities was the necessary addition
of Del Porter, who wanted no further involvement as a band leader.
Spike was, however, eager and happy to take the responsibility and
put up with the continuous headaches of starting and running a band.
      He patiently started rehearsing. To Porter's imaginative
instrumental scoring and ideas Spike added from his flotilla of
effects and his penchant for organization.
      He rehearsed not only potential show band repertoire, but
straight dance music as well, for which he needed a ballad singer, a
necessity in those days. Carl Grayson was another very important
figure in the early Jones saga. Having recorded and worked for Henry
Busse, he arrived in Los Angeles while on tour out of Chicago. Mea-
gerly sustaining himself until he became a full Union member, he became well known by leading a small but commercially successful society band in the area. Danny Van Allen (Van Allen, conversation with
author, 10 Sept 1983) remembers that Grayson, a good ballad singer
and a rather handsome individual, was touted as being a newly discovered romantic lead for films but failed the screen test because,
in profile, his nose was too prominent.
      In any case, Grayson (under the smoother, more suave stage
name of Donald Grayson) remained in Los Angeles. The Donald Grayson

Dance band featured his good, but at times, saccharine, vocal stylings and his violin. He was a good, but not serious, violinist. At
this time, no one knew of him beyond being a small group leader,
violinist and straight singer - and he was available to Spike for
rehearsing and gigs.

While rehearsing in his home, and the home of Del Porter,
as well as at an NBC transmission studio beside the Hollywood ceme-
tery, Spike had pretty well settled on the style he wanted to adopt
and the people who could and would help him get his idea under way.
Comedy had always been an attraction and Spike, having a history of
being a zany character, wanted to be a special kind of comedian and
leader - not so much in what he said but in the way he presented his
music. The music he chose to burlesque was theoretically the easiest
to make fun of: country/western music and its poorer cousin, hillbilly music. Any show put on by Spike with his new band had to be
properly choreographed, with the humor a visual stimulant in conjunction with any lyrical and musical humor that could be devised. Experience had shown that exaggeration of the obvious always brought a
laugh, and it was this emphasis that, with his percussion equipment
in exaggerated proportions - e.g., a set of chromatically tuned cowbells, washboards to emphasize rhythms, brake drums which produced
(sometimes) sympathetic vibrations to standard musical keys, bulb car
horns of different pitches and sounds, a pistol, many whistles and
sundry effects - slowly helped to develop an identifiable sound.
A great deal of time was spent fabricating a "corny" style.
Once a tune was selected, the arrangement was basically born of
Porter's fertile imagination and experience with a blend of everyone's ideas, including Spike's. At his home, Spike provided food and
drink while ideas were bounced around, then penciled (there were many
erasures as the various effects were indicated and written at pitch,
tried and continually re-worked) on a score by Porter. Choreography
was included as the chosen tune was continually rehearsed and edited,
with home recordings used for critical analysis. This process initially took days as they were creating, at a very high level, a composite of the many forms of entertainment they had encountered in
their considerable and varied careers which ranged from the silent
era comics to the current and very popular radio and stage comedians.
The '30s "Poet & Peasant" soundie and other movies of Milt Britton
were very influential to Spike for many years. Not all tunes chosen
made it to performance and not all that were performed made it to
commercial recording. Carl Hoefle attended all rehearsals and for
many years was their stand-by pianist. Spike was the monitor,
determining what was and what was not acceptable.
Everything was well rehearsed rather than spontaneous and
based loosely on the concept of the Feathermerchants and their shows,
which in turn was based on a format of the famous Mal Hallett show
band. Their own experiences in performing and accompanying all the
successful radio, movie and vaudeville comedians of the generation
told them that only those acts which were so well rehearsed as to
appear spontaneous had a chance of getting reaction from, and lasting
with, the paying public.
All of their show titles were primarily visual, built around
the actions and antics of each - the chief clown being Spike, trying
to get his pre-arranged sound effects in their proper and rehearsed
place. Their minimal dialogue was also scripted. His arsenal of effects was, it appeared, haphazardly placed around the bandstand -
seemingly out of reach. His washboards, important for the basic audible rhythm behind the melody, and a few of his auto horns were perch-
ed on a roughly built stand, while his set of tuned cowbells and
similar effects were laid out on a large flat stand, much in the
manner of a xylophone with a roughly built front and side cover. It
all looked as if it had been towed in from the hills.
The Jonathan Club in downtown Los Angeles was a private,
multi-storied, men-only (until 1984) club catering to the musical,
entertainment and business personalities of Hollywood - a professional club where the individual members of the group were well known.
"The Club" booked many bands for mixed dinner/dancing and through his

constant promotion, Spike secured a weekly booking. The audience were
his severest critics - or biggest fans. It was these week-end playdates which kept the group together initially and beyond their first
RCA session, as the members looked upon them as added income, or re-
compense for their many free rehearsals for Spike and, no doubt,
relaxation from their own demanding studio schedules.

Having learned from his failure with the Feathermerchants,
Spike, as agent/manager/player, was able to book the Donald Grayson
Dance Band into the Jonathan. Locally, Grayson was a well known band
leader and he "fronted" the band that Spike put together. The Grayson
band started with nine players late in 1940 but soon dropped to seven
(plus Spike as leader). He could see that this Saturday night combination of regular dance and show band outlet had the potential for
success. Their show was short, not more than 15 minutes at a time,
and was visually entertaining - the basic necessity. In tuxedos, and
later in rudimentary costumes, their effervescent performances were
slanted to the "corny", or hillbilly style from which the best were
honed for recording.

In the Jones estate files were a number of practice acetate
recordings. Some, with NBC labels, were done on professional equipment while the balance, with Cinematone labels or unlabled, were also
done on professional equipment, but at home.

All but one of the discs are undated and belong to the
late 1940 to '41 time period. Most of the 10" & 11" Cinematone and
NBC discs have typed labels: "Spike Jones Orchestra" or "Spike Jones
Band". Discs without labels were grease-penciled with abbreviated
song titles. A scant few had "7 men" & "9 men" penciled onto a paper
label. The following are "straight" titles from the Cinematone/blank
labeled discs, with the exception of the first two, which are NBC.
Having locked run-out grooves but no lead-in groove, these discs were
for home use only.

I Wonder Who's Kissing Her Now? - voc Donald Grayson (NBC)
Don't Talk To Me About Men - voc Cindy Walker (NBC)
Hot Lips - voc Del Porter
Caravan - inst
Fine and Dandy - inst
The Nearness of You - voc Donald Grayson
Medley No. 1:
    You're Driving Me Crazy - inst
    Am I Blue? - inst
    I Wonder Who's Kissing Her Now? - voc Donald Grayson
    Chant of the Jungle - inst
    Dream House - inst
Medley No. 2:
    I'll Never Smile Again - inst
    Make Believe Island - voc Donald Grayson
    Imagination - inst

While well played, the arrangements are archaic in style,
even for this era, and show that Spike would have had strong competition from the established bands working casuals had he decided to
run a straight band only. Personnel on these titles ranged from seven
to nine players. On a few, particularly Medley No. 2, there is evidence of strenuous but happy rehearsals as there are many breakdowns
in "I'll Never Smile Again" until it is acceptable. Their performance
standard was high and anything less, even for a home recording, was
personally unacceptable, regardless of their already having done a
full days "blowing" in the various studios.

King Jackson and Stan Wrightsman wrote most, if not all, of
the "straight" arrangements.

More of the "Spike Jones Band" practice discs of this period, preserved on a blank labeled 16" acetate and 12"-16" NBC acetates, show the following titles have been rehearsed in the new
style, with some almost ready for commercial recording:
    She Wouldn't Do - What I Asked Her To - voc Porter, Jackson.
        four takes (actually "straight"), nice Jackson trombone
        ala Teagarden - a good blues number (16" acetate)

I'll Lend You Everything I've Got (Except My Wife, and I'll
    Make You a Present of Her) - voc Jackson (2 takes), un-
    known voice (2 takes) - very corny succession of effects
    (16" acetate, very similar, but musically superior, to
    the Korn Kobblers transcription version)
Fix Up the Spare Room, Mother - voc Del Porter (sounds like
    a Porter/Hoefle song - humorous lyrics)
Red Wing - voc Del Porter (different intro to Bluebird)
Sweet Adeline - voc Del Porter (too corny to be commercially
    useful)
Behind Those Swinging Doors - voc Del Porter (extended
    verses, each concluding with a belch of increasing
    intensity)
Beautiful Eggs - voc Del Porter (actually "straight" -
    varied arr. and up-tempo from rejected Bluebird)
Barstool Cowboy from Old Barstow - voc Del Porter (identical
    to Bluebird release)
Covered Wagon Rolled Right Along - voc Del Porter
    (identical to Bluebird, but with extended verses)

    This small representation of the band's rehearsals is not in
chronological sequence and overlap with the "straight" titles previously listed. The quality of some performances also suggests that
these discs represent rehearsals into late 1941. The male choir heard
on some titles would be the trio of Porter, Grayson and Jackson. One
12" NBC acetate is dated 21 Jan 41 (TUES), indicating that it was cut
in the studio prior to rehearsal for, during a break, or, more likely
after the Fibber McGee and Molly show. "She Wouldn't Do..." is the
dated title, with "I'll Lend You.." on the flip side; both have been
been polished from the previous home attempts.
    Spike's musicians actually objected to being called "side
men" and in many respects, this was a cooperative venture with the
mutual idea of helping Spike make his first recording session. With
an average age of 30, the musicians had "paid their dues" - all were
thoroughly professional. Their unabashed drive and verve was derived
from the exceptional skill and quality of the musicians who performed: the energetic and staccato drive of the banjo, much like the
early jazz bands but more soloistic; Spike's rhythm on the washboard,
alternating with the drum trap set and other conspicuous effects; the
use of a tuba instead of string bass; the corny melodic and harmonic
phrasing of the front line trumpet, clarinet and trombone; the quick
melodic shifts among all instruments; the unusual trombone technique
called the "fonk" - humorously reminiscent of a flatulent faux pas;
and good muting effects with the brass. Spike seldom played drums
during these "corny" show pieces, but examples can be heard on the
Bluebird releases of "Barstool Cowboy", "Come Josephine" and "Clink
Clink".

    A dispute between broadcasters and ASCAP (American Society
of Composers, Authors and Publishers) over increased fees had come to
a head. Beginning 31 Dec 40, it became an infringement to broadcast
any ASCAP music, and in anticipation of this dispute, Broadcast Music
Inc. (BMI) was organized from 14 Oct 39. A truce was declared in August 1941, but in the meantime, only tunes licensed through BMI,
SESAC and the many public domain tunes (e.g., Stephen Forster songs,
adapted classics) were broadcast.
    A small group from the Trotter Orchestra, led by Spike,
provided rustic (corny) accompaniment to Crosby's regularly featured
Bob Burns, the "Arkansas Traveler", and his creation, the "bazooka".

27 March, 1941 (THURS) - KRAFT MUSIC HALL*
        NBC Hollywood   6:00 to 7:00 PM PST

        Bing Crosby, with John Scott Trotter's Orchestra
        (Spike Jones, audible drum effects)

        Peanut Vendor - inst, with Bob Burns, bazooka

                            16

3 April, 1941 (THURS) - KRAFT MUSIC HALL*
NBC Hollywood   6:00 to 7:00 PM PST

       Bing Crosby, with John Scott Trotter's Orchestra
       (Spike Jones, audible drum effects)

       Ta-Ra-Ra Boom-De-Aye! - Bob Burns, bazooka

10 June, 1941 (TUES) - FIBBER McGEE AND MOLLY
NBC Hollywood

       with Harlow Wilcox, announcer, and the Billy Mills
       Orchestra (Spike Jones, percussion effects)

       The Chewel Song - voc The Kings Men

     The rehearsals at the various studios brought Spike into
contact with Cindy Walker, who became one of Country Music's greatest
composers. Miss Walker, recently arrived in Hollywood from Texas, had
her first published song, "Lone Star Trail", recorded by Bing Crosby.
Dave Kapp of Decca Records was impressed and offered her a recording
contract, resulting in her first hit, "Don't Talk To Me About Men".
Her songs, though steeped in Western lore and tradition, show modern
melodic and harmonic invention while running the gamut of human
emotions and musical styles. They soon became the staple repertoire
for such artists as Gene Autry, the Sons of the Pioneers, Tex Ritter,
Roy Rogers and Dale Evans, etc, etc. She also wrote songs for Holly-
wood's Soundies, the studios of Universal, Republic and Monogram
Pictures. She has written the themes, songs and music for the Billy
Graham motion pictures and has found the time to write a hymn book.
Cindy Walker has always been a writer-member of BMI, as were Del
Porter, Carl Hoefle and Tune Towne Tunes.
     More recently, the Walker songs of "Distant Drums" in the
'50s and "Cherokee Maiden" of 1976, as recorded by Jim Reeves and
Merle Haggard respectively, were No. 1 country and western hits. She
also authored many of the Roy Orbison hits of the early '60's.
     The name of Spike's show band, should he actually be able to
keep it working, was a problem. Apparently there were several names
to choose from, as "Spike Jones Band/Orchestra" (as written on the
practice record labels) would not have had the needed or lasting
impact. "City Slickers" was but one name under consideration, but
Spike hesitated, as "city slicker" in '20's and '30's jargon was a
less than complimentary term. It was usually applied to a sly,
street-wise urbanite who took advantage of his not-so-wise country
cousins - not an endearing choice (at first thought). Miss Walker
heard Spike rehearsing in one of the studios and, liking what she
heard, asked Spike and his new group to back her on her first transcription and recording. Spike, who spent a good part of each day in
the various studios, met with Cindy Walker and her arranger, Dolor
(Dan) Michaud. They had to determine which of Walker's arms full of
songs were to be arranged, rehearsed and transcribed. One of her more
humorous, hillbillyish tunes was called "Gonna Stomp Those City
Slickers Down". Her suggestion to Spike that "City Slickers" would be
a good name for the group helped him to make up his mind.
     In the broadest sense of the term, they would truly be "City
Slickers" - street-wise urbanites, the cream of the musical crop, and
they were about to poke fun at what they considered their poorer
cousins - country/western and hillbilly music.
     Michaud, who had arranged extensively for vaudeville and then
movies, received his early musical training in Paris, France, and returned to the U.S. in the early 1900's. Well into his 50's by this
time, his effective charts for Miss Walker show economy bred of ma-
turity. Michaud's subsequent arrangement of "Gonna Stomp..." fit
Spike's original conception of the "City Slickers" like a glove.

7 July, 1941 (MON) - POINT SUBLIME*
NBC Hollywood   8:30 to 9:00 PM PST

with guests, "Duke Daniels and his City Slickers"

Blues My Naughty Sweetie Gave To Me - voc
    Del Porter
(A) Hot Time In the Old Town Tonight - inst

Spike used the "Duke Daniels" pseudonym not only for the value of testing unsuspecting colleages and friends reactions to his City Slickers music as broadcast, but still a cooperative group - the show band (formed mainly to help Spike get that first recording session) was not his - yet. "Duke Daniels" was a name pulled out of the air. Bruce Hudson has mentioned that he also played the slide whistle for Spike and did "Doowackadoo" solos. Hudson's slide whistle is prominent on this "Sublime" show.

Tune In Yesterday, a book on vintage radio by John Dunning, describes Point Sublime (produced by Robert Redd, who also produced the Kraft Music Hall for NBC) as a situation comedy-drama set in a fictitious little village on the Pacific coast, pop. 750. It portrayed a way of life all but lost in 20th century America, and was brought to NBC in December 1940. The characters on this West-coast-only show were built around the voices of Cliff Arquette, Earle Ross, Verna Felton, Harold Peary, Mel Blanc, Lou Merrill and Fred MacKaye. The program details are unknown and only these two titles in the Jones files have survived.

The personnel seldom varied from Grayson, Porter, Botkin, Stern and Wrightsman. When King Jackson was otherwise booked, Jimmy Thomasson, trombone, "subbed". While Bruce Hudson played the studio rehearsals (usually NBC), Frank Wylie, trumpet, did the home rehearsals and played the Jonathan from the start. Don Anderson (who worked the Fibber McGee show with Spike) replaced Wylie in the seven-piece Jonathan group on July 19, then replaced Hudson after August 8. Anderson's diary of this period shows that he was booked and paid by Spike while at "The Club".

There was always the certainty that due to their professional commitments elsewhere, his colleagues would not all be free for rehearsals and playdates. Spike had to have a reserve of musicians to fill these gaps when this occurred. Also advertising that he was starting a band, Spike auditioned many musicians, young and old. Two of the many instrumentalists/personalities who unsuccessfully tried out for the new band were Cecil Johnson (4'11") on tuba, and Marshall "Tiny" Rips (over 6') on clarinet and slide whistle.

Johnny Richards 18-piece band was playing nightly at the Trianon Ballroom in South Gate about this time. Remote b'casts also originated from there. Dan Michaud's daughter, Dorothy Rae, was a dancer in his show and vividly recalls Spike and his group (the nucleus of the Richards band) playing their new style of music on the dance floor during intermission while wearing mountaineer tall pointed hats, long beards and fake bare feet over their shoes (there is a known photo of this group). After the war, Horace Heidt bought and and successfully worked out of the Trianon and Miss Rae danced at the club for Heidt.

The Slicker "tag" or ending, became exclusively associated with Spike Jones.

All, or nearly all of their show tunes ended with this "tag", or a variation on it.

It did not show on record until the first RCA session of 1942 although it was put to good use on the 7 July Point Sublime show. Del Porter uses it to conclude his opening clarinet chorus in "Red Wing" on 8 Aug. In a much later interview, Porter acknowledges this "tag" evolving after being introduced during a home rehearsal by Frank Wylie. In later years, the famed composers/arrangers Henry Mancini and Billy May, among others, used this "tag" to capriciously conclude two of their specific arrangements: "Tico-Tico" from "The Latin Sound of Henry Mancini" RCA album, and May in "The Sheik of Araby" in his 1955 "Sorta-Dixie" Capitol album. Henry Mancini "had no clue as to the actual origin of the phrase" (Mancini, written communication, 28 Nov 1983). However, Billy May says "I guess I lifted it from Spike, but it is a phrase that goes back to the Ragtime era (early 20's). I remember a piano player named "Zez" Confrey that used that ending and its variations on old piano solo records" (May, written communication, 20 July 1983). Confrey wrote "Kitten on the Keys", "Stumbling" and "Dizzy Fingers".

Spike, no stranger to any studio or recording executive, could have recorded his group with any of the three major companies of Decca, Columbia or RCA Victor, and it is fortunate that he was able to interest RCA's A&R Representative, Harry Meyerson, with samples from among their home recordings. Meyerson, in turn, persuaded his boss and West coast RCA producer Leonard Joy to book Spike Jones and his City Slickers into RCA's Hollywood studios for August 8th. (The well-known Leonard Joy Orchestra backed such artists as Morton Downey, Kenny Baker, J. Fred Coots, Sam Coslow and Billy Daniels). The releases were to be on their budget label, Bluebird.

Meyerson is credited with producing such acclaimed hits of Freddy Martin as "Tonight We Love", "Symphony", "Bumble Boogie", "Warsaw Concerto" and many, many others.

It is sometimes difficult to imagine the schedules that musicians must keep, especially a very enterprising individual such as Spike. His own work calendar would have been full, and as well, there were meetings with Cindy Walker, promotion of the group (soon to be his own) with the major recordings studios and transcription services, and rehearsals, rehearsals, rehearsals. Each of the band had their own work calls, casuals, individual practice and constant rehearsals with Spike.

The following sketch of Don Anderson's career from 1941 to 1943 will give some indication of the types and extent of work a free-lance musician would be called upon to perform, assuming he (or she) was among this cadre of first-class musicians found in any of the world's big cities. A great diversity of styles and techniques and mental flexibility were necessary to be a "heavy" in this unique environment.

From Minnesota, Don Anderson settled in Los Angeles in 1936, having studied there a few years earlier. Continuing with the legendary Louis Maggio, Anderson kept meticulous accounts of his career and has kindly consented to their use. All of the leaders names that follow appear in Anderson's diaries covering the period 1941 to 1943. Very few of the following entries were singular bookings and most were continuous. Many of the names were known only locally while others were nationally and internationally famous. Work calls with Jones are not listed, as they follow in the statistical chronology.

Don Anderson worked for the movie studios of: MGM (for the Navy Show); RKO (Principal Artists Production); Hal Roach "Soundies"; Universal Studios, including Walter Lantz Productions; Republic Pictures; Paramount; "subbed" in the trumpet section for the soundtrack to Zenda; United Artists, with Abe Meyer: for the local radio shows from KHJ; KFWB; KECA; KMPC, with Don Hopkins; KNX "Hollywood Show Case": the national b'casts of Gildersleeve; Fibber McGee and Molly; Screen Guild; Al Jolson and Date with Judy, with Gordon Jenkins; Chase & Sanborn, with Paul Whiteman; Shirley Temple; Rudy Vallee summer series; Amos n' Andy, with Lud Gluskin; Abbott & Costello; Bank of America; "Over There" Treasury Show with Gordon Jenkins; Alec Templeton Show; Dick Haymes with Lou Bring: casuals and/or b'casts for the various sized groups of: Al Pierce; Gordon Jenkins; Hap Hazard; Muzzy Marcellino; Judy Canova (audition only); Mischa Russell; Bob Crosby on Swing Shift & Coke Show; Nat Young; Ransom Sherman; Eddie Miller; Phil Ohman; Rudy (Rudolph) Friml Jr; Lennie Conn; David Rose on auditions, dances, transcriptions; Tony Martin Show and KHJ b'cast; Freddie Slack, dances & recordings; Bill Gilcher; Johnny Richards at Casa Manana; Ray Bargy b'casts; Tommy Riggs; Lou Bring; Marty Malneck; Paul Martin: transcriptions for Lou Kosloff; Billy Mills and Paul Wetstein; Malcolm Beelby; "Cally" Holden; Mischa Levienne; Jimmy Dietrick; "Fuz" Menge; Garwood Van (for a 12 hour 20th Century Fox party!); Claude Sweetan; "Mickey" Whalen; Al Sack; Larry Kent; Ray Hendricks; Manny Harmon; John Boyd;

Art Whiting; Art Crippen (many dances at $8.82); Bob Mohr; Ballet at the Hollywood Bowl; Musicians Union benefit dance; plus these unknown musical bookings: Beechnut on NBC; "Campana"; Decca recording. There were also two tax refunds from Ray Noble during 1941. From 1937 to '39, Anderson had played and recorded with: Seger Ellis and his Choirs of Brass (along with King Jackson, John Stanley and Stan Wrightsman); Ray Noble (along with Frank Leithner); and Ben Pollack.

And now to the first recording session of Spike Jones and his City Slickers, but first a word about their transcriptions. Electrical Transcriptions, usually abbreviated as ET, were cut in the major studios during time leased by the various transcription companies. In Jones' case, Jack Richardson's Standard usually recorded though NBC or RCA facilities, using allotments of matrices, or recording numbers from RCAs daily sequence. ETs were usually recorded in a three-hour session, as were commercial discs, but were cut into 16" vinyl blanks playing at 33-1/3 RPM which were not microgroove. Ten titles, five per side, could be recorded, but inadequate time for rehearsal and balance per title usually resulted in "clinkers" (mis-pitched notes), poor instrumental balance and thin, often anemic sound - leaving much to be desired. Not for sale, ETs were leased to the individual broadcasting stations and presented the major artists performing alternate versions of their popular selections, introduced new songs to gauge public reaction and often gave fledgling groups not having recording contracts with major companies valuable exposure over the air.

Certain aspects of the Slickers first five ETs, excluding the three Cindy Walker discs, should be considered in light of the background presented. Each ET has a certain number of "straight" titles to fill out the required ten cuts. Spike could not put ten Slickers titles on each ET for the simple reason that the group did not have that many titles rehearsed to a recording standard. He had to "pad" each session. Some ardent collectors of purely Slickers music bemoan these "straight" titles but it is fortunate that they were recorded as they should be considered progressively representative of the type and style played at the important Jonathan Club dinner/dance dates.

The "straight" style shows noticable progress in all facets: the vocal trio, then quartet, known as the Boys in the Back Room are easily the best singing group within the Slickers to appear on record; the pleasant style of Carl (Donald) Grayson; the relaxed, bluesy and jazz-flavored style of King Jackson; the instrumental scoring becoming more intricate and interesting. If you can, make a dubbing of these "straight" titles - eighteen in all if you omit the flag-waver "Yankee Doodler". You will then have several dance sets that would have been played at the Jonathan!

Del Porter, showing excellent style, sings the basic but ever expanding Slickers repertoire (which were mostly his songs). This "corny" style shows increasing assuredness with each passing session. At no time during the course of these sessions did any of the members have an inkling of the eventual and phenomenal success of the group. In many respects, their efforts are unpretentious - professional musicians working hard, doing their job well, and having a good time.

The August RCA session was on a one-time only basis while the success and comment on them would determine if more sessions were to follow. The records sold, although sales were termed only mildly successful. Their local popularity at the Jonathan, ensured by the variety of slick arrangements to popular and jazz-flavored tunes, western ballads and swing, plus a goodly number of Porter-Hoefle songs and abetted by Spike's constant promotion (at which he was becoming very smooth), no doubt helped generate the succession of ETs starting in November and the new RCA contract which called for a session every three months starting early in 1942.

Having complete musical respect for each other, they worked well together. Del Porter and Carl Hoefle were less involved with the studios. Porter concentrated on creating for the Slickers and Hoefle became a booker, while both also composed and ran their publishing firm.

Although the following items are not in sequence, background on the two radio shows which sustained the Slickers and kept their name and music in the public mind during the years of the recording ban are now included. The last semi-final thought: Europe and the British Empire had been at war with Hitler's Germany since September 1939, and on December 7, 1941, the Japanese attack on Pearl Harbor brought the U.S. into World War II, a very important event in the ultimate success of Spike Jones and his City Slickers.

BOB BURNS SHOW

The Bob Burns Show started as "The Arkansas Traveler" show and later became "The Lifebuoy Show". Having been with Bing Crosby and the later Kraft Music Hall since 1935, after a very brief fling in films (The Cockeyed World, Rhythm on the Range), Burns tried on occasion to break away on his own, succeeding in 1941 with "The Arkansas Traveler". This comedy-variety show premiered on CBS, 16 Sept for Campbell Soups. Remaining in this Tuesday night slot for the season, the newly named "Bob Burns Show" moved to Wednesdays the following year for Lever Bros. before moving to NBC on Thursdays early in 1943.

The show developed its format around this tall-tale-teller whose legends and embellishments were the trademark and core of his act. Based on the theme "Arkansas Traveler", the Burns folksy comedy and rural monologues were ably abetted by the fast-talk delivery of Dick Lane on commercials and general topics. From the announcer's booth came the voice of Larry Keating to finish the show with a commercial for Lifebuoy, Vimms Vitamins or Rinso "White" (all Lever products), or promotion for the "Amos 'n Andy" show. Keating later appeared in the TV role of Harry, Burns and Allen's next door neighbor. On many of the 1942-43 season shows, the Memphis, Tennessee (Deep South) inflections of "Cousin" Luther Roundtree were a perfect foil to the Hollywood Hillbilly from Van Buren, Arkansas, Robin Burns.

In his earlier years with Bing and also as his summer replacement, Burns became somewhat famous with his "Bazooka", which was originally a gas pipe about 3 feet long with a whiskey funnel on one end - a very fat post-horn, or megaphone, with an extension. Music was produced by a combination of humming and vibrating ones lips into the small end (there was no mouthpiece), similar to wordless singing. Simple? Not really, as the performer still had to produce, as a singer would, the correct musical pitch. The pipe's short length, coupled with its large bore (about 2-1/2 inches in diameter), rendered it acoustically impossible to use as an open (or closed) ended tube, and having no fundamental tone or overtones (harmonic series), its range was limited to that of the soloist's voice. A tenor trombone played with a loose embouchure will give a good facsimile of the sound Burns produced.

Why Burns termed it a "Bazooka" is a matter of conjecture. However, the U.S. Army christened their over-the-shoulder rocket launcher of WWII after this unique Burns creation.

NBC produced two versions of each 30-minute broadcast, one for each coast. Spike Jones and his City Slickers provided all music for the two seasons 1942-44 - generally one feature selection and all necessary theme, cue, fill music and accompaniment. The pianist attended all rehearsals for two days prior and sketched arrangements. The show day consisted of a three hour rehearsal, then a dress rehearsal finishing with the 5:00 PM PST transmission for the East Coast. The West Coast version went out at 8:00 PM, with a noticable difference in the humor.

FURLOUGH FUN

Furlough Fun was first heard on NBC West Coast stations in November 1942 and ran to June '44. It featured music, comedy and interviews with servicemen on furlough. "Femmcee" was Earl Carroll's girl-friend, Beryl Wallace, and the announcer was Larry "Checks" Keating, so named as he did so many radio shows that his wallet was always full of un-cashed checks.

A topical comedy routine was developed by George Riley and all music was supplied by Spike Jones and his City Slickers, an integral part of the show, with the theme being "Pack Up Your Troubles".

The same day rehearsal/b'cast was sponsored by the Gilmore Oil Company, and Furlough Fun has occasionally been referred to as the Gilmore Oil Show. Two Gilmore commercials (written by Del Porter "for peanuts") were played each week; one being a parody on a different standard or public domain melody, while the other, in vaudeville or music hall style, was always:

"Don't use just any old gasoline in your machine,
'cause it might make your motor sound like this -
    (different effect each week)
Red Lion Gas you'll prefer, because it makes your
    motor purr like this--"
    (long trombone glissando-chord)

The show was very relaxed and loose, with weekly cash awards for articles (e.g., a used dog collar) motorists would submit on a Gilmore entry form. Cash prizes were also awarded for correctly answering skill-testing questions on popular subjects.

An interesting feature was a weekly on-the-air recording sent to an interviewed serviceman's wife or girl-friend. The recording was first dedicated by the person, then the Slickers played and sang a "straight" song, featuring many of the day's popular songs.

This "Furlough Fun" information has been taken from known 12" acetates mainly in the Jones estate files. Spike engaged International Artists, the same company that pressed the Burns shows, to provide him with copies of all Slickers music as played. This was for personal critical evaluation and to gauge the audience reaction, as new titles were auditioned on Gilmore before the national Burns shows.

The discs are marked part 1, or part 2, - up to four, and dated, establishing a sequence. However, only two shows have survived in their entirety and of the remaining dated discs, only a partial listing is possible. In many cases too, acetates are undated, lost or never existed and consequently the first three months are scarcely represented, with gaps appearing throughout the duration.

Interestingly, the acetates in the Jones files were dubbed from ETs, indicated by several having false starts - to change needles, perhaps. Possibly the entire "Furlough Fun" series is still on disc - somewhere.

Selected Bibliography

Alden, Ken. "Facing the Music", This Week, Nov 1943.

ASCAP. Biographical Dictionary (third edition), New York: Bowker, 1966. Compiled by Lynn Farnol Group.

Bergreen, Laurence. Look Now, Pay Later: The Rise of Network Broadcasting. New York: New American Library/Mentor Book, 1980.

Bernard, Tom. "Six Nights In a Madhouse", American, Jul 1949.

Berton, Ralph. Remembering Bix. New York: Harper and Row, 1974.

Bigsby, Evelyn. "Der Fuehrer's Face", This Week, 29 Nov 1942.

Broadcast Music Incorporated.
Performindex No. 3. copyright 1952 by BMI, New York.
Performindex No. 4. copyright 1954 by BMI, New York.
Performindex No. 5. copyright 1958 by BMI, New York.

Connor, D. Russell and Hicks, Warren W. BG - On the Record, a Bio-Discography of Benny Goodman. New Rochelle: Arlington House, 1969.

Delaunay, Charles. New Hot Discography. New York: Criterion Music Corporation, 1948.

Dorson, Art. Spike Jones interview, KNX Los Angeles, 14 Oct 1944.

Dunning, John. Tune In Yesterday: The Ultimate Encyclopedia of Old-Time Radio, 1925-1976. Englewood Cliffs, N.J.: Prentice-Hall, 1978.

Flower, John. Moonlight Serenade, a Bio-discography of the Glenn Miller Civilian Band. New Rochelle: Arlington House, 1972.

Gentile, Larry. Spike Jones interview, CKLW Windsor, Ont., 4 Apr 1948.

Gorner, Bob. Spike Jones interview, KQW San Francisco, 10 Mar 1944.

Henshaw, Laurie. "Chaos Comes to Town!", Melody Maker, 9 Sept 1944.

Hering, Ted. unpublished Spike Jones bibliography copyright 1965, 1982.

- - -   taped, unpublished Del Porter interview, 3 Jun 1971.

Katz, Mickey, as told to Hannibal Coons. Papa, Play For Me.
       New York: Simon and Schuster, 1977.

Kaye, Joseph. "Spike Jones Tells His Own Story", True Story, Jul 1949.

Kinkle, Roger D. The Complete Encyclopedia of Popular Music and Jazz
       1900-1950. New Rochelle: Arlington House, 1974.

Marshall, Jim. "A Night at the Uproar", Collier's, 10 Jan 1948.

Murrells, Joseph. The Book Of Golden Oldies. London: Barrie and
       Jenkins, 1978.

Othman, Frederick C. "He Plays Louder than Anybody", Saturday
       Evening Post, 10 Apr, 1943.

Robbins, Jhan. "Korn on the Kampus", Varsity, Apr 1949.

Rust, Brian. Jazz Records 1897-1942. Chigwell, England: Storyville
       Publications, 1970.

- - -   The American Dance Band Discography 1917-1942.
       New Rochelle, N.Y.: Arlington House, 1975.

- - -   The Complete Entertainment Discography.
       New Rochelle, N.Y.: Arlington House, 1973.

Sears, Richard S. V-Discs: A History and Discography. Westport,
       Conn.: Greenwood Press, 1980.

Shapiro, Nat. Popular Music (an Annotated Index of American
       Popular Songs). New York: Adrian Press,
              Volume 2, 1965
              Volume 4, 1968
              Volume 5, 1969

Stumpf, Charles K. "Spike Jones", World of Yesteryear, Apr 1978.

Spike with mother (Ada Jones), ca. 1918. Ted Hering collection.

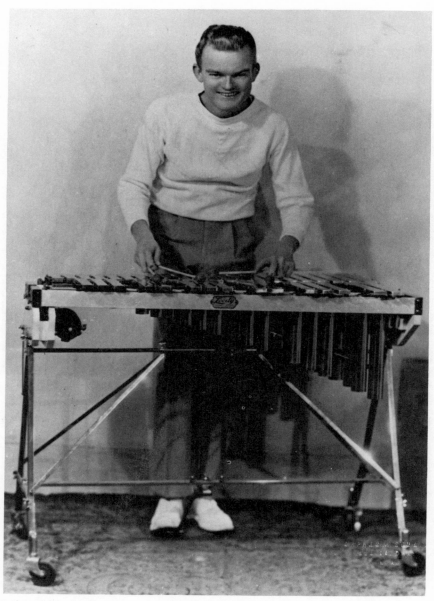

Spike with xylophone at Long Beach Polytechnical School, ca. 1929. Ted Hering collection.

"Command Performance" radio program, September 29, 1942. From left: Spike, Count Basie, Bob "Bazooka" Burns, Lionel Hampton, Tommy Dorsey. Ted Hering collection.

Thank Your Lucky Stars, November, 1942. From left: Country Washburn, Carl Hoefle, Spike, Ralph Dadisman, Luther Roundtree, Del Porter, John Stanley, Carl Grayson. Ted Hering collection.

Meet the People, ca. June, 1943. From left: Luther Roundtree, Carl Hoefle, John Stanley, Red Ingle, Spike, Country Washburn, Del Porter, Don Anderson. Ted Hering collection.

Milwaukee, ca. August, 1943. From left, front row: Beau Lee, Elsa Nilsson, Mr. Schlitz, Eileen Nilsson, Del Porter. Middle row: Red Ingle, Don Anderson, Spike. Back row: Irving (?), Luther Roundtree, Carl Hoefle, Country Washburn. Courtesy of Don Anderson.

Furlough Fun, ca. 1944. From left: Spike, Carl Grayson, Country Washburn, Joe Wolverton, Red Ingle, John Stanley, Beau Lee, Wally Kline, Frank Leithner, Del Porter, Nilsson twins. Courtesy of Wally Kline.

Bring on the Girls, ca. 1944. From left: Red ''Chloe'' Ingle, Wally Kline, Del Porter, Country Washburn, John Stanley, Spike, Beau Lee, Joe Wolverton, Carl Grayson, Herman Crone. Courtesy of Wally Kline.

"The Chamber Music Society of Lower Regent Street," BBC program for Allied forces, September 3, 1944. From left, front row: Herman Crone, Spike, Ron Waldman (R.A.F.), Carl Grayson, Red Ingle. Back row: Elsa Nilsson, Del Porter, Eileen Nilsson, Chick Dougherty, Nick Cochrane. By permission of the British Broadcasting Corporation.

Breakfast in Hollywood, ca. November, 1945. From left: Herman Crone, Zep Meissner, Carl Grayson, Candy Hall, Red Ingle, Chick Dougherty, Spike, Giggie Royce, George Rock, Dick Morgan. Ted Hering collection.

The Other Orchestra, Spring, 1946. From left, left side, front row: Bob Morrow, Theodore Norman, Theodore Klages, Truman Boardman, Al Saparoff, Myron Sandler. Middle row: Maurice Lahmeyer, Hans Bodendorfer, Jerry Jarnagan, Dick Morgan, Herman Crone. Back row: Doc Birdbath, Charlotte Tinsley, Frank Carlson. Right side, front row: Spike (covering Bob Poland), Don Brassfield, Zep Meissner, James Briggs, Red Ingle. Middle row: Willard Culley, Jr., Dick Noel, Chick Dougherty, Harry Rodgers. Back row: Slim Davis, Irving Lewis, Jack Mootz, George Rock. Ted Hering collection.

Spike's birthday on the road, Saint Joseph, Missouri, December 14, 1946. From left: Betsy Mills, Chick Dougherty, Candy Hall, Tommy Gordon, Spike, Zep Meissner, Joe Siracusa, Frankie Little, Joe Wolverton, Dick Morgan (partly hidden), Mickey Katz, Herman Crone, Doodles Weaver, Doc Birdbath, Dick Gardner. Courtesy of Joe Wolverton.

Variety Girl, ca. January, 1947. In foreground, from left: Chick Dougherty, Mary Hatcher, Spike, Dick Morgan. Ted Hering collection.

"The Musical Depreciation Review," ca. 1949. From left, front row: Joe Siracusa, Spike, Dick Morgan, Freddy Morgan, Roger Donley. Middle row: Bill King, Jack Golly, (unidentified woman), George Rock, (unidentified woman), Helen Grayco, Doodles Weaver, Frankie Little, J. L. ("Jr.") Martin. Back row: (?) Greco, Paul Leu, Earle Bennett, Joe Colvin, Purves ("Doc Birdbath") Pullen, (unidentified woman), Dick Gardner, (unidentified woman), Ed Metcalfe. Ted Hering collection.

The City Slickers, 1941–1965: Recordings, Playdates, Radio and Television Shows

8 August, 1941 (FRI) – Victor Studios, Hollywood   1:30 to
                    Harry Meyerson, A & R Rep, present   4:30 PM

              Leader/drums – Spike Jones
              Trumpet – Bruce (Robert) Hudson
              Trombone – King (Kingsley) Jackson
              Clarinet – Del (Delmar Smith) Porter
              Piano – Stanley Wrightsman
              Banjo – Perry Botkin
              Tuba – Hank (Henry) Stern
              Vocals – Del Porter, King Jackson, Carl Grayson
              Effects – Jimmy (James E.) Thomasson

PBS-061517-1   B-11282-B; HMV BD 1169; HMVSK BD 1169;
           (2:25)Red Wing – voc Del Porter
PBS-061517-2 (2:21)Unissued

PBS-061518-1   B-11364-A; V-Disc 125-A;
           (2:27)Barstool Cowboy From Old Barstow – voc
                  Del Porter

PBS-061519-1   B-11282-A; HMV BD 1168-B; 30-0821-B; 20-2507-A;
                44-0029-A/B; HMVS BD 1168; ET AFRS "Basic
                Music Library" P-877; AFRS "Purple Heart
                Album" 182;
           (3:11)Behind Those Swinging Doors – voc Del Porter
PBS-061519-2 (3:01)Unissued

PBS-061520-1   B-11364-B; HMV BD 1169; HMVSK BD 1169;
           (2:46)The Covered Wagon Rolled Right Along – voc
                  Del Porter

      Note: Harry Meyerson's position with RCA was as one of their A & R (Artist and Repertoire) representatives – talent scouts whose duties encompassed organizing and supervising recording sessions for established and new artists. B-11364 was issued 21 Nov 41.
      The names of Carl Grayson and Jimmy Thomasson, the latter a trombonist colleague of Spike's from the Johnny Richards (Cascales) band and the radio show band of Oscar Bradley for the Screen Actors Guild shows, do not appear on the RCA inst. Thomasson's effect, the 'belch' heard in "Behind Those Swinging Doors" and which was known from the earlier practice acetates, is heard in a mild form on the issued take only. Take 2, and the later transcription are 'belch-less'.
      Spike's check to Thomasson read "$30.00, for 3 belches at $10.00 each." Thirty dollars was the usual pay for a three-hour sess-ion. It would appear that non-instrumentalists, usually vocalists and on occasion, effects specialists, were hired by and paid directly by Spike rather than RCA with the consequence that their identities are rarely listed. This procedure is on file pertaining to sessions in later years.(Jimmy Thomasson correspondence, Spike Jones file letter)

Carl Grayson, Spike's dance band 'straight' singer was one of the vocal trio (Porter, Jackson, Grayson) in "Swinging Doors". It is assumed his presence was paid by Spike.

Arrangements attributable to Del Porter, who also plays all Sweet Potato/Penny-whistle solos. RCA double-sided issue 44-0029-A/B may not have been issued, although it is registered in BMI Perform-index No. 3 as having broadcast royalties paid.

"The first time in history that a pistol was fired as a note of music was in Hollywood in 1942(sic), the selection being 'Red Wing'" (Colliers, 10 Jan 49, p. 54)

In early 1941, Spike booked his dance band into the Jonathan as the house band. Playing for dancing, Spike also included a short "Slickers" show of their recorded material and 'rural' repertoire. The vocalists featured were Carl Grayson and King Jackson on the 'straight' titles and the rhythmic Del Porter on the 'Slickers' tunes. Although it is not yet technically correct for the "City Slickers" to be listed as the house band, in actuality - it was.

9 August, 1941 (SAT)

        Spike Jones and his City Slickers dance and
        show at the Jonathan Club
        8:15 PM to 1:00 AM (Pay scale: $10.00)

        Leader/contractor/drums - Spike Jones
        Trumpet - Don Anderson
        Trombone - King Jackson
        Clarinet/sax - Del Porter
        Violin - Donald (Carl) Grayson
        Piano - Stanley Wrightsman
        Guitar/bjo - Perry Botkin
        St bass/tuba - Hank Stern
        Vocals - King Jackson, Carl Grayson, Del Porter
        Arrangements - Del Porter, King Jackson,
           Stanley Wrightsman

Note: On this date, Don Anderson permanently replaces Bruce Hudson who had previously rehearsed with and recorded for Spike on the first Victor session. There is but slight audible difference in their trumpet abilities, so it is possible Spike preferred Anderson's stage personality. Victor recording sheets, and publications whose information is taken from those sheets are in error by listing Bruce Hudson beyond that date. Hudson writes:- "We were all free-lance musicians doing studios, radio shows, record dates, etc. I did several shows with Spike and Perry Botkin - we all decided to make the 1st session and had many rehearsals...That's all I ever did with the City Slickers."

Hudson, an inveterate golfer, briefly retired from music in the 50s' but returned, and as recently as 1982 had multi-tracked on trumpet and alto horn for an album with the great composer/arranger/conductor, Gordon Jenkins. Jenkins was a very individual musician and unusual musical director - he always conducted with his left hand - un-nerving until musicians became used to it. "I never had a better 'lip' in my life", now boasts a proud Hudson.

All of the following Slickers' dates to Sept 43, with the exception of Cindy Walker's first transcription/Decca sessions, as well as the first two Command Performance shows, have been culled from Anderson's diaries of this period. The casuals, including the Jonathan entries, were booked by (or for) Spike and paid as such.

15 August, 1941 (FRI) - Standard Transcription Library
        unknown studio, Hollywood

        Cindy Walker and the City Slickers

Personnel as 9 August, with <u>Ralph Dadisman</u>, tpt, replacing Anderson; delete <u>Stan Wrightsman</u>, add unidentified harmonica player, all for this occasion only.

PMS-061538   ET R-127-1;
(3:05)<u>Salt River Valley</u> - voc Cindy Walker

ET R-127-2;
(2:20)<u>Bear Cat Mountain Gal</u> - voc Cindy Walker

ET R-127-3;
(3:45)<u>Don't Talk To Me About Men</u> - voc Cindy Walker

ET R-127-4;
(3:05)<u>Hillbilly Bill</u> - voc Cindy Walker

ET R-127-5;
(2:30)<u>Don't Count Your Chickens</u> - voc Cindy Walker

PMS-061539   ET R-127-6;
(2:40)<u>I Want Somebody</u> - voc Cindy Walker

ET R-127-7;
(2:45)<u>Ridin' For the Rancho</u> - voc Cindy Walker

ET R-127-8;
(2:50)<u>Round Me Up and Call Me Dogie</u> - voc Cindy Walker

ET R-127-9;
(2:35)<u>Love Has Been the Ruin Of Many A Maid</u> - voc Cindy Walker

ET R-127-10;
(2:30)<u>Barstool Cowboy From Old Barstow</u> - voc Cindy Walker

Note: Arrangements by Dan Michaud. Occasional male chorus background assumed to be Porter, Jackson and Grayson.

"Spike Jones came to me in Hollywood and asked me to write some material for his newly formed combo. I was recording for Decca records at the time and he liked the material I was writing for myself. After hearing his music at a rehearsal hall, I liked it very much and convinced my record producer, Dave Kapp of Decca to let his group play for me on my next session, which I did. I was also slated to make several transcriptions for Standard and asked Spike to play behind me for these sessions also. (Note: Spike's approach to Miss Walker is an excellent example of PR/promotion producing tangible work for 'the Slickers') All 30 titles on these sessions were my compositions." "ET R-127 was released by 15 Sept 41." (Note that the back-up credit is "City Slickers" only, indicitive of a studio group)[★]
(Cindy Walker correspondence 28 Mar 82 & 23 Feb 83)
Don Anderson, previously booked at United Artists for today, could not make this work call with Spike. Ralph Dadisman has written, recalling 'subbing' for Anderson on occasion, but could not be specific on dating. Dadisman worked with Spike on the Kraft Music Hall series from 1937 and they remained close friends.

"Salt River Valley" has also been recorded by the Sons of the Pioneers, Decca 6035; "Don't Talk To Me About Men" has been recorded by Becky Barfield on Crystal 211 and Cindy Walker on Decca; "Hillbilly Bill" has been recorded by Texas Jim Lewis on Decca 5912, and "I Want Somebody" by Cindy Walker" for Decca.

Charlie Barnet recorded at Victor/Hollywood on 14 Aug 41, using the matrices PBS-061531/2/3 & 4.

16 August, 1941 (SAT)
           Jonathan Club dance/show
               (Ralph Dadisman, tpt, for Anderson)

23 August, 1941 (SAT)
           Jonathan Club dance/show

30 August, 1941 (SAT)
           Jonathan Club dance/show

5 September, 1941 (FRI) - Decca Studios, Hollywood

           Cindy Walker

           Personnel similar to 15 Aug, delete King Jackson,
           Carl Grayson

DLA 2730   Decca 6022-B;
        (2:44)He Knew All Of the Answers - voc Cindy Walker

DLA 2731   Decca 5992-A;
        (2:24)Waltz Me Around Again Willie - voc Cindy Walker

DLA 2732   Decca 6022-A;
        (2:22)I Want Somebody - voc Cindy Walker

DLA 2733   Decca 5992-B;
        Don't talk To Me About Men - voc Cindy Walker

Note: Timings are approximate. Date courtesy of Cindy Walker. Arrangements by Dan Michaud. The Slickers are not given label credit.

6 September, 1941 (SAT)
           Jonathan Club dance/show

20 September, 1941 (SAT)
           Jonathan Club dance/show

27 September, 1941 (SAT)
           Jonathan Club dance/show
           9:00 PM to 1:00 AM

4 October, 1941 (SAT)
           Jonathan Club dance/show
           (Pay scale now $12.00)

Note: The recent time and scale change at the Jonathan remain in effect for the next 13 months, with rare exceptions.

11 October, 1941 (SAT)
           Jonathan Club dance/show

18 October, 1941 (SAT)
           Jonathan Club dance/show

25 October, 1941 (SAT)
           Jonathan Club dance/show

27 October, 1941 (MON)
           Under this date in the Anderson diary is:-
           "KFWB 10:00--". Possible Slickers local b'cast

      "Caught Al Jervis's KFWB Make Believe Ballroom show. This is
supposed to be the original program of its kind. Freddy Slack, whose
new band is just getting started, was featured as the show along with
drummer Spike Jones, who, they told us, has most of the good work
sewed up around here - he's that good and that much in demand."
        (from the book "Simon Says" by George T. Simon (1971), p.
      292, re: Sat. in October 1941 - excerpted from the
         original Metronome article by George T. Simon)
      Note: Spike may have recorded for the Freddy Slack "Eight
Beats" on Decca at this time. Al Hendrickson, guit, who later recorded with Spike, also recorded with Slack around this time.

1 November, 1941 (SAT)
           Jonathan Club dance/show

9 November, 1941 (SAT)
           Jonathan Club dance/show

15 November, 1941 (SAT)
           Jonathan Club dance/show

22 November, 1941 (SAT)
           Jonathan Club dance/show
              (Ralph Dadisman, tpt, for Anderson)

24 November, 1941 (MON) - Standard Transcription Library
           NBC Hollywood   10:00 AM start
           Don Allen present

           Spike Jones and his City Slickers

           Personnel as 9 August; Spike Jones, leader; add
              Mel Blanc, Jack Owens for this occasion only

PMS-061925
           ET R-129-1;
    (1:45)Hil Neighbor - voc Jack Owens

           ET R-129-2;
    (3:15)Behind Those Swinging Doors - voc Del Porter
          and vocal quartette

           ET R-129-3; AFRS "Melody Round-Up" 37;
    (2:15)Clink Clink, Another Drink - voc Del Porter,
          Mel Blanc and vocal quartette

           ET R-129-4;
    (2:20)Barstool Cowboy From Old Barstow - voc
          Del Porter

           ET R-129-5;
    (2:25)Moo Woo Woo - voc Del Porter

29

PMS-061926   ET R-129-6; AFRS "Melody Round-Up" 37;
         (3:40)Fort Worth Jail - voc King Jackson
                        (straight)

                ET R-129-7;
         (2:55)Pass the Biscuits Mirandy - voc Del Porter

                ET R-129-8;
         (3:10)Last Horizon - voc Carl Grayson
                        (straight)

                LP GS 1754; ET R-129-9;
         (3:00)Don't Talk To Me About Women - voc Del Porter

                LP GS 1754; ET R-129-10;
         (2:10)Big Bad Bill - voc Del Porter

        Note: This, the Slickers first solo transcription, is note-
worthy on many accounts. It again shows that Spike will go to any
length and expense to ensure that the best available talents are
permanently represented with his band on record. Both associates of
Spikes', Jack Owens, who was one of the emminent singers and popular
song composers of the day, and Mel Blanc, whose unusual voice talents
have been the highlight of many radio programs and movie cartoons,
are both 'captured' on this ET. Here are eight titles that had been
featured during the Jonathan Club shows, and two 'straight' titles
displaying the best of King Jackson, whose voice and trombone are
reminiscent of Jack Teagarden, and the smooth, accurate ballad style
of Carl Grayson, whose comical and unique vocal attributes are as yet
unknown to the group.
        Don Allen, the Standard A&R Rep who signed Cindy Walker and
the City Slickers and now Spike Jones and his City Slickers was soon
to meet an unfortunate end, fatally shot through the heart upon returning home one night and surprising a burglar.
        Slickers arrangements attributable to Del Porter; 'straight'
titles by Stan Wrightsman. BMI Performindex No. 3 lists title as
"Over the Last Horizon". If the vocal quartet designation on R-129-
2/3 is correct, then the usual Slickers trio was augmented on this
occasion by either Owens or Blanc, with Owens the preferred choice.
"Clink Clink", as recorded, is listed by the National Archives, Wash.
D.C. as "manuscript", ie: as yet unpublished and was apparently written for the group and Mel Blanc by band leader Phil Ohman and cartoon
music composer/arranger/lyricist Foster Carling. Broadcast royalties
were not paid on unpublished recorded music.
        Of special interest is the fact that early releases of this
ET had two starts on "Barstool Cowboy". Spike plays one wrong note on
his cowbell chromatic intro and signals the band to stop, which they
do within four bars. Just barely audible before the second start are
the words - "new deal", or "new needle" (or perhaps "new bell"). Subsequent issues have this false start 'X'd out.
        The motif and trombone 'fonks' in the Jack Owens "Hi Neigh-
bor" are identical to their use in the later "Der Fuehrer's Face".
The motif, "Merrily We Roll Along", is the intro to Warner Bros. cartoons. The German band section is also similar in both arrangements.
        "Fort Worth Jail" was recorded in Hollywood by Woody Herman
28 Aug 41, DLA 2708, Decca 4293, and "Big Bad Bill" by Texas Jim
Lewis on Decca 6031.
        Alvino Rey recorded at Victor/Hollywood on 21 Nov, using the
masters PBS-061914/5/6/7 & 8 (with remake of 061914 on 25 Nov),
whereas on 24 Nov, Ozzie Nelson recorded in Hollywood using PBS-
061932/3/4 & 5

29 November, 1941 (SAT)
        Jonathan Club dance/show

30 November, 1941 (SUN)
                   Riverside Breakfast Club dance/show
                   8:00 to 11:00 PM

6 December, 1941 (SAT)
                   Jonathan Club dance/show

7 December, 1941 (SUN)
                   Pearl Harbour, Hawaii. The Japanese attack this
                   morning brings the United States into declared
                   war on Japan and Hitler's Germany

13 December, 1941 (SAT)
                   Jonathan Club dance/show

17 December, 1941 (WED) – Standard Transcription Library
              NBC Hollywood   6:30 to 9:10 PM
              Don Allen present

              Cindy Walker with Spike Jones' City Slickers

              Personnel as 15 Aug, with Don Anderson, tpt

PMS-061983
              ET R-131-1;
      (2:35) Travelin' In My Shoes - voc Cindy Walker

              ET R-131-2;
      (2:50) He Knew All Of the Answers - voc Cindy Walker

              ET R-131-3;
      (2:15) You've Got My Heart Doing a Tap Dance -
              voc Cindy Walker

              ET R-131-4;
      (2:30) The Old Wrangler - voc Cindy Walker

              ET R-131-5;
      (2:10) It's All Your Fault - voc Cindy Walker

PMS-061984
              ET R-131-6;
      (2:45) Song of the Cowboy - voc Cindy Walker

              ET R-131-7;
      (2:25) I Don't Trust the Men - voc Cindy Walker

              ET R-131-8;
      (3:15) Homesick - voc Cindy Walker

              ET R-131-9;
      (2:30) Now Or Never - voc Cindy Walker

              ET R-131-10;
      (2:20) It Never Can Be - vocv Cindy Walker

     Note: All titles composed by Cindy Walker and arranged by
Dan Michaud. "It's All Your Fault" was recorded by Bob Wills on OKEH
6598, and Cindy Walker on Decca 6082. "Now Or Never" recorded by
Walker on Decca 6057. The last two mentioned Walker releases were
probably recorded in New York (without the Slickers).

"Song of the Cowboy" male chorus by Porter, Grayson and Jackson.
RCA Hollywood used the matrices PBS-061985/6/7/8 on 17 Dec

19 December, 1941 (FRI)
Palos Verde Country Club dance/show

20 December, 1941 (SAT)
Jonathan Club dance/show

23 December, 1941 (TUES)
Jonathan Club Christmas dance/show

24 December, 1941 (WED)
Dance/show at, or for, 'Mona Lisa'

27 December, 1941 (SAT)
Jonathan Club dance/show

31 December, 1941 (WED)
Jonathan Club New Years' dance/show
(Pay scale for this occasion: $23.00)

3 January, 1942 (SAT)
Jonathan Club dance/show

Note: Anderson's diary indicates Spike Jones' "City Slickers" are now the official house dance band

10 January, 1942 (SAT)
Jonathan Club dance/show

12 January, 1942 (MON) - Victor Studios, Hollywood
2:00 to 5:00 PM
A & R Rep unlisted, Meyerson assumed

Leader/drums - Spike Jones
Trumpet - Don Anderson
Trombone - King Jackson
Clarinet/sax - Del Porter
Piano - Lou Bring
Banjo/guitar - Perry Botkin
Tuba - Hank Stern
Vocals - Del Porter, King Jackson, Carl Grayson,
    Mel Blanc
Effects - Mel Blanc

PBS-072020-1   BB 30-0818-B; HMVI NE 808;
                  ET AFRS "Downbeat" 105;
         (2:20)(The) Wild Wild Women - voc Del Porter

PBS-072021-1   B 11466-A; HMV BD 1099-B; 20-3338; HMVAU BD
                  1099-B; HMVSK BD 1099; RCADJ 642-A;
                  45 RCAG EPA 9720; LP RCAE HY 1006, INTS
                  5052; RCAG RCS 3217/1-2; ET AFRS "Basic
                  Music Library" P-1324, AFRS "Downbeat" 105;
         (2:20)Clink, Clink, Another Drink - voc Del Porter
                  and the Boys in the Back Room - Hiccups by
                  Mel Blanc

32

PBS-072022-1   Unissued
              (3:08)Beautiful Eggs - voc Del Porter

PBS-072023-1   B 11466-B; Musical Postcards(condensed) 409,
                      1008, 1802, 1803; ET AFRS "Basic Music
                      Library" W-10;
              (2:12)Pack Up Your Troubles - voc City Slickers

          Note: RCA inst do not credit Mel Blanc or Carl Grayson as
vocalists. Label info credits Blanc with the hiccups only on "Clink,
Clink", where in fact he sang and hiccuped one chorus, including the
'Lombardo' ending. Grayson, one of the 'Boys in the Back Room' and
Mel Blanc were, in all likelihood, personally paid by Spike for this
service.
          Lou Bring replaces Stan Wrightsman on this session only, as
in all probability, Wrightsman had a previous booking for this afternoon. Bring, well known conductor/arranger and one of RCA's musical
directors on the West coast, had conducted for recordings by Dorothy
Lamour, Kenny Baker, Allan Jones, Abbott & Costello. His wife was the
former Frances Hunt, one-time singer with Benny Goodman's band.
          "Beautiful Eggs" was never released as the nature of the
double-ententre lyrics did not meet with the RCA Morals Dept. approval, eg: 'She had such beautiful eggs' sounded much like 'beautiful
legs', and much was made of such word play. The song did remain as
part of Spike's show for a number of years. Stephen Sholes, as Division Vice President for RCA in 1967 indicated in a letter to the Jones
estate that the master of "Beautiful Eggs" had been destroyed. Dubbed
copies have surfaced among ardent collectors. "Beautiful Eggs" was
considered for, but unreleased on V-Disc.
          With the 1949 RCA issue 20-3338, "Clink Clink, Another
Drink" was retitled "Clink Clink Polka".

17 January, 1942 (SAT)
              Jonathan Club dance/show

24 January, 1942 (SAT)
              Jonathan Club dance/show

31 January, 1942 (SAT)
              Jonathan Club dance/show

6 February, 1942 (FRI) - Victor Studios, Hollywood
              Rudy Vallee and his Connecticut Yankees

              Leader - Lou Bring
              Brass - Manny Klein, Mickey Bloom, tpt;
                Eddie Kusby, trb
              Reeds - Jack Mayhew, Morton Friedman, Ryland
                Weston, Warren Baker
              Rhythm - Stan Wrightsman, pno; Artie Bernstein,
                bass; Spike Jones, drm
              Violins - Harry Bluestone, Mischa Russell

PBS-072075-2   RCAV 27823
                      A Letter From London - voc Rudy Vallee

33

PBS-072076-1   RCAV 27844
                    I'm Just a Vagabond Lover - voc Rudy Vallee

PBS-072077-1   RCAV 27841
                    My Time Is Your Time - voc Rudy Vallee

PBS-072078-1   RCAV 27823
                    I Just Couldn't Say It Before - voc Rudy Vallee

           Note: Information courtesy of Brian Rust

7 February, 1942 (SAT)
                    Jonathan Club dance/show

14 February, 1942 (SAT)
                    Jonathan Club dance/show

20 February, 1942 (FRI) - Hal Roach Studios, Culver City
                    Herbert Moulton Production, 9:00 AM to 2:15 PM

                    Spike Jones and his City Slickers,
                       personnel as 9 Aug 41; Spike Jones, leader

        Note: This date appears in Anderson's diary as a Soundies
work-call with Spike. "Come Josephine In My Flying Machine", according to an undated/unidentified clipping, was considered, if not planned and/or made. Cindy Walker made a Soundie about this time with
unidentified back-up personnel.
        SOUNDIES - short, short films distributed and projected via
vending machines. They featured many bands and were prominent in the
late 30's and early 40's. For Spike, this day continues:-

                    Columbia Studios, Hollywood
                    Ted Daffan's Texans

                    Steel guitar/leader - Ted Daffan
                    Rhythm guitar - Chuck Keeshan
                    Lead guitar - Buddy (Sidney) Buller
                    Violin - Leon Seago
                    Accordion - Freddy Courtney
                    Piano - Ralph Smith
                    Bass - Johnny Johnson
                    Drums - Spike Jones

H655   OKEH 6706-A
                    Born To Lose - voc Leon Seago

H658-1   OKEH 6719-A
                    Bluest Blues - voc Ted Daffan

H659   OKEH 6706-B
                    No Letter Today - voc Leon Seago, Chuck Keeshan

H660   OKEH 6729-A
                    Time Won't Heal My Broken Heart

H661   Col 20358
                    Long John

H662-1   OKEH 6719-B
              Look Who's Talkin' - voc Lean Seago

     Note: Personnel details courtesy Richard Sears. Masters
H656/657 are not Ted Daffan

21 February, 1942 (SAT)
              Jonathan Club dance/show

27 February, 1942 (FRI) - Standard Transcription Library
              NBC Studios, Hollywood

              Spike Jones and his City Slickers

              Personnel as 9 Aug 41; Spike Jones, leader; add
              Myrtle Horwin for this occasion only

PMS-072134   ET R-132-1;
        (2:00)Little Bo-Peep Has Lost Her Jeep - voc Del Porter

              ET R-132-2;
        (2:20)Trailer Annie - voc Del Porter

              ET R-132-3;
        (2:55)Siam - voc Del Porter, King Jackson, Carl Grayson

              ET R-132-4;
        (2:50)Hotcha Cornya - inst

              ET R-132-5;
        (2:05)Hey Mable - voc the Boys in the Back Room
                           (straight)

PMS-072135   ET R-132-6;
        (2:30)Boogie Woogie Cowboy - voc King Jackson
                           (straight)

              ET R-132-7;
        (2:25)Dodging a Gal From Dodge City - voc King Jackson
                           (straight)

              ET R-132-8;
        (2:45)Serenade To a Jerk - voc Myrtle Horwin
                           (straight)

              ET R-132-9;
        (3:00)Ridin' Home With You - voc Carl Grayson
                           (straight)

              ET R-132-10;
        (2:40)Now Laugh - voc Del Porter

     Note: Information from the US National Archives shows that
"Bo-Peep" and "Hotcha Cornya" of this session are in 'manuscript',
ie: unpublished. The first instance of the 'Slicker tag' is in "Bo-
Peep", although it appeared as a clarinet fill in the Bluebird issue
of "Red Wing". Cuts 1, 2, 4 and 10 are a light-hearted reflection of

the US war effort, with "Hotcha Cornia", often variously spelled, an adaption of several themes of the wartime ally, Russia. This cut of "Hotcha" has many inaccuracies, evidence of a new but under-rehearsed show number, however, the inept guitar in balalaika style is deliberate. Don Anderson recalls his contribution to "Hotcha" as the 'stop' chorus behind the cowbell melody near the end - 32 bars before the rim shots (later, sneezes), as developed at one of Spike's home 'think sessions'. This title evolves to become one of their most requested numbers during the war years.

"Siam" is the first recorded instance of Carl Grayson as a character vocalist. His additional talent as a 'glug' specialist is as yet unknown and he has yet to record with the violin. "Dodging A Gal" vocal assist (falsetto) to Jackson by Spike Jones.

Slickers arr. attributable to Del Porter; 'straight' arr. to Stan Wrightsman and King Jackson. "Hey Mable" (variously spelled) has been recorded by Tony Pastor on Bluebird 30-0802 and the Merry Macs on Decca 4265. "Boogie Woogie Cowboy" was recorded by Tex Ritter on Capitol 928 and Dude Martin on Mercury 6250.

28 February, 1942 (SAT)
           Jonathan Club dance/show

7 March, 1942 (SAT)
           Jonathan Club dance/show

14 March, 1942 (SAT)
           Jonathan Club dance/show

21 March, 1942 (SAT)
           Jonathan Club dance/show

27 March, 1942 (FRI) - Decca Studios, Hollywood
           Hoagy Carmichael Trio

           Leader/pno/celeste, whist - Hoagy Carmichael
           String bass - Artie Bernstein
           Drums - Spike Jones

DLA 2963-A   Decca 18396
                    Mr. Music Master

DLA 2964-A   Decca 18397
                    Old Man Harlem

Note: New World Records LP, NW 272 "And Then We Wrote.." have re-issued "Star Dust" with above personnel and presumably from this session. Original matrix and release number unknown.

28 March, 1942 (SAT)
           Jonathan Club dance/show
               (Ralph Dadisman, tpt, for Anderson)

4 April, 1942 (SAT)
           Jonathan Club dance/show

7 April, 1942 (TUES) - Victor Studios, Hollywood,   2:30 to
           Harry Meyerson, A & R Rep, present   5:30 PM

```
            Leader/drm - Spike Jones
            Trumpet - Don Anderson
            Trombone - King Jackson
            Clarinet - Del Porter
            Piano - Stanley Wrightsman
            Banjo - Perry Botkin
            Tuba - Hank Stern
            Vocalists - Del Porter, King Jackson,
              Carl Grayson
```

PBS-072236-1   B 11560-B; 20-2537-A; ET AFRS "Basic Music
                       Library" P-898, PGL 38; AFRS "Downbeat" 105;
                       AFRS "Purple Heart Album" 189;
               (2:56)Siam - voc Del Porter, King Jackson, Carl Grayson

PBS-072237-1   B 11530-A; HMV BD 1199-A; HMVAU EA 3450 & MH 133;
               (2:20)Little Bo-Peep Has Lost Her Jeep - voc Del Porter
                       with Willie Spicer at the Collidophone

PBS-072238-1   B 11560-A; 45 RCA EP "Platter Party" SPD6-
                       599 9049; ET AFRS "Remember" 318, 736;
               (2:44)Come Josephine In My Flying Machine - voc Boys
                       in the Back Room and King Jackson
PBS-072238-2 (2:43)Unissued

PBS-072239-1R   B 11530-B; HMV BD 1207-A; 20-2537-B; HMVAU BD
                       1207-A & EA 3450; ET AFRS "Basic Music Library"
                       P-898, PGL 38; AFRS "Downbeat"(excerpt) 82;
                       AFRS "Purple Heart Album" 184; AFRS "America's
                       Popular Music" 826;
               (3:00)Pass The Biscuits Mirandy - voc Del Porter

     Note: "Siam" is reportedly issued on Japanese 78 RPM, flip
"I Kiss Your Hand, Madame". RCA inst do not credit vocalists. "Siam"
timing, also not shown, from US Library of Congress. The RCA sheets
also show that the next day, 8 Apr, from 1:15 to 1:30 PM, "Mirandy"
was "rerecorded to correct gun shot wave shape. amplitude too high".
This service applied only to Spike. The previous take, -1 is now -1R,
and the re-recorded wave shape may have referred to the explosion on
the original which had a better chance of 'blasting out a wall' on
the master groove.
     Arrangements attributable to Del Porter. This session
produced the only two instances of King Jackson singing on Spike's
commercial recordings. Carl Grayson was, of course, one of the Boys
in the Back Room, his singing paid for directly by Spike. The
progress to note here is Grayson's recorded 'glugs' on "Siam", a
newly discovered facet of his talent.

     "Most of Spike Jones recordings (of this period) credit one
Willie Spicer at the sneezaphone, the birdaphone, the trainaphone and
the collidophone (etc), but Willie Spicer is a myth. His only good,
Spike reports, is that he holds the band together. He can't be
drafted."   (Saturday Evening Post, 10 Apr 43)
     "...it involves, among other things, the employment of one
Willie Spicer. Now Willie is the lad who pioneered on the birdaphone
in 'Der Fuehrer'...Willie, by the way, is draftproof - and nonexist-
ant."   (Newsweek, 20 Sept 43)

11 April, 1942 (SAT)
            Jonathan Club dance/show

16 April, 1942 (THURS) - KRAFT MUSIC HALL
            NBC Hollywood

Bing Crosby, with Mary Martin, Victor Borge,
the Music Maids and 'Hal', with the
John Scott Trotter Orch; ann: Ken Carpenter

Guests: Ronald Reagan; Sabu, the Elephant Boy
(Dastagir), and Spike Jones and his
City Slickers

Bing Crosby, Music Maids - "K-K-K-Katy"
Mary Martin - "Arthur Murray Taught Me
Dancing In a Hurry"
Bing Crosby, Sabu - comedy dialogue
Bing Crosby - "I Miss You"
Victor Borge, Music Maids - "He Comes From Timbuck
Three"(Upper, or inflationary language)
Bing Crosby, Mary Martin - dialogue
Bing Crosby - "Make Believe", "I'll Be With You
In Apple Blossom Time"
Little Bo-Peep Has Lost Her Jeep - voc
Del Porter
Pass the Biscuits Mirandy - voc Del Porter
Bing Crosby, Music Maids - (I'm Crazy About)"Mary"
Ronald Reagan, Bing Crosby, Mary Martin -
comedy soap opera
Mary Martin - "The Way You Look Tonight"
Bing Crosby - "The Song Of the Islands"

Note: Bing Crosby talks with 'Uncle' Spike and introduces
Perry Botkin, King Jackson, Don Anderson, Stanley Wrightsman, Hank
Stern and, "formerly of The Foursome", Del Porter. This one hour show
was issued by Spokane Records, Redmond, Wash.; LP Spokane 4. Some
early pressings of this album have Spokane 3 jackets. An NBC double
sided acetate of the Slickers show rehearsal was in Jones files.

18 April, 1942 (SAT)
Jonathan Club dance/show

Note: At this time, Perry Botkin leaves - his own very full
calendar scarcely able to keep up with Spike's increased work load.
He remains in the studios, working often with Bing. His son, Perry
Botkin Jr., is a free-lance musician in Los Angeles and in recent
times was the co-composer of such popular songs as "Nadia's Theme"
and "Bless the Beasts and the Children".
Joining Spike is the unique guitarist, Luther "Red" Roundtree. Although in Los Angeles for only two years, Texas born Roundtree spent most of his working life in the US South; working as a pro
musician in Shreveport, Louisiana, from 1924 to '32, then as staff
musician on radio in Memphis, Tennessee to 1940. He brought his
talents, on character voice and vocals as well as guitar and banjo,
to the fledgling Slickers.
Bearing in mind that all City Slickers dates from Anderson's
diaries indicate which play dates he was able to work within his own
professional schedule, it is highly likely there are Slickers 'gigs'
not covered due to Anderson's committments elsewhere, just as it is
possible that 'subs' on other instruments could have appeared on
Slickers dates listed. This would not be critical with their dance
music, but all 'subs' would have to have had some familiarity with
Spike's show routine.

20 April, 1942 (MON) - Standard Transcription Library
NBC Hollywood
Don Allen present

alias: "The Country Dodgers", personnel as 7 Apr;
Luther Roundtree, guit/bjo, voc, replacing
Perry Botkin

072248   (3:19)Your Morning Feature - voc King Jackson,
                        Carl Grayson

                (3:25)Virgin Mary Sturgeon - voc King Jackson,
                        Carl Grayson (see note following)

          Note: Timings approximate. On the "Standirt" label, "Morning
Feature" was issued on a 78 RPM ET, backed by Ann Shelton singing
"Gracie La Groove".
          "Virgin", an acetate in Skip Craig's files is virtually
identical to the risque "Morning Feature", with a fuller sound and
superior ambience. The penciled label designation is for the National
Association of Broadcasters (NAB). It was not cut at Standard but is
included here for reference. The vastly different acoustics of the
two discs indicate two separate facilities while the musical similarities suggest two takes from the same session. The female voice on
each is the admirable falsetto of Carl Grayson. The risque flip is an
unidentified non-Jones male quartet. This day's session continues:-

                  Standard Transcription Library
                  NBC Hollywood
                  Don Allen present (Pay scale: $57.00)

                  Spike Jones and his City Slickers

PMS-072254   ET R-138-6;
                (2:15)Three Little Words - voc King Jackson
                           (straight)

                    ET R-138-7;
                (1:50)When Buddha Smiles - inst
                           (straight)

                    ET R-138-8;
                (2:00)You're a Sap, Mr. Jap - voc Boys in the
                        Back Room

                    ET R-138-9; AFRS "Basic Music Library" W-10;
                (2:20)Pack Up Your Troubles - voc Boys in the
                        Back Room

                    LP GS 1754; ET R-138-10; War Dept "Melody
                        Round-Up" 233;
                (2:55)Never Hit Your Grandma With a Shovel - voc
                        Boys in the Back Room

PMS-072255   ET R-136-1; AFRS "Basic Music Library" P-1134;
                (2:50)That's What Makes the World Go 'Round - voc
                        Boys in the Back Room
                           (straight)

                    LP GS 1754; ET R-136-2; AFRS "Basic Music
                        Library" P-1134; AFRS "Melody Round-Up" 33;
                (2:32)Don't Give the Chair To Buster - voc Boys
                        in the Back Room

                                39

ET R-136-3; AFRS "Basic Music Library" P-1134;
(2:12)48 Reasons Why - voc Boys in the Back Room
(straight)

LP GS 1754; ET R-136-4; AFRS "Basic Music
Library" P-1134;
(2:45)De Camptown Races with Gestures - voc Luther
Roundtree and Uncle Spike

ET R-136-5; AFRS "Basic Music Library" P-1134;
(2:15)The Blacksmith Song - voc Boys in the Back Room

Note: Pay scale for transcription work was usually at the
rate of $36, and on occasion $39, per three-hour session. This days
rate indicates a longer and more productive session. Slickers arr
attributable to Del Porter, straight arr to Stan Wrightsman and King
Jackson. The guitar styling of Luther Roundtree is immediately evident in his solos on this ET, notably "Three Little Words". The Boys
in the Back Room are now a vocal quartet on the Slickers titles while
"...World Go 'Round" is still a trio. "When Buddha Smiles", not in
the realm of a jazz classic, had been also recorded by Benny Goodman
and Coleman Hawkins.
More titles bolstering the US war effort. "You're a Sap, Mr.
Jap" is a light-hearted look at the Pacific conflict while the old
"Blacksmith Song" has altered words to promote conservation at home.
"48 Reasons Why" is a flag-waver that is well played and displays
noteworthy ensemble work, including Spike's military drumming and
Porter's penny-whistle (ala piccolo) solo.

24 April, 1942 (FRI) - Standard Transcription Library
NBC Hollywood
Don Allen present

Leader/drm - Spike Jones
Trombone - King Jackson
Clarinet - Del Porter
Guitar/bjo - Luther Roundtree
Voices - Spike Jones, Del Porter, King Jackson,
Luther Roundtree, Myrtle Horwin (assumed)

AMO 2578/9   ET C.P. MacGregor
17 radio commericials on a 16" transcription
for "Butternut Bread"

Note: These short commercials, arranged by Del Porter to
familiar, classical and Public Domain melodies, are set to the verses
of John Gudell. The voices are in the role of actors/actress. The
matrix is hand-written on the label, which includes the following
information:- "Produced for R.J. Potts & Co., Kansas City Missouri
for C.P. MacGregor, 729 South Western Ave. Hollywood."
The dating of this ET is not conclusive, nor is the studio
identity. However, in the Anderson diary under this date is "City
Slickers transcription", which is crossed out, with the note: "...all
done April 20". This indicates the 20th and 24th were booked for
transcription sessions which would have included the "Standirt"
title(s), PMS-072254/5, and "Butternut". With their experience, all
was done on the 20th and a smaller group finished the booking with
"Butternut".

25 April, 1942 (SAT)
Jonathan Club dance/show
(Ralph Dadisman, tpt, for Anderson)

2 May, 1942 (SAT)
              Jonathan Club dance/show

11 May, 1942 (MON) - Standard Transcription Library
              NBC Hollywood

              Cindy Walker with Spike Jones' City Slickers

              Leader/drm - Spike Jones
              Trumpet - Don Anderson
              Trombone - King Jackson
              Clarinet/sax - Del Porter
              Guitar - Luther Roundtree
              Bass - Hank Stern
              Vocals - Cindy Walker

PMS-072270   ET R-136-6;
        (2:35) You're From Texas - voc Cindy Walker

        ET R-136-7; AFRS "Basic Music Library" P-1134;
        (2:45) The Farmer's Daughter - voc Cindy Walker

        ET R-136-8;
        (2:45) How Many Apples Does It Take To Make a Pie? -
             voc Cindy Walker

        ET R-136-9;
        (2:10) Sweet Something - voc Cindy Walker

        ET R-136-10;
        (2:40) The Rose of the Border - voc Cindy Walker

PMS-072271   ET R-143-6; War Dept "Melody Round-Up" 233;
        AFRS "Melody Round-Up" 33;
        (1:50) Gonna Stomp Those City Slickers Down - voc
             Cindy Walker

        ET R-143-7;
        (2:55) 'Til the Longest Day I Live - voc Cindy Walker

        ET R-143-8; AFRS "Melody Round-Up" 37;
        (2:05) That Big Palooka Who Plays the Bazooka - voc
             Cindy Walker (King Jackson, trombone)

        ET R-143-9;
        (2:30) Bye Lo Baby Bunting - voc Cindy Walker

        ET R-143-10;
        (3:10) Into the Sunrise - voc Cindy Walker

     Note: All titles composed by Cindy Walker, arranged by Dan
Michaud. It was "Gonna Stomp Those City Slickers Down" which helped
Spike decide on the name of his new band, thanks to a Cindy Walker
rehearsal in 1941.
     "You're From Texas" was recorded be Bob Wills and his Texas
Playboys on Okeh 6722; "The Rose of the Border" by Texas Jim Lewis
and his Lone Star Cowboys on Decca 6056. Cindy Walker commercially
recorded, sans Slickers, "'Til the Longest Day I Live" on Decca 6038.
AFRS "Melody Round-Up" 33 "Gonna Stomp Those City Slickers Down" is
erroniously titled, "We've Come To Town" - a line from the song.

16 May, 1942 (SAT)
                    Jonathan Club dance/show

18 May, 1942 (MON)
        There is reference among the Jones files of a Camel commer-
cial along with the notation "Drip, Drip, Drip" under the heading of
"Blondie, No. 151" on this date. Applicable only to Spike. There is a
"Blondie & Dagwood" radio script in a collector's possession with
Spike's name on it and while not personally appearing on the show,
Spike would use the script for music and/or effects cues.

23 May, 1942 (SAT)
                    Jonathan Club dance/show

30 May, 1942 (SAT) - U.S.O. SHOW*
                    NBC Red/MOB network, Hollywood

                    with Mary Martin, Don Ameche, Edgar Bergan and
                    Charlie McCarthy, Meredith Willson and his Orch-
                    estra, and Spike Jones and his City Slickers

24058/9B   Program details unknown

        Note: Pay scale ($36.00) indicates that two titles could
have been played on this program, one of which could have been
"Clink, Clink, Another Drink" with Mel Blanc the featured soloist.
AFRS "Basic Music Library" P-36, issued 30 June 1943 contains a live
performance of "Clink, Clink" with Blanc and the Slickers, but is
mislabeled as "Hasta Luego" - possibly from this broadcast.
        Information from the Library Of Congress file card reads:-
"AFRS LWO 15731, R 58 A1, Box T42-5, 24058/9B. Part one file card
missing". (There was no Slickers Jonathan dance/show this night)

6 June, 1942 (SAT)
                    Jonathan Club dance/show

13 June, 1942 (SAT)
                    Jonathan Club dance/show

17 June, 1942 (WED) - POINT SUBLIME*
                    NBC Hollywood, West Coast   Sponsor: Union Oil

                    with Cliff Arquette, Harold Peary, Verna Felton,
                    Mel Blanc and guests, Spike Jones and his
                    City Slickers

        Note: In the 5 July 1942 issue of Radio Life there is a
picture of Spike with Cliff Arquette, and mention of this being
Spike's second appearance on the Point Sublime show - the first being
the previous year (7 July 41) when he was but scarcely known, even
locally. The play dates of the Slickers have been increasing to the
point where it is obvious they are now a popular local group. The
rest of the world knows little, if anything, of Spike Jones and his
City Slickers.

20 June, 1942 (SAT)
                    Jonathan Club dance/show
                        (Ralph Dadisman, tpt, for Anderson)

23 June, 1942 (TUES) - FIBBER McGEE AND MOLLY*
                    NBC Hollywood   Sponsor: Johnson's Wax

with the Billy Mills Orchestra (Spike Jones, percussion)

The Blacksmith Song - voc the King's Men

Note: Spike adds very audible novelty percussion effects:-
anvil, cowbell, auto-horn etc, behind the vocal. "The Blacksmith
Song", an old chestnut, is heard with similar altered lyrics as the
Slickers recent Standard ET. The final chorus is pushing the concept
of salvage for recycling in the war effort.
Don Anderson played first trumpet with the Mills Orchestra
on the Tuesday Fibber McGee and the Sunday Gildersleeve Shows this
past and next season.

27 June, 1942 (SAT)
Jonathan Club dance/show
(Ralph Dadisman, tpt, for Anderson)

2 July, 1942 (THURS) - KRAFT MUSIC HALL*
NBC Hollywood

Bing Crosby, with John Scott Trotter's Orch.
Guests include Spike Jones and his City Slickers

Little Bo-Peep Has Lost Her Jeep - voc Del Porter
Hotcha Cornia - inst

Note: One double-sided NBC acetate of these titles was in
the Jones files.

3 July (FRI), 4 July (SAT) 1942
Jonathan Club dance/show
(Pay scale: $11.50 Fri; $12.00 Sat)

6 July, 1942 (MON) - Hal Roach Studios, Culver City
Herbert Moulton Production - Soundies

Spike Jones and his City Slickers, personnel as
7 Apr, with Luther Roundtree, guit/bjo,
replacing Perry Botkin. Add Mel Blanc, vocal

(2:45) Pass the Biscuits, Mirandy - voc Del Porter

(2:47) Clink, Clink, Another Drink - voc Del Porter,
Mel Blanc and the City Slickers

(2:23) The Blacksmith Song - voc Del Porter, King Jackson

(2:28) The Sheik of Araby - voc Del Porter, Carl Grayson

Note: Timings are approximate. The above titles were recorded for later filmed miming, lip-syncronization or, as it is called,
side-lining. One take of each is obviously known, and there is an
acetate from this session of "The Blacksmith Song" with a breakdown
after the typewriter solo. To the breakdown, this acetate is a copy
of the released soundtrack, which suggests editing to re-make this
faulty ending. (Music editing for films was an easy and common practise). This session lasted six hours.

43

The last three titles have been available on Official Film, No. 1030, for home projection. "Mirandy" has also been released, edited, for home projection, with unknown details. Production credits to Sam Coslow appear only on the original RCM (reverse image) prints. The pianist does not appear in the filming, and it is assumed that Wrightsman was still with the band, although Frank Leithner is to join the Slickers about this time.

10 July (FRI), 11 July (SAT), 1942
        Jonathan Club dance/show

12 July, 1942 (SUN)
        Show at Ft. McArthur

    Note: This is the first instance of the City Slickers booked for their show only. (Pay scale: $7.00)

13 July, 1942 (MON) - Hal Roach Studios, Culver City
        Herbert Moulton Production - Soundies

        Spike Jones and his City Slickers sidelining to
        6 July soundtrack. This session lasted eight hours

14 July, 1942 (TUES) - Hal Roach Studios, Culver City
        Herbert Moulton Production - Soundies

        Spike Jones and his City Slickers sidelining
        to 6 July soundtrack

    Note: About this time, Stan Wrightsman and Hank Stern leave, to be replaced by Frank Leithner and Joseph "Country" Washburn. Wrightsman, who much preferred their dance, or 'straight' music, opted out when the Slickers style became predominant, records with the Eddie Miller combo from 1945 to '46 and as well, teams up with Jack Teagarden for several Walter Lantz cartoons in 1944. Stern can be heard on the Capitol "History of Jazz" 78 RPM series with Paul Whiteman, with whom he had worked a decade earlier in New York, and on V-Disc with the Cookie Fairchild Orch. recorded 27 Feb 45. Perry Botkin and Frank Leithner also played on that V-Disc session.
    Frank Leithner had his own orchestra in New York in 1929. He was also the pianist for Frances Langford in 1931 and after moving to the West coast, became a successful free-lance pianist and arranger on most of the current radio shows. Joe, or 'Country' Washburn as he was more often referred, had been with the Ted Weems band, along with Red Ingle and Ormond Downes from the early 30's. An immense talent on bass, vocals and, as it turns out, arranging, he also composed in collaboration with Weems. Their biggest hit was "One Dozen Roses" while "Oh Monah" was also very popular.

17 July, 1942 (FRI) - Standard Transcription Library
        NBC Hollywood

        Spike Jones and his City Slickers, personnel
        as 28 July

PMS-072468   ET R-141-6;
        (2:10) John Scotter Trot - inst
                            (straight)

44

```
            ET R-141-7;
(2:40)Cheatin' On the Sandman - voc Boys in the
            Back Room
                    (straight)


            ET R-141-8;
(3:15)The Girl I Left Behind Me - voc Carl Grayson
                    (straight)


            ET R-141-9;
(2:40)Sailor With the Navy Blue Eyes - voc Boys
            in the Back Room
                    (straight)


            LP GS 1754; ET R-141-10;
(2:00)Camptown Races No. 2 - voc Luther Roundtree
            and Uncle Spike
```

PMS-072469

```
            ET R-143-1; AFRS "Basic Music Library" W-10;
            AFRS "Downbeat" 105;
(2:30)Come Josephine In My Flying Machine - vocal
            quartet and King Jackson


            ET R-143-2;
(2:40)Love For Sale - inst
                    (straight)


            ET R-143-3;
(2:20)Moanin' Low - voc King Jackson
                    (straight)


            ET R-143-4; AFRS "Melody Round-Up" 37; War Dept
            "Melody Round-Up" 233;
(2:00)Horsie Keep Your Tail Up - vocal quartet


            ET R-143-5; AFRS "Basic Music Library" W-9;
(2:55)Yankee Doodler - voc Del Porter and band
                    (straight)
```

      Note: Slickers arr attributable to Del Porter, with the
'straight' arr by King Jackson and Frank Leithner. The popular jazz
classics of "Love For Sale" and "Moanin' Low" are well played.
"Cheatin' On the Sandman" shows the development of the ensemble to
include Grayson's violin for harmonic support and melodic variation,
blending with the bari sax of Porter and trombone of Jackson - an
unlikely combination, but it works. This title was also recorded by
the Merry Macs on Decca 18361. "Moanin' Low" was soon to be a feature
of the incomparable Lena Horne, backed by the Lou Bring Orchestra on
Victor 27817.
      "John Scotter Trot", an unusual instrumental, was composed
by Scott, first name unknown. It sounds very like the avant-garde
style of Raymond Scott.

            Jonathan Club dance/show

18 July, 1942 (SAT)
            Jonathan Club dance/show

22 July, 1942 (WED) - Hal Roach Studios, Culver City
            Herbert Moulton Production - Soundies

                        45

Spike Jones and his City Slickers final
sidelining to 6 July soundtrack

24 July (FRI), 25 July (SAT), 1942
Jonathan Club dance/show

28 July, 1942 (TUES) - Victor Studios, Hollywood   8:30 PM to
                     Harry Meyerson, A & R Rep, present   12 :15 AM

                     Leader/drm - Spike Jones
                     Trumpet - Don Anderson
                     Trombone - King Jackson
                     Clarinet/sax - Del Porter
                     Violin - Carl Grayson
                     Piano - Frank Leithner
                     Banjo - Luther Roundtree
                     Tuba - Country Washburn
                     Vocals - Del Porter, Carl Grayson

PBS-072524-1   BB 30-0818-A; HMV BD 1099-A; HMVAU BD 1099-A
                     & EA 3464; HMVSK BD 1099; HMVI NE 808;
                     45 RCAG EPA 9720; LP RCAG LPM 10 013 & RCS
                     3211/1-2; RCAJ RVP 6300(m) & 5143(m); RCAF
                     PL 43197; ET AFRS "Downbeat" 105;
                (2:25)Hotcha Cornia(Black Eyes)(featured in the
                     Warner Bros.film "Thank Your Lucky Stars")
                     - arr. by Del Porter and Spike Jones,
                     Willie Spicer at the Sneezaphone

PBS-072525-1 (2:35)Unissued
PBS-072525-2   B-11586-A; HMV BD 5787; 20-2611-A; V-Disc 36-A;
                     LP LPM 2224; LPM 3849; LSP 3849(e); ANL1
                     1035(e); AYL1 3748; RCAE LSA 3084 & RD 7724;
                     RCAG LSP 10157 & RCS 3217/1-2; RCAJ 5143(m);
                     RCAAU CAS 7158; RCAIT CL 83748; RCA Special
                     Products "Good Music Record" DML1 0750;
                     Reader's Digest "Juke Box Saturday Night"
                     99945; New World "Praise the Lord and Pass
                     the Ammunition" NW 222; ET AFRS "Basic Music
                     Library" W-9; AFRS "Remember" 810; AFRS
                     "Jill's All-Time Juke Box" 17; AFRS "America's
                     Popular Music" 1298; AFRS "Sound Off" 34;
                (2:28)In Der Fuehrer's Face (from the Walt Disney film
                     "Nuttsey Land") - voc Carl Grayson and the Boys
                     in the Back Room, with Willie Spicer at the
                     Birdaphone

PBS-072526-1   BB 30-0812-A; LP RCAG PJM2-8021;
                (2:54)Oh By Jingo - voc Del Porter and the Boys in the
                     Back Room - Willie Spicer at the Anvilaphone

PBS-072527-1   BB 30-0812-B; 20-2507-B; HMVSK X8068;
                     LP RCAE INTS 5052; RCAG PJM2-8021; RCA
                     Special Products "Good Music Record" DML1
                     0570; ET AFRS "Basic Music Library" P-877 &
                     P-S-28; AFRS "Purple Heart Album" 183;
                (2:24)The Sheik - voc Del Porter and Carl Grayson -
                     Willie Spicer at the Hiccuphone

PBS-072528-1   B-11586-B; HMV BD 1199-A; 20-2611-B; HMVAU MH 133;
                     HMVSK X7245; ET AFRS "Basic Music Library"
                     PGL 38; AFRS "Downbeat" 123; AFRS "Remember"
                     249 & 806;

(3:08)I Wanna Go Back To West Virginia - voc Del Porter
       and the Boys in the Back Room - Willie Spicer
       at the Trainaphone

     Note: Issued titles are "Der Fuehrer's Face" and "The Sheik
of Araby". "Hotcha Cornia" was recorded several months prior to the
making of the Warner Bros. film. Movie credit, added to the RCA inst
13 Aug 43, is on the label as BB 30-0818 was issued in Oct 43, either
in conjunction with or after the movie release. Label information
perpetuates the mythical Willie Spicer.
     V-Disc 36-A was mastered from take 2 of this session.
     All arrangements by Del Porter. BMI Performindex No. 3
credits "Hotcha Cornia" arr to only Del Porter. The Encyclopedia of
Popular Music, entry 965, and the ASCAP Biographical Encyclopedia,
4th edition, P. 255 incorrectly credit Spike Jones as the composer of
"Der Fuehrer's Face". All composer credits go to Walt Disney com-
poser/conductor since 1936, Oliver Wallace.
     First editions read "From the Walt Disney Picture, Nuttsey
Land", and later, "From the Walt Disney film, Der Fuehrer's Face".
Certain editions reportedly read, "Donald Duck in Nuttsey Land".
Journalistic liberties have altered the "Nuttsey" spelling to "Nutzi"
or similar contractions. "Der Fuehrer's Face" was in rehearsal before
Frank Leithner joined - see 24 Nov 41 for arr origins.
     Carl Hoefle Jr. recalls that Wallace, a dour English compos-
er and known as Ollie to his colleagues, took his new tune "In Der
Fuehrer's Face" to Carl Hoefle, who lived a mere six houses away,
with the suggestion the tune could be suitable for Spike and his new
group. In a 1971 interview with Ted Hering, arranger Del Porter recalled no contractual problems with Disney regarding Spike recording
this song, but it did have to be published first. The Disney soundtrack with tubas blaring their insults to Hitler, was recorded 17
July 42.
     Spike's 'bird' to Hitler is a rubber razzer, or razor - not
to be confused with the similarly novel tongue effect as heard on
Rudy Vallee's "Sow Song" of 2 July 37, or Teddy Powell's "Serenade to
a Maid" of 4 Nov 41. The unissued take-1 of "Der Fuehrer's Face" is
birdless, with trombone 'fonks' in place of the take-2 'bird'.
     As "Beautiful Eggs" had been previously rejected, the filler
Spike needed to round out his issued sides was "I Wanna Go Back To
West Virginia", a song that Luther Roundtree remembers "got nowhere".
This title was also recorded by Jack McLean on Capitol 121; Milt
Hearth Trio on Decca 43708; the Merry Macs on Decca 18527A and Freddy
Martin on Victor 279651. BMI listing credits the arranger as Hathaway
(Charles Hathaway?) opposite all releases.
     "Der Fuehrer's Face" reached No. 3 position on the Hit
Parade by 15 Oct 42 and, according to Billboard Magazine, remained
there for ten weeks. See 17 Sept and 16 Oct notes.

31 July, 1942 (FRI) - Standard Transcription Library
                      NBC Hollywood

                    Spike Jones and his City Slickers, personnel
                    as 28 July

PMS-072577   ET R-141-1; AFRS "Basic Music Library" W-10;
             (3:10)I'm Going Back To West Virginia - voc Del Porter
                    and the Boys in the Back Room

                    ET R-141-2; AFRS "Downbeat" 123;
             (2:55)Water Lou (or Sloppy Lagoon) - voc Del Porter

                    ET R-141-3;
             (1:40)St-St-Stella - voc Del Porter

47

```
               ET R-141-4;
        (2:20)I Know a Story - voc Country Washburn
                            (straight)


               ET R-141-5; AFRS "Downbeat" 123;
        (3:00)Hi Ho My Lady - voc the Boys in the Back Room

PMS-072578     ET R-138-1; AFRS "Basic Music Library" W-9;
               AFRS "Downbeat" 105;
        (2:30)The Sheik of Araby - voc Carl Grayson


               ET R-138-2; AFRS "Basic Music Library" W-9;
               AFRS "Downbeat" 105;
        (2:50)Oh By Jingo - voc Del Porter and the Boys
                   in the Back Room


               ET R-138-3; AFRS "Basic Music Library" W-10 &
               P-465; AFRS "Melody Round-Up" 33;
        (2:15)Red Wing - voc Del Porter


               ET R-138-4; AFRS "Basic Music Library" W-9;
               AFRS "Downbeat"(excerpt) 105; War Dept "Melody
               Round-Up" 233;
        (2:40)Der Fuehrer's Face - voc Carl Grayson


               ET R-138-5;
        (2:10)I'm Going To Write Home - voc Carl Grayson
                            (straight)
```

Note: "Sheik of Araby" vocal credits omit Del Porter on ET label. "Der Fuehrer's Face" is 'birdless' and the sound is thin. "I'm Going Back To West Virginia" is a typo. American Music, Inc. and BMI list title as "Hi-Yo, My Lady". "St-St-Stella" was also recorded by Jack McLean on Capitol 112.

Slickers arr attributable to Del Porter, with King Jackson charting "I'm Going To Write Home". The Weems-Washburn "I Know a Story" was arranged by Washburn. Relaxed and loose - it swung!

THE RECORDING BAN

This schism between the recording industry and the American Federation of Musicians, James C. Petrillo, President, began at midnight on 31 July. RCA and Columbia settled by 11 Nov 44, while Decca and the new compamy of Capitol Records signed agreements with the AF of M in mid-43.

"Recording musicians long had been unhappy with the use of their records in jukeboxes and by disc jockeys on radio broadcasts without royalty payments. The AFM wanted the recording companies to pay a royalty for each record and transcription sold, with the fees going to a union unemployment fund (this fund would provide for musicians unemployed because of the competion of recorded music). The companies refused to pay and the ban was imposed."
                    (Richard S. Sears, V-Discs: A History and Discography)
                    (Greenwood Press, 1980)

          Jonathan Club dance/show

1 August, 1942 (SAT)
          Jonathan Club dance/show

7 August (FRI), 8 August (SAT), 1942
          Jonathan Club dance/show

                              48

9 August, 1942 (SUN)
                    Show at Warner Bros. Studios, Hollywood

        Note: The constant promotion of the City Slickers by Spike,
his agents, friends and associates, coupled with their fine musical
parody and humorous visual showings at the Jonathan where performances to his peers and the Hollywood establishment now included the
recorded but as yet unreleased "Der Fuehrer's Face", brought about
this private show which could be considered as the audition for
Warner Bros. "Thank Your Lucky Stars", one year and one day after
their initial recording session. Pay scale was $7.00

14 August (FRI), 15 August (SAT), 1942
                    Jonathan Club dance/show

        Note: About this time, John Stanley, trombone and vocals,
replaced King Jackson. Both had played the studios and often recorded
together, and Jackson had volunteered for the Coast Guard Band. After
the war, he was a regular with the Red Nichols band in L.A.

21 August (FRI), 22 August (SAT)
                    Jonathan Club dance/show

28 August (FRI), 29 August, (SAT), 1942
                    Jonathan Club dance/show

30 August, 1942 (SUN) - AFRS COMMAND PERFORMANCE 34
                    CBS Hollywood (b'cast/issue date: 7 Oct 42)

                    Master of Ceremonies - Cary Grant
                    announcer - Don Wilson

                    Spike Jones and his City Slickers, with John
                        Stanley, trb; and Ralph Dadisman, tpt,
                        replacing Don Anderson on this occasion

072363-1   Hotcha Cornia - inst
                    Joan Davis - "Jim"
                    Rise Stevens - "My Hero"
                    Ethel Waters - "A Woman Without a Man"
072364-1   Larry Adler - "Bolero"
                    Abbott & Costello - comedy routine
                    Ginny Simms - "Embracable You"

        Note: These two 16" discs were issued 7 Oct as a dubbed show
and are NBC pressings with the RCA logo on the reverse. This days
mammoth Command Performance also produced transcriptions for CP 31
bearing this date, and CP 30 which was issued 11 Sept. The Abbott and
Costello segment on CP 34 is the conclusion of their "Mustard Routine", with AFRS picking it up after the mustard dialogue. The yet
nationally unknown Spike leads off the show.

            CP 31, transcribed/dated 30 Aug:- Paul Douglas, ann;
                Bing Crosby, mc; Kay Kayser & Co.; Hedy Lamarr;
                Abbott and Costello; Dr. Frank Black & his Orch

            CP 30, transcribed 30 Aug/b'cast 11 Sept:- Paul Douglas,
                ann; Bing Crosby, mc; Connie Boswell; Bert Wheeler
                and Hank Ladd; Kay Kayser's Orch; James Cagney;
                Dr. Frank Black & his Orch

Details courtesy AFRTS/LA

"The best in radio - and a lot of it - goes to U.S. forces at the fighting fronts. They have received over 1,000 special programs which U.S. radio fans would give plenty to hear. Forty-odd shows a week are heard only by the Armed Forces. Command Performance gives the boys a variety show of anything they ask for ...G.I. (Gov't Issue) Jive is a steaming session of hot radio.
"The outfit responsible is the Radio Section of the War Department's Special Service Division, Services of Supply. Headquartered in Hollywood's old Fox studios, the Section is staffed by 20 officers, 25 enlisted men (all onetime radio producers, writers, executives) scattered from Alaska to North Africa.
"They also edit versions of 24 commercial radio shows for the troops. They cut out all advertising ballyhoo, delete painful adsurdities, like Eddie Cantor's "Mad Russian", which might be fine fodder for Axis propagandists.
"To make their programs available to troops all over the globe, the Radio Section had to develop many special facilities. The U.S. Army network now includes 19 short-wave stations; 138 standard-wave stations on United Nations soil and in the theatres of action; 37 U.S. expeditionary-force stations."
(Time, 8 Mar 43)

Note: Transcriptions of AFRS shows were pressed and labeled by NBC and CBS. AFRS shows from Jan 43 appear with their own labels and were pressed in their own facilities.

"Command Performance was described by Time as "the best war-time program in radio", but few Americans at home ever got to hear it ...beginning early in 1942...It was once estimated that a show like Command Performance might cost $75,000 a week, yet it had no budget and paid no money to anyone. All talent was donated. Both CBS and NBC donated their studios for production. The series was conceived and written by Glenn Wheaton of the War Department...directed by Vick Knight, who gave up a $1,000-a-week salary on The Fred Allen show to work for nothing on Command Performance...written to the specifications of homesick fighting men...the stars considered Command Performance part of their contribution to the war effort, and the show was booked solid throughout the war. On Christmas Eve, 1942 - a Command Performance was played on all four U.S. radio networks.
"The vitality of Command Performance was strictly a wartime phenomenon...continued on AFRS until December, 1949."
(John Dunning, Tune In Yesterday: An Encyclopedia of Old-Time Radio, 1925-1976, pub Hall 1978)

Note: Spike Jones and his City Slickers were paid for their 1942/43 appearances on Command Performance, bond rallies and USO shows, but the figure is basic, the Union minimum - surely applicable to all artists on these shows. AFRS agreements with the American broadcast industry provided that the use of programs was for military stations only. No other release or use could be considered.

4 September (FRI), 5 September (SAT), 1942
Jonathan Club dance/show

11 September (FRI), 12 September (SAT), 1942
Jonathan Club dance/show

17 September, 1942 (THURS)
This is the often printed release date for "Der Fuehrer's Face". While most contemporary and recent publications support this date, they differ on the surrounding events. Spike's own PR, starting in 1943 tells of miraculous results within a week, even 48 hours and

less of the record's release. Notice the date and time element errors in the 4 Apr 49 issue of Newsweek:- "Within 48 hours after its release on September 11, 1942, Jones was on his way to the top of the cornstalk."

Contrary to other popular suggestions, the group did not appear on the Bob Burns show on this date, nor is the publicity regarding the movie contract, the new RCA contract and the radio shows within 48 hours of "Der Fuehrer's" release, correct. See details after 16 October.

The following sales figures are commonly in print:- 500,000 (Sat. Evening Post, 10 Apr 43); 1,000,000 (Colliers, 10 Jan 48); 1,500,000 (Los Angeles Times, 5 Sept 82); 2,000,000 (World of Yesteryear, Apr 78).

"Spike...recorded the song at the last possible moment, once with a single trombone note ('fonk') blaring insults to Hitler and again with the bird, also known as the Bronx cheer, which never before had been heard on a standard phonograph record.

"It didn't seem like such a good song to me", Spike says, "but I got to thinking that if it were to get anywhere, it would have to be released with the bird included. So I drew a thousand dollars out of the bank and (my wife) Pat and I went to New York to talk the Victor Company's private board of Public Morals into letting us use the bird."

"He rushed...to the recording headquarters, ready to put up a fight, only to discover that Victor agreed with him. The bird was in.

"....he called upon Martin Block...known as the radio-turntable king of New York. Hour after hour Block spins phonograph records and intersperses them with sales chatter. Spike took along a sample...Block thought it was elegant, especially the bird."
(Saturday Evening Post, 10 Apr 43)

"The Disney studios turned out numerous documentary and instructional films using animation technique. They produced the well-known VICTORY THROUGH AIR POWER, based on the book by Major Alexander P. de Seversky, and featured Donald Duck in Der Fuehrer's Face, which contained a popular war time song of the same title, composed by Oliver Wallace. The film had considerable propaganda value, with European translations smuggled in by the underground - much to the chagrin of the Nazi High Command - and won an Academy Award in 1943..." (Adrian Bailey, Walt Disney's World of Fantasy)
(Everest House, 1982)

"Leading all war songs on the juke-box popularity poll was the season's wackiest satirical item, Der Fuehrer's Face, which sold out its initial edition of 100,000 records in ten days after its release three weeks ago. A medley of bronx cheers and polka-dottiness that has to be heard to be appreciated...last week seemed well on its way to become the comic theme song of World War II. The song, written...for a picture originally entitled Donald Duck in Nutzi-Land, skyrocketed so fast that Disney decided to change the title of the picture to that of the song."
(Time, 26 Oct 42)

"...is the biggest thing since "Beer Barrel Polka"...last issue had a story claiming that this record was going to come on like the Cards - and three weeks before that, the Beat played it on Alan Courtney's WOV show in NYC and repeated it twice on the same show! The next night, Martin Block cleaned up about $50,000, offering it in return for a $50 bond purchase.

"Victor has been caught flat-footed, and is racing desperately to catch up.

"This, brother, is the first big war-tune - and it fulfills every requirement that was put down here three months ago... it has an easy melody, with a refrain that a bunch of guys can scream at the top of their lungs. The lyrics are not only funny, but they also poke brutally at some of the Nazi's worst weaknesses.

"A good 50 per cent of what makes this look like the record of the year is the terrific job that the Spike Jones' gang do on it. I've been raving about their stuff for months and am certainly glad to see that they're going to pick up some chips now for their fine work.

"Listen to this disc and you'll hear not only terrific corn, but fine music as well. All the circus trombone and German tuba effects are perfectly played. The beat is cleaner and crisper than 99 per cent of the bands around, while the lead trumpeting is the kind section men dream about. Get the street band takeoff in the middle, with a touch of McCoy trumpet and Lewis clarinet. Gimme a record like this and I'll be permanently on the telephone when the Dear Moms come around."   (Downbeat, 15 Oct 42)

18 September (FRI), 19 September (SAT), 1942
          Jonathan Club dance/show

25 September (FRI), 26 September (SAT), 1942
          Jonathan Club dance/show

29 September, 1942 (TUES) - AFRS COMMAND PERFORMANCE 33
          CBS Hollywood

          Master of Ceremonies - Bob Burns

          Spike Jones and his City Slickers, with Ralph
          Dadisman, tpt, replacing Don Anderson for this
          occasion only.

072357-1   Count Basie Orchestra - "Boogie Woogie"
                  Der Fuehrer's Face - voc Carl Grayson
                  Tommy Dorsey, Dinah Shore - "He's My Guy"
072357-2   Lionel Hampton - "Flying Home"
                  Tommy Dorsey - "Song of India"
                  Basie, Dorsey, Hampton, Jones in 'jam session'
                      on tune "Dinah" (with Bob Burns on bazooka)

          Note: These two discs have NBC labels with the RCA logo on the reverse. Much is made by Burns of "...the latest juke-box sensation - just sweeping the country.." in his introduction of Spike and "Der Fuehrer's Face". The abrupt applause stop and improved acoustics on the jam session indicate a studio remake - difficult before the advent of tape.

1 October, 1942 (THURS) - GILMORE OIL SHOW
          NBC Hollywood

          Spike Jones and his City Slickers, incl Don
          Anderson, tpt. Musical Contractor for this
          series is Carl Hoefle (Pay scale: $17.50)

          Note: This is the audition for the house band position on this new, soon to be broadcast show, "Furlough Fun". An undated and uncredited acetate from the files of Skip Craig appears to have been from this audition, and the title played is:-

          Hotcha Cornia - inst

2 October, 1942 (FRI)
> Show at Pasadena Junior College

> Jonathan Club dance/show

3 October, 1942 (SAT)
> Jonathan Club dance/show

9 October (FRI), 10 October (SAT), 1942
> Pasadena Civic Theatre dance/show

14 October, 1942 (WED) - ARKANSAS TRAVELER (Bob Burns Show)*
CBS Hollywood

> Spike Jones and his City Slickers appear as
> guests. Program contents are unknown, but pay
> scale ($40:00) indicates two titles could have
> been played, one of which would have been:-

> Der Fuehrer's Face - voc Carl Grayson

16 October, 1942 (FRI)
> Show at the Hollywood Palladium, for

> RCA Victor party

> Jonathan Club dance/show

Note: This marks the signing of a new recording contract
between Spike and RCA commencing when the ban is over. His records
will now be the more expensive Black Popular RCA discs, with
royalties, instead of the flat-rate economy Bluebird.
Here now follow the first accountings in print relating to
the flurry of success now evident.

"Then everything happened at once! Sitting in Radio Life's
editorial office the other day (to escape from song pluggers), a wiry
little fellow who answers on formal occasions to the name of Lindley
Armstrong Jones, recited exactly what transpired.
"Monday", related the angular counterpart to Mr. Jimmie
Cagney, "I was signed by Warner Brothers for 'Thank Your Lucky
Stars'".
"Tuesday, the Slickers and I were signed by Gilmore Oil for
a new show."
"Wednesday we made a guest appearance on Bob Burns' show at
CBS."
"Thursday, they signed us for it."
"Friday, the Victor company notified me that sales for "Der
Fuehrer's Face" had passed the half million. They offered a new
contract."
"Saturday, we were approached for another picture deal."
"Sunday, my wife chained me to the garage to keep my feet on
the ground."   (Radio Life, 29 Nov 42)

"Jones...found himself suddenly thrust up among the top U.S.
bandleaders. Until then "Spike" had been modestly playing what he
calls "society music" (jazzed up Chopin and Debussy) at Los Angeles'
Jonathan Club. Now he is being fought over by several Hollywood
studios, is already signed up for a Warner Brothers musical called
'Thank Your Lucky Star'(sic)" (Time, 26 Oct 42)

"Hearing this record...Warner Brothers' producer Mark

53

Hellinger decided that here was the type of outfit he was seeking for
his coming production of "Thank Your Lucky Stars."
(Band Wagon, 46)

Note: Dating of listed events is supported, in part, by
Anderson's diaries re: Burns show (Wed), Victor party (Fri). Gilmore
could have confirmed successful audition (Tues) while the picture
deal (Sat) could have been the upcoming short for Movietone. PR liberties in the future place these events well out of proportion. All
Slickers personnel maintained their free-lance status for another
year, making their personal schedules unbelievably full.

Spike's business office (Business Administration) was expanded to handle the added furor caused this timely 'hit' while Spike
dropped most of his show and session work in order to devote himself
to the full-time manipulations of promotion and marketing. Although
the recording ban could have caught anyone less prepared without the
all-important second hit, Spike and RCA planned to slowly release the
balance of their recorded titles while Spike maintained a high profile with constant radio and public appearances, keeping the demand
for his show and music at a high level.

17 October, 1942 (SAT)
        Jonathan Club dance/show

21 October, 1942 (WED) - ARKANSAS TRAVELER (Bob Burns Show)*
            CBS Hollywood   Sponsor: Lifebuoy Soap

        with Spike Jones and his City Slickers now
            appearing as the regular house band

        Leader/drm - Spike Jones
        Trumpet - Don Anderson
        Trombone - John Stanley
        Clarinet/sax - Del Porter
        Violin - Carl Grayson
        Piano - Frank Leithner
        Banjo/guitar - Luther Roundtree
        Tuba/st bass - Country Washburn
        Vocals - Del Porter, Carl Grayson, Country
            Washburn and on occasion, Luther Roundtree
            and John Stanley
        Arrangers - Del Porter, Country Washburn,
            Frank Leithner

        Der Fuehrer's Face - voc Carl Grayson

Note: Pay scale $60.00 (Nat'l b'cast). Only the above title
survives on a dated Radio Recorders acetate. Radio Recorders, incidentally, was incorporated 26 Dec 34 and from 1941 to 1978 was located at 7000 Santa Monica Blvd., Los Angeles.

23 October, 1942 (FRI) - AFRS ARMY SHOW*
            CBS Hollywood

Note: Although this date appears in Anderson diaries, it may
have involved Anderson with another group - not the Slickers.

        Jonathan Club dance/show

24 October, 1942 (SAT)
        Jonathan Club dance/show

27 October, 1942 (TUES) - AFRS COMMAND PERFORMANCE 39*
            CBS Hollywood

            Master of Ceremonies - Rita Hayworth
            announcer - Don Wilson

            with Cass Daley, the Hall Johnson Choir, Frank
              Morgan, John Conte, Meredith Willson, Lena
              Horne, Lou Forbes and the Selznick Productions
              Orchestra, and Spike Jones and his City
              Slickers

        Note: Transcriptions of this show will likely bear NBC
labels as AFRS had not yet started to press their own. Artist listing
courtesy AFRTS/LA. Having enlisted in the Army, Meredith Willson
headed the AFRS music division during the war.

28 October, 1942 (WED) - ARKANSAS TRAVELER (Bob Burns Show)*
            CBS Hollywood

            with Spike Jones and his City Slickers

30 October (FRI), 31 October (SAT), 1942
            Jonathan Club dance/show

1 November, 1942 (SUN)
            Show at the Wilshire Country Club

2 November, 1942 (MON) - FURLOUGH FUN*
            NBC Hollywood   Sponsor: Gilmore Oil

            Beryl Wallace, "Femmcee"; George Riley, comedy
              dialogue; Larry Keating, Vern Smith, announc-
              ers; Carl Hoefle, music contractor, and
              featuring Spike Jones and his City Slickers

        Note: Broadcast time was 7:30 PM PST to 8 Feb 43. Pay Scale:
$30.00 (West coast b'cast only)

4 November, 1942 (WED) - 20th CENTURY FOX STUDIOS
            Hollywood

            Spike Jones and his City Slickers filming for
              "Movietone" wartime theatre news releases,

            Der Fuehrer's Face - voc Carl Grayson

        Note: Clips from this filming are still to be seen, the most
recent being "Life Goes To War" on television. Giving the 'finger' to
Hitler, as seen on this film, was part of the City Slickers show and
done on every performance. No fee involved.

            ARKANSAS TRAVELER (Bob Burns Show)*
            CBS Hollywood

            with Spike Jones and his City Slickers

5 November, 1942 (THURS) - WARNER BROTHERS STUDIOS
            Hollywood

For the next two weeks from this date, Spike Jones and his City Slickers appeared in the filming of THANK YOUR LUCKY STARS, 127 minutes, b/w

                      City Slickers personnel as 21 October, with
                        Ralph Dadisman, tpt, and Carl Hoefle, pno,
                        replacing Don Anderson and Frank Leithner.
                        Add Leithner, effects

1139-   Hotcha Cornia - inst
                      -I'm Ridin' For a Fall - voc Dennis Morgan and
                      Joan Leslie
                            (straight)

        Note: Carl Grayson's visual sneeze in "Hotcha Cornia" is actually sidelined to Frank Leithner's effect on the soundtrack. The Gower Gulch sequence, which includes the City Slickers and is of no consequence to the movie plot, is often omitted when "Stars" is shown on late night television.
        Additional songs and music for the film were composed by Frank Loesser and Arthur Schwartz. The studio orchestra is conducted by Cookie Fairchild. The music soundtrack was issued on Sandy Hook LP SH 2012, and Show Biz LP 5606. Vinylite 78 RPM soundtrack records were also available as Warner Bros.:- Exploitation Record, three record album; No. 1139 "I'm Ridin' For a Fall".
        The commonly seen PR photo of the Slickers appearing in tuxedos and jumping into the air with their instruments askew, as seen in the 10 Apr 43 Saturday Evening Post, is probably from an unreleased scene. Additional stills show Luther Roundtree with grotesque - fake feet, and Spike losing his fake hand to John Stanley. Their bandstand is a shambles. Anderson's diary entry for 6 Nov shows he was paid $200 for his participation in this feature. For reasons beyond recall, he was unable to continue.

6 November (FRI), 7 November (SAT), 1942
                Jonathan Club dance/show

8 November, 1942 (SUN)
                Show at the Riverside Breakfast Club

9 November, 1942 (MON) - FURLOUGH FUN
                NBC Hollywood

                      Pack Up Your Troubles - Theme
                      Beryl Wallace - Introductory comments
                      Siam - voc Del Porter, Country Washburn,
                        and Carl Grayson
                      Vern Smith and Spike - Gilmore purchase of an
                        old hunting hat
                      Commercial - Boys in the Back Room
                      Beryl - interview with three servicemen, cash
                        award to quiz winner
                      Vern and Beryl - Gilmore purchase of old golf ball
                      Sgt Al Hirsch - dedicates to his wife, this
                        'on-the-air' recording of
                      Come Josephine In My Flying Machine - voc Boys
                        in the Back Room and Country Washburn
                      George Riley - Comedy dialogue
                      Vern and Spike - Gilmore purchase of Grandfather's
                        old snuff box
                      Commercial - Boys in the Back Room
                      Beryl - interview with three servicemen, cash
                        award to quiz winner
                      Hotcha Cornia - inst

                    Vern – Gilmore purchase of old, toothless comb
                    Cash award to serviceman for sound effects
                    Pack Up Your Troubles – Theme

10 November, 1942 (TUES)
                    Show at the Pasadena Junior College

11 November, 1942 (WED) – ARKANSAS TRAVELER (Bob Burns Show)*
                    CBS Hollywood

                    with Spike Jones and his City Slickers

13 November (FRI), 14 November (SAT), 1942
                    Jonathan Club dance/show

15 November, 1942 (SUN)
                    Show at the Riverside Breakfast Club

16 November, 1942 (MON) – FURLOUGH FUN*
                    NBC Hollywood

                    with Spike Jones and his City Slickers

18 November, 1942 (WED)
                    Show at the Pasadena Civic Theatre

                    ARKANSAS TRAVELER (Bob Burns Show)*
                    CBS Hollywood

                    with Spike Jones and his City Slickers

21 November (FRI), 22 November (SAT), 1942
                    Jonathan Club dance/show

23 November, 1942 (MON) – FURLOUGH FUN*
                    NBC Hollywood

                    with Spike Jones and his City Slickers

25 November, 1942 (WED) – ARKANSAS TRAVELER (Bob Burns Show)*
                    CBS Hollywood

                    with Spike Jones and his City Slickers

        Note: There was also a play date at Long Beach this evening.
Don Anderson played not only with Spike (pay $15.00), but with Gordon
Jenkins (pay 13.50). Possible City Slickers show with Jenkins dance
band.

26 November, 1942 (THURS) – ELGIN WATCH SHOW*
                    CBS Hollywood

                    with Spike Jones and his City Slickers

27 November (FRI), 28 November (SAT), 1942
                    Jonathan Club dance/show

                                    57

30 November, 1942 (MON) - FURLOUGH FUN*
              NBC Hollywood

              with Spike Jones and his City Slickers

2 December, 1942 (WED) - ARKANSAS TRAVELER (Bob Burns Show)*
              CBS Hollywood

              with Spike Jones and his City Slickers

4 December (FRI), 5 December (SAT) 1942
              Shows at the Pasadena Civic Theatre

7 December, 1942 (MON) - FURLOUGH FUN*
              NBC Hollywood

              with Spike Jones and his City Slickers

9 December, 1942 (WED) - ARKANSAS TRAVELER (Bob Burns Show)*
              CBS Hollywood

              with Spike Jones and his City Slickers

14 December, 1942 (MON) - OLD GOLD SHOW*
              NBC Hollywood

              Audition for Spike Jones and his City Slickers
              for the position of house band (unsuccessful)

          FURLOUGH FUN
          NBC Hollywood

          Pack Up Your Troubles - Theme
          Beryl Wallace - introductory comments re:
             studio audience composed of over 300 guests
             with the surname 'Jones", invited in honor of
             this being Spike's birthday.
          Siam - voc Del Porter, Country Washburn,
             Carl Grayson
          Vern Smith, Spike, George Riley - Gilmore purchase
             of a wishbone from a 20lb. turkey
          Commercial - Boys in the Back Room
          Beryl - interview with two servicemen and one WAC,
             with cash award to quiz winner (one serviceman
             was Sgt Peter Linde-Hayes, impressionist, who
             had an act after the war)
          Vern, Spike, George - Gilmore purchase of a new
             necktie
          Seaman Leon Generon dedicates to his wife this
             'on-the-air' recording of
          I Know a Story - voc Country Washburn
                         (straight)
          George Riley - Comedy dialogue
          Commercial - Boys in the Back Room
          Beryl - interview with 3 servicemen, the cash
             award to quiz winner (Question: how many 'rasp-
             berries' in Spike's "Der Fuehrer's Face", which
             has just sold 700,000 copies?)
          Vern, Beryl - Gilmore purchase of a dog collar
          Vern - Gilmore purchase promotion
          Touch of Texas - voc Del Porter
          Pack Up Your Troubles - Theme

                          58

16 December, 1942 (WED) - ARKANSAS TRAVELER (Bob Burns Show)*
                        CBS Hollywood

                 with Spike Jones and his City Slickers

18 December (FRI), 19 December (SAT) 1942
                 Jonathan Club Christmas dance/show

          Note: Saturday was the final appearance at the Jonathan.
Their show is 'in', and regular dances will be phased out

21 December, 1942 (MON) - FURLOUGH FUN*
                         NBC Hollywood

                 with Spike Jones and his City Slickers

23 December, 1942 (WED)
                 Spike Jones and his City Slickers unknown
                 committment at, or for, 'Vega' (no fee involved)

                 ARKANSAS TRAVELER (Bob Burns Show)*
                 CBS Hollywood

                 with Spike Jones and his City Slickers

24 December, 1942 (THURS) - AFRS COMMAND PERFORMANCE
                 Special Christmas Show (un-numbered)
                 CBS, NBC Red, NBC Blue, Mutual-Don Lee

                 Master of Ceremonies - Bob Hope
                 Orchestra directed by Alfred Newman
                 announcer - Ken Carpenter

                 Elmer Davis (Chief of the Office of War
                   Information) - Message
                 Bob Hope - Comedy dialogue
                 Andrews Sisters - "Pennsylvania Polka"
                 Harriet Hilliard, Red Skelton - Comedy skit
                 Jingle Bells - City Slickers
                 Ginny Simms - "Savin' Myself For Bill"
                 Bing Crosby, Bob Hope - Comedy dialogue
                 Bing Crosby, Charioteers - "Basin Street Blues"
                 Ethel Waters - "Dinah"
                 Charles Laughton, Edgar Bergan, Charlie McCarthy
                   - Comedy skit
                 Kay Kayser - "Praise the Lord and Pass the
                   Ammunition"
                 Dinah Shore - "As Long As You're Not In Love
                   with Anyone Else"
                 Jack Benny and Fred Allen (on remote from New
                   York) - "Friendship", and comedy dialogue
                 Bob Hope - Narrative
                 "Over There"
                 National Anthem

          Note: This was the first AFRS Command Performance to be
broadcast to the civilian population. Photographs of Spike Jones and
Red Skelton on the NBC sound stage were taken during the dress
rehearsal. This one hour show was issued on cassette by Sandy Hook
"Radio Yesteryear" Listener's Digest 13

28 December, 1942 (MON) - FURLOUGH FUN*
                         NBC Hollywood

                    with Spike Jones and his City Slickers

30 December, 1942 (WED) - ARKANSAS TRAVELER (Bob Burns Show)*
                         CBS Hollywood

                    with Spike Jones and his City Slickers

         Note: This is the last Wed CBS b'cast of the "Traveler". It
emerges in eight days on NBC as the "Bob Burns Show"

31 December, 1942 (THURS)
                         "Swing Shift", Long Beach New Years dance/show

         Note: Feature articles on Spike Jones appeared during
               1942 in:-

               Radio Life, 5 July -
               Radio Life, 29 November - "Der Fuehrer's Face"
               Downbeat, 15 October - "Record Review"

4 January, 1943 (MON) - FURLOUGH FUN*
                       NBC Hollywood

                    with Spike Jones and his City Slickers,
                       personnel as 21 Oct 42

7 January, 1943 (THURS) - THE BOB BURNS SHOW*
                         NBC Hollywood

                    with Spike Jones and his City Slickers

         Note: NBC produced two versions of this national broadcast.
One early afternoon show for the East coast, then a later show for
the West. The two were basically identical with minute differences.
It is possible NBC and AFRS transcribed each show.(Pay scale: $72.00)

11 January, 1943 (MON) - FURLOUGH FUN*
                        NBC Hollywood

                    with Spike Jones and his City Slickers

14 January, 1943 (THURS) - THE BOB BURNS SHOW*
                          NBC Hollywood

                    with Spike Jones and his City Slickers

18 January, 1943 (MON) - FURLOUGH FUN*
                        NBC Hollywood

                    with Spike Jones and his City Slickers

21 January, 1943 (THURS) - THE BOB BURNS SHOW*
                          NBC Hollywood

                    with Spike Jones and his City Slickers

23 January, 1943 (SAT) - MARCH OF DIMES*
            NBC Hollywood

                    Spike Jones and his City Slickers participate
                        in this years March of Dimes b'cast (no fee)

            Alhambra High School dance/show

        "Spike...agreed to play for a dance at the Alhambra High
School... for half his usual fee if the students bought enough war
stamps to make up the difference. They bought $1500 worth of stamps
and presented Spike with a picture of Der Fuehrer's Face stamped out
with war stamps. The picture they used was the Post cover of January
23rd."   (Saturday Evening Post, 10 Apr 43)
        Note: The above picture was presented to Spike during the
March of Dimes show earlier this day.

25 January, 1943 (MON) - FURLOUGH FUN*
            NBC Hollywood

                    with Spike Jones and his City Slickers

28 January, 1943 (THURS) - THE BOB BURNS SHOW*
            NBC Hollywood

                    with Spike Jones and his City Slickers

        Note: For the Slickers, there was also an unexplained but
paid Bob Burns 'audition' at NBC today. Spike is trying to enlarge
his group to increase its versatility. New personalities tried out
for the Slickers, all temporary and mostly unidentified.

1 February, 1943 (MON) - FURLOUGH FUN*
            NBC Hollywood

                    with Spike Jones and his City Slickers

4 February, 1943 (THURS) - THE BOB BURNS SHOW
            NBC Hollywood

                    Bob Burns - monologue on tire inspection,
                        fly swatter, Mussolini's paratroopers
                    *Pass the Biscuits Mirandy - voc Del Porter
                    Dick Lane's vacation - fast talk commercial
                    The Lost Confession - skit
                    Bob Burns, Luther Roundtree - hogs
                    Bob Burns - "I'm Goin' Back To My Razorback
                        Down In Arkansas"
                    Larry Keating - Vimms Vitamins commercial

                    *issued on MF Distribution LPs MF 205/4,
                        947447, and GO 10016

        Note: The West coast version was used on the LP reissues,
and this show also contains the first known reference to Spike and
'Cornegie Hall'.

8 February, 1943 (MON) - FURLOUGH FUN*
            NBC Hollywood

with Spike Jones and his City Slickers

Note: This is the last Monday b'cast of Furlough Fun. It is next heard on Friday, 19 February

10 February, 1943 (WED)
              San Pedro dance/show

11 February, 1943 (THURS) - THE BOB BURNS SHOW
              NBC Hollywood

              Bob Burns - monologue on shoes
              Take the Door To the Left - voc Del Porter
                 and Boys in the Back Room
              Dick Lane - Little Red Riding Hood commercial
              Who Owns the Dog? - skit
              Sound Effects Man - commercial
              Public Service Announcement (PSA) - fat salvage
              Spike Jones chaser - Drip, Drip, Drip

18 February, 1943 (THURS) - THE BOB BURNS SHOW
              NBC Hollywood

              Guests: Burns and Allen

              Bob Burns - monologue on drunk uncle
              Sheik of Araby - voc Del Porter and Carl Grayson
              Dick Lane - Androcles and the Lion commercial
              Lost Letters - skit (Frank Nelson in cast)
              Boys in the Back Room - commercial on
                 "Mountain Gertie"
              Burns and Allen - comedy dialogue with
                 Bob Burns
              Larry Keating - Vimms Vitamins commercial

Note: Intro of Spike by Burns:- "...read in the morning paper that the City Slickers is 'the band that plays for fun'".

19 February, 1943 (FRI) - FURLOUGH FUN*
              NBC Hollywood   9:00 PM PST

              Red Wing - voc Del Porter
              Der Fuehrer's Face - voc Carl Grayson

25 February, 1943 (THURS) - THE BOB BURNS SHOW*
              NBC Hollywood

              Bob Burns - monologue on Victory gardens
              Hitch Old Dobbin To the Shay Again - vocal
                 Quartet
              Dick Lane - Little Red Riding Hood commercial
              Goat Hill protest - skit, with Cy Kendall
              Boys in the Back Room - commercial
              Bob Burns, Luther Roundtree - health
              Bob Burns - song "Life Story"

26 February, 1943 (FRI) - FURLOUGH FUN*
              NBC Hollywood

              with Spike Jones and his City Slickers

27 February, 1943 (SAT)
        Beverly-Wilshire dance/show

4 March, 1943 (THURS) - THE BOB BURNS SHOW
        NBC Hollywood

        Bob Burns with Dick Lane - monologue and
          questions from listeners
        Old McDonald Had a Farm - voc Del Porter
        Bob Burns, Dick Lane, Hans Conried - fast
          talk commercial
        Story of the Year award - skit
        B.O. Blues - commercial
        Bob Burns monologue, with piano - on piano
          playing and song writing
        Poems - Luther Roundtree
        Spike Jones fill - Clink Clink, Another Drink
        Larry Keating - Vimms Vitamins commercial

5 March, 1943 (FRI) - FURLOUGH FUN*
        NBC Hollywood

        Hotcha Cornia - inst
        Sweet Little You - voc Carl Grayson
                (straight)

7 March, 1943 (SUN)
        San Pedro show, on board a USN battleship

      Note: Larger than normal pay scale indicates the Slickers as
an accompanying 'pit' band - a bond rally, perhaps

9 March, 1943 (TUES)
        Club Del Rio, San Pedro, dance/show

11 March, 1943 (THURS) - THE BOB BURNS SHOW
        NBC Hollywood

        Bob Burns - monologue on Income Tax
        That's My Pop - voc Del Porter, Carl Grayson,
          Bryan Sisters, two unidentified male voices
        All's Fair in Love and War Bond Drives - skit
        B.O. Boys of History - commercial with
          vocal quartet
        Bob Burns, Luther Roundtree - taxes
        Bazooka solo - "Darktown Strutters Ball"
        PSA - Red Cross
        Fill music - Drip, Drip, Drip
        Larry Keating - Vimms Vitamins commercial

12 March, 1943 (FRI) - FURLOUGH FUN*
        NBC Hollywood

        Liebestraum - voc Carl Grayson, assisted by
          Spike (falsetto, hiccoughs), poems by Luther
          Roundtree

      Note: "Liebestraum", seemingly out of place in this early
pre-Ingle time slot, is correct at this date. A yet earlier take with
a different piano vamp and ukulele was in Jones' files and dubbed for
"Martin" (Block?). This is the first presentation of a full frontal
assault on a classic. The current public popularity of this classic

love song was brought about through the piano performances on radio
and film by Jose Iturbi. The 1945 RCA inst sheets credit Jones,
Porter and/or Hoefle as the arrangers.

18 March, 1943 (THURS) - THE BOB BURNS SHOW
                NBC Hollywood

                Bob Burns - More letters from listeners monologue,
                    with Dick Lane
                It's a Long Way From Minsk To Pinsk - voc
                    Carl Grayson
                Dick Lane - commercial (jealous of Spike Jones)
                Traveler hires an ex-convict - skit
                Bob Burns, Luther Roundtree - letter from
                    Grandma Snazzy
                Bazooka solo - "I Ain't Got Nobody"
                PSA - Red Cross
                Larry Keating - Vimms Vitamins commercial

19 March, 1943 (FRI) - FURLOUGH FUN*
                NBC Hollywood

                Take the Door To the Left - voc Del Porter
                    and the Boys in the Back Room
                Button Up Your Overcoat - vocal quartet
                            (straight)

24 March, 1943 (WED) - Fullerton Junior College*
                NBC Hollywood

                Bond Rally broadcast with
                Master of Ceremonies - Eddie Cantor

                *Der Fuehrer's Face - voc Carl Grayson

                *issued on MF Distribution LPs MF 205/4,
                    947447, and GO 10016

        Note: Details based on diary entry and surviving, but un-
dated, acetate

25 March, 1943 (THURS) - THE BOB BURNS SHOW*
                NBC Hollywood

                Bob Burns - monologue on butter shortage
                All-Truth Week - skit (possibly with Hans Conried)
                Dick Lane - commercial, with "professor"
                Bob Burns, Luther Roundtree - songs
                The Coon Hunt - Bob Burns with guitar
                PSA - fat recycling
                Fill music - Yankee Doodles Dandy
                Larry Keating - Vimms Vitamins commercial

26 March, 1943 (FRI) - FURLOUGH FUN*
                NBC Hollywood

                It's a Long Way From Minsk To Pinsk - voc
                    Carl Grayson
                Somebody Loves Me - voc Johnny Stanley
                            (straight)
                Hitch Old Dobbin To the Shay Again - inst

Note: This is one of the rare times that the straight vocal is not taken by Carl Grayson, nor is it certain the baritone is Johnny Stanley.

27 March, 1943 (SAT) - AFRS COMMAND PERFORMANCE 59*
       NBC Hollywood

            announcer Ken Carpenter, with Kay Kayser and
               his Orchestra, Lennie Hayton, Hedda Hopper,
               The Balalaika Gypsy Band, Ralina Zarova and
               Spike Jones and his City Slickers

Note: Pay scale $24.50. Artist listing courtesy AFRTS/LA

1 April, 1943 (THURS) - THE BOB BURNS SHOW
       NBC Hollywood

            Bob Burns - monologue on April Fools jokes and
               the military bazooka
            The Vamp - voc Del Porter
            The Honest Tire Thief - skit
            Spike Jones commercial - "A Pretty Girl Is
               Like a Melody"
            Bob Burns, Luther Roundtree - grammar, IQ test
            Bazooka solo - "April Showers"
            Fill music (short) - Spike Jones
            Larry Keating - Lifebuoy and Vimms commercial

2 April, 1943 (FRI) - FURLOUGH FUN*
       NBC Hollywood

            We Don't Want No Goose Step Over Here - voc Del
               Porter, Luther Roundtree, Beryl Wallace,
               George Riley
            The Blacksmith Song - voc Del Porter
            The Covered Wagon Rolled Right Along - voc
               Del Porter

7 April, 1943 (WED) - Compton Junior College*
       NBC Hollywood

            Bond Rally broadcast

Note: Pay scale indicates similarity to 24 Mar b'cast

8 April, 1943 (THURS) - THE BOB BURNS SHOW
       NBC Hollywood

            Bob Burns - monoloue on meat shortage
            Bob Burns - interview with Spike Jones
            Hotcha Cornia - inst
            Goat Hill Victory Parade - skit
            Commercial with vocal quartet - "Just a Song
               At Twilight"
            Bob Burns - monologue on gardens
            Bob Burns, Luther Roundtree - "I'm Goin'
               Back To My Razorback"
            PSA - War Bonds
            Commercial - Lifebuoy Shaving Cream

      Note: Burns announces that during this past week the new
U.S. Army secret weapon, the recoil-less rocket launcher has been

named after his "Bazooka". The Jones interview concerns the just
issued 10 April edition of the Saturday Evening Post which contained
the article "He Plays Louder Than Anybody". Mention is also made of
Spike recently winning the "King of Corn" award (for the first time).

9 April, 1943 (FRI) - FURLOUGH FUN*
                NBC Hollywood

                    *Wang Wang Blues - voc Del Porter
                     Brazil - voc Carl Grayson
                                (straight)
                     Red Wing - voc Del Porter

                    *issued on Corno LP 1001, Glendale LP 6005,
                     Sandy Hook LP SH 2073

11 April, 1943 (SUN)

        An unexplained but paid 'audition' at NBC for the City
Slickers for Lever Bros. This may mark the start of the expanded
Slickers to now include Beauregard Lee and Red Ingle.
        Little is known of Beauregard Wilmarth Lee and his back-
ground beyond that he was contemporary with Spike in the Everett
Hoagland band at Balboa, but he does emerge as an excellent rhythm
man, vocalist and, in the future, Spike's road manager. "There have
been a few changes in the original line-up since the band began, most
notable being the addition of a drummer. Of this, Spike says: "You
may think this silly, but I play washboards, horns and other effects
with the band, and while I'm wandering about lost - trying to think
of their social security numbers, when to take the fiddle player out
of the iron lung, and how the introduction of 'Old Black Magic' goes
- he can keep the rhythm going. Not only that, but he sings like mad
and played the part of Mussolini in the number we did in our second
film, M.G.M.'s 'Meet The People'". (Band Wagon 46. A similar narra-
tive appeared in Melody Maker, 9 Sept 44)
        With the addition of Lee, Spike is better able to 'front'
the band, conducting, which he could do quite well, without having to
be on top of the drum set-up. For Slickers conducting, his 'baton'
was a pistol, although he graduated to baseball bats and bathroom
plungers, which were also useful as a drum majors mace.
        The veteran Ernest Janzen "Red" Ingle had started with
pianist Joe Sullivan and drummer George Wettling, playing violin and
tenor sax. At 19, he joined Paul Whiteman's Kentucky Kernals and in
1926 he worked with Bix and Frankie Trumbauer in Jean Goldkette's
orch. With Ted Weems for more than 10 years from 1931, then a short
while with the CAA (Civil Aeronautics Administration) - he was a
flyer and joined the CAA as instructor at Trumbauer's urging just
before the U.S. became involved with the war, being director of
visual education with an office in Washington, D.C., with wife and
son in California. "He left to take an Air Force commission, but
failed the eye exam and got a 4-F rating, and headed back to California. Not there long when Country Washburn called and asked if he
would be interested in joining the Jones band. He was, did, and
that's history now."(Don Ingle, written communication, 21 Jun 83)
        Country Washburn, Red Ingle and the original Del Porter
proved to be an innovative, progressive and formidable trio at this
stage of the Slickers history.

        From this date or shortly afterwards, Spike Jones and
            his City Slickers personnel:-

                    Leader/effts - Spike Jones
                    Trumpet - Don Anderson
                    Trombone - John Stanley
                    Clarinet/saxophone - Del Porter, Red Ingle
                    Violin - Carl Grayson, Red Ingle (on occasion)

```
                    Piano - Frank Leithner
                    Banjo/guitar - Luther Roundtree
                    Tuba/st bass - Country Washburn
                    Drums - Beauregard Lee
                    Vocals - Del Porter, Carl Grayson, Red Ingle,
                       Country Washburn, Beauregard Lee. On special
                       occasions, add Luther Roundtree, Johnny Stanley


14 April, 1943 (WED)
                    Show at Hollywood High School; and
                    Manual Arts High School dance/show


15 April, 1943 (THURS) - THE BOB BURNS SHOW
                    NBC Hollywood

                    Bob Burns - monologue with Luther Roundtree on;
                       Hitler, Rommel, first aid
                    Oh By Jingo - voc Del Porter
                    The Rumor - skit
                    Spike Jones, Dick Lane - commerical
                    Bob Burns at piano - musical jokes, wartime
                    PSA - Bob Burns on War Bonds
                    Fill music - I'm Thinking Tonight of my
                       Blue Eyes
                    Commercial - Lifebuoy Shaving Cream


16 April, 1943 (FRI) - FURLOUGH FUN*
                    NBC El Toro Marine Base

                    Pass the Biscuits Mirandy - voc Del Porter
                    Sheik of Araby - voc Del Porter and Carl Grayson


        Note: Pay scale is reduced to $30 on Furlough Fun b'casts
for balance of season


22 April, 1943 (THURS) - THE BOB BURNS SHOW
                    NBC Hollywood

                    Bob Burns - monologue with Luther Roundtree on;
                       clothes, Easter Bunny
                    Wang Wang Blues - voc Del Porter
                    Spike Jones commercial - "There'll Be a Hot
                       Time in the Old Town Tonight", "Song of the
                       Volga Boatmen"
                    Bob Burns - monologue on 1943 bathing suits
                       and other styles
                    Bill Powell - promotion for War Bonds
                    PSA - fat recycling
                    Commercial - Lifebuoy Shaving Cream


23 April, 1943 (FRI) - FURLOUGH FUN*
                    NBC Hollywood

                    Guest: Ronald Coleman

                    The Sound Effects Man - voc Del Porter
                    Buy More Stamps and Bonds - voc Del Porter
                       and Boys in the Back Room
                    Little Bo-Peep Has Lost Her Jeep - voc Del Porter


24 April, 1943, (SAT)
                    Lick Pier, Los Angeles, dance/show
```

28 April, 1943 (WED)
           Show at Long Beach Polytechnical School

29 April, 1943 (THURS) - THE BOB BURNS SHOW
           NBC El Toro Marine Base

                Bob Burns - monologue on 'Easy Marine Life'
                Casey Jones - voc Del Porter and Country Washburn
                Dick Lane - fast-talk commercial on Marines
                Man-rationing - skit (with Arthur Q. Bryan)
                Bob Burns, Luther Roundtree - Romance
                PSA - fat recycling drive (with 'German Hausfrau')
                Fill music - Spike Jones
                Commercial - Lifebuoy Shaving Cream

30 April, 1943 (FRI)
           Show at Manual Arts High School

           FURLOUGH FUN*
           NBC Hollywood

                Oh By Jingo - voc Del Porter
                Row Row Row - voc Del Porter and Boys in
                   the Back Room
                I Love Coffee - voc Del Porter

      Note: The presence of Red Ingle is now noticable, particu-
larly with his effects (audibles) in the commercials. He may also be
on sax/clar in "Jingo" and "Row".

1 May, 1943 (SAT) - AFRS COMMAND PERFORMANCE*
           CBS Hollywood

      Note: This b'cast may not apply to the Slickers - perhaps
only to Don Anderson

6 May, 1943 (THURS) - THE BOB BURNS SHOW
           NBC Hollywood

                Bob Burns - monologue on meat shortage
                The Sound Effects Man - voc Del Porter
                Jury Duty - skit
                Hans Conried - commercial
                Bob Burns, Luther Roundtree - comedy with piano
                PSA - inflation, with Larry Keating

7 May, 1943 (FRI) - FURLOUGH FUN*
           NBC Hollywood

                I Want a Girl, Just Like the Girl - voc
                   Beauregard Lee
                Casey Jones - voc Del Porter and Country Washburn

12 May, 1943 (WED)
           Show at Alhambra High School; and
             show at South Pasadena High School

13 May, 1943 (THURS) - THE BOB BURNS SHOW*
           NBC U.S. Maritime Training Stat., Catalina Island

Bob Burns - monologue on Merchant Marine Base
Haunted House - skit (with Frank Nelson, Howard
    McNear)
Commercial - Bicycle Built For Two
Bob Burns, Luther Roundtree - Life story,
    with guitar
Fill music - I've Heard That Song Before

14 May, 1943 (FRI)
                 Show at Whittier High School

              FURLOUGH FUN*
              NBC Hollywood

                 Paddlin' Madeline Home - voc Beauregard Lee
                 Drip Drip Drip - voc Del Porter
                 Wang Wang Blues - voc Del Porter

15 May, 1943 (SAT)
                 Wilmington High School dance/show

17 May, 1943 (MON) - MGM STUDIOS
                 Hollywood

    Spike Jones and his City Slickers were entered on the
payroll of MGM for the production of the movie, MEET THE PEOPLE, 100
minutes, black and white.

                 Personnel as 11 April, with Carl Hoefle, pno,
                    replacing Frank Leithner

                 (0:45)Der Fuehrer's Face - inst
                 (4:23)Schicklegruber - voc Beauregard Lee and
                    MGM chorus

    Note: Timings are approximate. The filming of the City
Slickers sequences was to have finished by 24 June, but was extended
to 17 July. Vaughn Monroe and his Orchestra also appear in the movie.
Additional songs by Lee Wainer.
    In the film, the inroduction of "Schicklegruber" as by "the
Shipyard Symphony Orchestra" has given this opus the unofficial title
of "Shipyard Symphony". Curiously, just before Red Ingle sings, "What
you've done to our Benito?" is a voice sounding like that of Dick
Morgan, who will not become associated with the Slickers for another
year!

19 May, 1943 (WED)
                 Show at Pasadena College

                 Personnel as 11 April

20 May, 1943 (THURS) - THE BOB BURNS SHOW
                 NBC Ferry Command, Long Beach

                 Bob Burns - monologue on military flying
                 Bob Burns, Luther Roudntree introduce the
                    Frank Loesser tune of
                 In My Arms - voc Del Porter, effects by
                    Beauregard Lee
                 White Horse and Black Tail - skit, with
                    Mel Blanc in cast

Mel Blanc - commercial
Bazooka solo - "How Come You Do Me Like You
   Do, Do, Do"
PSA - "Praise the Lord and Pass the Ammunition"
   - Slickers and chorus on fat recycling

21 May, 1943 (FRI) - FURLOUGH FUN*
               NBC Hollywood

               *My Little Girl - voc Beauregard Lee

               *issued on Corno LP 1001, Glendale LP 6005,
                  Sandy Hook LP SH 2073

27 May, 1943 (THURS) - THE BOB BURNS SHOW
               NBC Hollywood

               Bob Burns - monologue on Spring and housework
               Sheik of Araby - voc Del Porter, Carl Grayson
               Trap for Black Marketeer - skit
               Commercial - Lifebuoy Bell introduced
               Bazooka solo, and Luther Roundtree - "Let's
                  Get Lost"
               Fill music - Drip Drip Drip

28 May, 1943 (FRI) - FURLOUGH FUN*
               NBC Hollywood

               with Spike Jones and his City Slickers

29 May, 1943 (SAT) - MGM STUDIOS
               Hollywood

               Spike Jones and his City Slickers recorded for
                  the film MEET THE PEOPLE, the soundtrack to
                  "Schicklegruber". Taping date of "Der Fuehrer's
                  Face" is unknown.

       About this time, Elsa and Eileen, the Nilsson Twins, join
the Slickers as vocalists. Having sung with the Ted Weems Band at age
fifteen, they had recently appeared in the filming of Universal's
"Hiya Sailor".

3 June, 1943 (THURS) - THE BOB BURNS SHOW
               NBC Hollywood

               Bob Burns - monologue on home redecorating
               Paddlin' Madeline Home - voc Beauregard Lee
               Persuading a miser to buy War Bonds - skit
               Commercial - Sonovox demonstrated
               Bazooka solo - "Three Little Fishies"
               PSA - fat recycling
               Fill music - "Don't Talk To Me About Women"

4 June, 1943 (FRI) - FURLOUGH FUN*
               NBC Hollywood

               Put Your Arms Around Me Honey - voc Beauregard
                  Lee and the Nilsson Twins
               brief fill - "Don't Talk To Me About Women"
               Pass the Biscuits Mirandy - voc Del Porter

10 June, 1943 (THURS) - THE BOB BURNS SHOW
                  NBC Hollywood and Camp Hood, Texas

                      Bob Burns and cast, with the WFAA (Dallas) Studio
                        Orchestra in Camp Hood, Texas, and Spike Jones
                        and his City Slickers on remote from Hollywood

                      Bob Burns - monologue on 'tough' Camp Hood
                      Liebestraum - voc Red Ingle, assisted by
                        Luther Roundtree and the Nilsson Twins
                      Bob Burns life story - skit
                      Bob Burns explains his bazooka, and plays -
                      "St. Louis Blues"
                      Fill music, WFAA orch - "Touch of Texas"

11 June, 1943 (FRI) - FURLOUGH FUN*
                  NBC Hollywood

                      Old MacDonald Had a Farm - voc Del Porter
                        and Carl Grayson
                      *I Want a Girl, Just Like the Girl - voc
                        Beauregard Lee
                      Blacksmith Song - voc Del Porter

                      *issued on Corno LP 1001, Glendale LP 6005,
                        Sandy Hook LP SH 2073

17 June, 1943 (THURS) - THE BOB BURNS SHOW*
                  NBC Hollywood

        "No comment from any source was forthcoming here (Los
Angeles) on recent action of AFM's Petrillo in ordering Spike Jones'
band off Bob Burns' airshow a short time before program went on the
air (17 June), forcing the show to go on for that broadcast with no
music of any kind, not even a snort from Bob Burns' bazooka.
        "Petrillo's order was prompted by his discovery that the
show was being transcribed for re-broadcast by a Chicago station
contrary to AFM regulations. Matter was ironed out in time for the
following week's show and Spike and his "City Slickers" were back on
the show minus a week's pay." (Downbeat, 15 July 43)

        Note: Program contents unknown. City Slickers personnel were
present and a rehearsal fee of $48.00 was paid.

18 June, 1943 (FRI) - FURLOUGH FUN*
                  NBC Hollywood

                    with Spike Jones and his City Slickers

24 June, 1943 (THURS)
                      Spike Jones and his City Slickers finish
                      their contract for filming MEET THE PEOPLE at
                      MGM, but remain on call to 17 July

                      Spike Jones and his City Slickers (sans Nilsson
                        Twins) are awarded a certificate from the Caravel
                        High School for "Schicklegruber Specialties"

                  THE BOB BURNS SHOW
                  NBC Hollywood

Bob Burns - monologue on Spike's absence from the
  last show
Take the Door To the Left - voc Del Porter
  and Boys in the Back Room
Griper gets taste of Army life - skit
Commercial - vocal quartet on Old Sol, the
  Summer Sun
Bob Burns - monologue
Summer replacement promo - Fred Brady
Bob Burns - comic song, with guitar

25 June, 1943 (FRI) - FURLOUGH FUN*
  NBC Hollywood

Mama's Makin' Bombers - voc Nilsson Twins
One Dozen Roses - voc Country Washburn
  (straight)
In My Arms - voc Del Porter, with Beauregard
  Lee, effects

28 June, 1943 (MON) - Treasury Department Transcription
  Unknown Studio, Hollywood

Spike Jones and his City Slickers, with
  narration/promotion by Spike Jones

Program
378   Theme: Pass the Biscuits Mirandy - inst
(3:12)   Take the Door To the Left - voc Del Porter
               and the Boys in the Back Room
             War Bond Jingle - voc Boys in the Back Room

379   Theme: Pass the Biscuits Mirandy - inst
(3:29)   Casey Jones - voc Del Porter and Country
               Washburn
             War Bond Jingle - voc Boys in the Back Room

380   Theme: Pass the Biscuits Mirandy - inst
(3:07)   *Put Your Arms Around Me Honey - voc Nilsson
               Twins and Beauregard Lee
             War Bond Jingle - voc Boys in the Back Room

381   Theme: Pass the Biscuits Mirandy
(3:22)   (That Old) Black Magic - voc Del Porter
             War Bond Jingle - voc Boys in the Back Room

*issued on Golden Spike LP 1754

Lyrics and music to War Bond Jingle by Del Porter:-
  "Buy more stamps and Bonds, they are really swell
  'Cause they buy the bombs to blow the Axis to
  Well, you know what we meant to say,
  So buy Bonds today,
  And we'll keep our country free!"

Note: Timings approximate. The four programs are on a 16"
transcription pressed by Allied Studios, Hollywood, under the title
"Treasury Song Parade". Each program was cut (mastered) as one take.
"That Old Black Magic" is introduced and labelled as "Black Magic".
Flip is Margaret O'Brian. Special AF of M permission would have been
obtained for this session as the recording dispute was still on.

1 July, 1943 (THURS) - THE BOB BURNS SHOW
                      NBC Aragon

                         Bob Burns - monologue on meat shortage, Hitler
                         Schicklegruber - voc Beauregard Lee
                         Preview of the Fred Brady Show, Burns' Summer
                           replacement (skit includes "Beulah")
                         Commercial - mixed vocal quartet on Old Sol,
                           the Summer Sun
                         Bazooka solo - "I Ain't Got Nobody"
                         PSA - withholding tax
                         Fill music - Spike Jones

        Note: In this, the season's last show, Bob Burns introduces
"Schicklegruber" as Spike's latest - from the movie MEET THE PEOPLE.
The appearance of 'Beulah' on the Summer replacement skit might be
considered her first on commercial radio.

        "Spike Jones, 30-0812, Bluebird. America's new King of Corn
sells his nonsense for Bluebird, with laughs for all guaranteed by
the whacky vocals and clowning instrumental work. Oh, by Jingo is on
the reverse of The Sheik of Araby, and either one could push the
plate into the big money." (Downbeat, 1 July 43)

2 July, 1943 (FRI) - FURLOUGH FUN*
                     NBC Hollywood

                         That Old Black Magic - voc Del Porter
                         That's My Pop - voc Del Porter, Carl Grayson
                           Red Ingle, Beauregard Lee, Nilsson Twins

                         This is the final show of the season

17 July, 1943 (SAT)
                         Spike Jones and his City Slickers complete
                         their committment for the MGM movie MEET THE
                         PEOPLE, nine weeks from their start

        "Some idea of the present corn market can be derived from
the fact that while other bandleaders here are literally squirming
for radio and picture deals, Spike Jones, of the very well known
"City Slicker" Jones, has calmly turned down two commercial radio
programs and a movie assignment in favor of a summer theatre tour.
        "When Spike and his fellow cornsters leave Hollywood for
their swing around the stage circuit they will be walking out on two
programs - "Gilmore Furlough Fun", and the summer replacement for the
Bob Burns program, on which they have been a regular feature.
        "The Jones Boys have completed two major picture assign-
ments, feature spots in Warner Brothers' Thank Your Lucky Stars and
in MGM's Meet the People, now in production. Another picture deal on
which they could have started immediately was side-tracked in favor
of the p.a. trek." (Downbeat, 15 July 43)

23 July (FRI) to 25 September (SAT), 1943
                         Spike Jones and his City Slickers ten-week
                         theatre tour, as advertised in the 15 July
                         Downbeat. Booked by Carl Hoefle

                         Personnel as 11 April, with Carl Hoefle, pno,
                         replacing Frank Leithner, adding Nilsson Twins
                         Road agent is Irving ?

73

Note: the following dates are a composite of the published Downbeat itinerary and the dates found in Anderson's diary - his final 'gigs' with Spike. In addition to their tour schedule which featured the City Slickers show, Spike arranged for War Bond promotional shows at every location.

23 July (FRI) to 29 July (THURS), 1943
                    Opened at the Orpheum in Omaha, Neb

30 July, 1943 (FRI)

This is the date that was decreed on 2 May, 1941 by James L. Fly, Chairman of the Federal Communications Commission, for RCA to divest itself of one of its two broadcasting subsidiaries, NBC Red or NBC Blue. The antimonopoly probe, begun three years before (in 1938) culminated in the purchase of the approximately 100 station NBC Blue Network by the "Lifesaver King" and owner of WMCA in New York, Edward J. Noble for $8 million:- the birth of the American Broadcasting Company - ABC

30 July (FRI) to 5 August (THURS), 1943
                    Shows at the Tower, Kansas City, Missouri

6 August (FRI) to 12 August (THURS), 1943
                    Shows (35) at the Oriental, Chicago, Ill

13 August (FRI) to 19 August (THURS), 1943
                    Shows (30) at Schuster's Riverside Theatre,
                    Milwaukee, Wis

20 August (FRI) to 4 September (SAT), 1943
                    Shows (30) at Keith's RKO Theatre, Boston, Mass

"Spike Jones...appearing in person on the stage of the RKO Boston Theatre...one of the newest band leaders to turn his hand to making movies...has a seven-year contract with M-G-M Studios...completed assignments in "Thank Your Lucky Stars" and "Meet The People" before coming east on tour...hasn't had a chance to see either of the films but reports they are filled with variety entertainment...for more than five years was the original "heard but not seen" musician with a number of large orchestras in various radio shows...like most band leaders is looking for the perfect script for a film about a band and thinks he has found it in a story written by a friend...with an eye to the future, he has added to his original group of musicians because he feels the present novelty angle won't last indefinitely."
                    (Prunella Hall, Boston Post, 1943)

5 September (SUN) to 11 September (SAT), 1943
                    Shows in New York City, New York

12 Septemeber, 1943 (SUN)
                    Shows in Springfield, Mass

13 September (MON) to 15 September (WED), 1943
                    Shows at the State Theatre, Hartford, Conn

"...will be the first headline attraction of the new fall and winter stage show season at the State Theatre which will get under way today. Billed as the "most unusual musical organization in the world", Spike Jones and his City Slickers employ such incongruous musical "instruments" as pistols, washboards, automobile horns, sirens, whistles, gongs and other equally fantastic contraptions. An

outstanding surrounding stage show headed by songstress Dolly Dawn
will augment Spike Jones during his three days appearance."
(<u>Hartford Daily Courant</u>, 13 Sept 43)

Note: Dolly Dawn and her Dawn Patrol Boys recorded for RCA's
Bluebird releases, and it is possible she sang with the Slickers for
the complete tour. "Dolly Dawn, who used to sing with George Hall's
band and then inherited the baton from George, will soon be the bride
of a Navy lieutenant." (<u>Radio Mirror</u>, Nov 43)

16 September (THURS) to 25 September (SAT), 1943
Shows at the Palace, Cleveland, Ohio

Note: All dates are to be considered as a guide only. During
this 10-week tour, the group played in theatres - five to six shows
per day between feature film showings, spending three to six days in
each major center. Travel time is unknown, and in many cases, shows
were performed enroute to the centers listed. An example is the above
listed play date for Springfield, Mass. Performances in Anderson,
Indiana, are also known.

"Hardly orthodox on a phonograph record, but highly
effective. So effective, indeed, that "Der Fuehrer's Face" made Spike
Jones the King of Corn overnight. Released a year ago this week, the
record has sold almost a million copies. It has also put the City
Slickers (1) on two radio shows...(2) in two movies (... yet to be
released), (3) on a three-month coast-to-coast personal appearance
tour, and (4) into the $5,000-a-week class.
"There is also the matter of thinking up new productions and
new instruments. A postwar vision - if the Slickers can stand the
strain - will present The Waterlude from Sloppy Lagoon (using canta-
loupe halves in a tub of water), the Sheik of Araby (with a live
horse), A Goose to the Ballet Russe (which will give the coup de
grace to The Dying Swan), and a piece de resistance to be titled
"I'll Give You Everything but My Wife and I'll Make You a Present of
Her". In order to realistically render this number it calls for one
member of the orchestra to crack English walnuts in his teeth,
another to rip a telephone book in half, and a .third and a fourth to
tear mustard plasters off each other's chests."
(<u>Newsweek</u>, 20 Sept 43)

"Spike Jones...the only bandleader that kids his own racket.
...is a musical joker. He has no illusions. For his dough Sibelius
could be a wrestler.
"We lay off the pop tunes", said Spike, explaining his meth-
od..."If we use 'em at all we purposely clown 'em because the people
want to laugh in war time. Soldiers just don't go for stuff like Over
There. They want sentimental stuff or strictly comic. We give 'em the
comedy, and it's what the public goes for, too."
"Spike's judgement was sound. He came up out of nowhere last
September...Now he has an M-G-M contract, more radio dates than he
can fill, more personal appearances than he can play.
"Why?", he asks, and then answers, "just a fluke. I'm not
kidding myself. I've got a novely and don't expect it to last. We'll
just keep going until people get sick to death of us and then it'll
be over. That's the music business..Nobody knows what makes a pop
tune. Take Pistol Packing Mama which is now right up there. There's
no reason for it. None that I can see. But there it is. I don't mess
with it much because it isn't my line. You can't burlesque a burlesque...My band's got rhythm - and to it we add a guffaw. We get
along by not taking anything serious."
"We made the record and it was broadcast by Martin Block....
Block long-distanced me...come to New York. Said we could play the
Paramount."
"I thought no. Let's just keep going as we are. And it

75

proved the right way. Now we are just finishing a coast-to-coast tour and we've cleaned up - broke records all over. Utterly unpredictable this music business." (<u>New York World Telegram</u>, 25 Sept 43)

"Spike Jones and his very charming wife drink a toast right in Der Fuehrer's Face during a visit to Cafe Society Uptown here. (New York) After a theatre tour that was slightly sensational, Spike and his boys have returned to California to resume their regular broadcasts for the winter." (<u>Downbeat</u>, 15 Oct 43)

The road tour just completed (politely dubbed "Musical Madness") and all indications point to its overwhelming success - the public acceptance of the personal appearance stimulus of "the Band That Plays For Fun", and the sales generated for War Bonds. The experience gathered opened the door to the possibilities of tours on a much more extensive basis, both in terms of personnel and itinerary. The endless succession of successes gave Spike the confidence to go ahead with his idea of the City Slickers as a full-time, professional musical organization. During the past two years, they could have performed more often had all of his regular musicians been free to do so. Many still had their radio, movie and casual dates, and considered Spike's new band as hard work, extra income and - fun.
Contracts were offered to all players. In addition to a modest pay increase for the Lifebuoy/Gilmore shows, he stipulated: "I must have first call on everything." Agreeing to the new contract could have curtailed most, if not all of their free-lance activities in and around Los Angeles.
As a consequence, Don Anderson and Luther Roundtree gave Spike their notice while in Cleveland and returned, after the tour, to their work in Hollywood. In 1944, Anderson played the "Johnny Mercer Music Shop" under Paul Weston, along with Matty Matlock, Stan Wrightsman & Nick Fatool, among others.

To some, Spike's handling of the Slickers was "pure genius". Whether the decision was popular or not, he had to have total control over all stages of their bookings, promotion - everything concerning PR and presentations. By now he was a shrewd businessman. Working ceaselessly to keep the Slickers alive and lucrative, he surrounded himself with the necessary talent - and devoted his life to the City Slickers.
"But Spike, shrewd business man and a realist, didn't give up his regular jobs until he had his own combination safely launched. He kept playing in studio orchestras and on occasional one-nighters, and kept up a relentless correspondance with juke box operators and show business executives, telling them about his unusual band. Because he worked doubly hard, Spike's City Slickers investment never once became a financial liability.
"Were a subtle burlesque of all corny, hill-billy bands," Spike insists. "Why, some of our best swing band musicians are our biggest rooters." Spike points out that Glenn Miller, Benny Goodman and other swing stars love to hear his band rib the dead-pan sweet orchestras with such curious instruments as tuned cowbells, washboards, auto horns, hiccup-o-phones, anvil-o-phones, sneez-o-phones, and that favorite outdoor Stradavarious - the guitarlet.
"I like playing this way because it pays good dough. That's all I'm in this racket for and when it stops paying dividends, I'll do something else" he says candidly.
(Ken Alden, <u>Radio Mirror</u>, Nov 43)

Note: Pay scale during the tour was $225 per week. Scale under the new contract was a minimum of $115 per week for Burns/Gilmore, with additional bookings extra. Scale during the previous season was a maximum of $105 ($72 + 33) for the two shows with additional services extra.
Spike is now a member of BMI and a partner with Hoefle,

Porter and the young country music composer, Fleming Allen, in Tune Town Tunes. As leaders often do, Spike could put his name as arranger to titles they performed, and less frequently as composer. His input varied in quantity, but was very real.

Dates, apart from the Burns/Gilmore shows, are sparse during this coming season. In fact, the final b'cast date of these shows is uncertain. Spike and his newly contracted City Slickers were busy up and down the California coast with War Bond rallies in theatres and schools; from Knott's Berry Farm in the South to the Golden Gate Theatre in San Francisco; U.S.O. committments; a launching at Cal Shipyards; Special Services V-Discs, and a movie.

Frank Leithner did not wish to travel and came to a special agreement with Spike in that he did only the weekly Furlough Fun show and no traveling. He also dabbled in booking the band. Herman Crone, also an excellent pianist and arranger, was approached and enticed away from the Roy Bargy Orchestra, which was at the Earl Carrol Theatre on the Durante/Moore shows, to do the Burns shows plus all movies and travelling appearances. Crone had also been with the Mike (Music Goes 'Round and 'Round) Riley band with the Teagarden Brothers, Jack and Charlie, and with Frank Trumbauer at the Hickory House, and had also been on the road with Red Nichols before the war. Carl Hoefle is still the stand-by pianist - involved with the Slickers as much as ever. Herman Crone remembers Hoefle as being "very methodical" with his booking and the paper work involved.

In Los Angeles since 1939, Joe Wolverton had worked out of Chicago since 1924. He and Les Paul later lived and worked together in St. Louis for four years before Joe started with Gene Austin. "Joe Wolverton and his Local Yokuls" appeared on NBC West at 11:30 AM on "Our Half Hour". With Art Wenzel on accordion/vibes/washboard, ex-Freddy Martin vocalist Gene Walsh on guitar/vocals and Eddie Snyder on bass, they lasted about nine months featuring Skitch Henderson and Margaret Whiting. Joe played all guitars, mandolin and violin. As a single, he played the Judy Canova, Burns and Allen, and Dinah Shore shows, keeping only the Canova show when Spike offered him a seven-year contract.

Trumpeter Wally Kline, colleague of Spikes from the Everett Hoagland band and recently working the studios, was invited to join this season.

The pianists were responsible for all cue and 'straight' arrangements used, and while all contributed to new Slickers material through the constant 'think' sessions, Porter, Washburn and Ingle take most of the credit (or blame) for new titles.

Tobe Reed takes over the announcing duties from Vern Smith in January, 1944 to be followed by Doug Goerlay in April.

5 October, 1943 (TUES)
      Spike Jones and his City Slickers commence
      rehearsals at NBC for the Burns/Lifebuoy show

        Leader/effts - Spike Jones
        Trumpet - Wally (Merle) Kline
        Trombone - John Stanley
        Clarinet/sax - Del Porter, Red Ingle
        Violin - Carl Grayson, Red Ingle on occasion
        Piano - Herman (Francis) Crone (on Burns only)
        Banjo/guit - Joe (Ralph) Wolverton
        Bass - Country Washburn
        Drums - Beauregard Lee
        Vocals - Nilsson Twins, Del Porter, Red Ingle,
           Carl Grayson, Country Washburn, Beauregard
           Lee, John Stanley on occasion

7 October, 1943 (THURS) - THE LIFEBUOY SHOW
      NBC Hollywood

Guest: Walt Disney

Bob Burns - monologue on the end of Summer
    vacation
Hotcha Cornia - inst
Radio listeners at home - commercial
Military training films - Walt Disney interview
    including talk on 'Victory Through Air Power'
I Wanna Go Back To West Virginia - voc Del
    Porter, with Bob Burns, bazooka
Radio listeners - commercial
The hypochondriac - skit
Promo of Amos 'n Andy show
Fill music - Clink Clink, Another Drink
Lipton Tea - commercial

8 October, 1943 (FRI) - FURLOUGH FUN*
    NBC Hollywood

    Spike Jones and his City Slickers, personnel as
      5 October with Frank Leithner, pno, arr,
      replacing Herman Crone (see notes preceding
      5 October)

    Down By the O-Hi-O - voc Beauregard Lee
    They're Either Too Young or Too Old - voc
      Nilsson Twins
              (straight)
    Take the Door To the Left - voc Del Porter
      and Boys in the Back Room

10 October, 1943 (SUN)
        Spike Jones and his City Slickers participate in
    "World's Funniest Baseball Game" - "Comedians vs Leading
    Men" at Wrigley Field, 2:00 PM. Other bands featured were:
    Xavier Cugat; Harry James; Freddie Martin; Frankie Masters;
    and Freddie Slack. Celebrities included Linda Darnell;
    Edward Arnold; John Charles Thomas; Mischa Auer; George
    Jessel and Deanna Durbin

14 October, 1943 (THURS) - THE LIFEBUOY SHOW*
    NBC Hollywood

    with Spike Jones and his City Slickers

15 October, 1943 (FRI) - FURLOUGH FUN*
    NBC Hollywood

    with Spike Jones and his City Slickers

21 October, 1943 (THURS) - THE LIFEBUOY SHOW*
    NBC Hollywood

    with Spike Jones and his City Slickers

22 October, 1943 (FRI) - FURLOUGH FUN*
    NBC Hollywood

    with Spike Jones and his City Slickers

28 October, 1943 (THURS) - THE LIFEBUOY SHOW
            NBC Hollywood

            Guest: "Klondike Kate" Rockwell

            Bob Burns - monologue on meat shortage,
              Grandpa's affair, unwanted advice
            Chloe, Part 1 - voc Red Ingle
            Klondike Kate interview
            Substitute teacher - skit
            Fill music - Hi Neighbor
            Commercial - Lipton Tea

        Note: Regarding "Chloe" Part 1, the later Part 2 and the
many other titles now starting to appear which later became successful recordings for Spike, Herman Crone gives descriptive background:-
"At that time we had a well rehearsed, very disciplined organization.
Our material was developed at meetings of several key members at
Spike's home. These meetings would last from several hours to several
days. We would have food, plenty to drink, a dip if you wanted to in
the pool. First we would select the number we hoped to use. I might
add that everyone contributed. Country W. of course was there and
would note when we got something good (our opinion)..."
        "You see basically everything had to have a visual potential
as that was our selling point and attraction. Country would then take
this skeleton outline and make the arrangement-sometimes as much as
six minutes. We would then rehearse it for weeks, cutting where weak
and then programmed it on the Gilmore Show. After a very careful review of the playback (plus audience reaction), the number was cut to
less than 3 minutes--this was now set up for recording. Actually
Country did such a wonderful job on arranging and refining down to
presentation size these numbers that I was constantly amazed. Spike
contributed the same as everyone but was the monitor and very sharp
indeed. He used excellent taste and discrimination, and knew where he
was going - and why." (Herman Crone correspondence 10 Oct 82)

29 October, 1943 (FRI) - FURLOUGH FUN*
            NBC Hollywood

            I'm Goin' Back To Whur I Come From - voc
                Del Porter
            You Can't Say No To a Soldier - voc
                Nilsson Twins
                          (straight)
            Hotcha Cornia - inst

4 November, 1943 (THURS) - THE LIFEBUOY SHOW
            NBC Hollywood

            Guest: John Brownlee

            Bob Burns - monologue on Burns' musical skills
            Chloe, Part 2 - voc Red Ingle
            Homecoming day in Van Buren - skit
            John Brownlee - "Waltzing Matilda"
            PSA - fats
            Commercial - Litpon Tea and Lifebuoy

5 November, 1943 (FRI) - FURLOUGH FUN*
            NBC Hollywood

            Down In Jungle Town - voc Del Porter, narration
                by Carl Grayson

Shoo Shoo Baby - voc Nilsson Twins
(straight)
Hitch Old Dobbin To the Shay Again - voc
Del Porter

Note: "Hitch Old Dobbin" is usually a Slickers instrumental
and this is one of the very rare occasions there is a vocal to this
Jud Conlon composition.
"The Joneses live for their home, but they haven't let it
intimidate them. It carries no fancy name. Realistically and with
humor they call it 'Cornegie Hall'" (Radio Mirror, Nov 43)

11 November, 1943 (THURS) - THE LIFEBUOY SHOW*
NBC Hollywood

Guest: Cliff Nazarro

Bob Burns - monologue on letters from Grandma
*I'm Goin' Back To Whur I Come From - voc
Del Porter
Cliff Nazarro, Bob Burns - skit
Serviceman interview - Major Joe Foss
Commercial - with Spike on cowbells
Fill music - Spike Jones

*issued on Corno LP 1001, Glendale LP 6005,
Sandy Hook LP SH 2073

12 November, 1943 (FRI) - FURLOUGH FUN*
NBC Hollywood

Best Of All - voc Beauregard Lee, Red Ingle
and Del Porter
Oh, Brother - voc Nilsson Twins
(straight)
That Old Black Magic - voc Del Porter

18 November, 1943 (THURS) - THE LIFEBUOY SHOW*
NBC Hollywood

with Spike Jones and his City Slickers

19 November, 1943 (FRI) - FURLOUGH FUN*
NBC Hollywood

with Spike Jones and his City Slickers

Note: Probably during the Lifebuoy dress rehearsal, but most
certainly during this next week, Special Services recorded the
Slickers for V-Disc.
In March 1942, the Army's Morale Services Division was
renamed Special Services. The recording ban and lack of current
recordings were contributing factors in the establishment of the
Special Services V-Disc program. Waiver of fees and royalties was
secured with the AF of M, MPPA (Music Publishers' Protective
Association), and AFRA (American Federation of Radio Artists), as the
discs were for military use only, with no commercial exploitation.
Headquartered in New York and under the non-commercial stipulation,
they were able to record many artists in their own setting.
Remastering of existing commercial recordings, including radio and
AFRS transcriptions was also done.
Under Capt. Robert Vincent were, among many others: from

RCA, Stephen Sholes and Walter Heebner; Morty Palitz from Decca; and from Columbia, Tony Janak. George T. Simon would join the group at a later date. All were members of the military at this time.

These 12" unbreakable 78 RPM records, of Formvar, Alvar or Vinylite (Columbia pressed with breakable shellac), were shipped to U.S. servicemen on every front of the war, and provided a playing time from 4:30 to 6:30 per side.

RCA and NBC used the new RCA custom pressing serial number sequence which was adopted in January 1943, and used with the V-Discs from October 1943 into 1947. The program terminated in May 1949.

A complete and thoroughly fascinating history of this program is the subject of Richard S. Sears V-Discs: A History and Discography , published 1980 by Greenwood Press.

D3-MC-442   V-Disc 113-A; ET AFRS "Basic Music Library"
                   P-77, P-S 28, P-424; AFRS "Surprise Package"
                   18; AFRS "Downbeat" 82, 123, 217;
            (2:18) That Old Black Magic - voc Del Porter

                   V-Disc 113-A;
            (2:06) You Can't Say No To a Soldier - voc
                   Nilsson Twins
                             (straight)

D3-MC-443   V-Disc 113-B; V-Disc (Navy) 115-A; ET AFRS
                   "Basic Music Library" P-77, P-S 28, P-424;
                   AFRS "Surprise Package" 18; AFRS "Downbeat"
                   82, 123, (excerpts on) 217;
            (4:29) Chlo-e - voc Red Tergall and the Saliva Sisters

      Note: V-Disc 113-A has a spoken introduction by Spike:- "Hi fellows, this is Spike Jones and the City Slickers here in Hollywood. The Nilsson Twins and all of us are happy to greet you with these numbers on a V-Disc". Red Ingle is Red Tergall - a typo, according to Red's son, Don. The Saliva Sisters, Spike's answer to the Andrews Sisters, were variously a trio or quartet of his male singers.

                   Shortly afterwards, another Special Services
                   session was held, resulting in the following:-

D3-MC-451   V-Disc 125-B; LP GS (edited) 1754; ET AFRS
                   "Basic Music Library" P-77(edited), P-424;
                   AFRS "Downbeat" (edited) 82; AFRS "Sound Off"
                   352;
            (2:18) Hotcha Cornia - inst

                   V-Disc 125-B; ET AFRS "Basic Music Library"
                   P-77; AFRS "Downbeat" 82;
            (2:13) (Down In) Jungle Town - voc Del Porter

      Note: After the cowbell cadenza in "Hotcha" is the yell, by Beau Lee, "Not So loud, you crazy you - this is a V-Disc". The V-Disc reference is removed on the GS LP and two AFRS 16" ETs.

25 November, 1943 (THURS) - THE LIFEBUOY SHOW
                   NBC Hollywood

                   Guests: Lt. Rudy Vallee, and the Chorus of
                   "Naval District, Coast Guard Band"

                   Bob Burns - monologue on health

D3-MC-486   V-Disc 125-A; LP GS 1754; ET AFRS "Basic Music
                 Library" P-424"; AFRS "Downbeat" 82;
          (2:38)As Time Goes By - voc Nilsson Twins, assisted
                 by Red Ingle (see notes below)

          Commercial - with Spike
          Lt. Rudy Vallee, Bob Burns - rivalry between
            Marines and Coast Gurad
          Naval Chorus - "The Girl of the Year"
          Rudy Vallee, Bob Burns - Thanksgiving dinner
          Rudy Vallee - solo, with chorus on
            "Whiffenpoof Song"
          Bob Burns - tribute to the Armed Forces

        Note: The above program information and V-Disc dating is
based on a dubbing of a transcription of the dress rehearsal, during
which there is a breakdown and mention of a recording in the process.
The issued V-Disc is not from this dress, nor from an air check of
the b'cast. Due to the mention of 'recording in the process', the
assumed issued disc would have been from a 'take' between rehearsal
and b'cast, or following the show. Special Services did allow for
'safties' to be taken and retained. Among Lt. Vallee's chorus were
Max Herman, Arthur Most and King Jackson.

26 November, 1943 (FRI) - FURLOUGH FUN*
              NBC Hollywood

          Casey Jones - voc Country Washburn
          St. Louis Blues - voc Nilsson Twins
                   (straight)
          Put Your Arms Around Me Honey - voc Nilsson
             Twins and Beauregard Lee

2 December, 1943 (THURS) - THE LIFEBUOY SHOW*
              NBC Hollywood

          Guest: Hedda Hopper

          I Know a Story - inst
                   (straight)
          Bob Burns - monologue on Hedda Hopper's hats
          Down on the O-Hi-O - voc Beauregard Lee
          Bob Burns, Hedda Hopper - comedy dialogue

3 December, 1943 (FRI) - FURLOUGH FUN*
              NBC Hollywood

          Wang Wang Blues - voc Del Porter
          The Dreamer - voc Nilsson Twins
                   (straight)

9 December, 1943 (THURS) - THE LIFEBUOY SHOW
              NBC Hollywood

          Guests: Mel Blanc (Bugs Bunny)
                  Arthur Q. Bryan (Elmer Fudd)
                  Florence Gill (Clara Cluck)

          Bob Burns - monologue on shortages;
            government; kids
          Liebestraum - voc Red Ingle

82

Red Ingle, Vern Smith - commerical
Clara Cluck - "Il Bacio"
Interview - War refugee from China
Bugs Bunny, Elmer Fudd - skit
Fill music - Spike Jones
Bob Burns - Amos 'n Andy promo
Commercial - Lifebuoy and Lipton Tea

10 December, 1943 (FRI) - FURLOUGH FUN*
             NBC Hollywood

             with Spike Jones and his City Slickers

16 December, 1943 (THURS) - THE LIFEBUOY SHOW
             NBC Hollywood

             Guests: Carole Landis and Dick Haymes

             Bob Burns - monologue on Christmas shopping;
                saving fats
             *People Will Say We're In Love - voc Nilsson
                Twins, assisted by Red Ingle
             Carole Landis interview - "Four Jills and a
                Jeep", and tour to entertain troops overseas
             Soldiers discuss entertainment - skit with
                Carole Landis, Dick Haymes
             Dick Haymes - "I Heard You Cried Last Night"
             Commercial - "Friendship", with Nilsson Twins
             Serviceman interview
             Promo of Dickens' Christmas Carol, with Lionel
                Barrymore
             Commercial - Lifebuoy and Lipton Tea

             *issued on Corno LP 1001, Glendale LP 6005,
                Sandy Hook LP SH 2073

     Note: The line by Red Ingle, 'Turn the page, you fathead'
which later became identified with "The Glow Worm", is heard here for
the first time. It was directed at the pianist, presumably Herman
Crone.

             Examiner Christmas Party
                "Spike Jones of City Slicker fame is the latest
                top-notcher added to the list of big name band
                leaders slated to play for the Examiner's
                Christmas Benefit."

     "The wizard of the Washboard will present his tuned cowbells
and other wierd music makers to the Hollywood Palladium, Thursday
evening, December 16th, to help provide Christmas gifts for disabled
service men.
     "He is cast as drummer in the greatest all-star band ever
assembled - Harry James, Alvino Rey, Les Brown, Teddy Powell and
Sammy Kaye - all in one orchestra."
     Note: Other bandleaders included that night were Lou Bring,
John Scott Trotter, D'Artega and Ray Noble. Undated Examiner clipping
courtesy of Wally Kline.

17 December, 1943 (FRI) - FURLOUGH FUN*
             NBC Hollywood

             Chloe, Part 1 - voc Red Ingle

Shoo Shoo Baby - voc Nilsson Twins
          (straight)
Chloe, Part 2 - voc Red Ingle

23 December, 1943 (THURS) - THE LIFEBUOY SHOW*
NBC Hollywood

Bob Burns - monologue on Christmas presents
Jingle Bells - voc Del Porter, Red Ingle
    and Nilsson Twins
Christmas story by Christopher Marley - skit,
    with Bea Benadaret
PSA - fats
Serviceman interview

24 December, 1943 (FRI) - FURLOUGH FUN*
NBC Hollywood

George Riley - Comedy dialogue
Cpl. Robert Spencer - interview with Beryl
    Wallace, dedicating this 'on-the-air'
    recording of
No Love, No Nothin' - voc Nilsson Twins
              (straight)
Commercial - Boys in the Back Room
    and Red Ingle
Beryl Wallace - interview with M/Sgt Stanley
    Lesqui
*Jingle Bells - voc Del Porter, Red Ingle
    and Nilsson Twins
Merry Christmas to all from Larry Keating
Jingle Bells - fade to Christmas greetings
    from Spike and George Riley

*issued on Corno LP 1001, Glendale LP 6005,
    Sandy Hook LP SH 2073

25 December, 1943 (SAT) - AFRS COMMAND PERFORMANCE 98
CBS Hollywood

Master of Ceremonies - Bob Hope

Bob Hope - comedy monologue
Kay Kayser - "St. James Infirmary"
Jimmy Durante, Bob Hope - comedy dialogue
Jimmy Durante - "The Strutaway"
Gen. George C. Marshall (Army Chief of Staff)
    - message
Frances Langford - "Night and Day"
Ed "Archie" Gardner, Bob Hope - comedy dialogue
Nelson Eddy - "Great Day"
Chloe - voc Red Ingle
Ginny Simms - "You'll Never Know"
Frank Fox (Secretary of the Navy) - message
The Christophers - "Ride, Ride, Ride"
Kay Kayser, Bob Hope, Ish Kabibble (Merwyn Bogue)
    - comedy dialogue
Henry L. Stimson (Secretary of War) - message
Dinah Shore - "Summertime"
Jack Benny, Fred Allen - comedy dialogue
Frances, Ginny, Dinah and the Ken Darby Singers
    - Christmas carols

84

Note: the CP number of this 90 minute show is not certain

30 December, 1943 (THURS) - THE LIFEBUOY SHOW
            NBC Hollywood

            Guest: Eddie Albert

            Personnel as 6 Oct, adding Aileen Carlisle,
               vocal, for his occasion only

            Bob Burns - monologue on the New Year; Hitler;
               train story
            Glow Worm - voc Aileen Carlisle, assisted by
               Red Ingle
            New Year's Eve phone call - skit, including music
               and voice by Spike (Howard McNear in cast)
            War Stories - Eddie Albert interview
            Commercial - Lipton Tea

31 December, 1943 (FRI) - FURLOUGH FUN*
            NBC Hollywood

            with Spike Jones and his City Slickers

      Note: Feature articles on Spike Jones appeared during
               1943 in:-

            Movie Radio Guide, March -
            Saturday Evening Post, 10 Apr - "He Plays
               Louder Than Anybody"
            Radio Mirror, Nov - "Facing the Music"

6 January, 1944 (THURS) - THE LIFEBUOY SHOW
            NBC Hollywood

            Guest: Jimmy Dodd

            Bob Burns - monologue on New Years' resolutions
            MacNamara's Band - voc Carl Grayson
            Getting a dog license - skit
            Jimmy Dodd - "Sinatra, Stay 'Way From My Gal"
            Fill music - Spike Jones
            PSA - fats

7 January, 1944 (FRI) - FURLOUGH FUN*
            NBC Hollywood

            Down By the O-Hi-O - voc Beauregard Lee
            Ain't Misbehavin' - voc Nilsson Twins
                     (straight)
            *There's a Fly on the Music - voc Del Porter

            *issued on Corno LP 1001, Glendale LP 6005,
               Sandy Hook LP SH 2073

13 January, 1944 (THURS) - THE LIFEBUOY SHOW*
            NBC Hollywood

            Guest: Ilka Chase

Bob Burns - monologue on Roosevelt's latest
    speech; essential war work
Bob Burns, the Peace-Maker - skit
Tobe Reed, Spike Jones - commercial
Ilka Chase, Bob Burns discuss smaller towns
    and big cities
Fill music - Sheik of Araby

14 January, 1944 (FRI) - FURLOUGH FUN*
    NBC Hollywood

    The Great Big Saw Came Nearer and Nearer - voc
        Del Porter
    The Kid With the Rip in his Pants - voc
        Nilsson Twins
                (straight)

15 January, 1944 (SAT) - AFRS COMMAND PERFORMANCE 101
    CBS Hollywood

    Master of Ceremonies - Frances Langford
    announcer - Ken Carpenter

    Frances Langford - "Shoo Shoo Baby"
    The Glow Worm - voc Aileen Carlisle, Red Ingle
    Phyllis Brooks - Greetings
    The Reviewers - "Tin Pan Alley"
    Jimmy Weakly - "Mexicali Rose"
    Virginia O'Brian - "Man on the Flying Trapeze"
    Snafu - voc Del Porter, Carl Grayson, Red Ingle
    Frances Langford - "No Love, No Nothin'"

20 January, 1944 (THURS) - THE LIFEBUOY SHOW*
    NBC Hollywood

    Guest: Billy Gilbert

    A room for Uncle Fudd - skit
    Commercial - "Bicycle Built For Two"
    Fill music - Red Grow the Roses
    Billy Gilbert - assorted sneezes

21 January, 1944 (FRI) - FURLOUGH FUN*
    NBC Hollywood

    Siam - voc Del Porter, Red Ingle, Carl Grayson
    I Never Knew - voc Nilsson Twins
                (straight)
    MacNamara's Band - voc Carl Grayson

27 January, 1944 (THURS) - THE LIFEBUOY SHOW*
    NBC Hollywood

    Guest: Jimmy Dodd

    Bob Burns - monologue on his Army dog
    Siam - voc Del Porter, Red Ingle, Carl Grayson
    When women have all the jobs - skit
    Jimmy Dodd - "Dear Mr. Crosby"
    PSA - fats

Note: Before playing "Siam", Spike is presented with the Downbeat "King of Corn" award for the second straight year

28 January, 1944 (FRI) - FURLOUGH FUN*
                NBC Hollywood

                    *Ragtime Cowboy Joe - voc Del Porter, Beauregard
                        Lee, Nilsson Twins

                    *issued on Corno LP 1001, Glendale LP 6005,
                        Sandy Hook LP SH 2073

3 February, 1944 (THURS) - THE LIFEBUOY SHOW*
                NBC Hollywood

                    Guest: Paul Mason

                    Bob Burns - monologue on war technology
                    The City Slicker Polka - voc Nilsson Twins,
                        Carl Grayson
                    More hogs, Mr. Burns - skit
                    Paul Mason - demonstrating jazz on the zither,
                        including duet with bazooka on "St. Louis
                        Blues"
                    Fill music - Red Grow the Roses
                    PSA - War Bonds

4 February, 1944 (FRI) - FURLOUGH FUN*
                NBC Hollywood

                    with Spike Jones and his City Slickers

9 February, 1944 (WED)
                Show at Anaheim Union High School, 9:00 PM

        "Each purchaser of a bond in Anaheim is entitled to one
ticket for each $25.00 in bonds purchased. Limit five tickets to any
one bond"   (ticket facimile courtesy Wally Kline)

10 February, 1944 (THURS) - THE LIFEBUOY SHOW*
                NBC Hollywood

                    Guest: Anna Lee

                    Bob Burns - monologue on Boy Scouts
                    Door-to-door Bond salesman - skit
                    Entertaining troops - Anna Lee interview
                    Fill music - Wang Wang Blues

11 February, 1944 (FRI) - FURLOUGH FUN*
                NBC Hollywood

                    Mairzy Doats - voc Nilsson Twins, Del Porter,
                        Carl Grayson
                    On the Sunny Side of the Street - voc
                        Nilsson Twins
                            (straight)
                    Down in Jungle Town - voc Del Porter, Larry
                        Keating

87

17 February, 1944 (THURS) - THE LIFEBUOY SHOW
            NBC Hollywood

            Bob Burns - monologue on breakfast cereal;
                stunt pilots; income tax; beaurocracy
            Mairzy Doats - voc Nilsson Twins, Del Porter
                Carl Grayson
            Filing income tax - skit
            Serviceman interview - Maj. Robert Westbrook

18 February, 1944 (FRI) - FURLOUGH FUN*
            NBC Hollywood

            Drip, Drip, Drip - voc Del Porter
            Red Grow the Roses - voc mixed quartet
                (Nilsson Twins, Porter, Grayson)
                    (straight)
            City Slicker Polka - voc Nilsson Twins,
                Carl Grayson

24 February, 1944 (THURS) - THE BOB BURNS SHOW*
            NBC Hollywood

            Bob Burns - monologue on California floods
            It Never Rains in Sunny California - voc
                Carl Grayson, Red Ingle
            Commercial - Toby Reed drops his script - he and
                Burns 'fake' it momentarily

25 February, 1944 (FRI) - FURLOUGH FUN*
            NBC Hollywood

            That Old Black Magic - voc Del Porter

2 March, 1944 (THURS) - THE BOB BURNS SHOW*
            NBC Hollywood

            Bob Burns - monologue on weather; war;
                celebrity books
            Serviceman interview - Lt. Laklin
            Bob Burns, Nilsson Twins - Bazooka, vocal on-the-
                air recording for Lt. Laklin on "Java Jive"

3 March, 1944 (FRI) - FURLOUGH FUN*
            NBC Hollywood

            Take the Door To the Left - voc Del Porter and
                the Boys in the Back Room
            Mary Lou - voc mixed quartet
                    (straight)
            Daughter of Mme. From Armentiers - voc Del
                Porter, Red Ingle, Shirley Mitchell

        Note: During this time, Spike Jones and his City Slickers
were performing in various Armed Forces hospital wards - entertaining
with short shows and conversation with the patients. It was after
such a show that the group was filmed at an outside set-up.

Ralph Staubs SCREEN SNAPSHOTS
U.S. Naval Hospital, Corona
Personnel as 5 Oct 43, deleting the Nilsson
Twins for this occasion

Series 24
No. 3
Columbia 1944

Hotcha Cornia - inst

intro by Spike:- "And thank you too, music lovers.
We'd like to start our show off this afternoon
with a beautiful symphonic arrangement, entitled
'Hotcha Cornia'"

6 March, 1944 (MON) - PARAMOUNT STUDIOS
Hollywood

From this date and for the next seven or eight weeks, Spike
Jones and his City Slickers appeared in the filming of BRING ON THE
GIRLS, 93 minutes, color

Personnel as 5 Oct 43, deleting the Nilsson
Twins for this occasion

Chloe - voc Red Ingle

Note: In a radio interview the next week, Spike mentioned a
possibility of "Black Magic" to be included in the movie, which featured, among others, Eddie Bracken and Veronica Lake. Additional
songs and music by Harold Adamson and Jimmy McHugh.
It is reported that Bob Hope showed up on the set during the
filming of "Chloe" one day and there was some horseplay between Hope
and Jones. The 'X' rated banter was recorded and is in the hands of a
private OTR collector. Further details unavailable

9 March, 1944 (THURS) - THE LIFEBUOY SHOW
NBC Hollywood

Bob Burns - monologue on romance
The Daughter of Mme. From Armentiers - voc
Del Porter, Red Ingle, unidentified female
Used car dealer - skit, with Frank Nelson in cast
Jimmy Dodd, Ruth Carol - "$32.50 a month"
Hotcha Cornia - inst

10 March, 1944 (FRI)
KQW, San Francisco

Interview by Bob Goerner with Spike Jones. Subject: the
"Spike Jones Stage Show" is discussed, with hilarious ad-
libbing between the two. Mention is made of bus travel from
Los Angeles this day, the start of Bring on the Girls, and
having done many 4-hour dances during the past year.

FURLOUGH FUN*
NBC Civic Auditorium, San Francisco

with Spike Jones and his City Slickers

Note: A dance is played this night at the Auditorium after
the b'cast.

89

11 March, 1944 (SAT)
        Civic Auditorium, San Jose, dance/show
        (A music store window display reads:-)

HAY!

STOP!   LOOK!   LISTEN!

        Spike Jones and his City Slickers are coming
        to town with a bag full of the 'Corniest'
        Musical tricks in the business.

        YOU'LL SCREAM! YOU'LL HOWL! You'll go berserk over
        the mad musical antics of the most sensational,
        the most talked about, the screwiest, nuttiest, in
        short

        THE MOST TERRIFIC BAND IN THE WORLD
        (copy courtesy Wally Kline)

12 March, 1944 (SUN)
        "Sweets" Ballroom, Oakland, dance/show

16 March, 1944 (THURS) - THE LIFEBUOY SHOW*
        NBC Hollywood

        Guest: Joe E. Brown

        Bob Burns - monologue on income tax; Joe. E.
          Brown; travel
        Henry Morgenthau Blues - voc Del Porter,
          Nilsson Twins, Carl Grayson, Red Ingle
        Commercial - selection of new foghorn
        Joe E. Brown, Bob Burns - comedy dialogue

   Note: Henry Morgenthau was Secretary of the Treasury

17 March, 1944 (FRI) - FURLOUGH FUN*
        NBC Hollywood

        The Blacksmith Song - voc Del Porter
        Sunday - voc Nilsson Twins
             (straight)
        Henry Morgenthau Blues - voc Del Porter,
          Nilsson Twins, Carl Grayson, Red Ingle

    About this time, two weeks into the filming of Bring on the
Girls at Paramount, Joe Wolverton was 'invited' to report to the Los
Angeles Induction Center. Because of the film's progress, he was
given a six-week deferrment.

23 March, 1944 (THURS) - THE LIFEBUOY SHOW*
        NBC Hollywood

        Guest: Hal Boyle (AP Reporter)

        Bob Burns - monologue on understanding women
        The Great Big Saw Came Nearer and Nearer - voc
          Del Porter and the Boys in the Back Room
        Baby sitting - skit

24 March, 1944 (FRI) - FURLOUGH FUN*
                 NBC Hollywood

            with Spike Jones and his City Slickers

30 March, 1944 (THURS) - THE LIFEBUOY SHOW*
                 NBC Hollywood

            Guest: Harry Barris

            Bob Burns - monologue on bathing suits and
                 beauty cream
            Commercial - military skit, including Spike
            Liebestraum - voc Red Ingle
            Locating a dentist - skit, with Howard McNear
                 in the cast
            Harry Barris, composer of "Mississippi Mud", I
                 Surrender Dear", "Wrap Your Troubles In Dreams"

        Note: Details as listed could belong to 6 Apr Burns show.
"Liebestraum" is announced but missing from the available ET.

31 March, 1944 (FRI) - FURLOUGH FUN*
                 NBC Hollywood

                 They Go Wild, Simply Wild Over Me - voc
                      Del Porter
                 *It's Love, Love, Love - voc Nilsson Twins
                                (straight)

                 *issued on AFRS ET "Downbeat" 82

1 April, 1944 (SAT) - COMMAND PERFORMANCE 113
                 CBS Hollywood

            Master of Ceremonies - Ginny Simms
            announcer - Ken Carpenter

            Ginny Simms - "San Fernando Valley"
            City Slicker Polka - voc Nilsson Twins
            Riders of the Purple Sage - "Sing Me a Song
                 of the Prairies", "Texas Blues"
            Lena Horne - "I Can't Give You Anything But
                 Love, Baby"
            Capt. Katherine Craig - greetings
            Irene Manning - "One Alone"
            Cocktails For Two - voc Carl Grayson, assisted
                 by Red Ingle
            Ginny Simms - "Can't Help Lovin' That Man"

        Note: Spike Jones did perform in a Command Performance this
day, however, the above details are from an unconfirmed source and
may be in error. The inclusion of "Cocktails For Two", introduced as
a recent hit by Spike is out of proportion to his known repertoire
and radio performances, lending doubt as to the actuality of the
listed contents.

6 April, 1944 (THURS) - THE LIFEBUOY SHOW*
                 NBC Hollywood

            with Spike Jones and his City Slickers

                              91

7 April, 1944 (FRI) - FURLOUGH FUN*
        NBC Hollywood

                *The Sound Effects Man - voc Del Porter
                San Fernando Valley - voc Nilsson Twins
                              (straight)

                *issued on Corno LP 1001, Glendale LP 6005,
                  Sandy Hook LP SH 2073

        Note: Reference is made of "Willie Spicer, our sound effects
man" at the end of this Billy Mills composition (See 7 April 42
notes). The actual sound effects men introduced after this tune on
the Fibber McGee & Molly shows, with possible aid from Spike were:
Virgil Rymer(Jun 41); Frank Pittman(May 42), and Monte Fraser(Apr 44)

13 April, 1944 (THURS) - THE LIFEBUOY SHOW*
        NBC Hollywood

                Guest: Rosita Morino

                Bob Burns - monologue, Be-Kind-To-Animals-Week
                Oh By Jingo - voc Del Porter
                Buying pink dress for daughter - skit

14 April, 1944 (FRI) - FURLOUGH FUN*
        NBC Hollywood

                Sailing on the Robert E. Lee - voc Country
                  Washburn, Nilsson Twins, Carl Grayson,
                  Del Porter
                              (straight)

        Note: This dated disc is broken and vocal credits have been
taken from the upcoming transcription.

        Personnel changes during the next short period occur at a
rapid rate and one in particular, for no apparent reason. Specific
dating of all changes is not possible and correspondence with George
Rock, Wally Kline, Joe Wolverton and Herman Crone has produced general dating only.

20 April, 1944 (THURS) - THE LIFEBUOY SHOW*
        NBC Camp Pendleton

                Guest: Cass Daley

                Bob Burns - monologue on the Marines
                Spike Jones - Song in honor of Hitler's
                    birthday
                Bob Burns, Cass Daley - Marines, movie career
                Cass Daley - "Willie the Wolf"
                It's Love, Love, Love - voc Nilsson Twins,
                  Bob Burns   (straight)
                PSA - fats
                Fill music - Sheik of Araby

        Note: Danny Van Allen, drums, replaces Beauregard Lee on
this and subsequent Burns shows for an indefinite period. There is no
known reason for Lee to be absent on Thursdays while making the Fri-

92

day Gilmore shows, unless it had to do with his working on details for the upcoming European trip.

On 10 Sept 83, Danny Van Allen, school chum of Spike's and formerly of the Feathermerchants, vividly recalled the trip to Camp Pendelton, the two show b'casts and the Officers' Club between shows where Spike had to borrow money until his next $50 weekly allowance.

21 April, 1944 (FRI) - FURLOUGH FUN*
       NBC Hollywood

           with Spike Jones and his City Slickers

   Note: Beauregard Lee is on drums

           KLINE SPENT DAY IN ARMY SERVICE

   "Los Angeles - Wally Kline, trumpet with Spike Jones, is now claimant to the record of shortest stint in the armed forces. Wally reported for induction the morning of Apr. 24, but was mustered out the same day with a medical discharge when he developed a severe asthma attack after a two-mile hike from the bus to the barracks. He has been a chronic victim of asthma for years."
           (unidentified clipping courtesy Wally Kline)

   Note: The fact that such an event would recieve newspaper mention is a sign of the popularity the Slickers had acheived. Joe Wolverton recalls George Rock and Chick Dougherty with the band before his six-week deferment ends.
   George was 'invited' to join, replacing Wally Kline. As Kline was medically classified 4-F, he was eligible to return to Spike, which he does after recovering from his asthma attack. Although Wally does not recall missing any b'casts, there is one undated Gilmore show on which the trumpet of George Rock is obvious - perhaps this is the week. Kline returns after this weeks absence
   The reason for the departure of John Stanley is unknown. Chick Dougherty (or 'Daugherty') had divided his professional time between Los Angeles and San Diego. Pianist Seth Storm, a long time friend of Spike's, recalls the young (17 yrs.) Dougherty playing the trombone with a big beautiful sound in Pomona in the early 30's - and playing into a megaphone on waltzs. He worked in Long Beach often, with many of the musicians who became the elite of Local 47.
   John Stanley played in the studio orchestra for the film biography "Moonlight Serenade", released as "The Glenn Miller Story".

   George Rock, a corpulent and powerful trumpet virtuoso from Farmer City, Ill., proved to be a durable personality with the Slickers. Only recently arrived on the Los Angeles scene, he had been on tour out of Chicago with Freddie "Schnicklefritz" Fisher, and subbed in the Charlie Barnet trumpet section. A unique trumpet stylist and possessor of a quality falsetto voice (Spike's falsetto was no longer needed), he soon became synonymous with the Slickers presentations - one of their widely acclaimed and indispensable personalities. One of his special effects was a 'burp' - anytime - anywhere.
   Kline's return put Rock on 'hold' for the time being. Spike's plans included extended traveling and as Wally perferred not to travel, it was a matter of time before George would be one of the Slickers.

27 April, 1944 (THURS) - THE LIFEBUOY SHOW
       NBC Hollywood

           Guest: Cass Daley

Personnel changes: <u>Chick (Harry J.) Dougherty</u>,
    trb, replaces Stanley; <u>George (David R.)
    Rock</u>, tpt, replaces Kline for this week only
    <u>add Charlotte (Laughton) Tinsley</u>, hrp, for
    this occasion only; Danny Van Allen 'subs'
    for Beau Lee

Bob Burns - monologue on Spring and romance
*<u>Holiday For Strings</u> - feat Charlotte Tinsley, harp
Bob Burns, Cass Daley - skit on hillbilly
    love story
Cass Daley - "My Maid" (parody on "My Man")
Serviceman interview
Burns, Daley, Nilsson Twins - "I'll Get By"
PSA - fats

*issued on AFRS ET "Downbeat" 105

        "I was the first harpist to play in the Spike Jones
organization. They had an arrangement on "Holiday for Strings" and
needed a harpist who could make up a part from a guitar chord sheet.
I had done (that type of work) before in radio and night club work.
After "Holiday For Strings", which was on the Bob Burns show, he
would usually turn to me and say "be queen for a day", depending on
the chords and number of bars needed." (Charlotte Tinsley communication 21 Oct 82). Herman Crone mentioned (letter of 10 Aug 82) the
'cackle chorus' in "Holiday" being developed at one of the 'think
sessions' and attributed it to Dick Morgan - "that was his style."
        Having had a six week warning of the departure of Wolverton,
Spike contracted the veteran musician and personality, Dick Morgan.
Morgan would have attended and contributed to Spike's home rehearsals
(those 'think sessions') on many occasions before Wolverton, soon to
celebrate his 38th birthday, departed for the 69th Infantry. In
Spike's files were many 10" shellac pressings of this premiere performance of "Holiday", with their exact purpose unknown.
        "My dear friend, Spike surprised me with his rendition of
HOLIDAY FOR STRINGS and as it had already been done, I could not have
done anything about it anyway--however, maybe someday someone will
record THE STRIPPER with a nice string quartet - to balance things
off."   (David Rose correspondence, 4 Aug 83)

28 April, 1944 (FRI) - FURLOUGH FUN*
            NBC Hollywood

            Personnel as 27 April; delete Charlotte Tinsley,
            Beau Lee on drums

            <u>Old MacDonald Had a Farm</u> - voc Del Porter
                Carl Grayson and Nilsson Twins

4 May, 1944 (THURS) - THE LIFEBUOY SHOW*
            NBC Hollywood

            Guest: Shirley Dinsdale and "Judy"

            Personnel changes: Wally Kline is back on tpt;
            <u>Dick (Richard Issac) Morgan</u>, guit/bjo/voc,
            replaces Wolverton; Danny Van Allen 'subs'
            for Beau Lee

            Bob Burns - monologue on messy house
            <u>By the Beautiful Sea</u> - voc Del Porter
            Bob Burns, Cass Daley - comedy dialogue

Shirley Dinsdale, Judy - ventriloquist skit
Production number - "Swingin' On a Star"
Cass, Bob - travelling saleslady and farmer's
    son (skit), with song "Don't Sweetheart Me"
PSA - War Labor Board
Fill music - Don't Sweetheart Me

Note: Cass Daley is now a regular on this show. Dick Morgan,
the seasoned show business vet was an individual who had worked with
most of the name bands in music. More often than not, he was called
"Icky" Morgan. This was brought about by a record he made in 1929
with the Benny Goodman (under a pseudonym) band called "Icky Blues",
on which Morgan performs the vocal. He was capable of a facial expression that was commonly termed "Icky". In 1935, his old friend
Glenn Miller (who was also on the above session), composed and arranged the song "When Icky Morgan Plays the Organ" as recorded by the
Clark Randall orchestra, in tribute to Dick. He had recently been
with Horace Heidt and Alvino Rey.

5 May, 1944 (FRI) - FURLOUGH FUN*
            NBC Hollywood

            Leader,effts - Spike Jones
            Trumpet - Wally Kline
            Trombone - Chick Dougherty
            Clar/sax - Del Porter, Red Ingle
            Violin - Carl Grayson, Red Ingle on occasion
            Piano - Frank Leithner (Herman Crone on Burns)
            Guit/bjo - Dick Morgan
            Bass - Country Washburn
            Drums - Beauregard Lee
            Vocals - Del Porter, Red Ingle, Carl Grayson,
                Beauregard Lee, Country Washburn, Nilsson Twins
            Arrangers - Porter, Washburn, Leithner, Crone

            Toot Toot Tootsie - voc Del Porter
            It's Love, Love, Love - voc Nilsson Twins
                        (straight)

11 May, 1944 (THURS) - THE LIFEBUOY SHOW
            NBC Hollywood

            Personnel as 5 May, except Danny Van Allen,
                drm, 'subs' for Beau Lee

            Bob Burns - monologue on Mother's Day
            *He Broke My Heart in Three Places - voc
                Nilsson Twins
            Bob Burns, Cass Daley - on Sinatra and
                record company
            Serviceman interview - with Jesse Jones,
                barber in the Coast Guard
            Daley, Burns, Nilssons - "You Are My Sunshine",
                with bazooka
            PSA - fats
            Fill music - Farewell Blues

            *issued on Corno LP 1001, Glendale LP 6005,
                Sandy Hook LP SH 2073

12 May, 1944 (FRI) - FURLOUGH FUN*
            NBC Hollywood

95

with Spike Jones and his City Slickers,
Beau Lee on drm

18 May, 1944 (THURS) - THE LIFEBUOY SHOW
NBC Hollywood

Bob Burns - monologue on speeches; slogans
*Besa Me Mucho - voc Carl Grayson, asst. by
Red Ingle, narration by Dick Morgan
Bob Burns, Cass Daley - comedy, songs
Serviceman interview
Daley, Burns - "I'm an Old Cowhand"
Fill music - I'm an Old Cowhand

*issued on Corno LP 1001, Glendale LP 6005,
Sandy Hook LP SH 2073

Note: This show was pressed on 16" discs by International
Artists, Inc, using the East coast edition, including commercials.
One notable difference between East/West discs is the East reference
of 'Shapiro' changed to 'Muntz' on the West coast b'cast of "Besa Me"

19 May, 1944 (FRI) - FURLOUGH FUN*
NBC Hollywood

I'm Goin' Back To Whur I Come From - voc
Del Porter
At Last I'm First With You - voc mixed quartet
(straight)

Note: Spike Jones and his City Slickers were at the 'Aragon'
in Ocean Park this weekend.

25 May, 1944 (THURS) - THE LIFEBUOY SHOW
NBC Hollywood

Guest: Frank Sinatra, with cameo appearance
by Bing Crosby

Bob Burns - monologue on the younger generation
*Cocktails For Two - voc Carl Grayson
Frank Sinatra, Bob Burns, Cass Daley - comedy
dialogue, including Bing Crosby
Frank Sinatra - "South of the Border"
Frank, Bob, Cass - musical skit

*issued on MF Distribution LPs MF 205/4,
947447, and GO 10016

Note: This is not the first performance of "Cocktails For
Two". If the details regarding the 1 April Command Performance are
correct, Spike had been playing this title as early as March. Also,
an undated acetate on a cardboard base, indicating it was dubbed from
a show prior to 14 April, has this title on it with an instrumental
coda - a Lombardo finish similar to "Clink Clink".
Charlotte Tinsley is the harpist on this b'cast and the
vocal chorus could be the Nilsson Twins, Del Porter and Red Ingle.
The arrangement as played here, and soon to be featured on what was
to become Spike's biggest selling record, is now ready for transcription and RCA recording when the ban is over. While the broadcast
version includes a harp, the undated acetate and upcoming ET feature,
respectively, a celeste and piano playing the opening harp arpeggios.

96

This Burns program was also the audition for Wally Kline to move on trumpet to the Frank Sinatra Show, the NBC Staff Orchestra, then to the Charlie McCarthy Show under Ray Noble, "one of the nicest gentlemen and good musicians I believe I ever worked for". The Sinatra Vimms Vitamins Show started broadcasting on 5 January 1944.

26 May, 1944 (FRI) - FURLOUGH FUN*
              NBC Hollywood

              with Spike Jones and his City Slickers

        Spike and his Beverly Hills business office, Business Admin-
istration at 360 North Camden, were totally involved with the promotion necessary in keeping the group working while building up a total
organization that could take advantage of any and all breaks. Spike
worked unceasingly at producing and promotion.
        Edward (Eddie) Brandt, budding song writer, pianist, had
been working for Spike for the past few months. They were actually
together while scouting the local night spots, catching the "Schnicklefritz" group at the Tropics, across from NBC. Both were impressed
by George Rock on that visit, with Spike quickly inviting Rock to
join the Slickers. Only recently arrived in Los Angeles, George could
not as yet accept a contract and as noted, 'subbed' for Wally Kline
in late April. Eddie Brandt was for many years a valued employee,
friend and associate of Spike's. In his first years, he was the 'go-
fer', the band boy, with many responsibilities. Although he was
'behind the scenes' and virtually anonymous for many years, Brandt
was thoroughly involved with the Slickers in all forms of production.
        The very talented reed man, James Joseph "Zep" Meissner,
becomes associated with the Slickers about this time. He now plays on
occasion, starting full-time in September.

1 June, 1944 (THURS) - THE LIFEBUOY SHOW
              NBC Hollywood

              Bob Burns - monologue on matrimony
              My (His) Rocking Horse Ran Away - voc Nilsson
                  Twins and Beauregard Lee
              Cass Daley, Bob Burns - paycheck skit
              Bob Burns, with guitar - "Life Story"
              Cass Daley - musical skit on "Life Story"
              PSA - inflation

2 June, 1944 (FRI) - FURLOUGH FUN*
              NBC Hollywood

              Oh! How She Lied To Me - voc Del Porter
              Snoqualimie Jo Jo - voc Nilsson Twins
                        (straight)

        Note: "Snoqualimie Jo Jo" had been recorded by the Town
Criers on ARA RM 108. This Slickers "Snoqualimie" is enhanced by a
good ad-lib chorus by Red Ingle, with all the sax shakes and nuances
associated with Charlie Barnet.

8 June, 1944 (THURS) - THE LIFEBUOY SHOW
              NBC Hollywood

              Guest: Shirley Ross

              Bob Burns - monologue on German propaganda; Summer
              Casey Jones - voc Country Washburn, Del Porter

Shirley Ross, Bob Burns - movie recollections
Shirley Ross - "Dear Old Donegal"
Serviceman interview
Shirley Ross - "Thanks For the Memory"

9 June, 1944 (FRI) - FURLOUGH FUN*
NBC Hollywood

with Spike Jones and his City Slickers

About this time, Spike recorded for Standard Transcriptions.
Matrices indicate two very close sessions, possibly a Friday/Monday
recording, at Columbia Studios

Personnel as 5 May, with Herman Crone, pno;
adding Zep Meissner, clar/sax, for this
session only

Standard Transcription Library
CBS Hollywood

YTH-985   ET R-150-1;
            (2:25) Down In Jungle Town - voc Del Porter, narrator:
                   Carl Grayson

                   ET R-150-2;
            (2:00) Whittle Out a Whistle - voc Mixed Quartet
                          (straight)

                   ET R-150-3;
            (2:15) By the Beautiful Sea - voc Del Porter

                   ET R-150-4;
            (2:45) At Last I'm First With You - voc Mixed Quartet
                          (straight)

                   LP GS 1754(edited); ET R-150-5;
            (3:20) Liebestraum - voc City Slickers

YTH-986   ET R-150-6;
            (3:10) City Slickers Polka - voc Nilsson Twins

                   ET R-150-7;
            (2:20) Red Grow the Roses - voc Mixed Quartet
                          (straight)

                   ET R-150-8;
            (2:45) Jamboree Jones - voc Nilsson Twins
                          (straight)

                   LP GS 1754; ET R-150-9;
            (1:55) Down By the O-Hi-O - voc Beauregard Lee

                   ET R-150-10;
            (2:00) Casey Jones - voc Country Washburn and the
                   City Slickers

    Note: The name of Zep Meissner is included at this time as
three reeds are used on the 'straight' titles at both sessions.

Possible Meissner clarinet solo on "Jamboree Jones". According to information in the U.S. National Archives, the new Washburn composition "At Last I'm First With You", and the Ohman-Carling (of "Clink, Clink" fame) tune, "City Slicker Polka", were manuscript - as yet unpublished.

The mixed quartet was the Nilsson Twins, Del Porter and Carl Grayson. Porter blends and phrases well with the trb on the bari sax on these sessions

Shortly afterwards, the following session:

YTH-995

       V-Disc 348A; V-Disc(Navy) 128-A; Standard 10"
          1028; 45 Verve (remastered) EPV 5056;
          LP Verve (remastered) MGV 4055; VAU (remaster-
          ed) MGV 4055; VF (remastered) 2304 436; VJ (re-
          mastered) MV 2119; GO (remastered) 10010;
          ET R-151-1; AFRS "Basic Music Library" P-590;
(2:50)Cocktails For Two - featuring Carl Grayson
          and the City Slickers

       ET R-151-2;
(2:35)Mary Lou - voc Mixed Quartet
                 (straight)

       ET R-151-3; AFRS "Basic Music Library" P-590;
(2:05)Paddlin' Madelin' Home(show: 'Sunny') - voc
          Beauregard Lee

       ET R-151-4;
(2:25)She Broke My Heart In Three Places - voc
          Nilsson Twins

       LP GS 1754; ET R-151-5;
(2:00)They Go Wild, Simply Wild Over Me - voc
          Del Porter

YTH-996

       ET R-151-6;
(2:40)Sailin' on the Robert E. Lee - voc Country
          Washburn and Mixed Quartet
                 (straight)

       V-Disc 348A; V-Disc(Navy) 128A; LP GS 1754;
          ET R-151-7; AFRS "Basic Music Library" P-590;
(2:40)The Great Big Saw Came Nearer and Nearer - voc
          Del Porter and the Boys in the Back Room

       ET R-151-8;
(1:50)It Had To Be You - voc Mixed Quartet
                 (straight)

       ET R-151-9;
(3:00)His Rocking Horse Ran Away(film: 'And The
          Angels Sing') - voc Nilsson Twins and
          Beauregard Lee

       LP GS 1754; ET R-151-10;
(2:10)Oh How She Lied To Me - voc Del Porter

       Note: V-Disc timing for "Cocktails" is given as 2:42, and "Great Big Saw..." as 2:33. The Nilssons sing "He Broke My Heart". This Standard "Cocktails For Two" and the later "Chloe" are the versions used by Spike for his audio demonstrations on his Verve

"Dinner Music" album, which has had wordwide distribution. See 15
Sept 56 for further information. The first note of the Standard ET
"Cocktails" is 'clipped' while the 10" issue 1028 is not.

During this week, Spike Jones and his City Slickers were
appearing at the Orpheum Theatre in Los Angeles.

"Spike Jones, who is to music what Dali is to painting - if
slightly more vigorous - is presenting his band in a concert of what
might be called symphonic spasms this week at the Orpheum, and on a
bill that boasts three additional top variety acts.
"If you happen to be in the downtown sector during the next
six days and you hear an unorthodox mixture of sound in the vicinity
of Seventh and Broadway, that will be Spike and his boys regaling the
Orpheum clientele. And you owe it to yourself to stop in and hear
musical history in the making.
"In David Roses's 'Holiday For Strings' for example, Spike
brings on a laughing chorus, although a special harpist, who knits
throughout the other offerings, manages to get in her two bits worth
also. But on 'Hotcha Cornia' no holds are barred, this being an
embalmed swing version of a famous Russian classic of a different
name.
"Assisting Spike on other renditions - including 'Clink,
Clink, Another Drink', 'Never Rains in Sunny California', and 'Glow
Worm' - is Red Ingle, who is himself a sort of walking instrument
capable of many werdi(sic) vocal sound effects. And in the 'Glow
Worm' number, Eileen Carlisle even reaches for a few bars of the
operatic with Ingle, to prove the Jones outfit has no prejudices.
"The attractive blonde Nilsson twins sing a chorus of
'Rocking Horse Ran Away' and Carl Grayson and Del Porter are handy
with any other form of vocalizing from baritone to alcoholic tenor.
In other words, the Jones menage is wired for anything in the field
of sound."
Sharing the billing with Spike were Low Hite and Stanley, a
midget and giant act; Simpson's Marionettes, and the pooch act of
Maxine and Bobby.   (unidentified clipping courtesy Wally Kline)

15 June, 1944 (THURS) - THE LIFEBUOY SHOW*
            NBC Hollywood

            Guest: Ella Logan

            Bob Burns - monologue on home economics
            Ella Logan, Bob Burns - comedy dialogue
            Serviceman interview
            PSA - fats
            Fill music - Pass the Biscuits Mirandy

16 June, 1944 (FRI) - FURLOUGH FUN*
            NBC Hollywood

            Paddlin' Madelin' Home - voc Beauregard Lee
            Texas Polka - voc Nilsson Twins
                        (straight(

17 June, 1944 (SAT) - AFRS MAIL CALL 95
            CBS Hollywood

            Master of Ceremonies - Carole Landis

            Holiday For Strings - feat Charlotte Tinsley
            Georgia Gibbs - "Amor"
            The Town Criers - "Straighten Up and Fly Right"

West and Lexing - comedy dialogue
Georgia Gibbs - "It Had To Be You"
Hotcha Cornia - inst

22 June, 1944 (THURS) - THE LIFEBUOY SHOW*
NBC Hollywood

with Spike Jones and his City Slickers

23 June, 1944 (FRI) - FURLOUGH FUN*
NBC Hollywood

with Spike Jones and his City Slickers

29 June, 1944 (THURS) - LIFEBUOY SHOW (final show of the season)
NBC Hollywood

Bob Burns - monologue
Holiday For Strings - feat Charlotte Tinsley
Bob Burns, Shirley Ross - life in 1950(skit)
Shirley Ross - "It Never Entered My Mind"
Serviceman interview - with Ray Maypole
Ross, Burns - "San Fernando Valley"
Fill music - San Fernando Valley

30 June, 1944 (FRI) - FURLOUGH FUN* (final show of the season)
NBC Hollywood

with Spike Jones and his City Slickers

International Artists, who dubbed most of Spike's personal
acetates for critical use, changed from a cardboard based acetate
disc to a glass based disc on 14 Apr 44. Originally, the cardboard
discs had a superior sound but have now disintegrated. Other 'dubbing' companies were also used, as noted:

The following titles are from undated Burns acetates:-
I'm Goin' Back To Whur I Come From - voc
    Del Porter
Chloe, No 1 - voc Red Ingle
You Can't Say No To a Soldier - voc Nilsson
    Twins   (straight)

The following titles are from undated Furlough Fun acetates,
cardboard and glass base with one and two sides dubbed:-

Cardboard base (before 14 Apr 44, mostly unlabled)
    The Last Shot Got Him - voc Del Porter and
        Carl Grayson
    Touch of Texas - inst (Presto label)
    Cocktails For Two - voc Carl Grayson
    Sailin' on the Robt. E. Lee - voc Country
        Washburn and Mixed Quartet
            (straight)
    Hitch Old Dobbin To the Shay Again - inst
    Whittle Out a Whistle - voc Del Porter
            (straight)

    Oh By Jingo - voc Del Porter
    I'm Just Wild About Harry - voc Nilsson Twins
            (straight)

101

In My Arms - voc Del Porter, with Beau Lee
Would You Rather Be a Colonel? - voc Nilsson Twins
            (straight)
I'm Goin' Back To Whur I Come From - voc Del Porter
Besa Me Mucho - voc Nilsson Twins
            (straight)
*The Vamp - voc Del Porter
Don't Blame Me - voc Nilsson Twins
            (straight)
People Will Say We're In Love - voc Nilsson Twins,
       assist Red Ingle
The Dreamer - voc Nilsson Twins (Vailco label)
            (straight)

Glass Base (after 14 Apr 44, Audiodisc except as noted)
       Charlie My Boy - voc Del Porter
       Whittle Out a Whistle - voc Mixed Quartet
Hotcha Cornia - inst
*Trolley Song - voc Nilsson Twins
       Gilmore commercial
       Holiday for Strings - inst
No, No, Nora - voc Del Porter
Swinging On a Star - voc Nilsson Twins
            (straight)
       As Time Goes By - voc Nilsson Twins (from Burns
       show - only instance of sharing w/Gilmore)
       St. Louis Blues - voc Nilsson Twins
            (straight)
       (both above titles on International label)
My Rocking Horse Ran Away - voc Nilsson Twins,
       Beauregard Lee
Mary Lou - voc Mixed Quartet
            (straight)
   *Row Row Row - voc Del Porter
   Take It Easy - voc Nilsson Twins
            (straight)

*Red Wing - voc Del Porter (single sided disc)
*G.I. Haircut - voc Del Porter (single sided)
   ("Haircut" courtesy of Skip Craig)

*issued on Corno LP 1001, Glendale LP 6005,
   Sandy Hook LP 2073

Preparations are well under way for the Special Services/USO sponsored European tour. Time is well spent with constant rehearsing, clearances and the overall logistics.
Details regarding who was the trumpet with Spike during the past weeks are confusing and somewhat contradictory. George Rock recalls following Wally, but that there was another for a very few weeks before George started. Herman Crone states that Rock was in the band when the USO approached Spike for the tour. Wally Kline is certain he completed the radio season, with Nick Cochrane following and Rock starting after the tour.
According to Herman Crone and local memories, George Rock could not go on the tour as he had not fulfilled the AF of M residency requirements. Curiously, Rock was a full Union member by 24 April and was eligible for any and all work. Both he and Nick Cochrane may have subbed for Kline during the past six weeks and as well, Rock may have been temporarily with Mike Riley during this summer.
During the month of August, Zep Meissner plays and records with the Charlie Barnet band, with such other musicians as Jack Mootz, tpt; Eddie Pripps and Bob Poland, sax. (Capitol and Decca had been recording since late 1943). Frank Leithner returns to the studios, which he never really left, but appears on record with Spike

in the future.

14 July (FRI) to 12 September (TUES), 1944
                USO (United Services Organization), Special
                Services Division war-zone tour

                Leader/effts - Spike Jones
                Brass - <u>Nick Cochrane</u>, tpt; Chick Dougherty, trb
                Reeds - <u>Del Porter</u>, Red Ingle
                Violin - Carl Grayson
                Rhythm - Herman Crone, pno; Dick Morgan, guit/
                    bjo; <u>Paul King</u>, bass; Beauregard Lee, drm
                Vocals - Nilsson Twins, Del Porter, Red Ingle,
                Beauregard Lee, Dick Morgan

        During this period, "The Band That Plays For Fun" traveled
overseas to England, then to France, meeting on the way with Bing
Crosby, Fred Astaire, Dinah Shore and Edward G. Robinson. They were
the first American entertainers to enter the European war zone.
        As the method of travel had yet to be determined, Country
Washburn, who was deathly afraid of flying, opted out and was replaced by Paul King. Nick Cochrane, a popular band leader in Los Angeles,
agreed to replace George Rock for the tour. Herman Crone recalls Paul
and Nick as "worthy subs". A curiosity regarding Paul King is the
fact that he never was a member of Local 47, AF of M. The explanation
may be that Union regulations were waived for this musically important but strictly military operation.
        After travelling to New York by train, they boarded a troop
ship bound to Scotland on which they played 21 two hour shows. Enroute to London, their train was halted due to the damage done hours
before by the Luftwaffe. Spike maintained a vivid recollection of the
utter devastation created by the bombing of London.
        While staying in the Strand Palace Hotel, Spike and his band
performed daily for the next two weeks in hospitals - up to 12 shows
per day (nine in wards and three for the walking wounded) which comprised 15 minutes of show, then 15 minutes of relaxed chat with as
many individuals as possible. They worked not in costume, but in the
uniform of the U.S. Army.
        The Liberty ship which landed them, on D-Day plus 62 (August
7), along with Dinah Shore and Edward G. Robinson at Omaha beachhead
in France was, by coincidence, the same ship the Slickers had helped
launch at Cal Shipyards only a few months before. That same day, a
platform was hastily rigged up the hill from the beach by engineers,
and their first show was to "acres of servicemen" (est. 16,000). Del
Porter recalled that as their platform was under construction and
many trucks were manouvering every which way, Dinah Shore, ("quite a
gal") sang to all from the side of a truck despite the clouds of dust
which choked everyone else.
        In France, the Slickers were quartered with the 9th Air
Corps, who were reponsible for the elevated platforms wherever Spike
was to play - which was mostly air strips.
        The daily routine encompassed three one-hour shows. Leaving
in the early morning, usually by jeep and truck with WAC drivers, and
on occasion by air, their first concert was at lunch hour. More
travel to a mid-afternoon concert, then travel again for an evening
performance. Robinson, Bing, Dinah and Fred were on their own entertainment circuit but occasionally joined with the Slickers.
        Returning to their quarters after night fall during a black-
out had its moments of excitement. In the book "<u>Hollywood Trivia</u>" by
Strauss and Worth (1981, Warner Books), it is reported that Bing
Crosby and his driver had actually driven in their jeep beyond the
front line and into German territory before realizing their error and
potential danger. They made it back with no incident!

In a 21 Jun 83 letter, Don Ingle, Red's son and who is presently a writer/photographer/PR man in Missouri, recalled his father's description:- "Bing was not the only one to get behind the German lines. Dad, Beau Lee, Icky Morgan and a G.I. jeep driver missed a road sign and ended up lost on a dark road at night. They passed several trucks full of German troops in the dark. They could hear the voices talking in German, but with the black out and all no one could see details. They thought later about being captured. It was rumored that Hitler did not think too much of the Jones band and their Der Fuehrer's Face - dad said he figured, rank cards or no, they would have been shot on the spot once it was learned who they were.

"He also said they went into one town about an hour after Patton's armor had swept through, buildings still burning, dead Jerry snipers hanging out of steeples where they'd been spotting and sniping, and what he recalled most were dogs running around and howling ...wild with their eardrums gone from the shelling. It was, apparently, a jolly good war to have missed, but they didn't". The Slickers entertained to within a mile of the front line and to within 40 miles of Paris.

The widow of Irving Lipschultz has written and included a description of him with Spike in France, leaving and returning home in the dark of night. Irving Lipschultz, first 'cellist at MGM for 15 years, loved comedy in music and had been called the "Victor Borge of the 'cello". This instance of a musician known to the Slickers and who had grounded his instrument for a chance to serve on the front, yet performed with the troupe is not unique. It is not beyond the realm of possibility that other musicians now in uniform joined Spike in England or France on what would have been termed a temporary/attached posting to the uniformed City Slickers.

Back in England, via a C-47, the City Slickers were aided by Vick Knight in the recording of 20 sides for broadcast to the Allied Forces in France. None of these titles are known to have survived, but an acetate of unknown origin with "Yankee Doodler" (Are We Going To Win This War?) may be from these 'lost' recordings. Vic Knight had been the director for the Command Performance shows before his overseas posting.

On September 3rd, the BBC broadcast and transcribed the show "The Chamber Music Society of Lower Regent Street" from the Queensberry All Service Club, John Harding, managing director. Along with Spike and the City Slickers were Sgt Dick Dudley, U.S. Army, announcer; Ronald Waldman of the BBC, master of ceremonies; Sgt Vic Knight, script; Cecil Madden, BBC producer and Colonel E.M. Kirby, Director of Broadcasting for SHAEF. The BBC program "Variety Band Box", which preceded Spike's show, featured the British band leaders John Blore and Edmundo Ros. BBC archives do not have the transcription of this show and indicated that it, like many other war-time ETs, were "wiped" for re-use. If a copy exists at all, or if any of the 20 sides for AEF broadcast remain, the possibilities are that either a private collector or the appropriate offices in the Pentagon have retained them.

"At 7:30 p.m. on Sunday, September 3, Chaos Came to Town - organized chaos... Spike Jones and his City Slickers. A laughter bombshell hit 3,600 men and women jammed together at the Queensberry Club, and the casualties rolled and writhed in the aisles.

"...Spike, who looks like James Cagney, packs a deadlier weapon than has ever been handled by the screen's tough guy. Spike wields the weapon of ridicule - and he employs it with deadly effect.

"When the curtain went up. so did a howl - from the audience. Jones' men were wandering, fumbling, tripping around the stage, dropping cowbells, hauling tubas around, upsetting music stands, and generally giving an impression of unprepared and embarassed confusion. Finally they managed to get straight, but...the floor of the stage looked like a hock-shop after a week's record business."

Their English programme started off with "Der Fuehrer's Face", its raspberries and parodied German band were well appreciated by the audience. Other titles "slayed"(sic) included "That Old Black Magic", "Hotcha Cornya", "Down By the Ohio", "Clink Clink, Another Drink", "Siam" and "Holiday For Strings".

"Something beautiful usually appears through every nightmare
...the eye-appeal of the Nilsson Twins, Elsa and Eileen...nineteen-
year-olds to render the saner musical moments in..."It's Love, Love,
Love" and "San Fernando Valley".
     "Spike says, "We've also added a new trio that were formerly
with Phil Spitalny, the Three Saliva Sisters"...three of the boys put
on girl's wigs and do a delicious parody of the usual "whoo-whoo"
mikeside close-harmony trios.
     "Despite their showmanship...Spike must be one of the most
modest men alive: there's definitely no bigtime bulldozing about him.
He sidles around on one foot when the gusts of applause hit him,
beckons to...all...to share in the bows.
     "Off stage he's just the same. I caught him in the wings...
before the act...running through his final routine...leaving most of
the talking to ideas man Del Porter and to the rest of the outfit.
The keynote to...success...seems to be wholehearted co-operation."
                    (Melody Maker, 9 Sept 44)

     Returning to New York aboard a troop ship loaded with German
prisoners-of-war, Spike recalled being asked for his autograph by one
German POW. Perhaps the most vivid memory Spike retained was the reaction of the French civilians on hearing their national anthem, "La
Marseillaise", when played (straight) by the City Slickers. After
four years of German occupation, during which time the anthem was
banned, the older citizens were brought to tears when they had to explain the significance of their anthem to the younger generation,
many of whom had never heard of, or could recall "La Marseillaise".
     Big band trumpeter, Zeke Zarchy, with the Glenn Miller AAF
Band stationed near London at this time, and who later records with
Spike, was not aware of any contact between musicians of either band.
However, from Don Ingle comes this additional information:- "You will
be delighted to learn that there was a contact between Glenn Miller
and at least some of the Jones gang. Dad and "Icky" Morgan spent several days with Glenn in England. In fact, they were together one
night when a buzz bomb fell nearby to where they were quartered, and
part of the ceiling fell on their beds (Dad and Dick bunked together
most of the time away from home - they were not in the room when it
fell). Dick had worked with Glenn in a college band (1920's) in Colorado (Dick was from Fort Morgan area originally) and later did casuals together in NY of '30s. So it was "old home week" for Dick and
Glenn, and of course, dad had known Glenn over the years from their
mutual big band days of the '30s." (Don Ingle letter 21 Jun 83)
     On AFRS "Downbeat" 105 transcription dated 12 Oct 44, Spike
dedicates "Holiday For Strings" to Maj. Glenn Miller and arranger
Jerry Gray, both still in London.
     Red Ingle developed a popular following in England and his
later recording success as leader of the "Natural Seven" is a highlight of the Melody Maker Feb 1949 issue.
     The following quote of Spike's, as printed in the Dec 44
issue of Tune In, while seemingly exaggerated, is probably not:-
"Spike Jones, leader of the City Slickers band, reports on overseas
entertaining. 'Five times we set up the bandstand to play for a show
for one frontline Army Group', he sighs, 'and five times the troops
advanced just as we were ready to start. We chased those boys halfway
across Europe, caught them on the sixth show and can report that not
a single man got away.'"
     Hotcha Cornia was their most requested number.
     All USO historical files were lost when a fire destroyed
their National headquarters in 1975.
     If there were clear-cut chapters to the Spike Jones saga,
then Del Porter agreed that the development and success of the City
Slickers to this point was "downright fun".

     The Nilsson Twins drop from sight after the tour. On return-
ing home. Spike found that the Slickers transcription of "Cocktails
For Two", released in July for radio b'cast only, had created an increased demand from the public for their brand of musical parody.

With characteristic and boundless energy, Spike consolidated the Slickers organization to include all personnel necessary for business administration, public relations and booking, arrangers, copyists, script writers and acts. The business office handled all financial affairs and kept inventory of available acts and Slickers auditionees (There were many who wanted to be part of the nation's hottest attraction); the booking office with national connections for local and interstate theatre tours (via chartered bus in California and chartered rail coaches elsewhere. Working with train schedules was to be an important factor with extended itineraries). All aspects of staging, costuming, lighting, music, promotion, local sponsors on tour (often the AMVETS), etc. was the responsibility of Spike's offices, with Spike having the first and last word on every detail in the marketing of the City Slickers.

City Slickers' referred to the instrumentalists who sang and played as was done on the recordings of 1941/42 - a style immediately identifiable aurally, becoming known in the trade as 'the City Slickers style'. Specialist acts, some of whom stayed for short lengths of time while others were contracted over many lengthy tours, embellished the basic group but were not considered by their instrumental counterparts as genuine 'Slickers', although many did become synonymous as such over the years.

Seemingly addicted to hard work, totally dedicated to his concept of the Slickers (which continually evolved) and regaling in the resultant accolades - and money, Spike rehearsed and rehearsed, constantly editing, refining timing, playing shows and dances locally with an exceedingly high standard of showmanship and, of course, musicianship. Each act and show feature was choreographed and all choreograhy was scripted. Nothing was left to chance. "I still say that people never realized what an organization this really was", reminisced Herman Crone. "They were great days tho'. Between Tommy Dorsey and ourselves we held and broke most of the theatre records. We held the respect of 'straight' musicians and the respect of our peers. We did I don't know how many 'Command Performances' where we always had to close the show as no one wanted to follow us...It made you kind of hold your head higher." (Herman Crone letter 10 Aug 82)

The Wonderful Era of the Great Dance Bands by Leo Walker (Howell-North Books, 1964) puts forward many statistics on the income breakdown from 1939 to 1951 of the Sammy Kaye, Bob Crosby, Freddy Martin, Ralph Flanagan and Harry James bands. A breakdown of the Slickers income is not available but would fit within the following parameters:- Location (hotels, dances) 10-23%; One-nighters 29-45%; Theatres 5-31%; Records 9-42%; Radio 1-14%; TV/radio (from '51) 28-33%.

Office and administration employees were full-time, whereas the performers were contracted for specific lengths of time, usually six months, renewable at Spike's option, and included a basic salary plus additional for services in excess of a specific number. Without Jones' actual files, it is impossible to identify most short term employees. Some left due to the excessively high pressure, others filled in temporarily when some were fired. In total control of all aspects of the Slickers, Spike did not hesitate in firing at whim or will any musician/act or personality who did not fit in - through excessive drinking, poor musicianship or attitude, personality conflict - regardless!

As agreed before the tour, George Rock replaces Nick Cochrane. Eddie Brandt has stated that Rock, a non-smoker and non-drinker, never missed one contracted performance in his entire career with Spike - a fantastic achievement in light of the schedules they followed.

27 September, 1944 (WED) - AFRS SPECIAL NEW YEARS' SHOW*
                          CBS Hollywood

                 with Spike Jones and his City Slickers

106

On, or shortly after October 1st, <u>Herschell Edison Ratliff</u>, tuba/string bass, replaced Country Washburn, who retired to the studios. Washburn remained good friends with the Jones' and continued to produce many fine adaptions for the Slickers.

Contemporary with Spike in Dwight Defty's Long Beach Poly Band and the 'Five Tacks', Ratliff had recently been tuba soloist with the Long Beach Municipal Band under the renowned Dr. Herbert L. Clarke. After six years of two concerts per day, 5-1/2 days per week and 50 weeks of the year, Ratliff left music for photo-finishing and cameras. Due to wartime lack of material, he was forced to sell his business, re-entering the music profession as a City Slicker.

Del Porter has put his clarinet away - permanently, and sings with Spike only on high profile occasion now. Settling in Hollywood, where he writes jingles and sings with studio groups, he also continues to write and occasionally arrange for Spike. Carl Hoefle is handling Spike's Hollywood office at this time, with occasional assistance from Porter.

Beauregard Lee is the road manager now, playing on those high profile occasions only. Spike does much of his own drumming, not only for the Slickers show, but for the dances that the troupe were booked for.

12 October, 1944 (THURS) - KRAFT MUSIC HALL
          NBC Hollywood

          Bing Crosby, on remote from New York City
          (just returned from Europe), and Marilyn
          Maxwell, George Murphy, "Ukie" (Leo Sherin),
          John Scott Trotter Orch.; ann: Ken Carpenter

          Guests: "Welcoming Home from Europe - Spike
          Jones and his City Slickers" (personnel as
          29 Nov) Cameo appearance by Bob Hope

          George Murphy, Marilyn Maxwell - "Thou Swell"
          <u>Cocktails For Two</u> - voc Carl Grayson
          Bing Crosby (from NY), dialogue with Murphy,
          Maxwell and Carpenter from Hollywood, including
          banter with Bob Hope
          Bing Crosby - "Swingin' On A Star", "White
          Christmas"

          Note: AFRS "Downbeat" 105, issued this day with Spike as "live" interview to his records/ETs, mentions returning from the E.T.O. On this disc, "Holiday For Strings" is introduced as "from the score 'A Goose to the Ballet Russe'".

14 October, 1944 (SAT) - AFRS COMMAND PERFORMANCE 142*
          CBS Hollywood

          with Spike Jones and his City Slickers

19 October, 1944 (THURS)
          Spike is interviewed on KHJ, Los Angeles. Subject:
the recently completed City Slicker European tour.

11 November, 1944 (SAT)
          This is the date of the end of what was called the recording strike. Although it had ended a year earlier for Decca and Capitol, RCA and Columbia did not come to an agreement with the AF of M until this date.

          Recording re-commences 12 November, and Spike is ready to start putting on 'wax' his acclaimed hits of the past two years.

23 November, 1944 (THURS) - THE ELGIN WATCH SHOW*
                          NBC Hollywood

                   Host: Don Ameche, with Spike Jones and his
                         City Slickers (personnel similar to 29 Nov)

                   *Holiday For Strings - feat Charlotte Tinsley
                   #It Never Rains in Sunny California - voc Carl
                         Grayson and Red Ingle

                   *issued on MF Distribution LPs MF 205/4,
                         947447, and GO 10016
                   #issued on Corno LP 1001, Glendale LP 6005,
                         Sandy Hook LP SH 2073

29 November, 1944 (WED) - Victor Studios, Hollywood,   11:00 AM to
                          Meyerson and Rush, A & R Reps, present 3:15 PM

                   Leader - Spike Jones
                   Brass - George Rock, tpt; Chick Dougherty, trb
                   Reeds - Del Porter, clar; Red Ingle, Zep
                         Meissner, sax
                   Violin - Carl Grayson
                   Rhythm - Herman Crone, pno; Dick Morgan, bjo;
                         Herschell Ratliff, tuba; Beauregard Lee, drm
                   Harp - Charlotte Tinsley
                   Voices - Carl Grayson, Del Porter and unknown
                         studio chorus

D4-AB-1056-1   20-1628-A; HMV BD 1107-A; 20-2092-A; HMVAU
(Band 7)   BD 1107-A, EA 3320 & EA 4238; 44-0012-A&B;
                   420-0173-A; Gramaphone SG43; 42-0030-A;
                   45 27-0030-A; 447-0173-A; EPA 5058; RCAE
                   RCX 1030; RCAAU EP 20017; RCAF EP 86233;
                   LP LPM 2224; LPM 2775; LSP 2775(e); LPM
                   3849; LSP 3849(e); ANL1 1035(e); AYL1 3748;
                   LPM 6059; VPM 6059; LPM 6088; RCAE LSA 3084 &
                   RD 7724; RCAAU ODLP 6024, ODLP 7503 & CAS 7158;
                   RCAG LPM 10 013 & RCS 3217/1-2; RCAJ RVP
                   6300(m) & 5143(m); RCAIT CL 83748; Camden CCL2
                   0620(e); Readers Digest "Hear Them Again"
                   640-ES-9; RCA Special Products "Good Music
                   Record" DML1 0570; RCA Special Products "Kalei-
                   doscope of Sound" DPL3-0095; ET AFRS "Basic
                   Music Library" P-8706 & P-S 28; AFRS "Downbeat"
                   123; AFRS "Remember" 7 & 127; AFRS "Turn Back
                   the Clock" 1061 & 1173; AFRS "Martin Block" 217
                   & 396; AFRS "Small World" 103; AFRS "Johnny
                   Green's World of Music" 6; AFRS "Ira Cook"
                   1096; AFRS "Eddie Cantor" 51; AFRS "Juke Box
                   USA" 252; Public Service Show "Here's To Vets"
                   (theme for) 227, 299 & 372; Guest Star Time-
                   Sister Kenny Foundation KBR-14;
                   (2:55)Cocktails For Two - voc Carl Grayson

D4-AB-1057-1   20-1733-A; HMV BD 1115-A; 20-2092-B; HMVAU
(Band 10)   BD 1115-A & EA 3342; HMVSK X7245; Gramaphone
                   SG43; 45 RCAG EPA 9720; LP RCAG LSP 10157 &
                   RCS 3217/1-2; RCA Special Products "Good
                   Music Record" DML1 0570; ET AFRS "Basic
                   Music Library" P-S 28 & P-465; AFRS "Downbeat"
                   105; AFRS "Remember" 331 & 927; AFRS "Variety
                   Album"(excerpts & complete) PA 144; AFRS
                   "Swingtime" 63; AFRS "G.I. Jive" 1116; AFRS
                   "Hot Off the Record Press" 98;

                    (3:05)Holiday For Strings

D4-AB-1058-1   20-1628-B; HMV BD 1158-A; 20-2093-B; HMVAU
(Band 1)   BD 1158-A & EA 3320; LP RCAE HY 1006;
                    ET AFRS "Downbeat" 123;
          (2:47)Leave the Dishes In the Sink, Ma - voc
                    Del Porter

        "Cocktails For Two": This is the best ballad burlesque ever
perpetrated. We pronounce it "wonderful" - without any kind of mental
reservations."   (Tune In, Record Review, May 45)

        Note: RCA inst do not credit vocalists or chorus. "Cocktails
For Two" was released in Dec 44 and reached number four on the hit
parade by 18 Jan 45 and, according to Billboard Magazine, remained in
the top ten for eight weeks. "Holiday For Strings" was released in
Oct 45 and, according to Billboard, rose to number 10 by 15 Nov, remaining in the top ten for one week. "Cocktails"/"Holiday" original
issues do not credit the later movie, Ladies Man.
        The 1951 RCA 'Collector's Issues' 42/27-0030, 78 & 45 RPM
respectively, erroneously show the recording date of "Cocktails" as 7
Mar 45. This is the date "Cocktails" was electrically transferred
from lacquer. RCA inst show the time as 1:30 to 1:45 PM. No further
details are given, but the overwhelming sales of the original issue
may have had some bearing.
        The record issues from this and Jones' next session are
among RCA's poorest for sound quality. It is a matter of amateur
conjecture, but RCA did change their recording technique during the
ban and where they had previously mastered directly onto wax, they
now cut directly onto 16-inch, 33-1/3 RPM, banded, lacquered discs,
mastering on transfer from these discs. A similar process was used by
pre-ban Columbia. However, on this date and 4 Jan 45, all rehearsal
time, including all takes, was recorded into bands with the satisfactory take of each title arbitrarily designated as take-1. The technically difficult "Holiday For Strings" issued take-1 was the tenth
attempt, with the satisfactory "Cocktails" the result of the seventh
attempt. "Leave the Dishes..." was from the first take. There could
have been more takes than the 'bands' listed for each title.
        Coin Operators release 44-0012-A&B had a reported issue of
150,000. The soprano sax of Red Ingle is prominent in "Leave the
Dishes". Though listed as clar, Del Porter did not play this session.
He was paid by RCA, not by Spike.

        The original concept of a 'straight' vocalist and accompani-
ment evolved during the years of the recording ban to include a
'straight' ballad singer with Slickers accompaniment - the innovation
of Washburn to Porter's original orchestrations and the multiple audibles of Red Ingle. Spike later auditioned 'straight' singers and
hopeful instrumentalists during the full mayhem of a Slickers rehearsal. Should they laugh or become distracted, the hopefuls were not
hired!

30 November, 1944 (THURS) - KRAFT MUSIC HALL
            NBC Hollywood

            Bing Crosby, with the Charioteers, John Scott
              Trotter's Orch; ann, Ken Carpenter and
              special guests, Spike Jones and his
              City Slickers

            Bing Crosby - "Is You Is, or Is You Ain't?"
            Bing Crosby, Henderson Choir - "I Promise You"
            Eugenia Baird - "The One I Love Belongs To
              Somebody Else"
            Charioteers - "Jeepers Creepers"

                            109

Bing Crosby, Spike Jones - banter on overseas
     tour and London
Glow Worm - voc Aileen Carlisle, Red Ingle
Bing Crosby - "I'm Making Believe"
Bing Crosby, Charioteers - "Love Is Just
     Around the Corner"
Bing Crosby - "June In January"

The complete show, less commercials and closing
     theme, has been issued on Lee-Bee LP, Specs 101

23 December, 1944 (SAT) - COMMAND PERFORMANCE 156
          CBS Santa Barbara

Master of Ceremonies - Bob Hope; announcer: Don
     Wilson; with Spike Jones Orchestra and the
     City Slickers

Bob Hope - Comedy monologue
Xavier Cugat - "Brazil"
Jerry Colonna - Comedy dialogue with Bob Hope
Virginia O'Brian - "Let's Be Sweethearts Again"
Holiday For Strings - feat Charlotte Tinsley
Ginny Simms - "Amor"
Jimmy Durante - Comedy dialogue with Bob Hope
     and as 'Patron of the Arts'
Harry Stimson, Sec. of War - Message
Xavier Cugat - "Babalu"
Dinah Shore - "I'll Be Seeing You"
Jack Benny, Fred Allen, Verna Felton and
     Frank Nelson - skit
Kay Kayser - "Dance With the Dolly"
Frances Langford - "It Had To Be You"
Kay Kayser - Comedy dialogue with sound effects
Dorothy Lamour - "Moonlight and Shadows"
Kay Kayser, Bob Hope - Comedy dialogue
Danny Kaye - Comedy song from "Up In Arms"
W.C. Fields - Temperance lecture
Judy Garland - "The Trolley Song"
Spencer Tracy, Lee Cobb, Skip Homier and
     Howard Duff - Christmas play
Virginia, Ginny, Dinah, Judy, etc, with the Ken
     Darby Singers - Christmas songs

          Note: This show may be un-numbered as CP 156 is uncertain.
The orchestra, which included a full complement of strings, numbered
approx. 35 and along with the Ken Darby chorus provided the cue music
and backed all performers. With the City Slickers as nucleus, Spike
was the musical director for this show.
          During this period, the Slickers were on a series of one-
nighters up and down the California coast. Herschell Ratliff cites
dances and shows at Monteray and San Jose, while Don Ingle, Red's
13-year old son, traveled to some of the performances and mentioned,
in his 21 Jun 83 letter, playing "3rd E-flat broken window pane at
the Golden Gate Theatre, Christmas week of 1944 in Sacramento". Carl
Hoefle Jr. also worked for Spike as a band-boy around this time.

          Note: Feature articles on Spike Jones appeared during
               1944 in:-

               Radio Life, 23 Apr
               Melody Maker (England), 9 Sept - "Chaos
                    Comes To Town"

110

1945 - New Years week
          Spike Jones and his City Slickers dances/shows in
          San Francisco, followed by several days in Oakland

1945 - AFRS*

                 My Home Town - voc Judy Manners
                             (straight)

        Note: At a military base and from an unknown AFRS broadcast,
Spike introduces Judy Manners, who sings with an unidentified orchestra this new Eddie Brandt/Sam Rones song. Acetate in Eddie Brandt
files.

11 January, 1945 (THURS) - KRAFT MUSIC HALL*
          NBC Hollywood

                 Bing Crosby, with John Scott Trotter's Orch. and
                 the Charioteers, Eugenia Baird and special
                 guests, Spike Jones and his City Slickers.
                 ann. Ken Carpenter

                 Cocktails For Two - voc Carl Grayson and his
                 Happy Nova Scotians

        Note: Only Jones portion is listed. AFRS pressed 30 min.
version as "Music Hall" 110. For the third straight year, Spike has
won the Downbeat "King of Corn" award, and it is presented by Bing.

13 January, 1945 (SAT) - Victor Studios, Hollywood, 8:30 to 12:00 PM
          Harry Meyerson, A & R Rep, present(assumed)

                 Leader - Spike Jones
                 Brass - George Rock, tpt; Chick Dougherty, trb
                 Reeds - Del Porter, Red Ingle, clar; Zep Meissner,
                 sax
                 Violin - Carl Grayson
                 Rhythm - Herman Crone, pno; Dick Morgan, guit;
                    Herschell Ratliff, tuba; Beauregard Lee, drm
                 Voices - Del Porter, Red Ingle, Judy Manners

D5-VB-1010-1 (NP) Unissued
          2 (NP)   Unissued
          3   20-1654-B; HMV BD 1158-B; HMVAU BD 1158-B;
          3A   HMVI NE 848; ET AFRS "G.I. Jive" 967;
             (3:10)A Serenade to a Jerk - voc Judy Manners and
                       Red "Jerk" Ingle

D5-VB-1011-1 (NP) Unissued
          2   20-1654-A; HMV BD 1107; HMVAU BD 1107-B, EA 3361
          2A   & 4238; 42-0030-B; 420-0173-B; 45-5165(Y 359);
                    HMVI NE 848; 45 27-0030-B; 447-0173-B;
                    47-0162-B(WY 359); EPA 5058; RCAE RCX 1030;
                    RCAAU EP 20017; LP LPM 2224; LPM 3849; LSP
                    3849(e); ANL1 1035(e); AYL1 3748; RCAE LSA
                    3084 & RD7724; PK ACL 7031(e); RCAAU CAS 7158;
                    RCAG LSP 10157 & RCS 3217/1-2; RCAIT CL 83748;
                    RCA Special Products "Good Music Record"
                    DML1 0570; ET AFRS "G.I. Jive" 951; AFRS
                    "Martin Block" 102; Guest Star Time-Sister
                    Kenny Foundation KBR 14;
             (3:05)Chloe (from the Paramount movie "Bring On The
                       Girls") - voc Red (Swamphead) Ingle

                             111

```
D5-VB-1012-1 (NP)    Unissued
        2            20-1733-B; HMV BD 1115-B; 20-2093-B; HMVAU 1115-B
        2A           & EA 3342; ET AFRS "Basic Music Library" P-645;
                     AFRS "Variety Album" PA 144;
              (3:09)Drip, Drip, Drip (Sloppy Lagoon) - voc Del
                    (Water-on-the-Brain) Porter
```

      Note: RCA inst neither credit the vocalists nor identify the
A & R Rep for this day. NP is uninterpreted. "Chloe" reached number
five on the Hit Parade by 26 Apr 45 and, according to <u>Billboard</u> Magazine, remained there four weeks.

      The RCA inst show the title as "A Serenade To A _____", and
the word 'Jerk' hand written with the parenthisized notation next to
it as "(per Record Committee 3/7/45)". Where Standard had unhesitat-
ingly issued this as a straight title in 1942, Spike waited nearly
two months for RCA to sanction the word "Jerk" for issue on their
label. As with the 29 Nov 44 session, these titles were mastered onto
acetate with only one copy of the issue take retained. "Chloe" 45 RPM
47-0162-B was originally slated to be 47-0163-B.

      Though listed as clarinet, Porter is featured vocalist only.
Bookings, by Carl Hoefle, are through the Wm. Morris Agency. Through
Tune Towne Tunes, the Slickers music (predominantly Porter/Hoefle
titles) are available to the public in sheet music and folios.

      Movies are in the offing for Spike during this period, but
as an undetermined dispute in the music business was raging in
Hollywood, Spike took to the road after the 13 Jan RCA session. A
promotional acetate, with four cuts and dated 27 Feb 45 is known.
Each short skit, which featured Carl Grayson and/or Red Ingle and
George Rock, composed by Del Porter, concluded with:- "For the love
of Mike, don't miss Spike", or "For laughs and snickers, don't miss
the Slickers!".

February to May, 1945

        "Spike Jones and his City Slickers Tour"

```
        Leader - Spike Jones
        Brass - George Rock, tpt; Chick Dougherty, trb
        Reeds - Red Ingle, Zep Meissner, clar/sax
        Violin - Carl Grayson, Red Ingle on occasion
        Rhythm - Herman Crone, pno; Dick Morgan, guit/bjo;
                 Herschell Ratliff, bass; Spike Jones,drm
        Vocals - Carl Grayson, Red Ingle, Aileen Carlisle,
                 Judy Manners
        Harp - Nancy MacDonald (assumed)
        Arrangers - Herman Crone, Zep Meissner
        Acts - Black Bros. (comedy, gymnastics)
        Additional - Eddie Brandt, Sammy Rones (band boys)
```

      The tour played up to a week in major center theatres and
one-nighters in between. In a 27 Oct 83 letter, Herschell Ratliff has
recalled the itinerary as:-

1.	Salt Lake City, Utah	12.	Pittsburgh, Penn
2.	Omaha, Neb	13.	Washington, D.C.
3.	Minneapolis, Minn	14.	Baltimore, Md
4.	Milwaukee, Wis	15.	Philadelphia, Penn
5.	Chicago, Ill	16.	Trenton, NJ
6.	Detroit, Mich	17.	Newark, NJ
7.	Toledo, Ohio	18	Boston, Mass
8.	Cleveland, Ohio	19.	Hartford, Conn
9.	Columbus, Ohio	20.	Buffalo, NY
10.	Cincinnati, Ohio	21.	Rochester, NY
11.	Louisville, KT	22.	Providence, RI

"In Milwaukee at the Riverside he set an attendance record during his first appearance (13 to 19 Aug 43). Returning recently to the same theatre he played before 35,000 in his week's stay."
(<u>Milwaukee Journal</u>, 5 Aug 45)

Beauregard Lee seldom performed. Lee was now the advance man to the tour - the road manager, ensuring hotels (when necessary), transportation/cartage, staging and adequate lighting, as well as advance P.R. and liason with local sponsors was proper. Early in the tour, <u>Gilbert A. (Giggie) Royce</u>, joins as drummer and comedy vocalist.

Travel was by chartered railway coaches. Sleeping was in the lower berth with the upper for personal belongings. On one-nighters the troupe slept on the mobile train between cities, but used hotels at stops of longer duration. Showers were usually available at the local 'Y', seldom at theatres.

Four to six one-hour shows were performed daily between feature film showings. The band boys set up the stage and unpacked/ packed all equipment/instruments, ensuring all were properly account- ed for. Spike's valet (probably <u>Ray Rubel</u>), secretary, librarian, office and wardrobe reps., traveled on the train as well - an exten- sive and expensive organization.

Their routine was set and there were no rehearsals while on the road. Spike wired all receipts back to the L.A. office, which in turn forwarded payroll checks and personal/business mail to the troupe. A hotel was contacted at each stop by the advance man, re- gardless of whether the Slickers stayed in the hotel or on the train, for the purposes of information sheet drop-off and mail pick-up. This procedure went on for many years.

Costuming at this time had been picked up in many stores in Main Street, L.A. Ratliff thought the garments 'cheap', certainly inferior to the subsequent quality tailoring.

Near the end of the tour, Herschell Ratliff 'folded' and was unable to continue, his place taken over by one of the band boys (Sammy Rones?). Despite the highly sophisticated comedy routines the Slickers were presenting, the pressure of travel and the uncomprom- isingly high standards of performance proved too much for Ratliff, who was himself no stranger to the pressures of professional perform- ance. On returning home, he spent many months in bed and it was many months yet before he could return to working - almost a year to re- cover, which he never fully did.

Spike Jones and Frances Langford were featured as Summer replacements for the Edgar Bergan and Charlie McCarthy show - the "Chase and Sanborn Program". Featured vocalist and guitarist, Tony Romano, had earlier been involved with Frances as band leader for a Bob Hope war-zone tour in 1943. Romano's guitar can be frequently heard accompanying Miss Langford's ballads.

Sponsored by Chase and Sanborn, the Purple Heart Circuit, (so called as it played in military hospitals and rehabilitation centers, usually converted hotels, throughout California) used a 25- piece orchestra and chorus, with the City Slickers as nucleus, and featured the arrangements of <u>Howard Gibeling</u>. <u>Eddie Pripps</u>, clar/sax, who may have been the musical director, ie: conducting the 'straight' titles and acts, had lately been in a similar capacity with 20th Century Fox and United Artists. The varied locale of the b'casts coincided with the Slickers Summer theatre bookings. The 1/2-hour b'cast was part of a longer Slickers show. The additional musicians were similar to those hired for the forthcoming recordings, pilot radio shows and the 1946 "Other Orchestra". Ken Carpenter was the series announcer, and Carl Hoefle the musical contractor.

"It took a bit of argument, a public statement by Bob Hope, permission from Hope's toothpaste sponsor, besides a final court decision to grant Frances Langford the go-ahead signal to head her own network air show this summer. But as Sunday night listeners know,

113

the little lady got her own way - as women generally do.

"The break goes down as Frances' first chance to stand up on her own and includes her in the steadily growing list of woman emcees of major variety shows. Assisted by Guitarist Tony Romano and the corn popping din of Spike Jones and his City Slickers, Francie is currently turning out the wit, glamor and vocals Sunday evenings at 7 over WTMJ-NBC."   (<u>Milwaukee Journal</u>, 5 Aug 45)

```
Leader - Spike Jones
Brass - George Rock, tpt; Chick Dougherty, trb
Reeds - Zep Meissner, alto/clar; Red Ingle,
     soprano/tenor/clar; Bob (Robert T.) Poland,
     bari/clar
Violin - Carl Grayson, Red Ingle on occasion
Rhythm - Herman Crone, pno; Dick Morgan, guit/
     bjo; Country Washburn(assumed), bass;
     Giggie Royce, drm
Harp - Mary Jane Barton
Vocals - Del Porter, Carl Grayson, Red Ingle,
     Giggie Royce
Additional - Irving Lipschultz, cel; remainder
     unknown. Occasional studio chorus, unknown
```

Bob Poland, an extremely fine sax man, had been with the Shep Fields band of 1939 and the Charlie Barnet band of '44. With Benny Goodman in 1942, he is on screen in "The Powers Girl". Many of the new and re-written Slickers charts called for the baritone sax, which Porter had played so well during his tenure with Spike. This instrument was sorely missed in the section for the past few months, and there could be none finer on bari that the new Slicker, Bob Poland.

Due to the Union's 'quota' ruling, Mary Jane Barton, under contract with Universal Pictures at this time, was hired for the balance of 1945. She recalls carrying on the harpists tradition of smoking a cigar during her "Holiday For Strings" performance. Nancy McDonald, a pupil of Miss Barton, toured with Spike starting in 1945. Under her married name of Nancy Youngman, she eventually remained in studio work with her trombonist husband.

Transcriptions of most, if not all of the following Chase and Sanborn shows were edited for AFRS release. See appendix iii for known AFRS shows. Medley titles played by the 'Big Band' are 'straight', with one Slickers exception.

3 June, 1945 (SUN) - CHASE AND SANBORN PROGRAM
                    NBC U.S. Naval Hospital, Corona

Starring Frances Langford, with Spike Jones
     and his City Slickers, and Tony Romano

Guest: Charlie Ruggles

Frances Langford - "On the Sunny Side of
     the Street"
<u>Laura</u> - voc Carl Grayson
Comedy skit - on "Accentuate the Positive"
Frances Langford - "All Of My Life"
<u>Leave the Dishes In the Sink, Ma</u> - voc
     Del Porter
Johnny Mercer medley:
     Tony Romano - "You Must Have Been a
                    Beautiful Baby"
     <u>Blues In the Night</u> - Big Band
     Frances Langford - "Tangerine"

114

Note: This is the first known performance/b'cast of "Laura", and featured Carl Grayson. The 'straight' exposition, or introduction to the Slickers adaption is by Howard Gibeling.

10 June, 1945 (SUN) - CHASE AND SANBORN PROGRAM
            NBC U.S. Naval Hospital, Long Beach

            Guest: Groucho Marx

            Frances Langford - "Sentimental Journey"
            Chloe - voc Red Ingle
            Comedy skit - Groucho and cast
            Frances Langford - "Embracable You"
            Down In Jungle Town - voc Del Porter, with
               Carl Grayson
            Jerome Kern medley:
               Tony Romano - "They Didn't Believe Me"
               Old Man River - Big Band
               Frances Langford - "Long Ago and Far Away"

17 June, 1945 (SUN) - CHASE AND SANBORN PROGRAM
            NBC Hoff General Hospital (US Army),
                                    Santa Barbara

            Guest: Garry Moore

            Frances Langford - "I'm Beginning To See
               the Light"
            The Choo Choo Polka - voc Carl Grayson
            Comedy skit - Moore and cast
            Frances Langford - "He's Home for a Little While"
            You Always Hurt the One You Love - voc Tony
               Romano and Red Ingle
            Rodgers and Hart medley:
               Tony Romano - "Blue Moon"
               Thou Swell - Big Band
               Frances Langford - "My Heart Stood Still"

24 June, 1945 (SUN) - MUSIC AMERICA LOVES BEST
            NBC Hollywood (Casino Gardens?) 4:30 to 5:00 PM

            Master of Ceremonies, Tommy Dorsey, with the
               Lou Bring Orch. and chorus, and guests,
               Spike Jones and his City Slickers

A-SSR-6-26-3   Tommy Dorsey, solo with orch - "So In Love"
   (AFRS)   Dave Street, voc - "I Don't Care Who Knows It"
                Lou Bring Orch/chorus - "I Should Care"
                Chloe - voc Red Ingle
A-SSR-6-26-4   I'm Getting Sentimental Over You - vocal chorus
   (AFRS)   with Tommy Dorsey, trombone
                Dave Street, voc - "We Lived a Dream" (by a
                   Blue Mountain Stream in Nevada"
                Tommy Dorsey, solo and chorus - "Body and Soul"
                Tommy Dorsey, solo and orch - unknown song

      Note: AFRS edited and issued the above as "Music America
Loves Best" 55. Spike gives a big 'dig' about T.D.'s theme being too
old-fashioned and proceeds to play the new Slickers version (as later
recorded). Dorsey plays the instrumental bridge, but fails to match
the intended humor.

Tommy Dorsey was Master of Ceremonies for NBC's RCA Victor "Music America Loves Best" series (Sundays 4:30/5:00 PM) in 1945: 29 Apr to 27 May from N.Y. with Jack Blackton's Orch; 3 June to 26 Aug from Hollywood with Lou Bring's Orch and 2 Sept to 25 Nov from N.Y., again with Blackton's Orch.

CHASE AND SANBORN PROGRAM
NBC Birmingham General Hospital (US Army) Van Nuys

Guest: Jack Carson

Frances Langford - "Just Say I'm a Friend
   Of Yours"
Cocktails For Two - voc Carl Grayson
Frances Langford - "Dream"
Comedy skit - Carson and cast
The Great Big Saw Came Nearer and Nearer - voc
   Del Porter
Irving Berlin medley:
   Tony Romano - "Blue Skies"
   Always - Big Band
   Frances Langford - "How Deep Is the Ocean?"

Note: The comedy skit featured, in part, the Langford/Carson duet on "Swanee River" and "Humoresque" - striking similarity to the 1959 Warner Bros. "Two Heads Are Better Than One"

1 July, 1945 (SUN) - CHASE AND SANBORN PROGRAM
NBC U.S. Naval Hospital, San Diego

Guest: Adolph Menjou

Frances Langford - "There, I've Said It Again"
By the Beautiful Sea - voc Carl Grayson
Frances Langford - "Night and Day"
Comedy skit - Menjou and cast
Holiday For Strings- feat Mary Jane Barton
George M. Cohan medley:
   Tony Romano - "I'm Strong For You"
   I'm A Yankee Doodle Dandy - City Slickers
   Frances Langford - "Mary's a Grand Old Name"

5 July, 1945 (THURS) - AFRS COMMAND PERFORMANCE 182
CBS Hollywood

Master of Ceremonies: G.I. Jill; Host: Bing Crosby

Bing Crosby - "Sentimental Journey"
Tommy Dorsey - "Stardust"
Ella Mae Morse - "Cow Cow Boogie"
Chloe - voc Red Ingle
Bing Crosby - "Don't Fence Me In", "Paper Doll",
   "I'll Walk Alone"
I'm Getting Sentimental Over You - vocal chorus
   with Tommy Dorsey, trombone
Bing Crosby - "I'll Be Seeing You"

Note: The uniquely sonorous bass voice of Harry Stanton is now becoming noticable on the chorus features.

116

8 July, 1945 (SUN) - CHASE AND SANBORN PROGRAM
                    NBC Army Air Force Regional & Convalescent
                                     Hospital, Santa Ana

          Guest: Vera Vague

          Frances Langford - "I Should Care"
          Oh By Jingo - voc Carl Grayson
          Frances Langford - "Stardust"
          Comedy skit - Vague and cast
          Liebestraum - voc Red Ingle
          Oklahoma medley:
               Surrey with the Fringe On Top - Big Band
               Langford, Romano - "Oh What a Beautiful
                    Morning", "People Will Say We're In Love"

15 July, 1945 (SUN) - CHASE AND SANBORN PROGRAM
                     NBC U.S. Army General Hospital, Menlo Park

          Guest: William Frawley

          Frances Langford - "Along the Navjo Trail"
          Sheik of Araby - voc William Frawley, Carl Grayson
          Frances Langford - (You Came Along From)
               "Out Of Nowhere"
          Comedy skit - Frawley and cast
          Hotcha Cornia - inst
          Styne and Cahn medley:
               Tony Romano - "I Finally Got That Kiss"
               Saturday Night is the Loneliest Night
                         of the Week - Big Band
               Frances Langford - "I'll Walk Alone"

22 July, 1945 (SUN) - CHASE AND SANBORN PROGRAM
                     NBC U.S. Naval Hospital, Santa Margarita Ranch

          Guest: Charles Kemper

          Frances Langford - "You Belong To My Heart"
          Casey Jones - voc Country Washburn
          Frances Langford - "There's No You"
          Comedy skit - Kemper and cast
          That Old Black Magic - voc Del Porter
          Jimmy McHugh medley:
               Tony Romano - "Don't Blame Me"
               Exactly Like You - Big Band
               Frances Langford - "I'm In the Mood For Love"

29 July, 1945 (SUN) - CHASE AND SANBORN PROGRAM
                     NBC A.A.F. Redistribution Center, Station 3,
                         (Edgewater Beach Club), Santa Monica

          Frances Langford - "On the Sunny Side of
               the Street"
          Toot Toot Tootsie - voc Del Porter
          Frances Langford - "Baia"
          Tribute to War correspondant, Ernie Pyle
          Comedy skit - cast, on surplus war equipment
          Gershwin medley:
               Tony Romano - "But Not For Me"
               I Got Plenty O' Nuttin' - Big Band
               Frances Langford - "The Man I Love"

117

5 August, 1945 (SUN) - CHASE AND SANBORN PROGRAM
                NBC A.A.F. Regional Hospital
                    (Vista Del Arroya Hotel), Pasadena

            Frances Langford - "Sentimental Journey"
            MacNamara's Band - voc Carl Grayson
            Frances Langford - "If I Loved You"
            Comedy skit - on "Gotta Be This Or That"
            Hawaiian War Chant - voc Giggie Royce
            Duke Ellington medley:
                Romano - "I Let a Song Go Out Of My Heart"
                It Don't Mean a Thing (If It Ain't Got
                            That Swing) - Big Band
                Langford - "I Got It Bad and That Ain't Good"

        Note: In view of the V-Discs soon to be recorded by Spike,
it is significant that the presence of Special Services Officer,
Laura Mack, is acknowledged during the program.
        Pending release from the Army and watching today's program
while convalescing, is an old colleague of Spike's - Russell (Candy)
Hall. After greeting each other, Candy is immediately hired as bass
player for the Slickers - when his release is final.

12 August, 1945 (SUN) - MUSIC AMERICA LOVES BEST*
            NBC Hollywood (Casino Gardens?) 4:30 to 5:00 PM

            Master of Ceremonies - Tommy Dorsey, with the
                Lou Bring Orch. and chorus, and guests
                Spike Jones and his City Slickers

            Tommy Dorsey - "On the Sunny Side of the Street"
            Mona Pauling - "Some Day"
            Tommy Dorsey, with chorus - "I'm a Yankee
                        Doodle Dandy"
            Holiday For Strings - feat Mary Jane Barton
            You Always Hurt the One You Love - voc Carl
                Grayson and Red Ingle
            Mona Pauling - "I've Got You Under My Skin"
            Tommy Dorsey - "If I Forgive You"
            Tommy Dorsey, Mona Pauling - "St. Louis Blues"

        Note: The above show was edited and issued by AFRS as "Music
America Loves Best" 62. "I'm Getting Sentimental...", a partial
dubbing from the 24 June Dorsey show, was added to the AFRS disc to
compensate for commercial deletions.

            CHASE AND SANBORN PROGRAM
                NBC A.A.F. Redistribution Center, Station 3,
                                    Santa Monica

            Frances Langford - "There, I've Said It Again"
            Siam - voc Del Porter, Red Ingle, Carl Grayson
            Frances Langford - "The More I See You"
            Comedy skit - Housing problems
            Blue Danube - voc Carl Grayson and Del Porter
            Gordon and Revel medley:
                Romano - "Did You Ever See a Dream Walking?"
                Wake Up and Live - Big Band
                Langford - "Goodnight My Love"

        Note: Special Services Officer, Capt. Wm E. Kaleth Jr., is
in the audience, indicative of the V-Discs about to be recorded.

                            118

13 August (MON) to 17 August (FRI), 1945
                NBC Studios, Hollywood

        "When Tony Janak (Sp. Ser. Recording Engineer) visited the
West coast in August 1945, he was given permission by Spike to record
dress rehearsals of these (Chase/Sanborn) programs. However, none of
these recordings (if made) was issued on V-Disc. Janak did record
Spike...at a special V-Disc session."
                (Richard Sears, <u>V-Discs: A History and Discography</u>)

D5-TC-1322   V-Disc 551-A;
              (2:45)<u>You Always Hurt the One You Love</u> - voc
                        Carl Grayson and Red Ingle

                      V-Disc 551-A;
              (2:41)<u>Siam</u> - voc Del Porter, Carl Grayson, Red Ingle

        Spoken intro by Spike:- "Hiya men, this is Spike Jones. Now
that the shooting is over we'd like to keep you entertained between
hops back home. Here we go with our impression of the Ink Spots doing
'You Always Hurt the One You Love' and Del Porter singing 'Siam'".
(Japan's formal surrender - V-J Day - 14 Aug 45)

D5-TC-1324   V-Disc 540-A;
              (3:09)<u>The Blue Danube</u> - narration by Carl Grayson

                      V-Disc 540-A;
              (3:10)<u>Toot Toot Tootsie</u> - voc Del Porter

        Spoken intro by Spike:- "Hello men, this is Spike Jones
coming to you on V-Disc. It certainly is a pleasure to be making some
more tunes for you. So, without further chatter, off we go with our
impression of Wayne King imitating us imitating him, imitating us in
a song called 'Blue Danube', and also Del Porter singing 'Toot Toot
Tootsie'".
        "Toot Toot Tootsie" as recorded by Mel Blanc on Capitol 57-
780 is often circulated as an authentic Jones version. Blancs' is a
hilarious parody on Al Jolson with frantic Slickerish backing.

                and shortly afterwards, the following:-

D5-TC-1336   V-Disc 570-B;
              (3:03)<u>Minka</u> - featuring George Rock, trumpet

                      V-Disc 570-B;
              (2:27)<u>McNamara's Band</u> - voc Carl Grayson

        Test approved on above two titles 10 Sept 45. Spoken intro
by Spike:- "Hello fellows, this is Spike Jones. Special Services has
asked us to do a record session for you, so we couldn't get here fast
enough, really. Here's some relaxation at 78 RPM".
        "Minka", the show-stopper solo of George Rock, was a carry-
over from his 'Schnicklefritz' days when he inherited the solo from
Fischer's previous trumpeter, Nels Laakso. Laakso had recorded it as
"Trumpet Blues" for the 'Korn Kobblers', a 'Schnicklefritz' spin-off
group (as were the 'Doowackadoodlers'). "Minka" was based upon a traditional melody with variations as featured and recorded as "Russian
Fantasie" (Levy) by Herbert L. Clarke. It is a fair and safe estima-
tion that Rock played his version of "Minka", variously arranged, an
average of once daily for the next ten years - from one to a high of
six performances per working day.

19 August, 1945 (SUN) - CHASE AND SANBORN PROGRAM
          NBC

          Frances Langford - "Long Ago and Far Away",
               "I'll Walk Alone"
          Tony Romano - "You're Mine You"
          Frances Langford - "I Cover the Waterfront",
               "Tangerine"
          Tony Romano - "Blue Skies"
          Frances Langford - "How Deep Is the Ocean?"
          Tony Romano - "Home"
          Langford, Romano - "Oh What a Beautiful
               Morning", "People Will Say We're In Love"
          Frances Langford - "Dream"
          Tony Romano - "Linda"
          Frances Langford - "The Man I Love"

     Note: The existing ET of this show sounds like a blend of
dress rehearsal and live show. The City Slickers are not b'cast, but
remain the nucleus of the accompaniment.
     On a tip from Zep Meissner, Spike scouted a young singer
just starting with the Hal McIntyre band at the Palladium - Helen
Greco. During this week, Beau Lee asked Miss Greco to make an appearance with the City Slickers at the Training Station of Catalina
Island where females, the likes of Helen, were seldom seen. "I never
dreamed I'd be the kind of singer Spike would want. I sing low, torch
type numbers. But one night a couple of years ago...I was approached
by a pleasant looking man who said his name was Beau Lee.
     "The name didn't mean a thing to me. That is until Mr. Lee
added that he was Spike Jones' manager.
     "'How would you like to come to Catalina and do a benefit
with the band next week?' Mr. Lee was asking me."
          (Radio and Television Mirror, NY, Jan 49)

26 August, 1945 (SUN) - CHASE AND SANBORN PROGRAM
          NBC U.S. Maritime Service Training Station,
                              Catalina Island

          Frances Langford - "More Than You Know"
          No, No, Nora - voc Del Porter
          Vincent Youmans medley:
               Tony Romano - "Sometimes I'm Happy"
               Great Day - Big Band
               Frances Langford - "Time On My Hands"
          Comedy skit - Hillbilly post war plans
          Laura - voc Carl Grayson
          Frances Langford - "I'll Be Seeing You"

     Note: The medley is interrupted for a news break re: Hiro-
shima. While these shows whetted the public appetite, the Slickers
b'cast performances during this series are not inspiring. Del Porter
commented that it seemed like "everyman for himself". Spike, now
handling an extended script, fumbles his characterizations and
frequently appears awkward. It will yet be many seasons of hard work
before he publicly overcomes this apparent self-consciousness (a
throw-back to the Chaffey College elocution contest?) to become adept
at handling radio script. He seldom, if ever, appeared on any show
without a script. For his own purposes, he hired the best that were
available, with a continuous supply of material from Eddie Brandt.
     Undoubtedly, Miss Greco sang 'straight' and looked 'great'
for the show, but was not involved with the b'cast. She sings
infrequently with the Slickers during the next few months.

     The following transcription session is included for reference only. On the basis of the V-Disc titles recorded and their presence on recent Chase and Sanborn shows, this ET could then be considered a dress rehearsal for the RCA session which follows. The quality of the performances, the presence of Miss Tinsley on harp, and the matrix (which shows a six to seven month gap from the June 1944 session) lends doubt to conclusive dating. Herschell Ratliff, whose memories of his Slickers days remain vivid, is certain he was not involved with any ET sessions. 'Doc' Birdbath, who starts later this year, does not recall participating on any ETs, despite the non-mechanical bird in "Row" and "Nora".

Standard Transcription Library
CBS Hollywood

Spike Jones and his City Slickers, personnel
similar to 3 June, with Charlotte Tinsley, harp

YTH-1757

     ET R-167-1;
(2:15)Toot Toot Tootsie - voc Del Porter

     Musical Postcard 1006(condensed); ET R-167-2;
(2:45)You Always Hurt the One You Love - voc Carl
     Grayson and Red Ingle

     ET R-167-3;
(3:10)The Glow Worm - voc Aileen Carlisle and
     Red Ingle

     45 Verve (remastered) EPV 5057; HMVAU (remastered)
     7EG 8286(EP); LP Verve (remastered) MGV 4005;
     VAU (remastered) MGV 4005; VF (remastered)
     2304 436; VJ (remastered) MV 2119; GO (re-
     mastered) 10010; ET R-167-4;
(3:45)Chloe (film: 'Bring on the Girls') - voc
     Red Ingle

YTH-1758

     ET R-167-5;
(3:00)The Blue Danube - voc Del Porter and the
     Boys in the Back Room

     ET R-167-6;
(2:35)That Old Black Magic (film: 'Star Spangled
     Rhythm') - voc Carl Grayson

     ET R-167-7;
(2:50)Holiday For Strings - featuring Charlotte
     Tinsley on the harp

     ET R-167-8;
(2:10)No, No, Nora - voc Del Porter

     ET R-167-9;
(2:10)Row, Row, Row - voc Del Porter

Note: See 15 Sept 56 for details on remastered use of the Standard 'Chloe'.

10 September, 1945 (MON) - Victor Studios, Hollywood   8:10 PM to
           Rush & Oberstein, A & R Reps, present   midnight

121

```
            Leader - Spike Jones
            Contractor - Carl Hoefle
            Brass - George Rock, tpt; Chick Dougherty, trb
            Reeds - Red Ingle, clar; Zep Meissner, Bob
              Poland, sax
            Violin - Carl Grayson
            Rhythm - Herman Crone, pno; Dick Morgan, guit;
              Country Washburn, bass; Giggie Royce, drm
            Vocals - Del Porter, Carl Grayson, Red Ingle,
              Dick Morgan, Giggie Royce
```

D5-VB-1127-1   20-1895-A(CP-4); HMV BD 1147-A; HMVAU BD 1147-A,
        1A   EA 3442 & EA 4242; 45 47-3287-A(WP 288);
              547-0069-A(EPA 288); RCA EPA 288; LP ANL1-
              2312(e); AYL1-3870; RCAE HY 1006; RCAG RCS
              3211/1-2; RCAAU ODLP 7503; RCAF PL 43197;
              ET AFRS "G.I. Jive" 565; Your Rhythm Revue-
              Sister Kenny Foundation KBAL-2;
        (2:25)That Old Black Magic - voc Carl Grayson

D5-VB-1128-1   20-1762-B; HMV BD 1139-B; HMVAU BD 1139-B,
        1A   EA 3409 & EA 4239; LP LPM 2224; LPM 3849;
              LSP 3849(e); ANL1 1035(e); AYL1 3748;
              PK ACL 7031(e); RCAE LSA 3084 & RD 7724;
              RCAAU CAS 7158; RCAG LSP 10157 & RCS 3217/1-2;
              RCA Special Products "Good Music Record" DML1
              0570; ET AFRS "Basic Music Library" P-514;
              AFRS "Turn Back the Clock" 386 & 1401; AFRS
              "Ira Cook" 2786;
        (2:51)You Always Hurt the One You Love - voc Carl
              Grayson and Red Ingle

D5-VB-1129-1   20-1762-A; HMV 1139-A; HMVAU BD 1139-A, EA 3361
        1A   & EA 4239; 45 RCAG EPA 9780; LP LSC 3235(e);
              AGL1 4142(e); PK ACL 7031(e); RCAAU ODLP
              7503; RCAE NL 42730(e); RCAG LPM 10 013 &
              RCS 3211/1-2; RCAJ 5142; RCAF PL 43197;
              ET AFRS "Basic Music Library" P-514;
        (2:54)The Blue Danube - voc Carl Grayson, Del Porter
              and the Boys in the Back Room

D5-VB-1130-1   20-1895(CP-4); HMV BD 1162; HMVAU EA 3409,
        1A   EA 4237 & MH 132; 45 47-3287-B(WP 288);
              547-0069-A(EPA 288); RCAG EPA 288; LP LSC
              3235(e); AGL1 2312(e); AYL1 3870; RCAE NL
              42730(e); RCAIT CL 83748; PK ACL 7031(e); RCAG
              RCS 3211/1-2; RCAJ 5142; RCAF PL 43197; RCA
              Special Products "Good Music Record" DML1 0570;
        (3:02)Liebestraum - voc Red Ingle, Narration by
              Richard Morgan

D5-VB-1131-1   Unissued
        1A(3:07)Hawaiian War Chant - Narration by Carl Grayson,
              voc Giggie Royce

     Note: RCA inst do not credit vocalists. HMVAU issued note
"Liebestraum" as take 2. Revised recording sheet from RCA lists
studio time as 9:10 PM to midnight. Curiously, the original RCA inst
credit "Danube" arrangers as Jones and Washburn, pencil corrected to
Jones, Porter. "Liebestraum" originally Jones and Porter but corrected to Jones, Hoefle. The revised sheet shows "Liebestraum" arranged
by Jones and Hoefle, then re-corrected(?) back to Jones, Porter.
     Sol Meyer is credited with the "Danube" lyrics. Meyer was
well known throughout the war years as composer/author to many
Hollywood movie scores, often in collaboration with Eddie Cherkose

(Maxwell). He had also written for the Glenn Miller AAF Band program
"I Sustain the Wings", and later was contracted by Spike for special
arrangements.

"Actually" says Herman Crone, "I don't remember too many
'Bombs'...one in particular - "THE DANUBE ISN'T BLUE, IT'S GREEN". We
thought it would top 'COCKTAILS FOR TWO'. Instead it layed an egg. I
guess we got too sophisticated." (10 Aug 82 correspondence)

27 September, 1945 (THURS) - Victor Studios, Hollywood   9:30 PM to
                    Cal Kuhl, A & R Rep, present   1:30 AM

                    Leader - Spike Jones
                    Conductor - Louis Adrian
                    Brass - George Rock, tpt; Chick Dougherty, trb
                    Reeds - Red Ingle, clar/b.clar/sax; Zep
                      Meissner, clar/sax
                    Violin - Carl Grayson
                    Rhythm - Herman Crone, pno; Dick Morgan, guit;
                      Country Washburn, bass

              additional musicians:-
                    Flutes - Luella Howard, Phillip Shuken
                    Bassoon - Jack Marsh
                    Harp - Mary Jane Barton
                    Drums - Ralph S. Hansell, mel perc; Ormond
                      Downes, trap set
                    Adaption(arrangements) - Country Washburn,
                      Foster Carling, Louis Adrian
                    Voices - Unidentified studio group, similar to
                      10 Feb 47

D5-VB-1134-1   20-1739-A(P-143); HMV BD 1182-A; HMVAU EA 3389-A;
      1A   HMVSK BD 1182-A; 45 47-2795-A(WP-143); EPA 143
                    (condensed); LP LSC 3235(e) (condensed); AGL1
                    4142(e) (condensed); RCAE HY 1006 (condensed);
                    RCAG PJM2-8021; RCAJ 5142; ET AFRS "Basic
                    Music Library" P-503; AFRS "Small World"
                    (Christmas '64);
            (3:28)Nutcracker Suite
                    "The Little Girl's Dream"
                    "Miniature March"
                    "March"

        Note: RCA inst neither credit the arrangers, the vocalists
(which include Harry Stanton, bass), nor give any clue regarding the
obvious re-recording. The last section, the "March", loses a 'genera-
tion' in sound and appears to be a transfer at increasing speed of
material recorded for that purpose.
        Ralph Hansell and Spike were old friends from the pre-
Slickers days when both free-lanced in radio and in the studios.
Leulla Howard was 1st flute with the Hollywood Bowl Symphony under
Stokowski and a member of the L.A. Philharmonic under Wallenstein.
She was also 1st, often solo flute on recordings, radio shows such as
Westinghouse/John Charles Thomas/Dinah Shore and many motion picture
studios, especially Columbia. Phil Shuken was a well-known woodwind
double, hired equally for clarinet, sax or flute.
        On this, and many occasions in the future, Spike wisely
leaves the coordination between orchestra, soloists and chorus to a
professional conductor. A colleague of Spike's from the radio days,
Louis Adrian also aided in the arranging of the chorus segments. Most
of this days session was spent in achieving proper balances for use
on all recorded sides.

28 September, 1945 (FRI) - Victor Studios, Hollywood   9:00 PM to
                        Cal Kuhl, A & R Rep, present   1:00 AM

                    Personnel as 27 September

D5-VB-1135-1   20-1739-B(P-143); 20-1740-A(P-143); HMV BD 1182-B;
        1A   HMVAU EA 3389-B; HMVSK BD 1182-B; 45 47-2795-B
                    (WP-143); 47-2796-A(WP-143); EPA 143(con-
                    densed); LP LSC 3235(e)(condensed); AGL1
                    4142(e)(condensed); RCAE HY 1006(condensed);
                    RCAG PJM2-8021; RCAJ 5142; ET AFRS "Basic Music
                    Library" P-505; AFRS "Small World"
                    (Christmas '64);
             (3:06)Nutcracker Suite
                    "Land of the Sugar Plum Fairy"
                    "Lemon Drop Waltz"
                    "Dance of the Sugar Plum Fairy"

D5-VB-1136-1   20-1740-A(P-143); 20-1741-A(P-143); HMV BD 1183-A;
        1A   HMVAU EA 3390-A; HMVSK BD 1183-A; 45 47-2796-A
                    (WP-143); 47-2797-A(WP-143); EPA 143(con-
                    densed); LP LSC 3235(e)(condensed); AGL1
                    4142(e)(condensed); RCAE HY 1006(condensed);
                    RCAG PJM2-8021; RCAJ 5142; ET AFRS "Basic Music
                    Library" P-503; AFRS "Small World"
                    (Christmas '64);
             (3:20)Nutcracker Suite
                    "The Chinese Dolls"
                    "The Fairy Ball"
                    "Chinese Dance"
                    "Dance of the Flutes"

D5-VB-1137-1   20-1740-B(P-143); 20-1741-B(P-143); V-Disc 640-B;
        1A   HMV BD 1183-B; HMVAU EA 3390-B; HMVSK BD
                    1183-B; 45 47-2796-B(WP-143); 47-2797-B
                    (WP-143); EPA 143(condensed); LP LSC 3235(e)
                    (condensed); AGL1 4142(e)(condensed); RCAE
                    HY 1006(condensed); RCAG PJM2-8021; RCAJ 5142;
                    FONIT VDL 1009; ET AFRS "Basic Music Library"
                    P-505; AFRS "Small World"(Christmas '64);
             (3:01)Nutcracker Suite
                    "The Mysterious Room"
                    "The Forbidden Room"
                    "Arab Dance"

29 September, 1945 (SAT) - Victor Studios, Hollywood   10:00 AM to
                        Cal Kuhl, A & R Rep, present   1:00 PM

                    Personnel as 27 Sept, except Larry Gomar, mel
                    perc, replaces Ralph Hansell

D5-VB-1138-1   20-1741-A(P-143); 20-1740-B(P-143); V-Disc 640-B;
        1A   HMV BC 1184-A; HMVAU EA 3391-A; HMVSK BD
                    1184-A; 45 47-2797-A(WP-143); 47-2796-B
                    (WP-143); EPA 143(condensed); LP LSC 3235(e)
                    (condensed); AGL1 4142(e)(condensed); RCAE
                    HY 1006(condensed); RCAG PJM2-8021; RCAJ 5142;
                    FONIT VDL 1009; ET AFRS "Basic Music Library"
                    P-503; AFRS "Small World"(Christmas '64);
             (3:24)Nutcracker Suite
                    "Back to the Fairy Ball"
                    "They Dance on the Seat of their Pants"
                    "Russian Dance"
                    "Waltz of the Flowers"

                              124

```
D5-VB-1139-1         20-1741-B(P-143); 20-1739-B(P-143); HMV BC 1184-B;
        1A           HMVAU EA 3391-B; HMVSK 1184-B; 45 47-2798-B
                     (WP-143); 47-2795-B(WP-143); EPA 143(con-
                     densed); LP LSC 3235(e)(condensed); AGL1
                     4142(e)(condensed); RCAE HY 1006(condensed);
                     RCAG PJM2-8021; RCAJ 5142; ET AFRS "Basic Music
                     Library" P-505; AFRS "Small World"
                     (Christmas '64)
                 (3:38)Nutcracker Suite
                     "End of the Little Girl's Dream"
                     "Waltz of the Flowers"(con't)
                     "Granny Speaks" by Susan Scott
                     "Goodnight, Sleep Tight"
```

Note: The "Nutcracker Suite" was released in Nov 45 and,
according to Billboard Magazine, reached number two in record sales
by 27 Dec. 78 and 45 RPM domestic issues of this suite had the couplings re-arranged for the three records to fall in sequence on auto-
matic changers - a new idea in phonographs. WP-143, authorized for
issue 26 Oct 48, changed it's sequence 13 Oct 49, while P-143 changed
as of 24 May 50.

     "Irving Berlin won't let Spike kid any of his songs, and
Cole Porter thinks melody manslaughter is unfunny. Spike wanted to
lampoon "Trees", but the line "Only God can make a tree" would create
a felling of bona-fide irreverence. And Jones is too good a musician
to laugh at anything but the truly laughable.
     "Together with the boys' choir from Going My Way, to be
known as the City Slickers, Jr., Spike plans a nursery album of
"Three Bears", "Three Little Pigs" and others.
     "His children's albums are not burlesque. They are sweet,
charming interpretations for youngsters. He often uses his big band
and plays the music straight. This side of Jones came to the front
when one of his boys, Country Washburn, inspired jealousy in Spike's
fatherly affection by entertaining Linda Lee (now seven) with sound
effects bed-time stories. Not to be outdone, Spike's pride made him
take the nursery apart, piece by piece, to entertain his daughter. A
direct result was the enchanting, full-orchestra story interpretation
of The Nutcracker Suite. A better Christmas present for a kid brother
or sister we cannot imagine." (Seventeen, Dec 46)

     An unfinished sequel to "Nutcracker" was a four-part version
of "The Three Bears". Practice acetates were among the Jones files.
The original music and lyrics are sung by a choir and soloists, with
Harry Stanton and George Rock the only identifiable voices. Rehearsal
support is piano only. The choir is similar to "Nutcracker" and the
November "Spike Jones" radio show voices.
     According to Richard Sears "V-Discs: A History and Discogra-
phy", Spike was to present a version of "Nutcracker Suite" on the 23
Oct 46 Philco Radio Show. Sears' information came from the show preview in a trade journal, possibly Metronome or Billboard. While planned, the performance did not take place.
     One of Spike's companies, Comedic Arts International at 360
N. Camden Drive in Beverly Hills, printed, circa 1960, the complete
lyrics and basic choreography to "Nutcracker" for distribution. The
reason:- "...this was recorded in 1945, before the use of audio tape
and also due to the lack of modern high fidelity and recording facilities...the lack of clarity on some of the lyrics will be noticed.
Because of this...a complete set of lyrics, as recorded."

12 October, 1945 (FRI)
     Russell (Candy) Hall is discharged from the Army and within
a week is working as bassist for Spike. Hall had worked extensively
with Gene Austin and before his Army service, with the "crazy" Mike
(Music Goes 'Round and 'Round) Riley band, and the "fabulous" Ken
Murray Black Outs. Hall and Spike were associates for many years.

Candy, a show in himself, was a slap-bass specialist who could play lying on his back, or dancing with it during a featured solo.

Hall recalls the two movies that featured Spike and the City Slickers being filmed shortly after he started, with the sequence being Ladies Man followed by Breakfast In Hollywood. They were released in reverse order.

PARAMOUNT STUDIOS
Hollywood

In the Fall of 1945, Spike Jones and his City Slickers appeared in the filming of LADIES MAN

Leader - Spike Jones
Brass - George Rock, tpt; Chick Dougherty, trb
Reeds - Zep Meissner, clar; Red Ingle, sax
Violin - Carl Grayson
Rhythm - Herman Crone, pno; Dick Morgan, guit;
   Candy Hall, bass; Giggie Royce, drm
Harp - Charlotte Tinsley
Voices - Spike Jones, George Rock, Carl Grayson

I Gotta Gal I Love (in North and South Dakota)
   voc Spike Jones, George Rock
Hotcha Cornia - inst
take HRD-1-   -Holiday For Strings - feat Charlotte Tinsley
Cocktails For Two - voc Carl Grayson

Note: Ladies Man starred Eddie Bracken, Cass Daley, Johnny Coy, Virginia Welles and Virginia Field. "I Gotta Gal..." and the additional songs were written by Sammy Kahn and Jule Styne. "Holiday For Strings" was transferred to 78 RPM acetate as a glass-based reference movie pre-record (dub) HTD-1. Copy in Jones' files is marked "movie production 11413D" with the envelope pencil dated November 45.

Spike Jones Song Folio No. 1 (1946) refers to the Slickers movie, "Manhatten Madness", the original working title to Ladies Man. Doodles Weaver appeared in the 1961 Jerry Lewis movie, Ladies' Man.

"When Spike and his Slickers checked off the Paramount lot, no one was happier than the studio prop man.

"The things these guys dream up - shouldn't happen all in one picture and to one prop man", he explained.

"Two 1912 car horns, a pair of rubber hands - one man's and one woman's, both for the right hand; a stethoscope, a works-less grandfather's clock, nine pairs of different sized cocktail glasses, 10 dozen imitation daisies, a harp with rubber balloons emerging from its top, and a three-foot loving cup...the order that almost threw the prop man was for three ping-pong balls, two regular size and one exactly two-thirds standard.

"The specially-built and small size ping-pong ball(sic) were required by Carl Grayson, vocal soloist, believe it ot not!"
(unidentified, undated newspaper)

7 November, 1945 (WED) - THE SPIKE JONES SHOW (pilot radio show)
NBC Hollywood

Spike Jones, the City Slickers, and augmenting orchestra and chorus

Personnel as "Ladies Man", adding Bob Poland, sax.
Additional: Al Saparoff, vln, remainder unknown
Cast: Carl Grayson, Red Ingle, Mary Anderson,
Mable Todd, Spike Jones

126

(30 minute show) Liza - Big Band
                  You Always Hurt the One You Love - voc Carl
                        Grayson and Red Ingle
                  Mable Todd - "I'm Breathless"
                  Chloe - voc Red Ingle

(15 Minute show) Great Day - Big Band
                  Bidin' My Time - voc Carl Grayson, with chorus
                                  (straight)
                  Holiday For Strings - feat Charlotte Tinsley

        A situation comedy totally involving the City Slickers, and
centering on Spike's "Sugar n' Spice and Everything Nice" Malt Shop
on the campus of "Sub Normal-Normal", their "Matter Alma". Slickers
characters Carl Grayson played Prof. Thadius Q. Derry-Derry (or
Derri-Berri) and Red Ingle was the football hero, Red Bagle.
        All shows were similar and sponsored by the final Victory
Bond/loan drive which ended Dec 8. These commercials were to show
potential sponsors (none picked up the shows) where their ads would
appear. Two editions were produced but never b'cast - a half-hour,
and a 15 minute show. The first two shows ran 40/45 minutes, and gags
which did not get audience reaction were later deleted. The series
was written by Charlie Isaacs and produced by Art Dailey. The announcer was Marvin Miller.
        The entire musical aspect of these pilot shows were of a
superior standard to the recently completed Chase and Sanborn series.
All big band titles are 'straight'.

14 November, 1945 (WED) - THE SPIKE JONES SHOW (pilot radio show)
                  NBC Hollywood

(30 minute show) Great Day - Big Band
                  *Hotcha Cornia - inst
                  Bidin' My Time - voc Carl Grayson, with chorus
                                  (straight)
                  Chloe - voc Red Ingle

                  *issued on MF Distribution LPs, MF 205/4,
                      947447, and GO 10016

(15 Minute show) Crazy Rhythm - Big Band
                  Mine - voc Carl Grayson, with chorus
                                  (straight)
                  Cocktails For Two - voc Carl Grayson

30 November, 1945 (FRI) - THE SPIKE JONES SHOW (pilot radio show)
                  NBC Hollywood

(30 minute show) Hotcha Cornia - inst
                  If I Loved You - voc Carl Grayson, with chorus
                                  (straight)
                  *Chloe - voc Red Ingle

                  *issued on MF Distribution LPs MF 205/4,
                      947447, and GO 10016

        After the completion of Ladies Man at Paramount, filming
starts on:-

                  GOLDEN PICTURES, INC (a United Artists release)
                  Hollywood

127

BREAKFAST IN HOLLYWOOD

> Personnel as Ladies Man, changing voices to Del
> Porter, Red Ingle and Judy Manners

M2 take 10	A Hat for Hedda Hopper - voc Del Porter
M2 rake 4	Glow Worm - voc Red Ingle, Judy Manners

Note: Breakfast in Hollywood also featured Bonita Gran-ville, Billie Burke, Zasu Pitts, Hedda Hopper, the King Cole Trio (Nat Cole, Marla Shelton, Louis Alter) and Tom Breneman, whose radio show of the same name this film is based on.

The above titles were transferred to 78 RPM acetates and were available as movie pre-records as numbered.

The presence of Del Porter may indicate a Carl Hoefle booking, and the song "A Hat for Hedda Hopper" sounds like a Porter/Hoefle collaboration. The film also introduces Spike's brief-lived straw hat and the Slickers new, expensively tailored and soon to be well-known costuming - loud, with seemingly uncoordinated color and pattern, and the anachronistic high button shoes. (Seen also in the following Army-Navy short feature)

ARMY-NAVY SCREEN MAGAZINE, No. 70, Signal Corps

> "presenting Spike Jones and his City Slickers",
> personnel as Ladies Man, deleting Charlotte
> Tinsley.

111 SM 70	Cocktails For Two - voc Carl Grayson and
(Reel two)	the City Slickers (see note below)
	Alexander's Ragtime Band - gang sing-along
	(straight)
	Hotcha Cornia - inst (edited arr)

Note: This short, 10 minute film is the second of two reels as designated. Side-lining was used, with full-enactment to "Cock-tails". Spike's mannerisms in the "Hotcha" intro are identical to those later used in the 1953 intro to "Poet and Peasant" as seen in "Fireman, Save My Child". "Cocktails" is extended with a brief 'straight' bouncing ball sing-along into "Alexander's". The Slickers are not on screen for the sing-along. "Hotcha" is side-lined and done as a show performance.

Exact dating has not been possible on the two feature films and the Signal short.

Late this year, E. Purves Pullen auditions at Spike's home and many hours later, emerges as the newly christened Dr. Horatio Q. Birdbath, known to many as simply 'Doc'. Doc had spent 10 years in the Ben Bernie band with colleague Bruce Hudson, and on Bernie's death in 1941, remained in Hollywood where his sound effects became well known and in demand on many radio shows (Rinso White Bird) and films (Ray Milland's 'Lost Weekend' "bat", Tarzan's Cheetah). He made guest appearances on the shows of Jack Benny, Carveth Wells, the Screen Guild, Amos n' Andy, Bing Crosby, Jimmy Durante and countless others. Doc has been responsible for the sound effects in motion pictures with most of the major companies.

Adept at imitating virtually any bird or animal call, as well as being a ventriloquist, made him a natural for the City Slickers and was heavily featured for many years. Linda Lee recalls crying when the audition was over and Doc put his dummy, 'Johnny' in a trunk - she thought Johnny was real.

The most difficult part of the audition was the creation, or invention, of a new stage name, and the end result was:-

Dr. - of ornithology (birds)
Horatio - symbolic of success ala Horatio Alger
Q. - for quinine, as he is so hard to take!
Bird - because of the imitations
bath - for the 'dousing' he is liable to get
      on every show

Although Doc admits to not being a trained musician, his longevity amongst the excellent musicians of the Bernie band and the Slickers is a testimonial to his natural abilities. Doc starts to incorporate his act before the year is out.

Late in 1945, Spike went 'on the wagon', and remained a tee-totaler. In the past, he was known to have drunk his share of alcohol and may have realized continuance would adversely affect continued success. Herman Crone feels that Spike's physician advised its discontinuance. There are also some who feel that Helen Greco, singing increasingly on the Slickers personal theatre appearances, tremendously influenced Spike on drinking. That he was able to do so in a profession where alcohol is rife, was, and still is, a measure of ones' supreme resolve.

13 December, 1945 (THURS) - KRAFT MUSIC HALL*
              NBC Hollywood

                      with John Scott Trotter's Orch, the Charioteers, Lina Romay, Larry Storch, Skitch Henderson; Special guests Spike Jones and his City Slickers, Vera Vague and Frank Morgan; ann: Ken Carpenter

                      You Always Hurt the One You Love - voc Carl Grayson and Red Ingle
                      Blue Danube - Carl Grayson

Note: the above details have been taken from an undated AFRS transcription titled "Music Hall" 158, which has no Bing Crosby involvement. Date courtesy of the Library of Congress.

"Nearly 10,000 ballots were cast in the 1945 poll.....The voters have chosen Spike Jones, the King of Corn, by the unheard of margin of three-to-one for four consecutive years."
                (Downbeat souvenir program, 1946)

"Like all new trends, corn itself is difficult to define. A decade ago, collegians...trying to tell one another what "swing" was and how it differed from its ancestral "jazz". But even those who played it weren't sure...the same is true of corn...it's not just plain hillbilly music, dusted off and resurrected from the day of the Sorghum Sextette. Nor is it related to the current Burl Ives-led mountaineer balladry.
"Deceptively simple, with...primitive instruments and mawkish performers, corn is quite possibly the most sophisticated musical style ever to reach popularity. It amounts...to an audacious satire on the moon-June-croon school of composition.
"Spike Jones...the country's leading corn exponents, literally rends...numbers...by incorporating auto horns, cop's whistles, cider jugs, shotguns and slamming doors.. ..however sentimental a song may be, no one who has heard it played by Spike's "Musical Depreciation Revue" will ever take it seriously again.
"One of the most appealing aspects of corn...is its air of

happy spontaneity. No matter how long a corn band has rehearsed......
over-all effect is that of a gang of musically inclined screwballs on
the loose in a hardware store".
(<u>Varsity</u>, Apr 49)

Note: Feature articles on Spike Jones appeared during
1945 in:-

Tune In, Mar - "Spike Jones"
Band Leaders, May - "Keeping Up With the Jones"
Time, 17 Dec - "Spike Jones, Primitive"

"...a lot of big record names and big acts. The biggest was
Spike Jones and his City Slickers, at the time the hottest record and
road attraction in the country. His smash-hit...Der Fuehrer's Face...
had vaulted Spike...into superstardom. By 1946, after a string of hit
records, he was an American institution."
(Mickey Katz, Hannibal Coons: <u>Papa Play For Me</u>,
Simon and Schuster, 1977)

Early in the New Year, Giggie Royce leaves - the drum chair
temporarily filled by <u>John DeSoto Jr.</u> "I had just been released from
the Service. Spike was looking for some one for the Slickers - pay
was good - so went with it for the time being. We did a series of
theatre dates etc, and this (11 Feb) record date. That was it for the
Slickers." (John DeSoto correspondance, 6 Jun 83)

8 February, 1946 (FRI)
NBC New York

"Bill Stern Sports Newsreel of the Air", interview with
Spike Jones in Hollywood. Subject: unknown

10 February, 1946, (SUN) - REQUEST PERFORMANCE*
CBS Hollywood 9:00 PM (Sponsor: Campbell Soup)

Master of Ceremonies - Red Skelton

Spike Jones and his City Slickers, personnel
similar to 11 Feb

Glow Worm - voc Aileen Carlisle, Red Ingle
(A) Hot Time in the Old Town Tonight - inst,
feat Sir Aubrey Smith, washboard

"...last week an economy-size...(Command Performance) called
Request Performance was well along on its way...
"Since it began four months ago, Request Performance has
attracted new listeners by presenting famous people in the act of
doing something out of character...Next week: Dame May Whitty playing
a washboard in Spike Jones' orch...after a suitable build-up, the
famed stage-&-screen dowager with the impeccable enunciation will
address the mike in a slightly Yiddish accent: 'You were expecting
maybe Mrs. Nussbaum?'" (<u>Time</u>, 11 Feb 46)

11 February, 1946 (MON) - Victor Studios, Hollywood,   3:00 to
Eli Oberstein, A & R Rep, present   8:00 PM

Leader - Spike Jones
Brass - George Rock, tpt; Chick Dougherty, trb
Reeds - Red Ingle, Zep Meissner, Bob Poland,sax

130

Rhythm - Herman Crone, pno; Dick Morgan, guit;
Candy Hall, bass; John DeSoto Jr, drm
Voices - Carl Grayson, Aileen Carlisle, Red
Ingle, Purves Pullen, unidentified chorus

D6-VB-2024-1   20-1894-A(CP-4); HMV BD 1145-A; HMVAU BD 1145-A
     1A   & EA 3491 & EA 4240; HMVSK 1145; 45 RCAE
                RCX 1030; LP ANL1 2312(e); AYL1 3780; RCAE
                NL 42730(e); RCA Special Products "Good Music
                Record" DML1 0570; ET AFRS "Remember" 4221;
                AFRS "G.I. Jive" 1349;
          (3:05)I Dream of Brownie with the Light Blue Jeans - voc
                Carl Grayson and the Barefooted Pennsylvanians

D6-VB-2025-1   20-1836-B; HMV BD 1164-B; HMVAU BD 1164-B &
     1A   EA 3384; Y-465; 45 47-0180-B; WY-465;
                LP RCAE HY 1006; ET AFRS "Downbeat" 217;
          (3:20)Mother Goose Medley
                Into: Brahms Lullaby, Farmer in the Dell,
                Hi Diddle Diddle, Sing a Song of Sixpence,
                Little Boy Blue, Hickory dickory Dock, Jack
                and Jill, Old King Cole, London Bridge is
                Falling Down, Brahms Lullaby
                - animals and birds by Dr. Horatio Q. Birdbath

D6-VB-2026-1   20-1893-A(CP-4); HMV BD 1162; HMVAU MH 132,
     1A   EA 3464 & EA 4237; HMVSK X7244; 420-0174-B;
                45 447-0174-B; EPA 5080; RCAE RCX 1037;
                RCAAU EP 20050; LP LPM 2224; LPM 3849; LSP
                3849(e); ANL1 1035(e); AYL1 3748; PK ACL
                7031(e); RCAE RD 7724 & LSA 3084; RCAAU CAS
                7158; RCAG LSP 10157 & RCS 3211/1-2; RCAJ
                5143(m); RCAIT CL 83748; RCAF PL 43197;
                RCA Special Products "Good Music Record" DML1
                0570; ET AFRS "Remember" 733;
          (3:06)The Glow Worm - voc Red Ingle and Aileen
                Carlisle with chorus

D6-VB-2027-1   20-1836-A; HMV BD 1164-A; HMVAU BD 1164-A &
     1A   EA 3384; HMVSK X7244; 45-5164-A(Y-359);
                45 47-0162-A(WY-359); 47-0180-A; RCAG EPA
                9780; LP RCAE INTS 5052; RCAG RCS 3217/1-2;
                ET AFRS "Turn Back the Clock" 929;
          (3:05)Old MacDonald Had a Farm - with chorus

D5-VB-1131-2   20-1893-A(CP-4); HMV BD 1145-B; HMVAU BD 1145-B,
     2A   EA 3442 & EA 4240; HMVSK BD 1145; 420-0174-A;
                45-5165-A(Y-359); V-Disc 709-A; 45 447-0174-A;
                47-0163-B(WY-359); EPA 5058; RCAAU EP 20050;
                RCAF EP 86233; LP LPM 2224; LPM 3849; LSP
                3849(e); ANL1 1035(e); AYL1 3748; RCAE RD 7724
                & LSA 3084; RCAG LSP 10157 & RCS 3211/1-2;
                RCAAU ODLP 7503 & CAS 7158; RCAJ RVP 6300(m)
                & 5143(m); RCAIT CL 83748; RCAF PL 43197; RCA
                Special Products "Good Music Record" DML1 0570;
                ET AFRS "Remember" 721; AFRS "Ira Cook" 907;
                AFRS "Turn Back the Clock" 1108; AFRS "Juke
                Box USA" 46; U.S. Pacific Fleet "Across the
                Blue Pacific";
          (2:33)Hawaiian War Chant - Spike Jones and his
                Wacky Wakakians

       Note: RCA inst do not list vocalists or Purv Pullen. The
uncredited chorus would be similar to "Nutcracker" voices. "Hawaiian
War Chant" 45 RPM 47-0163-B was originally intended as 47-0163-A.

"Hawaiian" was issued in June 1946 and, according to Billboard Magazine, reached No. 8 on the Hit Parade during the week of 25 July, re-
"Hawaiian" take-2 is a remake of the previously rejected 10 Sept 45
take-1. Remakes usually retain the matrix and are done within days or
mere weeks of the date in question. The anomaly here is that Victor
assigned the same matrix as 10 Sept 45 - five months previous -
instead of a new sequential number, such as D6-VB-2028-1.
        RCA inst and release labels erroneously spell 'London
Bridges..' and 'Brahm's...' on "Mother Goose". "Foster Follies" is a
reported title from the Burns/Gilmore shows, and speculation is that
it was re-worked and re-titled as "I Dream Of Brownie..."

        Note: On AFRS ET "Downbeat" 217, issued in March 46, Spike,
as co-host, talks about "Ladies Man", "Breakfast in Hollywood", the
recent overseas tour and soon to be released (near Easter) "Mother
Goose Medley". Also mentioned is the Other Orchestra opening soon at
the Trocadero.

23 (SAT) to 25 (MON) February, 1946
                        Spike Jones, his City Slickers and a large group
                        of studio and dance band musicians start re-
                        hearsing for the upcoming Trocadero engagement
                        as the 'Other Orchestra'

                Leader - Spike Jones
                Contractor - Carl Hoefle
                Brass - George Rock, Jack Mootz, Irving (Irv) Lewis,
                        Tommy (Slim) Davis, tpt; Chick Dougherty, Dick
                        Noel, Harry H. Rodgers, trb; Willard Culley Jr.
                        fr hrn
                Reeds - Zep Meissner, clar/alto sax; Red Ingle, clar/
                        b.clar/tenor sax; Bob Poland, bari sax/b.clar;
                        Don Brassfield, clar/tenor sax; James Briggs, fl/
                        clar/alto sax
                Rhythm - Herman Crone, pno; Dick Morgan, guit/bjo;
                        Candy Hall, bass; Frank Carlson, drm
                Harp - Charlotte Tinsley
                Strings - Theodore Klages(leader), Truman Boardman, Al
                        Saparoff, Myron Sandler, Theodore Norman, Bob
                        Morrow, vln; Hans Bodendorfer, Maurice Lahmeyer,
                        vla; Jerry Jarnagan, cel
                Effects - Purves Pullen
                Vocals - Jimmy Cassidy (Cassity), Helen Greco
                Arrangers - Howard Gibeling, Harry Rodgers, Zep
                        Meissner, Herman Crone

        Note: Some of the musicians designated as appearing here for
the first time had augmented the Slickers in past broadcast performances. Carl Grayson did perform for an undetermined length of time at
the Troc and it is possible he was intended as the ballad singer for
this series, as he sang remarkably well on the NBC pilots of Nov. 45.
But he was having personal problems.
        Helen Greco, who sang on occasion with the troupe during the
past six months in their theatre appearances, now "...came to work as
a permanent member...This didn't happen...until six months after the
Catalina date."   (Radio and TV Mirror, NY, Jan 49)
        Having completed a long stint with Alfred Newman at 20th
Century Fox studios, Don Anderson sat in on the first Troc rehearsal
with a view to re-joining Spike, but was almost immediately drafted,
ending up in Ft. Lewis, Washington, in charge of a military bugle
band.

26 February, 1946 (TUES)
>Spike Jones, his City Slickers and Other Orchestra
>dance/show at Pacific Square Ballroom,
>San Diego

O.O. dates to 16 March courtesy Dick Noel. Rehearsals for
both the Slickers and O.O. continue, with the Slickers playing
regional theatre dates. The next public appearance of the big band
is:-

16 March, 1946 (SAT)
>Spike Jones, his City Slickers and Other Orchestra
>dance/show at Municipal Auditorium, Long Beach

Brief biographies on but a few Other Orchestra musicians:

Howard Gibeling, arranger/trombone - recorded with Glenn Miller,
>Larry Clinton and Hal McIntyre (along with Bob Poland);
>in the Goodman film, "The Powers Girl". Zep Meissner es-
>timated 90% O.O. arrangements were Gibelings. He was trb
>'sub' on this engagement.
Harry H. Rodgers, trombone/arranger - played and recorded with Les
>Brown, Glenn Miller, Artie Shaw, Harry James, Charlie
>Barnet, Jan Savitt. Arranged for most of these plus Glen
>Gray, Hal McIntrye, Bob Hope and many others.
Dick Noel, trombone - previously with Tommy Dorsey, soon to go
>with Harry James.
Frank Carlson, drums - because of his use of two bass drums, nick-
>named "club-foot-Carlson" by Candy Hall. Played with
>Mills Cavalcade orch. in '35; Woody Herman from 1937 to
>'42 (the original "Golden Wedding" of Herman's featured
>Carlson); recorded "Moonlight Serenade" on 4 Apr 39 with
>Glenn Miller orch, along with Paul Tanner, Hal McIntyre
>and Allan Reuss; with the Raphael Mendez Orch. in '45;
>appeared in Goodman's "The Powers Girl"; more recently a
>student in Hawaii, studying the criminal justice system.
Jack Mootz, trumpet - with Charlie Barnet in 1944 and '45, as were
>Eddie Pripps and Bob Poland.
Irv Lewis, trumpet - recorded with Benny Carter and Woody Herman
>during 1945.
Willard Culley Jr., French horn - recorded with Harry James in '42.
Theodore Klages, violin - with all recording bands, from Jan
>Savitt to Artie Shaw (incl "Frenesi"), Richard Himber to
>Ray Noble - all as strings leader.
Theodore Norman, violin - with Los Angeles Philharmonic 1935 to
>'42; three years in 377th Army Corps Band. Since '67 has
>been head of UCLA guitar dept, having adapted and had
>published many classical violin solos, notably the 24
>Caprices of Paganini, for the guitar literature.
Trueman Boardman, violin - experienced in all phases of studio
>string playing; later on violin with the Liberace Orch.
Al Saparoff, violin - recorded with Harry James in '42.
Hans Bodendorfer, viola - with Ted Norman in 377th Army Air Corps;
>with Spike's O.O. on release; presently with Guadalajara
>Symphony Orch., Mexico.

21 March, 1946 (THURS)
>GALA PREMIERE - SPIKE'S AT THE TROC

>Spike Jones, his City Slickers and
>Other Orchestra

>32 piece band, including the City Slickers
>(advance PR indicated 32 plus 10 Slickers)

Note: There were two shows nightly. Broadcasting a portion of each 'modern dance stylings' show began Friday, 22 March. Charlotte Tinsley mentions b'casts five nights per week but there may have been more, with the b'cast time variable. Only known b'casts are listed for the duration of the engagement and the length of each was, in most cases, 15 minutes.

    The Slickers changed into costume during intermission but their show was never on the air. The dressing rooms, like the stage, was very small for this size group. The series announcer was Jim Byron. The opening and closing theme, "Spike Speaks", a Gibeling arrangement of the Arab Dance from Tchaikovsky's "Nutcracker Suite", was heard on each b'cast. The series remained un-sponsored and commercially unsuccessful.

22 March, 1946, (FRI) - SPIKE'S AT THE TROC
              KHJ Mutual-Don Lee, Trocadero

              Heat Wave - inst
              My Home Town - voc Jimmy Cassidy
              Personality - voc Helen Greco
              Warsaw Concerto - feat Charlotte Tinsley
              I Only Have Eyes For You - inst

Note: Over the opening theme, "Spike Speaks", Jim Byron turns the mike over to Spike, the only known instance of Jones speaking to the radio audience. "Warsaw Concerto" was arranged by Melvin A. Tinsley.

            SPIKE'S AT THE TROC
              KHJ Mutual-Don Lee, Trocadero
              2nd show, 11:15 PM PST

              This Can't Be Love - inst
              Rhumba Rhapsody - inst
              E-Bop-O-Lee-Bop - voc Helen Greco
              You're Blase - voc Jimmy Cassidy

Note: Spike, now 'on-the-wagon', had to let Carl Grayson go as a regular Slickers performer due to, what Herman Crone referred to as, 'uncontrolled drinking'. Candy Hall recalls leading Grayson from a San Francisco stage after a solo number earlier this year, with Grayson unaware of where he was. Spike's ballad singer since 1941, he was followed by a succession of 'straight' vocalists, the present one being Jimmy Cassidy.

    Al Saparoff was with Spike when, from the Troc, he telephoned Cleveland and auditioned Mickey Katz, a virtuoso clarinettist, vocalist and 'glug' specialist. Having met the previous year in Cleveland, Spike recalled these talents. Joining the Slickers very quickly, Katz was to be with them for the next 18 months.

29 March, 1946 (FRI) - SPIKE'S AT THE TROC
              KHJ Mutual-Don Lee, Trocadero
              2nd show, 11:15 PM PST

              Jealousy - inst
              Pico Pick Up - inst
              Medley:
                  Oh What It Seemed To Be - voc Jimmy Cassidy
                  Day By Day - inst
                  Shoofly Pie and Apple Pan Dowdy - voc
                      Helen Greco

Note: Sunday nights were designated as 'guest' nights, but

personalities were frequently mentioned on the air. This evening, George Jessel, June Haver, Dorothy Lamour, Lois Andrews, Madman Muntz and Jerry Colonna are mentioned.

3 April, 1946 (WED) - SPIKE'S AT THE TROC*
KHJ Mutual-Don Lee, Trocadero

Lovely - voc Jimmy Cassidy

6 April, 1946 (SAT) - AFRS COMMAND PERFORMANCE
in honor of Army Day, 1946
CBS Hollywood (assumed)

Host - Bob Hope, with the orch and chorus of
Meredith Willson. ann: Harry Von Zell

Bob Hope - Comedy dialogue
Dinah Shore - "Shoofly Pie and Apple Pan Dowdy"
Bette Davis talks with Dinah Shore, Bob Hope,
Bing Crosby and Frank Sinatra
Frank Sinatra - "Oh What It Seemed To Be"
Sinatra, Crosby, Hope - "You're the Top"
You Always Hurt the One You Love - voc Carl
Grayson and Red Ingle
Andrews Sisters - "Chickery Chick"
Bob, Bing introduce the Chief of Staff, U.S.
War Department -
General Dwight D. Eisenhower - message
Medley: special settings and lyrics to-
Chorus - "Aura Lee"
Frank - "What Do You Do In the Infantry?"
Dinah - "This Is the Army, Mr. Jones"
Bing - "Caisson Song"

Note: The date of Army Day 1946 has never been specified. As advertised in 1 April 49 Newsweek, "Army Day" was 6 April and assuming the date to be an annual constant, 6 Apr has been applied to 1946. This is the last known appearance of Carl Grayson with the Slickers, although he does appear on record in the future. On the side and when he had the time, Herman Crone was writing vocal and background arrangements for the Merry Macs vocal group.

14 April, 1946 (SUN) - SPIKE'S AT THE TROC
KHJ Mutual-Don Lee, Trocadero

Dardanella - inst
September Song - voc Jimmy Cassidy
E-Bop-O-Lee-Bop - voc Helen Greco
Perfidia - inst

Note: Guests introduced this evening were: William Powell, Diana Lewis and Clark Gable

16 April, 1946 (TUES) - SPIKE'S AT THE TROC*
KHJ Mutual-Don Lee, Trocadero

Medley:
I'm Always Chasing Rainbows - inst
Come To Baby, Do - voc Helen Greco
Jealousy - inst
Over the Rainbow - inst
Heat Wave - inst

135

Note: Once the series was established, Spike allowed 'subs'. Red Nichols, the well known and respected band leader and an early idol of Spikes' - now a studio musician, often 'subbed', as may be the case this evening with an alternate trumpet soloist on "Heat Wave".

18 April, 1946 (THURS) - CHESTERFIELD SUPPER CLUB*
                        NBC Hollywood

            Starring Perry Como, with Master of Ceremonies
            Martin Block, Lloyd Shaeffer's Band, and
            guests, Paula Kelly and the Modernaires, and
            Spike Jones and his City Slickers

            Perry Como, Modernaires - "I Don't Know Enough
              About You"
            The Glow Worm - voc Aileen Carlisle and Red Ingle
            Perry Como - "Song of Songs"
            Perry Como, Modernaires - "Sittin' and Rockin'"

     Note: The above information is based on the 15 minute AFRS ET of this show, pressed as "Supper Club" 198. The troupe return to the Troc after their appearance

19 April, 1946 (FRI) - SPIKE'S AT THE TROC
                       KHJ Mutual-Don Lee, Trocadero
                       1st show, 9:45 PM PST

            Jungle Drums - inst
            I've Got the World on a String - voc Helen Greco
            September Song - voc Jimmy Cassidy
            Hardly Ever Amber - inst
            East of the Sun - inst

     "The thought occurred to me to create a two-headed drummer. My wife, Ruth Norman is a fine arts painter and sculpter. I asked her to create another head exactly like Frankie Karl(sic) the drummer. The head was mounted on a football pad (shoulder) and my wife sewed two shirts together. The jacket belonged to Rolmo Falk, the well-known band arranger.
     "To try it out, Frankie and his other head and I walked into the dimly lit bar of the Trocadero. I asked for 3 beers, was serverd three beers and I knew it would work.
     "The photograph you see was taken...at the club. One (patron) was drunk and thought he was seeing double! He tried to squint Frankie into one head. He couldn't...so he asked the (club) photographer to take a picture of Frankie. When she returned with the picture and put it on the table, he gave one look at it, saw two heads and fled! I paid the girl $1.50 for the picture.
     "I'm happy I did because many years later my wife met a man at a party who claimed he had invented it. I found this rather annoying since Spike had never paid me for it. It was a lark for me."
                       (Theodore Norman correspondence, 15 Jan 83)

     Ted Klages recalls:- "Ted Norman's wife made the shirt for the two-headed drummer. I understand it was a helluva hard job. (Can you imagine designing and making a shirt, complete with collars for a two-headed man?). Frankie had a lot of fun talking to himself. When the customers saw him, they used to die laffing! I used to break up everytime I saw the show - which was nearly every night." Klages, a friend of Spike's from the radio days of '37, also knew Carl Grayson as a good violinist and talented with his voice. "I know that (Grayson) would have liked to have played violin in the 'Troc' and

136

also have participated in the (Slickers) floor show...but he never made it. I felt very sorry for him." (Klages communication, 5 Feb 83)

21 April, 1946 (SUN) - SPIKE'S AT THE TROC
KHJ Mutual-Don Lee, Trocadero
1st show, 10:00 PM PST

Rhumba Rhapsody - inst
Medley:
  Oh What It Seemed To Be - voc Jimmy Cassidy
  Day By Day - inst
  Shoofly Pie and Apple Pan Dowdy - voc
    Helen Greco
Pico Pick Up - inst
I'll Never Be the Same - inst

SPIKE'S AT THE TROC
2nd show, 11:30 PM PST

Jealousy - inst
I've Got the World on a String - voc Helen Greco
September Song - voc Jimmy Cassidy
Hardly Ever Amber - inst

Note: Guests introduced this evening were: Alan Ladd, Forrest Tucker, Ellen Rains

24 April, 1946 (WED) - SPIKE'S AT THE TROC
KHJ Mutual-Don Lee, Trocadero

Jungle Drums - inst
I've Got the World on a String - voc Helen Greco
September Song - voc Jimmy Cassidy
Hardly Ever Amber - inst
I Only Have Eyes For You - inst
E-Bop-O-Lee-Bop - voc Helen Greco
Medley:
  Oh What It Seemed To Be - voc Jimmy Cassidy
  Day By Day - inst
  Shoofly Pie and Apple Pan Dowdy - voc
    Helen Greco

26 April, 1946 (FRI) - Victor Studios, Hollywood
Standard Transcription Library

Spike Jones and his Other Orchestra, personnel
23/25 Feb, with added strings. Additional:-
Louis Adrian, vln

HD6-MM-7124   LP HSR 185(edited); ET Z-213-1;
          (3:05)Spike Speaks(Spike Jones Theme) - inst

               ET Z-213-2;
          (3:20)Rhumba Rhapsody - inst

               LP HSR 185; ET Z-213-3;
          (2:55)E-Bop-O-Lee-Bop - voc Helen Greco

               LP HSR 185; ET Z-213-4;
          (3:30)Minka - featuring George Rock, trumpet

137

HD6-MM-7125   LP HSR 185; ET Z-213-5;
                (2:45)Laura - voc Jimmy Cassity

                     ET Z-213-6;
                (1:55)Lovely - voc Jimmy Cassidy

                     ET Z-213-7;
                (2:50)Warsaw Concerto - featuring Charlotte Tinsley

                     ET Z-213-8;
                (2:45)September Song - voc Jimmy Cassidy

                     LP HSR 185; ET Z-213-9;
                (2:45)Hardly Ever Amber - inst

        Note: Date/location courtesy of Dick Noel. Neither Mickey
Katz nor 'Doc' were present on this or the next ET session. "E-Bop
-O-Lee-Bop" was recorded by Charlie Barnet in Hollywood on 6 Dec 45,
L4020, Decca 18761. Tommy Pederson and Eddie Pripps were in that
Barnet band, while Jack Mootz and Bob Poland had just left. The
Barnet band on 3 Aug 44 had amongst its musicians Jack Mootz, Zep
Meissner, Eddie Pripps and Bob Poland.

27 April, 1946 (SAT) - TRIBUTE TO THE SHRINERS
                ABC Hollywood   5:30 PM PST

             the entertainment profession salutes "the Shriners"
                Bob Hope, Dinah Shore and George Montgomery,
                    Roy Rogers and Trigger, the King Cole Trio,
                    Tom Harmon and featuring the music of
                    Spike Jones, his Other Orchestra and the
                    City Slickers

                    Holiday For Strings - brief intro
                    Introducing co-announcers - Harry Von Zell
                        and Don Wilson
                    King Cole Trio - "Paper Moon"
                    Roy Rogers - dialogue on Shriners aid to
                        crippled children
                    Laura - voc Jimmy Cassidy
                    Wm. H. Whitfield - Imperial Potentate for
                        North America, introduces
                    Bob Hope - Comedy monologue
                    George Montgomery, on wire recording, speaking
                        for an ill Dinah Shore
                    Tom Harmon, All-American - dialogue on
                        Shriners and their childrens work
                    Hawaiian War Chant - feat Mickey Katz
                    sign off before finish

        Note: This show, pressed with NBC labels although it is ABC,
is the first known b'cast performance to feature Mickey Katz

29 April, 1946 (MON) - Victor Studios, Hollywood
                Standard Transcription Library

                    Personnel as 26 April, adding Country Washburn,
                    tuba soloist

HD6-MM-7196   LP HSR 185; ET Z-214-1;
                (2:40)I Only Have Eyes For You (show: 'Dames') - inst

                                138

                    LP HSR 185; ET Z-214-2;
          (2:35) When Yuba Plays the Rhumba on the Tuba(show
                    'The Third Little Show') - featuring
                    Country Washburn on the Tuba

                    LP HSR 185; ET Z-214-3;
          (2:10) Spike Rocks the Troc - inst

                    LP HSR 185; ET Z-214-4;
          (2:15) I've Got the World on a String - voc Helen Greco

                    LP HSR 185; ET Z-214-5;
          (2:00) Pico Pick Up - inst

HD-MM-7197   ET Z-214-6;
          (3:25) Chameleon - inst

                    ET Z-214-7;
          (3:30) Perfidia - inst

                    LP HSR 185; ET Z-214-8;
          (3:30) Young Man with a French Horn - featuring
                    Willard Culley on the French Horn

                    LP HSR 185; ET Z-214-9;
          (2:55) I'll Never Be the Same - inst

30 April, 1946 (TUES) - SPIKE'S AT THE TROC*
               KHJ Mutual-Don Lee, Trocadero

                    On the Sunny Side of the Street - voc Helen Greco
                    Dardanella - inst
                    Lovely - voc Jimmy Cassidy
                    Spike Rocks the Troc - inst

1 May, 1946 (WED) - SPIKE'S AT THE TROC
               KHJ Mutual-Don Lee, Trocadero

                    Perfidia - inst
                    I've Got the World on a String - voc Helen Greco
                    September Song - voc Jimmy Cassidy
                    Warsaw Concerto - feat Charlotte Tinsley
                    Sophisticated Lady - inst
                    E-Bop-O-Lee-Bop - voc Helen Greco
                    East of the Sun - inst

2 May, 1946 (THURS) - CHESTERFIELD SUPPER CLUB*
               NBC Hollywood

                    Starring Perry Como, with Master of Ceremonies
                      Martin Block, Lloyd Shaeffer's Band, and
                      guests, Paula Kelly and the Modernaires and
                      Spike Jones and his City Slickers

                    Perry Como, Modernaires - "Shoofly Pie and
                      Apple Pan Dowdy"
                    Laura - Perry Como with Shaeffer's Band, then
                      with the Slickers
                    Perry Como - "Laughing on the Outside"
                    Perry Como, Modernaires - "You Won't Be Satisfied"

                              139

Note: Information based on the 15 minute AFRS ET pressed as "Supper Club" 307. The original NBC show may have had more Jones involvement and Block material. Occasional pressings erroniously show 3 May as show date.

SPIKE'S AT THE TROC
KHJ Mutual-Don Lee, Trocadero

Warsaw Concerto - feat Charlotte Tinsley
September Song - voc Jimmy Cassidy
E-Bop-O-Lee-Bop - voc Helen Greco
Sophisticated Lady - inst

4 May, 1946 (SAT) - SPIKE'S AT THE TROC
KHJ Mutual-Don Lee, Trocadero

Medley:
     It Might As Well Be Spring - voc Jimmy Cassidy
     Autumn Serenade - inst
     I'm Gonna Love That Guy - voc Helen Greco
Medley:
     It's Been a Long Long Time - voc Jimmy Cassidy
     Symphony - inst
     Waitin' For the Train To Come In - voc
                         Helen Greco
Medley:
     I Can't Begin To Tell You - voc Jimmy Cassidy
     I'm Always Chasing Rainbows - inst
     Come To Baby, Do - voc Helen Greco

5 May, 1946 (SUN) - SPIKE'S AT THE TROC
KHJ Mutual-Don Lee, Trocadero

Jungle Drums - inst
Medley:
     Oh What It Seemed To Be - voc Jimmy Cassidy
     Day By Day - inst
     Shoofly Pie and Apple Pan Dowdy - voc
                         Helen Grayco
Spike Rocks the Troc - inst
East of the Sun - inst

Note: This is Dick Noel's last night with Spike, as he starts with Harry James in the morning.

6 May, 1946 (MON) - Victor Studios, Hollywood, 9:30 to 10:30 PM
                    Eli Oberstein, A & R Rep, present

Leader - Spike Jones
Brass - George Rock, tpt; Chick Dougherty, trb
Reeds - Zep Meissner, Red Ingle, sax
Rhythm - Herman Crone, pno; Dick Morgan, guit;
     Candy Hall, bass; Frank Carlson, drm
Vocal - Mickey Katz, Jimmy Cassidy
Effects - Red Ingle, Purves Pullen

D6-VB-2063-1   20-1894-B(CP-4); HMV BD 1147-B; HMVAU BD 1147-B,
       1A   EA 3491 & 4242; V-Disc 709-A; ET AFRS "G.I.
                   Jive" 1378;
              (2:34)Jones Polka - voc Mickey Katz

Note: RCA inst do not credit vocalists/effects

140

Additional musicians to above:-
Brass - Clyde Hurley Jr.. Ray Linn, Rubin(Zeke)
Zarchy, tpt; Harry Rodgers, Edward Kusby
(Kuesborski), Howard Gibeling(assumed), trb;
Willard Thorpe Culley Jr, fr hrn; Country
Washburn, tuba soloist
Reeds - Bob Poland, Don Brassfield, James Briggs,
sax
Harp - Charlotte Tinsley
Strings - Theodore Klages(leader); Al Saparoff,
Myron Sandler, Theodore Norman, Pepe Landeros,
Frederick J. Wolff, vln; Maurice Lahmeyer,
Hans Bodendorfer, vla; Jerry Jarnagan, cel

D6-VB-2064-1   20-2118-A; HMVAU EA 3600; LP LPM 2224; LPM 3849;
1A   LSP 3849(e); ANL1 1035(e); AYL1 3748; PK ACL
7031(e); RCAE LSA 3084 '& RD 7724; RCAAU CAS
7158; RCAG LSP 10157 '& RCS 3217/1-2; RCAJ
5143(m); RCAIT CL 83748; RCA Special Products
"Good Music Record" DML1 0570; ET AFRS "Basic
Music Library" P-736; AFRS "Purple Heart Album"
153;
      (2:56)Laura - Spike Jones and his Other Orchestra with
the City Slickers and vocal by Jimmy Cassidy,
Red Ingle and Dr. Horatio Q. Birdbath

D6-VB-2065-1   20-1983-A; HMV BD 1174-A; HMVAU BD 1174;
1A   ET AFRS "Basic Music Library"(condensed)
P-769;
      (3:16)Minka - Spike Jones and his Other Orchestra,
featuring George Rock

D6-VB-2066-1   20-1983-B; HMV BD 1174-B; HMVAU BD 1174;
1A   ET AFRS "Basic Music Library"(condensed)
P-769; AFRS "America's Popular Music" 771;
      (3:23)Lassus Trombone - Spike Jones and his Other
Orchestra, featuring Eddie Kusby

D6-VB-2067-1   20-2118-B; HMV EA 3600; ET AFRS "Basic Music
1A   Library" P-S 28 '& P-715; AFRS "Remember"
858;
      (2:30)When Yuba Plays the Rhumba on the Tuba - Spike
Jones and his Other Orchestra, featuring
Joe "Country" Washburn

Note: RCA inst do not credit vocalist on "Laura". Country
Washburn and Ed Kusby played only their respective solos on this
session. Three 'bones are scored for in O.O. orchestrations. Dick
Noel had left for James and Kusby played only the solo. It is assumed that Howard Gibeling, who 'subbed' for Noel on the Troc series,
sat in on this session. Domestic issues of "Minka" credit the arranger as John Niles.
      Dick Noel had played "Lassus" at non-broadcast Troc dances
and was understandably miffed when Spike asked Ed Kusby to record the
solo. In retrospect, Noel concedes that no one would have done it
better than Kusby - praise indeed!
      Mickey Katz leaves after his part in the session for about
ten days due to a family crises in Cleveland. Although he is not
credited on the RCA sheets, Katz does sing and play the clarinet on
"Jones Polka".
      Standard ET spelling is 'Cassity', RCA is 'Cassidy'. The
three studio trumpets who temporarily replaced the Troc section were

among the current Hollywood 'heavies', with careers touching most of the big and small bands that ever recorded.

7 May, 1946 (TUES) - SPIKE'S AT THE TROC
                    KHJ Mutual-Don Lee, Trocadero

                    Personnel as 23/25 Feb, with Howard Gibeling,
                        trb, replacing Dick Noel

                    Jealousy - inst
                    I've Got the World on a String - voc Helen Greco
                    September Song - voc Jimmy Cassidy
                    Spike Rocks the Troc - inst

9 May, 1946 (THURS) - KRAFT MUSIC HALL*
                    NBC Hollywood

                    featuring Bing Crosby

                    I Dream of Brownie with the Light Blue Jeans -

        Note: East coast b'cast interrupted during "Brownie" to announce a power 'brown-out'

                    SPIKE'S AT THE TROC
                        KHJ Mutual-Don Lee, Trocadero
                        8:30 to 8:55 PM PST

                    Jungle Drums - inst
                    I've Got the World on a String - voc Helen Greco
                    September Song - voc Jimmy Cassidy
                    Spike Rocks the Troc - inst
                    I Only Have Eyes For You - inst
                    E-Bop-O-Lee-Bop - voc Helen Greco
                    Lovely - voc Jimmy Cassidy
                    Hardly Ever Amber - inst

        Note: This was the final b'cast and playdate at the Troc. "I'll never forget Spike Jones...a complex and little-understood man...we were playing the Trocadero on Hollywood's famed Sunset Strip. Spike spent a lot of money and hired about thirty extra musicians, fine ones, to have himself a symphonic jazz orchestra like Paul Whiteman. Conducting his symphonic orchestra, Spike was in seventh heaven. No funny stuff, just beautiful music." In his autobiographical 'Papa Play For Me', Mickey Katz continues, "And do you know what the crowds who came in said? They said 'What kind of crap is this? If we want a symphony, we'll go to the Hollywood Bowl. We came to hear Spike Jones, not Stokowski.'"
        The Other Orchestra, despite its artistic excellence, was a commercial flop. This culmination of Spike's dream as a leader of good music and great musicians was a bitter disappointment. In a 21 Oct 82 letter, Charlotte Tinsley looked at it from yet another point of view:- "...the big band he put together at great personal expense ...it should be noted that the big band was going great and on nightly network radio from the Trocadero...when the Union decided that he had to pay the same amount to each musician for each broadcast (five nights a week) as a sponsored broadcast. END THE BIG BAND, the Trocadero and Spike's ambition which was never the same after that."

                    MUSICAL DEPRECIATION REVUE

        The first tour to be known as the "Musical Depreciation

Revue" is ready for the road at the conclusion of the Troc engagement. As far as can be determined, the following personnel list is
correct for this phase of the City Slickers

        Leader - Spike Jones
        Brass - George Rock, tpt; Chick Dougherty, trb
        Reeds - Zep Meissner, Red Ingle, Bob Poland
        Violin - Red Ingle
        Rhythm - Herman Crone, pno; Dick Morgan, guit/bjo;
              Candy Hall, bass; Richard Petersen, drm
        Harp - Nancy Mcdonald
        Voices/acts - Purves Pullen(effts); Helen Greco, Eileen
              Carlisle(vocals); Bill King(juggler/comic); Tommy
              Gordon(vocal/dancer); Dorese Midgley(acrobat;
              Bettyjo Huston(contortionist); Frankie Little
              (midget); Kaye Ballard (Ballad)(comedienne)
        Band Boy - Eddie Brandt
        Additional - Jack Egan, PR; Ray Rubel, valet

      Note: During the initial absence of Mickey Katz, the 'glugs'
so necessary in certain Slickers titles would be supplied by Spike
and 'Doc'. Bob Poland started the "very enjoyable" tour while filling
in for Katz who re-joined in mid-May. When the Revue played in Yuma,
Arizona, Joe Wolverton joined, again, on bjo/guit. Rhythm was a prime
ingredient in the Slicker style and it suffered when Dick Morgan
became increasingly involved with singing and skits. Spike needed two
players. After his release from the Army, Joe had spent the past
seven months with Noel Boggs at the Palladium.
      International Artists, Inc. of Hollywood recorded on a 12"
acetate, three radio ads for the Revue. Each skit promulgated the
Slickers show (five to six per day) and "plays good dance music". Cut
in early 1946, these short skits featured the voices of George Rock
and Carl Grayson.

      "The band that plays for fun"
      "For laughs and snickers, don't miss the Slickers"
      "If we have to hike, we're gonna see Spike"

      Itinerary is not available for this four month tour, but
would be similar in detail to 1947.

12 July (SAT) to 18 July (FRI), 1946
      RCA decreed this to be "Musical Depreciation Week" and
provided all dealers with large colorful poster and promotional
material, as well as issues of new Jones titles.

      "Therefore when Spike Jones conceived his idea of "Musical
Depreciation Week" RCA Victor cooperated with him by placing on the
market several new releases and a raft of standard favorites. The new
records are: "Glow Worm" and "Hawaiian War Chant", "I Dream Of
Brownie..." and "Jones Polka" while "That Old Black Magic" is coupled
with "Liebestraum". The standard favorites: "Chloe" and "Serenade to
a Jerk", "Holiday For Strings" and "Drip Drip Drip", "The Blue
Danube" and "You Always Hurt..." and "Mother Goose Medley" and "Old
MacDonald...".   (RCA promotional literature)

      Note: The RCA "Musical Depreciation Album", which was also
part of this promotion, was designed to accomodate five-78 RPM
unspecified records. The Canadian album with the same cover was
numbered CP-4 and held three records, presumably the first three
titles listed above: 20-1893/4/5.
      The cover of the 15 July 46 issue of Downbeat featured
Spike, Dorese Midgley and Helen Greco.

20 July, 1946 (SAT) - HI! JINX
          NBC

          Jinx Falkenburg interview with Spike Jones from the
Strand Theatre (New York?). NBC files specify that an ET
was made. Subject: unknown

          "We were in a taxi...between shows at the Oriental theatre
to Jim Sherman's National Magic Shop in the Palmer House, where the
leader of the City Slickers bought:
                    (1) One stuffed white rabbit.....$16.50
                    (2) One magic pitcher............ 2.50
                    (3) One kitchen sink.............   ?
                    (4) One cigar store indian.......   ?
          "No price quotation on the last two items, because ...a se-
lection...between a strictly prop kitchen sink and a genuine used
article...the Indian remained to be picked up at an undetermined
price. More props are carried by his band than by any other on tour.
          "It keeps us on the prowl all the time, looking for new
effects and new sounds", Spike explained. "We have one prop boy that
does nothing but search for blank cartridges in every town we hit."
(Spike fires one of three revolvers several times in the course of a
show.)
          "On the last day of the Oriental engagement, the white
rabbit (a complete skin, not just a patched job) was reposing on a
shelf in the...dressing room. Spike hadn't written him into his
scenario yet.
          "Rubel, the colored valet, had filled the magic pitcher with
something more interesting than milk or red water - ice, for the
highballs of visitors (Spike has been on the wagon for six months).
          "We'd like to see the amazing City Slickers during their
current Strand theatre engagement in New York. We're curious about
what Spike is doing with the white rabbit."
                    (Downbeat 46 - 15 July possible)

          Note: The Revue also toured into Western Canada, playing
Edmonton, Saskatoon, Calgary and Banff. Candy Hall still recalls the
Canadian Rockies from this trip. To relieve personal boredom while
stopped for a playdate on the train, Hall made it a ritual to workout
at every local YMCA. Others found card games their 'relaxation' on
tour.

28 September, 1946 (SAT) - Victor Studios, Hollywood,   10:00 AM to
                    Walt Heebner, A & R Rep, present   1:00 PM

                    Leader - Spike Jones
                    Trombone - Tommy Pederson
                    Piano - Frank Leithner
                    Effects - sneezes, Frank Leithner; Laughing,
                       George Rock, Dick Morgan, Red Ingle and others

D6-VB-2163-1   20-2023-A; HMV BD 1207-B; HMVAU BD 1207-B &
         1A   EA 3772; 45 RCAG EPA 9062; LP LSC 3235(e);
                    AGL1 4142(e); RCAE HY 1006 & NL 42730(e);
                    RCAG LSP 10157 & RCS 3211/1-2; RCAJ RVP
                    6300(m) & 5142; RCAF PL 43197;
          (2:46)The Jones Laughing Record(Introducing The
                    Flight of the Bumble Bee)

          Note: RCA inst list only Pederson and Leithner. An earlier
take, probably a test recording, was among Jones' files.
          Spike had approached the formidable trombonist Tommy
Pederson, to make a satirical recording of a trombone soloist with
hay fever. Unaware of Spike's proposed format, Pederson showed up

that morning and under a double handicap - he had a hang-over and there was no music, he and Leithner ("a beautiful sneezer - the best") masterfully put "The Bee" onto record. Pederson recalls four professional Hollywood laughers (plus George Rock) hired by Spike. They were as 'wiped' as he was - they could hardly speak, and his usually impeccable double-tonguing showed definite signs of wear and tear. The other 'laffers' as listed are also possible.

Harry Meyerson, the 'discoverer' of Spike and his Slickers for RCA, had recently left for Decca, with the A & R position finally resting with Walter Heebner.

One of the original stalwart members of the V-Disc staff in 1943, Walt Heebner, who had been a professional sax/clar man with Lester Lanin before his Army days, was now back at RCA, but in Hollywood. Moving to Los Angeles after his 14 Aug 45 discharge, Heebner becomes A & R Rep to Spike (and many other class artists), an association lasting four productive years.

7 October, 1946 (MON) - Victor Studios, Hollywood,   10:00 PM to
               Walt Heebner, A & R Rep, present   1:00 AM

        Leader - Spike Jones
        Brass - George Rock, tpt; Chick Dougherty, trb
        Reeds - Zep Meissner, Red Ingle, Mickey Katz, sax
        Rhythm - Herman Crone, pno; Dick Morgan, Joe
          Wolverton, guit; Candy Hall, bass; Richard
          Peterson, drm
        Voices - Gil Mershon, Art Davies, Frank Holiday,
          Harry Stanton
        Effects - Gene Conklin, Purves Pullen

D6-VB-2175-1   20-2023-1; HMV BD 1168-A; HMVAU EA 3586; HMVS BD
      1A   1168; RCADJ D6-VB-2175 & D7-CB-416; 45 RCAG
             EPA 9780; LP RCAG RCS 3217/1-2; ET AFRS "Basic
             Music Library" P-695; AFRS "Remember" 856;
      (2:53)Pretty Girl - voc Boys in the Back Room
            (Whistling by Dr. Horatio Q. Birdbath)

Note: Re-titled to "My Pretty Girl" 28 Oct 46. RCA inst show the studio vocal group to have been labeled as "The Foursome" and the the composers of this adaption of a Scandanavian Clog dance are Ray Johnson and Del Porter, 50% of the original "Foursome". Original issue label credit was to Gene Conklin but later changed to credit only 'Doc', whose name is not on the RCA inst. The whistling duet was done by 'Doc' and Conklin. BMI Performindex No. 3 also credits Howard Gibeling as co-composer.

"My Pretty Girl" (publisher Tune Towne Tunes) was also recorded by Dick Jurgens, Lawrence Welk and Cliffie Stone.

About this time, Kaye Ballard (Ballad) leaves the tour, as does Red Ingle. Finally retiring, he thought, after almost a lifetime on the road, he tried to concentrate on painting, leather-work and the training of his son, Don, as a cornettist being reared on Bix recordings. Artistically gifted, he made many caricatures of Spike, several of which were used in Slickers PR. The most commonly seen drawing is of a 'Zoot-suited' Spike conducting while his hands are encased in boxing gloves.

Country Washburn and some other musical cronies tempted him back into music and worked out an arrangement (with the addition of Jo Stafford giving forth in her best Judy Canova style vocal) of "Tim -Tay-Shun". Success followed its release and many more flowed from their fertile imaginations,

Never in serious competition with Spike, Ingle did enjoy success as a leader and made a respectable showing on the 'corn-polls' of Downbeat and Billboard. The Feb 49 English Melody Maker carries on:- "To create an authentic sound that would appeal to

rustic rhythm fans, I hired musicians like 'Red' Roundtree(guitar),
Art Wenzel(accordion), Herman the Hermit(banjo), Ray Hagan (drums),
Dandy(sic) Hall(bass), and Noel Boggs(steel guitar). This is the band
that made "Tim-Tay-Shun" - (with Red singing and fiddling and Country
Washburn whisking the suitcase)"

October, 1946
        In this month, Spike and Pat Jones divorce

23 October, 1946 (WED) - PHILCO RADIO TIME (broadcast date)
                ABC Hollywood

                Bing Crosby, with John Scott Trotter and his
                Orch, the Charioteers, Lina Romay, Skitch
                Henderson. ann: Ken Carpenter. Spike Jones
                and his City Slickers (personnel similar to
                7 Oct 46, chorus similar to 10 Feb 47)

                Bing Crosby - "My Heart Goes Crazy"
                *Hawaiian War Chant - feat Mickey Katz,
                    narration Ken Carpenter
                Love In Bloom - voc Bing Crosby with the City
                    Slickers and chorus
                Skitch Henderson - "Fascinating Rhythm"
                Lina Romay - "Little Surplus Me"
                Bing Crosby, Skitch Henderson - "All By Myself"
                Charioteers - "On the Boardwalk In Atlantic City"
                Bing Crosby - "The Things We Did Last Summer"

                *issued on MF Distribution LPs MF 205/4,
                    947447, and GO 10016. The complete show
                    issued on AFRS "Bing Crosby" 89; excerpts
                    on AFRS "To the Rear March"

        "The Philco-sponsored show was the first major transcribed
network show, and many people were apprehensive about its (transcribed series) chances. Recording allowed (Bing) to edit out flat sections and produce a smooth 30-minute package. Rehearsals and recording sessions could be scheduled at everyone's convenience.
        "Philco Radio Time started with a bang on October 16... with
Bob Hope. Spike Jones appeared on the second show and trumpet virtuoso, Raphael Mendez, following." (John Dunning, Tune In Yesterday,
                the Ultimate Encyclopedia of Old-Time Radio,
                1925-1976, pub Hall, 1978)

7 November, 1946 (THURS) - SEALTEST VILLAGE STORE*
                NBC

                with Spike Jones and his City Slickers

        The late Fall tour of the Revue through the mid-West started
about this time and carried on to mid-December.
        Red Ingle had been responsible for much of the Slickers
visual and audible effects and it took at least three personalities
to eventually replace him. Taking over on sax, clar and the comedy
violin that Ingle did so well is, from Utah, Dick (Richard Booth)
Gardner. Gardner, who had been a pilot with the AAF during the war,
makes his first appearance this Fall on sax/clar/vln.
        Already a notable young comic, Winstead (Doodles) Weaver
joins for a lengthy stay. From L.A., he had played leading roles in
such Broadway shows a "Marinka", "Meet the People" and did night club
work on a national scale. He also appeared on NBC's 1946 "Hour Glass"
television presentation and had been on the new 1946 "Kraft Music
Hall" series. Spike had caught his act, a car-race routine with the

146

winner - 'Twirl-A-Way', in the "Band Box" earlier this year. The audition was by 'phone. For many years, Doodles' brother, Sylvester (Pat) was a top executive with NBC.

From Cleveland, Joe Siracusa, drums, also very inventive and artistically creative, joins Spike's Slickers. Over the next six years, he is responsible for producing many of the troupe's special effects.

Another to join the troupe is the 7'7" giant, Junior Martin, who, along with midget Frankie Little, take part in a great many of the show acts. (Probably similar routines to Low and Hite who shared the billing with Spike in 1944)

Everyone in the troupe were totally involved with the stage presentation - never confined to the singular definition of singer, musician, comic or dancer.

The six-week tour saw the beginning of a natural extension to the vaudeville style Revue by the augmenting of the Slickers 'corn' with quality acts and comedians. In Beverly Hills, Spike set up his own company, Arena Stars, an MCA agency with branch offices in New York and Chicago, which phased out the one-hour, 'between showings' Revue (but which still occur on rare occasions into 1947) and put on a full evenings entertainment (2 to 2-1/2 hrs.) in the various larger arenas, forums and auditoriums throughout the United States and Canada. Ralph Wonders was hired as General Manager of the new company. At one time, Arena Stars handled Marian Richmond (Richman) on a radio audition for the justifiably short-lived "Old Hockum Bucket" show.

Betsy Mills is now the harpist and Aileen Carlisle remains the magnificent diva and Tommy Gordon is the 'straight' singer and dancer. Dorese Midgley is still with the troupe.

Ted Hering recalls Mickey Katz referring to a radio theme recorded by the Slickers while on tour, titled "Louisville Calls America". Apparently made in 1946 in Louisville, Kent., but there are no further details.

From late 1946 and into January 1947, Spike Jones and his City Slickers were involved with the filming of the Paramount movie VARIETY GIRL, 93 min. black/white

> PARAMOUNT STUDIOS
> Hollywood
>
> Leader - Spike Jones
> Brass - George Rock, tpt; Chick Dougherty, trb
> Reeds - Zep Meissner, Mickey Katz, Red Ingle
> Rhythm - Herman Crone, pno; Dick Morgan, bjo;
>   Joe Wolverton, guit; Candy Hall, bass;
>   unidentified drummer
> Strings - Dick Gardner, two unidentified vln
> Effects - Doodles Weaver, Purves Pullen
> Vocal - Mary Hatcher
>
> I Hear Your Heart Calling Mine - voc
>   Mary Hatcher

Note: Variety Girl starred Mary Hatcher, Olga San Juan, Deforest Kelley and William Demerest. Doodles Weaver is seen as a flautist, clarinettist and trumpeter. Red Ingle's presence is quite low-profile. Bob Hope and Bing Crosby made cameo appearances.

Note: Feature articles on Spike Jones appeared during
    1946 in:-

    Band Leader, Jun - "From Corn to Ham"
    Seventeen, Dec - "Is It Music Or Is It Mayhem?"

Completion of Variety Girl saw, for a variety of reasons, the departure of Zep Meissner, Chick Dougherty, Herman Crone, Joe Wolverton and Candy Hall.

Meissner, a very serious musician, remained in L.A. as a studio reed man, arranger and composer, Some of his dixieland publications, composed in collaboration with Eddie Pripps, are still in use (Blizzard Head Blues, Randolph St. Strut). Herman Crone played and arranged locally before returning to Cleveland, and Chick Dougherty joined the touring Russ Morgan Orchestra. Joe Wolverton returned to Arizona where he ran his own club for many years. Of late, Wolverton has been working in the Orient and Western Pacific area for the USO. Candy Hall remained in L.A. before settling in Reno, Nevada. As Entertainments Director at Harrah's in Reno, Hall was responsible for hiring the band of Leighton Noble for a ten-year stay starting in 1957.

6 January, 1947 (MON) - Victor Studios, Hollywood   3:00 to
          W.Heebner, A'& R Rep, present   6:00 PM

> Leader - Spike Jones
> Brass - George Rock, tpt; <u>Victor Hamann</u>, trb
> Reeds - Mickey Katz - clar
> Rhythm - <u>Stanley Bridges</u>, pno; Dick Morgan,
>   bjo; <u>Martin Kaplan</u>, bass; <u>Charlie Cantor</u>,
>   drm
> Vocalists - Del Porter, Frank Holiday Jr.,
>   <u>Allan Watson</u>, <u>Stewart Bair</u>, <u>Raymond Clark</u>,
>   <u>Sydney Pepple</u>, <u>Tudor Williams</u>, <u>Robert</u>
>   <u>Priester</u>, <u>Richard Davis</u>, Purves Pullen

D7-CB-416-1   RCADJ D7-CB-416
      1A (3:00)<u>All Hail Coinegie Tech</u> - voc the Boys in
           the Back Room

Note: Recorded for "the Coin Operators Association" and coupled with D6-VB-2175, "My Pretty Girl", this title was written by Spike Jones, Mickey Katz and Howard Gibeling.

From the band at the Biltmore Hotel, where Spike used to play with the Al Lyons band, came Paul Leu, piano and arranger.

7 February, 1947 (FRI)
      NBC Jersey City, New Jersey

> Bill Stern interview with "one of the most famous orchestra leaders in the world", Spike Jones, on 'remote' from Hollywood. Subject: Spike's favorite sport, midget auto racing

10 February, 1947 (MON) - Victor Studios, Hollywood   9:30 PM to
          Oberstein, Heebner, A'& R Reps, present 12:30 AM

> Leader - Spike Jones
> Brass - George Rock, tpt; John Stanley, trb
> Reeds - Dick Gardner, Mickey Katz, <u>Ding (Eugene</u>
>   <u>Walla) Bell</u>, sax
> Rhythm - <u>Paul Leu</u>, pno; Dick Morgan, bjo;
>   <u>Roger Donley</u>, bass; Joe Siracusa, drm
> Harp - Charlotte Tinsley
> Vocalists - <u>Elizabeth K. Newburger</u>, Arthur R.
>   Davies, Harry Stanton, <u>Faith Kruger</u>, Frank
>   Holiday Jr., Gil Mershon, <u>Camille Holiday</u>,
>   <u>Ruth Clark</u>
> Effects - Purves Pullen

D7-VB-455-1	20-2245-A; HMV BD 1177-A; HMVAU BD 1177-A &
1A	EA 3586; 45 47-3288-A(WP-288); 547-0069-B

D7-VB-455-1
1A

20-2245-A; HMV BD 1177-A; HMVAU BD 1177-A &
EA 3586; 45 47-3288-A(WP-288); 547-0069-B
(EPA 288); RCAG EPA 288; LP ANL1 2312(e);
AYL1 3870; RCAE HY 1006; RCAG RCS 3211/1-2;
RCAAU ODLP 7503; RCAF PL 43197; RCA Special
Products "Good Music Record" DML1 0570;
ET AFRS "Basic Music Library (condensed)
P-807; AFRS "Purple Heart Album" 150; AFRS
"G.I. Jive" 1695; AFRS "Remember" 696, 777 &
885;
(3:26)Love In Bloom - voc the Barefooted Pennsylvanians,
Dr. Horatio Q. Birdbath and the Saliva Sisters

D7-VB-456-1
1A

20-2245-B; HMV BD 1177-B; HMVAU BD 1177-B;
45-5269-B(Y-407); 45 47-0221-B(WY-407;
RCAG EPA 9720; LP ANL1 2312(e); AYL1 3870;
RCAE NL 42730(e); RCAG RCS 3217/1-2;
ET AFRS "Basic Music Library" P-807; AFRS
"Purple Heart Album" 158; Public Service
Show "Here's To Vets" 227;
(3:18)I'm Forever Blowing Bubble Gum - voc
George Rock

Note: RCA inst do not list Purves Pullen, but he is given
label credit. Vocalists as listed could be similar to the various
uncredited chorus' on previous sessions. On a suggestion by Mr.
Oberstein, "I'm Forever Blowing Bubble Gum" was changed as a title to
"Blowing Bubble Gum" and later, "The Bubble Gum Song". Johnny Stanley
returns on these two days sessions.

11 February, 1947 (TUES) - Victor Studios, Hollywood   9:30 PM to
                  Oberstein, Heebner, A & R Reps, present 12:30 AM

                  Spike Jones and his City Slickers, personnel as
                  10 Feb, deleting harp, vocalists and effects

D7-457-1
1A

20-2820-B; RCADJ 232; ET AFRS "Basic Music
Library"(condensed) P-994;
(3:25)Ugga Ugga Boo Ugga Boo Boo Ugga - voc Ding Bell

Unslated   I Wuv a Wabbit - voc Elmer Fudd (Arthur Q. Bryan)

      Note: Some release labels denote "with Vocal Refrain". In
scripts for his radio show, Mel Blanc belonged to the Loyal Order of
Benevelent Zebras, whose password "Ugga Ugga Boo Ugga Boo Boo Ugga"
was one of the shows catch phrases. It ran on CBS from 1946 for one
year.
      "I Wuv a Wabbit", a one-of-a-kind cutting, was among the
many demo acetates in the Jones files. Originally thought to have
been rejected RCA titles because of the labels and pressing, they
have never shown in any RCA listing, official or otherwise. Walter
Heebner recalls: "Spike used to try to record (really personal demos)
whenever he was near an RCAV studio, then he would study, ponder,
worry, worry, worry about the impact of his presentation. Quite frequently the entire concept of his work would be changed in the studio." This use of studio time accounts for the frequent occasions
where, officially, one or two titles were produced in a three hour
session instead of the common four. Of the many cuttings to ponder
and worry over, two have survived. (See also 5 Nov 47)

      Arena Stars, Spike's company that set up the total marketing
of the Depreciation Revue, also published Spike Jones sheet music.
From the now multi offices at 360/366 N. Camden in Beverly Hills,

first Arena Stars Inc., then Oakhurst Music Publishing Co. (both were BMI, and Spike lived at 708 No. Oakhurst Dr., Beverly Hills); then from 1952, the Lindley Music Company (ASCAP) handled Jones' and related artists music. Lindley Music is still operational, according to ASCAP.

As traveling PR rep for the Revue, Doc helped maintain a detailed itinerary with the years 1947 and up 24 Sept 48 surviving. Double-sheeted, they were left at a hotel by the advance rep, with basic local info filled in, then picked up on the troupe's arrival. The wealth of information is staggering and editing was a personal judgement. It is all representative of their daily schedule for 1946 and, to a lesser extent, 1945.

Details were maintained on: Location (date, weather, incl. population, promotors and arena mangagers); Auditorium(Aud)(capacity, ticket price scale, box offices and un-salable seats); Stage (lighting, footlights, overheads & spots, switchboards, curtains, dressing rooms, line voltage and microphones); Transfer Co. for baggage and props; Employees (ushers, cashiers, police, stage hands and musicians demanded by the local Unions' offices); Opposition in the area; Concessions; Acts; Transportation to and from town(with hotel and manager names - for mail pick-up or stay); Newspaper; Radio stations and DJs; Personal appearances slated or made(incl. interviews); Special exploitation; RCA Distributors and General remarks.

Not every heading was completed but in many cases additional info was entered, such as attendance; cost of cabs to and from bubble gum (BG) contests; newpaper cost(for reviews and ads); phone calls, both local and long distance - all the bits of trivia that helps to put this now massive touring show into perspective.

Hopefully, the information edited is of interest. Included are: Date, City(and current population); Perf(performance time, where logged); Arena capacity, where logged; Seat price scale, where logged. When they occurred, Interviews (most were transcribed onto tape, wire recordings or disc and may still exist in radio station archives) and special exploitation are lumped as one, plus some of the good and bad comments. Jargon and abbreviations have been left as printed which will account for variations in spelling.

A universal Musicians' Union by-law prevalent for many years required traveling musical organizations to hire local musicians when performing within a particular local's jurisdicion. The minimum number of these 'stand-by' musicians required was a ratio more dependant upon the number of AF of M members in the troupe than the size of the Union. Each jurisdiction had its own guidelines. Every traveling band, from Henry Busse to Louis Armstrong; Count Basie to Tex Beneke had 'stand-by' bands which may or may not have played. On the road, Spike's utilization of this by-law was to have the required musicians, augmenting from the Slickers when necessary, play the specially written Overture and exit music. The band was rehearsed and conducted by one of Spike's musicians, who also conducted for the on-stage acts. Mickey Katz handled these chores in 1947.

"For three years The City Slickers toured the theatres playing five and six shows a day as part of a vaudeville bill, until Jones set up the Revue, a two-and-a-half-hour show with a $1.20 to $3.00 ticket range." (Newsweek, 4 Apr 49)

MUSICAL DEPRECIATION REVUE 1947

Leader - Spike Jones
Brass - George Rock, tpt; Robert Robinson, trb
Reeds - Ding Bell, Dick Gardner, Mickey Katz
Violin - Dick Gardner
Rhythm - Paul Leu, pno; Dick Morgan, guit/bjo;
        Roger Donley, bass; Joe Siracusa, drm
Harp - Nancy McDonald
Vocalists - Helen Greco, Aileen Carlisle, Ding Bell,

150

George Rock, Mickey Katz
Act/effts - Purves Pullen, Doodles Weaver, Bill King,
Bettyjo Huston, Ward Ellis(dancer), Frankie
Little, Junior Martin, Gloria and Gladys Gardner
(Slickerettes)
Additional - Eddie Brandt, Les Calvin(carpenter),
Johnny Mattison(choreographer), Maxine Thomas
(secretary), Eddie McCarthy(band boy), Jack Egan,
Ray Rubel

12 February (WED) to 14 February (FRI), 1947
        Revue final rehearsals, packing and traveling

15 February, 1947 (SAT)
                Auditorium, Denver, Colo (370,000)
                    2:30 '& 8:30 PM (sold out)
                    Capacity: 3300
                    Scale: 3.00, 2:40, 1:80, 1.20, .90

        Interviews: Doodles and Doc, 4:15 to 4:30 on Fri 14 Feb on
        "Record Show". Spike on KMYR "Had to leave train and give
        up our two pullmans - making reservations at Albany Hotel"

        "Delegates attending the Denver Country Democratic Conven-
tion yesterday unanimously passed a mild resolution endorsing the
'true leadership demonstrated by President Truman'.
        "All business had to be conducted hurridly because the
Democrats had to vacate the City Auditorium by noon to make way for
Spike Jones and his City Slickers."
                (unidentified, undated newspaper)

16 February, 1947 (SUN)
                To Sioux City, Iowa (lv. Union Station 2:00 PM)

17 February, 1947 (MON)
                Orpheum Theatre, Sioux City, Iowa (83,364)
                    8:30 PM (sold out)
                    Capacity: 2648
                    Scale: 3.66, 3.05, 2.44, 1.83, 1.22, .92

        Interview: Spike, Helen '& Doc on KTRI with Shel Singer,
        3:30 to 4PM

18 February, 1947 (TUES)
                St. Paul Theatre, St. Paul, Minn (287,736)
                    Capacity: 2800 (fair attendance)
                    Scale: 3.60, 3.00, 2.40, 1.80, 1.20

        Interviews: Spike, Helen '& Doc on KSTP with Sev Widman,
        11:30 PM; on WCCO with Geo. Johnson, 12:30 AM; on WLOL with
        Glenn Harris 1:20 AM "above build up for Minneapolis appear-
        ance Thurs Feb 20, 1947"(Lighting - generally not good)

19 February, 1947 (WED)
                Field House, Fargo, ND (32,580)
                    8:30 PM (full house)
                    Capacity: 4100
                    Scale: 3.50, 3.00, 2.50, 2.00

        "Jack Frost Band met train at 3:30 PM on arrival"(Could
        not put overhead light off during entire show - very bad)

151

20 February, 1947 (THURS)
                    Auditorium, Minneapolis, Minn (492,370)
                    8:30 PM (average)
                    Capacity: 10,000
                    Scale: 3.60, 3.00, 2.40, 1.80, 1.20

        Interviews: done 18 Feb

21 February, 1947 (FRI)
                    Mayo Civic Aud, Rochester, Minn (26,312)
                    Capacity: 3700
                    Scale: 2.40, 1.80, 1.20

22 February, 1947 (SAT)
                    Memorial Aud, Burlington, Ia (25,832)
                    Capacity: 2500
                    Scale: 3.05, 2.44, 1.22

23 February, 1947 (SUN)
                    Civic Aud, Chicago, Ill (3,396,808)
                    3:00 PM (sold out), evening time not logged
                    Capacity: 3800
                    Scale: main floor - 3.60, 3.00, 2.40
                        1st balcony - 3.00, 2.40, boxes 3.60
                        2nd balcony - 1.80, 1.20

        Interviews: none, although 12 radio stations were listed
        for future contact (Pullman cars parked at Ill. Central
        Station 3 nights - Charter bus to/from next engagement)

24 February, 1947 (MON)
                    Bus travel to Sheboygan

25 February, 1947 (TUES)
                    Auditorium, Sheboygan, Wis (40,638)
                    Capacity: 3945 (2/3 filled)
                    Scale: 3.00, 2.40, 1.80, 1.20

        (Lighting inadequate; Dressing rooms, no toilets - water
        or mirrors)

26 February, 1947 (WED)
                    Jr. High Aud, Champaign, Ill (23,302)
                    7:00 PM (sold out), 9:00 PM (2/3 full)
                    Capacity: 2900
                    Scale: 3.00, 2.40, 1.80

        Interview: Spike & Doc 3:30 to 4PM on WDWS with Marc
        Howard, Program Director

27 February, 1947 (THURS)
                    Coliseum, Ottumna, IA (31,570)
                    Dance & show: 8 to 10 '& 10 to 12
                    (10 pice orch played for dancing 9 to 10
                    PM - Attendance V.G.)
                    Capacity: 2900
                    Scale: 1.56 (advance), 2.04 (at door)

        Interview: Spike, Helen, Aileen Carlyle, Doc on KBIZ,
        6:30 to 7PM - Warren Anderson(small stage inadequate;
        dressing rooms too small; microphones poor; crowd asked

152

to sit on dance floor - confusion throughout first half
of show. People seated in the balcony okay!)

28 February, 1947 (FRI)
>> Armory, Peoria, Ill (105,187)
>> Capacity: 5000
>> Scale: 3.00, 2.40, 1.80

Interviews: 5:30 PM on WWXL, Myles Foland Prog. Autograph
session at 4:00, Beverly Music Store, 106 N. Adams
(Platform inadequate - no stage; lighting poor; dressing
rooms very poor)

1 March, 1947 (SAT)
>> Masonic Aud, Davenport, IA (66,039)
>> 3:00 PM (2/3 full), 8:00 PM (sold out)
>> Capacity: 2500
>> Scale: 2.00, 1.50, 1.00 (matinee)
>> 3.60, 3.50, 1.80 (evening)

2 March, 1947 (SUN)
>> Kinter Gym Aud, Decatur, Ill (59,305)
>> Capacity: 4153
>> Scale: 3.60, 3.00, 2.40, 1.80, 1.20

3 March, 1947 (MON)
>> County Aud, Jackson, Mich (47,656)
>> Capacity: 1900 (fair response)
>> Scale: 3.60, 2.40, 1.80

(dressing rooms not so good - small aud)

4 March, 1947 (TUES)
>> Kellogg Aud, Battle Creek, Mich (43,453)
>> Capacity: 2500
>> Scale: 3.60, 3.00, 2.40, 1.80, 1.20

"Afternoon benefit show at Percy Jones General Hospital
3:30 to 4:30 PM. KPJ(?) on the air"

5 March, 1947 (WED)
>> I.M.A. Aud, Flint Mich, (151,543)
>> Capacity: 6000
>> Scale: 3.00, 2.40, 1.80, 1.20

Interviews: 3PM Spike & Doc on WFOF with Ted Taylor; 5PM
Spike & Doc on WMRP with Ed Berryman plus record store
appearance at 4PM

5 March, 1947 (THURS)
>> Prudden Aud, Lansing, Mich (78,753)
>> Capacity: 2400
>> Scale: 3.00, 2.40, 1.80, 1.20

Interview: 4 to 4:30 PM Gardner Twins, Spike & Doc on
WJIM. 6:30 to 6:45 PM, wired b'cast on WILS. Record autographing at Grinnell's 4PM(Auditorium tonight too small.
Try Michigan State College Aud for future booking - new -
fully equipt - seats over 4000)

7 March, 1947 (FRI)
                  Coliseum-Armory, Louisville, Ky (319,217)
                     9:30 PM
                     Capacity: 7500
                     Scale: 3.00, 2.50, 1.80, 1.30

Interviews: midnight on WHAS with Jim Lownsberry(Train arrived - show scheduled at 8:30, did not go on until 9:30. Standby orch played fill in until we got set up)

8 March, 1947 (SAT)
                  Murat Temple, Indianapolis, Ind (386,972)
                     Capacity: 1975 (2121 on eve show)
                     Scale: 3.60, 3.00, 2.50, 1.80 (evening)
                               3.00, 2.50, 2.00, 1.80 (matinee)

9 March, 1947 (SUN)
                  Memorial Aud, Columbus, Ohio (306,087)
                     Capacity: 3800
                     Scale: 3.00, 2.40, 1.80, 1.20

10 March, 1947 (MON)
"Spike Jones and Doc Birdbath did 2 radio interviews in Indianapolis: 3 to 3:30 PM on WIBC - news bldg. with Easy Gynn; 4 to 4:30 WISH with Ozzie Osborne and Bill Landrum. Build up for Bloomington, Ind. and other Indiana dates"

11 March, 1947 (TUES)
                  Indiana University Aud, Bloomington, Ind (20,870)
                     7:00 & 9:00 PM
                     Capacity: 3788
                     Scale: 1.20, .90

Interview: 5 to 5:30 Doc on WSUA with Bill Harlow and Milt Bohard(to and from town via chartered Greyhound)

12 March, 1947 (WED)
                  Memorial Aud, Dayton Ohio (210,718)
                     Capacity: 2700 (sold out)
                     Scale: 3.39, 3.10, 2.45, 1.85, 1.23

Interviews: 12:15 to 12:35 AM Spike & Doc on WING with Gene Barry. Build-up for Ft. Wayne, Ind and Springfield Ohio dates

13 March, 1947 (THURS)
                  Quimby Aud, Ft. Wayne, Ind (118,410)
                     Capacity: 2000
                     Scale: 3.60

14 March, 1947 (FRI)
                  Civic Aud, Toledo, Ohio (283,349)
                     Capacity: 2200
                     Scale: 3.00, 2.40, 1.80, 1.20

Interviews: 5:45 to 6PM WTOL with Russ Perry; 4PM autograph deal at Grinnell's Record Shop, wire recording of interview at Grinnell's - on air 4:45 to 5 on WTOD

15 March, 1947 (SAT)
                  Music Hall(Public Aud), Cleveland, Ohio (878,336)

                    3:00(very poor), 8:30 (sold out)
                    Capacity: 3300
                    Scale: 3.60, 3.00, 2.40, 1.80

    "Appearance at record store on Prospect. Luncheon by Coin
    Operators at Carter Int, on WHK with Bud Wendell 1:15 to
    1:30 PM" (Possible use for "Coinegie Tech"?)

16 March, 1947 (SUN)
                    Masonic Temple, Detroit, Mich (1,623,452)
                    Capacity: 5000
                    Scale: 3.60, 3.00, 2.40, 1.80

    "Temple Cathedral - seats 1586 - complete staging. Did
    3PM matinee only - Pullman cars SJ1-SJ2-baggage car spotted
    in Detroit until Mon eve."

17 March, 1947 (MON)
                    Detroit, Mich - day off

18 March, 1947 (TUES)
                    Scottish Rite Cathedral, Newcastle, Pa (47,638)
                    Capacity: 2400
                    Scale: 3.60, 2.40, 1.20

    Interviews: 6 to 6:30 PM Dick Morgan, Spike & Doc on WKST
    with Geo. Varnum; Autograph session at Fleming Music
    Store 4:30 to 5PM

19 March, 1947 (WED)
                    Syria Mosque, Pittsburg, Pa (671,659)
                    Capacity: 3800
                    Scale: 3.60, 3.00, 2.40, 1.80, 1.20

    Interviews: 6:30PM on WCEA with Chet Clark; 5:30 Nat'l
    Record Mart presentation of tickets, albums to winners,
    WWSW - on air; 4:30 record dept Kaufman's Dept. Store

20 March, 1947 (THURS)
                    Memorial Hall, Springfield, Ohio (70,662)
                    Capacity: 2596
                    Scale: 3.60, 3.00, 2.40, 1.80, 1.20

    (Lighting, in general - bad, could not lower stage lights
    or spots would go out)"Up to tonite we have completed:-
    30 cities, 37 performances, 37 days on the road since we
    left Calif Feb 12, 1947"

21 March, 1947 (FRI)
                    Hill Aud, Ann Arbor, Mich (29,815)
                    7:00 & 9:45 PM
                    Capacity: 4578
                    Scale: 1.80, 1.20

    Interviews: 4:45PM on WPAG with Ed Burrows; 4:30 at
    Grinnell's Music Store

22 March (SAT), 23 March (SUN), 1947
                    Civic Opera House, Chicago, Ill
                    Details as 28 Feb

                                 155

24 March, 1947 (MON) - Victor Studios, Chicago, Ill, 2:00 to 6:00 PM
A.E. Hindle, A & R Rep, present

                    Leader - Spike Jones
                    Brass - George Rock, tpt; Robert Robinson, trb
                    Reeds - Dick Gardner, Mickey Katz, Ding Bell,
                        clar/sax
                    Rhythm - Paul Leu, pno; Dick Morgan, bjo/guit;
                        Roger Donley, tuba; Joe Siracusa, drm
                    Vocals - George Rock, Doodles Weaver

D7-VB-356-1   Unissued
    1A (3:10)My Cornet - voc George Rock

D7-VB-357-1   20-2861-B; HMV BD 1212; 420-0175-B; 45-5269-A
    1A   (Y-407); HMVAU BD 1212 & EA 3811; 45 47-0021
                     (WY-407); 447-0175-A; EPA-5080; RCAE RCX 1037;
                     RCAAU EP 20050; RCAF EP 86233; LP LPM 2224;
                     LPM 3849; LSP 3849(e); ANL1 1035(e); AYL1
                     3748; RCAE LSA 3084 & RD 7724; RCAAU CAS 7158;
                     RCAG RCS 3217/1-2 & LSP 10157; RCAIT CL 83748;
                     RCA Special Products "Good Music Record"
                     DML1 0570; ET AFRS "Remember" 963
            (3:05)The Man on the Flying Trapeze - voc Doodles
                     Weaver

        Note: RCA inst do not credit Rock or Weaver as vocalists.
Joe Twirp(really!), comic, on the 30 Jul 35 "Comedy Caravan" does a
'spoonerized' version of "Flying Trapeze" - perhaps the model for
Weaver's successful act at almost successfully singing a song. His
use of a choir tuner to constantly help find his starting note
(pitch) was a comic device Weaver used extensivly during the Revue
and on the later radio broadcasts of his 'lyrical renditions'.

25 March, 1947 (TUES)
                    Auditorium, Grand Rapids, Mich (164,292)
                    Capacity: over 5000 (sold out)
                    Scale: 2.00, 1.50, 1.25, 1.00

        Interviews: 5:30 to 6 PM at Grinnell's - carried on WLAV;
        Spike 7 Doc on WJEF with Vic Lundberg "Train arrived late
        - 50 min. - 5:30PM"

26 March, 1947 (WED)
                    Central H.S. Aud, Kalamazoo, Mich (54,079)
                    Capacity: 2700
                    Scale: 3.00, 2.80, 2.10, 1.80

        Interviews: 4:55 to 5PM on WKZO, made transcription -
        rebroadcast at 7:05; record autograph session at
        Grinnell's - 4:00 to 4:30PM

27 March, 1947 (THURS)
                    Field House Aud, Muncie, Ind (49,720)
                    Capacity: 6500
                    Scale: 3.00, 2.40, 1.80, 1.20

        Interviews: 5PM Doc & Mickey Katz autograph session at
        Muncie Music Centre (WLBC would not cooperate)"train
        leaves at 1:20 NYC RR"

28 March (FRI), 29 March (SAT), 1947

Purdue University, Lafayette, Ind (28,798 +
        7:00 & 9:00 PM both nights   student pop.
        Capacity: 6200   11,500)
        Scale: 1.20, .76

Interviews: 2:15 to 3:45PM Doodles Weaver & Doc Birdbath
on WASK(Fri); 4:05PM Doodles, Doc & Gardner Twins on WASK
Teen Age show(SAT)"Like Music Hall in NYC"

30 March, 1947 (SUN)
        Market Aud, Wheeling, W. Va (61,099)
                Capacity: 1700
                Scale: 3.60, 2.40, 2.00

(no stage - inadequate platform - very poor)

31 March, 1947 (MON)
        Memorial Aud, Charleston, W. Va (67,914)
                Capacity: 3517
                Scale: 3.07, 2.46, 1.34

1 April, 1947 (TUES)
        Carmichael Aud, Clarksburg, W. Va (30,574)
                Capacity: 2400
                Scale: 3.60, 2.40, 2.00

Interviews: 6:15 to 6:30PM Spike & Doc on WHAR(sound very
poor - short circuit - system went off & on while acts
were performing - no spotlights all night)(stopped show
with 'Glow Worm' - audience and aud impossible to work)
"Try Robinson Grand Theatre next time - they would like
to play Spike for 2 shows"

2 April, 1947 (WED)
        City Hall Aud, Huntington, W. Va (78,836)
                Capacity: 2370
                Scale: 3.66, 3.06, 1.53

3 April, 1947 (THURS)
        Memorial Aud, Gary, Ind (111,719)
                Capacity:3900
                Scale: 3.00, 2.40, 1.80, 1.20

4 April, 1947 (FRI)
        Travel to Milwaukee, Wis

5 April, 1947 (SAT)
        Auditorium, Milwaukee, Wis (587,472)
                3:00 & 8:30 PM
                Capacity: 6700
                Scale: 3.60, 3.00, 2.40, 1.80, 1.20

6 April, 1947 (SUN)
        KRNT Radio Theatre Aud, Des Moines, Ia(159,819)
                9:15 PM
                Capacity: 4200
                Scale: 3.00, 2.50, 1.50, 1.00

"Train late - arrived at KRNT Aud exactly 8:30 curtain
time - theatre packed - sell out. Spike made appearance -
introduced Mickey Katz who led a community sing. Paul at

157

the piano. Then Dr. H.Q. Birdbath did a 12 min. skit of imitations - and Geo. Rock played two cornet solos - a local orch. in the pit played several selections and by 9:15PM the stage was set and the regular show began"

7 April, 1947 (MON)
            Auditorium, La Porte, Ind (16,100)
                Capacity: 3000
                Scale: 3.60, 2.40, 1.80, 1.20

    Interviews: none(no radio station) - (mics: 1st half show no volume; 2nd half show fair volume)

8 April, 1947 (TUES)
            Jaffa Mosque, Altoona, Pa (80,214?)
                Capacity: 3400
                Scale: 3.60, 3.00, 2.40, 1.80, 1.20

    Interviews: 6PM Spike '& Doc on WJSW with Skip Miller

9 April, 1947 (WED)
            Strong Vincent H.S. Aud, Erie, Pa (116,955)
                Capacity: 1500
                Scale: 3.60

    Interview: 3:45 to 4:15PM Spike, Doc, Doodles, Helen Kramer & Twins on WLEW(2PM EST gave up our 2 Union Pacific Pullmans; also lost porters: Wm. Jones, car SJ1; Henry Gale, car SJ2)

10 April (THURS) to 16 April (WED), 1947
            Shea's Buffalo, Buffalo, NY (575,901)
                perf between showings of "Fear in the Night"
                Capacity: 3500
                Scale: .50(before 6PM) .70(after 6PM)
                       .25(children)

    Interviews: Fri 6:10 PM Spike '& Doc wire recording on WKBW; Fri 9PM Spike '& Doc live on Carl's Army Show on WBNY; Mon 12:45PM Spike, Doodles '& Doc on WKBW with Lillian Kirk(transcribed); Tues 8AM Spike on WEBR wire recording; Wed 7:45 to 8AM Doodles & Doc on WEBR wire recording. "stay Statler Hotel"

17 April, 1947 (THURS)
            Mosque, Harrisburg, Pa (83,893)
                Capacity: 2500
                Scale: 3.60, 2.40, 1.80

18 April (FRI) to 24 April (THURS), 1947
            Earle Theatre, Philadelphia, Pa (1,931,334)
                perf between showings of "Dance Band" (which
                    featured Frances Langford) except Sunday
                Capacity: 2831
                Scale: .60(to 1PM) .80(to 6PM) .99(to close)
                       Children .25, .35

    Interviews: none, although all pertinent personnel at every station are listed for:- "Mon 5th show, Spike had Disc Jockeys(26) in the orch. pit - later they were guests at the Click Club - Doodles Weaver '& Doc went to the Ocean Room at Drake Hotel over WFIL as guests of Mary Biddle 11:15

to 11:30PM" "Stay Drake Hotel"

20 April, 1947 (SUN)
Stanley Aud, Camden, NJ (125,000)
3:35, 6:35 & 9:35 PM, between showings of
"Lady in the Lake"
Capacity: 2213
Scale: .95, .30(children)

Interviews: none, and the newspaper was on strike. Camden,
home of the RCA factory, had many good Jones promo displays

25 April (FRI) to 27 April (SUN), 1947
State Theatre, Hartford, Conn (165,272)
perf between showings of "Philo Vance's
Capacity: 4000   Gamble"
Scale: .80, .45, .30(Fri); .85, .45, .30
(Sat); .85, .50(Sun)

Interviews: Spike & Doodles Fri; Helen Greco & Doc on
WTIC "Teen Star Time" with S. Allen Sat; Doc on WRIC with
Glenn Rowell on his children program Sun

28 April, 1947 (MON)
Mosque Aud, Richmond, Va (193,042)
Capacity: 4600
Scale: 3.00, 2.50, 2.00, 1.50

Interviews: Doc on WOL(Wash) at 2:15 with Bill Brundadge,
between trains Hartford, Conn to Richmond, Va (as far as
attendance goes NSG. Crowd that did show up - very recep-
tive)

29 April (TUES), 30 April (WED), 1947
Travel to and set up 'legitimate' show in
Washington, DC

1 May (THURS) to 7 May (WED), 1947
Capitol Theatre, Washington, DC (862,000)
Four shows first day, then five daily
between showings of "Temptation"
Capacity: 3434
Scale: .80, .50(.60 Sat), .44, Child .30

Interviews: (Sat)8:15 to 9:00AM, Doc, Doodles with
"Uncle" Bill Jenkins on WTOP (wired recording) "Thurs-May
1st after 4 shows, our opening day - entire cast entertains
Mexican Delegation on 13th floor of Lowes Theatre Bldg -
Sun eve. Spike invited all the local Disk Jockeys to see our
show. They filled the orch. pit during the last show - Pres.
Truman & the US Asso. Press accepted Spike Jones and Revue
to appear the first Sat in March 1948, at the National Thea-
tre(guns were OK'd)" - "stay Willard Hotel"

9 May (FRI) to 15 May (THURS), 1947
Fox Theatre, Atlanta, Ga (302,288)
perf 4 shows daily, between showings of
"Fear in the Night"
Capacity: 4562
Scale: .80, .65(matinee), Child .30

Interviews: 10:45 to 11PM Spike on WSB with Bob Watson

159

(record show) Fri; Wired recording on WGST Fri & WAGA Sat
(stay Grady Hotel) - under Special exploitation, by local
RCA dealers: window cards; banners; bumper strips;
imprint napkins

16 May, 1947 (FRI)
Auditorium, Atlanta, Ga (65,919)
Capacity: 4000
Scale: 3:66, 3.05, 2.44, 1.83, 1.22

Interviews: 6PM on WGAC with Lonnie Moore (lighting in-
complete, no spots, no power, to use ours - dressing
rooms, no mirrors, toilets unsanitary, no warm water,
paper towels)

17 May, 1947 (SAT)
Municipal Aud, Birmingham, Ala (287,583)
Capacity: 5540
Scale: 3.05, 2.44, 1.85, 1.22

Interviews: Spike, Greco & Doc 2:45PM on WTNB with Joe
Ford; 3:15 on WBRC with Davenport Smith; 4:00 on WSGN
with Dick Hawley; 4:30 on WKAX with Frank Hamilton
"Trailers in 8 movie houses in regards to Spike Jones
appearance" (lighting inadequate, not enough power)

18 May, 1947 (SUN)
Ft. Whiting Aud, Mobile, Ala (78,770)
Capacity: 3000
Scale: 3.70, 2.45, 1.85, (with tax)

Interviews: 6:15PM Doc on WMOB

19 May, 1947 (MON)
Travel to and set-up in Memphis, Tenn

20 May, 1947 (TUES)
Auditorium, Memphis, Tenn (292,942)
8:30 PM
Capacity: 6500
Scale: 3.00, 2.50, 2.00, 1.50, 1.00, .75

Interviews: 3:15 to 4PM Doc on WMPS with Bill Gordon;
4 to 4:30 Spike, Doc & Helen on WHHM with Ted Harding and
Milton Q. Ford; 4:30 to 4:45PM Doc on air with Tom
Reardon(WHBQ) "show started promptly at 8:30, curtain
closed show at 10:15. Cast on train by - 11PM. Train left
station - 11:50PM"

21 May, 1947 (WED)
Ryman Aud, Nashville, Tenn (167,402)
Capacity: 3000
Scale: 3.00, 2.50, 2.00, 1.50

22 May, 1947 (THURS)
City Auditorium, Montgomery, Ala (78,084)
Capacity: 2500
Scale: 2.95, 2.44, 1.83, 1.22

Interviews: 3:15 to 3:45 PM Doc, Spike, Greco, Syracusa
and Frank Little on WSFA with Knox Holman; 3:50 to 4:15

Doc, Spike, Greco and Little on WMGY with Ed Brown

23 May, 1947 (FRI)
                    Travel to and set-up in Beaumont, Tex

24 May, 1947 (SAT)
                    City Aud, Beaumont, Tex (59,061)
                         Capacity: 2376
                         Scale: 2.95, 2.60, 1.95, 1.30

Interviews: 1:30 to 2:30 Doc on KPBX with Hugh Herrington
& Frank Boardman; 3:45 to 4 Spike & Doc on KRIC with Roy
Dixon; 4:15 to 4:45 Doc on KRIC with Ed Henry (KPBX was a
new station - on the air for one week) "Air Conditioned"

"In 1946 Freddy was back in America...playing night-clubs
and theatres. A year later, while he was appearing in a club at West
Palm Beach, Fla., Freddie recieved a telephone call from Beaumont,
Tex. 'This is Spike Jones', said the voice on the phone. 'Sure',
Freddy replied, 'and this is Napoleon III'. Once these preliminaries
were done with, Spike went on to say that he had heard a lot about
Freddy and now he'd like to have Freddy show him, on the phone, what
he could do. 'So', as Freddy recalls, 'I did some imitations of
Edward G. Robinson and barking and sang in a Japanese dialect. People
sitting at the bar near the phone thought I had gone off my rocker.
But Spike apparently liked what he heard. He signed me on the spot'.
Freddy has been with Spike Jones ever since."
                    (Freddy Morgan, Mr. Banjo, Verve MGV 2065)

25 May, 1947 (SUN)
                    Auditorium, New Orleans, La (494,537)
                         Capacity: 4947
                         Scale: 3.00, 2.50, 2.00, 1.50, 1.25

Interviews: "Made 2 transcriptions which were used 2
different nights on Bob Poole's show WWL 12PM to 1AM. WNOE
- Spike, Doc on with Bill Elliot (Fri); WJBW - Doc on
with Harry Nigocia 1:15 to 1:45 (Fri)" "Air Conditioned"

26 May, 1947 (MON)
                    City Aud, Houston, Tex (384,514)
                         Capacity: 4232
                         Scale: 2.95, 2.60, 1.95, 1.30

Interviews: Aileen Carlyle & Doc: 3:30 to 4PM on KTHT
with Bill Guy(recording); 4 to 4:30 on KXYZ with Bob
Blaze(recording); 4:30 to 5 on KATL with Larry Blieden
(recording); 5:15 to 5:25 on KTRH with Tom Jacobs(orch?)

27 May, 1947 (TUES)
                    City Aud, Galveston, Tex (60,862)
                         Capacity: 4000
                         Scale: 2.95, 2.60, 1.95, 1.30

28 May, 1947 (WED)
                    Fair Ground Aud, Dallas, Tex (294,734)
                         Capacity: 4300
                         Scale: 2.40, 1.80, 1.20, .75(3rd balcony)

Interviews: 4:05 to 4:35 Doc on KRLD with Melvin Munn;
4:55 to 5:15 Doc on KIXL with Louis Quince (what may be
of interest is the Auditorium manager's name - Jack Ruby,

a name to become infamous 15-1/2 years later)

29 May, 1947 (THURS)
                    Auditorium, Shreveport, La (98,167)
                       9:00 PM
                       Capacity: 3700
                       Scale: 2.95, 2.40, 1.80, 1.20

Interviews: 4:30 to 4:45 Doc on KTBS with Mike Rapollo; 4:15 to 4:30 Doc on KRMD with Brice Dickson (under 'Opposition in the area' is mention of Midget Races and the Byrd H.S. graduation. "show started 9PM to allow graduation class to arrive")

30 May, 1947 (FRI)
                    Baylor University Aud, Waco, Tex (55,982)
                       Capacity: 2418
                       Scale: 2.95, 2.60, 1.95, 1.30

Interviews: 4:45 to 5PM Doc on KWTX with Gerry Lansing "Memorial Day" (Bus strike 30 days old, and we're 2 miles from town)

31 May, 1947 (SAT)
                    Will Rogers Mem. Aud, Fort Worth, Tex (177,662)
                       Capacity: 2900
                       Scale: 2.95, 2.60, 1.95, 1.30

Interviews: 3 to 3:30 Doc Birdbath on KWBC with Tom Allen; 4 to 4:30 on KCNC with Jerry Hahn; 4:30 to 5 on KXOL with Jim Lowe and Norman Alden

1 June, 1947 (SUN)
                    Municipal Aud, Oklahoma City, Ok (265,000
                       Capacity: 5600   in '45)
                       Scale: 2.44, 1.83, 1.22

"Matinee 3PM Amphitheatre - show for US Army. Train arrival 2PM Santa Fe - parade of cars and Army bus met troop(sic) of Spike Jones Revue and drove thru town out to open air theatre - 'Tinker' Okla. City Air Material Area, Tinker Field, Okla - attendance 7500"

From this slightly jumbled sequence of words, a special show was performed for the U.S. Army that afternoon. Tinker Field was the Transfer company handling the baggage & equipment in Oklahoma City.

2 June, 1947 (MON)
                    Memorial Aud, Wichita Falls, Tex (60,000)
                       Capacity: 3148
                       Scale: 2.95, 2.60, 1.95, 1.00

3 June, 1947 (TUES)
                    Municipal Aud, Amarillo, Tex
                       Capacity: 2500
                       Scale: 2.95, 2.40, 1.80, 1.20

Interviews: 1 to 1:15PM Doc with Bernie Howell & "Linda" on KGNC; 4:30 to 5 Doc KFDF (or KFDA) with Ken Duke

4 June, 1947 (WED)

        Convention Hall, Hutchison, Kan (30,013)
          Capacity: 2700
          Scale: 2.95, 2.40, 1.80, 1.20

5 June, 1947 (THURS)

        Stadium, Chicago, Ill (3,396,808)
          Capacity: 18,000
          Scale: Private tickets

A private function where the promotor and manager are listed as "Hawthorne Club" and "Western Electric Co", with 10,000 tickets given out

6 June, 1947 (FRI)

        Capitol Theatre, Manitowoc, Wisc (24,404)
          Capacity: 1400
          Scale: 3.00, 2.40, 1.80, 1.20

Interviews: 5PM Spike, Greco '& Doc on WOMT with Frank Pollack

7 June, 1947 (SAT)

        Armory, Mankato, Minn
          Capacity: 2400
          Scale: 3.00, 2.40, 1.80, 1.20

(stage too small, lighting inadequate, dressing rooms NG) "Ballroom (more modern) High School aud. 1800 seats"

8 June, 1947 (SUN)

        Armory (Aud), Omaha, Neb (223,844)
          Capacity: 5000 (3235 attended)

Interviews: Mon 12 noon, Doc, Spike, Greco, Rock & Doodles wire record on KDIL with advance adv. for Sioux City - Lincoln, Neb. dates. (Eight RCA stores are listed, each having good SJ displays)

9 June, 1947 (MON)

        Orpheum Theatre, Sioux City, Ia (82,364)
          details as 17 Feb 47

Interviews: 4PM Spike & Doc on KSCJ; 4:30 on KTRI

10 June, 1947 (TUES)

        Coliseum, Lincoln, Neb (81,984)
          Capacity: 6000
          Scale: 3.00, 2.40, 1.80, 1.20

Interviews: 3:30 to 3:45 Spike '& Doc on KFOR with Lee Berg; 5 to 5:30 Spike, Doc & Greco on KFAB with Don French

11 June, 1947 (WED)

        Fairgrounds, Davenport, Ia (66,039)
          Capacity: 5000
          Scale: 2.50, 2.00, 1.50, 1.25

Interviews: 5:15 to 5:45 Doc on KSTT

163

12 June, 1947 (THURS)
                    Coliseum, Grand Rapids, Ia (62,120)
                        Capacity: 3100
                        Scale: 2.45, 2.05, 1.85, 1.43

        Interviews: 12 noon Doc on WMT "Man in the Street" with
        Dean Langear; 12:15 to 1:15 PM Doc went to Lions Club
        luncheon & gave short talk about show tonight; 5:15 to
        5:30 Spike, Doc & Linn (Lynn Johnson) on WMT with Gene
        Ellston "Gene Ellston wants tie" (stage hands did not
        work show accurately)

        Lynn Johnson is on record with Spike c.1960. He is an
impressionist-writer and comic as well as vocalist. His appearance
now suggests that the featured 'straight' vocalist, Ding Bell, has
left with Johnson as temporary vocalist. Instrumentally, Merle Howard
replaces Bell.

13 June, 1947 (FRI)
                    Coliseum Aud, Marshalltown, Ia (19,240)
                        7:00 & 9:30 PM
                        Capacity: 1800
                        Scale: 3.00, 2.75, 2.50, bleachers 1.50

        Interviews: 4:15 to 5PM Spike & Linn Johnson on KFJB -
        FLOOD APPEAL. "Flood and heavy rains - lower valley no
        roads in(all blocked!)"

14 June, 1947 (SAT)
                    Coliseum, Sioux Falls, S. Dak (45,000)
                        7:05 & 9:30 PM
                        Capacity: 2400
                        Scale: 3.65, 3.05, 2.44, 1.83, 1.22

        Interviews: 5:30 to 6PM Doc on KSOO with Erv Kult; 6:15 to
        6:30 Spike, Lynn & Doc on KELO with Dick Harris. "Due to the
        floods in Iowa our train was late - left our cars (Pullman)
        in Worthington, Minn. Took bus to Sioux Falls, SD. Arrived
        5:30PM - did 2 b'casts - until 6:30 - show started 7:05 -
        second show - 9:30 PM"

15 June, 1947 (SUN)
                    Municipal Aud, Norfolk, Neb (10,439)
                        Capacity: 2400
                        Scale: 3.60, 3.00, 2.40

        Interviews: 5 to 5:15 PM Lynn Johnson & Doc on WJAG with
        Dennis Ballant. "Left our Pullman cars in Columbus, Neb.
        Took bus to Norfolk, Neb"

16 June, 1947 (MON)
                    City Aud, Hastings, Neb (15,145)
                        7:00 & 9:30 PM
                        Capacity: 1800+
                        Scale: 3.60, 3.00, 2.40, 1.80, 1.20

        Interviews: Spike, Lynn & Doc on KHAS (Diane Watts);
        4:15 to 4:45 PM Spike & Doc autograph records at Radio
        Electronics Music Store. (7PM - P.A. did not work at
        start of show. Mike short - fixed for 2nd half - P.A.
        system picked up a local b'cast that went out to the
        audience. System inadequate for our show)

17 June, 1947 (TUES)
    Enroute to Pueblo, Colo

18 June, 1947 (WED)
    Memorial Hall Aud, Pueblo, Colo (52,162)
     7:00 (full) '& 9:30 PM (3/4 full)
     Capacity: 1958
     Scale: 3.00, 2.40, 1.80, 1.20, .90

  Interviews: Spike, Lynn '& Doc on KGHF with Cliff Hendricks.
 "KCSJ (MBS) station to go on air July 14 - wants 78 RPM
 saluting their opening - send to Bob Price, Coronado Lodge,
 Pueblo"

19 June, 1947 (THURS)
    Auditorium, Colorado Springs, Colo (36,789)
     Capacity: 2900
     Scale: 3.60, 3.00, 2.40, 1.80, 1.20

  Interviews: 5 to 5:30 Spike, Lynn '& Doc on KRDO with Cecil
 Davey(?); Spike, Lynn & Doc on KVOR with Max Morath "side-
 walk stencils read- "For the Love of Mike, Don't miss Spike"

20 June (FRI) to 24 June (TUES), 1947
    Travel to and prepare for Pasadena

25 June, 1947 (WED)
    Civic Aud, Pasadena (111,000)
     Capacity: 1969
     Scale: 2.40, 1.80, 1.20

  Acts listed:- "same, plus trampoline act - Paul and Paulette

26 June, 1947 (THURS)
    Municipal Aud, Long Beach (300,000)
     Capacity: 3600
     Scale: 2.40, 1.80, 1.20

  "On Holiday to August"

25 July, 1947 (FRI) - Victor Studios, Hollywood, 1:30 to 6:10 PM
    W. Heebner, A & R Rep, present

    Leader - Spike Jones
    Brass - George Rock, tpt; John Stanley, trb
    Reeds - Mickey Katz, clar
    Violin - Dick Gardner
    Rhythm - Paul Leu, pno; Dick Morgan, guit;
     Roger Donley, bass; Ormond Downes, drm;
    Actor - Paul Frees
    Actress - Loulie Jean Norman
    Vocalists - Harry Stanton, Arthur Davies,
     E. Newton, J. Martin, Purves Pullen
    Musical Saw - John A. Rinehart

D7-VB-1303-1 20-2375-B; HMV BD 1188-B; HMVAU BD 1188-B &
   1A   EA 3710; LP RCAE INTS 5052; RCAG PJM2-8021;
      ET AFRS "Basic Music Library" P-840;
  (2:58)Pop Corn Sack - voc the Boys in the Back Room
      and Sir Frederick Gas
  -2   Unissued
  -2A(3:00)Pop Corn Sack

```
D7-VB-1304-1      20-2375-A; HMV BD 1188-A; HMVAU BD 1188-A &
         1A          EA 3710; 45-5164-B(Y-359); 45 47-0163-A
                     (WY-359); RCAG EPA 9635; LP RCAE INTS 5052;
                     RCAG RCS 3217/1-2; ET AFRS "Basic Music
                     Library" P-840; AFRS "Purple Heart Album" 168;
               (3:27)Our Hour(The Puppy Love Song) - voc Tailwaggers,
                     Dr. Horatio Q. Birdbath, George Rock, Sir
                        Frederick Gas
         -2          Unissued
         -2A(3:27)Our Hour
```

Note: RCA inst indicate John Rinehart booked from 2:30 to
6:10 PM. Sir Frederick Gas is no one in particular - a humorous name
quickly invented for the label credits (reminiscent of the mythical
Willie Spicer). "Our Hour" duet is George Rock - done before conver-
sion to tape. 45 RPM "Our Hour" was originally slated as 47-0162-B.
The trombone chair is still unsettled and John Stanley makes another
recorded appearance with his old boss.
    Paul Frees, a unique imitator of voices, is responsible for
most of the "Pop Corn Sack" characters, including the Hepburn lines:-
"the Calla Lillies will soon be back...". Voice specialists Loulie
Jean Norman and Frees work often and successfully for Spike in the
future. One clarinettist is listed, two appear in "Pop Corn Sack".

    Phillip Morgenstern, better known as Freddy Morgan, is now
one of the Slickers. From Cleveland, via New York, he had played the
Palace in NY when it was known as "Actor's Paradise". With Leo Stone,
he toured as the team "Morgan and Stone". As a single, Morgan had
played in Europe, Asia and Australia, helping to organize the "American Overseas Artists", a forerunner of the U.S.O., and entertained in
Europe until V-E day, when he went to the Orient with the U.S.O.
    Earle Bennett, one of the actors/comedians hired to replace
Red Ingle, starts about this time but quickly establishes his own
character and humor - and fills the nebulous form of Sir Frederick
Gas. From Kansas City, Missouri, he is an accomplished portrait artist and had been with the famous Ken Murray "Blackouts" and in the
movie "The Egg and I". Visually, his 'fright-wig' of real hair was a
development with Spike, as was his ability to imitate a violin
(Stradivarius, of course) using a tree branch as a prop. Bennett used
a strip of leather around his tongue and blew over it as a reed. Sen-
sative, his meek, sad-sack humor was a departure from the normal
boisterous Slickers presentations, and he shared the "Chloe" vocals
with Doodles Weaver, as well as soloing on comedy 'violin' routines.
    Joe Colvin, trombonist, starts about this time. From Okla-
homa, Colvin had worked with many bands in his career, from Rudy
Vallee to the Frank Sinatra show with Jan Savitt, and many others.

1 August, 1947 (FRI)
                High School Stadium, Tucson, Ariz (145,000)
                   8:30 PM
                   Capacity: 4500 (3800 admitted)
                   Scale: 2.75, 2.10, 1.50

        Interviews: 2:45 to 3PM Spike & Doc on KVOA with Jim
        Hayes; 3:15 to 3:30 on KTUC with Scott Henderson; 4:30
        Spike, Doc & Jr. Martin autograph session at Grabes
        Record Shop and b'cast in conjunction with Al Morris on
        KCNA. "Rehearsal room for (vocal) quartette - piano
        available" (Lighting inadequate)

        "Acts listed for this tour"
            Betty Jo Huston - Acrobatic dancer
            Dick Gardner - violin solo
            Dick Morgan - singer comedian
            Mickey Katz - Comedian
            George Rock - Comedian

                         166
```
```

Freddy Morgan - Comedian - banjoist
Dr. H.Q. Birdbath(P. Pullen) - imitator
Gardner Twins - Slickerettes - Dancers
Bill King - Juggler-comedy
Aileen Carlyle - Prima Donna comedienne
Frankie Little - Midget
Jr. Martin - Giant
Sir Fredric Gas(Earl Bennett) - Comedian
                                      novelty

Doodles Weaver - Comedian
<u>Jim Cook</u> - Vocalist
Helen Grayco - Popular Singer

Note: "Grayco" is now appearing as Helen's name

2 August, 1947 (SAT)
                 Isaac Men's Park Stadium, Phoenix, Ariz
                 8:30 PM   (200,000)
                 Capacity: 4500 (4200 attended)

Interviews: 4:15 to 4:30PM Spike & Doc on KPHO with Lou
King; 5 to 5:30 on KOV with Andy Wilson; 1/2-hour interview,
Doc with Gil Lee (KOOL) transcribed, to be played Mon Aug
4 at 8PM "Out-doors platform built to our plans"

7 August (THURS) to 20 August (WED), 1947
                 Flamingo Hotel, Las Vegas, Nev (25,000)
                 8:30(for 75 min.), 11:15(for 90 min.) PM
                 Capacity: 450
                 Scale: no cover-minimum or admission

Interviews: Fri Aug 8 4PM, Spike autograph session at
Music Store; Billboards along hi-way; 4-one minute spots
each day over KENO - "For the love of Mike, Don't miss
Spike" - "Two weeks of our engagement surpassed all records
at the Flamingo or any club in Las Vegas"

"...as West Coast Recording Director for RCAVictor, I used
to go regularly to Vegas to catch the acts", recalled Walt Heebner in
a 12 May 83 letter. "Spike was playing at the Flamingo, and, after
seeing and hearing a few of his shows, I suggested he merge Doodles'
solo race track routine with the band's version of the Wm. Tell Overture. He liked the idea, and we did it on a subsequent recording date
...Incidentally, I also signed, on the same visit, Mickey Katz...to
do Jewish comedy and dance music for the RCAV International label as
it was called."

    <u>Emilio Malione</u>, sax/clar, replaces Mickey Katz

21 August (THURS),   22 August (FRI), 1947
                 Jerry Jones Rainbow Randevu, Salt Lake City, Ut
                 Capacity: 1200   (175,000)
                 Scale: 2.50 at tables, 2.00 on floor

Interviews: Spike & Doc 3:35 to 4:00PM on KALL with Jim
Hamlett; 4:15 to 4:30 on KSL with Paul Alexander; 5:05 to
5:15 on KDYL with Chas. Berry(all on Fri); 5:30 to 6PM
Spike on KNAK Thurs "Center Theatre - gave us prefiew of
'Variety Girl' showing 12:30AM Sat. ending at 2:30" -
"no sleep - had to catch train for Elko 6:30AM - coach -
no pullman" - "Bob Krueger(RCA Dist.) gave us 25 Our Hour/
Pop Corn Sack" - Nancy MacDonald & Jim Cook left review to
to return to L.A."

Betsy Mills, harp, and <u>Irving Franklin (Paul) Judson</u>,
vocalist, start with the troupe after this day

23 August (SAT) to 1 September (MON), 1947
                Commercial Hotel, Elko, Nev (4,094)
                Capacity: 275
                Scale: no cover, no minimum

        Interviews: Pep Rally, Mon Aug 25 (1 hr. show) 2000
        attended. "left new Victor "Our Hour" & "Pop Corn Sack"
        with Juke Box Operators" - "Local orch. played for dancing
        Lou Math(4)" (lighting inadequate: dressing rooms - none,
        boys had to take suits home every night)

2 September (TUES), 3 September (WED), 1947
                California State Fair Grounds, Sacramento(119,994)
                Grandstand show 75 min.
                Capacity: 15,000
                Scale: 1.20 reserve, .60 gen. ad.

        "Extra 45 min. show each night at Governor's Casino -
        in conjunction with a dance"

                "Routine - Grandstand Show acts:-"
                1. Hotcha Kornya
                2. Chloe
                3. Dr. H.Q. Birdbath
                4. Always Hurt the One You Love
                5. Bettyjo Huston
                6. Doodles Weaver
                7. Geo. Rock - Minka
                8. Hawaiian War Chant
                9. Liebestraum
                10. Bill King
                11. Sheik of Araby
                12. Cocktails
        "30 Helen O'Neill Girls - Dancers Gay Ninety routines
                opened show"

5 September (FRI) to 4 October (SAT), 1947
                Curran Theatre, San Francisco (634,536)
                evening shows with Saturday matinee
                Capacity: 1767
                Scale: 3.60, 2.40, 1.80, 1.20
                      mat 2.40, 1.80, 1.20

        Interviews: were many and frequent, including p.a. "Gang
        went to Marine Hospital to ent(ertain) patients there!" -
        "Made appearance before RCA sales meeting Spike & Doc -
        Sat 12 noon Sept 13th" - "Robert & Renee in Sept 17, out
        Sept 24"

        "...Coca Cola bought a refined version of the Revue for the
radio audience." (<u>Newsweek</u>, 4 Apr 49)

        Spotlight Revue, produced by Hal Finberg for Coca-Cola, was
to have been co-hosted by Martin Downey, the popular vocalist and
former accompanist to Hildegarde. He was now a 'Coke' executive and
the host position was shared by Spike with the Columbia recording
star, Dorothy Shay, the 'Park Avenue Hillbilly'.
        The Big Band titles played on the initial b'casts were from
the 1946 'Spike's At The Troc' library, arranged mainly by Howard
Gibeling. Local musicians augmented the Slickers on brass, reeds and

strings for the big band features and to accompany Miss Shay.

Eddie Pripps, sax/reed/arr in many famous big bands was the conductor of the 'legitimate' Revue show. In cities where the show ran longer than the 'one-nighter', Pripps would handle the 'straight' music and conduct the acts. He was also responsible for most of the Spotlight Revue music, along with Paul Leu. Leu and Dick Gardner were responsible for most of the 'Slickers' b'cast arrangements.

Miss Shay was on her own personal appearance (p.a.) club circuit. The b'cast day consisted of rehearsal, dress, audience warm-up to the 1/2 hr. b'cast, followed, after a short break, by the regular Revue show.

The Coca-Cola employee's pamphlet, the "Red Barrel", carried occasional Spike Jones articles during the course of his radio shows.

AFRS released 15 minute segments of most, if not all shows, in a series called "Corn's a Poppin'". A known listing appears in appendix iii.

3 October, 1947 (FRI) - SPOTLIGHT REVUE
                CBS San Francisco   ann: Marvin Best

                Guest: Victor Borge

                This Can't Be Love - Big Band
                Dorothy Shay - "Feudin' and Fightin'"
                Perfidia - Big Band
                Victor Borge - "Clair de Lune"
                Dorothy Shay - "Near You"
                William Tell Overture - Doodles Weaver

        The Spike Jones Fan Club mimeographed magazine available at this time, reviewed the Borge solo "Warsaw Concerto" as part of this b'cast. It may have been included in the dress for the show, then dropped due to time restrictions. After this tenuous start, which relied more on the talents of Miss Shay and quality guests, the series became a natural extension of the Slickers p.a. shows. The Slickers reached a zenith of zaniness lasting well into the early 1950's.

        Two baggage cars of props were now part of the road tours and consisted of all music, stands, instruments, wardrobe and the neon-lit backdrop curtain. It was obvious that all arenas were not created equal and they must carry their own lighting, mikes, and staging material. Their one-night set-up was more economical than the 'legitimate', or broadcast show and the longer duration stops.

        During 1947 and '48, these shows were b'cast live from the nearest CBS facility.

5 October, 1947 (SUN)
                Civic Aud, Fresno (84,000)
                3:00 PM and evening
                Capacity: 3200
                Scale: 3.60, 2.40, 1.80

        (Our mike set went off for opening of show. Went on after "Hotcha Cornya", Chloe & Betty Jo acts. Used emergency local aud. set during Birdbath number. Our mike set not tested before show. This must be done in future)

6 October (MON) to 11 October (SAT), 1947
                Philharmonic Aud, Los Angeles (1,805,657)
                8:30 + 2:30 Sat matinee (9:00 PM Fri)
                Capacity: 2670
                Scale: 3.60, 3.00, 2.40, 1.80, 1.20

"Reh. 3PM Mon Oct 6 - Record RCA Tues afternoon - made pic
for C.C. Thurs afternoon - Variety Girl preview 9 Oct" in-
person movie stars" (no prop tables, stagehands missed cues)

Ina Souez, Prima Donna, Diva-comedianne replaces Eileen
Carlyle. Ina (Eena) had been featured in Grand Opera in France,
Vienna, Holland, Berlin, Budapest and throughout England. A matchless
voice and an appreciation of comedy.
Temporarily on sax/clar for the Los Angeles show was 'Tiny'
Rips, who had done a lot of practising and practical work since his
audition for Spike in 1940/41.

7 October, 1947 (TUES) - Victor Studios, Hollywood, 1:00 to 6:00 PM
              Walt Heebner, A & R Rep, present

              Leader - Spike Jones
              Brass - George Rock, tpt; Joe (Joseph Frederick)
                Colvin, trb
              Reeds - Emilio Malione, Merle (Sydney) Howard,
                clar
              Rhythm - Paul Leu, pno; Dick Morgan, guit;
                Roger Donley, bass; Joe Siracusa, drm
              Harp - Betsy Ann Mills
              Strings - Dick Gardner, Nicholas Pisani*, Felix
                Slatkin*; Theodore Klages*, vln; Paul
                Robyn*, vla; Arthur Kafton*, cel
              Actors - Winstead Weaver, Paul Frees, Paul
                Judson, Freddy Morgan, Purves Pullen

D7-VB-1367-1   20-2592-A; HMV BD 1200; HMVAU MH 134 & EA 3817;
       1A   45 47-3288-B(WP-288); 547-0069-B(EPA 288);
                    EPA 5080; RCAG EPA 288; RCAE RCX 1037;
                    LP LPM 2224; LPM 3849; LSP 3849(e); ANL1
                    1035(e); AYL1 3748; PK ACL 7031(e); RCAE
                    LSA 3084 & RD 7724; RCAAU CAS 7158; RCAG LSP
                    10157 & RCS 3217/1-2; RCAJ 5143(m); RCAIT
                    CL 83748; RCA Special Products "Good Music
                    Record" DML1 0570; ET AFRS "Basic Music
                    Library" P-912; AFRS "Remember" 841; AFRS
                    "Hot Off the Record press" 155; AFRS "Martin
                    Block" 217;
              (3:22)My Old Flame - voc Paul Judson and Peter Gory
                    by Paul Frees
NP   2 (3:38)Unissued
NP   2A
NP   3 (3:38)Unissued
NP   3A

     * designated musicians were booked 2:30 to 5:30 PM

D7-VB-1368-1   20-2861-A; HMV BD 1212; 420-0175-A; HMVAU BD 1212
       1A   & EA 3772; HMVSK X72298; RCADJ 334;
                    45 47-3289-A(WP-288); 447-0175-A; 74-0532;
                    EPA 415; EPA 5058; RCAG EPA 415; RCAAU EP
                    20050; RCAF EP 86233; LP LPM 2224; LPM 3128;
                    LPM 3849; LSP 3849(e); ANL1 1035(e); AYL1 3748;
                    LSC 3235(e); AGL1 4142(e); RCAE RD 7724; RCAAU
                    ODLP 6024, ODLP 7503 & CAS 7158; RCAG 10 013
                    & RCS 3211/1-2; RCAJ RVP 6300(e) RCAIT CL
                    83748; RCAF PL 43197; RCA Special Products
                    "Good Music Record" DML1 0570; ET AFRS "Basic
                    Music Library" PGL 38 & P-1024; AFRS "Remember"
                    906; AFRS "Martin Block" 196 & 396; AFRS
                    "Carroll"(condensed) 875;

                              170

(3:14)<u>William Tell Overture</u> - Commentary by
Doodles Weaver

Note: "My Old Flame" label voc credits were changed by Mr.
Oberstein to read simply:- "voc Paul Frees and Paul Judson". Paul
Frees created, recorded and then auditioned his "Flame" material. The
only alterations on Spike's RCA issue were references to Jones' hits
- "Laura" and "Chloe", and the audible flames at the end. "William
Tell Overture" was issued in April 1948 and, according to <u>Billboard</u>
Magazine, reached No. 6 on 4 June and remained on the Hit Parade for
15 weeks.

On 3 Jan 1950, Spike sent a check to Walter Heebner to the
amount of $1984.42 to acknowledge his contribution towards the
creation of the successful "Wm. Tell Overture". As Doodles had taken
the entire composer's share of royalties to "Wm. Tell", Spike felt
Heebner should have one-third the composer's royalty on "Flying
Trapeze". (see 7 Aug 47) "...oh yes, it was my idea on the session to
bury Doodles last 'Feitlebaum' in the echo chamber", Heebner writes,
"...however, any participation by an A&R man in those days with an
Artist or Publisher was strictly verboten, hence Spike wrote his
letter for transmittal to the then VP of the RCAV Division (J.W.
Murray) for his approval." (Walt Heebner correspondence 12 May 83)
'Twirl-A-Way', Doodles' previous race winner had given way
to 'Feetlebaum', a mythical nag who wins every race, and who became a
national catch phrase to vie with the older 'Kilroy Was Here' in nonsense usage. As 'Professor Feetlebaum', Doodles Weaver virtually became a national celebrity.

Doodles often named his horses after friends as an 'inside'
joke. The RCA "Wm. Tell" contains "Beautiful Linda" (Spike's daughter), "Flying Sylvester" (Weaver's brother Sylvester (Pat), President
of NBC-TV 1953), "Lady Evelyn" (his wife). On b'casts, there were
also the obvious references to "Flying Spike" and "Little Helen",
among many others. For his own amusement and the bands', Weaver would
also mention the "Greeper" (eg: Green Briar Greeper) - a nonsense
code best left alone. In a 1950 b'cast, one horse's name was "Skip
Craig", and in 1949 did we hear a horse named "Walt Heebner" (as
thanks for his aid in helping the record go 'gold'?)

10 October, 1947 (FRI) - SPOTLIGHT REVUE
                CBS Hollywood   ann:

                Guest: Burl Ives

                <u>Thou Swell</u> - Big Band
                <u>Dorothy Shay</u> - "Flat River, Missuri"
                <u>Caravan</u> - Big Band
                Burl Ives - "On Top of Old Smokey",
                    "Old Dan Tucker"
                Dorothy Shay - "Tallahassee"
                <u>Pop Corn Sack</u> - City Slickers

        Note: Program info is based on a published review appearing
in the Spike Jones Fan Club magazine. No ETs or dubbings of any
portion of this show are known.
        Additional musicians hired in Los Angeles for this radio
series were: Tommy Jones, Red Nichols and Jimmy Hardy, tpts. Tom
Jones later coached Danny Kaye on the cornet for the Kaye role in
"Red Nichols and the Five Pennies"

12 October, 1947 (SUN)
                "9:30 AM leave L.A."

13 October, 1947 (MON)
                University of Wyoming Aud, Laramie, Wyo(10,627)

                        171

                              Capacity: 1996
                              Scale: 3.60, 2.40, 1.50

14 October (TUES), 15 October (WED), 1947
                    City Aud, Denver, Colo (375,000)
                    Details as 15 Feb 47

          Interviews: Tues 2PM Spike on KFEL with Ray Perkins; 2:30
          Spike & Doc on KLZ with Clark Thorton; 3 to 4 autograph
          session at Daniels & Fishers Record show; 5:15 on KMYR
          with Gene Amoli; 6 to 6:30 on KOA "These Kids of Ours";
          Wed 12:30 PM Doc on KMYR with Gene Amoli "Man in the
          Street"; 2PM Doc on KFEL with Ray Perkins. "Both evenings
          sold out. 3400 each night - matinee on Wed just fair about
          1000" (Accomodations very poor, Albany Hotel, some of cast
          turned away)

15 October, 1947 (THURS)
                    Travel to Chicago

17 October, 1947 (FRI) - SPOTLIGHT REVUE
                    CBS Chicago   ann: John McCormick

          Guest: Frankie Laine

                    I've Found a New Baby - Big Band
                    Dorothy Shay - "I've Been to Hollywood"
                    Laura - voc Doodles Weaver, Dr. H.Q. Birdbath,
                       Sir Frederick Gas, Paul Judson
                    Frankie Laine - "That's My Desire",
                       "Two Loves Have I"
                    Dorothy Shay - "I Wish I Didn't Love You So"
                    Johnny Mercer medley:
                       Frankie Laine - "Small Fry"
                       Dorothy Shay - "Accentuate the Positive"
                    That Old Black Magic - voc Paul Judson

          This complete show has been issued on Mar-Bren
                    Records LP, MBR 743 (thin sound on LP suggests
                    dub from wire recording instead of ET)

18 October, 1947 (SAT)
                    Municipal Arena, Kansas City, Mo (399,178)
                    Capacity: 11,500 (sold out)

19 October, 1947 (SUN)
                    Memorial Aud, Dayton, Ohio (210,718)
                    Details as 12 Mar 47

          Interviews: Sun midnight Spike, Doodles & Doc transcription
          (15 min) with Gene Barry - to be played on WING midnight
          Mon Oct 20

20 October, 1947 (MON)
                    Memorial Hall, Columbus, Ohio (306,087)
                    Details as 9 Mar 47

21 October, 1947 (TUES)
                    Masonic Temple, Detroit, Mich (1,623,452)
                    Details as 16 Mar 47

                              172

22 October, 1947 (WED)
                    Quimby Aud, Ft. Wayne, Ind (118,410)
                    7:30 & 10:20 PM
                    Details as 13 Mar 47

23 October, 1947 (THURS)
                    Taft Theatre Aud, Cincinnati, Ohio (455,610)
                    8:30 PM
                    Capacity: 2500
                    Scale: 3.60, 3.00, 2.40, 1.80, 1.20

24 October, 1947 (FRI) - SPOTLIGHT REVUE
                    CBS Chicago   ann: Mike (Myron)
                                                        Wallace
                    Guest: Tex Williams

                    *Toot Toot Tootsie, Goodbye - City Slickers
                    Dorothy Shay - "Efficiency"
                    *Down In Jungle Town - voc Paul Judson and
                         Freddy Morgan; narration, Mike Wallace
                    Them There Eyes - Big Band
                    Tex Williams - "Smoke, Smoke, Smoke",
                         "That's What I Like About the West"
                    Dorothy Shay -"So Far"
                    Oklahoma medley:
                         Entire cast - "Oklahoma"
                         Dorothy Shay - "Oh What a Beautiful Morning"
                    People Will Say We're In Love - voc Paul Judson

                    *on Public Service Show ET "Here's To Vets" 91;
                     The complete show issued on Mar-Bren Records
                     LP, MBR 743

25 October, 1947 (SAT)
                    Purdue Music Hall, Lafayette, Ind
                    7:00 & 9:00 PM
                    Details as 28/29 Mar 47

Interviews: Spike & Doc autograph session at Foster's
Music Store. "Entire cast went to Purdue(14)-Illinois(7)
football game in the afternoon"

26 October, 1947 (SUN)
                    Murat Temple, Indianapolis, Ind
                    8:30 PM
                    Details as 8 Mar 47

27 October, 1947 (MON) to 3 January, 1948 (SAT)
                    Studebaker Theatre, Chicago, Ill (3,396,808)
                    2:30 Sat/Sun; 8:30 PM nightly (10:30 Fri)
                                  2:30 PM Spec. perf Thanksgiving
                                  8:30 & 11:30 New Years Eve
                    Capacity: 1270
                    Scale: eve 3.60, 3.00, 2.40, 1.80, 1.20
                           mat 3.00, 2.40, 1.80, 1.20

Interviews: innumerable on DJ programs but none on television. "Coca Cola show every Fri at 9:30 to 10PM CST.
Banners used on 1000 trucks announcing Coke show & our
appearance at Studebaker" - "Doorman: Gus Neville(87)" -
"Stopped Mon night shows starting Mon Dec 8th" (Cast
spread out among nine hotels)

173

30 October, 1947 (THURS) - Victor Studios, Chicago   2:15 to
         A.E. Hindle, A & R Rep, present   5:00 PM

           Leader - Spike Jones
           Brass - George Rock, tpt; Joe Colvin, trb
           Reeds - Dick Gardner, Emilio Malione, Merle
             Howard, clar/sax
           Rhythm - Paul Leu, pno; Dick Morgan, Freddy
             Morgan, guit/bjo; Roger Donley, tuba;
             Joe Siracusa, drm
           Vocalists - Paul Judson, Purves Pullen, Freddy
             Morgan

D7-VB-1113-1   20-2820-A; RCADJ 231; ET AFRS "Basic Music
    1A   Library" P-994;
      (2:55)Down In Jungle Town - voc Paul Judson, Freddy
           Morgan assisted by the Head Hunters

      Note: RCA inst do not list Freddy Morgan as vocalist

31 October, 1947 (FRI) - SPOTLIGHT REVUE
         CBS Chicago   ann: Mike Wallace

         Guest: Jan August

         No, No, Nora - City Slickers
         Dorothy Shay - "Say That We're Sweethearts Again"
        *My Old Flame - voc Paul Judson and Paul Frees
         Jan August - "Miserlou"
         Dorothy Shay - "It Was Just a Friendly Feeling"
         South American medley:
            Jan August - "Oye Negra"
            Dorothy Shay - "Besa Me Mucho"
            Las Chiapanecas - City Slickers

        *excerpt on Public Service Show ET "Here's To
          Vets" 91

5 November, 1947 (WED) - Victor Studios, Chicago   2:00 to
         A.E. Hindle, A & R Rep, present   6:00 PM

           Personnel as 30 October, adding Dick Morgan
            on vocal

D7-VB-1140-1   20-2592-B; HMV BD 1207-A; HMVAU MH 134;
    1A   45 RCAG EPA 9062; LP RCAE INTS 5052; RCAG
           RCS 3217/1-2; ET AFRS "Basic Music Library"
           P-912;
      (3:05)People Are Funnier Than Anybody - voc Dick Morgan
           and Freddy Morgan

unslated   MacNamara's Band

      Note: RCA inst do not list either Morgan as vocalist, only
Judson and Pullen. This as yet unpublished composition was written by
Eddie Brandt and the Spotlight Revue producer, Hal Finberg.
"MacNamara's Band" details, see 11 Feb 47 - "I Wuv a Wabbit".

7 November, 1947 (FRI) - SPOTLIGHT REVUE
         CBS Chicago   ann: Mike Wallace

Guest: Jack Owens

Alabamy Bound - City Slickers
Dorothy Shay - "You Do"
Three Little Words - Big Band
*I'm Getting Sentimental Over You - voc Dr. H.Q.
   Birdbath, George Rock, Sir Frederick Gas and
   the Barefooted Pennsylvanians
Jack Owens - "How Soon", "All Dressed Up With
   a Broken Heart"
Dorothy Shay - "Feudin' and Fightin"
Jack Owens medley:
   Jack Owens - "Hut Sut Song"
   Dorothy Shay - "Louisiana Lullaby"
   Hi Neighbor - City Slickers

*issued on MF Distribution LPs MF205/4,
   947447, and GO 10016

Note: Chorus in "I'm Getting Sentimental" similar to RCA 4
Dec session. "Hi Neighbor" is an excerpt of the 1941 Del Porter arr.

13 November, 1947 (THURS) - Victor Studios, Chicago   1:00 to
   A & R Rep unlisted, A. Hindle assumed   5:30 PM

      Personnel as 30 Oct, with Betsy Mills, harp;
      vocalists Paul Judson, Purves Pullen, Earle
      Bennett, George Rock, Dick Morgan and
      unidentified chorus

D7-VB-1162-1   20-2861-B; HMV BD 1238; RCADJ 335; ET AFRS
     1A   "Basic Music Library" P-1024; AFRS
                  "Remember" 904;
        (3:10)By The Beautiful Sea - voc the Salt Water
                  Tuffies:(credits: Barker, Dick Morgan;
                  interruptions, George Rock)

D7-VB-1163-1   20-2949-B; HMV BD 1214-B; HMV BD 1214-B,
     1A   EA 3811 & EA 4241; RCADJ 449; 45 RCAG EPA 9062;
                  LP RCAE HY 1006 & INTS 5052; RCAG LPM 10 013 &
                  RCS 3217/1-2; RCAJ 5143(m); ET AFRS "Basic
                  Music Library" P-1104; AFRS "Remember" 981;
        (3:30)I'm Getting Sentimental Over You - voc the
                  Barefooted Pennsylvanians, credits: Sir
                  Frederick Gas, Dick Morgan and George Rock

      Note: RCA inst do not list Rock or Morgan as vocalists. RCA
release 20-2861, "Wm. Tell"/"By The Beautiful Sea", was issued in
April 1948 but quickly withdrawn and replaced with, using the same
catalog number, "Wm. Tell"/"...Flying Trapeze". The original coupling
does not show on RCA inst. There were objections from some quarters
over the enunciation of certain words in the "Beautiful Sea" lyrics,
('Over and under and then up for air') causing RCA (always sensitive
to public opinion) to withdraw the original issue very quickly. The
offending words, not audible to everyone, were not intentional, according to 'Doc' and Weaver, and the problem stemmed from certain
voice patterns not being cleanly reproduced by the recording techniques of the day. The English HMV BD 1238 was issued in March 1949
and kept in their catalogs (catalogues!) for many years.
      Choir credits on "Sentimental" similar to 4 Dec session.

14 November, 1947 (FRI) - SPOTLIGHT REVUE
              CBS Chicago   ann: Mike Wallace

Guest: Francis Craig

San - City Slickers
Dorothy Shay - "It's the Little Things You
   Do That Count"
By The Beautiful Sea - voc Dick Morgan and
   George Rock
Francis Craig - "Near You", voc Bob Lamm
Dorothy Shay - "How Lucky You Are"
The Man on the Flying Trapeze - Doodles Weaver
Politeness medley:
   Francis Craig - "Beg Your Pardon"
   Dorothy Shay - "Pardon My Southern Accent"
*Who's Sorry Now - City Slickers

*on Public Service Show ET "Here's To Vets" 91

        Possibly from the 19 Nov 47 issue of Downbeat:- "SPIKE JONES
AND HIS CITY SLICKERS SLATED FOR BRITISH TOUR - handled by MCA,
leaves N.Y. in late June for a date at London's Palladium. Booked 6
to 8 weeks at the theatre, stricly on a guarantee basis, through July
and August. Spike plans to return to N.Y. immediately after the
engagements conclusion, hitting various theatres in the vicinity of
NYC to open in the big city during Sept. or Oct. 1948."
        Due to continuing disagreement between the Musicians' Unions
concerned, neither this nor any other UK tour, materializes. Each
country's Union insisted on exchanges of equal tour length, equal
personnel and approx. the same dates. Eg: it was easier for Benny
Goodman or Stan Kenton to exchange with Humphrey Lyttelton or Ted
Heath, but difficult for Spike with nearly 40 in his troupe.

21 November, 1947 (FRI) - SPOTLIGHT REVUE
                 CBS Chicago   ann: Mike Wallace

        Guests: the Dinning Sisters

        *Near You - City Slickers
        Dorothy Shay - "Mountain Lullaby"
        Blowing Bubble Gum - voc George Rock
        Dinning Sisters - "Brazil"
        Love In Bloom - Sir Frederick Gas, Dr. H.Q.
           Birdbath and the Barefooted Pennsylvanians
        Dorothy Shay - "Smile Right Back at the Sun"
        Home on the Range - Doodles Weaver
        Time medley:
           Dinning Sisters - "Once In A While"
           Dorothy Shay - "Time On My Hands"
           As Time Goes By - City Slickers

        *issued (edited with 16 Jan 48 version) on
           MF Distribution LPs MF 205/4

Note: Chorus on "Love in Bloom" similar to 4 Dec session

28 November, 1947 (FRI) - SPOTLIGHT REVUE
                 CBS Chicago   ann: Mike Wallace

        Guests: Jack Smith and the Clark Sisters

        Running Wild - City Slickers
        Dorothy Shay - "The Style To Which I'm Accustomed"
        Old MacDonald Had a Farm - feat Dr. H.Q. Birdbath

Holiday For Strings - feat Betsy Mills, harp
Jack Smith - "Civilization"
Dorothy Shay - "White Christmas"
When You and I Were Young, Maggie - Doodles Weaver
Irish medley:
    Dorothy Shay - "That's An Irish Lullaby"
    Jack Smith - "Peggy O'Neil"
    MacNamara's Band - City Slickers

4 December, 1947 (THURS) - Victor Studios, Chicago   1:00 to
    A.E. Hindle, A & R Rep, present   5:30 PM

Personnel as 30 Oct, adding Betsy Mills, harp;
Vocal - Paul Judson, Purves Pullen, Earle Bennett
Chorus - A. Trendler, G. McCarthy, B. LaFrandre
    soprano; Emma Kay Bowers contralto; William
    Cole, John Halloran tenor; Tom Yeakle baritone;
    Arwin Schweig bass
Sound Effects - Ed Wojtal

D7-VB-2341-1   20-2949-A; HMV BD 1214-B; HMVAU BD 1214-B, EA
    1A   3817 & EA 4241; HMVSK X7298; RCADJ 448;
    45 47-3289-B(WP-288); RCAG EPA 9062;
    LP RCAG LPM 10 013 & RCS 3211/1-2; RCAJ RVP
    6300(m) & 5143(m); RCAF PL 431.97; ET AFRS
    "Basic Music Library" P-1024;
(3:35)I Kiss Your Hand Madame - voc Paul Judson and
    the Ben Ghost Singers

D7-VB-2342-1   20-3177-A; HMV B 9855; 20-4315-B; 420-0172-A;
    1A   45-5285-B(Y-417); RCADJ 592-A & D7-VB-2342;
    HMVAU EA 3849; 45 47-2963-A; 47-4315-B;
    447-0172-A; 47-0254-B(WY-417); EYA 18;
    Luniverse 107(excerpt); LP RCAG PJM2 8021; RCA
    "Special Products" DPL1 0177; RCAAU 6LP set
    "Wishing You a Merry Christmas"; UA-LA 669-R;
    Scotch Tape "The Magic of Christmas" RD4-57-4;
    Rori RLP 3301(excerpt); Rhino RNLP 888(ex-
    cerpt); IX Chains NCS 9000(excerpt); Cash
    OR6000(excerpt); ET AFRS "Basic Music Library"
    P-1324; AFRS "Pewter"(Christmas'72); AFRS
    "Christmas" 325; AFRS "Martin Block" 196;
(3:05)All I Want For Christmas(Is My Two Front Teeth)
    Voc George Rock

    Note: The second recording ban of the decade was looming and
all recording artists were in the studios as often as possible to
build up a catalog of unissued titles for the duration. "All I Want
For Christmas" had been recorded too late for 1947 seasonal issue and
is held by Victor until late 1948. On 8 Dec 48, the title was changed
to "My Two Front Teeth" (All I Want For Christmas), with subsequent
releases reflecting this change. The 1949 78RPM re-issues had picture
sleeves.
    RCA inst indicate the chorus were to be paid directly by
Spike. RCA issued two DJ "Front Teeth", first with "Happy New Year"
then "Rudolph" on flip. Curiously, an RCA correction dated 7 Jan 48
changes "Two Front Teeth" credits to read: "Toy Band: Spike Jones and
his Junior City Slickers". All known issues credit George Rock.
    "All I Want For Christmas" reached No. 1 on the Hit Parade
on 19 Nov 48 and, according to Billboard Magazine, remained there for
eight weeks. It's re-issue, one year later, reached 18th position on
30 Dec 49, remaining there for one week.
    "I Kiss Your Hand Madame" has been reportedly issued on a
Japanese 78 RPM, "Siam" on flip. (Japanese PR poster in Jones files)

5 December, 1947 (FRI) - SPOTLIGHT REVUE
       CBS Chicago   ann: Mike Wallace

            Guests: the Three Suns

            Yes, We Have No Bananas - City Slickers
            Dorothy Shay - "The Man in the Stanley Steamer"
            People Are Funnier Than Anybody - voc Dick
                Morgan, Joe Siracusa, Freddy Morgan
            Three Suns - "Dardanella"
            What Is This Thing Called Love - Big Band
            Listen To the Mocking Bird - feat Dr. H.Q.
                Birdbath
            Dorothy Shay - "Feudin' and Fightin'"
            My Blue Heaven - Doodles Weaver
            Cold Storage medley:
                Three Suns - "Let It Snow, Let It Snow"
                Dorothy Shay - "June In January"
                Winter Wonderland - City Slickers

        Note: Itinerary lists Betsy Mills as leaving this day. After
the Birdbath solo, Dorothy Shay is presented the Cashbox (Magazine)
Award for the best hillbilly record by a popular artist in 1947 - her
Columbia "Feudin' and Fightin'".
        CBS ET of this show was not in the Jones estate files.
Existing dub is poor in quality. A CBS promo disc with a variety of
artists 'pushed' their Friday night line-up (eg: Francis Langford,
Don Ameche, Ozzie and Harriet). It contains a brief instrumental of
"Der Fuehrer's Face", but may be a studio band with no Jones involve-
ment and dates from late '47 or early '48. Label info unknown.
        There were no Monday shows at the Studebaker after 1 Dec.

11 December, 1947 (THURS) - Victor Studios, Chicago   1:00 to
        A.E. Hindle, A & R Rep, present   6:00 PM

            Personnel as 30 Oct, with Spike Jones,
                narrator; Edward R. Pripps, conductor;
                Paul Judson, Purves Pullen, voices, and;
            W.A. Mercier Jr., fr hrn; F.S. Walker, b.clar;
            T.D. Robinson, fl; J.A. Turso, bsn; D.R.
            Knapp, drm; Ed Wojtal, sound effts

D7-VB-2366-1   45-5224-A(Y-377/Y-387); 45 47-0192-A(WY-387);
        1A(3:20)How the Circus Learned To Smile, Part 1

        Note: Eddie Pripps wrote the music to a story by Frank
Tashlin, a Hollywood scripter and director. Albums Y/WY 387 are
picture book albums. (Y-377 is not)

12 December, 1947 (FRI) - SPOTLIGHT REVUE
        CBS Chicago   ann: Mike Wallace

            Guest: Mel Torme

            Five Foot Two, Eyes Of Blue - City Slickers
            Dorothy Shay - "Flat River, Missouri"
            I Kiss Your Hand Madame - voc Paul Judson
            Mel Torme - "Makin' Whoopee"
            Three Little Words - Big Band
            Dorothy Shay - "How Soon"
            Shortnin' Bread - Doodles Weaver
            Wet medley:
                Dorothy Shay - "Singin' In the Rain"
                Mel Torme - "September In the Rain"

*Over the Rainbow - City Slickers

*issued on MF Distribution LPs MF 205/4

15 December, 1947 (MON) - Victor Studios, Chicago   1:00 to
                        A.E. Hindle, A & R Rep, present   6:00 PM

                        Personnel as 11 Dec

D7-VB-2367-1   45-5225-A(Y-377/Y-387); 45 47-0193-A(WY-387);
    1A(3:30)How the Circus Learned To Smile, Part 2

D7-VB-2368-1   45-5225-B(Y-377/Y-387); 45 47-0193-B(WY-387);
    1A(3:30)How the Circus Learned To Smile, Part 3

D7-VB-2369-1   45-5224-B(Y-377/Y-387); 45 47-0192-B(WY-387);
    1A(3:40)How the Circus Learned To Smile, Part 4

        Note: In the Jones files is a copy, perhaps a test record-
ing, of Part 2 with a breakdown. The character voices of many Slickers appear on this childrens album.

19 December, 1947 (FRI) - SPOTLIGHT REVUE
                        CBS Chicago   ann: Mike Wallace

        Guests: the Dinning Sisters, Jerry Murad
                and his Harmonicats

        Kate - City Slickers
        Helen Grayco - "Ca-Ca-Caramba"
        All I Want For Christmas - voc George Rock
        Harmonicats - "Peg O' My Heart"
        This Can't Be Love - Big Band
        Dinning Sisters - "I Love My Love"
        Deck the Halls - Doodles Weaver
        Transportation medley:
            Harmonicats - "Chattanooga Choo Choo"
            Helen Grayco - "The Trolley Song"
            Bicycle Built For Two - City Slickers

        Note: Helen Grayco stands in for an ill Dorothy Shay. "Ca-Ca
Caramba", featured with the Revue, was written for Miss Grayco by
Eddie Brandt and Rene Tuzete. Tuzete (or Touzet) had recorded a Latin
album for RCA Victor in 1947 and recorded (Unison Riff 22 Sept 47)
with Stan Kenton. "Made For Each Other", featured by popular organist
Ethel Smith, is a Tuzete composition. Jack Egan, associated with the
Revue PR, has left for a position with Downbeat Magazine.

23 December, 1947 (TUES) - Victor Studios, Chicago   1:20 to
                        A.E. Hindle, A & R Rep, present 6:20 PM

                        Personnel as 30 Oct, with voices: Purv Pullen,
                            Earle Bennett, Ina Souez, Paul Judson,
                            Doodles Weaver, George Rock

D7-VB-2408-1   20-4125-B; 20-3010-B(un-released); HMV BD 1214-B;
    1A   HMVAU EA 3789; RCADJ D7-VB-2408; 45 47-4125-B;
                     LP LSC 3235(e); AGL1 4142(e); RCAG PJM2 8021;
                     RCAJ 5142; ET AFRS "Basic Music Library" P-1104
                     & P-2202; AFRS "Turn Back the Clock" 162;

179

                    (3:25)Ill Bacio(Il Bacio) - voc Ina Souez and
                          Horatio Q. Birdbath

D7-VB-2409-1   20-3177-B; HMV B 9855; HMVAU EA 3849; RCADJ
     1A   592-B; 45 47-2963-B; ET AFRS "Basic Music
                      Library" P-1024;
                    (3:20)Happy New Year - voc Sir Frederick Gas, Doodles
                          Weaver, George Rock, Spike Jones

          Note: RCA inst do not credit Weaver or Rock as vocalists,
and indicate that Pullen, Bennett, Souez and Judson were paid
directly by Spike. "Ill Bacio" title was changed to, and released as
"Ill Barkio" after consideration by Eli Oberstein in May 48. "Il
Bacio" originally was, and still is, a well known solo belonging to
the soprano recital repertoire. To have been released in June 1948,
"Ill Barkio" finally was available in April 1951. The English HMV was
issued in March 1949.
          Original matrices were 2370/2371. These were changed on 7
Jan 48 to 2407/2408, and finally 2408/2409. "Happy New Year" became
"New Years Resolution" on the AFRS ET.
          Eddie Brandt, as composer/arranger/scripter is now very
prominent on many Revue, b'cast and recorded titles.

26 December, 1947 (FRI) - SPOTLIGHT REVUE
                  CBS Chicago   ann: Mike Wallace

                  Guests: the Golden Gate Quartet

                  Near You - City Slickers
                  Dorothy Shay - "I've Been To Hollywood"
                  The Glow Worm - voc Ina Souez and Dick Morgan
                  Golden Gate Quartet - "Shadrack"
                  Dorothy Shay - "What Are You Doing
                     New Years Eve?"
                  Jingle Bells - Doodles Weaver
                  Three-Directional medley:
                     Golden Gate Quartet - "Carry Me Back To
                                Old Virginny"
                     Dorothy Shay - "Georgia On My Mind"
                  California, Here I Come - City Slickers

30 December, 1947 (TUES) - Victor Studios, Chicago   1:00 to
                  A.E. Hindle, A & R Rep, present   5:00 PM

                  Personnel as 30 Oct, adding Dick Gardner, vln;
                  voices: Purves Pullen, Earle Bennett, Paul
                  Judson, Helen Greco

D7-VB-2380-1   Unissued
     1A(2:57)Rum Tee Diddle Dee Yump - voc Sir Frederick Gas

D7-VB-2381-1   20-3516-B; 20-3010-A(un-released); HMVAU EA 3789;
     1A   420-0171-B; RCADJ 746-B; 45 47-2992-B; EPA 415;
                      447-0171-B; EPA 5080; RCAE RCX 1037; RCAG EPA
                      415; RCAAU EP 20017; LP LPM 2224; LPM 3128;
                      LPM 3849; LSP 3849(e); ANL1 1035(e); AYL1
                      3748; LSC 3235(e); AGL1 4142(e); RCAE LSA 3084
                      & RD 7724; RCAAU CAS 7158; RCAG LSP 10157 &
                      RCS 3211/1-2; RCAJ 5142; RCAIT CL 83748; RCAF
                      PL 43197; RCA Special Products "Good Music
                      Record" DML1 0570; ET AFRS "Basic Music
                      Library" P-1104; AFRS "Remember" 964;

                                   180

(3:12)<u>None But the Lonely Heart</u> (A Soaperetta) -
voices: Girl - Gilda Fish,
Boy - Maurice Matzah

Note: RCA inst do not credit Dick Gardner on vln. On 15 Jun
48, the label credits were changed to read "Cast: Girl: Helen Grayco,
Boy: Spike Jones, Violin solo: Dick Gardner". 20-3010, backed with
"Ill Barkio", was withdrawn as of 23 June 48 and it is doubtful if
any were actually released. RCA inst indicate the four vocalists were
paid directly by Spike, and the spelling was 'Greco' rather than the
now familiar 'Grayco'.

The decade's second recording ban, affecting all AF of M
members and the recording industry, comes into effect the last day of
December 1947, and lasts until 13 Dec 48.

2 January, 1948 (FRI) - SPOTLIGHT REVUE
                CBS Chicago   ann: Mike Wallace

            Guest: Buddy Clark

            <u>Yes, We Have No Bananas</u> - City Slickers
            <u>Dorothy Shay</u> - "The Sample Song"
            <u>Happy New Year</u> - City Slickers and Dorothy Shay
            <u>Buddy Clark</u> - "Ballerina"
            <u>I've Found a New Baby</u> - Big Band
            <u>Dorothy Shay</u> - "Two-Gun Harry"
            <u>Loch Lomond</u> - Doodles Weaver
            Triangular medley:
                Buddy Clark - "There's a Small Hotel"
                Dorothy Shay - "Penthouse Serenade"
                <u>Home on the Range</u> - City Slickers

Note: "New Years Resolution" is the listed title on a reference acetate in Jones' files, cut by Kay Studios, Chicago

<u>Downbeat</u> Magazine has just voted Spike Jones "King of Corn"
for the sixth consecutive year. The December poll results:-

            1. Spike Jones   699
            2. Guy Lombardo   331
            3. Sammy Kaye   95
            4. Red Ingle   90
            5. Vaughn Monroe   44

"Some of these, like Phil Harris, may be former swing bands
that have climbed on the corn wagon. Their total income will be well
over three million dollars...they will use up, in the course of their
corn-certs, 1200 hats, including turbans, helmets, umpires' masks...
turkish towels, fire 3,000 rounds of phony stage ammunition, wear out
eight dozen stuffed ducks, 450 pairs of red flannel underwear, fifty
washboards and a rubber bird cage. They will play...to about 12 million fans, and their most requested number...will be a tender little
love lyric called 'Pass the Biscuits, Mirandy'".
                (<u>Varsity</u>, Apr 49)

Emilio Malione leaves the Revue after the final Chicago
performance of 3 Jan 48, and is replaced by John E. Gollobith, (<u>Jack
Golly</u>) on sax/clar. Golly contributes 'straight' arrangements for the
Revue and possesses a quality character voice.

1948 tour personnel, see 9/10 Feb 48

181

4 January, 1948 (SUN)
                    KRNT Aud, Des Moines, Iowa (159,819)
                    Details as 6 Apr 47 (sold out)

          "4PM - at Walgreens SJ bubble gum (BG) appearance, no
          newspaper ads - 80 people"

                    "Routine of show for one nighters:"

                                        Act II
    1. Hotcha Cornya   1. Shiek
    2. Chloe   2. Bill King juggler
    3. Dr. Birdbath   3. Flashbulb Freddy
    4. Bettyjo Huston   4. Helen Grayco
    5. Always Hurt   5. Doodles Weaver
    6. Geo. Rock - Minka   6. Czardas
    7. Black Magic(Gas bucket bit)7. Hawaiian
    8. Holiday   8. Glow Worm
    9. Stalin - F. Morgan   9. Sir Fredric Gas
    10. Baseball   10. Finale - Cocktails
    11. Robert '& Renee - King ball bit
                        - Little - Martin
                        - dual
                        - Gas Oxydol
    12. Geo. Rock - Bubble Gum
    13. Liebestraum

          "Concessions - pitched (1) Sax-a-phones, (2) Programs,
                    (3) Bubble Gum"

          Note: see appendix i re: Sax-a-phones

5 January, 1948 (MON)
                    Auditorium, Omaha, Neb (223,844)
                    Details as 8 June 47 (good house)

          "4PM Walgreens, SJ BG contest (100 people) no ad in news-
          paper; World Herald - took Little, Martin, Birdbath & 3
          contest SJ BG pict for Tues. paper (Lighting inadequate)

6 January, 1948 (TUES)
                    High School Aud, Quincy, Ill (40,469)
                    8:30 PM
                    Capacity: 2020 (sold out 2 weeks before)
                    Scale: 3.60, 3.00, 2.40, 1.80, 1.20

          Interviews: 11AM Roger (?) on WGEM; 3PM Spike '& Doc on
          WTAD with Hal Bartin; 3:30 Doc on WGEM with Warren Clark;
          4PM Walgreens - SJ BG contest (1000); 4:30 Harris' Music
          Store (800) Roger Donley, Doc, Martin, Little; 8PM Doc,
          Spike, Doodles, Roger, Freddy Morgan, Rock int(erview)
          backstage (wire recorded) to be B'cast 5PM Wed WQDI(FM)

7 January, 1948 (WED)
                    Municipal Aud, Burlington, Ia (25,832)
                    Details as 22 Feb 47 (sold out)

          Interviews: 4PM SJ BG contest at Walgreens (700); 4:15 to
          4:45 Spike & Doc on KBUR with Dick Mosens

8 January, 1948 (THURS)

                              182

Masonic Temple, Davenport, Ia (66,039)
8:30 PM
Details as 11 June 47 (sold out)

Interviews: 4PM Walgreens SJ BG contest - wire recorded
by KSTT; 4PM Parkers Rec. Dept. - wire recorded by WOC;
4:30 RCA - party reception at auditorium

"If Spike Jones ever decided to look for a new home, he
could do worse than locate in Davenport.
"The folks in these parts like the young man who has made
his first million via corn.
"They proved it Thursday night...they packed the Masonic
Temple to the chandeliers...
"No matter how thin you cut it, you still get corn - and
it's corn the thousands like because at 11:00, they still hung around
and asked for more.
"Spike had an added number Thursday night...the birthday of
business manager (Ralph Wonders)...he was presented with a cake on
which the candles glowed.
"It's something to pack the Masonic Temple once, but when a
fellow can do that in his fourth appearance and his sixth show in one
year's time - well, it looks as if vaudeville is here to stay."
(undated, unidentified Davenport newspaper)

9 January, 1948 (FRI) - SPOTLIGHT REVUE
              CBS Chicago   ann: Mike Wallace

        Guest: Nellie Lutcher

        Charlie My Boy - City Slickers
        Dorothy Shay - "It Was Just a Friendly Feeling
          On My Part"
        People Are Funnier Than Anybody - Joe Siracusa,
          Dr.Birdbath, Freddy & Dick Morgan
        Nellie Lutcher - "Do You or Don't You Love Me?"
        Lullaby of Broadway - Big Band
        Dorothy Shay - "My Song"
        Ragtime Cowboy Joe - Doodles Weaver
        Conversation medley:
            Nellie Lutcher - "Three Little Words"
            Dorothy Shay - "Say It Isn't So"
            Whispering - City Slickers

10 January, 1948 (SAT)
              Armory, Springfield, Ill (75,508)
              Capacity: 5480 (sold out)
              Scale: 3.60, 3.00, 2.40, 1.80, 1.20

        Interviews: 4PM Walgreens Drug Store BG contest (300);
        4PM Spike autograph sessin Myers Dept. Store (Mayor present-
        ed Spike with Key to City) wire recorded and b cast on WTAX
        at 5:15; 3:45 Fire Chief & City Comm. made Spike an Honorary
        Fire Chief. Fire Engine - hook & ladder - went to train &
        took Spike to (4PM) rec. sessions. "Taxi to BG contest .50
        - Calls to radio stations .20 - newspapers 1.25" Pullman
        cars - Red Fork SJ1 & McPherson SJ 2 remained in Springfield
        - took chartered bus to Decatuer date on Sunday"

11 January, 1948 (SUN)
              High School Aud, Decatur, Ill (59,305)
              Capacity: 4153 (sold out)

183

"Phone calls to R Station .10" - "papers .10"

12 January, 1948 (MON)
            Armory, Peoria, Ill (205,187)
            Capacity: 5000 (sold out)

    Interviews: 2PM Doc on WWSL with Myles Foland; 3:30 on
WMMJ with Berne Enterline; 4:40 on WMBD with Glenn Ken-
singer; 4PM Walgreen BG contest. "Calls to R. Stat. .40"
"Taxi from contest to Aud. .75" - "Papers .25"

13 January, 1948 (TUES)
            Municipal Aud, Grand Rapids, Mich (164,292)
            Details as 25 Mar 47 (sold out)

    Interviews: 4:30 BG contest at Walgreens; 7PM George
Rock, Joe Siracusa & Doc on WJEF with Nat Bryant

14 January, 1948 (WED)
            C.H.S. Aud, Kalamazoo, Mich (54, 079)
            Details as 26 Mar 47

    Interviews: 4PM Walgreens BG contest; 4:30 to 5:00 Doc,
Doodles & Spike on WKZO with Bob Tazelaar; 5:45 to 6 on
WJFG with Warren Anderson

15 January, 1948 (THURS)
            Murat Temple, Indianapolis, Ind (386,972)
            Details as 26 Oct 47

16 January, 1948 (FRI) - SPOTLIGHT REVUE
            CBS Chicago   ann: Mike Wallace

        Guest: Jan August

            Baby Face - City Slickers
            Dorothy Shay - "Mountain Lullaby"
            *Ballerina - voc Paul Judson
            Jan August - "Hungarian Rhapsody"
            Get Happy - Big Band
            Dorothy Shay - "Please Don't Play Number
                Six tonight"
            *Near You - Doodles Weaver
            Hawaiian medley:
                Jan August - "Sweet Leilani"
                Dorothy Shay - "Blue Hawaii"
                On the Beach at Waikiki - City Slickers

        *issued on MF Distribution LPs 205/4 ("Near You"
            edited with 21 Nov 47 version)

    Note: "Ballerina" uses themes which are later incorporated
in "Dance of the Hours" and "Rhapsody From Hunger(y)"

17 January, 1948 (SAT)
            Armory, Duluth, Minn (101,065)
            7:15 & 9:45 PM
            Capacity: 3700
            Scale: 3.60, 3.00, 2.40, 1.80, 1.20

                        184

Interviews: 4PM BG contest (train late, due 11AM, arr.
5:20PM) - appeared at 5:30, 200 kids still on hand; 4PM
b'cast of contest scheduled on KDAL - "We couldn't make it
train 5-1/2 hrs. late"

18 January, 1948 (SUN)
Municipal Aud, Minneapolis, Minn (402,307)
Details as 20 Feb 47 (7,000 attended)

"4PM BG contest - Walgreens"

"The secret of Jones' success is vulgarity and noise in
about equal - and heaping - proportions. The comedy is slapstick with
no holds barred...some of the buffoon-musicians...funny as Ringling
clowns. The sound effects, as before, ranged from honking auto horns
to plates smashed with a hammer to pistol shots. Musical instruments
ranged from tubas that gushed water to harps made from toilet seats.
"The Jones' entertainment takes the form of a wild and weird
vaudeville show, the music is reminiscent of Olsen and Johnson. The
effect is reminiscent of Vesuvius in eruption."
(Minneapolis Star, 19 Jan 48)

19 January, 1948 (MON)
Coliseum, Sioux Falls, S.D. (40,832)
9:00 PM (sold out)
Details as 14 June 47

20 January, 1948 (TUES)
Orpheum Theatre, Sioux City, Ia (82,364)
Details as 19 June 47 (two shows - sold out)

Interviews: 12:15 to 12:30 Doc on KSCJ with Don Stone;
4PM Walgreens BG contest. "Taxi from train to b'cast
interview .50"

21 January, 1948 (WED)
Paramount Theatre, Waterloo, Ia (51,743)
4:00 (1200), 7:00 (1900), 9:40 (1900)
Capacity: 1843(1)

Interviews: Wire recordings: KAYX - meet at station on
arrival (with Ray Starr and Erling 'Jorgey' Jorgensen);
KWWL - Spike's dressing room

"...here by rail from Sioux City only two hours and 10 min-
utes ahead of show time, and Water Street between East Fourth and
Fifth streets...blocked off until cars have been unloaded.
"Evening performances of the Revue are at 7 and 9:30 p.m.
All seats have been sold for both shows."
(unidentified newspaper, 19 Jan 48)
"No one knows for sure what went on at the Paramount theatre
from about 4 p.m. to midnight yesterday...A sign outside said that
Spike Jones was inside on the stage with his Amvets-sponsored Musical
Depreciation revue.
"Guns were shot, and ducks fell from the ceiling...Doves, or
reasonable facsimiles thereof, flew around the joint. Two guys spent
most of the show sitting with the orchestra, one guy reading
Collier's and the other knitting.
"A skunk was thrown out of a big horn.
"A midget and a giant kept running across the stage at in-
decent intervals, and even got down into the audience, the midget to
whack customers on the head and the giant to sell bubble gum. Automobile horns, cow bells, old tomato cans, washboards and a formidable

185

array of improbable objects served as musical instruments.

"Musicians were squirted with seltzer bottles, and the giant broke eggs into a frying pan held by the midget as integral parts of a Rube Goldberg chain reaction.

"Everyone wore strange and wonderful suits. A man called Sir Frederic Gas played tunes on a crooked tree branch.

"There probably isn't much like it anywhere around today... their zestful type of humor is reminiscent of an old and better day at burlesque. Jones never lets things get dull, even though it wasn't all strictly tomfoolery. Watching a Jones performance is a lot like watching a three ring circus. Lots of things happen. He had the crowd in the aisles most of Wednesday afternoon and night.

"He can come back anytime" K.M.
(unidentified, undated newspaper)

22 January, 1948 (THURS)
              Armory, Rockford, Ill (84,637)
              Details as '30 Nov' (46)

    Interviews: 4PM BG contest - Walgreens; 5PM made trans. int. with Herb Anderson for WROK

23 January, 1948 (FRI) - SPOTLIGHT REVUE
              CBS Chicago   ann: Mike Wallace

              Guest: Jack Owens

              I'm Looking Over a Four Leaf Clover - City
                Slickers
              Dorothy Shay - "It's the Little Things You
                Do That Count"
              My Old Flame - Paul Judson, Sir Frederick Gas
              Jack Owens - "How Soon"
              Dorothy Shay - "Somebody Loves Me"
              Comin' Through the Rye - Doodles Weaver
              Wonderful Gals medley:
                Jack Owens - "Cynthia"
                Dorothy Shay - "Mary"
                Kate - City Slickers

24 January, 1948 (SAT)
              Travel to Flint, Mich

25 January, 1948 (SUN)
              IMA Aud, Flint, Mich (151,543)
              Details as 5 Mar 47

    Interviews: 6:45PM Spike & Doc on WWOK

26 January, 1948 (MON)
              Prudden Aud, Lansing, Mich (78,753)
              7:00 & 9:30 PM
              Details as 6 Mar 47

    Interviews: 4PM BG contest at Walgreens (400), wire recorded for b'cast on WILS at 5PM; Gladis Gardner & Doc on WJIM with "Wee Willie" Dougherty - B'cast Mon night "Taxi to BG .50" (Lighting inadequate)

27 January, 1948 (TUES)
              Municipal Aud, Saginaw, Mich (82,794)
               7:00 & 9:30 PM

                    Capacity: 2800
                    Scale: 2.40, 1.80, 1.20, (500 seats @.25 ea)

    Interviews: 5 to 5:15 Spike, Doc, Doodles, Joe S., Gas on
WKNX with Bob Maxwell; 5:15 to 5:30 Doc & Joe Syracusa on
WSAM "Taxi to b'cast with Joe Syracusa .75"

28 January, 1948 (WED)
                    Sports Arena, Toledo, Ohio (282,349)
                    Capacity: 8000 (new arena)
                    Scale: 3.00, 2.40, 1.80, 1.20

    Interviews: 4PM BG contest @ Walgreens; Doodles on WTOD;
Transcribed interview on WTOL, b'cast 7PM on Sat. "Telegram
to CJBC Toronto Canada .73" - "Taxi to BG contest, .50"
(no footlights, no curtains)

29 January, 1948 (THURS)
                    College Aud, Terra Haute, Ind (62,693)
                    7:00 & 9:30 PM
                    Capacity: 1732
                    Scale: 2.50, 2.08, 1.75, 1.00

    Interviews: 4PM Doc & Doodles on WTHI with Lee Kennedy;
5:20 to 5:30 on WBOW with Don McCarthy "Taxi to radio
int. .50" - "Newspapers .80"

30 January, 1948 (FRI) - SPOTLIGHT REVUE
                    CBS Chicago   ann: Mike Wallace

          Guest: John Laurenz

          Hindustan - City Slickers
          Dorothy Shay - "Flat River, Missouri"
          There's No Business Like Show Business
             (Cavalcade of Vaudeville)
          John Laurenz - "All Dressed Up With a
             Broken Heart"
          Dorothy Shay - "How Lucky You Are"
          Oh Suzannah - Doodles Weaver
          Round-up medley:
             John Laurenz - "Sierra Madre"
             Laurenz, Dorothy Shay - "Don't Fence Me In"
             San Antonio Rose - City Slickers

31 January, 1948 (SAT)
                    Municipal Aud, Milwaukee, Wisc. (587,472)
                    Details as 5 Apr 47

    "4PM BG contest @ Walgreens - called off, crowd too big
(however, we visited there)" - "Doodles missed entire show -
accident in Chicago" - "FAKE"

    Following the Friday night b'cast and show, Doodles visited
a bar in the theatre area, bragging about the $100,000 ring on his
finger . He was later badly beaten and robbed in the theatre parking
lot. "FAKE", written in another's handwriting next to the PR-Doodles
reference, referred to Weaver's ring, worth about $1. He called after
the muggers, "Don't you want my watch too?". They did, running off
with his Mickey Mouse watch.

    "Spike Jones and his City Slickers...coming to the Aud. Jan

                              187

31, feel that through their tomfoolery they are helping add to the
world what is sadly lacking - real honest to goodness hearty laughter
..."

"The genuine slot machine on the stage gives out the sweetest music of all, however, right before the very eyes of the audience. It gives out with the 'jack-pot', some $24.35 rolls out of it
every night when George Rock...hits a higher note than Harry James
calling Betty Grable to dinner...on his dinner horn."
(Milwaukee Sentinel, 28 Dec 47)

1 February, 1948 (SUN)
                Coliseum, Evansville, Ind (97,682)
                Capacity: 3500

        Interviews: Cut Rec. for WDEA to be played Mon AM Feb
        2nd; 4PM BG contest at Walgreens. "Taxi to BG contest .75
        - taxi to & from int. $1.00"

2 February, 1948 (MON)
                Memorial Aud, Louisville, Ky (319,277)
                Capacity: 2340

        Interviews: 1:30 PM Doc on SHAS "Man in the Street"
        B'cast; 3:15 on WGRC record show; 4PM Walgreen BG contest

3 February, 1948 (TUES)
                Taft Theatre Aud, Cincinnati, Ohio (455,610)
                Capacity: 2500 (one show)
                Scale: 3.60, 3.00, 2.40, 1.80, 1.20

4 February, 1948 (WED)
                Memorial Aud, Springfield, Ohio (70,662)
                Details as 20 Mar 47

        Interviews: 4:15 to 4:30 Doc & Joe Syracusa on WIZE with
        Wendell Brakefield(by transcription); 4PM BG contest at
        Walgreens

5 February, 1948 (THURS)
                Memorial Aud, Dayton, Ohio (210,718)
                Details as 23 Oct 47

        Interviews: Spike, Doodles & Doc made wire recording with
        Gene Barry at R.R. Union Sta. - played on WING at 1:30AM
        as we left Dayton

6 February, 1948 (FRI) - SPOTLIGHT REVUE
                CBS Chicago   ann: Mike Wallace

        Guests: the Mills Brothers

                I'm Just Wild About Harry - City Slickers
                Dorothy Shay - "Feudin' and Fightin'"
                I Kiss Your Hand Madame - voc Paul Judson
                Mills Bros. - "Across the Alley From the Alamo"
                Liza - Big Band
                Dorothy Shay - "So Far"
                Peg O' My Heart - Doodles Weaver
                Toyland medley:
                    Mills Bros. - "Paper Doll"
                    Dorothy Shay - "Dance With the Dolly"
                    Oh, You Beautiful Doll/Wedding Of the
                                Painted Doll - City Slickers

7 February, 1948 (SAT)
                Coliseum, Marion, Ind (26,767)
                    Capacity:6000

    Interview: 2:30 to 3:00 PM Doc & Doodles on WBAT with
    Dick Aker. "Newspapers .10 - call to station .10 - taxi
    fares to & from RR sta. with Spike 3.50" - "Doc - ill
    here, missed show completely. 1st time since Hartford,
    Conn April 1947

8 February, 1948 (SUN)
                Adams H.S., South Bend, Ind (101,268)
                    Capacity: 3000

    "1:30 BG appearances at Walgreens (N.S.G.). "Roger(?)
    left show - Bruno(?) has baby 7lb 6oz" - "Opposition -
    Tommy Dorsey at Palais Royale Ballroom"

9 February (MON), 10 February (TUES), 1948
                (Arena) Coliseum, Toronto, Ont (804,349)
                    Capacity: 12,000
                    Scale: 2.25, 1.75, 1.25

    Interviews: 1:30 to 2:00 PM Doc on CJBC with Byng Whittaker.
    "Calls to R. station .40 - taxi to radio int. & return 1.50"

        Note: The following dated personnel listing, copied verbatim
but not part of the itinerary, is of interest in that it shows the
entire troupe on SJ1 & SJ2. Possibly used to facilitate border cross-
ing

                                Feb. 9 1948

    Spike Jones (Lindly A. Jones) 36 Long Beach, Cal.
    George Rock 28 Farmer City, Ill
    Dick Morgan (Richard Morgan) 43 Boulder, Colo.
    Jack Golly (John E. Gollobith) 25 Hanover, Illinois
    Dr. Horatio Q. Birdbath (A. Purves Pullen) 38
                                Philadelphia, Pa.
    Roger Donley 25 Quincy, Ill
    Dick Gardner (Richard B. Gardner) 29 Mintvale, Utah
    Paul Leu 34 Delta, Ohio
    Joe Siracusa 25 Cleveland, Ohio
    Joe Colvin 27 Oilton, Okla.
    Merle Howard 34 Winona, Minn.
    Ina Souez (Ina Rains) Windsor, Colo.
    Helen Grayco (Helen Greco) 23 Tacoma, Wash.
    Gladis Gardner 18 Lansing Mich.
    Gloria Gardner 18 Lansing Mich.
    Paul Judson (Irving Judson) 31 Seattle, Wash
    Doodles Weaver (Winstead Weaver) 34 Los Angeles, Calif.
    Frankie Little (Frankie Little Scalia) 47 Palermo, Italy
    Bill King (Wm. King) 28 Muncie, Ind.
    Jr. Martin (J. Lockhard Martin) 31 Wst. Bridge Water, Pa.
    Freddy Morgan (Phillip Morgenstern) 37 New York, NY
    Paulette Paul (Loraine Y. Paul) 26 Oakland, Cal.
    Rubel Ray 40 Waterloo, Iowa
    Clarence Robert Prey 29 Wilmington, Cal
    Earl Bennett 28 Kansas City, Ks
    Lester Calvin (Lester Calvin Vesey) 52 Council Bluffs, Ia
    Jack McNaughton 24 Butte, Mont.
    Eddie McCarthy 21 Oakland, Calif.
    O.L. Corkum (Othel Loranzo Corkum) 42 Walla Walla, Wash.

                            189

Ralph Wonders 52 Gettysburg, Pa.
Nina Moore 30 Indianapolis, Ind.
Charles Browne 45 Camden, Maine
Betty Browne 32 Minneapolis, Minn.
Betty Jo Huston 22 Bakersfield, Calif.
Martin M. Yaeger (McCan) 51 Chicago, Ill.
Henry Taylor 40 Brooklyn, N.Y.
Edward A. Brandt 25 Chicago, Ill

Note: Betty Browne and her husband were a knife throwing act
and sold programs in the theatres at this time. Nina Moore was
Spike's secretary.

11 February, 1948 (WED)
    Arena, London, Ont (76,250)
     Capacity: 4317
     Scale: 2.25, 1.75. 1.25

(Could not hear in back of Aud)

12 February, 1948 (THURS)
    Arena, Niagara Falls, Ont (22,000)
     Capacity: 4500
     Scale: 2.25, 1.75, 1.25

Interviews: 6PM Doc & Jr. Martin on CHCV with Gordie Tapp
"4PM Walgreens BG (no adv. - a complete flop) "All personnel
on train by 1:15 AM for customs clearance - Whata hassel!"

13 February, 1948 (FRI) - SPOTLIGHT REVUE
    CBS Statler Ballroom, Buffalo, ann: Martin Tobyn

    Guest: Vic Damone

    Shuffle Off To Buffalo - City Slickers
    Dorothy Shay - "The Sample Song"
    Ill Barkio - Ina Souez with Dr. H.Q. Birdbath
    Vic Damone - "Love Is Just Around the Corner"
    In a Little Spanish Town - Big Band
    Dorothy Shay - "This Can't Be Love"
    How Soon - Doodles Weaver
    Valentine medley:
     Vic Damone - "I Love You"
     Dorothy Shay - "Sweetheart Of All My Dreams"
    I Love You/Spring Song - City Slickers

14 February, 1948 (SAT)
    Cochran H.S. Aud, Johnstown, Pa
     7:00 & 9:00 PM
     Capacity: 1900
     Scale: 3.60, 3.00, 2.40, 1.80

Interviews: Doc, Doodles and Spike on WARD with Bob
Bressler, wire recorded for later b'cast

15 February, 1948 (SUN)
    Armory, Akron, Ohio (244,791)
     7:00 & 9:30 PM
     Capacity: 3700

"4PM BG contest @ Walgreens - good turn out"

190

16 February, 1948 (MON)
                    Kleinhans Aud, Buffalo, NY (575,901)
                         Capacity: 2900
                         Scale: 4.80, 3.60, 3.00, 2.40, 1.80

        Interviews: 2:45 to 3PM Doc on WEBR with Bud Hulich

17 February (TUES), 18 February (WED), 1948
                    Lincoln Aud, Syracuse, NY (225,000)
                         Capacity: 1900

        Interviews: 1:30PM Doc & Spike on WSYR; 2:15 on WAGE; 4
        to 4:30 Doc on WNDR(all on Tues.); Wed. - 4:30 BG contest
        at Walgreens; 4PM Doodles on WFBL; 3PM Doc, Spike, Martin
        & Little appear at Johnson Memorial Hospital

19 February, 1948 (THURS)
                    Armory, Troy, NY (70, 304)
                         Capacity: 4500
                         Scale: 1.90 advance, 2.20 at door

        "Taxi to radio station .50" (WTRY would not cooperate)

20 February, 1948 (FRI) - SPOTLIGHT REVUE
                    CBS New York   ann: Joe King

                    Guest: Buddy Clark

                    Somebody Stole My Gal - City Slickers
                    Dorothy Shay - "The Style To Which I'm Accustomed"
                    Ballerina - voc Paul Judson
                    Buddy Clark - "I'll Dance At Your Wedding"
                    Dorothy Shay - "Bill"
                    I'm Looking Over a Four Leaf Clover - Doodles
                         Weaver
                    George Washington medley:
                         Buddy Clark - "Little White Lies"
                         Dorothy Shay - "They Didn't Believe Me"
                         It's A Sin To Tell A Lie - City Slickers

21 February, 1948 (SAT)
                    Columbus Civic Aud, Rochester, NY
                         7:00 & 9:30 PM
                         Capacity: 2180
                         Scale: 3.60, 3.00, 2.40, 1.80, 1.20

        Interviews: 1 to 1:30 Doc, Merrill & Doodles on WVET;
        3 to 3:30 Doc, Doodles & Spike on WARC; 4:30 to 5:00 on
        SHEC; 4PM BG contest at 5&10 store

22 February, 1948 (SUN)
                    Stambaugh Aud, Youngstown, Ohio (190,000)
                         Capacity: 2604

        Interviews: WFMJ wire recorded backstage to be broadcast
        Mon. night

23 February, 1948 (MON)
                    Jaffe Mosque, Altoona, Pa (80,000?)
                         Details as 8 Apr 47

                              191

24 February (TUES) to 27 February (FRI), 1948
                    Syria Mosque, Pittsburg, Pa
                    Details as 19 Mar 47

         Interviews: Midnight to 12:30 AM Wed. Martin '& Doc on
         KOKA with Bill Brandt. "Eve. taxi to radio int. .75"

27 February, 1948 (FRI) - SPOTLIGHT REVUE
                    CBS Syria Mosque, Pittsburg, ann: Bob Clayton

              Guest: Eddy Arnold

              No, No, Nora - City Slickers
              Dorothy Shay - "Flat River, Missouri"
              *Liebestraum - City Slickers
              Eddy Arnold - "I'll Hold You In My Heart"
              Dorothy Shay - "But Beautiful"
              Sioux City Sue - Doodles Weaver
              Golden West medley:
                  Eddy Arnold - "I'm Thinking Tonight Of
                               My Blue Eyes"
                  Arnold, Dorothy Shay - "Don't Fence Me In"
              San Antonio Rose - City Slickers

              *issued on MF Distribution LPs 205/4,
                  947447, and GO 10016

28 February, 1948 (SAT)
                    Mosque, Harrisburg, Pa (83,893)
                    Details as 17 Apr 47

29 February, 1948 (SUN)
                    Lyric Theatre, Baltimore, Md
                    Capacity: 2600
                    Scale: 3.60, 3.00, 2.40, 1.80, 1.20

1 March, 1948 (MON)
                    Royal Theatre, Reading, Pa (110,568)
                    7:00 '& 9:30 PM
                    Capacity: 2200

         Interviews: 5 to 5:30 PM Doodles on WRAW with Chas. Adams
         and 6 to 6:20 on WHUM "Lost SJ1, SJ2 & baggage car in
         Phila today Mar 1, 1948 - checked in Penn-Sheraton Hotel
         W. Phila, came by bus to Reading, returned to Phila"

2 March, 1948 (TUES)
                    War Memorial Bldg, Trenton, NJ (124,697)
                    7:00 & 9:30 PM
                    Capacity: 1926

         "Cars SJ1 & SJ2 returned to us in Trenton, NJ. To be used
         on & off until Mar. 14"

3 March, 1948 (WED)
                    Lyric Theatre, Bridgeport, Conn (150,000)
                    7:00 & 9:30 PM
                    Capacity: 2400

         Interviews: WNAG Doc & Doodles with Jack Scanlon; WLIZ

                              192

Doc & Doodles with Jack Dahlby; 4:30 BG contest at Walgreens (750)(Mr. Lambo) "Taxi to BG contest .50 - taxi to
radio int. .50 - phone to R. station .20"

4 March, 1948 (THURS)
                    Mosque, Newark, NJ (429,760)
                    Capacity: 3365

Interviews: 3:30 to 4PM Doc on WAAT with Mel Tunis; 4:30
to 4:45 Doc on WHJR with Fred & Alois Harville

5 March, 1948 (FRI) - SPOTLIGHT REVUE
                    CBS New York, NY   ann: Joe King

                    Guest: Francis Craig

                    Please Don't Talk About Me When I'm Gone -
                        City Slickers
                    Dorothy Shay - "It's the Little Things You
                        Do That Count"
                    My Old Flame - Paul Judson, Joe Siracusa, Sir
                        Frederick Gas
                    Francis Craig - "Beg Your Pardon", voc Bob Lamm
                    Dorothy Shay - "The Gentleman Is a Dope"
                    Whiffenpoof Song - Doodles Weaver
                    Keeping Warm medley:
                        Feancis Craig - "Near You"
                        Dorothy Shay - "Close To Me"
                        Side By Side - City Slickers

6 March, 1948 (SAT)
                    for The White House Correspondants' Association
                        for President Truman (Washington, D.C.)

        Note: For this occasion, the Revue is called "Virgin Island
Vertigo or Haphazard Harmonies of 1948". As well, Margaret Truman
entertained this evening, but not accompanied by the Slickers. Eddie
Pripps was the Musical Director.

7 March, 1948 (SUN)
                    War Memorial Aud, Worcester, Mass (193,694)
                        7:00 & 9:20 PM
                        Capacity: 3500
                        Scale: 2.40, 1.80, 1.20

8 March, 1948 (MON)
                    Symphony Hall, Boston, Mass (770,816)
                        Capacity: 2631

Interviews: 3 to 3:30 Doc on WMEX with Jay McMasters;
3:45 to 4PM on WNAC with Verne Williams; 5 to 5:40 on
WEGI with Pricilla Fortesque.

9 March, 1948 (TUES)
                    Springfield Aud, Springfield, Mass (149,554)
                        3:00 & 8:30 PM
                        Capacity: 3600
                        Scale: Mat 1.80(adults), 1.20, .75(kids)
                              Eve 4.20, 3.60, 3.00, 2.40, 1.80

        (Lighting - not ample, inadequate)

193

10 March, 1948 (WED)
                    Atlantic City, NJ

     "Coca Cola Convention, radio show and ent. for dealers"

11 March, 1948 (THURS)
                    Arena, New Haven, Conn (160,645)
                       8:30 PM
                    Capacity: 5400

     "Cars SJ1 & SJ2 left in Stamford, Conn. Took coaches to
     NYC & back"

12 March, 1948 (FRI) - SPOTLIGHT REVUE
                    CBS New York, NY   ann: Joe King

          Guests: Jack Smith and the Clark Sisters

               After You've Gone - City Slickers
               Dorothy Shay - "Responsibility"
               Hawaiian War Chant - City Slickers
               Jack Smith - "Shawnee O'Shay"
               Dorothy Shay - "Love Is So Terrific"
               Sonny Boy - Doodles Weaver
               New York medley:
                    Jack Smith - "Broadway Rhythm"
                    Dorothy Shay - "42nd Street"
                    Give My Regards To Broadway - City Slickers

13 March, 1948 (SAT)
                    Westchester County Center, White Plains, NY
                       Capacity: 4200   (40,327)
                       Scale: 3.00(box), 2.40, 1.80, 1.20

     "Train leaves Stamford Conn for Wash D.C. - lose SJ1 &
     SJ2 & baggage car"

14 March (SUN) to 27 March (SAT), 1948
                    National Theatre, Washington, D.C. (930,000)
                       Capacity: 1660 (3 perf sold out)

     Interviews: Mon Mar 15 11:30 to midnight Doc on WWDC with
     Jackson Lowe; Tues Mar 16 1:30 to 2AM Doodles on WWDC
     with Les Sands; WTOP trans Spike, Doodles & Doc with Bill
     Jenkins - to be used Wed Mar 17; 2:30 to 3Pm Doodles &
     Spike 16 Mar on WINX; Wed Mar 17 1:15 to 1:45 AM Doc &
     George Rock on WWDC with Les Sands; Wed Mar 17 2PM Spike
     on WQQM; 2:15 to 2:30 PM Tues Mar 23 Doc on WWDC Tony
     Wakeman; Wed Mar 24 3to4PM Martin, Little & Doc ent. Boys
     Reform School; 10:30 to 11AM Martin, Little & Doc on WOL;
     Landsburgh Dept. Store - Gardner Twins & Helen Grayco
     modeling; Thurs Mar 25 2to3PM at Landsburgh record auto-
     graph session - Spike, Doc, Rock, Martin & Little

          Note: Programs at this time credit Jeff Griffith, vocal/act,
     among the Slickers personnel

19 March, 1948 (FRI) - SPOTLIGHT REVUE
                    CBS National Theatre, Washington, ann: Joe King

               Guests: the Milt Herth Trio

                              194

<u>Missouri Waltz</u> - City Slickers
Dorothy Shay - "Grandpa's Getting Younger
    Every Day"
<u>Morpheus</u> - feat Freddy Morgan and Spike Jones
<u>Milt Herth Trio</u> - "Herthquake Boogie"
Dorothy Shay - "Just One Of Those Things"
<u>When the Red Red Robin Comes Bob Bob Bobbin'</u>
    <u>Along</u> - Doodles Weaver
Salute To Spring medley:
    Milt Herth Trio - "Bye Bye Blackbird"
    Dorothy Shay - "The Saucy Little Bird
        On Nellie's Hat"
    <u>Listen To the Mocking Bird</u> - feat Dr. H.Q.
        Birdbath

29 March, 1948 (FRI) - SPOTLIGHT REVUE
        CBS National Theatre, Washington, ann: Joe King

    Guest: Jan August

    <u>Ain't She Sweet</u> - City Slickers
    Dorothy Shay - "The Sample Song"
    <u>Slap 'Er Down Again Pa</u>(Rhythm Opera) - feat
        Jones, Gas, Rock, Siracusa, Freddy Morgan
    Jan August - "Oye Negra"
    Dorothy Shay - "Horray For Love"
    <u>When It's Springtime In the Rockies</u> - Doodles
        Weaver
    Spring medley:
        Jan August - "Love Your Magic Spell Is
            Everywhere"
        Dorothy Shay - "Blue Skies"
        <u>April Showers</u> - City Slickers

    Note: The rhythm opera was a soap-opera set to a re-occur-
ing chant, a device often used by Spike to extend feature skits for
radio and, later, television.

28 March (SUN) to 1 April (THURS), 1948

    "Off - cast went home or other cities"

2 April, 1948 (FRI) - SPOTLIGHT REVUE
        CBS Fairgrounds, Indianapolis, ann: Mike Wallace

    Guests: the Ten Harmonaires

    <u>When My Sugar Walks Down the Street</u> -
        <u>City Slickers</u>
    Dorothy Shay - "The Old Apple Tree"
    <u>Down In Jungle Town</u> - voc Paul Judson, Freddy
        Morgan
    Harmonaires - "Kentucky Babe"
    Dorothy Shay - "What Is This Thing Called Love?"
    <u>Beg Your Pardon</u> - Doodles Weaver
    Slang medley:
        Harmonaires - "Jeepers Creepers"
        Dorothy Shay - "Goody Goody"
        <u>Oh By Jingo</u> - City Slickers

    "Meet @ Coliseum Ill. Fairground for B'cast & show. Int.
Harvester & Coca Cola. 10,000 attended. 1-1/2 hour warm-

195

up show"

3 April (SAT) to 17 April (SAT), 1948
                    Music Hall, Detroit, Mich (1,623,452)
                    Capacity: 1900
                    Scale: Eve 3.60, 2.40, 1.20
                         Mat 2.40, 1.80, 1.20

          Interviews: Spike with Larry Gentile on "Dawn Patrol"
          CKLW (MBS stat.) Windsor, Ont

          "Spike, I don't know when I've seen a better show!"
          "Why - thank you Larry"
          "Spike, I'd like to get into some of the background of your
show. Now, I saw the show Sunday afternoon at the Music Hall and I
noticed all of your contraptions look like they would fill a couple
of rail-road cars. I was wondering how you managed to get around the
country and even play one-nighters with all that?"
          "Your guess is exactly right, Larry. It does (fill complete-
ly with equipment) two baggage cars and the cast fill two pullmans...
We were in Indianapolis doing our Coca-Cola show before we came in
here to open at the Music Hall. Now our stage hands came straight
over from Washington...We kept two stage hands with us, then we sent
three of our own men over here on Friday evening. They started
setting all the electrical equipment, focusing the lights and hanging
the back-drops along with a local crew of around eleven or twelve.
We've never hung our show in less than 12 hours. It takes that long
to hang our legitimate (Revue) show...about five hours to break it
down...
          "When we do our Friday night Coca-Cola show, we augment our
band in order to accompany Miss Shay, and in order to play the Coca-
Cola theme - that beautiful theme...and also we have a band in the
pit when we play longer than one-night stands. It's the band that
plays an overture while the Milt Gross curtain lights up and plays an
exit march...However, what you saw on the stage, that is our band
that we carry with us. We have 26 people on the stage, including all
the acts..."
          The interview, similar to many others at this time, gave
good insight into the total organization of the staging, traveling
and set-up of the Revue. The importance of each employee on lighting
and sound is emphasized. No gag - from the lyrics of each song; the
doves that fly out of Miss Souez' hat in "Glow Worm"; the pigs that
come down the slide in "Black Magic"; the water that pours from Doc's
tuba; to the exact amount of gunpowder in each cartridge (for exact
tuning) - was to be missed.
          Along with the secretary, valet and carpenter, there are em-
ployees in charge of sound, lighting, electricity, setting up the
show and breaking down the stage with its stands, instruments, lights
and the fragile, neon-lit Milton Gross back-drop curtain.
          Although factual and serious, Spike concluded with:- "It's
quite a 'clambake', not like Vaughn Monroe where he just gets out and
sings "Racing For the Moon", and everybody faints - we do it the hard
way!"   (Spike Jones/Larry Gentile, Dawn Patrol, CKLW, Windsor, Ont)

9 April, 1948 (FRI) - SPOTLIGHT REVUE
                    CBS Olympic Stadium, Detroit,   ann: Mike Wallace

          Guest: Mel Torme

          Yes Sir, That's My Baby - City Slickers
          Dorothy Shay - "Just a Friendly Feeling
              On My Part"
          When a Gypsy Makes His Violin Cry - feat Sir
              Frederick Gas
          Mel Torme - "The Best Things In Life Are Free"

                              196

Dorothy Shay - "I May Be Wrong"
April Showers - Doodles Weaver
Dream medley:
    Mel Torme - "Wrap Your Troubles In Dreams"
    Dorothy Shay - "Did You Ever See a Dream
               Walking?"
    You Tell Me Your Dream - City Slickers

     Note: 15,000 employees of Ford Motor Co. and their families
attended this b'cast, which was preceded by a 1-1/2 hr. warm-up show.
The lengthy Gas feature, "When a Gypsy..." contains themes which are
later adapted as "Rhapsody From Hunger(y)"

16 April, 1948 (FRI) - SPOTLIGHT REVUE
              CBS Music Hall, Detroit,   ann: Mike Wallace

      Guests: the Dinning Sisters

     Don't Bring Lulu - City Slickers
     Dorothy Shay - "Two-Gun Harry"
     There's Nothing Like a Circus - City Slickers
     Dinning Sisters - "Harlem Sandman"
     Dorothy Shay - "Too Marvelous For Words"
     Take Me Out To the Ball Game - Doodles Weaver
     Dance medley:
         Dinning Sisters - "Papa, Won't You Dance
               With Me?"
         Dorothy Shay - "Dancing In the Dark"
         Stumbling - City Slickers

     Note: 1900 employees of Packard Motor Co. and their families
attended this b'cast, which was preceded by a 1-1/2 hr. warm-up show.

19 April (MON) to 24 April (SAT), 1948
              Music Hall, Cleveland, Ohio (878,336)
              Eve show Mon to Sat(except Fri), Mat on Sat
              Capacity: 3300
              Scale: 3.70, 3.00, 2.50, 1.80

     Interviews: 1PM 21 Apr, Doc on WTAM with Joe Zohn; 8:30
to 9:30 AM 22 Apr on WJMO with Gene Carroll; BG contest
at Gray Drug Store 4PM (Wed 21 Apr) Doc, Little, Martin

23 April, 1948 (FRI) - SPOTLIGHT REVUE
              CBS Little Theatre, Cleveland,   ann: Ed Stokes

      Guest: Vic Damone

     Down By the O-Hi-O - City Slickers
     Dorothy Shay - "Joan of Arkansas"
     Take Me Out To the Ball Game - feat Dick and
        Freddy Morgan, Joe Siracusa
     Vic Damone - "Lillibollero"
     Dorothy Shay - "You Are So Thoughtless Of Me"
     Down By the Old Mill Stream - Doodles Weaver
     Wonderful Gals medley:
         Vic Damone - "Theresa"
         Dorothy Shay - "Peggy O'Neil"
         Martha - City Slickers

     Note: 900 attended this 'Little Theatre' broadcast.

25 April, 1948 (SUN)
                    Memorial Hall, Columbus, Ohio (306,087)
                       3:00 & 8:30 PM
                       Capacity: 3350

        "Dr. Birdbath replaced "Old MacDonald" with "Mockingbird"
        - SJ1 & SJ2 + baggage started again here for our concert
        tour" - "Newspapers .30 - new prop fish pole 1.00"

26 April, 1948 (MON)
                    County Aud, Jackson, Mich (47,656)
                       7:00 & 9:00 PM
                       Capacity: 1900
                       Scale: 3.00, 2.50, 2.00, 1.50

27 April, 1948 (TUES)
                    Municipal Aud, Saginaw, Mich (82,794)
                       7:00 & 9:30 PM
                       Capacity: 2800
                       Scale: 3:00, 2.50, 2.00, 1.50

        "BG contest 5PM at Cunningham Drugstore" - "Train to
        Detroit, bus to Saginaw & ret to Detroit"

28 April, 1948 (WED)
                    Sports Arena, Toledo, Ohio (282,349)
                       8:30 PM
                       Capacity: 8000 (sold out)

        "Phone call to Cleveland regarding purchase of a prop
        skunk 1.50" (platform too high. Trampoline & acrobatic
        acts worked on floor)(could not sell BG)

29 April, 1948 (THURS)
                    Kellogg Aud, Battle Creek, Mich (43,453)
                       7:00 (sold out), 9:30 PM (G.)

        "B'cast to Percy Jones Hosp. from stage of our 2nd show"

30 April, 1948 (FRI) - SPOTLIGHT REVUE
                    CBS Medinah Temple, Chicago,   ann: Mike Wallace

                    Guests: the Page Cavanaugh Trio

                    Baby Face - City Slickers
                    Dorothy Shay - "I'm My Own Grandma"
                    None But the Lonely Heart - Helen Grayco,
                       Spike Jones
                    Page Cavanaugh Trio - "I Would Do Anything
                       For You"
                    Dorothy Shay - "Love Is So Terrific"
                    My Old Kentucky Home - Doodles Weaver
                    Blue Mood medley:
                       Page Cavanaugh Trio - "Blue Moon"
                       Dorothy Shay -"Am I Blue?"
                       Blues My Naughty Sweetie Gave To Me -
                          City Slickers

        Note: 4750 employees of Illinois Bell Telephone Co. and
their families attended this show, which was preceded by a 1-1/2 hr.
warm-up show. "Rehearsal @ 1PM"

                              198

1 May, 1948 (SAT)
                          Armory (Mun. Aud), Sheboygan, Wisc (40,638)
                          8:30 PM (sold out)
                          Details as 25 Feb 47

"SJ1 & SJ2 + parked without steam or elec. lights"

2 May, 1948 (SUN)
                          John Adams H.S. Aud, South Bend, Ind (101,268)
                          2:30 & 8:30 PM
                          Details as 8 Feb 48

3 May, 1948 (MON)
                          Masonic Aud, Davenport, Ia (66,039)
                          Details as 8 Jan 48

Interviews: on WOC Tues AM "Left Chicago 11AM CST by
coach - SJ1 & SJ2 to join us later in Rock Island, Ill."

4 May, 1948 (TUES)
                          Wharton Field House, Moline, Ill (34,608)
                          8:30 PM
                          Capacity: 6500

Interviews: Doc, Doodles on WHBF Rock Island 11:15 to
midnight 3 May with John O'Connor; 5:15 to 5:45PM on WOC
4 May with Harold; on KSTT with Gegg Dunn; 5PM Spike on
WQUA "left cars in Rock Island, Ill"

5 May, 1948 (WED)
                          Municipal Aud, Cedar Rapids, Ia (62,120)
                          8:30 PM
                          Capapcity: 3150

Interviews: 12 noon Doc on WMT with Dean Lanfear; 4:15 to
5PM on KCRG with Wally Pearson - contest party, 200 teen-
agers, Doc & Doodles - Spike could not make it

6 May, 1948 (THURS)
                          Day off in Chicago

7 May, 1948 (FRI) - SPOTLIGHT REVUE
                          CBS Medinah Temple, Chicago,   ann: Mike Wallace

                          Guest: Burl Ives

                          Row, Row, Row - City Slickers
                          Dorothy Shay - "Making Love Mountain Style"
                          There's No Business Like Show Business -
                              City Slickers Production
                        Burl Ives - "It Takes a Worried Man"
                        Dorothy Shay - "A Couple of Stay-At-Homes"
                        Chicago - Doodles Weaver
                        Matrimony medley:
                              Burl Ives - "I Wish I Were Single Again"
                              Ives, Dorothy Shay - "I Wanna Get Married"
                          Wedding Bells Are Breaking Up That Old Gang
                                  Of Mine - City Slickers

Note: 5000 employees of the Electro-Motive Division of
General Motors and their families attended this broadcast, which was

199

preceded by a one-hour show

8 May, 1948 (SAT)
                    Danville H.S. Aud, Danville, Ill (36,919)
                      7:00 & 9:00 PM
                      Capacity: 1700
                      Scale: 3.60, 3.00, 1.80, 1.20

Interviews: 12 noon parade with local orch. from train to
town - Doc & Eddie (Brandt); 2:30 to 3PM Doc on WDAN with
Joan Henry; 4PM record auto. session @ Block & Kuhl new
record store

9 May, 1948 (SUN)
                    Armory, Galesburg, Ill (28,976)
                      3:00 & 8:30 PM
                      Capacity: 2800

Interviews: 1:30 to 1:45PM Doc on WGIL with D.B. (Bunk)
Olson; 7 to 7:30PM Weaver on WGIL with Kermit Allen
(lighting inadequate)

10 May, 1948 (MON)
                    Armory, Peoria, Ill (105,187)
                      8:30 PM (sold out)
                      Details as 12 Jan 48

Interviews: 3:30 to 4:30PM rec. session @ Jay!, Spike &
Doc(autograph session) "Taxi to autograph session .75 -
R.R. strike settled - keep SJ1 & SJ2"

11 May, 1948 (TUES)
                    Jr. H.S. Aud, Champaign, Ill (23,050)
                      Details as 24 Feb 47

Interviews: 4:30 to 4:45 Doc on WDWS with Mark Howard

12 May, 1948 (WED)
                    H.S. Aud, Decatur, Ill (59,305)
                      Details as 11 Jan 48

Interviews: 1:30 to 1:45 Doc on WSOY with Tom Richards;
4:30 to 5PM on WSOY with John B. Guy "Taxi to int. .75"

13 May, 1948 (THURS)
                    Armory, Springfield, Ill (75,508)
                      Details as 10 Jan 48

13 May, 1948 (FRI) - SPOTLIGHT REVUE
                    CBS Municipal Aud, St. Louis, Mo,   ann: Mike
                                                        Wallace
                    Guests: the Eddy Heywood Trio

Shine - City Slickers
Dorothy Shay - "Finishin' School Was the
    Finish of Me"
Haunted Heart(Rhythm Opera) - feat Judson,
    Jones, Rock, Gas
Eddy Heywood - "Begin the Beguine"
Dorothy Shay - "Horray For Love"
In the Merry Month of May - Doodles Weaver

Travelogue medley:
                Eddy Heywood Trio - "Chicago"
                Dorothy Shay - "St. Louis Blues"
                San Fernando Valley - City Slickers

        Note: 3565 supervisors and personnel of Union Power & Light
attended this broadcast, which was preceded by a 1-1/2 hr. warm-up
show. Stanley Daugherty was the local music contractor.

15 May (SAT), 16 May (SUN), 1948
                Kiel Aud, St. Louis, Mo
                8:30 PM Sat(sold out), 3:00 & 8:30 Sun

        "Fri 4:30PM BG contest @ Walgreens (200); Sat 12:15 @
        Chase; 2:00PM Spike, Doc, Doodles, Twins, Martin & Little
        at Roth____ Rec. store" "Cars SJ1 & SJ2 at Union Station-
        Opposition - Count Basie at the Arena Sun. night"

17 May, 1948 (MON)
                Auditorium, Burlington, Ia (25,832)
                8:30 PM
                Details as 7 Jan 48

        Interviews: 4:15 to 5PM Spike, Doodles & Doc on KBUR with
        Dick Mosens

18 May, 1948 (TUES)
                Armory, Ottumna, Ia (31,570)
                Capacity: 2900 (1900 sold)
                Scale: 3.65, 3.05, 2.55, 1.25

        Interviews: 4:30 to 5PM Spike, Doodles, Doc, Golly, Dick
        Gardner, Siracusa etc. on KBIZ with Del Donahue(fire des-
        troyed all records, only have 4 Spike Jones recordings)
        "Skippy Anderson's 13 piece orch. played for dancing
        11:45 PM to 1:00 AM"

19 May (WED), 20 May (THURS), 1948
                KRNT Aud, Des Moines, Ia (159,819)
                8:30 PM
                Capacity: 4200
                Scale: 3.65, 3.05, 2.44, 1.83, 1.22

        Interviews: On KRNT 3:30 to 4PM Wed Spike & Doc with Gene
        Emerald; Wed RCA Victor Reception for Spike Jones in East
        Room of Savoy Hotel; BG contest (Fri) Doc, Little &
        Martin at 4:30 @ Katz Drug Store (100)

21 May, 1948 (FRI) - SPOTLIGHT REVUE
                CBS Ivanhoe Temple, Kansas City,   ann: Mike
                                                              Wallace

        Guest: Ken Griffin

        Missouri Waltz - City Slickers
        Dorothy Shay - "He Didn't Ask Me"
        Ill Barkio - Ina Souez, Dr. H.Q. Birdbath
        Ken Griffin - "You Can't Be True Dear"
        Dorothy Shay - "Somebody Loves Me"
        Nature Boy - Doodles Weaver
        Radio Personalities medley:

Ken Griffin - "Love In Bloom"
Dorothy Shay - "Where the Blue Of the Night
Meets the Gold Of the Day"
If You Knew Suzie - City Slickers

Note: 1000 employees of Coca-Cola and their families were in
the audience. The following note from the itinerary is intriguing:-
"No CBS outlet in K.C., on air 8:30 to 9:00 PM CST 'El- Bascio"(sic)

22 May, 1948 (SAT)
            Municipal Aud, Oklahoma City, Ok (204,424)
            9:05 PM
            Details as 1 June 47

        "Train arrived late: Free show started at 8:30 PM - 9:05
        reg. show began"

        "All Oklahoman and Times carriers in Oklahoma City will be
guests of the Oklahoman Publishing Co. at the Spike Jones show.......
more than 300 will attend the show, where a special section is being
reserved for them. The Jones show will be the full 'musical depreciation' treatment which has rocketed the noisy, clowning band to the
top of the entertainment ladder"
                    (Oklahoman-Times, undated)

23 May, 1948 (SUN)
            Convention Hall, Tulsa, Ok (142,157)
            8:30 PM
            Capacity: 2700

        (slanting stage - all acts lost balance unless careful)

        "'The King Of Corn' has labeled the 14 act of his show as
160 minutes of musical madness. sensations, surprises, songs, dances, blackouts and novelties were promised by beyond that "we're not
telling a thing", said Spike, "simply warning you folks to be ready
for anything.
        "An indication as to what may come, however, is in the
'prop' list sent to Tulsa in advance of the show.
        "According to the list, to help Spike set back music 2,000
years, he needs such 'instruments' as 'three 12-inch dinner plates
per performance, three washtubs, 12 quart whisky or dark beer
bottles, three hall trees, two kitchen tables, one seltzer water
(MUST be in syphon bottle), two live pigs, six pigeons and four
washboards.
        "The list, however, it was pointed out, omitted one detail.
It didn't mention in which key Spike wants these tuned."
                    (Tulsa newspaper, unidentified, undated)

24 May, 1948 (MON)
            Auditorium, Oklahoma City, Ok

        "Private Party for Ford Motor Co. Entire cast invited to
        Beverly Osborn for 6PM dinner"

        Note: The Musical Depreciation Revue was a superb family
show, but infrequently, the entire revue would be hired to present an
'adult' oriented show in which the acts would remain but the dialogue
and lyrics would be altered to match the nature of a private party,
as may or may not have been the case on this occasion.

25 May, 1948 (TUES)
            Wichita, Kan (180,000)

```
                 7:00 & 9:45 PM
                 Capacity: 1975
                 Scale: 3.65, 3.05, 2.44, 1.80


     Interviews: 4 to 4:30PM Doc & Martin on KFBI with Vern
     Nydegger; 5 to 5:30 Spike, Doc, Doodles, Freddie Morgan
     contest show on KFH "Taxi to radio int. .35"


26 May (WED), 27 May (THURS), 1948
                 Music Hall, Kansas City, Mo (399,178)
                 8:30 PM
                 Capacity: 2600


     "4PM Wed RCA Victor window contest winner - Goldman's
     K.C. Kans." - "Dressing Rooms(10) excellent" (SJ1 & SJ2 -
     no water or air comp. - changed 27 May 1948 12 Noon)


28 May, 1948 (FRI) - SPOTLIGHT REVUE
                 CBS AK-SAR-BEN Aud, Omaha, Neb,        ann: Mike
                                                              Wallace
                 Guest: Frankie Laine


                 When the Midnight Choo Choo Leaves For Alabam -
                      City Slickers
                 Dorothy Shay - "Why Won't Someone Marry Mary Ann?"
                 Hotcha Cornia - City Slickers
                 Frankie Laine - "Baby, That Ain't Right"
                 Dorothy Shay - "Mean To Me"
                 Lazy Bones - Doodles Weaver
                 Travel medley:
                      Frankie Laine - "Sentimental Journey"
                      Dorothy Shay - "Waitin' For the Train
                             To Come In"
                 Dream Train - City Slickers
```

     Note: 8500 employees of Union Pacific R.R. Co. and their
families attended this show. Local musicians augmenting the Slickers
were:- Julie Hornstein, Nuncio Pomidoro and Art Randall.

```
29 May, 1948 (SAT)
                 Auditorium, St. Joseph, Mo (75,711)
                 Capacity: 3200


     Interviews: 1:15 to 1:30 Doc on KRES with Bud Pratt; 5:15
     to 5:30 Doc, Doodles & Martin on KRES with contest winners;
     4:30 BG contest at Katz Drug Store with Doc, Doodles and
     Martin


30 May, 1948 (SUN)
                 Memorial Hall, Joplin, Mo (37,144)
                 8:15 PM
                 Capacity: 2500


     Interviews: 6:30 to 7PM Doodles and Doc with Noel Ball on
     KSWM, contest awards with audience "Fireworks celebration
     at station SJ1 & SJ2" (microphones(3) very poor)


31 May, 1948 (MON)
                 Memorial Hall, Salina, Kan (21,073)
                 8:30 PM (sold out)
                 Capacity: 2700
```

Interviews: 4:45 to 5:15 Doc & Doodles on KSAL with Jack
Hines "Record Shack had good windows on S.J. records" -
"Tues. 1st June off, vacation - Hurrah!"

1 June, 1948 (TUES)
                        No show this day (but travel to Emporia)

2 June, 1948 (WED)
                    Civic Aud, Emporia, Kan (13,811)
                    8:30 PM

        Interviews: 11:05 to 11:30PM(Tues) Spike, Doc, Freddie
Morgan on KTSW; 4:15 to 4:45PM Doodles & Doc on KTSW
contest winners of Pop Corn Sack; 1:00 spot ann. on KTSW
"Rehearsal 1 to 5:00PM, My Old Flame, Slickerettes, Stalin
No., Laura" - "Excellent aud" (Mic system very poor)

        Note: The rehearsal may have been called for the benefit of
Jud Conlon, vocalist, composer, arranger who replaces Paul Judson
about this time.

3 June, 1948 (THURS)
                    Hutchison, Kan (30,013)
                    Details as 4 June 47 (sold out)

        Interviews: 5PM Doc & doodles on KWBW, contest winners;
5:15 Doc & Doodles on KWHK, contest winners

4 June, 1948 (FRI) - SPOTLIGHT REVUE
                    CBS YMCA, Pueblo, Colo   ann: Bob Petrie

        Guest: Buddy Clark

        San - City Slickers
        Dorothy Shay - "No Ring On Her Finger"
        William Tell Overture - Doodles Weaver
        Buddy Clark - "My Gal Is Mine Once More"
        Dorothy Shay - "I Don't Know Why"
        Chloe - Doodles Weaver
        Indian Legends medley:
            Buddy Clark - "Cherokee"
            Dorothy Shay - "Pass That Peace Pipe"
            Pale Moon - City Slickers

        Note: 1000 employees of Colorado Steel & Iron Corp. and
their families attended this broadcast, which included a 30 minute
warm-up prior. The regular Revue show followed the b'cast

5 June, 1948 (SAT)
                    City Aud, Denver, Colo (375,000)
                    3:00 & 8:30 PM (sold out)
                    Details as 15 Feb 47

    "Gave up our SJ1 & SJ2 at 8AM on arrival"

        "We are going to start a couple of campaigns. Our civic and
social indignation was aroused...where M. Spike Jones was presenting
his second Musical Depreciation Revue of the day.
        "Henceforth, M. Jones should have to pay at least four times
as much as anyone else for auditorium rental. Wear and tear on the
stage, induced by such antics as shooting down wild ducks in flight,

handling viciously a trampoline, and putting on a full-scale baseball game, must be enormous.

"M. Jones has not changed his revue very much. One or two musical(?) items were added; several of the stalwarts, notably Doodles Weaver and George Rock, have slipped even farther from the human plane - but, by and large, it's the same show.

"To judge by the reaction of the throngs who stood four deep in precious unreserved space, he can keep the same Revue forever."
(<u>Rocky Mountain News</u>, 6 June 48)

6 June, 1948 (SUN)
                    "Sun. off - leave 5:20PM for Salt Lake City"

7 June (MON), 8 June (TUES), 1948
                    Capitol Theatre, Salt Lake City, Utah (175,000)
                    2:30 & 8:30 PM
                    Capacity: 2000
                    Scale: Mat 1.83, .90, .75
                           Eve 3.65, 3.05, 1.83, 1.22

        Interviews: Mon - Jazzbo on KNAK, sire recorded Spike,
        Doodles, Doc, F. Morgan, Gas, Twins etc; 5:30 to 5:45 Doc
        & Doodles on KSL; 8PM Bill King on KDYL Television; Tues
        - Doc & Doodles made trans. on (1) KALL 5:15 PM, (2) 5 to
        6 on KDYL "Robert Perry & Rene - Trampoline act left troupe
        here to join Judy Canova show" (Note: The Judy Canova show
        will be in Las Vegas and in opposition to Spike from 19 Jun)

        "...Spike Jones publicity agent was in our editorial offices
seeking some advance notices of...appearance at the Rainbow Randevu.
That was before the dance hall burned to the ground. On the day after
the big blaze a package of Spike's recordings arrived in the office
in appreciation of the publicity. Ironically enough, one of them was
titled: 'My Old Flame'"
                    (Salt Lake newspaper, unidentifed, undated)

9 June, 1948 (WED)
                    Travel to Las Vegas

10 June (THURS) to 23 June (WED), 1948
                    Flamingo Hotel, Las Vegas, Nev
                    8:30, 11:30 PM, and (Sat) 2:00 AM
                    Details as 7-20 Aug 47

        Interviews: 3 to 3:15 June 14 Doodles on KLAS with Bill Guy;
        3 to 3:15 15 June Doc on KLAS with Bill Guy; 3:45 Doodles &
        Doc @ Harris-Warden Music Store autograph session 'on-the-
        air'

        Note: In the magazine <u>True Story</u> of July 1949, Spike talks
of the death of his father in a Pasadena hospital, which would have
occured during this Las Vegas engagement

11 June, 1948 (FRI) - SPOTLIGHT REVUE
                    CBS Las Vegas, Nev   ann: Michael Roy

                    Guests: the Delta Rhythm Boys

                    <u>Jingle, Jangle, Jingle</u> - City Slickers
                    Dorothy Shay - "Hootenest Gal In Town"
                    <u>Wild Bill Hiccup</u> (A Quiet Town) - City Slicker
                        Rhythm Opera

Delta Rhythm Boys - "My Blue Heaven"
Dorothy Shay - "Love Somebody"
Give a Man a Horse He Can Ride - Doodles Weaver
Western Panorama medley:
    Delta Rhythm Boys - "Ole Buttermilk Sky"
    Dorothy Shay - "Wa-Hoo"
    Home On the Range - City Slickers

18 June, 1948 (FRI) - SPOTLIGHT REVUE
        CBS Las Vegas, Nev   ann: Michael Roy

        Guest: Buddy Clark

        California, Here I Come - City Slickers
        Dorothy Shay - "Two-Gun Harry"
        When a Gypsy Makes His Violin Cry - feat Sir
            Frederick Gas
        Buddy Clark - "Blue Shadows On the Trail"
        Dorothy Shay - "Got That Feathery Feeling"
        The Man On the Flying Trapeze - Doodles Weaver
        Scenic Route medley:
            Buddy Clark - "Lazy River"
            Dorothy Shay - "Blue Skies"
            Over the Rainbow - City Slickers

        Note: "When a Gypsy..." details, see 9 Apr 48

24 June, 1948 (THURS)
        Travel to Los Angeles

25 June, 1948 (FRI) - SPOTLIGHT REVUE
        CBS Hollywood   ann: Michael Roy

        Guest: Andy Russell

        That Old Gang Of Mine - City Slickers
        Dorothy Shay - "I've Been To Hollywood"
        I Kiss Your Hand Madame - voc Jud Conlon
        Andy Russell - "Yours"
        Dorothy Shay - "What's Good About Goodbye?"
        I'll Be Seeing You - Doodles Weaver
        Thanks to Listeners medley:
            Andy Russell - "Thanks a Million"
            Dorothy Shay - "I'll See You Again"
            Thanks For the Memory - City Slickers

        Note: "Coca-Cola Salutes Firestone". The summer replacement
for Spotlight Revue was Dick Jurgens and his Orchestra

25 June to 26 August, 1948
        "Band lay-off in L.A., Two months vacation"

18 July, 1948 (SUN)
        Spike Jones and Helen Grayco (Greco) wedding at the
        Beverly Hills Hotel. Their honeymoon was in Honolulu,
        Hawaii, and while there, Spike appeared on Mutual's
        "Hawaii Calls"

        "I just recalled a story about Spike and me in Honolulu in
1948. I was there playing the "Far East Rice Relief Show" with Frank
DeVol. Spike was there on his honeymoon...we were staying at the
Royal Hawaiian Hotel and every day I'd go out on a catamaran ...ride

on the tip of one of the pontoons and was submerged each time a wave
would come directly into the tip. I convinced Spike to try it warning
him that he must hold onto the ropes on the side of the pontoon or
he'd be washed overboard. We hit the first wave and Spike was not on
the tip...he'd gone overboard...I jumped in and pulled him back to
the boat. He was very grateful..."
                        (Milton Holland correspondance 28 Nov 83)

        Other husband and wife teams within the troupe were:- Betty
Jo Huston/George Rock and Gladys (Pat) Gardner/Joe Colvin.

        During the course of living out of a train, a creative
pattern developed which greatly enhanced all acts. Generally, when
the evening show was completed, broken down and the train moved
through the night to its next destination, this is the time of day
that entertainers are on a 'high' from the level of energy expended
during their show. In their mobile 'home-away-from-home', performance
post-mortems invariably led to miniature rehearsals which would
change, not for the sake of change, a word - a line - timing - and
creation of potential skits. At these times, no two shows were ever
the same although the changes would have been more subtle than
obvious.

        Dick Baldwin, vocalist, replaced Jud Conlon at this time as
the 'straight' singer. Conlon remains in Hollywood and is responsible
for the chorus backings in concert, b'casts and recordings for many
West coast artists, including Spike.

25 August, 1948 (WED) - AFRS COMMAND PERFORMANCE 346
                        CBS Hollywood

                "A special edition of the Spotlight Revue
                 starring Spike Jones, the City Slickers, and
                 Dorothy Shay, with guest Marie MacDonald and
                 announcer Larry Thorr". Master of Ceremonies
                 Spike Jones

H18-346   (1:11)Yes Sir, That's My Baby - City Slickers
D30729   (2:43)Dorothy Shay - "It's the Little Things You
                      Do That Count"
              *(2:16)William Tell Overture - Doodles Weaver
                     #Dorothy Shay - "What's Good About Goodbye?"
H18-346   Marie MacDonald, Dorothy Shay, Spike Jones -
D30730   Comedy routine
                     #Documentary - "Shot Machine Paying Off"
                (2:26)Sidewalks of New York - Doodles Weaver
                (4:41)Limehouse Blues - City Slickers

                *issued on MF Distribution LPs MF 205/4,
                    947447, and GO 10016
                #deleted from the AFRS ET (issued 2 Nov 48)

27 August (FRI) to 4 September (SAT), 1948
                Cal-Neva Resort Hotel, Crysal Bay, Nev
                            (160,000 around entire lake)
                8:30 & 11:00 PM
                Capacity: 450
                Scale: 4.50 minimum

        Interviews: Doc & Jack Golly transcribed on KOLO with Art
        Laboe, on air 8AM 2 Sept;(KOLO in Reno was nearest CBS
        station); "Ralph 5-1/2 trout" (Wonders?)

                                207

```
            1st show - 8:30 PM              2nd show - 11 PM
            1.  Black Magic                1.  Hotcha Cornia
            2.  Chloe                      2.  Laura
            3.  Birdbath - Old MacDonald   3.  Stalin "Uncle Joe"
            4.  Betty Jo                   4.  Betty Jo
            5.  Sheik                      5.  Minka
            6.  Gas bucket Bit             6.  My Old Flame
            7.  Bill King                  7.  Helen Grayco
            8.  Helen Grayco               8.  Doodles Weaver
            9.  Doodles Weaver             9.  Hawaiian War Chant
            10. Dick Gardner violin        10. Gas (act)
            11. Baseball Game              11. Cocktails
            12. Twins..dance
            13. Bubble Gum
            14. Liebestraum
```

5 September, 1948 (SUN)
```
                    Auditorium, Oakland (600,000 area)
                    8:30 PM
                    Capacity: 6500
```

6 September, 1948 (MON)
```
                    Civic Aud, San Jose (60,000)
                    Capacity: 5000
```

7 September (TUES), 8 September (WED), 1948
```
                    State Fair Grounds, Sacramento (125,000)
                    Details as 2-3 Sept 47
```

Interviews: Tues PM Doodles Weaver on KROY

```
                    Grandstand - 1 hr. show
            1.  Hotcha Cornia       8.  Minka
            2.  Chloe               9.  Twins (dance)
            3.  Birdbath            10. Sheik
            4.  Bettyjo Huston      11. Hawaiian War Chant
            5.  Bill King           12. My Old Flame
            6.  Helen Grayco        13. Cocktails
            7.  Doodles Weaver
```

"Pit Band - Jim Greer" - "Gasoline strike affected those
driving to Canada - all went by train from Davis, Cal"

10 September (FRI) to 21 September (TUES), 1948
```
                    The Cave Supper Club, Vancouver, BC (335,000)
                    7:00 & 11:00 PM, Mat. Sat 1:30 (no show Sun)
                    Capacity: 750
                    Scale: 3.75, 2.50, 1.25; 4.50 Sat nite
```

Interviews: 3:30 to 4PM 15 Sept Spike & Doc on CJOR with
Wally Peters; Board of Trade Luncheon 13 Sept Dr. Birdbath
2 min. skit "Forum - 8000 to 10,000 where Crosby played Wed
Sept 22"

22 September, 1948 (WED)
```
                    Armory, Bellingham, Wash (30,000)
                    Capacity: 4200
                    Scale: 2.80, 2.50
```

Interviews: 3:45 to 4:30PM Doc, Doodles & Dick Baldwin
on WPUG (MBS station) "This date in Bellingham had only
5 day promotion. Turn-out just fair but okay"

23 September, 1948 (THURS)
> Civic Aud, Seattle, Wash (365,000)
> Capacity: 5000
> Scale: 1.25 to 3.13

"3:30 to 4:30 Spike, Doodles, Doc, Little, Martin, Twins record autographing session at Bon Marche; 5:30 Cocktail party at Press Club" -" Note: KELA (MBS/1000W) came to cut Spike & gang backstage from Centralia, Wash - Lloyd Hannah, Lyle Sellards" - "17 excellent RCA windows in downtown stores" (audience too far away from band)

24 September, 1948 (FRI)
> Auditorium, Portland, Oregon (305,000)
> Capacity: 5000 (sold out)

"Record autographing session 4 to 5PM Myer & Franks Dept Store - Spike, Doc, Doodles, Gloria, Little, Martin" - "Football Inter High School Game - Opposition" - "Crosby had just been here & played to 10,000 at outdoor stadium" "This ends our tour which started Aug. 27th. Return to LA leaving Portland 8:30AM PST" (25 Sept)

Note: Daily itinerary to Jan 49 is missing but all activities, as usual, are up and down the California coast

The new season of "Spotlight Revue" was to feature increased Slickers involvement within the shows format. Ina Souez leaves for her own solo concert circuit and is replaced by Eileen Gallagher, operatic star. Vocalist Jay Meyer augments, as does the well-known and versatile writer/arranger/composer Eddie Maxwell (Cherkose). Eddie McCarthy and George Green are band boys while Eddie Pripps remains the Musical Director and chief arranger for the 'Coke' shows, with additional arrangements by Frank DeVol, Bob Ballard and Paul Leu.

Paul Leu handled Helen Grayco's stage arrangements until 1954. Exceptions are, among others, "John's Other Wife" and "El Cumbanchero" by Dick Gardner and "You Came a Long Way From St. Louis" by Jack Golly.

Eddie Maxwell was well known in the radio and movie studios of Hollywood. For BMI (and the Tune Towne Tunes "Ugga Ugga Boo..."), his published name was Eddie Cherkose, whereas for ASCAP, he established himself as Eddie Maxwell. Under either name, he was a respected writer and lyricist, contributing to such shows as "Danny Thomas", "Donald O'Connor Show", "Abbott & Costello", "Beany & Cecil", "Jimmy Durante" and many others. He wrote special material for Homer & Jethro, and one of his many songs, "Pico & Sepulveda" is currently the theme of a popular Los Angeles radio show under Barry Hansen, who is better known as Dr. Demento.

Eddie Maxwell, Jay Sommers and the ever-present Eddie Brandt noticably improve the comedy dialogue throughout the season.

During this season, each opening Slicker title contained a 'gag' interruption. Dick Gardner and Jack Golly demonstrated "outrageous" flights of virtuosity this past and next season, noticably on the opening Slickers titles. It is hard to believe that what they played was written, and harder to believe that what was written could be played! Their use of all saxophones (soprano, alto, tenor, baritone and Spike's personal bass sax) and clarinets (bass, Bflat and small Eflat), coupled with the prestissimo speed of these opening titles is impressive!

Most, if not all, shows have been issued on AFRS 15 minute transcriptions "Corn's-a-Poppin'", a known listing to be found in appendix iii.

1 October, 1948 (FRI) - SPOTLIGHT REVUE
                CBS Hollywood   ann: Dick Joy

            Guest: Frank Sinatra

            12th Street Rag - City Slickers
            Dorothy Shay - "You'll Be Just Another Notch
                on Father's Gun"
            Hair of Gold, Eyes of Blue - Doodles Weaver
            The Best Things In Life Are Free (quiz shows) -
                City Slickers
            Dorothy Shay - "You Call Everybody Darling"
            Frank Sinatra - "Everybody Loves Somebody"
            Frank, Spike & Dorothy - "Love Somebody"

        Note: Frank Sinatra's rendition of "Everybody Loves Some-
body" predates the Dean Martin hit by 16 years.

8 October, 1948 (FRI) - SPOTLIGHT REVUE
                CBS Hollywood   ann: Dick Joy

            Guest: Gene Kelly

            *Tiger Rag - City Slickers
            Dorothy Shay - "A Man Around the House"
            Rhapsody In Blue - Dick & Freddy Morgan(banjos)
                (straight)
            William Tell Overture - Doodles Weaver
            Dorothy Shay - "Buttons and Bows"
            Entire cast - "Take Me Out To the Ball Game"

            *issued on MF Distribution LPs 205/4,
                947447, and GO 10016; Public Service Show
                ET "Here's To Vets" 139

13 October, 1948 (WED) - AFRS COMMAND PERFORMANCE 352
                CBS Hollywood (assumed)

            with Spike Jones, the City Slickers, Dorothy Shay,
                Doodles Weaver, with guest Dane Clark and
                announcer Bob Shannon. Master of Ceremonies
                Spike Jones

H18-352   (1:26)12th Street Rag - City Slickers
RL8501   (2:43)Dorothy Shay - "You'll Be Just Another Notch
                On Father's Gun"
            *(2:23)Nature Boy - Doodles Weaver
H18-352   (1:35)Dorothy Shay - "You Call Everybody Darling"
RL8502   #*(5:03)You Can't Be True Dear - City Slickers
                Comedy routine with Dane Clark, Spike, Dorothy,
                Dane, Spike & Dorothy - "Love Somebody"

            *issued on MF Distribution LPS MF 205/4,
                947447, and GO 10016
            #On Coast Guard Memorial 16" ET (pressed by
                Allied Record Co., L.A.)

        Note: The issue date of the AFTS ET was 16 Nov 48. Harry
Stanton's bass voice is apparent in "You Can't Be True Dear"

15 October, 1948 (FRI) - SPOTLIGHT REVUE
                CBS Hollywood   ann: Dick Joy

            Guest: Don Ameche

            *That's A Plenty - City Slickers
            Dorothy Shay - "Finishing School Was the
                Finish Of Me"
            It's Magic - Doodles Weaver
            Limehouse Blues (Rhythm Opera) - City Slickers
            Dorothy Shay - "Only With You"
            *Quartet From Rigor Mortis - Entire cast

        *issued on MF Distribution LPs MF 205/4

        Note: The RKO-Goldwyn movie "A Song Is Born", filmed in
Hollywood during July and August 1948, used a similar device on the
operatic "Quartet from Rigoletto" with Virginia Mayo and the 'square'
professors at the Music Academy where Danny Kaye and Benny Goodman
'taught'. The famed Verdi quartet had many adaptions this year.

21 October, 1948 (THURS)
        Spike Jones is a guest on the Steve Allen radio talk
    show this evening

22 October, 1948 (FRI) - SPOTLIGHT REVUE
                CBS Hollywood   ann: Dick Joy

            Guest: Jack Carson

            Hindustan - City Slickers
            Dorothy Shay - "Rootinest Tootinest Gal In Town"
            Put 'Em In a Box - Doodles Weaver
            I Kiss Your Hand Madame - voc Dick Baldwin
            Dorothy Shay - "What Did I Do?"
            Jack Carson & Slickers - Disc Jockeys

29 October, 1948 (FRI) - SPOTLIGHT REVUE
                CBS Hollywood   ann: Dick Joy

            Guest: Tony Martin

            Yes Sir, That's My Baby - City Slickers
            Dorothy Shay -"Why Won't Someone Marry Mary Ann?"
            You Call Everybody Darling - Doodles Weaver
            You Can't Be True Dear - City Slickers
            Dorothy Shay - "When the Right Man Comes,
                You'll Know"
            Tony Martin - "This Is the Moment", "Galway Bay"
            Tony, Spike & Dorothy - "Underneath the Arches"

        Note: Spike Jones and his City Slickers were appearing in
the Florentine Gardens, L.A., at this time

5 November, 1948 (FRI) - SPOTLIGHT REVUE
                CBS Hollywood   ann: Dick Joy

            Guest: Jerry Colonna

211

#<u>Blues My Naughty Sweetie Gave To Me</u> - City
   Slickers
Dorothy Shay - "Joan Of Arkansas"
<u>Sidewalks of New York</u> - Doodles Weaver
#*<u>Barber of Seville</u> - feat Sir Frederick Gas
Dorothy Shay - "I Get A Thrill Thinking of You"
Jerry Colonna & Slickers - "The Life Of a
   Sailor For Me"

*issued on MF Distribution LPs MF 205/4
#On Public Service Show ET "Here's To Vets" 139

Note: 350 Marines were invited guests this evening

         Spike had caught the society band of colleague Leighton
Noble at the Catalina Casino many months before and, impressed by the
singing and instrumental skills of <u>Edwin C. Metcalfe</u>, invited
Metcalfe to join the Slickers for the pending English tour. The tour
never materializes and due to his own committments, Metcalfe was
unable to join Spike until this time. Metcalfe replaces Merle Howard.

8 November, 1948 (MON)
         Spike Jones and his City Slickers opened at
         Slapsy Maxie's Night Club, Los Angeles

         "Spike Jones says if Slapsie Maxie's restraunt re-opens
tonight (15 Nov) it will do so without his band. He said the check
was for $10,500 - one weeks wages for the madcap musicians. The
contract called for a four-week appearance."
                  (<u>News-Tribune</u>, Tacoma, Wash., 15 Nov 48)
         "Spike Jones, who recently announced that the one 'instru-
ment' his City Slickers will not play is a rubber check, is asking
the Superior Court to confirm his stand.
         "The orchestra leader, suing under the corporate name of
Arena Stars, Inc., filed a complaint for collection of $9000 against
Slapsy Maxie's, Inc. (owner Charles Devere)...payment has not been
received, the complaint says, for performances given by the Jones
musicians...from Nov .8 to Nov. 13. It was on the latter day that
Jones walked out of the club, complaining this its check for this
orchestra's services had bounced."
                  (<u>Times</u>, Los Angeles, 6 Dec 48)

12 November, 1948 (FRI) - SPOTLIGHT REVUE
         CBS Hollywood   ann: Dick Joy

         Guest: Dick Haymes

         <u>Please Don't Talk About Me When I'm Gone</u> -
            City Slickers
         Dorothy Shay -"Pappy's Predicament"
         <u>Buttons and Bows</u> - Doodles Weaver
         <u>The Newsreel</u> - City Slickers
         Dorothy Shay - "You Were Only Fooling"
         Dick Haymes - "Just a Little Bit More"
         Dick, Spike & Dorothy - "Feudin' and Fightin'"

19 November, 1948 (FRI) - SPOTLIGHT REVUE
         CBS Hollywood   ann: Dick Joy

         Guest: Morton Downey

Pale Moon - City Slickers
Dorothy Shay - "Sage Brush Sadie, the
    Bearded Lady"
You Can't Be True Dear - Doodles Weaver
The Courtship of Miles Standish - City Slickers
    Rhythm Opera
Dorothy Shay - "The Money Song"
Morton Downey - "A Tree In the Meadow"
Downey, Spike & Dorothy - "MacNamara's Band"

26 November, 1948 (FRI) - SPOTLIGHT REVUE
            CBS Hollywood   ann: Dick Joy

        Guest: Harold Peary

        Sweet Georgia Brown - City Slickers
        Dorothy Shay - "That's Stretchin' Things Too Far"
        On a Slow Boat To China - Doodles Weaver
        *All I Want For Christmas - George Rock
        Dorothy Shay - "My Darling, My Darling"
        Hal Peary, cast - "School Days"

        *issued on MF Distribution LPs MF 205/4,
            947447, and GO 10016

        Note: Itinerary this week includes Los Angeles, San Diego,
Long Beach, San Francisco and Oakland

3 December, 1948 (FRI) - SPOTLIGHT REVUE
            CBS Hollywood   ann: Dick Joy

        Guest: Frank Sinatra

        *Football Medley(Notre Dame "Victory March" - USC
            "Fight On") - City Slickers
        Dorothy Shay - "Dear Mr. Sears and Roebuck"
        A Tree In the Meadow - Doodles Weaver
        It's Magic - City Slickers
        Dorohy Shay - "A Little Bird Told Me"
        Frank Sinatra - "Once In Love With Amy"
        Sinatra, Slickers & cast - "Prisoner of Love"

        *issued on MF Distribution LPs MF 205/4

10 December, 1948 (FRI) - SPOTLIGHT REVUE
            CBS Hollywood   ann: Dick Joy

        Guest: Peter Lorre

        *After You've Gone - City Slickers
        Dorothy Shay - "The Old Apple Tree"
        Cuanto Le Gusta - Doodles Weaver
        Tiger Rag - Dick and Freddy Morgan
        Dorothy Shay - "What Are You Doing New Years?"
        My Old Flame - Dick Baldwin, Paul Frees
        Peter Lorre, Slickers & cast - "My Old Flame"

        *On Public Service Show ET "Here's To Vets" 139

11 December, 1948 (SAT) - TRUTH OR CONSEQUENCES
                  NBC Hollywood   Sponsor: Duz Soap

                  Host - Ralph Edwards, ann: Harlow Wilcox
                     Mystery guests - Spike Jones and his
                     City Slickers

                  Glow Worm - with contestant, Mrs. Florence
                     Andrews, assisted by Dick Morgan

13 December, 1948 (MON)
                  The end of the recording ban, in effect since
                     1 Jan 48

17 December, 1948 (FRI) - SPOTLIGHT REVUE
                  CBS Hollywood   ann: Dick Joy

                  Guest: Ralph Edwards

                  *Jingle Bells - City Slickers
                  Dorothy Shay - "I Don't Rhyme With No Place"
                  April Showers - Doodles Weaver
                  Happy New Year - City Slickers
                  Dorothy Shay - "Until"
                  Ralph Edwards, cast - Truth or Consequences

                  *Excerpt issued on Rainbo Record Co. paper 78
                     RPM and titled "Happy New Year", with the
                     Red Ingle caricature of Spike in boxing
                     gloves under the lamination

24 December, 1948 (FRI) - SPOTLIGHT REVUE
                  CBS Hollywood   ann: Dick Joy

                  Guests: the Harry Stanton Choir

                  Winter Wonderland - City Slickers
                  Dorothy Shay - "Santa Claus Is Coming To Town"
                  Deck the Halls - Doodles Weaver
                  All I Want For Christmas - George Rock
                  Dorothy Shay - "White Christmas"
                  How the Circus Learned To Smile - City Slickers

            Note: Feature articles on Spike Jones appeared during
                     1948 in:-

                  Colliers, 10 Jan - "A Night At the Uproar"
                  Juke Box Comics, Mar - "Music Was Never Like This"
                  Radio Album, Fall - "Spotlight Revue"
                  Movie Stars Parade, Dec - "Spike Jones"

        In January, Dorothy Shay starts at New York's Waldorf Hotel
and the Spotlight Revue is now "The Spike Jones Show". The format is
exclusively Slickers with popular guests. Eddie Brandt recalls this
series as the high point in Spike's creativity for radio. To accommo-
date the touring schedule, all half-hour b'casts were transcribed for
6:30 PM EST airing.
        Generally, there was a one-hour rehearsal, a half-hour break
followed by the taping, editing and pressing. Occasionally the shows
were transcribed and b'cast the same day (trans/b'cast), but more
often than not, they were delayed a day or more before airing (delay-

214

ed/b'cast). The network 'feed' may have been from tape, with ET as a safety back-up. Transcribing accounts for the Revue appearing in one locale while a b'cast originates from another. These differences are noted where known and all shows are listed by their b'cast date.

In all likelihood, Jay Sommers was now an additional script writer for this series and like many of the personnel added by Spike and Coca-Cola for this series. Sommers did not travel on the train but worked with the guests in advance in the city the broadcasts originated from. One of Sommers creations, the 'Roundtable Discussions' featured Gas and Jones dialogue and had similarities to his later 'Green Acres' TV show. Sommers created similar characters for radio in the late '40s which were never broadcast.

Helen Grayco, while starting this series, did not complete the tour due to her pregnancy.

2 January, 1949 (SUN) - THE SPIKE JONES SHOW* (trans/b'cast)
                 CBS Hollywood   ann: Dick Joy

              Guests: Joan Davis and Buddy Clark

              Sunday - City Slickers
              Liebestraum - Sir F. Gas, Freddy Morgan
                 George Rock
              My Darling, My Darling - Doodles Weaver
              Joan Davis - "'Tisn't Rain"(tune "Let It Snow")
              Joan Davis, cast - The Hollywood Story

        Note: This programs details have been pieced together from several sources and is possibly incomplete. There was no copy in Jones files. "Sunday", featuring special lyrics to promote the new CBS line-up, contained:- "Remember, Jack Benny follows on Sunday, then comes Amos n' Andy". The song is interrupted by Sir F. Gas (ala Jack Benny) playing the familiar Kreutzer finger exercise, and Spike saying, "I'm sorry Mr. Benny, but you don't come on for a half-hour yet".

        The Benny show of this date drops plugs for Amos n' Andy and Spike. Jack Benny:- "I had my (Maxwell) car tuned just yesterday", Mary Livingston:- "Who tuned it - Spike Jones?"

6 January, 1949 (THURS) - Radio Recorders, Hollywood
                 Client: RCA Victor   7:30 PM to 2:00 AM
                 Walter Heebner, A & R Rep, present

              Leader - Spike Jones
              Brass - George Rock, tpt; Joe Colvin, trb
              Reeds - Dick Gardner, Jack Golly, sax
              Rhythm - Paul Leu, pno; Dick Morgan, guit; Freddy
                 Morgan, bjo; Roger Donley, bass; Joe Siracusa,
                 drm
              Actors - Doodles Weaver, Purves Pullen,
                 Earle Bennett
              Vocal - Harry Stanton, Art Davies, Gil Mershon,
                 A. Markussen

D9-VB-500-1   LP RCAG PJM2 8021(1974)
        1A (3:29)Rum Tee Diddle Dee Yump - voc Sir Frederick
                       Gas, featuring his Sadavarious
NP   2 (3:22)Unissued
NP   2A

D9-VB-501-1   20-3338-B; HMV BD 1241; HMVAU EA 3853-A; RCADJ
        1A   642-B; 45 RCAG EPA 9780; LP RCAE HY 1006;
                       RCAG RCS 3217/1-2; ET AFRS "Basic Music
                       Library" P-1324; AFRS "Remember" 1119;

215

```
                   (2:39)MacNamara's Band - voc I.W. Harper and the
                        Four Fifths
NP        2    (2:38)Unissued
NP        2A


D9-VB-502-1         20-3359-B; HMVAU EA 3853-B; RCADJ 655-B;
         1A           45 47-2894-B; ET AFRS "Basic Music Library"
                     P-1324;
                   (3:23)Knock Knock (Who's There?) - voc Doodles
                        Weaver, Sir Frederick Gas, George Rock,
                        Freddy Morgan, Dick Morgan and the Four
                        Fifths


D9-VB-503-1         20-3359-A; HMV BD 1241; HMVAU EA 3950; RCADJ
         1A           655-A; 45 47-2984-B; LP WB BS 2855;
                     ET AFRS "Basic Music Library" P-1324;
                   (3:16)Ya Wanna Buy A Bunny? - voc George Rock
```

        "We knew this one would never be issued when we did it!"
Earle Bennett to Ted Hering in 1965, in reference to the nonsense
song "Rum Tee Diddle...". "Ya Wanna Buy a Bunny" reached 24th on the
Hit Parade by 8 April 1949 and, according to Billboard magazine,
remained there for two weeks.
        I.W. Harper, but one of the many voices of Dick Morgan, fits
beautifully in an Irish scenerio. After many years of trying to
'Slicker' "MacNamara's Band", Spike finally came up with this
recorded version, far superior to previous b'cast attempts. The basic
difference is a change in the opening rhythms (from 2/4 to a 6/8),
the bel canto trumpet solo now on "Danny Boy" instead of "My Wild
Irish Rose", and the voice of experience ("under the influence of
money"), Dick Morgan.
        It is assumed that RCA now contracted the superior Radio
Recorders facilities for the majority of their artists, and all
sessions are now taped.

                        1949 Tour Personnel

```
        Leader - Spike Jones
        Brass - George Rock tpt; Joe Colvin, trb
        Reeds - Dick Gardner, Jack Golly, Eddie Metcalfe,
            all sax/clar
        Rhythm - Paul Leu, pno; Dick Morgan, Freddy Morgan, bjo/
            guit; Roger Donley, bass; Joe Siracusa, drm
        Harp - Nancy McDonald Youngman
        Vocalists/effects - Eileen Gallagher, Helen Grayco,
            Dick Baldwin, Eddie Metcalfe, Jay Meyer, Earle
            Bennett, Purv Pullen, Doodles Weaver
        Acts - Gloria & Gladys Gardner, Bettyjo Huston; Bill
            King, Frankie Little, Jr. Martin
        Writers/arrangers/copyists - Eddie Brandt, Paul Leu,
            Dick Gardner, Jack Golly
        Band Boys - Eddie McCarthy, George Green
        General Staff - Ralph Wonders; Faith Thomas, Anne
            Wilson(secretaries); Ray Rubel(valet); Jack
            McNaughton, Harry Coberly(electricians); Marshall
            Alderson(traffic); Richard King(props); Lester
            Calvin(carpenter); Bert Lang(PR)
```

8 January, 1949 (SAT)
        Evening travel to Calipatria

9 January, 1949 (SUN)
        Calipatria

THE SPIKE JONES SHOW (delayed b'cast)
CBS Hollywood   ann: Dick Joy

Guests: Dinah Shore and Fred Astaire

Oh By Jingo - City Slickers
Dinah Shore - "Buttons and Bows"
You Were Only Fooling - Doodles Weaver
*The Funnies Aren't Funny Anymore - City Slickers
Dinah Shore, Fred Astaire - "Cheek To Cheek"
Fred Astaire, Spike - Dance contest

*issued on MF Distribution LPs MF 205/4

Note: Spike's washboard accompaniment to Astaire's dancing is, ironically, very similar to their pre-Slicker duet, "Dig It", on Columbia - almost a decade earlier.

"It's a far cry from the cold in Winter, hot in Summer second floor of the Niland depot, to the luxurious modern special Pullman that will stand under the eaves of the depot Saturday night and Sunday.
"...and that is what makes the story. A quarter of a century or more ago Spike Jones lived in that second floor while his father was Agent of the Southern Pacific.
"Saturday night a fast Southern Pacific train will pull into the depot at Niland and the luxurious special Pullman will be shunted off and rest quietly under the shelter of the Niland depot...Sunday, January 9th, Spike Jones will fill an engagement with his orchestra at Calipatria and that evening his staff will board the special car and go east.
"Spike has had many audiences that paid fabulous sums to hear him and will unquestionably have more, but the large audience at Caliaptria will probably be the one that he will never forget after the others have long since passed from memory."
(Imperial Valley Democrat, Brawley, CA, 6 Jan 49)

Shows in Phoenix, Tucson, El Paso, Albuquerque, Amarillo
and Oklahoma City this week

16 January, 1949 (SUN) - THE SPIKE JONES SHOW (delayed b'cast)
CBS Hollywood   ann: Dick Joy

Guests: Bob Crosby and Celeste Holme

Down In Jungle Town - City Slickers
Bob Crosby - "Say It Isn't So"
What Did I Do? - Doodles Weaver
You Can't Be True Dear - City Slickers
Celeste Holme - "It's What You Do With What
     You've Got"
Celeste & cast - Inspector Spike Mal de Mer

23 January, 1949 (SUN) - THE SPIKE JONES SHOW (trans/b'cast)
CBS Dallas, Texas   ann: Johnny Hinks

Guests - Peggy Mann and Alec Templeton

*In a Persian Market - City Slickers
A Little Bird Told Me - Doodles Weaver
Peggy Mann - "I've Got My Love To Keep Me Warm"

217

Alec Templeton - "I Wonder Who's Kissing Her Now?"
    (pno solo with Slickers style effects)
Alec Templeton - "2nd Prelude" (Gershwin)
Alec, Spike, cast - "1812 Overture" (Rhythm Opera)

*issued on MF Distribution LPs MF 205/4,
    947447, and GO 10016

Note: The CBS ET of this show starts with the Slickers
production number, "Persian Market", instead of the usual instrumental opening - evidence of unusual editing.
    Downbeat Magazine has voted Spike Jones as "King of Corn"
for the 7th straight year. The April issue of Varsity explains:- "...
national recognition...the ability to command big money...Jones is
'way out in front. He puts on a terrific show, no two of which, he
boasts, are ever the same ...
    A recent poll by Billboard showed the following bands scram-
bling for the runners-up positions to Spike's No. 1:- Red Ingle,
    Korn Kobblers, Al Trace, Phil Harris, Bob Willis and the
    Hoosier Hot Shots

Shows in Ft. Worth, Austin, Tyler, Galveston, San Antonio,
    Houston and Beaumont this week

30 January, 1949 (SUN) - THE SPIKE JONES SHOW (delayed b'cast)
        CBS Hollywood   ann: Dick Joy

        Guests: Basil Rathbone and Lina Romay

        By the Beautiful Sea - City Slickers
        Roundtable discussion - The Samba
        Lina Romay - "Tico Tico"
        Say Something Sweet To Your Sweetheart -
            Doodles Weaver
        When a Gypsy Makes His Violin Cry - Sir F. Gas
        *Portia and the Hollywood Wolf - narrator, Basil
            Rathbone; DJ, Spike; Portia, Romay; villian,
            Dick Morgan; and Dr. H.Q. Birdbath

        *issued on MF Distribution LPs MF 205/4,
            947447, and GO 10016

        "Spike Jones...Sunday was named "man of the year" by the
National Retail Hardware Association...he received a scroll honoring
him as the Wagner of the Washboard and the Haydn of the hammer" for
lifting kitchen utensils, horns and tools to "the high cultural level
of the music room." (Evening World News, Omaha, Neb. 31 Jan 49)

        Shows in Lake Charles, Shreveport, Ruston, Baton Rouge
        and New Orleans this week

6 February, 1949 (SUN) - THE SPIKE JONES SHOW (delayed b'cast)
            CBS Roosevelt Hotel, New Orleans, La. ann: John
                                                        Kent
            Guests: Eddy Arnold and Janice Paige

            'Way Down Yonder In New Orleans - City Slickers
            Cast - Tour of New Orleans
            Eddy Arnold - "Heart Full Of Love"
            Say It Isn't So - Doodles Weaver
            Chloe (Rhythm Opera) - Joe Siracusa, Sir F.
                Gas, George Rock

218

Janice Paige - "A Little Bird Told Me"
Cast - Showboat

Note: Local musicians augmenting the Slickers included;
David Winstein, reeds; Marion Suter, tpt; "Bubba" Castigliola, con-
tractor/trb. As well, Al Hirt, tpt, recalls augmenting the Slickers
for this show, though memory of his participation is lost to the
contractor and others. Shows in Starkville, Montgomery, Tampa, Miami,
Jacksonville and Orlando this week

13 February, 1949 (SUN) - THE SPIKE JONES SHOW (delayed b'cast)
                    CBS Jacksonville, Fla.   ann: Harold Cohen

                    Guests: Tony Martin and Cyd Charisse

                    My Gal Sal - City Slickers
                    Tony Martin - "No Orchids For My Lady"
                    Lavender Blue (Dilly Dilly) - Doodles Weaver
                    Far Away Places - feat Spike, Dick Morgan(as
                         Ralph Wonders), Geo. Rock, Jack Golly,
                         Freddy Morgan
                    Cast - Carmen

        Note: "Carmen" punch-line is buried by commercial:- "cancel
the operation Doctor, Carmen just blew her top!" An oddity is that
"Carmen" is piano accompaniment only and is made up of arias from
other operas.
        The following itinerary, through to 7 Nov courtesy of Ed
Metcalfe.

14 February, 1949 (MON)
                    University of Florida, Gainsville, Fl
                         7:00 & 9:30 PM

15 February, 1949 (TUES)
                    Municipal Aud, Savannah, Ga
                         7:00 PM

16 February, 1949 (WED)
                    Auditorium, Birmingham, Ala
                         8:30 PM

17 February, 1949 (THURS)
                    University of Alabama Gym, Tuscaloosa, Ala
                         8:30 PM

18 February, 1949 (FRI)
                    Municipal Aud, Chattanooga, Tenn
                         8:30 PM

19 February, 1949 (SAT)
                    Auditorium, Atlanta, Ga
                         8:30 PM

20 February, 1949 (SUN) - THE SPIKE JONES SHOW (trans/b'cast)
                    CBS Fox Theatre, Atlanta, Ga. ann: Bill McKane

                    Guests: Alec Templeton and Monica Lewis

                    Is It True What They Say About Dixie? -
                    City Slickers

219

                    Entire cast - Tour of Atlanta
                    Alec Templeton - Impromptu medley
                    Monica Lewis - "The Tree With the Red Red Leaves"
                    Powder Your Face With Sunshine - Doodles Weaver
                    Alec Templeton - "Prelude in a minor" (Debussy)
                    The Unoriginal Amateur Hour - feat Spike, Alec,
                         F. Morgan, Sir F. Gas, Joe Siracusa

        Note: Local musicians augmenting the Slickers included
Johnny Dilliard, tpt.

21 February, 1949 (MON)
                    N.C.C.S. Aud, Columbus, Ga
                       7:00 & 9:30 PM

22 February, 1949, (TUES)
                    Ryman Aud, Nashville, Tenn
                       8:30 PM

23 February, 1949 (WED)
                    Auditorium, Macon, Ga
                       8:30 PM

24 February, 1949 (THURS)
                    City Aud, Augusta, Ga
                       8:30 PM

25 February, 1949 (FRI)
                    County Hall, Charleston, S.C.
                       8:30 PM

26 February, 1949 (SAT)
                    Columbia, S.C.
                       8:30 PM

27 February, 1949 (SUN) - THE SPIKE JONES SHOW (trans/b'cast)
                    CBS Armory, Charlotte, N.C.   ann: John Trimble

                    Guest: Hildegarde

                    Carolina In the Morning - City Slickers
                    Entire cast - Tour of North Carolina
                    Hildegarde - "S'Wonderful"
                    Carolina Moon - Doodles Weaver
                    I Dream Of Brownie With the Light Blue Jeans -
                         feat Sir Frederick Gas
                    Hildegarde - "Oh My Darling, Won't You
                         Play, Play, Play"
                    Hildegarde, cast - Inspector Spike Mal de Mer

28 February, 1949 (MON)
                    Greenboro, N.C.
                       8:30 PM

1 March, 1949 (TUES)
                    Chillowee Park Admist, Knoxville, Tenn
                       9:00 PM

2 March, 1949 (WED)
                    Reynolds H.S. Aud, Winston Salem, N.C.
                       6:30 & 9:00 PM

                               220

3 March, 1949 (THURS)
                    Municipal Aud, Raleigh, N.C.
                       8:00 PM

4 March, 1949 (FRI)
                    City Aud, Danville, Va
                       8:30 PM

5 March, 1949 (SAT) - THE SPIKE JONES SHOW (trans/b'cast)
                    CBS Mosque, Richmond, Va.   ann: Scott Jerrett

                    Guests: Burgess Meredith and Peggy Mann

                    Carry Me Back To Old Virginny - City Slickers
                    Entire cast - Travel
                    Peggy Mann - "So In Love"
                    Blue Danube - City Slickers
                    Far Away Places - Doodles Weaver
                    Burgess Meredith, cast - The Pocahontas Story

        Note: From this point on to 25 June, the b'cast dates
according to the original itinerary, do not always coincide with the
transcribing dates or originating facilites, and as well, ETs seem to
have been scheduled with no apparent broadcast. Ed Metcalfe (letter
of 28 Sept 83) gives some clarification:- "Shortly after appearing in
Atlanta in early '49 (where we appeared at a special performance for
Coca-Cola corporate officers)...a problem developed with the sponsor.
As nearly as we can determine, the sponsor wanted us to "tone down"
our music and antics, suggesting that our brand of tomfoolery was not
appropriate for a Sunday afternoon musicale. I remember that Spike
vehemently refused to compromise (a position I have always admired)
and we were replaced on the Coca-Cola Hour shortly thereafter by
Percy Faith and his Orchestra. My itinerary records show that we
produced only six additional Coca-Cola shows beyond Atlanta."

6 March, 1949 (SUN)
                    Mosque, Richmond, Va
                       8:30 PM

7 March, 1949 (MON)
                    Municipal Aud, Norfolk, Va
                       8:30 PM

8 March, 1949 (TUES)
                    Lyric Theatre, Baltimore, Md
                       8:30 PM

9 March, 1949 (WED)
                    Academy of Music, Philadelphia, Pa
                       8:30 PM

10 March, 1949 (THURS)
                    McCaskey H.S., Lancester, Pa
                       7:00 & 9:30 PM

11 March, 1949 (FRI)
                    Mosque, Harrisburg, Pa
                       8:30 PM

12 March, 1949 (SAT)
     Convention Hall, Washington, D.C.
      Cut ETs for re-broadcast (show included)

    THE SPIKE JONES SHOW (delayed b'cast)
    CBS Philadelphia, Pa.   ann: Joe King

    Guest: Gene Tierney

    Pennsylvania Polka - City Slickers
    Entire cast - Tour of Philadelphia
    Minka - George Rock
    The Pussycat Song - Doodles Weaver
    We're Out Of Money (parody on "We're In the Money")
     - Spike, D. Morgan, Eileen Gallagher
    Gene Tierney, cast - Smellbound (movie:
     "Spellbound")

   Note: During the course of this show, Dick Morgan realistically simulates the sound of the 'theremin', an electronic oscillator
which interferes with radio-frequency waves, on his Hawaiian guitar.

13 March, 1949 (SUN)
     Convention Hall, Washington, D.C.
     8:30 PM

14 March, 1949 (MON)
     Lyric Theatre, Allentown, Pa
     7:00 '& 9:30 PM

15 March, 1949 (TUES)
     Rajah Theatre, Reading, Pa
     7:00 '& 9:30 PM

16 March, 1949 (WED)
     Lakewood Park, Mahanoy City, Pa
     8:30 PM

17 March, 1949 (THURS)
     Armory, Wilkes-Barre, Pa
     8:30 PM

18 March, 1949 (FRI)
     War Memorial, Trenton, N.F.
     8:30 PM

19 March, 1949 (SAT)
     Mosque Theatre, Newark, N.J.
     8:30 PM

    THE SPIKE JONES SHOW (delayed b'cast)
    CBS Washington, D.C.   ann: Joe King

    Guest: Jack Carson

    Missouri Waltz - City Slickers
    Entire cast - Tour of Washington
    Jack Carson - "I Never Met a Texan Who Won't
     Love Texas 'Til the Day He Dies"
    Careless Hands - Doodles Weaver
    Minstrel Show - City Slickers

Jack Carson, cast - Music Easy as A-B-C

20 March, 1949 (SUN)
        New York, NY
          Cut ETs for re-broadcast

21 March, 1949 (MON)
        Westchester County Center, White Plains, NY
          8:30 PM

22 March, 1949 (TUES)
        Bridgeport, Conn
          7:00 & 9:30 PM

23 March, 1949 (WED)
        Arena, New Haven, Conn
          8:30 PM

24 March, 1949 (THURS)
        Bushnell Memorial Aud, Hartford, Conn
          8:30 PM

25 March, 1949 (FRI)
        R.I. Aud, Providence, R.I.
          8:30 PM

26 March, 1949 (SAT)
        City Aud, Worcester, Mass

      THE SPIKE JONES SHOW (delayed b'cast)
      CBS New York, NY   ann: Joe King

        Guest: Madeline Carroll

        Cruising Down the River - City Slickers
        Entire cast - Tour No. 1 of New York
        Jay Meyer - "Just a Song At Twilight"
        Brush Those Tears From Your Eyes - Doodles Weaver
        *Ya Wanna Buy a Bunny? - George Rock
        The Best Things In Life Are Free (production)
        Madeline Carroll, cast - The Knockwursts

        *issued on MF Distribution LPs MF 205/4

27 March, 1949 (SUN)
        Worcester, Mass
          Cut ET for re-broadcast

"...Spike Jones...and the City Slickers expect to wind up their cross-country tour in New York sometime around Easter... in town long enough to get five or six video appearances under their belts...as a sort of barometer to test the public's reaction..... Spike's gone at the TV thing in dead earnest. He's been planning this debut for months and with the aid of Ralph Wonders...he's gathering everything from special colored and checked bow ties and turkey feathers, to suits, instruments and other props created just for the purpose. He's even rented a warehouse to house the the collection until he needs it." (Movie Stars Parade, Mar 49)

28 March (MON), 29 March (TUES), 1949
                    Symphony Hall, Boston, Mass
                    8:30 PM both nights

30 March, 1949 (WED)
                    H.S. Aud, Manchester, N.H.
                    6:30 & 9:00 PM

31 March, 1949 (THURS)
                    Armory, Lewiston, Ma
                    8:30 PM

1 April, 1949 (FRI)
                    City Hall, Bangor, Ma
                    6:30 & 9:00 PM

2 April, 1949 (SAT)
                    City Aud, Portland, Ma
                    6:30 & 9:00 PM

                    THE SPIKE JONES SHOW (delayed b'cast)
                    CBS New York, NY   ann: Joe King

                    Guests: Charles Boyer and Kitty Kallen

                    Sidewalks of New York - City Slickers
                    Entire cast - Tour No. 2 of New York
                    Kitty Kallen - "Kiss Me Sweet, Kiss Me Simple"
                    Down By the Station - Doodles Weaver
                    Morpheus - City Slickers
                    Charles Boyer, cast - Inspector Spike Mal de Mer

3 April, 1949 (SUN)
                    Portland, Ma
                    Cut ET for re-broadcast

        Note: This is the final listing in Metcalfe's itinerary
showing CBS transcription dates

4 April, 1949 (MON)
                    Forum, Montreal, Que
                    8:30 PM

5 April, 1949 (TUES)
                    Auditorium, Ottawa, Ont
                    8:30 PM

6 April, 1949 (WED)
                    Arena, Peterboro, Ont
                    8:30 PM

7 April, 1949 (THURS)
                    Arena, London, Ont
                    8:30 PM

8 April, 1949 (FRI)
                    Coliseum, Toronto, Ont
                    8:30 PM

9 April, 1949 (SAT)
                    Arena, Niagara Falls, Ont
                       8:30 PM

          THE SPIKE JONES SHOW (delayed b'cast)
          CBS Boston, Mass   ann: Joe King

          Guest: Boris Karloff

          Charlie My Boy - City Slickers
          Entire cast - Tour No. 1 of Boston
          Aileen Gallagher - "Love is Where You Find It"
          Down Among the Sheltering Palms - Doodles Weaver
          Wild Bill Hiccup (All Right Louie, Drop the
             Gun) - City Slickers
          Boris Karloff, cast - Paul Revere's Other Horse

10 April, 1949 (SUN)
                    Col. Civic Center, Rochester, N.Y.
                       3:00 & 8:30 PM

11 April, 1949 (MON)
                    Lincoln Aud, Syracuse, N.Y.

12 April, 1949 (TUES)
                    Armory, Utica, N.Y.
                       8:30 PM

     "Account keeping is almost a full-time job. For, sold out 99
per-cent of the time, the Revue is grossing about $25,750 a week -
less operating expenses of $10,000 to $11,000. In addition there are
printed programs, sold by a 7 foot 7 inch giant and a pint-sized
midget at 50 cents a piece. They cost Jones 14 cents each."
                    (Newsweek, 4 Apr 49)
     "Spike Jones' troupe...has just wound up six-Canadian key-
city concerts, which grossed walloping $65,971, after taxes. The
$17,934 reaped in Toronto...is biggest gross of any one-niter in
Jones' whole tour this year. The $12,042 in Ottawa and $13,619 in
Montreal are among best takes troupe has registered. On all dates,
Jones got straight 60 percent of gross."
                    (unidentified Schenectady newspaper, 13 Apr 49)

13 April, 1949 (WED)
                    Armory, Schenectady, NY
                       8:30 PM

14 April, 1949 (THURS)
                    Kleinham Aud, Buffalo, NY
                       8:30 PM (sold out)

     Temporarily 'joining' the Slickers at Niagara Falls, Ont. (9
Apr) is Tom Bernard, journalist for the American Magazine.
     "I have just returned from playing six consecutive one-night
stands with Spike Jones and his City Slickers, that band of uninhibi-
ted screwballs who sincerely believe that music is something to be
murdered rather than played for purposes aesthetic or cultural. In
another week of so I should be able to struggle from my oxygen tent
and out of my bandages, and renew, at least physically, my previous
peaceful existence. My bruises, contusions, and abrasions will have
disappeared. The pneumonia will be gone. My deafness will gradually
abate. With concerted effort with shampoo and currycomb I should be
able to remove the bubble gum from my hair. My mental future, how-

225

ever, is in doubt."
         Bernard's entertaining account of his brief Slicker career
started when he was handed a gaudy green, yellow and red plaid suit,
a battered black derby, "a sorry excuse for a trombone", then assigned a seat on the bandstand - all with the promise he would be well
looked after. "...Six nights later I collapsed in a hotel room, convinced that never in the history of music had such a zany collection
of entertainers been assembled to masquerade as an orchestra."
         "In those six nights I learned something of how Spike Jones
has taken unadulterated idiocy, mixed it with generous portions of
good music and broad satire, and sold the whole concoction for well
over a million dollars a year. In doing so, he has hired otherwise
sane and talented entertainers and paid them handsomely to join him
in the nuthouse and help him prove that corn and music can pay off
with a laugh-loving public.
         "They work twice, three times, four times harder than the
average bandsman, and when the opportunity to relax presents itself
they grab it with both hands and make the most of it. Their work is
never done, because they are continually working on new arrangements
of production numbers and planning fresh musical madness for their
radio show."   (Tom Bernard, American Magazine, July 1949)

15 April, 1949 (FRI)
                    Open date (Good Friday)

16 April, 1949 (SAT)
                    Stambaugh Aud, Youngstown, Ohio
                    7:00 & 9:30 PM

                    THE SPIKE JONES SHOW (delayed b'cast)
                    CBS Boston, Mass   ann: Joe King

                    Guests: Basil Rathbone and Fran Warren

                    Knock, Knock, Who's There - vocal quartet
                    Entire cast - Tour No. 2 of Boston
                    Fran Warren - "What's My Name?"
                    Galway Bay - Doodles Weaver
                    Ya Wanna Buy a Bunny? - George Rock
                    The Barber of Seville - Sir Frederick Gas
                    Basil Rathbone, cast - Television show medley

17 April, 1949 (SUN)
                    Arena, Cleveland, Ohio
                    8:30 PM

         Note: Window posters advertise the Revue's appearance in
Akron, Ohio on this date

18 April, 1949 (MON)
                    Wills Gym, Kent, Ohio
                    8:15 PM

19 April, 1949 (TUES)
                    Municipal Aud, Columbus, Ohio
                    8:30 PM

20 April, 1949 (WED)
                    Memorial Aud, Dayton, Ohio
                    8:30 PM

226

21 April (THURS), 22 April (FRI), 1949
               Civic Opera House, Chicago, Ill
               8:30 PM both nights

        "Now on the last lap of his nationwide and northern Canadian
one-niters, Jones returns here next month for three-week stand at
Biltmore theatre downtown, starting May 15 at 70 percent of gross. He
gets same deal for date starting June 6 at another legit house, the
Curran, Frisco. Troupe vacashes during July, then plays three frames
at Flamingo, Las Vegas, opening Aug. 4 at flat $12,000 per week."
               (unidentified, undated trade journal)

23 April, 1949 (SAT)
                    Field House, Beloit, Wis
                    8:30 PM

               THE SPIKE JONES SHOW (delayed b'cast)
               CBS Chicago, Ill   ann: Mike Wallace

               Guest: Marlene Dietrich

               Chicago - City Slickers, with vocal refrain
               Czardas - feat Dick Gardner, vln
                         (straight)
               Rabbits, Rabbits, Rabbits (story) - Doodles Weaver
               Take Me Out to the Ball Game (skit) -
                    City Slickers
               Marlene Dietrich - "Want To Buy Some Illusions?"
               Marlene, Slickers - Cowbell lesson

24 April, 1949 (SUN)
                    Municipal Aud, St. Paul, Minn
                    8:30 PM

25 April, 1949 (MON)
                    Arena, Aberdeen, S.D.
                    8:30 PM

26 April, 1949 (TUES)
                    Corn Palace, Mitchell, S.D.
                    8:30 PM

28 April, 1949 (WED)
                    Orpheum Theatre, Sioux City, Iowa
                    7:00 & 9:30 PM

29 April, 1949 (THURS)
                    Field House, Iowa City, Iowa
                    8:30 PM

30 April, 1949 (SAT)
                    Field House, Moline, Ill
                    8:30 PM

               THE SPIKE JONES SHOW (delayed b'cast)
               CBS Chicago, Ill   ann: Mike Wallace

               Guests: Don McNeill and the Dinning Sisters

               Five Foot Two, Eyes Of Blue - City Slickers

                              227

Entire cast - History of Chicago
Dinning Sisters - "Oh, Monah"
Cruising Down the River - Doodles Weaver
There's Nothing Like a Circus - City Slickers
Don McNeil, cast - The Wake-Up Club

Note: Tape editing has become sloppy, cutting from one word to the middle of another sentence on this ET

1 May, 1949 (SUN)
Auditorium, Waterloo, Iowa
8:30 PM

2 May (MON), 3 May (TUES), 1949
KRNT Theatre, Des Moines, Iowa
8:30 PM both nights

4 May, 1949 (WED)
University of Nebraska, Lincoln, Neb
8:30 PM

5 May, 1949 (THURS)
Auditorium, Denver, Colo
3:00 & 8:30 PM

6 May, 1949 (FRI)
Travel

7 May, 1949 (SAT)
Arrive Los Angeles 7:00 PM

THE SPIKE JONES SHOW (delayed b'cast)
CBS KRNT Theatre, Des Moines, Ia,   ann: Tom
                                                Lewis
Guest: Frances Langford

Knock, Knock, Who's There? - vocal quartet
Entire cast - Tour of Des Moines
Frances Langford - "Just One Of Those Things"
I've Got My Love To Keep Me Warm - Doodles Weaver
California Here I Come - City Slickers
Frances Langford - "That Old Black Magic"
Frances, cast - The Knockwursts (in the style
     of the "Bickersons", which Frances and Don
     Ameche took to fame)

Note: During "California...", the network line is interrupted for several seconds. At the conclusion of this tour, Nancy McDonald put out her cigar, hung up the serape and went into the studios. Local musicians augmenting the Slickers on this (3 May) show included, among others; Robert Bagley, James Selland, tpt; Karl Killinger, trb; Dave Kever, reeds.

8 May to 14 May, 1949
Off, according to original itinerary

13 May, 1949 (FRI)
NBC New York

Bill Stern interview with Spike Jones in Hollywood.
Subject: racing car accidents.

14 May, 1949 (SAT) - THE SPIKE JONES SHOW
                CBS Hollywood   ann: Michael Roy

                Guests: Richard Widmark and Kay Starr

                Sweet Georgia Brown - City Slickers
                Kay Starr - "How It Lies"
                *Dance of the Hours - Doodles Weaver
                Richard Widmark, Spike - The Killers

                *issued on MF Distribution LPs MF 205/4,
                    947447, and GO 10016

        Note: "The Killers" script verbatim from "The Jack Kirkwood
Show" of 1 July 46 (also written by Jay Sommers)

15 May (SUN) to 4 June (SAT), 1949
                Biltmore Hotel Theatre, L.A. (see below)

        "Spike Jones is breathing easier today...The zany comic
three months ago booked his troupe into Biltmore for three weeks and
put up bond of $1,250 for each week, in case he cancelled. He did and
was on the hook for the coin ($3,750) until house nabbed another at-
traction ('Cabalgata' Revue from Mexico City) for the period. Yesterday, Jones' luck still holding, he got out from under a $2,900 bill
for 62 24-sheet stands he had ordered. Bill-posting firm of Foster &
Kleiser took the order off his hands for another client. All the can-
cellation now costs Jones is $65 for a lobby display he had ordered
for the Biltmore. Reports of Jones' illness on road were greatly mag-
nified. He missed three one-nite stands due to flu bugs. He had planned to break in four new acts and new "slicker" routines at Biltmore,
but now will dust off new material and turns during date at Curran,
Frisco, starting June 5. His rep. here, Dick Webster, is digging up
new acts for tryout, prior to troupe's arrival back May 8"
                (unidentified, 'Hollywood Inside' column, 26 Apr 49)

        Paul and Paulette, trampoline stars who work often with the
Revue, are replaced by the Herzogs.

19 May, 1949 (THURS)
                Son, Lindley Armstrong Jones Jr., born to Spike Jones
        and Helen Grayco (Mrs. Jones). Weight 7 lbs, 12 oz., at
        the Hollywood Presbyterian Hospital

21 May, 1949 (SAT) - THE SPIKE JONES SHOW
                CBS Hollywood   ann: Michael Roy

                Guest: Dorothy Lamour

                By the Beautiful Sea - City Slickers
                Roundtable discussion - Tchaikovsky
                Dorothy Lamour - "What Is This Thing Called Love?"
                Pootwaddle Car Polish - Doodles Weaver
                *Riders In the Sky - Dick Morgan, Earle Bennett
                Dorothy Lamour, cast - South Pacific

                *issued on MF Distribution LPs MF 205/4,
                    947447, and GO 10016

        Note: This performance of "Riders In the Sky", a dress for
the recording, went well - smoother than the history of the recorded

                                229

version.

24 May, 1949 (TUES) - Radio Recorders, Hollywood   8:45 PM to
                   Client: RCA Victor   3:00 AM
                   W. Heebner, A & R Rep, present

                               Leader - Spike Jones
                               Brass - George Rock, tpt; Joe Colvin, trb
                               Reeds - Jack Golly, clar; Dick Gardner, Eddie
                                 Metcalfe, sax
                               Rhythm - Paul Leu, pno; Dick Morgan, Freddy
                                 Morgan , bjo; Roger Donley, bass; Joe Siracusa,
                                 drm
                               Harp - Charlotte Tinsley
                               Flute - Phillip Shuken
                               Vocalists - Jay Meyer, J. Brown, Dick Morgan
                               Actors - Doodles Weaver, Earle Bennett, Purves
                                 Pullen, Dick Baldwin, George Rock, Jack Golly,
                                 Freddy Morgan

D9-VB-643-1   20-3620-B; HMV B 9816; HMVAU B 9816 & EA 4258;
     1A   HMVS B 9816; RCADJ 827-B; VSM SG 206;
                   45 47-3126-B; LP RCAAU ODLP 7503; RCAG PJM2-
                   8021; ET AFRS "Basic Music Library" PGL-37;
        (3:19)Wild Bill Hiccup - voc Spike Jones, Jack Golly,
                   Freddy Morgan, George Rock and the Four
                   Fifths

D9-VB-644-1   20-3516-A; 420-0171-A; HMVAU EA 4178; RCADJ
     1A   746-A; 45 47-2992-A; 74-0532-B(condensed);
                   447-0171-A; EPA 415; RCAG EPA 415; RCAAU
                   EP 20017; LP LPM 2224; LPM 3128; LPM 3849;
                   LSP 3849(e); ANL1 1035(e); AYL1 3748; AGL1
                   4142(e); RCAAU CAS 7158, ODLP 6024 & ODLP 7503;
                   PK ACL 7031(e); RCAE LSA 3084 & RD 7724; RCAG
                   LSP 10157 & RCS 3211/1-2; RCAJ 5142; RCAIT
                   CL 83748; RCAF PL 43197; RCA Special Products
                   "Good Music Record" DML1 0570; ET AFRS "Basic
                   Music Library" P-1423 & PGL-37; AFRS "Martin
                   Block" 396; AFRS "Carroll" 875(condensed);
                   Public Service Show "Here's To Vets" 372; Your
                   Rhythm Revue-Sister Kenny Foundation KBAL 2;
        (3:30)Dance of the Hours - Commentator: Doodles
                   Weaver

D9-VB-645-1   20-3741-B; HMV B 9816; HMVAU B 9816 & EA 4258;
     1A   HMVS B 9816; RCADJ 943-B; VSM SG 206;
                   LP RCAE NL 42730(e); RCAG PJM2 8021; RCAJ
                   RVP 6300(m) & 5143(m);
        (3:22)Riders in the Sky
                   (MADE ON APPROVAL) "a parody on Vaughn Monroe"

      2   20-3741-B; 45 47-3741-B; LP ANL1-2312(e);
     2A   AYL1 3870;
        (3:22)Riders in the Sky - voc I.W. Harper, Sir
                   Frederick Gas and the Sons of the Sons of
                   the Backwoodsmen

      Note: The RCA inst do not list as voc/act:- Dick Morgan
(I.W. Harper), George Rock, Jack Golly or Freddy Morgan. BMI registry
lists the title and Arena Stars published the music as "....Hickup".
"Dance of the Hours" reached No. 13 position on the Hit Parade on 19
August 1949 and, according to Billboard Magazine, remained there for
nine weeks.

"Riders in the Sky" takes -1 and -1A contained an ending that was offensive to Vaughn Monroe, popular band leader/vocalist, major RCA recording artist and spokesman for their Victrola line. An altenate ending was intercut 13 Mar 50 and "Riders" was then released and backed with "Chinese Mule Train". In Jones' files were breakable 78 RPM dubs of "Riders..." from the 21 May b'cast - undoubtedly for friends as RCA would not release the studio version. A 12" 78 RPM vinyl dub of "Riders..." from the same show, with a plain label is also known, with a Red Skelton version of "Mule Train" on flip

Some issues of 20-3741 did contain the original, unaltered ending on "Riders", and these are believed to have originated from a West Coast distributor. These original issues, very rare, are iden- tifiable by the bright gold lettering on the label. They were hastily recalled and take -2 is the common North American issue. As far as can be determined, take -1 (-1A) was issued on all discs outside of Canada and the U.S., being virtually identical to the "Riders" as b'cast. It is the final few seconds of this "parody on Vaughn Monroe" that was offensive and subsequently altered to the sound effect of the rider being shot off of his horse.

("Riders" ending:-)
        Chorus:- "For all I hear is Ghost Riders sung
                Vaughn Monroe,"
        I.W. Harper:- "I can do without his singing-" (deleted)
        Ghost:- "But I wish I had his dough" (deleted)

"Monroe has frowned upon RCA...plans to release Spike Jones' version of "Riders in the Sky", the disc recorded for the same company by Vaughn Monroe which has sold more than 1,000,000 copies. Issue of the zany platter is temporarily halted until Monroe has heard the Jones version."
                         (Evening Star-Telegram, Ft. Worth, 3 June 49)
"Don't be too concerned about the budding feud between Vaughn Monroe and Spike Jones, it's a phony.
"This department was warned by a press agent some time ago to expect a 'feud' to break out to draw more attention to the radio shows - one of those Jack Benny-Fred Allen things.
"However, there was a little bad feeling between the two a while back. Monroe's recording of 'Riders in the Sky' was at the top of the heap when Jones recorded a burlesque version of the tune. Monroe insisted that RCA-Victor hold up release of Jones' version, which the company did. Monroe was said to be afraid the Jones record would hurt the sale of his recording.
"It was reported the publisher of the tune threatened to sue Jones if the record were released.
"If how a tune is performed is basis for a suit, we can think of several singers and orchestras that would be in jeapardy."
                    (unidentified, Kansas, 21 Aug 51)

        Walt Heebner, RCA's A & R Director at that time, writes:- "I remember the Vaughn Monroe reference very well...we all broke up because of the ending when we played it back; however, I remember vividly explaining Vaughn's character traits that he would not permit any humor about his voice--he hated the comics who burlesked his voice. I remember speaking to my boss, Eli Oberstein, (the 'grand- daddy' of all A&R men...) in NY...and (alerting) him to the VM end- ing--rushing a 78 dub to him, then calling Spike at home to again "suggest" he make a new ending. As I remember, the ending was record- ed and cut into (mine) in Chicago." (Walt Heebner letter 2 Jun 83)

28 May, 1949 (SAT) - THE SPIKE JONES SHOW
                CBS Hollywood   ann: Michael Roy

        Guests: Eddy Arnold and Lassie

Runnin' Wild - City Slickers, with voc refrain
Roundtable discussion - Schubert
Eddy Arnold - "One Kiss Too Many"
*Pootwaddle Cigarettes - Doodles Weaver
*When Knighthood Goes To Pot(Rhythm Opera on
    A Connecticut Yankee In King Arthur's Court)
    - feat Spike, Dick Morgan, Sir Frederick Gas
Ill Barkio - Aileen Gallagher, Dr. H.Q.
    Birdbath and Lassie

        *issued on MF Distribution LPs MF 205/4,
            947447, and GO 10016

        Note: Lassie goes berserk during "Ill Barkio" with the
operatic singing, Doc's barking and the sound effects. Trainer Rudd
Weatherwax is noticably shaken after the song, mis-reading his
closing lines.

4 June, 1949 (SAT) - THE SPIKE JONES SHOW
        CBS Hollywood   ann: Michael Roy

        Guest: Dan Dailey

        *Barney Google - City Slickers, voc refrain
        Roundtable discussion - Wedding March (Wagner)
        Dan Dailey - "Beautiful Blonde From Bashful Bend"
        Pootwaddle Hair Tonic - Doodles Weaver
        People Are Funnier Than Anybody - City Slickers
        Dan Dailey, cast - Spike Jones' life story

        *issued on MF Distribution LPs MF 205/4,
            947447, and GO 10016

6 June, 1949 (MON)
        Curran Theatre, San Francisco, for three weeks

        "Since I've become acquainted with Spike Jones, I've come to
know what a really nice person he is. He sent me a cable about the
arrival of his son and this is the first chance I've had to congrat-
ulate him and his wife, Helen.
        "I have just heard that the baby had a pretty hard time.
Last Monday it was rushed to the Hollywood Hospital in a critical
condition. Three doctors were in attendance. Helen didn't want to
ruin Spike's opening in San Francisco, so she didn't tell him anything about the illness, but when the baby became terribly sick Spike
had to be told. He planed home and remained until Spike Jr. was out
of danger. The little one went home yesterday."
        (unidentified, undated newspaper)

10 June, 1949 (FRI)
        KCBS, San Francisco, "Curfew Club"

        Interview by Bob Goerner with Spike Jones. Subject:
stage show presentation (transcribed)

11 June, 1949 (SAT) - THE SPIKE JONES SHOW (delayed b'cast)
        CBS San Francisco   ann: Michael Roy

        Guests: Kay Starr and Kirk Douglas

                            232

Wang Wang Blues - City Slickers, voc refrain
Roundtable discussion - Beethoven
Kay Starr - "The Lonsomest Gal in Town"
Pootwaddle Vitamins - Doodles Weaver
*That Old Black Magic - voc Dick Baldwin
Kirk Douglas, cast - The Schlemiel (in the
    style of "The Champions" movie)

    *issued on MF Distribution LPs 205/4,
        947447, and GO 10016

18 June, 1949 (SAT)
        KROW, Oakland, "Boyd's Nest"

    Interview by Lex Boyd with Spike, Doc, Doodles and
Frankie Little. Subject: stage show promotion (on 16" ET)

        THE SPIKE JONES SHOW
            CBS San Francisco   ann: Michael Roy

        Guest: Diana Lynn

        Charlie My Boy - City Slickers, voc refrain
        Roundtable discussion - Schubert
        Diana Lynn - "You've Got That Thing"
        *Pootwaddle Toothpaste - Doodles Weaver
        #Want Ads - feat Spike, Jack Golly, George
            Rock, Dick Morgan

        *issued on MF Distribution LPs 205/4
        #issued (edited) on MF Distribution LPs
            205/4, 947447, and GO 10016

    Note: Dick Morgan is "Horse Trader Ed", and his song, "I Got
'Em" has been published "as featured by Spike Jones and his City
Slickers". Apart from this show, just when and where it was featured
is unknown. Opener was to have been "San Francisco"(Open Up Your
Golden Gate) according to script. George Rock's vocal, "the Puppy
With the Patent-Leather Ears" was deleted from the ET.

25 June, 1949 (SAT) - THE SPIKE JONES SHOW
        CBS San Francisco   ann: Michael Roy

        Guest: Don Ameche

        My Gal Sal - City Slickers, voc refrain
        Roundtable discussion - Opera
        Dick Baldwin - "It Happens Every Spring"
        Dance of the Hours - Doodles Weaver
        Don Ameche, cast - This is your F.B.Aida

    The entire show was issued (with some of the Roundtable
dialogue edited) on Radiola Records LP MR-1010. The "Spike
Jones Show" theme from this b'cast was issued on Viva LPs
VV-2572 & V-36020, "Themes Like Old Times"; and Warner Bros.
LPs SP 2504, "I Remember Radio"

    Note: Spike thanks all Slickers by name, although he omits
Jack Golly. Audience reactions (eg: laughter) were later edited into
the comedy dialogue of the 18/25 June CBS ETs, to the surprise of the
recording engineer, Paul Courtland Smith.

3 July, 1949 (SUN) - LOUELLA PARSONS SHOW*
                    CBS(?) Hollywood

            Guests: Spike Jones and his City Slickers

            Dance of the Hours - Doodles Weaver

        Typical of the annual rumors in trade journals about Spike
doing another movie is the following:- "Deal is cooking for Spike
Jones'...crew to make a picture to be produced by Harry Sherman.
Jones and Sherman have had several meetings but no script has been
settled upon. If papers are inked, picture won't be made until next
April, at the earliest, because Jones' upcoming string of personals..
.."   (unidentified newspaper, 6 June 49)

31 July (SUN), 1 August (MON), 1949 - Radio Recorders, Hollywood
                    Client: RCA Victor   6:00 to 9:00 PM
                    Walter Heebner, A & R Rep, present

                    Leader - Spike Jones
                    Brass - George Rock, tpt; Joe Colvin, trb
                    Reeds - Dick Gardner, Jack Golly, Eddie
                        Metcalfe, sax/clar
                    Rhythm - Paul Leu, pno; Dick Morgan, Freddy
                        Morgan, bjo; Roger Donley, bass; Joe Siracusa
                        drm
                    Harp - Charlotte Tinsley
                    act/voc - Earle Bennett, Carl Grayson, Frank
                        Leithner, Helen Grayco, Freddy Morgan

D9-VB-685-1   20-3620-A; RCADJ 827-A; HMV B 10009;
        1A   45 47-3126-A; LP LSC 3235(e); AGL1 4142(e);
                        RCAG PJM2 8021; RCAJ RVP 6300(m) '& 5142;
              (2:45)Orpheus Overture - voc Freddy Morgan; sneezes,
                        Sir Frederick Gas

D9-VB-686-1   Unissued
        1A (3:14)A Goose to the Ballet Russe - voc Freddy Morgan
                        and Helen Grayco
        2   20-4055-B; RCADJ D9-VB-686; 45 47-4055-B; EPA 415;
        2A   RCAG EPA 415; LP LPM 3128; LSC 3235(e);
                        AGL1 4142(e); RCAE INTS 5052; RCAAU ODLP 6024;
                        RCAG LPM 10 013 & RCS 3211/1-2; RCAJ RVP
                        6300(m) & 5142; RCAF PL 43197; ET AFRS "Basic
                        Music Library" P-2202 & PGL 37; AFRS "Juke Box
                        USA" 96;
              (3:14)Rhapsody From Hunger(y) - voc Freddy Morgan
                        and Helen Grayco

        Note: RCA inst do not include the names of Freddy Morgan and
Helen Grayco as vocalists. "Orpheus" issued title is "Morpheus", and
the oft advertised "Goose to the Ballet Russe" is "Rhapsody From
Hunger(y)", a title which suffers further metamorphosis in 1950 when
re-recorded for a special occasion and retitled "Ballet For Bosuns'
Mate". Varying standards between recording companies are to be noted.
Columbia issued "Don't Give Me No Goose For Christmas, Grandma" years
before Spike tried to put a 'Goose' on the RCA label. The Canadian
issues of "Morpheus", 78/45 RPM, lack the final triplet, chord and
sneeze. "Morpheus" label credit is given to Sir F. Gas for all sneezes, but they belong to Spike's long time colleague, Frank Leithner,
and the 'glugs' are those of the original Slicker, Carl Grayson.
        RCA addition/correction sheets dated 31 July and 13 December
give the take no. for the issued "Rhapsody" as -2 & -2A. 13 Dec sheet

also notes:- "...that the above take (-2 and -2A was electrically transferred from the -1 and -1A take with certain deletions, etc)". This days session continues:

Radio Recorders, Hollywood, 10:00 PM to 1:00 AM, &
1:15 to 4:15 AM (1 Aug)

Personnel as listed, deleting Paul Leu, Carl
Grayson and Frank Leithner, and adding

Conductor - Charles Hathaway
Narrator - Spike Jones
Brass - W.R. (Bobby) Guy, tpt
Reeds - Phillip Shuken, Art Fleming, sax
Rhythm - George Greely, pno; Ralph Hansell, perc
Voc/act - Eileen Gallagher, Elizabeth Rinker,
Loulie Jean Norman, Virginia Rees, Faith
Kruger, D. Knight, W. Reeve, Harry Stanton,
A. Markussen
Adaption - Jay Sommers, Eddie Brandt

D9-VB-687-1   45 EPA 440; RCAG EPA 440; RCAAU EP 20015;
        1A   LP LPM 3128; LSC 3235(e); AGL1 4142(e);
                    RCAG LPM 10 013 & RCS 3211/1-2; RCAAU ODLP
                    6024; RCAJ RVP 6300(m) & 5142; RCAF LP 130216
                    & PL 43197;
          (3:27)Carmen (side 1)
                    1. Overture (Bizet Gets the Business)
                    2. The Bubble Gum Girls Stick Together
                    3. Carmen (A Square in Seville)
                Spike Jones, narrator; Eilleen Gallagher,
                Messy-Soprano, and the Hollywood Bowling
                Choral Group

D9-VB-688-1   All releases identical to Carmen side 1 listing
        1A (2:49)Carmen (side 2)
                    1. Don Schmozay and Soldiers
                    2. March (April, May, June and July)
                    3. Carmen Kills a Cadenza
                Spike Jones, narrator; Eileen Gallagher,
                Messy-Soprano; Harry Stanton, Bass Barracuda

        Note: Carmen may have been intended for 78 RPM issue but was
held by RCA for almost four years before issuing on their new 45 RPM
extended play disc (which was not issued in Canada). The arrangers,
Brandt and Sommers are identified on the album jacket only. Carl
Grayson 'glugs' on side 2, "March", although RCA inst indicates he
was not there.

1 August, 1949 (MON) - Radio Recorders, Hollywood   1:00 to
                Client: RCA Victor   6:30 PM
                Walter Heebner, A & R Rep, present

                Conductor - Charles Hathaway
                Narrator - Spike Jones
                Brass - George Rock, Bobby Guy, tpt; Joe
                Colvin, trb
                Reeds - Dick Gardner, Jack Golly, Ed Metcalfe,
                Phillip Shuken, Art Fleming
                Rhythm - Paul Leu, pno; Dick Morgan, Freddy
                Morgan, bjo; Roger Donley, bass; Joe Siracusa,
                Ralph Hansell, perc
                Harp - Charlotte Tinsley

```
                    Actor - Earle Bennett
                    Actress/voc - Eileen Gallagher
                    Vocalist - Elizabeth Rinker, Loulie Jean Norman,
                      Virginia Rees, Faith Kruger, Harry Stanton,
                      D. Knight, W. Reeve, A. Markussen
                    Adaption - Jay Sommers, Eddie Brandt

D9-VB-689-1            All releases identical to Carmen side 1 listing
     1A (3:15)Carmen (side 3)
                         1. The Giggle Song
                    Spike Jones, narrator; Eileen Gallagher,
                      Messy-Soprano; Sir Frederick Gas, base

D9-VB-690-1            All releases identical to Carmen side 1 listing
     1A (3:12)Carmen (side 4)
                         1. Typewriter Song for Twelve Fingers
                         2. Toreador Song (It's the Bull)
                         3. Finale (also End)
                    Spike Jones, narrator; Eilleen Gallagher,
                      Messy-Soprano, The Hollywood Bowling
                      Choral Group, and Bull
```

Note: The bassoon heard on side 3 was very likely played by Art Fleming.

"Coincidence often plays a great part in success.
"And it was an odd circumstance that resulted in Spike Jones receiveing one of the biggest publicity promotions of modern times, appearing in the Dick Tracy comic strip for eight consecutive weeks.
"Playing in Chicago for two nights only (21/22 Apr) Spike invited Chester Gould, creator of Dick Tracy, together with his family to a performance. Tickets were reserved but the Gould family did not arrive. A mistake had been made, they thinking it was the second peroformance. The next night the Gould party arrived and the auditorium was completely sold out, not unusual for Spike, but unfortunate for the Goulds.
"However Spike did the next best thing. He placed four chairs in the wings for the family to view the show, put a slicker and a derby on Gould, handed him a trombone, and sat him on the band stand with his musical maniacs.
"Following the performance Gould told Spike he might have a surprise for him but did not explain further. Weeks went by and Spike had all but forgotten the incident. Playing in Las Vegas he picked up a paper, and after a cursory digest of the news, sports page and other features turned to the comics to see what was happening to Dick Tracy - and received the surprise of his life.
"Spike 'Dyke' Jones was being introduced to the detective. The strip appeared for eight weeks while the famous sleuth solved a murder mystery climaxed by Tracy shooting the culprit from Spike's band stand while wearing a disguise and ostensibly playing a trombone!".   (Colorado Morning Press, Colorado Springs, Colo, 21 Jan 51)

Note: Spike 'Dyke' Jones met Dick Tracy 7 Aug 49. Audrey Haas, dancer, starts with the troupe. Gilda Fish starts to appear on programs at this time, another ficticious name that applied to many actress', but no one in particular. Dick Baldwin has left, and the 'straight' singing is now well handled by Eddie Metcalfe.

```
D9-CB-1346            RCADJ D9-CB-1346;
                    Spike Jones, in a Roundtable Discussion, describes
                      the musical instruments used in "Dance of the
                      Hours", with Dick Morgan and selected clips
                      from the issue disc, and one effect clip from
                      the 18 June 49 Coke show.
```

3 August, 1949 (WED)
>   Spike Jones appeared as guest on the NBC produced
>   UNITED STATES COAST GUARD 159th Anniversary
>   show transcription. Details unknown (WNBC only)

"MUSICAL DEPRECIATION REVUE OF 1950"

4 August (THURS) to 24 August (WED), 1949
>   Flamingo Hotel, Las Vegas, Nev

17 August, 1949 (WED)
>   KLAS(CBS), Las Vegas

>   Interview by Chubby Johnson with Spike, as heard on
>   the "Old Timers Program". Subject: Spike Jones Day at the
>   Las Vegas Animal Shelter

25 August (THURS) to 27 August (SAT), 1949
>   Lagoon Park Ballroom, Salt Lake City, Utah
>   9:30 & 11:30 PM

28 August, 1949 (SUN)
>   Travel

29 August, 1949 (MON)
>   Memorial Aud, McCook, Neb
>   8:30 PM

30 August, 1949 (TUES)
>   Orpheum Theatre, Omaha, Neb 7:00 & 9:30 PM

31 August, 1949 (WED)
>   Travel

1 September (THURS) to 4 September (SUN), 1949
>   Coliseum, Indianapolis, Ind

5 September, 1949 (MON)
>   Evansville, Ind

6 September, 1949 (TUES)
>   N. High School Aud, Ft. Wayne, Ind
>   8:30 PM

7 September, 1949 (WED)
>   Municipal Aud, Kalamazoo, Mich
>   8:30 PM

8 September, 1949 (THURS)
>   Prudden Aud, Lansing, Mich
>   8:30 PM

9 September, 1949 (FRI)
>   Municipal Aud, Saginaw, Mich
>   7:00 & 9:30 PM

10 September, 1949 (SAT)
>   Kellogg Aud, Battle Creek, Mich
>   8:30 PM

11 September, 1949 (SUN)
                    Sports Arena, Toledo, Ohio
                    8:30 PM

12 September, 1949 (MON)
                    I.M.A. Aud, Flint, Mich
                    8:30 PM

13 September, 1949 (TUES)
                    County Aud, Jackson, Mich
                    7:00 & 9:30 PM

        "Ever wonder where Spike Jones finds the material for those
fantastic suits he and his "City Slickers" wear? Spike says he makes
it a point of dropping into the little 'general stores' in the rural
areas of the country through which he travels on his p.a. tours.
Often he unearths old bolts of cloth which have been gathering dust
for 30 years and lo, the Slickers have new suits.."
                    (unidentified, undated newspaper)
        "The zany musical group's weird sound effects are almost
equaled by the crazy checks and 'ice cream' tints of their flamboyant
wardrobe. Spike pays a Hollywood tailor $350 apiece for the Gay Nine-
ties suits the boys wear. But it took the Truman Inauguration for
Spike to really go overboard - to the tune of $500 for a white
gabardine suit, cross-braided with gold."
                    (unidentified, 20 May 49)

14 September, 1949 (WED)
                    H.S. Gym, Ponitac, Mich
                    8:30 PM

15 September (THURS) to 23 September (FRI), 1949
                    Music Hall Theatre, Detroit, Mich

24 September, 1949 (SAT)
                    Fair Grounds, Ashland, Ohio

25 September, 1949 (SUN)
                    High School Aud, South Bend, Ind
                    8:30 PM

        Note: The knife-throwing act of Gordon and Olivia join the
troupe this day

26 September, 1949 (MON)
                    Arena, Grand Rapids, Mich
                    8:30 PM

27 September, 1949 (TUES)
                    Municipal Aud, Gary, Ind
                    8:30 PM

28 September, 1949 (WED)
                    Shrine Aud, Peoria, Ill
                    7:00 & 9:30 PM

29 September, 1949 (THURS)
                    High School Aud, Champaign, Ill
                    8:30 PM

30 September, 1949 (FRI)

                    Orpheum Theatre, Springfield, Ill
                         8:30 PM

1 October, 1949 (SAT)
                    High School Aud, Decatur, Ill
                         8:30 PM

2 October, 1949 (SUN)
                    High School Aud, Quincy, Ill
                         8:30 PM

3 October, 1949 (MON)
                    City Aud, S. Joseph, Mo
                         8:30 PM

4 October, 1949 (TUES)
                    Open booking, originally to have been
                         Topeka, Kan

5 October, 1949 (WED)
                    Municipal Aud. Music Hall, Kansas City, Mo
                         8:30 PM

6 October, 1949 (THURS)
                    A & M College, Stillwater, Ok
                         7:00 & 9:00 PM

7 October, 1949 (FRI)
                    Travel

8 October (SAT) to 23 October (SUN), 1949
                    "State Fair of Texas"
                    Fair Park Aud, Dallas, Tx

     "At the State Fair Auditorium...Musical Depreciation Revue
of 1950. Curtain times in the evenings are at 8:30 p.m. Mondays through Saturdays and 9 p.m. Sundays. Matinees are scheduled at 2:30
p.m. Thursday, at 1:30 and 4:30 Saturdays and at 2:30 and 6 p.m. Sundays.
     "Among the zany madcaps are Doodles Weaver, Freddie and Dick
Morgan, Sir Fredric Gas, Bill King, Dr. Horatio Q. Birdbath, George
Rock, Joe Siracusa, Roger Donley and Dick Gardner. Helen Grayco is
principal soloist. Other performers include Eileen Gallagher, The
Slickerettes, Eddie Metcalfe and Audrey Haas."
                    (News, Dallas, Tex, 9 Oct 49)

     "...Spike is hopeful that his visit will turn up at least
one new instrument for his band.
     "He says he hasn't added a new gadget to the fabulous array
of zany instruments since the Gazola-phone...was a musical monstros-
ity cooked up by Don Ameche, combining the most obnoxious features of
the alarm clock and the telephone.
     "Jones has however added a lot of new numbers to the Revue
since his last visit here. These include 'Dance of the Hours', which
for automobile racing did what Professor Feetlebaum does for nags;
'Wild Bill Hiccup', a departure for the Jones troupe; and 'Spike
Jones Amateur Hour'.
                    (News, Dallas, Tex, 30 Aug 49)

     "Winner of one contest was a young man whose instrument
included rubber hose, a locomotive whistle and parts of an egg beat-

                              239

er. No one else has been able to play the thing yet."
(Colliers, 10 Jan 49)

"George Rock, 280 pounds of man, did the falsetto vocal in
'...Two Front Teeth'. The record made platter history, selling over a
million copies in three weeks. Mr. Rock encases his robust frame in a
Little Lord Fauntleroy suit, plays a mean trumpet when given a chance
to go straight.
"Another stellar member...is Dr. Horatio Q. Birdbath, whose
real name is Purv Pullen. Purv can assemble a full barnyard via the
imitation route , but his real boast is that he's 'World bubble-gum
champion'. In Elko, Nevada, he once used 14 sticks of the nauseating
stuff to blow a bubble larger than a basketball. One of the Jones
bedlam specialists is Joe Siracusa, drummer. When he played with sym-
phonies in El Paso and Cleveland they called him a percussionist.
'Now', says Mr. Siracusa gleefully, 'I make more noise in one night
than I could make in a whole year with a symphony'.
(Times Herald, Dallas, Tex, 15 Sept 49)

"Musical Depreciation Revue of 1950...breaking box office
records in ninety per cent of the huge auditoriums and theatres in
which it has appeared this year..."
"The crazy antics of Spike and the company of forty-four
assorted madmen and pretty girls are said to appeal to music lovers,
music haters, farmers, city folk, socialites, anti-social people,
financiers, people without any money in the bank, and the plain guy-
-in-the-street.
"The show starts off with forty-four people on the stage
each trying to be nuttier than the other, and bit by bit new instruments appear on which the Slickers and Spike create bedlamic music
(you should pardon the expression)
"There are pistols, gongs, washboards, tin cans of all sizes
and battered water buckets. There's a 'pianothirty' for student music
musicians not expert enough to play the pianoforte, and the 'juke-
elele' which plays Hawaiian music when Spike drops a nickel into it.
'Ideal for musicians with broken hands'.
"And the genuine slot machine on the stage gives out the
sweetest music of all during each performance, when a jackpot of
$24.35 rolls out."   (Light, Waxahachie, Tex, 25 Aug 49)

"His brain teeming with ideas for further assaults on music.
...Jones, No. 1 mangler of music, flew in from Oklahoma City via
American Airlines. Accompanying him was Mrs. Jones...featured as
Helen Grayco in the Musical Depreciation Revue...
"Spike had a problem when he took on the Auditorium show, he
confessed. This was the matter of keeping old fans pleased with...
perennial favorites...while avoiding the charge that nothing new has
been added.
"The solution, he said has been in restaging the old ones,
engaging a knife-throwing act, two black pigs, and adding latest
instrumental creations...Spike refused to be pinned down...he might
even give Dallasites a preview of 'Goose to the Ballet Russe' and 'El
Barkio', two Jones inspirations that are to be issued by RCA Victor
in January."   (Times Herald, Dallas, Tex, 9 Oct 49)

RCADJ-613
Trailers (skits) for use in promotion of "My Two
Front Teeth", featuring Spike, George Rock,
Earle Bennett, Doodles Weaver, Freddy and Dick
Morgan. Recording date unknown

Note: Christmas promotion on "Two Front Teeth" is now very
evident. Reissued on 78 RPM (in picture sleeves) and the new 45 RPM,
it reached No. 18 on the Hit Parade by 30 Dec 49, and remained there
one week, according to Billboard Magazine.

240

24 October, 1949 (MON)
                        Municipal Aud, Shreveport, La
                        8:30 PM

25 October, 1949 (TUES)
                        Neville High School, Monroe, La
                        7:00 & 9:30 PM

26 October, 1949 (WED)
                        Robinson Memorial Aud, Little Rock, Ark
                        8:30 PM

27 October, 1949 (THURS)
                        Auditorium, Memphis, Tenn

28 October (FRI) to 10 November (THURS), 1949
                        Chase Hotel, St. Louis, Mo
                        2 shows per night

"The Chase Hotel in St. Louis is paying top dough of any hotel operating without shaking the dice or spinning roulette. Spike Jones is getting $12,500 a week for his two-week engagement."
(undated trade journal)

30 October (SUN), or
6 November (SUN), 1949 - SUNDAY AT THE CHASE*
            CBS Chase Hotel, St. Louis, Mo (KMOX)

                  Hindustan - City Slickers
                  Shortnin' Bread - Doodles Weaver
                  Sir Frederick Gas - "Souvenir"(monologue)
                  My Two Front Teeth - George Rock
                  Dance of the Hours - Doodles Weaver

"Whenever Spike Jones moves into a dressing room, his name plate on the door is a large nail.
"They offer two shows a night, running an hour each. A house band fills in for dancing between shows.
"Spike's crew used to play dance music - every member is a Grade A musician as well as a comedian - but hasn't in several years. "We put too much into our shows", said George Rock, the double-voiced trumpeter. "We just wouldn't have time to rehearse new numbers".
"I (Paul Hochuli) got an offer from Spike to 'join' the band. "Now that you are a movie star, I can use you", he said. "I'll put you on for a one-nighter when we get to Houston in January."
(Press, Houston, Tex, 1 Nov 49)

11 November, 1949 (FRI)
                        Evansville, Ind

12 November, 1949 (SAT)
                        Owensboro, Kent

13 November, 1949 (SUN)
                        Memorial Aud, Louisville, Kent
                        8:30 PM

14 November, 1949 (MON)
                        Taft Aud, Cincinnati, Ohio
                        8:30 PM

15 November, 1949 (TUES)
              High School Aud, Kokomo, Ind
                 8:30 PM

16 November, 1949 (WED)
              Anderson, Ind

17 November, 1949 (THURS)
              Indiana University Aud, Bloomington, Ind
                 8:15 PM

18 November, 1949 (FRI)
              Memorial Aud, Dayton, Ohio
                 8:30 PM

19 November, 1949 (SAT)
              Municipal Aud, Columbus, Ohio
                 8:30 PM

20 November, 1949 (SUN)
              Milwaukee, Wis

21 November (MON), 22 November (TUES), 1949
              Opera House, Chicago, Ill
                 8:30 PM both nights

23 November, 1949 (WED)
              Municipal Aud, Burlington, Iowa
                 8:30 PM

24 November (THURS) to 27 November (SUN), 1949
              Municipal Aud, Davenport, Iowa

28 November, 1949 (MON)
              Coliseum, Ottumna, Iowa
                 6:.30 & 9:30 PM

29 November, 1949 (TUES)
              Convention Hall, Tulsa, Ok
                 8:30 PM

30 November, 1949 (WED)
              Chanute, Kan

1 December, 1949 (THURS)
              Municipal Aud, Salina, Kan
                 8:30 PM

2 December, 1949 (FRI)
              Arcadia Theatre, Wichita, Kan
                 7:00 '& 9:30 PM

3 December, 1949 (SAT)
              Municipal Aud, Hutchinson, Kan
                 8:30 PM

4 December, 1949 (SUN)
              Municipal Aud, Puelo, Colo
                 8:30 PM

5 December, 1949 (MON)
                    Municipal Aud, Denver, Colo
                    8:30 PM

6 December, 1949 (TUES)
                    University Aud, Laramie, Wyo
                    8:30 PM

7 December, 1949 (WED)
                    Travel - arrive Los Angeles 8 Dec

    Eddie Metcalfe comment written at end of his itinerary:-

                            WHOOPEE!

        "Even the reindeers will go zany tonight when Spike Jones
and his "Music Depreciation" gang accompany Santa Claus down Christmas Tree Lane.
        "Spike and his beautiful bride, Helen Grayco, the not-so-
beautiful Dr. Horatio Q. Birdbath and George...Rock will be along.
        "The mad maestro and his troupe...recently returned from a
five-month tour of the country...hit the road again on Jan. 6.
        "Santa's sleigh leaves Argyle Ave. and Hollywood Blvd. at
7:30 p.m."   (unidentifed L.A. newspaper, 10 Dec 49)

        "There is no such thing as "corny music", according to Kay
Kayser, the "Professor of Musical Knowledge", who has been on the
radio for more than a decade. Reversing his usual position of dispen-
ser of musical information, 'Professor' Kayser, as guest star last
Saturday, asked his audience of high school musical scholars, who met
with him at the Herald Tribune Record Review Party, to quiz him regarding his knowledge of things musical.
        "'Do you consider Spike Jones's music corny?' was the init-
ial question. "Indeed Not!" Mr. Kayser said. "Spike Jones does his
type of musical nonsense extremely well - so it isn't corny. Now if I
tried to imitate Spike I'd be corny, because I'd be a poor imitation
of the original.
        "'Take Ted Lewis. He's great in his style with his clarinet,
but if he tried to play like Benny Goodman, he'd be corny. As long as
a man is good, and he stays himself - he's never corny'".
                    (Herald Tribune, N.Y. 17 Dec 49)
        (The student audience rated six current discs, and placed
Spike's "Happy New Year" second at 91, with Johnny Desmond the winner
at 92)

17 December, 1949 (SAT) - Radio Recorders, Hollywood   2:30 to
                    Client: RCA Victor   6:30 PM
                    W. Heebner, A & R Rep, present

                    Leader - Spike Jones
                    Brass - George Rock, tpt; King Jackson, Arthur
                        Most, trb
                    Reeds - Arthur 'Doc' Rando, b.clar/clar/sop sax
                    Rhythm - Paul Leu, pno; Freddy Morgan, bjo; Roger
                        Donley, tuba; John Cyr, drm; Lou Singer, xyl
                    Vocals - Del Porter, Eddie Maxwell

D9-VB-2611-1   20-3675-A(P-277); HMV B 9912; HMVSK B 9912;
        1A   HMVAU EA 3964; RCADJ 891-A; 45 47-3198-A
                    (WP-277); 547-0068-A(EPA-277); RCAG EPA 277;
                    RCAF 45308; LP LPM 18; ANL1 2312(e); AYL1
                    3870; RCAE HY 1006; RCAG RCS 3217/1-2;
                    ET AFRS "Basic Music Library" P-1512;

                            243

```
            (2:44)The Charleston  - voc Gil Bert and Sully Van
                  (from "Runnin' Wild")
        -2 (2:44)Unissued
        2A


D9-VB-2612-1    20-3676-B(P-277); RCADJ 892-B;
        1A      45 47-3199-B(WP-277); 547-0068-B(EPA-277);
                RCAG EPA 277; LP LPM 18; RCAG RCS 3217/1-2;
                ET AFRS "Basic Music Library" P-1512;
            (2:50)Doin' The New Raccoon - voc Gil Bert and
                  Sully Van


D9-VB-2613-1    20-3677-A(P-277); RCADJ 893-A;
        1A      45 47-3200-A(WP-277); LP LPM 18; RCAG PJM2
                8021; ET AFRS "Basic Music Library" P-1512;
            (2:42)I Wonder Where My Baby Is Tonight - voc
                  Gil Bert and Sully Van
        -2 (2:42)Unissued
        2A


              Radio Recorders, Hollywood      9:30 PM to 12:30 AM


D9-VB-2614-1    20-3677-B(P-277); RCADJ 893-B;
        1A      45 47-3200-B(WP-277); LP LPM 18;
                ET AFRS "Basic Music Library" P-1512;
            (2:40)Varsity Drag - inst
        -2 (2:43)Unissued
        2A


18 December, 1949 (SUN) - Radio Recorders, Hollywood    10:00 PM
              Client: RCA Victor                        to 3:00 AM
              Walter Heenber, A & R Rep, present


              Personnel as 17 December


D9-VB-2615-1    20-3675-B(P-277); 20-3827-B; RCADJ 891-B &
        1A      D9-VB-2615; 45 47-3198-B(WP-277); 547-0068-A
                (EPA 277); RCAG EPA 277; LP LPM 18; RCAG
                RCS 3217/1-2; RCAJ 5143(m); ET AFRS "Basic
                Music Library" P-1512; AFRS "Take a Record
                Please" 13;
            (3:02)Charlestono-Mio - voc Gil Bert and Sully Van


D9-VB-2616-1    20-3676-A(P-277); HMV B 9912; HMVSK B 9912;
        1A      RCADJ 892-A; 45 47-3199-A(WP-277); 547-
                0068-B(EPA 277); RCAG EPA 277; RCAF 45308 &
                430286; LP LPM 18; RCAE NL 42730(e); RCAG
                3211/1-2; RCAF LP 400.286 & PL 43197;
                ET AFRS "Basic Music Library" P-1512;
                Public Service Show "Here's To Vets" 227;
            (2:31)Black Bottom - inst
```

Note: RCA inst do not credit Porter, Maxwell or Donley. Although Porter did not recall the particulars in his interview with Ted Hering, he was certain overdubbing was not used on the vocals. Ed Metcalfe states that Eddie Maxwell could have easily sung the duet with Porter; Arthur Most recalls two vocalists and 'Doc' Rando remembers Eddie Maxwell as the other vocalist. All titles were complete on one take with no overdubbing.

This was the Slickers Christmas break and not all of the regulars were available for this session. Arthur Most, who remembers Spike as a soda jerk at the Balboa Ballroom c.1928, and who played for many years with the Abe Lyman band, then later with the war-time

Coast Guard band (with King Jackson), is the "gabba-gabba" trombone soloist on these sides. Most and Jackson split the parts, each doing what he did the best - either "gabba-gabba" or "fonk", both non-academic techniques which go back in time into the '20s and its experiments with jazz and novelty. As a plunger mute doesn't "gabba" too well, Most fitted a trumpet buzz-wow mute into the bell which was then 'fanned' with an actors make-up tin by the left hand. At times, the humor displayed by these musicians is reminiscent of a 'cutting' contest, to see who can make the others 'break-up'.

There were no arrangements at this session. Only a lead sheet (melody and chord symbols) was provided by Eddie Maxwell and the format for each was methodically rehearsed. Spike later had certain titles copied from the recordings, slightly altered, for use with the Revue, and not all of these copied titles were played out.

Eminently dancable, this set of Charleston titles was part of the current Victor 'Perfect For Dancing' series which featured all of their bands and orchestras in a variety of dance styles. The Jones set reportedly reached 10th position of top selling LPs by 2 Jun 50.

Del Porter and Arthur Most were old friends, having worked together in Oregon before "The Foursome". 'Doc' Rando and Spike were old friends from the radio days of Bing's Kraft Music Hall under John Scott Trotter. Lou Singer had worked in many studio bands, and with Spike's old friend, Ralph Hansell, had performed on many Billy May recordings of the '50s. Arena Stars sheet music and BMI Performindex list title as "Charlestona-Mio".

Feature articles on Spike Jones appeared during 1949 in the following magazines:-

Radio Mirror, Jan - "Just the Two of Us"
Look, 15 Feb - "Spike Jones Spends a Wacky Weekend"
Newsweek, 4 Apr - "Cornecopia Jones"
Varsity, Apr - "Korn on the Kampus"
True Story, July - "Spike Jones Tells his Own Story"
American, July - "Six Nights in a Madhouse"
Quick News Weekly, 29 Aug - "Happy Hollywood Family"

Bill DePew follows Jack Golly. DePew, an excellent reed man with experience in many stellar bands, from Bob Crosby to two years with Benny Goodman - 1935 to '37 - the years of the 'triumvirate'.

EO-CC-1299   RCADJ EO-CC-1299
                  (0:46)Andre Koroshovsky to his Foster Parent, Spike Jones
                  (1:07)Spike Jones response, for use with 20-3934-A - Mommy Won't You Buy a Baby Brother

Note: RCA inst do not show the session that produced this public service spot/promo. 13 yr. old Koroshovsky "thanks his American Papa Spike Jones for his financial support", with response from Jones on the worthiness of the Foster program. A 12" disc, with a Mindy Carson 'Rain' medley (5:14) on the flip (EO-CC-1298)

4 January, 1950 (WED) - Radio Recorders, Hollywood   8:00 PM to
                  Client: RCA Victor   1:00 AM
                  Walter Heebner, A & R Rep, present

                  Leader - Spike Jones
                  Brass - George Rock, tpt; Joe Colvin, trb
                  Reeds - Dick Gardner, clar; Ed Metcalfe, sax
                  Rhythm - Paul Leu, pno; Dick Morgan, guit;

                    Freddy Morgan, bjo; Roger Donley, bass;
                    Joe Siracusa, drm
                    Voices - George Rock, <u>Betty Allen</u>, unknown
                    choir

EO-VB-3506-1   Unissued
        1A(3:31)<u>Mommy, Won't You Buy a Baby Brother</u> (or Sister
                    For Me) - voc George Rock and the <u>Mitchell</u>
                    Choirboys (contains "Happy Birthday" intro)
        -2   Unissued
        2A
        -3   Unissued
        3A

EO-VB-3507-1   20-3934-A; HMV B 10004; RCADJ EO-VB-3507;
        1A   45 47-3934-A;
            (3:31)<u>Mommy, Won't You Buy a Baby Brother</u> (or Sister
                    For Me) - voc George Rock and the <u>Mitchell</u>
                    <u>Choirboys</u> (contains "Merry Christmas" intro)
        -2   Unissued
        2A
        -3   Unissued
        3A

EO-VB-3508-1 (3:07)Unissued
        1A
        -2M   20-3827-A; RCADJ EO-VB-3508; 45 47-3827-A;
        2A(3:07)<u>I Know a Secret</u> - voc George and Betty

        Note: RCA inst do not list the vocalists, while the chorus
sound like a full studio group, probably the Jud Conlon Singers which
sound quite unlike the Mitchell Choirboys, or any boy choir for that
matter. Betty Allen was a member of the Conlon choir at this time. On
the original RCA sheet, the "Merry Christmas" intro was take -3/3A of
EO-VB-3506, and corrected that day with a new matrix...3507 with its
various takes encompassing this alternate version. Both versions are
identical after the intro.
        "I Know a Secret" was authorized for issue after take -1/ 1A
was changed to 2M/2A on 31 May (M refers to the take a master is made
from). RCA correction sheet gives no further clarification than:
"Elec. transf. from EO-VB-3508-A with live additions by Henri Rene".
        "Mommy, Won't You Buy..." DJ issue as listed had two issues;
one with "Rudolph" on flip, and the other for use in "Mommy..." pro-
gramming (EO-QB-13282), a schoolroom skit featuring Spike and intro-
ducing the voices of Ralph Wonders, Eddie Maxwell, Joe Siracusa,
<u>Mickey Cole</u>, Dick and Freddy Morgan, Earle Bennett, 'Ingrid Blast'
and George Rock. It's details do not show on RCA files.

        This was the last session in which Walter Heebner supervises
Spike. He leaves RCA shortly but remains on the West coast, and is
presently associated with Recorded Treasures, Inc., which transfers
vintage classical rolls onto LP, and of which Time magazine says:-
"They are hi-fi's first completely successful encounter with a golden
age of piano and they well become towering endorsements..."
        In his last months, Heebner was grooming, through RCA and
for the public, a new face and voice - that of the yet unknown Mario
Lanza.
        Henri Rene, the internationally known composer, arranger,
producer and conductor became the A & R director to many RCA West
coast artists, including Spike. Rene began his career with RCA in
1936 and his total career has successfully touched every aspect of
musical performance, nationally and internationally.

                    1950 Tour Personnel

                            246

Leader - Spike Jones
Brass - George Rock, tpt; Joe Colvin, trb
Reeds - Dick Gardner, Bill DePew, Ed Metcalfe
Violin - Dick Gardner
Rhythm - Paul Leu, pno; Dick Morgan, Freddy Morgan, bjo/
     guit; Roger Donley, bass; Joe Siracusa, drm
Harp -
Vocal/effts - Ed Metcalfe, Helen Grayco, Purv Pullen,
     Earle Bennett, Doodles Weaver
Acts - Bill King, Frankie Little, Jr. Martin, Lucille
     and Betty Barton (Twins), Lois Ray, Mickey Cole
Writers/arrangers/copyists - Eddie Brandt, Paul Leu,
     Dick Gardner, Bill DePew
Band Boys - Eddie McCarthy, George Green
General Staff - Ralph Wonders, Faith Thomas, Anne
     Wilson, Bert Lang, Les Calvin, Jack McNaughton,
     Richard King, Marshall Alderson

"The cash register's steady jingle is drowning out the cowbells, doorbells, trolley gongs, ringing anvils, bicycle pumps and
tuned flitguns of the world's noisiest orchestra.
"Spike Jones, the comic bandleader with the concave face,
has made musical depreciation an art. And how this...pays off is a
wonder to behold:...last year, Jones' outfit commanded $120,000 for
16 days at the Texas state fair...$12,500 a week in big hotels at Las
Vegas and St. Louis. The smallest stops...guaranteed $3,500 a night.
"The 1948 tour...grossed over $1,000,000. Spike's junket in
1949 nearly matched that figure although the band 'took it easy' by
staying longer in some cities.
"This is big business for a guy who started with a washboard
and a $10 set of cowbells. The revenue isn't all gravy...Spike takes
about 40 people on tour, augmenting the band with singers, acrobats
and comedy acts. They travel in a chartered train of two pullmans and
baggage car...estimated travelling expenses at $700 per day...Spike's
side men are expensive. They have to be good musicians to kick a
piece around the way they do. Jones' travesties may sound like uproar
to the uninitiated, but they are very carfully arranged.
"His style is corn, but it's sharp. His most steadfast ad-
mirers are sophisticates - not hillbillies. Among Spike's fans are
conductors Arthur Fiedler and Leopold Stokowski. In Boston last year,
the entire...symphony orchestra attended Spike's concert. Fiedler has
every record Spike has made. In Austin, Tex., Spike's appearance was
a benefit for the local symphony orch.
"Jones is forever adding weird props to his band. One of the
newest is a mechanical miracle: Six fake frogs pop up from the bass
saxophone. He also has a tuba from which white doves flutter upward
on cue."   (Star, Kansas City, Mo. 18 Dec 49)

        "THE SPIKE JONES MUSICAL DEPRECIATION REVUE"
            (Itinerary to 4 Oct courtesy Ed Metcalfe)

6 January, 1950 (FRI)
                    Civic Aud, Pasadena
                    8:30 PM

7 January, 1950 (SAT)
                    Municipal Aud, Long Beach
                    8:30 PM

8 January, 1950 (SUN)
                    Travel

247

9 January, 1950 (MON)
                        Municipal Aud, Phoenix, Ariz
                        8:30 PM

10 January, 1950 (TUES)
                        Municipal Aud, Tucson, Ariz
                        8:30 PM

11 January, 1950 (WED)
                        Municipal Aud, El Paso, Tx
                        8:00 PM

12 January, 1950 (THURS)
                        Coliseum, Albuquerque, N. Mex
                        8:30 PM

13 January, 1950 (FRI)
                        Paramount Theatre, Amarillo, Tex
                        7:00 & 9:30 PM

14 January, 1950 (SAT)
                        Municipal Aud, Oklahoma City, Ok
                        8:30 PM

15 January, 1950 (SUN)
                        Municipal Aud, Enid, Ok
                        8:30 PM

16 January, 1950 (MON)
                        Civic Aud, Bartlesville, Ok
                        6:45 & 9:15 PM

17 January, 1950 (TUES)
                        Municipal Aud, Shawnee, Ok
                        8:30 PM

18 January, 1950 (WED)
                        Municipal Aud, Wichita Falls, Tx
                        8:30 PM

19 January, 1950 (THURS)
                        Texas A & M University, Bryan, Tx
                        7:00 & 9:30 PM

20 January, 1950 (FRI)
                        Baylor Aud, Waco, Tx
                        8:30 PM

21 January, 1950 (SAT)
                        High School Aud, Tyler, Tx
                        7:00 & 9:30 PM

22 January, 1950 (SUN)
                        Municipal Aud, San Antonio, Tx
                        8:30 PM

23 January, 1950 (MON)
                        Auditorium, Victoria, Tx
                        7:00 & 9:30 PM

24 January, 1950 (TUES)
           University Gym, Lake Charles, La
           7:00 & 9:30 PM

25 January, 1950 (WED)
           Neville High School, Alexandria, La
           8:30 PM

26 January, 1950 (THURS)
           Municipal Aud, Beaumont, Tx
           8:30 PM

27 January, 1950 (FRI)
           Municipal Aud, Galveston, Tx
           8:30 PM

28 January (SAT), 29 January (SUN), 1950
           City Aud, Houston, Tx
           8:30 PM both nights; 3:00 Sun

30 January, 1950 (MON)
           Municipal Aud, New Orleans, La
           7:00 & 9:30 PM

31 January, 1950 (TUES)
           Municipal Aud, Montgomery, Ala
           8:30 PM

1 February, 1950 (WED)
           Ryman, Nashville, Tenn
           8:30 PM

2 February (THURS), 3 February (FRI), 1950
           Day off, then travel

4 February, 1950 (SAT)
           Arrival, set-up in Chicago

5 February (SUN) to 11 March (SAT), 1950
           Great Northern Theatre (new), Chicago, Ill
           8:30 PM (except Mon)
           2:30 PM Sat & Sun
           11:30 PM Sat
           Scale: 3.71, 3.10, 2.50, 1.85, 1.25
               Mat: 2.50, 1.85, 1.25

28 February, 1950 (TUES) - DON MCNEIL'S BREAKFAST CLUB*
           ABC Chicago, Ill   Sponsor: Philco

           Spike conducts the Breakfast Club orchestra in:

           Crocodile Tears

10 March, 1950 (FRI) - Victor Studios, Chicago   12:30 to
           Client: RCA Victor   6:30 PM
           A.E. Hindle, A & R Rep, present

           Leader - Spike Jones
           Conductor - William Levitt
           Brass - George Rock, tpt; Joe Colvin, trb

```
                    Reeds - Dick Gardner, Bill DePew, sax/clar
                    Violin - Dick Gardner
                    Rhythm - Paul Leu, pno acc; Dick Morgan, Freddy
                        Morgan, bjo/guit; Roger Donley, bass/tuba;
                        Joe Siracusa, drm
                    Vocals - John Halloran, H.D. (Homer) Haynes,
                        K.C. (Jethro) Burns, Freddy Morgan
                    Effects - Earle Bennett

EO-CB-3401      (0:25)Musical Depreciation Revue of 1950
                        featuring George Rock and Mike Wallace
                        on this 10" transcription

EO-VB-3402-1        45 RCA "Platter Party" 599-9049-B, SPD-6(1955);
         1A         LP RCAG PJM2-8021(1974);
                (3:20)Fiddle Faddle - voc Homer and Jethro

EO-VB-3403-1        20-5472-B; RCADJ EO-VB-3403; 45 47-5472-B;
         1A         LP LPM 1560; LSC 3235(e); AGL1 4142(e); RCAG
                    PJM2-8021; RCAJ 5142; ET AFRS "Basic Music
                    Library" P-3324;
                (3:20)Pagliacci - voc Homer and Jethro, assisted by
                        Sir Frederick Gas

EO-VB-3404-1        20-3741-A; RCADJ 943-A; 45 47-3741-A;
         1A         LP ANL1 2312(e); AYL1 3870; PK ACL 7031(e);
                    RCAE NL 42730(e); RCAG PJM2-8021; RCAJ RVP
                    6300(m) & 5143(m); ET Public Service Show
                    "Here's To Vets" 227;
                (3:10)Mule Train - voc Fleddy Morgan
```

Note: Issued titles to above are "Pal-Yat-Chee" and "Chinese Mule Train". Earle Bennett and Freddy (Fleddy) Morgan are not listed on the RCA inst on vocal or effects. RCA inst list Dick Morgan as trombonist and his namesake, Freddy, as vln/sax/guit. John Halloran is the operatic singer on "Pal-Yat-Chee", which is conducted by William Levitt. Promo disc EO-CB-3401 does not show on the RCA inst. "Chinese Mule Train" reached to 16 on the Hit Parade on 21 Apr 50 and remained there for three weeks, according to Billboard Magazine. Although only one take (plus safety) of each title was retained by RCA, both issues of "Fiddle Faddle" have slight differences and an alternate, presumably previous take/test recording titled "Mule Train B take-hold" was in Jones' files.

Freddy Morgan, in conversation with Ted Hering, recalled that authentic Chinese were hired to open "Mule Train". They either refused to show, or walked off the job after discovering the nature of the recording and Morgan ad-libbed his own psuedo-Chinese dialect. Eddie Maxwell co-authored many songs with Homer and Jethro.

12 March, 1950 (SUN)
                Travel, set-up in Minneapolis

13 March (MON) to 25 March (SAT), 1950
                Lyceum Theatre, Minneapolis, Minn

Note: Ed Metcalfe recalls that Skip Craig replaced George Green about this time. Skip, "a young chap who until he was hired as band boy, would meet our train each time we played in his area, and would be bedecked in a crazy "slicker-type" suit and derby hat, with a trombone."

26 March, 1950 (SUN)
                Travel, set-up in Duluth

27 March, 1950 (MON)
                Armory, Duluth, Minn
                8:30 PM

28 March, 1950 (TUES)
                Mayo Aud, Rochester, Minn
                8:30 PM

29 March, 1950 (WED)
                Municipal Aud, Eau Claire, Wis
                7:00 & 7:30 PM

30 March, 1950 (THURS)
                Memorial Aud, Racine, Wis
                8:30 PM

31 March, 1950 (FRI)
                Coliseum, Marion, Ohio
                8:30 PM

1 April, 1950 (SAT)
                Music Hall, Cleveland, Ohio
                8:30 PM

2 April, 1950 (SUN)
                Armory, Akron, Ohio
                8:30 PM

3 April, 1950 (MON)
                Palace Theatre, Canton, Ohio
                7:00 & 9:30 PM

4 April (TUES), 5 April (WED), 1950
                Syria Mosque, Pittsburg, Pa
                8:30 PM

6 April, 1950 (THURS)
                V.P.I. College, Blackburg, Va
                8:30 PM

7 April, 1950 (FRI)
                Greensboro, N.Car
                7:00 & 9:30 PM

8 April, 1950 (SAT)
                Municipal Aud, Norfolk, Va
                7:00 & 9:30 PM

9 April, 1950 (SUN)
                Mosque, Richmond, Va
                8:30 PM

10 April, 1950 (MON)
                Constitution Hall, Washington, D.C.
                8:30 PM

11 April, 1950 (TUES)
                Rajah Theatre, Reading, Pa
                8:30 PM

12 April, 1950 (WED)
                Lyric Theatre, Allentown, Pa
                7:00 & 9:30 PM

13 April, 1950 (THURS)
                High School Aud, Pottsville, Pa
                7:00 & 9:15 PM

14 April, 1950 (FRI)
                Zambo Mosque, Harrisburg, Pa
                8:30 PM

15 April, 1950 (SAT)
                McCaskey High Aud, Lancaster, Pa
                3:00 & 8:30 PM

16 April, 1950 (SUN)
                War Memorial Aud, Trenton, N.J.

17 April, 1950 (MON)
                Academy of Music, Philadelphia, Pa
                8:30 PM

18 April, 1950 (TUES)
                William Penn Hi Aud, York, Pa
                7:00 & 9:30 PM

19 April, 1950 (WED)
                Lyric Theatre, Baltimore, Md
                8:30 PM

20 April, 1950 (THURS)
                Day off

21 April, 1950 (FRI)
                Shrine Aud, Scranton, Pa
                8:30 PM

22 April, 1950 (SAT)
                Geo. F. Pavillion, Johnson City, N.Y.
                8:30 PM

23 April, 1950 (SUN)
                Kleinham's Aud, Buffalo, N.Y.
                3:00 & 8:30 PM

24 April, 1950 (MON)
                Batavia Theatre, Batavia, N.Y.
                7:00 & 9:30 PM

25 April, 1950 (TUES)
                Lincoln Aud, Syracuse, N.Y.
                7:00 & 9:15 PM

26 April, 1950 (WED)
                Bushnell Aud, Hartford, Conn
                8:30 PM

27 April, 1950 (THURS)
>> Arena, New Haven, Conn
>> 8:30 PM

28 April, 1950 (FRI)
>> Arena, Providence, R.I.
>> 8:30 PM

29 April (SAT), 30 April (SUN), 1950
>> City Aud, Worcester, Mass
>> 8:30 PM

1 May, 1950 (MON)
>> Municipal Aud, Springfield, Mass
>> 8:30 PM

2 May, 1950 (TUES)
>> Veteran's Aud, Lynn, Mass
>> 8:30 PM

3 May, 1950 (WED)
>> High School Aud, Manchester, N.Hamp
>> 6:30 & 9:00 PM

4 May, 1950 (THURS)
>> Auditorium, Lowell, Mass
>> 8:30 PM

5 May, 1950 (FRI)
>> Auditorium, Bangor, Ma
>> 8:30 PM

"In the solo acts the well-known antics of Dr. Horatio Q. Birdbath, Sir Frederick Gas and Doodles Weaver added to the enjoyment of the audience which applauded the noisy take-offs of the classics as the band presented them. Feminine attractions in the stellar line included the Slickerettes in the "Hawaiian War Chant", Helen Grayco and Lois Ray.

"The audience's approval of Freddy Morgan was climaxed when he appeared as a Chinese laundryman to sing as Asiatic version of Mule Train. The feats of Bill King in his juggling act were well received.

"Spike Jone himself appeared more bored with the show than anyone else at the auditorium. His flashy suits, which he changed between appearances did not match his glum mood.

"The troupe appeared on the auditorium stage without benefit of curtain or backdrop. The audience, which was smaller than antici- pated, was made up mostly of children and students.

"The Spike Jones show arrived in town yesterday and expected to leave on the early morning train. Doodles Weaver spent the after- noon bicycling around Bangor and attending the Babst-Bar baseball game.

"Jones was presented the key to the city by members of the city council. The Chamber of Commerce delegation was also on hand to welcome the troupe to Bangor." (unidentified newspaper, Bangor, Ma)

6 May, 1950 (SAT)
>> Armory, Lewiston, Ma
>> 8:30 PM

7 May, 1950 (SUN)
>> City Aud, Portland, Ma
>> 8:30 PM

8 May, 1950 (MON)
>
> City Hall Aud, Burlington, Vt
> 8:30 PM

9 May, 1950 (TUES)
>
> Forum, Montreal, Que
> 8:30 PM

10 May, 1950 (WED)
>
> Forum, Ottawa, Ont
> 8:30 PM

11 May, 1950 (THURS)
>
> Arena, Oshawa, Ont
> 8:30 PM

12 May, 1950 (FRI)
>
> Brock St. Gardens, Peterboro, Ont
> 8:30 PM

13 May, 1950 (SAT)
>
> Memorial Gardens, Guelph, Ont
> 8:30 PM

14 May, 1950 (SUN)
>
> Day off

15 May, 1950 (MON)
>
> Maple Leaf Gardens, Toronto, Ont
> 8:30 PM

16 May, 1950 (TUES)
>
> Arena, Niagara Falls, Ont
> 8:30 PM

17 May, 1950 (WED)
>
> Arena, London, Ont
> 8:30 PM

18 May, 1950 (THURS)
>
> Waterloo, Ont
> 8:30 PM

19 May, 1950 (FRI)
>
> Arena, Hamilton, Ont
> 8:30 PM

20 May, 1950 (SAT)
>
> Arena, Windsor, Ont
> 8:30 PM

21 May, 1950 (SUN)
>
> Day off

22 May, 1950 (MON)
>
> Arena, Sarnia, Ont
> 8:30 PM

23 May, 1950 (TUES)
>
> Owen Sound, Ont
> 8:30 PM

24 May, 1950 (WED)
>
> Barrie, Ont
> 8:30 PM

25 May, 1950 (THURS)
>
> North Bay, Ont
> 8:30 PM

26 May, 1950 (FRI)
>
> Sudbury, Ont
> 8:30 PM

27 May, 1950 (SAT)
>
> Sault Ste. Marie, Ont
> 8:30 PM

28 May, 1950 (SUN)
>
> Travel

29 May, 1950 (MON)
>
> Grand Fork, N.D.
> 8:30 PM

> Note: This was originally a Winnipeg, Man. booking

30 May, 1950 (TUES)
>
> Field House, Fargo, N.D.
> 8:30 PM

31 May, 1950 (WED)
>
> Travel

1 June, 1950 (THURS)
>
> Shrine Aud, Billings, Mont
> 8:30 PM

2 June, 1950 (FRI)
>
> Fox Theatre, Butte, Mont
> 7:00 & 9:30 PM

3 June, 1950 (SAT)
>
> Civic Center, Great Falls, Mont
> 8:30 PM

4 June, 1950 (SUN)
>
> Civic Center, Helena, Mont
> 8:30 PM

5 June, 1950 (MON)
>
> Highland Park, Missoula, mont
> 8:30 PM

6 June, 1950 (TUES)
>
> High School Aud, Pocatello, Idaho
> 8:30 PM

7 June, 1950 (WED)
>
> Rainbow Rendezvous, Salt Lake City, Utah
> 8:30 PM (show in two parts, with dancing
> between halves)

8 June (THURS), 9 June (FRI), 1950
                    Travel, arrive Union Station,L.A.

10 June (SAT) to 18 June (SUN), 1950
                    "Los Angeles Home Show" at Pan-Pacific Auditorium,
                    Mon - Fri: 5:00 & 7:00 PM
                    Sat, Sun: 5:00 7:00 & 10:00 PM

July, 1950 - JERRY FAIRBANKS STUDIOS
             San Francisco

             Musical Depreciation Revue (TV Pilot Film)

             Slickers personnel identical to Jan 1950 list,
                 with voc/act: Barton Twins, Billy Reed, Earle
                 Bennett, Bill King, Helen Grayco, Frankie
                 Little, Jr. Martin. "Mata Herring" unidentified

             FOREIGN LEGION
             Charlestono-Mio
             Morpheus (Fr. Foreign Legion)
             Caravan - inst
                        (straight)

             WILD BILL HICCUP
             Pass the Biscuits Mirandy
             Wild Bill Hiccup
             Chinese Mule Train
             One For My Baby - voc Helen Grayco
                        (straight)
             Square Dance

        Note: Sidelining was used, except on the rhythm opera, "Wild
Bill Hiccup". "Mule Train" has live vocal although the instrumental
chorus is spliced in. Both of Eddie Maxwell's skits were also avail-
able on 16mm b/w film with sound, at 1200' and 1000 ' respectively.
        Label reads "One for the Road" instead of "... My Baby".
Produced by Audio/Visual Recorders, 418 South Robertson Blvc., Los
Angeles, serial no. TVl MV-7(5) and is dubbed from 35mm optical film.

9 August, 1950 (WED) - Radio Recorders, Hollywood   10:00 AM
                    Client: RCA Victor   to 1:00 PM
                    Henri Rene, A & R Rep, present

             Leader - Spike Jones
             Brass - George Rock, tpt; Joe Colvin, trb
             Reeds - Bill DePew, clar
             Rhythm - Stan Wrightsman, pno; Dick Morgan, guit;
                 Freddy Morgan, bjo; Roger Donley, bass; Joe
                 Siracusa, drm; Lou Singer, drm (xyl)
             Voices - Terry Housner, King Jackson, Freddy
                 Morgan, Joe Siracusa, Earle Bennett, Harry
                 Stanton, Marion Richmond, Jud Conlon Singers

EO-VB-3756-1   20-3939-B; HMVAU EA 3999, HMVSK X7286; RCADJ
      1A   EO-VB-3754; 45 47-3939-B; ET AFRS "Turn Back
                    the Clock" 657;
             (2:26)Baby Buggie Boogie - with Baby Terry Housner,
                    voc by the Rhythmaires

EO-VB-3755-1   Unissued
      1A(2:28)Come Josephine In My Flying Machine - voc Boys
                    in the Back Room and King Jackson

Note: This re-make of "Josephine", with three of the original Slickers; Jones, Wrightsman and Jackson, while an interesting
idea, does not have the same unpretentious feeling as the 1942 version - particularly noticable in the solo vocal accompaniment. RCA
inst do not credit any vocalists. "The Rhythmaires" was Jud Conlon's
studio group at this time. This days session continues:-

Radio Recorders, Hollywood, 2:00 to 8:00 PM

Personnel as above, with Paul Leu, pno, replacing
Stan Wrightsman

EO-VB-3756-1   20-3912-B; HMVAU EA 3978; RCADJ EO-VB-3756;
        1A   45 47-3912-B;
        (3:04)Yaaka Hula Hickey Dula - voc the Rhythmaires
              (Ukelele solo by Freddy Morgan)

EO-VB-3757-1R   20-3912-A; HMV B 9988, HMVAU EA 3964; HMVSK B
        1AR   9988; RCADJ EO-VB-3757; 45 47-3912-A; LP ANL1
                          2312(e); AYL1 3870; RCAE NL 42730(e); RCA
                          Special Products "Good Music Record" DML1 0570;
        (3:14)Yes! We Have No Bananas - voc Joe Siracusa, Freddy
              Morgan and Sir Frederick Gas

EO-VB-3758-1   20-4209-B; RCADJ EO-VB-3758; 45 47-4209-B;
        1A   ET AFRS "Basic Music Library" P-2202;
        (2:45)So 'Elp Me - voc Freddy Morgan

EO-VB-3743-1   20-3934-B; HMV B 9988; HMVAU EA 3999; HMVSK
        1A   B 9988; 20-4315-A; 45-5285-A(Y-417); RCADJ
                          EO-VB-3743; 420-0172-B; 45 47-3934-B;
                          47-4315-A; 447-0172-B; 47-0254-A(WY-417);
                          EYA 18; ET AFRS "Martin Block" 196;
        (3:29)Rudolph, the Rednosed Reindeer - voc Rudolph and
              the Reindeers

        Note: RCA inst do not list vocalists. Marion Richmond is
"Rudolph" and Harry Stanton is Santa. Eddie Maxwell wrote the special
lyrics to "Rudolph" and "Bananas". Additional RCA sheets show that
"Bananas" was "Elec. transf. with speed frequency changes per Charlie
Grean" on 24 Aug, with the matrix altered. Canadian issues had no
frequency variations in the first chorus (ie: take -1/-1A issued)
        "Rudolph", the final listing on the RCA inst, has a matrix
suggesting an earlier session time, perhaps 10 a.m. to 1 p.m. It is
possible "Rudolph" comprised entire morning session time with balance
of titles taped in the afternoon. A further anomaly is that Wrightsman was paid for 3-1/2 hrs and Paul Leu for 6 hrs.
        "Rudolph" reached No. 11 on the Hit Parade by 15 Dec 50 and,
according to Billboard Magazine, remained there for three weeks.
"Rudolph" had two DJ releases, with either "Mommy, Won't You Buy..."
or "Two Front Teeth" on flip.

11 August (FRI) to 24 August (THURS), 1950
        Cal-Neva Lodge, Crystal Bay, Nev

        Note: About this time, an unusual character known only as
'Gypsy Boots' joins the Slickers. The band called him 'Nature Boy'
and he would have been the original 'hippie'. Evidently he was the
'fall guy' for the show and in one of the skits, Spike would slap
him. Skip Craig recalled that for some reason, Spike would slap Gypsy
hard - just for kicks! A '60s 'Gypsy Boots' LP may be related.

25 August, 1950 (FRI)
                Civic Aud, Sacramento
                8:30 PM

26 August, 1950 (SAT)
                Civic Aud, San Jose
                8:30 PM

27 August, 1950 (SUN)
                Shasta Union High School Aud, Redding
                8:30 PM

28 August, 1950 (MON)
                Armory, Klamath Falls, Ore
                4:30 & 8:00 PM

29 August, 1950 (TUES)
                University of Oregon, Eugene, Ore
                8:30 PM

30 August, 1950 (WED)
                Jantzen Beach BR, Portland, Ore
                9:00 & 11:30 PM (one show in two parts)

31 August, 1950 (THURS)
                Airplane Hanger, Moses Lake, Wash
                8:30 PM

1 September, 1950 (FRI)
                Fox Theatre, Spokane, Wash
                6:30 & 9:00 PM

2 September, 1950 (SAT)
                Arena, Trail, B.C.
                8:30 PM

3 September, 1950 (SUN)
                Travel to Vancouver, B.C.

4 September, 1950 (MON)
                Arena, Nanaimo, B.C.
                8:30 PM

5 September, 1950 (TUES)
                Memorial Arena, Victoria, B.C.
                8:30 PM

6 September, 1950 (WED)
                Kerrisdale Arena, Vancouver, B.C.
                8:30 PM

7 September, 1950 (THURS)
                Armory, Bellingham, Wash
                8:30 PM

8 September, 1950 (FRI)
                Civic Aud, Everett, Wash
                8:00 PM

9 September, 1950 (SAT)
     Field House, Tacoma, Wash
      8:15 PM

10 September, 1950 (SUN)
     Seattle, Wash

11 September, 1950 (MON)
     High School Aud, Salem, Ore
      8:30 PM

12 September, 1950 (TUES)
     Egyptian Theatre, Coos Bay, Ore. (Coquille)
      6:30 & 9:30 PM

13 September, 1950 (WED)
     High School Aud, Medford, Ore
      6:30 & 8:00 PM

14 September, 1950 (THURS)
     Municipal Aud, Eureka
      6:30 & 9:00 PM

15 September, 1950 (FRI)
     Civic Aud, Berkeley
      8:30 PM

16 September, 1950 (SAT)
     Civic Aud, Salinas
      6:30 & 9:00 PM (scheduled)
      2:30 & 9:00 PM (performed)

17 September, 1950 (SUN)
     Civic Aud, Fresno
      8:30 PM

18 September, 1950 (MON)
     Civic Aud, Stockton
      8:30 PM

19 September, 1950 (TUES)
     Harvey Aud, Bakersfield
      6:30 & 9:00 PM

20 September, 1950 (WED)
     Travel

21 September (THURS) to 4 October (WED), 1950
     Flamingo Hotel, Las Vagas, Nev
      9:00 & 11:00 PM (show in two parts)

   "All of the Slickers are back, with new members added to the cast, and the whole aggregation makes for two full hours of enter-tainment as they go from the sublime to the ridiculous.
   "One of the most spectacular portions of the entertaining show is the 'Hawaiian War Chant', staged in technicolor. It is one of the most beautiful bits of musical art that has been presented in Las Vegas in many months. That goes also for Spike's own technicolor suit job. It's really tops.
   "There's a cute trick by the name of Lois Ray who presents a tap routine which keeps the ringsters pop-eyed, not only because of

the excellence of her dancing by because of the beauty of her face
and figure." (unidentified newspaper, Las Vegas, Nev)

25 September, 1950 (MON) - Radio Recorders, Hollywood 1:00 to
                        Client: RCA Victor   4:00 PM
                        H. Rene, A & R Rep, present

                        Leader - Spike Jones
                        Brass - George Rock, tpt; King Jackson, trb
                        Reeds - Arthur 'Doc' Rando, clar
                        Rhythm - Frank Leithner, pno; Luther Roundtree,
                           bjo; P.G. (Lofty) Smearer, tuba; John Cyr, drm;
                           Earl W. Hatch, xyl
                        Voices - S. McKean, J. Cady, N. Murdock, Betty
                           Allen, Marion Richmond, George Rock

EO-VB-5562-1   20-3939-A; HMV B 10004; HMVAU EA 3950; HMVSK
                           X7286; RCADJ EO-VB-5562; 45 47-3939-A;
                 (3:17)Molasses, Molasses - voc George Rock, Henrietta
                           Pootwaddle and Ingrid Blast

     Note: RCA inst do not list George Rock as vocalist or iden-
tify 'Henrietta' and 'Ingrid', who are assumed to be Marion Richmond
and Betty Allen. Frank Leithner was allowed 1/2-hr. overtime on this
session for the purpose of adding his sneezes to the taped tracks.
     Spike and George Rock came in from the Flamingo, the balance
of the personnel are from the L.A. studios.

     "Social note: Spike Jones played "O Promise Me" on the organ
for the Joan Barton-Madman Muntz welding(sic)..."
                   (Variety, "Just for Variety", 4 Oct 50)

September/October, 1950 - Universal Recorders, Hollywood

                        The U.S. Navy Presents:

                        THE LAND'S BEST BANDS

                        Leader - Spike Jones
                        Brass - George Rock, tpt; Joe Colvin, trb
                        Reeds - Dick Gardner, Bill DePew, Eddie Metcalfe
                        Violin - Dick Gardner
                        Rhythm - Paul Leu, pno; Dick Morgan, Freddy
                           Morgan, bjo/guit; Roger Donley, bass; Joe
                           Siracusa, drm
                        Voices - Del Porter, George Rock, Doodles Weaver,
                           Freddy Morgan, Ed Metcalfe, Don Wilson, unknown
                           female voices and chorus

2-A   (14:10)Theme: Dance of the Hours
UR 161358   Oh! By Jingo - voc Del Porter
D 69680   Mommy, Won't You Buy a Baby Brother - voc
                         George Rock
                      There's Nothing Like a Circus - Del Porter and
                         the City Slickers
                      April Showers - Doodles Weaver
                      Chaser: Anchors Aweigh
                         (flip: prog. 1A Elliot Lawrence)

5-A   (14:10)Theme: Dance of the Hours
UR 161360   Way Down Yonder In New Orleans - voc Del Porter
D 69683   Man On the Flying Trapeze - Doodles Weaver

Morpheus - Freddy Morgan and the City Slickers
Charlestono-Mio - Del Porter
Chaser: Anchors Aweigh
        (flip: prog. 6A Harry James)

8-A   (14:10)Theme: Dance of the Hours
UR 162045   My Gal Sal - Del Porter
D 70346   Molasses, Molasses - voc George Rock and the
                       Carbohydrate Sisters
                    Dance of the Hours - Doodles Weaver
                    Yaaka Hula Hickey Dula - Freddy Morgan, ukulele:
                       voc Del Porter, Eddie Metcalfe
                    Chaser: Anchors Aweigh
                       (flip: prog. 7A Elliot Lawrence)

11-A   (14:10)Theme: Dance of the Hours
UR 162044   Charlie My Boy - Del Porter
D 70349   Shortnin' Bread - Doodles Weaver
                    Ballet For Bosun's Mate - City Slickers
                    Five Foot Two - Del Porter
                    Chaser: Anchors Aweigh
                       (flip: prog. 12A Harry James)

        Note: These four 16" ETs have U.S. Navy Department, Navy Re-
recruiting Service labels. The dialogue is necessarily heavy with
Naval promotion, which has been carefully deleted on the LP release
of all titles as "Musical Depreciation Revue", Silver Swan LP 1002, a
bootleg record.
        One disc is dated 29 Nov 50. This is likely the issue date
of the disc, but may also be the pressing or session date. Correspondence with Harry James in an effort to fix the dates of his participation turned up a blank in his files. The dialogue was recorded at
Universal Recorders Studios, and the music may have been taped in
four sessions, with guest vocalist Del Porter.
        Ed Metcalfe has no recollection of this set and feels it was
done after he had left the Slickers, late in 1950, despite Spike's
introduction of Metcalfe in "Yaaka Hula". It is doubtful if any
titles are alternate RCA takes. George Rock overdubs himself in
"Molasses".
        There are no files to refer to for accurate personnel list-
ing or dating. The following Departments of the U.S. Navy and other
installations have no knowledge of or information on these four
discs:- Naval Historical Center; Navy Internal Relations Activity;
U.S. Navy Band, Washington; AFRTS/LA; Defence Audiovisual Agency at
Norton AFB, CA; Library of Congress; National Archives; USO.

8 December, 1950 (FRI) - Radio Recorders, Hollywood   1:00 to
                         Client: RCA Victor   5:30 PM
                         H. Rene & C. Grean, A & R Reps, present

                         Leader - Spike Jones
                         Brass - George Rock, tpt; Joe Colvin, trb
                         Reeds - Bill DePew, Eddie Metcalfe, clar
                         Violin - Dick Gardner
                         Rhythm - Paul Leu, pno; Freddy Morgan, bjo; Noel
                            Boggs, guit; Roger Donley, bass; Joe Siracusa,
                            drm
                         Vocals - Sara Berner, Earle Bennett, Dick Morgan

EO-VB-5051-1   20-4011-A; HMV B 10049; HMVAU EA 3978; RCADJ
        1A   EO-VB-5051; 45 47-4011-A; LP RCAG PJM2-8021;
                        Bandstand LP 7118; ET AFRS "Basic Music
                        Library" PGL-37; AFRS "Juke Box USA" 94;
                        AFRS "Take a Record Please" 38;

```
            (2:48)Tennessee Waltz - voc Sara Berner, assisted by
                  Sir Frederick Gas

EO-VB-5052-1       20-4011-B; HMV B 10049; RCADJ EO-VB-5052;
      1A           45 47-4011-B; LP RCAE INTS 5052; RCAG PJM2-
                   8021; ET AFRS "Basic Music Library" P-2202;
            (3:00)I Haven't Been Home For Three Whole Nights - voc
                  Dick Morgan
```

      Note: RCA inst do not credit vocalists and curiously, Earle
Bennett is listed with George Rock on trumpet. Dick Morgan is listed
on guitar, but with the presence of Freddy and Noel Boggs, it is unlikely Dick did more than sing his solo this day.

      A contract between Arena Stars and Sara Berner shows that
she was paid directly by Spike for her services, a situation known
from the earliest Bluebird recordings. Sara Berner and Bea Benaderat
appeared as Mabel and Gertrude in many Jack Benny radio shows.

      "Tennessee Waltz" reached No. 16 on the Hit Parade by 12 Jan
51, remaining there for five weeks according to Billboard Magazine.

December 1950

```
EO-QB-6792    (0:20)Musical Depreciation Revue of 1951
                   10" transcription featuring George Rock and
                   Dick Lane (of the Bob Burns shows)
```

      Ed Metcalfe leaves at, or very near the end of 1950 to
begin a career in broadcasting. Starting with KTTV in Los Angeles in
1951, he has since become the vice-president of WPTA-TV in Ft. Wayne,
Indiana.

```
3 January, 1951 (WED) - Radio Recorders, Hollywood       10:00 AM to
                  Client: RCA Victor                      1:00 PM
                  Henri Rene, A & R Rep, present

                  Leader - Spike Jones
                  Brass - George Rock, tpt; Joe Colvin, trb
                  Reeds - Dick Gardner, Bill DePew, clar
                  Rhythm - Paul Leu, pno; Dick Morgan, Freddy
                    Morgan, bjo; Roger Donley, bass; Joe Siracusa,
                    drm
                  Voices - Harry Stanton, Gil Mershon, Art
                    Markussen, G. Latham, Marion Richman

E1-VB-500-1        20-4055-A; HMV BD 1188; Y-465-A; RCADJ E1-VB-500;
      1A           45 47-4055-A; WY-465-A; LP RCAG PJM2-8021;
                   ET AFRS "Basic Music Library" P-2202;
            (2:40)Peter Cottontail - voc Peter Cottontail (Marion
                  Richman) and the Four Long Hares
```

      Note: Discrepancies in personnel spellings at times are
obvious, as in this case where Richman is better known as Richmond

      Before the Musical Depreciation Revue of 1951 takes to the
road again, Bernie Jones joins on sax/clar and 'straight' vocals.
Jones had been with CBS, the Jimmy Grier and Ozzie Nelson bands
before "turning professional".

19 January, 1951 (FRI) - Radio Recorders, Hollywood   2:00 to
                Client: RCA Victor   5:00 PM
                H. Rene, A & R Rep, present

                Leader - Spike Jones
                Brass - George Rock, Bobby Guy, tpt; Joe Colvin,
                    trb
                Reeds - Dick Gardner, Bernie Jones, sax; Bill
                    DePew, clar
                Rhythm - Paul Leu, pno; Dick Morgan, guit; Roger
                    Donley, bass; Joe Siracusa, drm
                Vocal - George Rock

El-VB-529-1   20-4125-A; RCADJ El-VB-529; 45 47-4125-A;
    1A (3:03) My Daddy Is a General To Me

        Note: Neither the RCA inst nor issue label credit the
vocalist, George Rock. During the final editing, an instrumental
chorus of "When Johnny Comes Marching Home" was deleted.

        Two extracts from PR material used by Jones:- one giving an
inkling to Spike's long-standing and total preparedness, - the latter
showing the 'tougue-in-cheek', or 'gag letter' approach to public
expectations of Jones.
        "Spike Jones' high place in the entertainment world today
was achieved through a mercurial start accelerated by a wartime
novelty number recording which captivated the nation overnight.
        "Previous to this, the early records didn't sell as fast as
he hoped they would. The subtle clash of corn and sophistication
needed something else to jell public taste into a mass response.
        "Initial failure didn't discourage Jones. He hired a girl to
answer fan mail. When comments dribbled in Spike analyzed them to
find out what made people laugh. He tried to work them into his
novelty numbers - one laugh for every four bars.
        "The analysis and application paid off in his novelty arr-
angement of 'Der Fuehrer's Face'. The nation's juke boxes and disc
jockeys spread the fame of Spike Jones and his City Slickers, and the
formula of classic sophistication and corn finally clicked.
        "In five years of personal appearances with his own stage
show, Spike Jones has never ventured forth unprepared, for he knows
that ideas and expert planning have made his musical lunatics favorites of the American public."
                    (Press & Dakotan, Yankton, S.D., Jan 51)

        "Musical Depreciation Revue of 1951" - "The musicians will
report ten minutes before curtain time. Spike insists upon this so he
can have an advance check-up to see if all are present. This is easy
to accomplish. He says he counts the heads and divides by two. Next
he checks the instruments. When he started out he had sixty-five, he
swears - two .32-calibre pistols and a washboard. Today there are
more than 300 instruments, ranging from a cowbell to a bathtub.
        "The curtain is about to rise and Spike bangs his sink-
plunger as a cue. Meanwhile the orchestra has seated itself in an
arrangement similar to that used by Toscanini. There similarity ends.
Farthest away from the conductor's stand and facing it is the brass
section. This is composed of four instruments - two trumpets, a trombone and an ashtray. The latter is played by Spike's first ashtrayist
Sir Frederick Gas.
        "In front of the brass section are the woodwinds. These
seats are generally empty since no one in the band knows what a woodwind is. To the right is the most important part of the orchestra,
the first aid section. It is always ready for action.
        "By that time the audience should be prepared for two and
one-half hours of zany entertainment."
                    (Star, Kansas City, Mo. Jan 51)

Leader - Spike Jones
Brass - George Rock, tpt; Joe Colvin
Reeds - Dick Gardner, Bill DePew, Bernie Jones
Violin - Dick Gardner
Rhythm - Paul Leu, pno; Dick Morgan, Freddy Morgan,
    guit/bjo; Roger Donley, bass; Joe Siracusa, drm
Harp -
Vocalists/effects - Bernie Jones, Helen Grayco, Doodles
    Weaver, Purv Pullen, Earle Bennett, Laverne
    Pearson
Acts - Bill King, Frankie Little, Jr. Martin, Lois Ray,
    Bob & Diane Anderson, Wayne Marlin Trio
Writers/arrangers/copyists - Eddie Brandt, Dick Gardner,
    Bill DePew, Paul Leu, Bernie Jones
Band Boys - Eddie McCarthy, Skip Craig
General Staff - Ralph Wonders, Faith Thomas, Anne
    Wilson, Lester Calvin, Jack McNaughton, Richard
    King, Marshall Alderson

The Revue played twenty-five states during this four-month tour. Itineraries will not be included from this point on. Only recording sessions, radio and television b'casts, commericals, interviews - any medium that has produced tangible or suspected Spike Jones/City Slickers involvement, plus suitable magazine/newspaper extracts.

"These guys may be nuts, but they don't grow on trees", says the Jones boy.
"Musical satirists are a rare breed...first of all - and this is what most persons don't realize - they have to be terrific musicians, with flawless technique and a sound musical background.
"...has to hire the best musicians obtainable...no mediocre performers could possibly play his wild arrangements. Any serious musician who ever tackled one of Spike's fantastic satires concedes ...it is much tougher to play than the number which is being satirized."

(Star-Journal, Pueblo, Colo. 26 Jan 51)

"Supporting Jones will be The City Slickers, The Wayne-Marlin Trio, Eddie Metcalfe(sic), Doodles Weaver..." Eddie Metcalfe, just recently left, is gathering some of the advance publicity that should have gone to Bernie Jones on this tour.

11 February, 1951 (SUN) - COLGATE COMEDY HOUR
    NBC TV Chicago, Ill   ann: Mike Wallace

Guest - Gale Robbins

In a Persian Market - City Slickers
My Heart Cries For You - Sir Frederick Gas
Laura - voc Ron Beatty
Sheik Of Araby - Dick Morgan
Dave Garroway - Cameo appearance
Gale Robbins - "I Am Loved"
Gale, Spike, string section - "Be My Love"
Poet and Peasant Overture - City Slickers
Interview with Laverne Pearson
Glow Worm - Laverne Pearson, Dick Morgan, with
    Bill King, Frankie Little
Pootwaddle Portable Sink - Doodles Weaver
'Million Seller' Medley:

Holiday For Strings - inst
Chloe - Sir F. Gas, Freddy Morgan
My Two Front Teeth - George Rock
Cocktails For Two - Ron Beatty, City Slickers

Note: This one hour show, written by Jay Sommers, has been available on Video Yesteryear cassette 642. The 'string section' was comprised of the Morgans and Earle Bennett with yo-yos, similar to the photo seen on the recent Goldberg & O'Reily re-issue of "Dinner Music For...". Ron Beatty was hired for this show only. The cameo by Dave Garroway is reciprocated. "GARROWAY AT LARGE" is b'cast from an adjacent studio and Spike, after appearing in his own show, is then seen sweeping out the studio.
        Gale Robbins throws a broken prop into the empty orchestra pit, but it lands in the audience, with the result:- "A woman who claims her face was disfigured by a fragment from a fractured fiddle during a Spike Jones TV program has filed a $10,000 damage suit.
        "Mrs. Rita Morgan, 25, filed the Circuit Court suit Monday against National Broadcasting, the Colgate-Palmolive-Peet Corporation, sponsor of the show, and Studebaker Corporation, owner of the theatre where the incident occurred Feb. 11, 1951."
                (unidentified, undated newspaper, Chicago)

        "In addition to restaging some of their most popular numbers ...Jones self-styled musicians have added some new ones that reach a new high in unique interpretation.
        "The personality of every individual member of the cast is so distinct as to virtually constitute a trademark. No Spike Jones show would be complete without the inimitable Doodes Weaver...added a new and hilarious performance in a bit of buffoonery billed as 'Beethoven's Unfinished Fifth'.
        "Triple threat entertainers were a roller skating due, Bob and Diane, who thrilled and chilled the spectators as they did sensational feats on a raised platform only a few feet in diameter. Also spectacular was perpetual motion juggler, Bill King...Hawaiian War Chant...was staged in darkness with instruments and costumes in fluorescent relief.
        "The Slickers played a mean flit gun number as they accompanied the gravel-voiced Sir Frederick Gas in an impromptu and weird recitation.
        "A new gimmick was added to the amateur hour with an applause meter that measured the popularity of some of the zaniest stars of the show."   (Tribune-Journal, Sioux City, Iowa, 1 Feb 51)

12 March, 1951 (MON)
                WHAS, Louisville, Ky

        Spike Jones 'cameo' appearance on 'Ladies Day'.
    Subject: promotion of Depreciation Revue

24 March, 1951 (SAT) - SATURDAY AT THE CHASE
                CBS KMOX, Chase Hotel, St. Louis, Mo

                Missouri Waltz(theme)
                Peter Cottontail - City Slickers
                Ya Wanna Buy a Bunny? - George Rock
                My Little Grass Shack - Ole Svenson
                Shortnin' Bread - Doodles Weaver
                Fiddle Faddle - Dick Gardner
                        (straight)
                William Tell Overture - Doodles Weaver

        Note: Bernie Jones' character vocal style, Ole Svenson, had been introduced previously with the Ozzie Nelson band

31 March, 1951 (SAT) - SATURDAY AT THE CHASE
CBS KMOX, Chase Hotel, St. Louis, Mo

Missouri Waltz(theme)
Rhapsody From Hunger(y) - City Slickers
Barber of Seville - Sir Frederick Gas
Big Bad Knute(Big Bad Bill) - Ole Svenson
My Daddy Is a General To Me - George Rock
April Showers - Doodles Weaver
Dance of the Hours - Doodles Weaver

Note: Program material is based on partial information supplied by an enthusiast. The dates at the Chase could have been 23 Mar
to 5 Apr(see excerpt below), while local 2-197 AF of M have the dates
on file as from 30 Mar for two weeks (to 12 Apr). The Revue alternat-
ed with Wm. Blair's four-piece unit during that time.

"Patrolman Aloysius Nelke, paralyzed by a burgler's bullet,
will recieve a collection of Spike Jones phonograph records and a new
record player today as a gift from the band leader.
"Jones, whose engagement at the Chase Hotel ended Thursday
night, visited Nelke in the Hospital while he was here and played a
benefit for the wounded officer."
(Star-Times, St. Louis, Mo. 7 Apr 51)

"Spike Jones and his Mrs...honeymooned in Hawaii in '48 -
so, to celebrate their third annvy, he booked an engagement next
month in the Islands. Howsomever, he'll be observing it alone. She'll
have to stay behind here to become a mama for the second time."
(unidentified newspaper, 10 Apr 51)

Note: During this May tour in Hawaii at the 49th State Fair,
Spike is interviewed on the show, "Across the Blue Pacific", a United
States Pacific Fleet Production and the RCA recording of "Hawaiian
War Chant" is b'cast. The available dub of this show sounds as from
an actual b'cast, but pre-production and dubbed background suggests a
transcribed show.
'Doc' Birdbath recalls that Frankie Little was terrified of
flying, and on this trip to Hawaii, Billy Barty took his place - the
first of many appearances with Spike for the talented Mr. Barty. On
return from the Moana Hotel, the troupe were off for the month of
June and part of July.

13 June, 1951 (WED)
Daughter, Leslie Ann, born to Helen and Spike Jones

9 July, 1951 (MON) - Universal Recorders, Hollywood   8:30 to
Client: RCA Victor   11:30 PM
Henri Rene, A & R Rep, present

Leader - Spike Jones
Brass - George Rock, tpt; Joe Colvin, trb
Reeds - Dick Gardner, sax; Bill DePew, clar
Violin - Dick Gardner
Rhythm - Paul Leu, pno; Dick Morgan, guit; Freddy
Morgan, bjo; Roger Donley, bass; Joe Siracusa,
drm
Vocal- Eddie Maxwell

E1-VB-662-1   20-4209-B(unissued); LP RCAG PJM2-8021(1974);
1A (3:02)Alto, Baritone and Bass - voc Eddie Maxwell

266

Note: RCA inst do not list Eddie Maxwell as vocalist. Issue 20-4209 was authorized 12 July to be coupled with "Too Young", but "Alto, Baritone and Bass" was withdrawn on 19 July and only recently issued by RCA Germany. It's words, while humorous, were cutting, in that they took the recording companies to task for the now common practise of overdubbing to the extent that musicians and singers were doing "three times the work for one-third the pay". Issued ending is "...tenor on radio" with ultra-short "Be My Love" play-off. A known alternate ending is "...tenor named Mario" (Lanza). This days session continues:-

Universal Recorders, Hollywood, 11:50 PM to 2:50 AM

in addition to the above personnel:-
Steel Guitar - Noel Boggs
Vocalists - Loulie Jean Norman, Gloria Wood, Betty Allen, Sue Allen, C. Schrouder, E. Newton, Mac McLean, R. Wacker
Vocal arr - Jud Conlon

El-VB-663-1   20-4209-A; RCADJ El-VB-663; 45 47-4209-A;
      1A   LP RCAE INTS 5052; RCAG PJM2 8021; ET AFRS
                  "Basic Music Library" P-2202; AFRS "Juke Box
                  USA" 224;
            (3:47)Too Young - voc Sara Berner, Paul Frees and the
                  the Jud Conlon Choir

Note: RCA inst indicate Noel Boggs was hired from 10:00 PM, overlapping both sessions. Paul Frees was hired to originate the literary material, gags and to perform, repeating his earlier success of "My Old Flame".
Gloria Wood had previously sung with Kay Kayser; her most memorable recording being "The Woody Woodpecker Song" of 31 Dec 47 on Columbia.

13 July, 1951 (WED) - SPIKE JONES' SYMPHONY HALL (Radio pilot)
              Universal Recorders, Hollywood

Spike Jones, with Dick Morgan, Freddy Morgan and Sir Frederick Gas give a "Roundtable discussion" to classical records with a canned audience. Written and produced by Jay Sommers, and designated as the first of a series.

"Spike Jones has been inked for a two-weeker at the Flamingo Hotel, Las Vegas, starting July 20, and will follow that with a concert tour."   (unidentified newspaper, 23 May 51)

24 July, 1951 (TUES) - Radio Recorders, Hollywood   8:00 to
                 Client: RCA Victor   9:30 PM
                 C. Grean, H. Rene, A & R Reps, present

Spike Jones Without his Orchestra

Organ - Milton Charles
Narration - Ross Mullholland

El-VB-700-1   HMVAU EA 4178;
      1A (3:35)What Is a Disc Jockey - narrator: Ross Mulholland:
                  with unoriginal far-in-the-background music by
                  Winter Hugohalter

267

Note: This title has remained unissued in North America, its only issue coinciding with Spike's 1955 tour of Australia. Flip is "Dance of the Hours" and neither title is cataloged A or B side. Issued title credits read 'with Organ Accompaniment'. Popular RCA issues at this time were "What Is a Boy" and "What Is a Girl" with background music by Hugo Winterhalter. BMI registry lists the composer/performer for "Disk Jockey" as Larry Monroe.

Milton Charles was a free-lance organist dividing his time between CBS and NBC. Many years before, he had recorded in Chicago with Guy Lombardo. The final exhortation - "Good Morning" - is one of the many voices of Dick Morgan. As Spike Jones and his City Slickers were performing in Las Vegas at this time, Spike contracted the session out, mixing then overdubbing Morgan's voice at a later time.

An undated transcription of a Spike Jones, Helen Grayco interview by Paula Stone in Hollywood is from this time period. Subject: a staged recording session

New Musical Depreciation Revue of 1952

        Leader - Spike Jones
        Brass - George Rock, tpt; Joe Colvin, trb
        Reeds - Dick Gardner, Bill DePew, Bernie Jones
        Violin - Dick Gardner
        Rhythm - Paul Leu, pno; Dick Morgan, Freddy Morgan, bjo/
            guit; Roger Donley, bass; Joe Siracusa, drm
        Harp -
        Vocalists/effects - Bernie Jones, Helen Grayco,
            Laverne Pearson, Peter James, Earle Bennett,
        Acts - Frankie Little, Jr. Martin, Bill King, Ruth
            Foster(Mrs. P. James), Wayne-Marlin Trio, Paul
            and Paulette, Barton Twins
        Writers/arrangers/copyists - Eddie Brandt, Jay Sommers,
            Paul Leu, Dick Gardner
        Band Boy - Skip Craig
        General Staff - Ralph Wonders, Faith Thomas, Anne
            Wilson, John J. Hill, Les Calvin, Richard King,
            Jack McNaughton, Marshall Alderson, Eddie Cline

Note: Doodles Weaver and 'Doc' have retired from the Revue. Weaver carried on in night clubs and occasional movies. 'Doc' moved north near San Francisco, but remained in touch with the studios and can be heard putting his talents to good use in movies, radio shows and recordings - those exotic natural backgrounds to the many Martin Denny discs. Both reappear with Spike on occasion in the future.

Eddie Cline, already a retired veteran of many screen successes, joins the traveling troupe. Involved mostly with the visual aspect of the shows and the TV productions (and the TV pilot films of 1950), his experience with shows ranging from the early comedies of Mack Sennett to W.C. Fields to Olson and Johnsons' "Crazy House" of 1943 (which also included the talents of Eddie Cherkose, Cass Daley, Hans Conried, Dick Lane, Billy Gilbert, the Herzogs, among many others, and the orchestras of Leighton Noble and Nick Cochrane) was an example of talent Spike could not overlook.

16 September, 1951 (SUN) - COLGATE COMEDY HOUR
            NBC TV New York, NY

        Guest - Jan Peerce

        Pass the Biscuits Mirandy - inst
        English Movie
        Hotcha Cornia - inst
        The Pelican Club

Helen Grayco - "Mad About the Boy"
Hawaiian Medley - City Slickers
The Wayne-Marlin Trio
Jan Peerce - "What Is a Boy?"
<u>Foreign Legion</u> - City Slickers
<u>Morpheus</u> - City Slickers

Note: A rather sad testimonial to "the show must go on" axiom:- the chief electrician runs to the control room and dies of a heart attack, the rest of the crew having to work around his body for the rest of the show. "Mad About the Boy" is the last live solo as the background is very noisy with stagehands, dancers and police. Pre-recorded tracks (lip-sync) will be used until the 'live' solos re-occur in 1955.

"Spike Jones, who can't get his comedy band into England because of a musicians union hassle, yesterday sent a big bundle of his records to the British union to prove he's no musician."
(unidentified, undated newspaper)

Catching the Revue in their act between showings of "A Millionaire for Christy", (harkening back to their vaudeville show days) <u>Christian Science Monitor</u> writer Harold Rogers, wrote in the 21 Sept 51 issue a comprehensive review of Jones and his current show:-
"Music lovers who feel that their education has been one-sided, that their constant listening to the Boston Symphony Orchestra...may cause them to swell in an artistic atmosphere that is over-refined, now have an opportunity to round out their background in less subtle areas of musical thought by attending the RKO-Boston where Spike Jones, regular conductor of a chamber ensemble known as "The City Slickers", is devoting his efforts to the standard repertoire.
"...opens his program with a somewhat unconventional..."In a Persian Market"...Jones has a tendancy to whip the tempo to a point beyond credibility...his allegros into vivaces...vivaces into prestissimos. His musicians...seem equal to almost any demand.
"Jones is a master of the unexpected. His most impressive effects are...through a...musical "shock treatment" that relies upon sudden dynamic contrasts...sometimes take the form of explosions (as when a gun goes off) or thunder (as when a musician...dives through the head of the tympani).
"Bernie Jones, baritone soloist, sings a moving rendition of ..."One(sic) Enchanted Evening", while diversion is supplied by two headless gentlemen appearing in an accompanying tableaux.
"...sustains the listener's interest... with certain non-musical artists, such as Ruth Foster (a charming devotee of the dance) or Bill King (who juggles with lighted torches) or Paul and Paulette (who cavort on the trampoline) or the Wayne-Marlin Trio (acrobats par excellence).
"William Saroyan's latest..."Come On-A-My House", is sung... impressively by Helen Grayco, who...demonstrates remarkable versatility by quickly changing the mood to Noel Coward's impassioned "Mad About the Boy"."

"Spike Jones is the sponsor of a unit which will open a three-month cross-country tour at Carnegie Hall next month. The unit will be composed of Duke Ellington, his band, Sarah Vaughn and the King Cole Trio."   (unidentified magazine, copyright 1951)
The above unit was booked into Washington's National Guard Armory for two performances on Sunday, 21 Oct 51.

"Spike Jones and his City Slickers soon to become comic book characters. Two comic books, "Spike Jones on Mars" and "Spike Jones Goes West" will be published next month."
(unidentified, undated newspaper)

269

The comic book, "Youthful Romances, No. 3", published in Melbourne, Australia, featured "the ever-popular Spike Jones" in its first of four short 'stories'.

"It was a quiet Spike Jones who arrived in town yesterday to arrange additional bookings...quiet because he was alone and had left his troupe of 40 of the world's loudest musicians and their 600 strange musical instruments waiting for his return in Florida.
'"Last week we went through Tampa..and put on a joint concert with Martha Raye, who was appearing at the Bayshore Royal Hotel. We played as loud as we could and we still heard her".
"Spike will fly back to Florida tonight and begin a series of one-night stands. Thirty-one to be exact, which were planned to get the band back to California for the Christmas vacation.
(<u>World-Telegram</u>, New York, 17 Nov 51)

"My rigouous schedule of one-nighters through the south was really rugged. Despite such formidable competition as playing day and date with the Ringling Bros. Circus, my band did sellout business in every town we bucked the oppostion. When we were the only entertainment troupe in other towns, we found the...Revue had sold out weeks in advance.
"Joe Siracusa, my drummer, who invents all those wacky noises, is busy perfecting a harp which will 'pop' pop corn, shoot ping pong balls and arrows, and has a factory whistle, a cuckoo bird, a stop and go signal, and a rubber octopus plays eight instruments. For the latter, Petrillo demands that it carry eight separate Union Cards" (In his 1952 Revue press release kit, Spike mentions being thrilled by 'sitting in' with the Ringling Bros. Circus band during a performance - possibly during this tour)
(unidentified magazine, Dec 51)
"Spike Jones last month purchased a $20,000 portable machine shop for his drummer, Joe Siracusa, who invents all the wacky musical props for the band." (unidentified newspaper, 11 Dec 51)
"Incidentally, it became definite yesterday that Spike Jones' troupe will not supply game half-time entertainment - outfit's long-woolen underwear routine - as planned. Publisher's Association weeks ago contacted Jones in Florida and he promised to work game, which at that time was carded for Jan. 13. Game subsequently was shifted to Saturday Jan 12. to facilitate telecast. Game sponsors continued to believe Jones was 'in', although it apparently occurred to no one to notify comedian of date shift.
"Yesterday, NBC-TV learned of proposed Jones Coliseum caper and promply nixed it. The night of game Jones' troupe will do network's 'Saturday Night Revue' and hence must rehearse. Also network did not want to be carrying comic in afternoon, sandwiched into a grid-cast, then repeat him the same night.
"Jones' troupe....returns here Dec 14."
(<u>Daily Variety</u>, Hollywood, 7 Dec 51)
"...Jones' troupe trains in this morning...outfit will lay-off till Jones' NBC-TV spread...Jan. 12. No definite plans for another road tour have crystallized, though MCA has been contacting promotors in Pacific northwest anent proposed trek through that territory, starting late in February.
"Ralph Wonders, Jones' manager returns with troupe..."
(<u>Daily Variety</u>, Hollywood, 13 Dec 51)

"Other repeaters in their categories were George Shearing's Quintet, vocalists Billy Eckstine and Sarah Vaughn, the Mills Brothers vocal Quartet, and Spike Jones, the (<u>Downbeat</u>) poll's perennial 'King of Corn'".
"King of Corn Poll": 1. Spike Jones 2. Guy Lombardo
3. Ralph Flanagan
(<u>Chronicle</u>, San Francisco, 13 Dec 51)

Note: Feature articles on Spike Jones appeared during
1951 in the following magazines:-

Melodyland, No 1 -
Tab, Nov - "King of Corn"

12 January, 1952 (SAT) - ALL-STAR REVUE
NBC-TV El Capitan Theatre, Hollywood, 8:00 PM

Guests: Billy Eckstine and Hugh Herbert

City Slicker Medley:
   In a Persian Market
   Scheherazade (augmented by studio band)
   Whispering - feat Jimmy Vey
Paul and Paulette - trampoline act
City Slicker Production: "Cold Cold Heart"
      around the world:
   Germany - City Slickers, Mellomen
   Italy - Spike, Dick Morgan, Barton Twins
   Cuba - Helen Grayco
   Alaska - Spike, George Rock
Billy Eckstine - "Song of India", "You
   Are My Dream"
City Slicker Production: "The Witching Hour"
   It's Tough To Be a Girl Musician -
   12th Street Rag - inst
   Sugar Blues - George Rock
   He's Funny That Way - Peter James, Mac Pearson
   Wild Wild Women - inst
Cocktails For Two - City Slickers

        Note: Billy Eckstine and Spike swap Downbeat awards after
"Song of India". The Mellomen personnel, a studio group and favorite
of Disneys', is similar to 25 Jan listing. The sponsors were:
Kellogg, Pet Milk, Snow Crop. Al Goodman provided the incidental and
production music.
        Some observations on the hazards of 'live' television: Thurl
Ravenscroft stood behind Freddy with a hot-water bottle on "Cold Cold
Heart" number, was supposed to squeeze it, causing water to flow
through unseen hose attached behind Freddy's ears. Thurl squeezed and
the stopper came out! Embarrassed silence followed as Spike tried to
figure out how to save the gag, finally pouring contents of empty
prop mug over Freddy's head. Other problems: blanks in Spike's gun
didn't fire; break-away statue (plaster bust of a famous composer)
didn't break; break-away drinking mugs didn't break when 'clinked';
the toaster in the commercial didn't pop up!

25 January, 1952 (FRI) - Radio Recorders, Hollywood   1:00 to
               Client: RCA Victor   4:00 PM
               H. Rene, A & R Rep, present

        Leader - Spike Jones
        Brass - George Rock, tpt; Joe Colvin, trb
        Reeds - Dick Gardner, Bill DePew, Bernie Jones, sax
        Violin - Dick Gardner
        Rhythm - Paul Leu, pno; Dick Morgan, bjo;
           Roger Donley, bass; Joe Siracusa, drm;
           Ernest Felice, acc
        Vocalists - Del Porter, Thurl Ravenscroft,
           Maxwell Smith, Robert Hamlin, William Lee
        Flute - Henry Mandel
        Harp - Charlotte Tinsley

271

E2-VB-5230-1   20-4731-B(P-3054); RCADJ E2-VB-5230;
   1A   <u>45</u> 47-4731-B(WP 3054)(unissued); 547-0008
       (EPB 3054); <u>LP</u> LPM 3054; RCADJ TAS-4;
       RCAF 100255; <u>ET</u> AFRS "Basic Music Library"
       P-2635; Your Rhythm Revue-Sister Kenny
       Foundation KBAL-2;
   (3:00)<u>Gesundheit Polka</u> (German Polka) - voc Del
       Porter and the Mellomen

    Radio Recorders, Hollywood   7:00 to 11:00 PM

     Personnel, in addition to above, add Paul
     Frees, Larry Cotton, Dick Morgan, Bernie
     Jones, vocals

E2-VB-5239-1   20-4731-A(P-3054); RCADJ E2-VB-5239; 20-5320-B;
   1A   HMVSK X8130; <u>45</u> 47-4731-A(WP 3054)(unissu-
       ed); 547-0007(EPB 3054; 47-5320-B; RCAIT
       B72V 0014; <u>LP</u> LPM 3054; RCAF 100255;
       <u>ET</u> AFRS "Basic Music Library" P-2635; Public
       Service Show "Here's To Vets" 227; Your
       Rhythm Revue-Sister Kenny Foundation KBAL-2;
   (3:07)<u>A Din Skal, A Min Skal</u> (Swedish Polka) - voc
       Ole Svenson and the Yumpin' Yimminy Fans

E2-VB-5240-1   20-4546-A; RCADJ E2-VB-5240; HMVSK X8068;
   1A   <u>45</u> 47-4546-A; <u>LP</u> RCAG PJM2 8021; <u>ET</u> AFRS
       "Basic Music Library" P-2374; Public Service
       Show "Here's To Vets" 299; Guest Star Time-
       Sister Kenny Foundation KBR-14; 1952 Cancer
       Crusade(spot announcement, cut 1); 1952
       Cancer Crusade "Morning Musicale Miniature"
   (3:23)<u>Deep Purple</u> - voc Paul Frees

E2-VB-5241-1   20-4546-B; RCADJ E2-VB-5241; <u>45</u> 47-4546-B;
   1A   <u>LP</u> RCAG PJM2 8021; <u>ET</u> AFRS "Basic Music
       Library" P-2374; Public Service Show "Here's
       To Vets" 299;
   (3:07)<u>It Never Rains In Sunny California</u> - voc
       <u>Larry Cotton</u> and Dick Morgan

Note: RCA inst do not credit Larry Cotton, Dick Morgan, Paul
Frees or Bernie Jones as vocalists. WP 3054 and its four single
records was authorized for release 5 May 52, with no reason given for
it remaining unreleased.
   The album notes to EPB 3054 credit the conception and
writing of these polkas to Freddy Morgan, Bernie Jones and Sol Meyer.
Meyer is also credited as Spike's television and script writer.
   The Ernest Felice Quartet, with vocals by Felice, had
recorded for Capitol Records. Larry Cotton had sung with the Four
King Sisters in the Horace Heidt Band of 1937, and before that with
the band of Jimmy Grier.
   "A Din Skal" had two DJ releases: one with "I Saw Mommy" on
flip and the other with "Three Little Fishies". In "Deep Purple", the
bridge between the Cotton and Morgan vocals is the intro as used on
the Standard ET/V-Disc "Chloe" - a segment of the "William Tell Overture" which was omitted from the RCA "Chloe" due to time limitations.

4 February, 1952 (MON) - Radio Recorders, Hollywood   1:30 to
     Client: RCA Victor   5:00 PM
     Henri Rene, A & R Rep, present

     Spike Jones and his Country Cousins

```
                    Leader - Spike Jones
                    Trumpets - George Rock, Bobby Guy
                    Rhythm - Marvin Ashbaugh (Ash), pno; Eddie Kirk,
                        Speedy West, guit; Cliffie Stone (Snyder),
                        bass; Joe Siracusa, drm
                    Vocal - Wesley L. (Minister) Tuttle

E2-VB-5252-1       20-4568-A; RCADJ E2-VB-5252; 45 47-4568-A;
        1A            EPA 456; ET AFRS "Basic Music Library"
                      P-2374; AFRS "Juke Box USA" 367;
               (2:45)Down South - Country Cousins


E2-VB-5253-1       20-4669-A; RCADJ E2-VB-5253; 45 47-4669-A;
        1A            ET AFRS "Basic Music Library" P-2374;
               (2:15)There's a Blue Sky 'Way Out Yonder -
                      Country Cousins


E2-VB-5254-1       20-4669-B; RCADJ E2-VB-5254; 45 47-4669-B;
        1A            ET AFRS "Basic Music Library" P-2374;
               (2:29)Stop Your Gamblin' - Country Cousins


E2-VB-5255-1       20-4568-B; RCADJ E2-VB-5255; 45 47-4568-B;
        1A            EPA 456; ET AFRS "Basic Music Library"
                      P-2374; Guest Star Time-Sister Kenny
                      Foundation KBR-14;
               (2:39)I've Turned a Gadabout - Country Cousins


     Note: RCA inst indicate Bobby Guy worked until 4:30 PM. C.
Stone is listed as guit, instead of bass. Jimmy Bryant (see 1 July
52), Speedy West and Cliffie Stone recorded country/western and
square dance titles for Capitol Records. Wesley Tuttle also recorded
for Capitol. The second voice (duet) is George Rock.
     The P.R. stills of "Spike Jones Country Cousins", showing
two females dressed Daisy Mae fashion, bear no resemblance (in any
respect) to the recorded "Country Cousins"


12 February, 1952 (TUES) - Radio Recorders, Hollywood       1:00 to
                    Client: RCA Victor                      5:00 PM
                    Henri Rene, A & R Rep, present


                    Leader - Spike Jones
                    Brass - George Rock, tpt; Joe Colvin, trb
                    Reeds - Dick Gardner, Bill DePew, sax;
                        Henry Mandel, picc
                    Rhythm - Paul Leu, pno; Dick Morgan, Freddy
                        Morgan, bjo; Roger Donley, bass; Joe Siracusa,
                        drm; Earl Hatch, xyl; Ernest Felice, acc
                    Vocalists - William Lee, Thurl Ravenscroft,
                        Maxwell Smith, Robert Hamlin, Freddy Morgan


E2-VB-5268-1       20-4730-B(P-3054); 45 47-4730-B(WP 3054)(un-
        1A            issued); 547-0008(EPB 3054); LP LPM 3054;
                      RCAF 100255;
               (2:36)Slanthe (Irish Polka) - voc Bob Stevens and
                      the Mello Men


E2-VB-5269-1       20-4729-A(P-3054); RCADJ E2-VB-5269;
        1A            45 47-4729-A(WP 3054)(unissued); 547-0007
                      (EPB 3054); RCAIT B72V 0014; LP LPM 3054;
                      RCAF 100255; ET AFRS "Basic Music Library"
                      P-2635;
```

                    (3:14)<u>Sante</u> (French Polka) - voc Freddy Morgan and
                         the Mello Men

E2-VB-5270-1   <u>20-4728-B</u>(P-3054); <u>45</u> 47-4728-B(WP 3054)(un-
          1A   issued); 547-000<u>8</u>(EPB 3054); <u>LP</u> LPM 3054;
                         RCAF 100255;
                    (3:04)<u>Cheerio</u> (English Polka) - voc Freddy Morgan
                         and the Mello Men

        Note: RCA inst do not credit Freddy Morgan nor identify Bob
Stevens, which could be a pseudonym for one of the Mello Men. The uncredited violinist on "Slanthe" is Dick Gardner

17 February, 1952 (SUN) - Radio Recorders, Hollywood   1:00 to
                    Client: RCA Victor   5:30 PM
                    Henri Rene, A & R Rep, present

                    Leader - Spike Jones
                    Brass - George Rock, tpt; Joe Colvin, trb
                    Reeds - Dick Gardner, sax; Bill DePew, clar
                    Rhythm - Paul Leu, pno; Dick Morgan, bjo;
                         J. Rose, mandolin; Roger Donley, bass;
                         Joe Siracusa, drm; Ernest Felice, acc
                    Bagpipes - <u>W. Jones</u>
                    Vocalists - Thurl Ravenscroft, Maxwell Smith,
                         Robert Hamlin, William Lee, Del Porter,
                         <u>D. Hood</u>

E2-VB-5271-1   <u>20-4729-B</u>(P-3054); <u>45</u> 47-4729-B(WP 3054)(un-
          1A   issued); 547-000<u>8</u>(EPB 3054); <u>LP</u> LPM 3054;
                         RCAF 100255; <u>ET</u> AFRS "Basic Music Library"
                         P-2635;
                    (2:45)<u>Salute</u> (Italian Polka) - voc Del Porter and
                         the Mello Men

E2-VB-5272-1   <u>20-4730-A</u>(P-3054); <u>45</u> 47-4730-A(WP 3054)(uniss-
          1A   ued); 547-0007(EPB 3054); RCAIT B72V 0014;
                         <u>LP</u> LPM 3054; RCAF 100255; <u>ET</u> AFRS "Basic
                         Music Library" P-2635;
                    (2:50)<u>Drink to the Bonnie Lassies</u> (Scotch Polka) -
                         voc <u>Alec Kelvin</u> and the Mello Men

E2-VB-5273-1   Unissued
          1A(2:39)<u>Bottoms Up</u> (American Polka) - voc Del Porter
                         and the Mello Men

        Note: RCA inst indicate: J. Rose as booked to 3:00 PM; W.
Jones and D. Hood (Alec Kelvin) to 5:00 PM. George Rock has a brief
interjection in "Salute". EPB album notes mention J. Rose as Helen
Grayco's third cousin. RCA matrices run consecutively from 12 Feb.

26 February, 1952 (TUES) - Radio Recorders, Hollywood   1:00 to
                    Client: RCA Victor   4:00 PM
                    Henri Rene, A & R Rep, present

                    Leader - Spike Jones
                    Brass - George Rock, tpt; Joe Colvin, trb
                    Reeds - Dick Gardner, sax; Bill DePew, clar;
                         Henry Mandel, picc
                    Rhythm - Paul Leu, pno; Dick Morgan, guit;
                         Roger Donley, bass; Joe Siracusa, drm;
                         Ernest Felice, acc

                         274

                Vocalists - Thurl Ravenscroft, Maxwell Smith,
                Robert Hamlin, William Lee, Dick Morgan,
                George Rock, Bernie Jones

E2-VB-5273-2   20-4728-A(P-3054); 45 47-4728-A(WP 3054)(un-
        2A   issued; 547-0007(EPB 3054); RCAIT B72V 0014;
                  LP LPM 3054; RCAF 100255; RCADJ TAS-4;
                  ET AFRS "Basic Music Library" P-2635;
          (2:14)Bottoms Up (American Polka) - voc Mello Men

E2-VB-5279-1   20-4839-B(unreleased); 20-5107-B; RCADJ
        1A   E2-VB-5279; 45 47-4839-B(unreleased);
                  47-5107-B; ET AFRS "Basic Music Library"
                  P-2566;
          (2:36)I'll Never Work There Any More - voc Mello Men,
                  George Rock, Ole Svenson and Dick Morgan

        Note: RCA inst do not credit George Rock, Bernie Jones or
Dick Morgan as vocalists. An unusual 10" 78RPM of "I'll Never Work.."
is known. With Perry Como's "Wild Horses" on the reverse, this multi-
colored vinyl record bears the correct artist label on each side (and
the mis-matched release numbers). A very rare RCA issue of unknown
use.

        The "New Musical Depreciation Revue of 1952" traveled
through the 'heartland' of America, Western Canada and California.
Personnel similar to Sept 51 listing, adding Don Dodge, (secretary).

E2-CB-1357   Musical Depreciation Revue of 1952
                  10" transcription (edited from spot for
                  Mus. Dep. Revue of 1951)

        "Derailment of a 70-foot baggage car delays the S.J. Special
for three hours. Troupe arrives at its destination, Grand Forks,
N.D., at 9:45 PM.
        "While stage hands and personnel set up, band members give
an impromptu show from numbers that were squeezed out of revue by
lack of time.
        "At 10, Spike greets 8000 fans, says: "We had a wreck, but
relax. It was nothing on the DeMille scale. There'll be a show when
we get organized."
        "Frank Little (like many of the group, he's been with show
several seasons) was a show stopper as he recalled bits he did in
walkathons 15 years ago.
        "The regular show goes on at 10:30. At finale, Spike sighed
with relief. His seven-year record of never having missed a performance remained intact." (Look, 1 July 52)

31 May, 1952 (SAT) - ALL-STAR REVUE
                NBC-TV El Capitan Theatre, Hollywood

                Guests: Liberace and Jim Backus

                The Evolution of Music
                City Slicker Medley:
                    Tchaikovsky Piano Concerto
                    String of Pearls - Jimmy Vey, xyl
                    I Love To Sock Myself On the Chin - P. James
                    Melody In F -
                The Hustrei Sisters - Trampoline act
                Cry - Sir Frederick Gas
                Helen Grayco - "Kiss of Fire"
                Down South - gang sing to Billy Reed dinner
                    plate solo

City Slicker Medley:
    Holiday For Strings
    Chloe - Sir Frederick Gas
    My Two Front Teeth - George Rock
    You Always Hurt the One You Love
    Liberace - "Ritual Fire Dance"
    Liberace, brother George - "September Song"
    <u>Poet and Peasant Overture</u> - City Slickers
    Lenny Kent - Summary of the show

       Note: The sponsors were: Pet Milk, Kellogg, Snow Crop. On occasional listings, this show is erroniously dated 7 June 52

       About this time, Dick Gardner, whose virtuosity on reeds added so much to the Slickers style during the past five years, leaves. His reed chair is ably filled by a succession of players, while Bernie Jones now appears on violin.

14 June, 1952 (SAT) - Radio Recorders, Hollywood   1:00 to
           Client: RCA Victor   3:00 PM
           Henri Rene, A & R Rep, present

           Leader - Spike Jones
           Organ - Milton Charles
           Voice - Freddy Morgan

E2-VB-5290-1   20-4839-A(unreleased); <u>45</u> 47-4839-A(unreleased);
     1A   ET AFRS "Basic Music Library" P-2566;
   (2:50)(All Of A Sudden) <u>My Heart Sings</u> - voc by
           Freddy Morgan, the Contented Mental

       Note: Although authorized for release on 23 June and appearing in RCA catalogs, "My Heart Sings" was never issued commercially. The final line "..must be the crap suzette" was edited from the master. Inspired by the Charles Boyer style "My Heart Sings" of the 'Continental' on Capitol, which also inspired little interest, this parody was thought not worthwhile.

1 July, 1952 (TUES) - Radio Recorders, Hollywood   8:00 PM to
           Client: RCA Victor   1:00 AM
           Henri Rene, A & R Rep, present

           Spike Jones and his Country Cousins

           Leader - Spike Jones
           Trumpet - George Rock
           Rhythm - Marvin Ash, pno; Eddie Kirk, <u>Jimmie</u>
           <u>Bryant</u>, guit; Speedy West, electric <u>guit</u>;
           <u>Cliffie</u> Stone, bass; Joe Siracusa, drm
           Vocal - Eddie Kirk

E2-VB-5358-1   <u>20-4875-A</u>; HMV B 10355-A; HMVSK X8096;
     1A   RCADJ E2-VB-5358; <u>45</u> 47-4875-A; EPA 456;
           ET AFRS "Turn Back the Clock" 212;
   (2:07)<u>Hot Lips</u> - voc Eddie Kirk,
           Trumpets, George Rock

E2-VB-5359-1   Unissued
   1A(2:23)<u>Keystone Kapers</u> - Country Cousins,
           Trumpets, George Rock

```
E2-VB-5357-1        Unissued
        1A(2:20)Under the Double Eagle - Country Cousins,
                Trumpets, George Rock

E2-VB-5356-1        20-4875-B; HMV B 10355-B; RCADJ E2-VB-5356;
        1A          45 47-4875-B; EPA 456; ET AFRS "Bud's
                    Bandwagon" 156;
        (2:12)Hotter Than a Pistol - voc Eddie Kirk,
                Trumpets, George Rock
```

      Note: Matrices appear in this illogical order on the RCA
inst. Trumpet overdubbing of all titles was performed on 7 July, 1:00
to 5:30 PM. George Rock was listed as Trumpet Leader, no doubt to
financially compensate for the preparation necessary. RCA inst do not
list Eddie Kirk as vocalist.

      Stephen Sholes indicated to the Jones estate in 1967 that
RCA could not locate the unissued masters to "Keystone Kapers" and
"Double Eagle". Curiously, sheet music to "Double Eagle" as published
by Spike has the notation - "as recorded by Spike Jones..."

      "...Musical Depreciation Revue of 1953 (daylight saving
time louses everything up!)"

```
        Leader - Spike Jones
        Brass - George Rock, tpt; Joe Colvin, trb
        Reeds - Bill DePew, Bernie Jones, Len Doty(?),sax/clar
        Violin - Bernie Jones
        Rhythm - Paul Leu, pno; Dick Morgan, Freddy Morgan, bjo/
                guit; Roger Donley, bass; Joe Siracusa, drm
        Harp -
        Vocal/effts - Helen Grayco, Bernie Jones, Earle Bennett,
                Peter James, Laverne Pearson, Mack Pearson
        Acts - Frankie Little, Wayne-Marlin Trio, Lottie Brunn,
                Janie Kringle, Robert Bell, Bill King, Ruth Foster
        Writers/arraners/copyists - Eddie Brandt, Bill DePew,
                Paul Leu, Bernie Jones
        General staff - Ralph Wonders, Faith Thomas, Anne
                Wilson, John J. Hill, Jack McNaughton, Marshall
                Alderson, Art Rummert, Lester Calvin, Eddie Cline,
                Skip Craig
```

      July to September club dates for Slickers at Lake Tahoe
(Cal-Neva), Las Vegas (Flamingo Hotel) and Los Angeles (Home Show)

```
E2-CB-6685          Musical Depreciation Revue of 1952
                    10" ET (edited from spot for Mus. Dep. Revue
                    of 1951 - identical to E2-CB-1357)

E2-KB-6686/7        Promo ET for "I Saw Mommy Kissing Santa Claus"
                    One skit featuring Spike and George Rock; and
                    "Only ___ days 'til Christmas", George Rock
                    countdown, 15 to one day, continued on flip
```

16 September, 1952 (TUES) - Radio Recorders, Hollywood   9:00 to
            Client: RCA Victor   11:30 PM
            H. Rene and A. Miller, A & R Reps, present

```
        Leader - Spike Jones
        Organ - Milton Charles
        Guitar - Dick Morgan
        Vocal - Earle Bennett
```

```
E2-VB-6980-1        20-5107-A; HMV B 10452; HMVSK X8096; RCADJ
       1A           E2-VB-6980; 45 47-5107-A; RCAG EPA 9635;
                    RCAE RCX 1030; LP RCAE INTS 5052; RCAAU
                    ODLP 6024; RCAG RCS 3211/1-2; RCAF PL 431975;
       (3:26)I Went to Your Wedding - voc Sir Frederick Gas
```

Note: RCA inst do not credit Jones as leader or Earle
Bennett as vocalist. "I Went To Your Wedding" reached 20th position
on the hit parade by 24 Jan 53 and, according to Billboard Magazine,
remained there for one week.

19 September, 1952 (FRI) - Radio Recorders, Hollywood
                Client: RCA Victor

                Leader - Spike Jones
                Brass - George Rock, tpt; Joe Colvin, trb
                Reeds - Bill DePew, Len Doty, clar; Bernie Jones,
                    sax
                Rhythm - Paul Leu, pno; Dick Morgan, Freddy
                    Morgan, guit; Roger Donley, bass; Joe Siracusa,
                    drm
                Effects - Purves Pullen
                Vocalists - Bell Sisters

E2-VB-6984   20-5015-B; Y-461-B; RCADJ E2-VB-6984;
                    45 47-5015-B; WY-461-B; ET AFRS "Basic
                    Music Library" CH-40;
                    Barnyard Christmas - featuring the Bell Sisters

E2-VB-6985   20-5015-A; Y-461-A; RCADJ E2-VB-6985;
                    45 47-5015-A; WY-461-A; EYA 18;
                    ET AFRS "Basic Music Library" CH-40;
                    Socko, the Smallest Snowball - featuring
                    the Bell Sisters

        Note: RCA inst for this session are missing from RCA New
York files. The above information has been passed through many gener-
ations of collectors and errors could exist.

4 November, 1952 (TUES) - Radio Recorders, Hollywood   10:00 AM to
                Client: RCA Victor   2:00 PM
                A. Miller, H. Rene, A & R Reps, present

                Leader - Spike Jones
                Brass - George Rock, tpt; Joe Colvin, trb
                Reeds - Bernie Jones, Clyde Hylton, Bill DePew,sax
                Rhythm - Paul Leu, pno; Dick Morgan, Freddy
                    Morgan, bjo; Roger Donley, tuba; Joe Siracusa,
                    Lou Singer, drm
                Vocals - Robert Hamlin, Maxwell Smith, William
                    Lee, Thurl Ravenscroft, George Rock,
                    Mitchell Boychoir

E2-VB-6990-1   Unissued
       1A(1:59)Winter - voc Mello Men

E2-VB-6991-1   Unissued
       1A(2:38)I Saw Mommy Kissing Santa Claus - voc George
                    Rock and the Mitchell Boychoir

        Note: RCA inst do not credit Rock or the Mitchell Boychoir
on vocals.

6 November, 1952 (THURS) - Radio Recorders, Hollywood   4:00 to
                Client: RCA Victor   7:30 PM
                A. Miller, H. Rene, A & R Reps, present

                Leader - Spike Jones
                Brass - George Rock, tpt; Joe Colvin, trb
                Reeds - Bernie Jones, Clyde Hylton, Bill DePew,sax
                Rhythm - Paul Leu, pno; Freddy Morgan, bjo;
                    Roger Donley, bass; Joe Siracusa, drm
                Voices - Betty Allen, Dorothy McCarthy; Elizabeth
                    Rinker, Thurl Ravenscroft, William Lee, Maxwell
                    Smith, Robert Hamlin, Loulie Jean Norman,
                    Gloria Wood, Sue Allen, Virginia Reese, Betty
                    Noyes

E2-VB-6990-2   20-5067-A; HMV B 10580; RCADJ E2-VB-6990;
        2A   45 47-5067-A; HMV 7M160; LP RCAE LSA 3084;
                        ET AFRS "Basic Music Library" CHR-40;
                (2:57)Winter - voc Mello Men

E2-VB-6991-2   20-5067-B; HMV B 10580; RCADJ E2-VB-6991;
        2A   45 47-5067-B; HMV 7M160; EYA 18;
                        ET AFRS "Basic Music Library" CHR-40;
                (3:02)I Saw Mommy Kissing Santa Claus - voc
                      George Rock

        Note: "I Saw Mommy Kissing Santa Claus" reached No.7 on the
Billboard Hit Parade on 13 Dec 52 and remained there for three weeks.
RCA releases of this record credit the Mitchell Boy Choir, while RCA
inst indicate they participated in the unissued takes only. "I Saw
Mommy..."ıhad two DJ releases; one coupled with "Winter" and the
other with "A Din Skal". This days session continues:

                Radio Recorders, Hollywood   8:30 PM to midnight
                A. Miller, H. Rene, A & R Reps, present

                Leader - Spike Jones
                Brass - George Rock, tpt; Joe Colvin, trb
                Rhythm - Marvin Ash, pno; Wesley West, Edward
                    Kirk, Jimmy Bryant, guit; Clifford Stone
                    (Snyder), bass; Joe Siracusa, drm
                Voices - Loulie Jean Norman, Betty Noyes,
                    Gloria Wood, Mack McLean, Charles Parlato,
                    Charles Schroeder

E2-VB-7000-1   20-5239-B; RCADJ E2-VB-7000; 45 47-5239-B;
        1A   ET AFRS "Bud's Bandwagon" 15; AFRS "Turn
                        Back the Clock" 193;
                (2:21)The Boys in the Back Room - Country Cousins

        Note: In all likelihood, Norman, Noyes and Wood were at this
later session for additional overdubbing to this day's earlier take
of "Mommy...". More evidence of routine overdubbing - George Rock
sings X-rated Freddy Morgan lyrics to "I Saw Mommy Screwing Santa
Claus" to the tracks of the released background. On acetate, it is an
embarrassment to the Jones estate.

10 December, 1952 (WED) - THIS IS YOUR LIFE* (Hazel Bishop)
                NBC TV Hollywood

                Spike Jones: guest on show honoring Sara Berner

                            279

"How can you burlesque burlesque? Some of the sounds coming out of legitimate musical instruments these days make my autohorns sound like a string quartet!" Spike Jones groaning about the novelty song craze - songs which he can't murder because they're being murdered without his help.

"A few years ago we could take any popular song and murder it", Spike said. "Now we're limited because of tunes like 'Hock Shop', 'Come On'a My House', 'Wheel of Fortune', 'Slow Poke', 'Hambone', and all the other novelty numbers."

"Spike's still in there with his horns, guns and cowbells on standard and classic tunes, but he's also unveiling a new hillbilly format - straight instrumentation by Spike Jones' Country Cousins."
(unidentified L.A. newspaper, 7 Jul 52)

"You may wonder why in the past few years I have branched out in different styles of music on recordings. It was strictly in self-defense, because some of the so-called pretty records nowadays are almost as funny as "Chloe". For example, I'm sure you've heard one of the most popular records on the air today beautifully sung by one of the top girl vocalists, but they made the poor girl record it at a dog pound.

"And of course, there's the man singing with only his guitar about the Happiest Day of His Life and sounding about as happy as Freddy Martin if he found out Tchaikowsky was alive and had a good lawyer.

".......However, they can't scare me, because every once in a while a beautiful ballad beautifully done breaks through and after it has been heard for awhile, just invites a satirical rendition, so I call the Slickers and away we go to the studios in our bullet-proof vests."
(Downbeat, 22 Apr 53)

Joining the Slickers in January for the tour are: Abe Nole, trombone; Joe Guerrero, drums, and Jack Currance on reeds, replacing Joe Colvin, Joe Siracusa and Clyde Hylton

11 February, 1953 (WED) - Premier Radio Enterprises, St. Louis, Mo
Client: RCA Victor   12:00 to 5:30 PM
H. Grill, A & R Rep, present

Leader - Spike Jones
Brass - George Rock, tpt; Abe Nole, trb
Reeds - Bill DePew, clar; Jack Currance,
    Bernie Jones, sax
Rhythm - Paul Leu, pno; Dick Morgan, guit;
    Freddy Morgan, bjo; Roger Donley, bass;
    Joe Guerrero, drm
Voices - Freddy Morgan, Earle Bennett, George
    Rock
Bells - Elmer Boyd Schwartzbeck

E3-VB-0560-1   Unissued
    1A(3:13)Oh Happy Day - voc Sir Frederick Gas

E3-VB-0561-1   20-5239-A; HMV BD 1241; HMVSK X8130; RCADJ
    1A   E3-VB-0561; 45 47-5239-A;
        (2:12)Lulu Had a Baby - voc Freddy Morgan and
              the Slickers

E3-VB-0570-1   20-5320-A; HMV B 10535; RCADJ E3-VB-0570;
    1A   45 47-5320-A; LP RCAE INTS 5052; RCAG
              PJM2 8021; ET AFRS "Basic Music Library"
              P-5447; AFRS "Bud's Bandwagon" 594;
        (2:02)Three Little Fishies - voc George Rock

280

Note: RCA inst do not credit the vocalists, nor is there any explanation for the matrix gap: 0561 to 0570. Original "Lulu" and "Fishies" was to have been 20/47/5239 but was withdrawn as such on 5 Mar 53. Stephen Sholes, as RCA Divisional Vice President, indicated to Spike Jones Jr. on 3 Mar 67 that RCA could not locate the master to "Oh Happy Day".

Dick Morgan, the multi-talented guitar, banjoist and character vocalist with Spike since 1944, died of a heart attack at home on 17 May. From the Red Ingle and Harry James bands, Hayden Causey now joins the Slickers for a few seasons on guitar and banjo.

22 June, 1953 (MON) - Radio Recorders, Hollywood   12:00 to
               Client: RCA Victor   3:30 PM
               A. Miller, A & R Rep, present

               Leader - Spike Jones
               Brass - George Rock, tpt; Abe Nole, trb
               Reeds - Bill DePew, Jack Currance, Bernie
                 Jones, sax
               Rhythm - Paul Leu, pno; Freddie Morgan,
                 Hayden Causey, bjo; Roger Donley, bass;
                 Joe Guerrero, drm
               Voices - Jud Conlon, Loulie Jean Norman, Tora
                 Matthiason, Betty Noyes, Gloria Wood, Betty
                 Allen, Donna Manners, Ruth Clark, Dorothy
                 McCarthy, Mary (Marion) Richmond, George Rock

E3-VB-0116-1   20-5392-A(un-released); Y-472-A(un-released);
     1A   45 47-5392-A(un-released); WY-472(un-released);
            ET AFRS "Basic Music Library" CH 78;
    (2:15)Are My Ears On Straight - voc Mary Richmond

E3-VB-0117-1   20-5392-B(un-released); Y-472-B; 45 47-5392-B
     1A   (un-released); WY 472-B; ET AFRS "Basic Music
            Library" CH-78;
    (2:19)Captain of the Space Ship - voc George Rock

Note: RCA inst do not credit Marion Richmond or George Rock as vocalists. The unissued couplings, 20/47-5392 and Y/WY 472 were authorized for issue on 1 July and 21 Aug, with 5392 withdrawn as of 29 Sept. "Captain" was reinstated, coupled with "Toot-Boom" for issue with picture sleeves on 29 Sept, the same day as "Ears" was withdrawn
    "Are My Ears On Straight" was recorded by Lawrence Welk, (with Marion Richmond on vocal) as a Christmas feature, "... go home Christmas Day", whereas the Jones version finishes "...go home right away". A cute song with no known reason for it remaining unissued. There was an additional 1-1/2 hrs. for Spike, Donley, Leu and Rock according to a notation on the employees listing attached to the AF of M contract by Dick Webster, Spike's office manager.

22 July, 1953 (WED) - Radio Recorders, Hollywood   11:00 AM to
               Client: RCA Victor   2:30 PM
               Henri Rene, A & R Rep, present

               Spike Jones with the Jud Conlon Choir

               Leader - Spike Jones
               Rhythm - Buddy Cole, pno; Vince Terri, guit;
                 Phil Stephens, bass; Nick Fatool, drm
               Voices - Jud Conlon, Thera Matthiason, Loulie
                 Jean Norman, Betty Noyes, Gloria Wood,
                 Betty Allen, Dorothy McCarthy, Mack

McLean, Charles Parlato, Charles Schrouder,
Gil Mershon, George Rock, Marian Richmond

E3-VB-0154-1   20-5413-A; HMV B 10566; RCADJ E3-VB-0154;
    1A   45 47-5413-A; ET AFRS "Basic Music Library"
       CH-78;
    (2:49)God Bless Us All - voc George Rock

E3-VB-0155-1   20-5413-B; HMV B 10566; RCADJ E3-VB-0155;
    1A(3:10)I Just Love My Mommy - voc Marian Richman

Note: The RCA inst do not credit Rock or Richmond as
vocalists.

July and August saw Spike Jones and the City Slickers star in the
filming of FIREMAN, SAVE MY CHILD, 80 min. b/w (Prod. No. 1754)

      UNIVERSAL STUDIOS
      Hollywood

         Leader - Spike Jones
         Brass - George Rock, tpt; Abe Nole, trb
         Reeds - Bill DePew, Bernie Jones
         Rhythm - Paul Leu, pno; Freddy Morgan, Hayden
            Causey, bjo; Roger Donley, tuba; Joe
            Guerrero, drm
         Actors - Earle Bennett, Billy Barty, Peter James

         Poet and Peasant Overture - inst
         Pass the Biscuits, Mirandy -
         In a Persian Market -
         Dance of the Hours -
         (A) Hot Time In the Old Town Tonight

This Mack Sennett/Keystone Kops style slapstick movie, an
alternative to the proposed Jones/Abbott/Costello "Phantom of the
Opera", also starred Buddy Hackett, Hugh O'Brian, Adele Jergens and
Tom Brown. Originally intended as an Abbott & Costello feature,
"Fireman..." is occasionally mentioned in A/C movie books. O'Brian
and Hackett were chosen as look-alikes to match completed stunt
shots. A/C dropped this project in favor of "...meet Dr. Jekyll and
Mr. Hyde"
      Castle Films have released home movie editions:-
         No. 1029 "Fireman, Save My Child"
         No. 1031 "No Fires, Please!"
              8mm 12 min edition
              8mm 4 min edition
              8mm magnetic sound edition
              Super-8 12 min edition
              Super-8 4 min edition
              Super-8 sound 12 min edition
              16mm 12 min edition
              16mm sound 9 min edition

9 September, 1953 (WED) - Radio Recorders, Hollywood   1:00 to
           Client: RCA Victor   4:30 PM
           Harry Geller, A & R Rep, present

         Leader - Walter Schumann
         Contractor - Cliff (Dick) Webster
         Brass - George Rock, tpt; Abe Nole, Harold
            Diner, Simon Zentner, trb

Reeds - Bill DePew, Bernie Jones, Donald
     Lazenby, Louis Palange, Leonard Hartman, sax
Rhythm - William Sabransky, pno; Freddy Morgan,
     guit; Roger Donley, bass; Ralph Hansell, drm
Sound Effects - Victor Livoti, Ray Erlenborn
Actor - Jerry (Terry) Housner, Spike Jones

E3-VB-0191-1   20-5472-A; RCADJ E3-VB-0191; 45 47-5472-A;
     1A   ET AFRS "Basic Music Library" P-3324;
                  AFRS "Bud's Bandwagon" 151;
          (3:16)Dragnet - Spike Jones as Jim Saturday

     Note: RCA inst do not list the name of Spike Jones. Harry
Geller, an RCA representative at this time, was well known in the big
band and studio circles throughout North America, having been with
George Hamilton before joining the Benny Goodman band of 1935, the
band that also included Bill DePew among its stellar members.

25 September, 1953 (FRI) - Radio Recorders, Hollywood   1:00 to
                     Client: RCA Victor   5:45 PM
                     Harry Geller, A & R Rep, present

               Leader - Spike Jones
               Brass - George Rock, tpt; Abe Nole, trb
               Reeds - Bill Depew, Bernie Jones, Red Mandell,
                    sax
               Rhythm - Paul Leu, pno; Freddie Morgan, bjo;
                    Roger Donley, bass; Joe Guerrero, drm
               Chimes - Edgar Forrest
               Voices - Parky Parkinson, Linda Strangis,
                    George Rock, St. Mary Magdalen Children's
                    Choir, unidentified Mello Men quartet

E3-VB-2002-1   Y-472-A; RCADJ E3-VB-2002; 45 WY 472-A;
     1A   ET AFRS "Basic Music Library" P-3324;
                  AFRS "Bud's Bandstand" 220; AFRS "Martin
                  Block" 196;
          (2:00)A Toot and a Whistle (and a Plunk and a Boom) -
                  voc Mello Men

E3-VB-2003-1   Unissued
          (2:39)Gerald McBoing Boing - voc Mello Men

E3-VB-2004-1   20-5497-A; RCADJ E3-VB-2004; 45 47-5497-A;
     1A   ET AFRS (Frankfurt local recording) 3139;
          (2:20)Where Did My Snowman Go? - voc Linda Strangis
                  accompanied by St. Mary Magdalen's
                  Children's Choir

E3-VB-2005-1   20-5497-B; RCADJ E3-VB-2005; 45 47-5497-B;
     1A   ET AFRS (Frankfurt local recording) 3139;
          (2:56)Santa Brought Me Choo Choo Trains (But Daddy's
                  Having Fun) - voc George Rock

     Note: RCA inst do not credit as vocalists George Rock, the
St. Mary Magdalen Choir and "Mello Men" identities, or Linda
Strangis, one of Spike's many talented nieces. The "Mello Men" would
be similar to male quartet of 25 Jan, 4/6 Nov 52.
     "Toot and a Whistle and a Plunk and a Boom", from a Walt
Disney cartoon of the same name and a Jack Elliot tune (he also wrote
"It Never Rains in Sunny California" among many others), won the
Academy Award in 1953 as best song. The DJ release of "Toot-Boom" is
coupled with Paul Smith's "Living Desert".

        Edgar Forrest, on chimes for this session, is not the
Firehouse Five plus 2 drummer of the same name.

                 Spike Jones' "Musical Insanities of 1954"
                 (revised Musical Depreciation Revue)

        As nearly as can be determined, the following personnel were
involved with this Fall tour throughout California, and possibly to
Las Vegas, Nevada.

                 Leader - Spike Jones
                 Brass - George Rock, tpt; Abe Nole, trb
                 Reeds - Bill DePew, Bernie Jones, Jack Currance
                 Violin - Bernie Jones
                 Rhythm - Paul Leu, pno; Freddy Morgan, Hayden Causey,
                      bjo/guit; Roger Donley, bass; Joe Guerrero, drm
                 Harp -
                 Vocals/effects - Helen Grayco, Bernie Jones, Theron
                      Nay, Earle Bennett, Freddy Morgan, Laverne Pearson
                 Acts - Frankie Little, Paulette, Wayne-Marlin Trio,
                      Bill King, Bill Muir, Dolores Gay, Amin Brothers
                      (Mustafa and Abdou), Frank D'Amore, Arthur Walsh
                      Jimmy Kennedy
                 Band Boys - Skip Craig
                 Writers/arrangers/copyists - Eddie Brandt, Paul Leu,
                      Bernie Jones, Bill DePew
                 General staff - Ralph Wonders, Faith Thomas, Anne
                      Wilson, Arthur Wenzel, Lester Calvin, Jack
                      McNaughton, Art Rummert, Marshall Alderson,
                      Eddie Cline

November, 1953 - MARTIN AND LEWIS TELETHON*
                 ABC-TV

                 Guests: included Spike Jones and his City Slickers
                 and Phil Silvers

        Note: Aired before the U.S. Thanksgiving weekend, the Jones
portion included a performance of "Poet and Peasant", identical
(almost) to the "Fireman, Save My Child" version.

21 December, 1953 (MON) - Radio Recorders, Hollywood   8:00 PM
                 Client: RCA Victor   to midnight
                 Harry Geller, A & R rep, present

                 Leader - Spike Jones
                 Brass - George Rock, tpt; Joe Colvin, trb
                 Reeds - Bernie Jones, Bill DePew, William
                      (Willie) Martinez, sax/clar
                 Rhythm - Paul Leu, pno; Freddy Morgan, Hayden
                      Causey, bjo; Roger Donley, bass; Joe Guerrero,
                      drm
                 Vocals - Betsy Gay, Margery Ray(burn)

E3-VB-2043-1   20-5602-A(unreleased); 45 47-5602-A(unreleased)
                 (2:00)My Heart Went Boom Boom - voc Betsy
                      and Margie Sorghum

E3-VB-2044-1   20-5602-B(unreleased); 45 47-5602-B(unreleased)
                      LP RCAG PJM2 8021(1974);
                 (2:13)Rickeyshaw - voc Betsy and Margie Sorghum

                                284

Note: "Boom Boom" and "Rickeyshaw" were back to back on DJ
78 RPM acetate with limited distribution by Bob Stern. A small stick-
er on the un-numbered Electrovox label reads:- "many thanks, BOB
STERN". Abe Nole left when the tour finished in December. Joe Colvin
returned briefly for the recording and initial television shows.

Note: Feature articles on Spike Jones appeared during
1953 in the following magazines:

Downbeat, 22 Apr - "Spike Jones...not playing
Dance Music"
Screen Stars, Apr - "Givin' the Stork the Bird'
Downbeat, 20 May - "A Whacky Wax Date" (Carmen)
Look, 8 Sept -

2 January, 1954 (SAT) - THE SPIKE JONES SHOW
NBC-TV Burbank   5:00 PM PST

Guest: George Gobel

Leader - Spike Jones
Brass - George Rock, tpt; Joe Colvin, trb
Reeds - Bill DePew, Bernie Jones, Bill
  Hamilton, sax/clar
Rhythm - Paul Leu, pno; Freddie Morgan, Hayden
  Causey, guit/bjo; Roger Donley, bass; Joe
  Guerrero, drm; John DeSoto, xyl

Note: For this TV series: - Dick Webster, manager; David
Forester and/or Lou Bring, cond; Joe Krechter, Paul Leu, arr; Bill
DePew, Bernie Jones, copyists; Bill DePew, librarian. (Krechter, as
you recall, played clarinet with the Perry Botkin studio band of 22
Sept 40) Helen Grayco used pre-recorded music for her solos. The
first six shows were sustaining, Liggett and Myers sponsored the
remainder from 13 Feb.

Sabre Dance - feat Wayne Marlin Trio
City Slicker Production - "The Story of
  Spike Jones" (Cast: Spike, Earle Bennett,
  Freddy Morgan, Helen Grayco, George Rock)
  Helen Grayco - "I've Got the World On a String"
George Gobel - monologue
That Old Black Magic - voc Peter James

Stills from an undated show in this series show the childrens TV personality "Pinky" Lee with the City Slickers. He does not
appear on screen, however. Network time expires during "Black Magic"

"Square-jawed, gum-chewing, flamboyant Spike Jones is
practically a household word thoughout this continent, and he has
built this reputation the hard way - on one-night concerts which
annually draw millions of people from all walks of life.
"Perhaps one reason for Spike's amazing success is his
intense desire to give the live customer his full measure of show for
money spent at the boxoffice. However, in a few previous attempts
Spike did not seem to have developed this formula for the new medium.
"This new NBC series is a different story...Spike obviously
has given the format of his new show a lot of thought and the results
results are as abvious as sneakers with tails. The initial show was a
smoothly-run half-hour with a story line explaining how the City
Slickers were born, the chirping of Helen...Grayco, who sounded and
looked better than ever, and interrupted only by Georgie Gobel, an

NBC prodigy who is getting a lot of attention as a coming comic.
         "Spike appeared far more at ease on this show than on his
previous attempts to wrestle with TV, and even the over-all show was
slightly less tempestuous than is normal with this crew.
         "If Spike can maintain the pace (and there's no reason why
he shouldn't after his personal appearance records of the last decade
or so) he should be around the nation's living rooms for a long while
to come."   (Downbeat, 10 Feb 54)
         Note: Another Downbeat TV review on the same page covered
the Bing Crosby CBS-TV debut of 3 Jan, and in the course of the
article is mention of solo guitarist, Perry Botkin

9 January, 1954 (SAT) - THE SPIKE JONES SHOW
                NBC-TV Burbank   5:00 PM PST

         Guest: Harpo Marx

         Personnel as 2 Jan, deleting John DeSoto

         Tchaikovsky Piano Concerto - City Slickers
         City Slicker Production - "Panel Shows"
            (Cast: Spike, Harpo, Earle Bennett, Freddy
            Morgan, Peter James, Ruth Foster, Betty Serpico
            Helen Grayco, Harpo - "My Heart Went Boom Boom"
            Helen Grayco - "Somewhere With a Nowhere Guy"
         Melody In F - City Slickers (tuned 'flit-guns')

         Note: Harpo laughs loudly during game show. A short show
allows Harpo one minute of pantomime after "Melody In F"

16 January, 1954 (SAT) - THE SPIKE JONES SHOW
                NBC-TV Burbank   5:00 PM PST

         Guests: Bob Smith and Howdy Doody

         Leader - Spike Jones
         Brass - George Rock, tpt; Ray Heath, trb
         Reeds - as 2 Jan
         Rhythm - Paul Leu, pno; Freddy Morgan, Jad Paul,
            guit/bjo; Roger Donley, bass; Dick Shanahan, drm

         That's Amore - voc Bill Hamilton
         City Slickers Production - "Snow White"
            (Cast: Billy Barty, Helen Grayco, Spike,
            Freddy Morgan, Earle Bennett, Peter James,
            George Rock, Billy Reed, Purves Pullen)
            Helen Grayco - "Some Day My Prince Will Come"
            Billy Reed - Dinner Plate solo
            'Dwarfs' - Alphabet Soup Serenade (comp. Jay
                Meyer)
         Howdy Doody, Slickers - "Bye Bye Blackbird", with
            Clarabel (Bob Keeshan), trb

23 January, 1954 (SAT) - THE SPIKE JONES SHOW
                NBC-TV Burbank   5:00 PM PST

         Guest: Paul Gilbert

         Leader - Spike Jones
         Brass - George Rock, tpt; Ted Vesley, trb
         Reeds - Bill DePew, Bernie Jones, Eddie Rosa
         Rhythm - Paul Leu, pno; Freddy Morgan, Jad Paul,

guit/bjo; Roger Donley, bass; Dick Shanahan,
John DeSoto, drm

Opener - Spike introduces Bill DePew, Bernie Jones
    and Peter James
City Slicker Production - "Ricochet Romance
    Around the World"
    Germany - City Slickers
    Japan - Freddy Morgan, Betsy Gay, Margie
                Rayburn
    Cuba - Helen Grayco
    India - Sir Frederick Gas
    Hollywood - Paul Gilbert
Holiday For Strings - feat Reginald Rymal,
                paddle-ball solo on prop chimes

30 January, 1954 (SAT) - THE SPIKE JONES SHOW
            NBC-TV Burbank   5:00 PM PST

        Guests: Dick Contino, Peggy Ryan and
            Ray McDonald

        Personnel as 23 Jan, deleting John DeSoto

        Hindustan - City Slickers
        City Slicker Production - "Variety"
            Bill King - Juggler
            Peggy Ryan, Ray McDonald - Tap dancing
            Helen Grayco - "Blue Pacific Blues"
            Dick Contino - "Cumana", "Oh, Marie",
                    "Lady Of Spain"
        I'm In the Mood For Love - Billy Barty

6 February, 1954 (SAT) - THE SPIKE JONES SHOW
            NBC-TV Burbank   5:00 PM PST

        Guest: William Woodson

        Personnel as 16 Jan

        Opener - Trumpet playing by George Rock and
            Billy Barty
        City Slicker Production - "This Is Your Life,
            Peter Ilyich Spikovsky"
        Helen Grayco - "Tonight We Love"
        Texas Concerto - voc George Rock, Jad Paul
                (Tchaikovsky Piano Concerto melody)
          *Tchaikovsky Medley:
                    1812 Overture; Love theme(Romeo and
                    Juliet); Chinese Dance(Nutcracker
                    Suite); None But the Lonely Heart;
                    Piano Concerto No.1

        *issued on MF Distribution LPs MF 205/4,
            947447, and GO 10016

13 February, 1954 (SAT) - THE SPIKE JONES SHOW
            NBC-TV Burbank   5:00 PM PST

        Guests: Arthur Q. Bryan and the Arthur
            Murray Dancers

287

Personnel as 16 Jan

Pass the Biscuits, Mirandy - City Slickers
City Slicker Production - "Cinderella"
    (Cast: Cinderella, Helen Grayco; Ugly Sisters,
    Morgan & Bennett; Fairy Godmother, Arthur Q.
    Bryan; Prince Charming, Spike; Squeeky(mouse),
    Billy Barty; Page, Peter James)
    Helen Grayco - "Secret Love"
That's Amore - voc Bill Hamilton

20 February, 1954 (SAT) - THE SPIKE JONES SHOW
            NBC-TV Burbank   5:00 PM PST

    Guest: Eddy Arnold, Joe Besser

    Personnel as 16 Jan

    *Farandole - City Slickers
    City Slicker Production - "Prison Life"
        (Cast: Spike, Eddy Arnold, Joe Besser,
        City Slickers)
        Eddy Arnold - "I Really Don't Want To Know"
            (lip-sync)
        Flashbuld Freddy - Spike, Freddy Morgan
        Helen Grayco - "Somebody Bad Stole De
                    Wedding Bell"
    Changing Partners - voc Bill Hamilton

    *issued on MF Distribution LPs MF 205/4,
        947447, and GO 10016

27 February, 1954 (SAT) - THE SPIKE JONES SHOW
            NBC-TV Burbank   5:00 PM PST

    Guest: Margaret Truman

    Personnel as 16 Jan

    Charlestono-Mio - inst
    City Slicker Production - "Margaret Truman visits
                    Spike Jones"
        Poet and Peasant Overture - F. Morgan, J. Paul
        Helen Grayco - "Mad About the Boy", "From This
                    Moment On"
        Margaret Truman, Spike - To Be a City Slicker
    Cocktails For Two - Margaret Truman with the
        City Slickers

    Note: Actors/actresses are now joining the cast, with fewer
Slickers in every role. The Jones estate kinescope of this show was
destroyed by fire.

6 March, 1954 (SAT) - THE SPIKE JONES SHOW
            NBC-TV Burbank   5:00 PM PST

    Personnel as 16 Jan, add Jimmy Vey, xylophone

    San - City Slickers

288

City Slicker Production - "Foreign Legion"
  (Cast: Spike, George Rock, Freddy Morgan,
  Mack Pearson, Bernie Jones, Helen Grayco,
  Billy Barty, Peter James, Earle Bennett)
  Helen Grayco - "Young At Heart"
  *Minka - George Rock, tpt; Spike Jones, drm
City Slicker Medley:
  Whispering - Jimmy Vey, xyl solo
  I'm Forever Blowing Bubbles - Bill Hamilton
  My Gal Sal - Banjo duet
  Runnin' Wild - Spike, with drumsticks

    *issued on MF Distribution LPs MF 205/4,
       947447, and GO 10016

13 March, 1954 (SAT) - THE SPIKE JONES SHOW
         NBC-TV Burbank   5:00 PM PST

    Guest: Hal Peary

    Personnel as 16 Jan, adding Jacques Gasselin,
    Murray Kellner, Israel Baker, Joseph Quadri, vln

    MacNamara's Band - City Slickers
    City Slicker Production - "Movie Session"
      (Cast included Hal Peary)
      Helen Grayco - "Little Girl Blue"
    Slanthe - voc Jad Paul

    Note: Helen Grayco lip-sync during this series is quite 're-
markable'. She produces genuine tears during this live TV solo.

20 March, 1954 (SAT) - THE SPIKE JONES SHOW
         NBC-TV Burbank   5:00 PM PST

    Guests: Frankie Carle, Joe Houston,
      Artie James

    Personnel as 16 Jan

    Siam - voc Bill Hamilton
    City Slicker Production - "Tribute To the Piano"
    Joe Houston, Frankie Carle;
    Helen Grayco, Artie James - Rodgers
           and Hart medley
    Helen Grayco - "The Lady Is a Tramp"
    I'm In the Mood For Love - Billy Barty, City
              Slickers

    Note: From Spike's PR kit for 1956:- "Barty's 'Liberace bit'
("I'm In the Mood For Love") created such a furore when it first was
introduced on TV that Liberace, himself, phoned Spike long distance
to say he was sorry he'd missed it and to ask if it couldn't be
repeated. Spike, and little Billy, obliged, and Liberace wrote the
midget a fan letter saying he thought it was simply great..."

27 March, 1954 (SAT) - THE SPIKE JONES SHOW
         NBC-TV Burbank   5:00 PM PST

Personnel as 16 Jan, adding Jacques Gasselin,
        Murray Kellner, Joe Quadri, <u>Emil Briano</u>, vln

<u>Charlie My Boy</u> - City Slickers
City Slickers Production - "Rumplestiltskin"
    (Cast: Helen Grayco, Billy Barty, Spike,
    Freddy Morgan, Earle Bennett)
    Spike, Gas, Freddy - "Nothing To Eat"
    Helen Grayco - "Over the Rainbow"
    Billy Barty - "Rumplestiltskin Is My Name"
            (tune: "Glow Worm")
    Spike, Helen, Gas - "What Can the Name of
            the Little Man Be?"
*<u>Yes Sir, That's My Baby</u> - voc Freddy Morgan
    (additional lyrics: Harry 'Hari Kari' Stewart)

*issued on MF Distribution LPs MF 205/4,
    947447, and GO 10016

3 April, 1954 (SAT) - THE SPIKE JONES SHOW
        NBC-TV Burbank   5:00 PM PST

        Guest: Zasu Pitts

        Personnel as 16 Jan

        *<u>San Antonio Rose</u> - voc Bill Hamilton
        City Slicker Production - "Charity Bazaar"
            (Cast: Zasu Pitts, Spike, Freddy Morgan,
            George Rock, Jad Paul, Earle Bennett,
            Laverne Pearson, Peter James)
            George Rock - "I Don't Know Why"
            Sir F. Gas, Laverne Pearson - "The Giggle Song"
        *<u>Love In Bloom</u> - Zasu Pitts and City Slickers

        *issued on MF Distribution LPs 205/4,
            947447, and GO 10016

    Note: An example of the excellent City Slickers organization
was the fact that the touring troupe were able to carry on working
almost as per usual. Not only were they involved with the music and
script consultations/rehearsals for the television shows but they
performed throughout southern Calfornia, and Lake Tahoe, Nevada,
during this period.

10 April, 1954 (SAT) - THE SPIKE JONES SHOW
        NBC-TV Burbank   5:00 PM PST

        Guests: Beany and his Gang

        Personnel as 16 Jan

        <u>William Tell Overture</u> - Doodles Weaver
        City Slicker Production - "Easter Party"
            (Cast: Billy Barty, Spike, Helen, Beany and
            his Gang, celebrities' children)
            Helen Grayco - "You Do Something To Me"
            Billy Barty - "Peter Cottontail" (lip-sync
                    Spike's RCA recording)
            Mr. Wolf (from Beany show) - "Rhapsody From
                    Hunger(y)" (lip-sync to RCA disc)

Note: The voices of Beany & Cecil were Stan Freberg and Daws Butler. "Wm. Tell" used the Revue comedic film clips for the horse race

14 April, 1954 (WED) - Radio Recorders, Hollywood   1:00 to
                Client: RCA Victor   6:00 PM
                Harry Geller, A & R Rep, present

        Leader - Spike Jones
        Contractor - Dick Webster
        Brass - Chico Alvarez, Conrad Gozzo, George Rock, tpt; Ray Heath, trb
        Reeds - Bill DePew, Bernie Jones, Bill Hamilton
        Rhythm - Eddie Cano, Frank Leithner, pno; Jad Paul, guit; Roger Donley, bass; Dick Shanahan, drm; Wally Ferguson, conga drm; Eddie Gomez, maracas; Eddie Aparicio, timbales
        Strings - Jacques Gasselin, Israel Baker, Mischa Russell, Marshall Sosson, Nick Pisani, Joe Quadri, Walter Edelstein, Murray Kellner, vln; Dave Sterkin, Louis Kievman, vla; Cy Bernard, Eleanor Slatkin, cel
        Vocalist - Billy Barty, Tony Martinez
        Effects - Earle Bennett
        Arrangers - Joe Knechter, Chico Alvarez
        Copyist - Bernie Jones

E4-VB-3144-1   20-5742-B; HMV POP 110; RCADJ E4-VB-3144; 45 47-5742-B; HMV 7M 324; RCAG EPA 9635; LP RCAE HY 1006; RCAG RCS 3217/1-2; RCAJ RVP-6300(m), 5143(m); ET AFRS "Bud's Bandwagon" 416;
        (2:32)Secret Love - voc Tony Martinez

E4-VB-3145-1   20-5742-A; HMV POP 110, RCADJ E4-VB-3145; 45 47-5742-A; HMV 7M 324; RCAG EPA 9635; LP ANLI 2312(e); AYLI 3870; RCAE NL 42730(e); RCAG RCS 3211/1-2; RCAJ 5143(m); RCAF PL 43197; ET AFRS "Martin Block" 102, 217, 396;
        (3:00)I'm In the Mood For Love - voc Billy Barty

Note: The RCA inst sheet for this session is complete even to the matter of specifying Radio Recorders. 78 & 45 RPM issues were in picture sleeves. Not all domestic releases credit Billy Barty as vocalist on "Mood for Love", although he is credited on the RCA sheets. The presence of two pianists leads one to correctly conclude Leithner was hired for his sneezing artistry and was paid by RCA (as an instrumentalist) rather than by Spike.

17 April, 1954 (SAT) - THE SPIKE JONES SHOW
        NBC-TV Burbank   5:00 PM PST

        Guests: Art Tatum, the Asia Boys

        Personnel as 16 Jan, adding Jacques Gasselin, Joe Quadri, Murray Kellner, Nick Pisani, vln

        Five Foot Two, Eyes Of Blue - City Slickers
        Ya Wanna Buy a Bunny? - George Rock
        The Asia Boys - Acrobatics
        Helen Grayco - "I Concentrate On You"
        Art Tatum - Jazz At the Philharmonic
        Stranger In Paradise - Peter James (lip-sync to Bill Hamilton)

24 April, 1954 (SAT) - THE SPIKE JONES SHOW
                    NBC-TV Burbank   5:00 PM PST
                    Sponsor: Liggett and Myers

                    Guest: Leonid Kinskey

                    Personnel as 17 Apr

                    <u>Bye Bye Blues</u> - City Slickers
                    City Slicker Production - "Pinocchio"
                        (Cast: Spike, Helen, Billy Barty, Freddy
                        Morgan, Leonid Kinskey)
                        Helen Grayco - "Answer Me"
                        Spike, Helen - "When a Puppet Falls In Love"
                    City Slicker Medley:
                        To Rags From Riches - Freddy Morgan, Peter
                                  James (adapted by Bernie Jones)
                        Oh, My Pa-Pa - George Rock
                        The Song From Moulin Rouge -
                        Changing Partners - voc Bill Hamilton

1 May, 1954 (SAT) - THE SPIKE JONES SHOW
                    NBC-TV Burbank   5:00 PM PST

                    Guest: Perez Prado

                    Personnel as 16 Jan

                    <u>Linger Awhile</u> - City Slickers
                    Perez Prado -
                    Helen Grayco - "Easy Come, Easy Go, Lover"
                    Battle of the Bands:-
                        Spike Jones vs. Perez Prado
                        Billy May Mambo - Perez Prado
                        <u>Secret Love</u> - voc Tony Martinez

6 May, 1954 (THURS) - (pilot radio show)*

                    with Spike Jones and his City Slickers

8 May, 1954 (SAT) - THE SPIKE JONES SHOW
                    NBC-TV Burbank   5:00 PM PST

                    Personnel as 16 Jan, except <u>Joe Yukl</u>, trb,
                      replaces Ray Heath

                    <u>That Old Black Magic</u> - voc Billy Barty
                    Helen Grayco - "I'll Be Seeing You", "Ridin' High"
                    RCA Favorites Medley:
                      Captain of the Space Ship - George Rock
                      Chloe - Sir Frederick Gas
                      Holiday For Strings - inst
                    *You Always Hurt the One You Love - Freddy
                      Morgan, Sir F. Gas, Bernie Jones
                    Cocktails For Two - voc Bill Hamilton (Eddie
                      Cline in skit)

                    *issued on MF Distribution LPs 205/4,
                    947447, and GO 10016

Note: After the farewell speech, entire cast exits via the studio fire-doors. Quite moving, as, in light of hindsight, many favorites would not re-appear on subsequent shows and never again would the band achieve the same height of Slicker-ness.

"A weekly television show is tougher, Spike believes, than seven nights a week of one-night stands..."When I'm on the road, I seem to have time to sit down with some of my key men and work out new numbers", he explains, "but during the television season there simply wasn't any time for idea sessions and conferences"....."We do numbers on our personal appearances that we could never think of televising. They're simply too big."

"Television and personal appearances constitute two entirely different media and I try to present material that is hand-tailored for each one. TV, great as it is, is still governed by the restrict- ions imposed by a small screen -- and even a 27-inch screen is a small area in which to encompass a production number of the type that we present. The close-up is still the big thing in TV, and we try to devise numbers which will utilize this technique."

"In personal appearances, however, Spike can shoot the works with lavish production numbers, beautiful girls, and sketches in which a dozen things are going on at once...all things visibly simul- taneously to the human eye of the in-person spectator.

"For example, we've never felt we could do an adequate job on TV with production numbers like our "Sabre Dance", "Indian Love Call", "Lover", "Caravan", "Blue Danube", and "Hall of the Mountain King". They're just too big and there's too much production involved"
(Arena Stars/Spike Jones 1956 PR/Information sheet)

"Spike Jones' Musical Insanities" tour personnel similar to the Sept 53 listing, with the following changes: Billy Barty, voc/ tpt/act added; Bill Jacoby replacing Jack Currance; Jad Paul, guit/ bjo/voc replacing Hayden Causey; Carl (Ziggy) Elmer, trb; replacing Abe Nole; Mark Barnett, drm, replacing Joe Guerrero; Dick Webster and Verne McLeod replacing Art Wenzel and Jack McNaughton.

An inventory of the tour, dated 20 May, 1954, is reprinted, giving an excellent look at the individual props and those picked up over the years for use on tour. Spike Jones Souvenir Programs for this season still contain photos of past members, such as Dick Gardner, Dick Morgan, Joe Siracusa and Lottie Brunn, while the group photo is the 1949 pose with a now bearded Doodles Weaver.

INVENTORY

"SPIKE JONES' MUSICAL INSANITIES"

DEPARTMENT - PROPERTY, WARDROBE, ELECTRICAL, CARPENTER

ARENA STARS, INC.
366 N. Camden Drive
Beverly Hills, Calif.   May 20, 1954

Compiled by Ray Harrison
Approved by Ralph Wonders, Mgr.

INVENTORY OF ELECTRICAL DEPARTMENT

QUANTITY	DESCRIPTION	MAKE & SERIAL NO.
1	Seventy Amp. Arc Lamps & Stands	Kleigel Brothers
1	Eight Inch Irises	" "
1	Electric Polarized Bell	Faraday
1	Electric Horn	"
2	Telephone Bells	Western Electric
9	Music Stand lights	

```
9          Music Stands
1          Tilt sign
1          Piano Lamp
1          Feeder cable for Music Stand Stage Proper
1box       Various lengths of cable and plugging boxes
50         Trims of carbon for Arc Lamps - National Carbon Co.
75         Pieces of colored gelatin
8          Color frames
8          Caster boxes for Electrical Equipment
1          Personal caster box with tools, etc.
4          Ultra violet lights for stage show
4          Transformers                          General Electric
1          8 volt Plugging Box
2          Spare 250 volt Ultra Violet lights
1          Flash Pot
2          All State 6 volt Auto Batteries
1          Electrically operated prop boat
1          Box flash powder, Spare Lamps, Fuses, Plugs,
                                           Battery Cable, etc.
2          Electric Cannons
1          Electric Guitar
```

INVENTORY OF SHOW WARDROBE

QUANTITY	DESCRIPTION	MADE BY
15	Ties	Miscellaneous
25	Slicker suits	Max Koltz of Hollywood
40	Slicker shirts	Max Koltz of Hollywood
4	Black Tail Coats	Miscellaneous
1	Lord Fauntleroy Suit	Jack's of Hollywood
1	Boy Scout Uniform	George Rock
4	Headless Man Suits	Miscellaneous
1	Flannel Nightgown	Earle Bennett
1	Indian Costume	Miscellaneous
1	Tail Suit	Mack Pearson
3	Smocks	" "
1	Halman Pants	Frankie Little
1	Tuxedo	Earl Bennett
3	High Silk Hats	Miscellaneous
1	Boy Scout Hat	"
1	Lord Fauntleroy Hat	"
1	Russian Hat	"
2	Sailor Straw Hats	"
1	Towel Turban	"
1	Straw Boomerang Hat	"
2	Large Round Checked Hats	"
18pr.	Costume Shoes	"
2	Bottles shoe polish	"
1	Clothes Brush	
2	Upside men costumes	

WAYNE MARLIN TRIO

```
6pr.    Ragged duck white pants      1  Wardrobe bag
6       Supporters                   1  Raincoat
1pr.    Slippers                     2  Womens suits
8pr.    Sandals                      1  White dress
6pr.    Ballet shoes                 1  Robe
6pr.    Swim trunks                  5  Short costumes
1box    Misc. drugs - oil & peroxide 1  Bathing suit
2pr.    White wardrobe pants         1  Nurse outfit
1       Sewing machine, Portable - Sew Right
```

```
2       White Gowns                  Helen Grayco
1       Pink Gown                         "
1       Gold and black lace gown          "
1       Beige and gold lace gown          "
1       Red Gown                          "
```

1	Green Gown	"
1	Black Pring(sic) Gown	"
1	Purple Gown	"
1	Rust Gown	"
1	Black Net Gown	"

1	Brown lace and net gown	Laverne Pearson
1	Purple Street Dress	"
1	Green street dress	"
2	Bags	"
4pr.	Shoes	"

BOXES

2	Large grey boxes containing Slicker suits, hats
2	Large grey boxes containing women's wardrobe, feature
1	Large Black - Feature wardrobe
1	Caster box containing musical scores and arrangements
1	Metal shoe trunk

Amount of Souvenir programs on Hand _____

Above statement verified by _____

INVENTORY OF PROPERTY DEPARTMENT

BILL KING

1	Large black suitcase containing:		
3	Juggling clubs	1	Large rubber ball
3	Juggling axes	9	Juggling Hoops
1doz.	La Crosse balls	1	Glass spinning ball
5	Mouth pieces		Misc. small props

1	Large metal fire box containing:		
3	Firebrands	1	Red gas can
1	Spinning hoop	1	Fire extinguisher
1	Headpiece		

1	Prop guitar	6	Prop wooden clarinets
3	Axes		

BILLY BARTY

2	Bartender aprons	1	Top Hat
1	Change apron	2	White shirts
1	Chef's cap	1	Towel
3	Comedy shirts		

EARL BENNET

1	Stradavarious and case	1	Prince Albert coat
1	Hot water bottle	1	Table cloth
2	Stocking caps, red and blue	1	Tympani Hammer
3	Spare Stradavarious bows		
2	Spare Stradavarious instruments		

Note: Had Earle Bennett's props been Stradivarius, they
would not have been subjected to such baggage handling.

MAGIC PROPS

1	Box - contents: Magic carpet		
1	Crate - Levitation table		
2	Prop saxes	1	Pop machine pistol
2	Prop derbies	1	Wood Block
1	Bicycle pump	1	Prop mirror

ADDITIONAL PROPS

12	Hand chimes		
1	Prop bass violin in case		
1	Prop teeter board (red) with wooden horse		
1	Box prop chicken feathers		
1	Prop canteen	1	Prop bugle
1	Prop hatchet	2	Prop Red Cross boxes
12	Prop flit guns (Musical)	1	Fur coat
1	Box of strob light props	1	set prop bagpipes
1	Prop Xylophone	1	Crate (Liberace piano)
1	Bird cage with 1 live dove		
1 box	Contents: Bass drum, tom-tom & stand, beep horns on mounting		

Taken by Lester Calvin

1	Woodblock	2	Washboards & stand, consisting of 9 auto horns
1	Mop		
1	Broom		
2	Anvils	1	Breakdrum
2	Police whistles	1	Musical ratchet
1	Telephone	1	String of sleigh bells
1	Toilet seat	1	Bell set consisting of 10 pieces
2	Klaxton horns		
2	Tom-Toms	1	Brass gong
2	Sink plungers	1	Train bell
2	Rubber hands		
2	Baseball bats	2	Rubber ball bats

LIVE PROPS

1	Stethescope	1	Train whistle
1	Rope	2	Wash tubs - assorted cowbells
2	Chrome stools		
1	Bouquet of magic glowers	2	Hot Water bottles
		1	Wooden bench
12	Prop ducks	1	Black cloth
1	Dressed Dummy	2	Gongs
1	Frying pan & hammer	1	Red hand truck
1	Bird cage	1	Red wig
1	Rubber hammer	1	Billiard chalk line
2	Prop trombones	1	Rubber hose - assorted or plastic drumsticks
2pr.	Maracas		
2	Yo-Yos	1	Truck rubber hose
1pr.	Prop eyeglasses	2	Wigs
1	Trench coat	1	Brass dinner bell
1	Slap stick	1	Wooden train whistle
1	Bucket	3	Wigs
1	Fish pole, line & one rubber fish	1	Wooden plunger for water effect
2	Red velvet covers	2	Horn racks
5	Rubber syringes	1	Washboard with mount horns
1	Drum top		
1	Broken telephone	1	Prop saw
1	Silk "Bang" flag	10	Flit guns
1pr.	Claves	1	Grey trunk for bell
3	Wooden swords	1	Trunk for wasboards & horns
1	Prop lantern		
1	Fur coat	1	Junk box
2pr.	Cymbals	3	Boxes for musical instruments
1	Prop mute		
1	Seltzer bottle	1	Black barrel for instruments & instrument stands
1	Rain coat		
2	Prop horns (Inst)		
2	Soft felt hats	1	Large brass gong
1	Red ladder	1	Prop shotgun
1	Rubber glove	2doz.	Sparklets
5	Song whistles	1	Large misc. prop box

1	Box assorted whistles	1	Long box for pipes, etc.
2	Leather whistles	1	Box for prop heads
1	Round mirror	1	Box for large horn
1	Extra "Bang" flag	1	Trunk for Tympani, casters
1	Tool box	1	Large wooden tray
1	Ironing board		

GUNS

1	38 cal. black Smith & Wesson	Serial No. S-916065
1	38 cal. black Smith & Wesson	" 667994
1	38 cal. black Smith & Wesson	" 33171
1	38 cal. Nickel Smith & Wesson	" 143896
1	22 cal. black Smith & Wesson	" 0672932
1	Prop 22 cal. small gun	
1	Sawed off double barrel shotgun	
2	Nickel plated Smith & Wesson	" S-098304
		S-098285

SHELLS ON HAND
150	Blanks shot gun shells	
2500	"38" blanks	100 "22" blanks

JAD PAUL
1	Gibson Guitar	L7-No. 94990
1	Banjo Vega Vox	No. 99010
1	Gibson Amplifier	

ROGER DONLEY
1	Martin Recording Tuba	No. 113008
1	Kay String Bass	No. 3409

BERNIE JONES
1	Selmer Clarinet	No. L-2952
1	Selmer Tenor	No. 28511
1	Pruefer Bass	No. CL 21245

BILL DEPEW
1	Selmer Alto sax	No. 19714
1	Selmer B Flat Clarinet	No. M 7010

BILL JACOBY
1	Baritone Sax, Buescher	No. 25817
1	Conn Sax	CL 444NB290177L
1	Armstrong Flute	No. 21467
1	German Violin	
1	Martin Alto	No. 164900

CARL ELMER
1	Williams Trombone	No. 911

MARK BARNETT
1	Bass drm (14" x 22") Slingerland
1	Snare drum (3-1/2" x 14") Leedy and Ludwig
2	Tom-Toms (9" x 13" and 16" x 20") Slingerland
4	Cymbals (All Zildjian) 2-14"; 17" and 19"
5	Stands for accessories
4 Cases	Fibre

GEORGE ROCK
1	Blessing Trumpet (Special model)	No. 52841
1	Blessing Trumpet " "	No. 43151

```
1       Selmer Trumpet              No. 25214
```

FREDDY MORGAN
```
1       Vega electric Tenor Banjo    No. 92610
1       Vega Tenor Banjo             No. 98998
```
SPIKE JONES
```
1       Bass Sax, Lyon and Healy     No. 81697
1       Saxcello B Flat, King        No. 74477
1       Clarinet B Flat, G Vallette  None
1       Clarinet B Flat, G Vallette  None
1       Saxophone Baritone,King      No. 140575
   Drums:
1       Complete set of Slingerland red drums
1       24" x 24" Bass Drum (with spurs and pedal)
1       7" x 14" Snare drum (with stand)
1       9" x 13" tom-tom with stand
2       16" Zildjian cymbals with holders
2       15" Zilco Cymbals with sock stand
1       Cowbell with holder
1       Woodblock with holder
1       9" x 11" Tom-tom with holder
3       Painted B Flat Clarinets, Metal, ABC Special
1       Trombone, miniature King     No. 220707
```

MUSICAL INSTRUMENTS (Other than those named by players)
```
1Box    Music library               1Trunk Tympani drum
1       Small box (tuba, Roger Donley)
2       Complete sets of drummers traps and trap cases
3       Crates of musical instruments
```

Note: In addition to the above inventory, each show required the following props to be supplied by the host:-

```
        1/2 dozen eggs per performance
        One grand piano - must be in perfect concert pitch
        15 wooden back chairs (not kitchen or folding chairs)
```

Touring is now by chartered, air-conditioned bus with a 32-foot trailer and cab carrying 16,000 pounds of props, costumes and instruments. Spike and Helen usually traveled by car (Cadillac), with Helen driving (fast). Bill Jacoby recounts; Spike - "My God! Helen! You are driving so fast even the radio won't come in!".
Jacoby also recalls some of the unusual Slickers presentations of this tour: the three saxs playing the "Sabre Dance" (2 Jan arr.) with arms wrapped like an octopus - each man playing a section of the others horn; playing "Glow Worm" on flit-guns - each having a different note on his spray; and accidentally falling off a 9-ft stage in Canada during a black-light Dixieland presentation. The next night Spike said it got such a laugh to do it again! The baritone sax around his neck was destroyed.
Around this time, Ralph Wonders retires as General Manager and Dick Webster, who had been the West coast office representative then the touring PR agent, is now the Arena Stars General Manager. Earle Bennett, who filled the shoes of the ficticious Sir Frederick Gas, leaves but remains in Hollywood. A semi-serious artist, his paintings, particularly the pseudo "Great Masters" series, are treasured by his colleagues.

12 August, 1954 (THURS) - THE BETTY WHITE SHOW*
              NBC-TV Hollywood

```
```

Guest: Spike Jones

7 September, 1954 (TUES) - Radio Recorders, Hollywood
Client: RCA Victor (see note following)

alias: 'Go-Go Joe's' & 'Go-Go Jones'

Unissued
(2:07)Cool Yule (master on take 6)

Unissued
(2:20)No Dough Blues (master on take 15, start take 7)

Unissued
(2:22)Zippity Zum (master on take 8)

Note: RCA files do not indicate these titles or this days session. Explanation could be that these were for Spike's personal and critical use, and the recording engineer, out of habit, wrote on the recording sheets, 'Client: RCA Victor' instead of 'Client: Spike Jones'. These titles featured a 'straight' male vocal quartet with jazz combo backing. While assumed never issued commercially, many acetate copies and the recording sheets were retained by Spike.

September, 1954 - JUKE BOX JURY*
ABC (radio)

Spike Jones appeared on this one-hour show as one of four panelists (including Dennis Morgan) reviewing current records, (eg: Louis Armstrong's "Skokiaan"). Helen Grayco's latest was also reviewed and voted a 'hit'. Copy in Jones files with network unidentified.

18 September, 1954 (SAT) - PLACE THE FACE*
NBC-TV   Sponsor: Toni Co.

Guest Contestant: Spike Jones

"Musical Insanities" 1955 started in Phoenix, Ariz. on 20 Sept, and while on tour, recorded in Oklahoma City.

17 October, 1954 (SUN) - Victor Studios, Oklahoma City, Okla
9:00 PM to 2:00 AM

Leader - Spike Jones
Brass - George Rock, tpt; Ray Heath, trb
Reeds - Bill DePew, Bernie Jones, William
    Martinez, sax
Rhythm - Paul Leu, pno; Freddy Morgan, bjo;
    Kenny Burt, guit; Roger Donley, bass;
    Joe Guerrero, drm
Vocals - J.B. Dreadfulwater, Mitchell Beaver,
    James Anderson, Richard Anderson

E4-VB-5784   20-5920-B; 45 47-5920-B; RCADJ E4-VB-5784;
                    LP ANLI 2312(e); AYLI 3870; RCAE NL 42730(e);
                    RCAF 130216; ET AFRS "Bud's Bandwagon" 494;
                    Japanese Skokiaan - voc Freddy Morgan

Note: Timing, take numbers and A&R Rep. are absent from the RCA inst. The domestic LP issue is an alternate take to the 78/45 RPM original release, and the original matrix E4-VB-5279 was changed according to Los Angeles instructions. ("California nos. 2/18/55")

The vocalists, a professional Oklahoma City group, appear on the recording sheet as the "Ocsola Four". RCADJ releases are now believed to be exclusively on 45 RPM.

22 October, 1954 (FRI)

1955 "Musical Insanities" perform in Wichita, Kansas, and a Hollywood recording session has been arranged for in Spike's name.

<pre>
        Radio Recorders, Hollywood,   7:30 to
            Client: RCA Victor   9:30 PM
        Harry Geller, A & R Rep, present

            Leader - Harry Geller
            Contractor - Milton Holland
            Trumpet - Cecil Read
            Rhythm - Paul Smith, pno; Al Hendrickson, guit;
                George (Red) Callender, bass; Earl Hatch,
                Ralph Hansell, Lou Singer, marimba;
                John Cyr, Milton Holland, drm
            Harp - Ann Mason (Stockton)
            Voices - Linda Strangis
</pre>

E4-VB-4560-8   20-5920-A; 45 47-3920-A; RCADJ E4-VB-4560;
                   LP RCAF 130216; ET AFRS "Basic Music Library"
                   CHR-84; AFRS (Frankfurt Local Recording)
                   LR 3402;
          (2:52)I Want Eddie Fisher For Christmas - Spike Jones
                   and solo by Linda Strangis and the St.
                   Mary Magdalene Choir

Note: The presence of Spike, his niece Linda Strangis and the choir are not credited on the RCA inst. As he was on tour and not personally at this session, it is highly possible the voices were overdubbed and mixed to the studio take-8 by Spike on his return. A similar session occurred 22 Jul 53.

Milton Holland, who worked on as many as four dates a day for 30 years, has little recollection of this session, except - "I've just had a flash on Harry (Geller) conducting the date and have slight recall that he did the charts. I don't recall the name, Linda Strangis". (Milton Holland correspondence 28 Nov 83)

24 November, 1954 (WED)
One commercial for Robert Hall Clothing Stores: Empire Broadcasting Corp., New York City; 10" 78 RPM acetate featuring George Rock and the City Slickers

Note: This date is not definite

November, 1954 - PETER POTTERS JUKE BOX JURY*
ABC-TV Hollywood

Cameo appearance by Spike on this one hour show, which discussed the merits of various popular records played to mimed singers and dancers. This date is indefinite, and there may have been more Juke Box Jury radio and TV show with Jones appearances.

"Last fall Jones completed a million miles of US barnstorming. After resting and making what he calls an album of low fidelity

records, Jones starts out next week on his second million miles."
(<u>Life</u>, 31 Jan 55)

       With reference to the above stated album of low fidelity music, the cover art work (with an eerie Charles Adams flavor) for "A Study in Low Fidelity - Music for Leasebreakers", a 10" RCA Victor long play album LPM 3216 was completed, however, RCA have no knowledge on any details surrounding this cover or its contents, nor do the recording sheets from Radio Recorders with RCA as the client give any hint of the studio time being used for any other purpose than the listed titles. Spike may have contracted a studio such as Radio Recorders and started to lay the basics for an album produced entirely by himself.

       During the time he was with the Slickers, Eddie Metcalfe remembers being involved with re-recording such standards as "Cocktails For Two", "Laura", "That Old Black Magic" and "My Old Flame". RCA files have no information on these and the explanation seems that, as evident over the years and as time permitted, Spike used studio facilities for his own purposes, such as making Revue promo discs or personal demos. On many occasions lately, RCA sessions produced only one or two registered titles instead of the average four - indicative of time spent on personal projects. Metcalfe's copies of the incomplete re-makes were stolen many years ago.

       The recording industry had lately been offering its artists new techniques to produce full-frequency range recordings (commercial stereo will soon be a reality) and Spike was at the vanguard in their utilization. The Slickers music of the '40s would certainly have been a natural test for the improvements in sound via taping, even with its primitive splicing, which evolved to inter-cutting, overdubbing, multi-tracking or over-laying. The days of one-take performances for recordings had gone the way of the Edison cylinder. 'Direct-to-Disc' one-take recordings would be a comparison to pre-tape techniques, with stereo and full-frequency sound the audible improvement.

       LPM 3216 would not have been issued at this time. The catalog number places it c.1957.

6 February, 1955 (SUN) - COLGATE COMEDY HOUR
                 NBC-TV Hollywood, San Diego, Tijuana Mexico

             with Bobby Van, Nat King Cole, Senor Wences
             and Paul Gilbert. Orchestra under Gordon
             Jenkins. Spike Jones and his City Slickers
             personnel similar to 15 Feb 55

             <u>Sabre Dance</u> - inst
             <u>I'm In the Mood For Love</u> - voc Billy Barty,
               with <u>Mousie Garner</u>
             Helen Grayco - "Please Don't Freeze", "Teach
               Me Tonight", "Just Say the Word"
             City Slicker medley:
               Japanese Skokiaan - Freddy Morgan
               Mr. Sandman - Spike lip-sync Helen
               Shake, Rattle and Roll - Billy Barty
               Open Up Your Heart (and Let the Sun Shine In)
                 - George Rock
               Sh-Boom - Spike as 'One-Man-Band'

       Note: Only Jones portions listed as b'cast from San Diego.
Helen Grayco sings 'live'.

15 February, 1955 (TUES) - Radio Recorders, Hollywood   1:30 to
                 Client: RCA Victor   6:00 PM
                 Henri Rene, A & R Rep, present

```
              Leader - Spike Jones
              Brass - George Rock, tpt; Ray Heath, trb
              Reeds - Bill DePew, Bernie Jones, Bill Hamilton
              Rhythm - Paul Leu, pno; Freddie Morgan, bjo;
                  Roger Donley, bass; Joe Guerrero, drm
              Voices - Paul Ely, Rex Dennis, William Hood,
                  Wayne Hoff, George Rock
              Effects - Dorothy Lloyd (Clara Cluck), Purves
                  Pullen
```

```
F2-PB-0444-M        20-6064-A; 45 47-6064-A; RCADJ F2-PB-0444;
                    LP RCAF 130216; ET AFRS "Basic Music Library"
                    P-5448; AFRS "Bud's Bandwgon" 604;
              (1:58)Hi Mister - voc George Rock's Little Monsters
```

```
F2-PB-0445-G        20-6064-B; 45 47-6064-B; RCADJ F2-PB-0445;
                    LP RCAF 130216; ET AFRS "Basic Music Library"
                    P-5447; AFRS "Bud's Bandwagon" 594;
              (2:05)This Song Is for the Birds - voc Clara Cackle,
                    Dr. Birdbath and Sam Quentin and his Quails
```

        Note: Takes are indicated only by letters, M and G. George
Rock (multi-tracked) is not credited as vocalist on the RCA inst.
Dorothy Lloyd is given two pseudonyms, Clara Cluck on the RCA inst
and Clara Cackle on the label. Florence Gill was the original Clara
Cluck. An alternate version of "Hi Mister", in the Jones files, has
an additional opening vocal refrain. Sam Quentin refers to no one
particular. The studio time of George Rock and Spike was to 6:00 PM,
while the others were booked to 5:00 PM.

        After nearly 14 years and, reportedly, 30 million RCA re-
cords sold, Spike and Victor parted and Spike tried to produce his
own records. Henri Rene, the very highly respected composer, conduc-
or and arranger who worked for RCA for many years gives a hint of the
background prevalent in music at this time. "RCA, as well as Spike
Jones...many other legitimate artists and recording companies, were
all victims of their time, ie: the Rock Revolution. Most entertainers
- and many record producers - thought they could join the cult, only
to get killed in the process. Even Spike experimented and thought he
could join the do-it-yourselvers."

4 March, 1955 (FRI) - USE YOUR HEAD (radio pilot)
              NBC Hollywood

        A quiz show, with Spike as M.C. The Slickers gave the con-
testants audio and visual clues on the prize of a $100 War Bond. A
small band provided cue music, with George Rock much in evidence.
Also mentioned are Billy Barty, Bernie Jones and Mousie Garner.

March to April, 1955
              Spike Jones and his City Slickers tour to
              Australia.

```
              Leader - Spike Jones
              Brass - George Rock, tpt; Ray Heath, trb
              Reeds - Bill DePew, Bernie Jones, Bill Hamilton
              Rhythm - Paul Leu, pno; Freddy Morgan, Jad Paul, guit/
                  bjo; Roger Donley, bass; Joe Guerrero, drm
              Vocals - Helen Grayco, Bernie Jones, Billy Barty,
                  George Rock, Mousie Garner, Laverne Pearson
              Acts - Bill King, Wayne-Marlin Trio, Dolores Gay
              Writers - Eddie Brandt
```

        Note: This engagement, booked through Arena Stars by Pacific

Stars of Melbourne, Australia, carried 21 members of Spike's usual 40-plus personnel. Freddie Morgan had a tape dub of a "Poet and Peasant" segment. There are no other known tapings from this tour.

"The craziest show ever seen in Sydney - THE SPIKE JONES SHOW - thrilled and "split the sides" of more than 16,000 fans who saw the first two performances at the Sydney Stadium on Tuesday (29 Mar) night.
"Without a doubt this is the maddest, most zany, yet astoundingly clever show ever staged here.
"No words can adequately describe the scenes of madness crossed with musical genius seen at the Stadium Tuesday night. Tom Farrell wrote in the "Telegraph": 'The National Anthem was the only tune which came out straight in the Spike Jones Show at the Stadium last night. Jones musical lunacy and the astonishing versatility of his troupe made it the best of any of the recent American shows.'"
(Kings Cross Advertiser, Sydney, Aust., 31 Mar 55)

The Slickers were the entire game-show line-up (as contestants) on the AMPOL radio show, with Jack Davie. There was much tour promotion. The 30 minute show is heavily edited from the original hour show. AMPOL was the Australian Atlantic Richfield Oil Company.

Note: In apparent honor of this visit, HMV at Wellington, New Zealand and Sydney, Australia, whose 78 RPM issue catalog numbers were identical to the parent English company, released new discs and re-issued vintage Jones with the special prefix of EA.

9 May, 1955 (MON) - THE SHEILAH GRAHAM SHOW*
                    NBC-TV

          Guest: Spike Jones

19 May, 1955 (THURS) - Radio Recorders, Hollywood
               Client: Spike Jones

          alias: "Davey Crackpot and the Mexican
                 Jumping Beans". Personnel similar to 15 Feb.

K9-101-A   ST 1371-B; 45 ST45 1371-B; LP TST 535; TMT 7535;
(composite) (2:46)No Boom Boom In Yucca Flats - voc Billy Barty

K9-101-4   ST 1371-A; 45 ST45 1371-A; LP TST 535; TMT 7535;
(composite) (2:34)Cherry Pink and Apple Blossom White - featuring
                   George Rock

          alias: "Banjo Maniacs"
                 (with Freddy Morgan, Jad Paul, George Rock)

K9-102A-8   Decca 29623-B; 45 Decca 9-29623-B;
(take 8)   (2:12)Double Eagle Rag - inst

K9-102B-5   Decca 29623-A; 45 Decca 9-29623-A;
(take 5,   (2:28)Pick-It-You-Peasant - inst
insert for
take 5)

Note: Starlite, whose most successful artists were the Hi-Lo's, is the original and very rare issue of "Davey Crackpot". The Tiara LPs (c. '64), feature the original Hoosier Hot-Shots', with the two Jones titles 'pirated' and poorly pressed. The Leithner

303

sneezes are spliced in from previous RCA recordings. "Maniacs" was
issued in Canada. K9 nos. (non-matrix) were used for studio slating.

25 May, 1955 (WED) - THIS IS YOUR LIFE* (Hazel Bishop)
                     NBV-TV

                     Spike Jones: guest on program honoring Van Heflin

30 October, 1955 (SUN) - COLGATE VARIETY HOUR*
                         NBC-TV

                     Guest: Spike Jones performs, and accepts Colgate
                         Achievement Award for his contributions(???)
                         to music

                Note: Feature articles on Spike Jones appeared during
                      1955 in the following magazine:-

                      Life, 31 Jan - "Speaking of Pictures"

24 January, 1956 (TUES) - Radio Recorders, Hollywood
                          Client: Spike Jones

                     Personnel similar to 15 Feb 55, with Gil
                         Bernal, sax/voc replacing Bill Hamilton and
                         adding Paul Frees, Tony Martinez voc;
                         Purves Pullen, effts

                     45 V EPV 5057; LP V MGV 4005; VAU MGV 4005;
                         VF 2304 436; VJ MV 2119; GO 10010;
                  (1:37)Little Child (master, take 13) - voc George
                         Rock and Paul Frees (see also 15 Sept 56)

20,059   V-2003-B; 45 V-2003x45-B; VK V-2003x45;
                         VAU EP V-5003; ET AFRS "Basic Music Library"
                         P-5447;
                  (1:29)16 Tacos (take 8) - voc Tony Martinez

20,060   V-2003-A; 45 V-2003x45-A; VK V-2003x45;
                         VAU EP V-5003; ET AFRS "Basic Music Library"
                         P-5447;
                  (1:43)Love and Marriage (take 2) - voc George Rock

20,060   V-2003-A; 45 V-2003x45-A; VK V-2003x45;
                         VAU EP V-5003; ET AFRS Basic Music Library"
                         P-5447;
                  (1:34)The Trouble With Pasquale (take 6) - voc
                         Freddy Morgan, Sax solo Gil Bernal

20,059   V-2003-B; 45 V-2003x45-B; VK V-2003x45;
                         VAU EP V-5003; V EPV 5057; LP V MGV 4005;
                         VAU MGV 4005; VF 2304 436; VJ MV 2119;
                         GO 10010; ET AFRS "Basic Music Library"
                         P-5447;
                  (1:54)Memories Are Made Of This (composite) - voc
                         Gil Bernal and Ole Svenson's Canine 9

     Note: The Verve label, also pressed in Melbourne for Aus-
tralian distribution, was long associated with jazz impresario Norman
Granz. VAU catalog listing for EP V-5003 does not include "Love and

Marriage" title. The American "Spike Spoofs the Pops", released as "No. 1" indicated that sequals were considered. Bernie Jones reportedly taped at a dog pound with his results edited into sequence on "...Memories" (originally to have been "Love Is a Many Spendored Thing"). 'Doc' recalls adding to this session - the dog whines are human. There is a reported but unconfirmed issue of this EP with "Little Child" replacing "Love and Marriage". As each title is so short, this is not really an EP!

After a much longer than usual Winter break, Spike found that several of his personnel had signed with other bands and clubs. Bernie Jones now starts with Horace Heidt, then later leads his own club band. Spike used to introduce Bernie as "being with Horace Heidt before he turned professional". The scope of band business was indeed narrowing to those few still active. By 1960, Harry James work/income was derived from: Clubs (Reno & Las Vegas) 71.6%; one-nighters(mostly private) 21.9%; records 6.5%. A drastic change from a decade earlier.

12 June, 1956 (TUES) - QUEEN FOR A DAY*
              NBC-TV

              Guest: Spike Jones

15 June, 1956 (FRI) - IT COULD BE YOU*
              NBC-TV

              Guest participant: Spike Jones

25 July, 1956 (WED) - Radio Recorders, Hollywood
              Client: Verve Records

              Personnel - unknown, but including George Rock,
                  Freddy Morgan, Jad Paul, Gil Bernal, Linda
                  Strangis, Jud Conlon singers

              V-2026-A; 45 V-2026x45-A; VK V-2017x45, VEP 5011;
                  EPV 5026; LP V MGV 2021; V MGV 8654; MGM SE
                  4731(s); VAU MGV 2021; GO 10011; ET AFRS
                  "Basic Music Library" CHR-112;
              (2:08)Wouldn't It Be Fun To Be Santa Claus' Son
                  (master, take 2) - the City Slickers and
                  George Rock

              V-2026-B; 45 V-2026x45-B; VK VEP 5011; EPV
                  5024; LP V MGV 2021; V MGV 8654; MGM SE
                  SE 4731(s); VAU MGV 2021; GO 10011;
                  ET AFRS "Basic Music Library" CHR-111;
              (2:08)My Birthday Comes On Christmas (take 3) -
                  the City Slickers and George Rock

              (2:03)Unissued (take 1-2)
                  45 EPV 5023; LP V MGV 2021; V MGV 8654; MGM
                  SE 4731(s); VAU MGV 2021; GO 10011;
                  ET AFRS "Basic Music Library" CHR-110;
              (1:58)Rudolph, the Red Nosed Reindeer (take 3-4) -
                  the City Slickers and the City Slicker
                  Juniors

                  45 EPV 5024; LP V MGV 2021; V MGV 8654; MGM
                  SE 4731(s); VAU MGV 2021; GO 10011;
                  ET AFRS "Basic Music Library" CHR-111;
              (1:38)(I'm Getting) Nuttin' For Christmas (take 9) -
                  the City Slickers and the City Slicker
                  Juniors

```
            (0:15)Voice spot for Spike: "Musical Insanities" promo
                  (Opening 8 Aug at 'Chez Paris')
```

        Note: "Santa Claus' Son" on domestic MGV LPs are condensed
by one verse. Possible all LP versions are condensed. Two 7" HMV
extended play albums are known - "Christmas Fare for the Entire
Family" 7EG 8196, and "Carols for the Fireside" 7EG 8197. However
their specific contents are unknown. See 25 Feb 57 for additional
"Nuttin' For Christmas" information.
        From the album jackets to MGV 8654 and 2021 comes this vari-
able information:- "It is interesting to note that the City Slicker
Juniors include a part of Helen and Spike Jones' 27 neices and
nephews...the solos were sung by Linda Strangis and Cathy Bissutti.."
"Silent Night, sung reverently by my twenty-five piece choir...by the
City Slicker Juniors (seven of my thirty-one neices and nephews.)"
This has remained one of the finer family Christmas albums - a show-
case for the excellent Jud Conlon arrangements and choir, with a good
blend of Slickers and 'straight' adaptions.

26 July, 1956 (THURS) - Radio Recorders, Hollywood
                Client: Verve Records

                Personnel similar to 25 July

                45 EPV 5025; LP V MGV 2021; V MGV 8654; MGM
                   SE 4731(s); VAU MGV 2021; GO 10011;
                   ET AFRS "Basic Music Library" CHR-112;
        (2:47)(I'm the) Angel In the Christmas Play (master,
                   take 4) - the City Slickers and George Rock

                45 EPV 5025; VK VEP 5011; LP V MGV 2021;
                   V MGV 8654; MGM SE 4731(s); VAU MGV 2021;
                   GO 10011; ET AFRS "Basic Music Library"
                   CHR-112;
        (1:28)Frosty, the Snow Man (take 8) - the City
                   Slickers and the City Slicker Juniors

                45 EPV 5026; VK VEP 5011; LP V MGV 2021;
                   V MGV 8654; MGM SE 4731(s); VAU MGV 2021;
                   GO 10011; ET AFRS "Basic Music Library"
                   CHR-113;
        (1:41)Here Comes Santa Claus (take 7) - the City
                   Slickers and the City Slicker Juniors

                45 EPV 5023; VK V-2017x45;VK VEP 5011;
                   LP V MGV 2021; V MGV 8654; MGM SE 4731(s);
                   VAU MGV 2021; GO 10011; ET AFRS "Basic
                   Music Library" CHR-110;
                   All I Want For Christmas Is My Two Front Teeth
                   (composite) - the City Slickers and
                   George Rock

        Note: See 4 Aug for additional info re: "Two Front Teeth"

27 July, 1956 (FRI) - Radio Recorders, Hollywood
                Client: Verve Records

                Personnel similar to 25 July

                45 EPV 5023; LP V MGV 2021; V MGV 8654; MGM
                   SE 4731(s); VAU MGV 2021; GO 10010;
                   ET AFRS "Basic Music Library" CHR-110;
                   AFRS (Frankfurt Local Recording) LR 3996;

                              306
```
```

(3:50)Jingle Bells Medley (master: composite) - the
         City Slickers, Jud Conlon Singers and
         City Slicker Juniors

         45 EPV 5025; LP V MGV 2021; V MGV 8654; MGM
            SE 4731(s); VAU MGV 2021; GO 10011;
            ET AFRS "Basic Music Library" CHR-111; AFRS
            "Johnny Green's World of Music" 6; AFRS
            "Ira Cook"(Christmas '64);
(3:50)White Christmas Medley (take 3) - the City
         Slickers, the Jud Conlon Singers and
         the City Slicker Juniors

         45 EPV 5023; LP V MGV 2021; V MGV 8654; MGM
            SE 4731(s); VAU MGV 2021; GO 10011;
            ET AFRS "Basic Music Library" CHR-110;
(2:35)Silent Night (composite) - the Jud Conlon
         Singers (a cappella)

         45 EPV 5024; LP V MGV 2021; V MGV 8654; MGM
            SE 4731(s); VAU MGV 2021; GO 10011;
            ET AFRS "Basic Music Library" CHR-111;
(2:30)Away In a Manger Medley (take 4) - the Jud
         Conlon Singers (a cappella)

         Note: A comment on the recording sheet: "remake Mel Torme
bit from bar 29" (Christmas Song) opposite Jingle Bells Medley. See 1
Aug for additional info. This session also finished with an "Insanit-
ies" voice spot/promo by Spike.
         "Deck the Halls Medley" is the issue title of "Away In a
Manger Medley", containing "Deck the Halls", "Away In a Manger", "It
Came Upon a Midnight Clear" and "The First Noel".
         "White Christmas Medley" titles:- "Winter Wonderland",
"Silver Bells" and "White Christmas".
         "Jingle Bells Medley" titles:- "Santa Claus Is Coming To
Town", "The Christmas Song" and "Jingle Bells".

1 August, 1956 (WED) - Radio Recorders, Hollywood
         Client: Verve Records

         Personnel similar to 25 July, including
         Frank Leithner

         45 EPV 5026; VK VEP 5011; LP V MGV 2021;
            V MGV 8654; MGM SE 4731(s); VAU MGV 2021;
            GO 10011; ET AFRS "Basic Music Library"
            CHR-112; AFRS "Date With Christmas" 13;
            AFRS "Small World" No. 3; AFRS "Grant"
            (Christmas '68);
(3:26)Christmas Alphabet Medley (master: composite)
         the City Slickers, the Jud Conlon Singers,
         the City Slicker Juniors

         45 EPV 5024; VK VEP 5011; LP V MGV 2021;
            V MGV 8654; MGM SE 4731(s); VAU MGV 2021;
            GO 10011; ET AFRS "Basic Music Library"
            CHR-111;
(3:52)Snow Medley (composite) - the City Slickers and
         the Jud Conlon Singers

         Insert for 27 July
(1:55)Jingle Bells Medley

45 EPV 5024; VK VEP 5011; LP V MGV 2021;
V MGV 8654; MGM SE 4731(s); VAU MGV 2021;
GO 10011; ET AFRS "Basic Music Library"
CHR-110;
(2:15)Sleigh Ride (composite) - the City Slickers
and the Jud Conlon Singers

45 EPV 5026; LP V MGV 2021; V MGV 8654; MGM
SE 4731(s); VAU MGV 2021; GO 10011;
ET AFRS "Basic Music Library" CHR-113;
(1:46)What Are You Doing New Years Eve? (take 6) -
the City Slickers and the Jud Conlon Singers

Note: This "Jingle Bells" insert may be the "Mel Torme bit"
referred to on 27 July.
"Christmas Alphabet Medley" titles:-"Merry Christmas Polka"
and "Christmas In America"
"Snow Medley" titles:- "The First Snowfall" and "Let It
Snow, Let It Snow" (in which George Rock uses three voices)

2 August, 1956 (THURS) - Radio Recorders, Hollywood
Client: Verve Records

Personnel similar to 25 July

45 EPV 5026; LP V MGV 2021; V MGV 8654; MGM
SE 4731(s); VAU MGV 2021; GO 10011;
ET AFRS "Basic Music Library" CHR-113;
(1:33)Christmas Island (master: take 4) - the
Allie-Kai Malahinis (Jud Conlon Choir)

45 EPV 5023; LP V MGV 2021; V MGV 8654: MGM
SE 4731(s); VAU MGV 2021; GO 10011;
ET AFRS "Basic Music Library" CHR-110
(1:35)The Night Before Christmas (take 7) - the
Saint Victor Boys Choir

Unissued
(3:30)The Story of Christmas Medley (composite of
7 takes)

4 August, 1956 (SAT) - Radio Recorders, Hollywood
Client: Verve Records

Personnel similar to 25 July

45 EPV 5025; LP V MGV 2021; V MGV 8654; MGM
SE 4731(s); VAU MGV 2021; GO 10011;
ET AFRS "Basic Music Library" CHR-112;
(2:53)Hark Medley (master: take 4) - the Jud
Conlon Singers (a cappella)

Unissued
The Spirit of Christmas (take 1)

45 EPV 5026; LP V MGV 2021; V MGV 8654; MGM
SE 4731(s); VAU MGV 2021; GO 10011;
ET AFRS "Basic Music Libary" CHR-113;
(1:31)Sleep Well, Little Children (composite) -
the Jud Conlon Singers (a cappella)

<u>45</u> EPV 5026; <u>LP</u> V MGV 2021; V MGV 8654; MGM
   SE 4371(s); VAU MGV 2021; GO 10011;
   ET AFRS "Basic Music Library" CHR 113;
It's Christmas Time (composite)
   Jud Conlon Singers (a cappella)

Intro
Christmas Cradle Song (take 8)

<u>45</u> EPV 5025; <u>LP</u> V MGV 2021; V MGV 8654; MGM SE
   4731(s); GO 10011; ET AFRS "Basic Music
   Library" CHR-112;
Christmas Cradle Song (master: composite take 3)
   Jud Conlon Singers (a cappella)

Final composite
Alphabet Medley of 1 Aug
The First Snowfall of 1 Aug
White Christmas of 27 July
Sleep Well, Little Children

"Look Ma, No Hands" intro to 26 July
My Two Front Teeth

"Hark Medley" titles:- "Hark the Herald Angels Sing", "O
Little Town of Bethlehem", "Joy To the World" and "O Come All Ye
Faithful". "Sleep Well, Little Children" and "It's Christmas Time"
belong to the Victor Young (style) Medley.

Note: Spike Jones Jr. wanted to re-issue the Verve Christmas
LP through Goldberg & O'Reily Productions in time for Christmas 1983.
A 15 ips protection dub of the original master was located and Randy
Morris, a Florida pianist/banjoist and ardent Spike Jones fan, was
available for supervising its remastering in a florida recording
studio. During the transfer, Randy was suddenly aware that something
was missing from "Nuttin' For Christmas" - the two frogs glugs,
supplied by Spike Jones! Evidently these effects were added by Spike
at the last minute (on 4 Aug), even after the final protection dubs
were made. The solution? Randy stepped up to a nearby microphone and
the engineer overdubbed Randy's impromptu "replacements"! Did anyone
notice the difference?

23 August, 1956 (THURS) - Universal Recorders, Chicago
               Client: Spike Jones

               alias: "Mr. Banjo, Freddy Morgan"

               Personnel unknown

56823-1   LP V MGV 2065;
           (2:37)Melody In F (master, take 10) - inst

56823-2   LP V MGV 2065;
           (2:27)Nobody's Sweetheart Now (take 3) - inst

56823-3   LP V MGV 2065;
           (2:12)Bye Bye Blues (take 8) - inst

56823-4   LP V MGV 2065;
           (2:12)Sweet Sue (composite takes 1 & 6) - inst

Note: The instrumentation for the above album is: sax, bjo, pno, tuba and drm. The issued title is "Pickin' Melody In F". See 3 Sept 56 and 5 Apr 57 for additional info. Verve, France, has reportedly issued most of these titles on a 10" LP.

The following titles from this album are as yet undated:-

Somebody Stole My Gal
Yes Sir, That's My Baby
Five Foot Two, Eyes Of Blue
Why Did You Let Me Leave You?

3 September, 1956 (MON) - Universal Recorders, Chicago
Client: Spike Jones   2:00 PM to ?

alias: "Mr. Banjo, Freddy Morgan"

Personnel unknown

(56)936-1   LP V MGV 2065;
                 The World Is Waiting For the Sunrise (master,
                    take 5) - inst

(56)936-2   LP V MGV 2065;
                 Ain't She Sweet (take 4) - inst

(56)936-3   LP V MGV 2065;
                 Pretty Posie (take 8) - inst

(56)936-4   LP V MGV 2065;
                 Chinatown, My Chinatown (take 3) -inst

                 45 EPV 5066; HMV 7EG 8286; HMVAU 7EG 8286;
                    LP V MGV 4005; VAU MGV 4005; VF 2304 436;
                    VJ MGV 2119; GO 10010; ET AFRS "Johnny Green's
                    World of Music" 6;
                 Ramona (drum/sax solos; master take 3 of 4)

                 unspecified
                    piano solo (Liebestraum - one take)
                    tuba solo (4 takes - Black & Blue Danube?)

15 September, 1956 (SAT) - Radio Recorders, Hollywood   8:30 AM
                 Client: Spike Jones

                 Personnel unknown

                 45 EPV 5057; VF 2009 039; HMV 7EG 8286;
                    HMVAU 7EG 8286; LP V MGV 4005; VAU MGV
                    4005; VF 2304 436; VJ MGV 2119; GO 10010;
                 Flight of the Bumble Bee (master: composite)

                 45 EPV 5057; LP V MGV 4005; VF 2304 436;
                    VJ MGV 2119; GO 10010;
                 (2:15)Wyatt Earp Makes Me Burp (composite) - Mousie
                    Garner, Sir Frederick Gas and the Sons of
                    the Sons of the Pioneers

                 45 EPV 5056; VF 2009 039; HMV 7EG 8286;
                    HMVAU 7EG 8286; LP V MGV 4005; VAU MGV
                    4005; V 2304 436; VJ MGV 2119; GO 10010;
                 Black and Blue Danube (composite) - inst

<u>45</u> EPV 5056; HMV 7EG 8286; HMVAU 7EG 8286;
HMVAU 7EG 8286; LP V MGV 4005; VAU MGV
4005; VF 2304 43̄6̄; V̄J̄ MGV 2̄1̄1̄9; GO 10010;
The Old Sow Song (take 3) - George Rock and
Assorted Birds

<u>45</u> EPV 5057; LP V MGV 4005; VAU MGV 4005;
VF 2304 43̄6̄; V̄J̄ MGV 2̄1̄1̄9; GO 10010;
How High the Fidelity (take 2) - Electronics
Professor, SUB NORMAL NORMAL

Intro insert to 24 Jan 56
Little Child - inst

Note: Tommy Pederson and Frank Leithner recreate their 1946
"Laughing Record", retitled as "Sneezin' Bee". "Black and Blue Danube
Waltz, Paris Symphony(Texas)" is the issued title.
Thurl Ravenscroft is one of the voices in "Wyatt Earp" while
Mousie Garner is credited on the label as Sir Frederick Gas. Earle
Bennett, the original Sir Frederick, had left the previous year and
Spike's line, "I guess he ran out of gas" certainly has a double
meaning. George Rock can be credited with the burps. "How High the
Fidelity" is Freddy Morgan monologue only, with intro by Spike. Under
the pseudonym of "Jay Bird", George Rock later recorded the "Sow
Song" for Harmad Records, issue 108.
In a Jan 55 interview, Spike mentioned his doing a "low
fidelity" album, (a parody on the Hi-Fidelity albums of the 50s')
which could have been the "Music for Leasebreakers" Victor LPM 3126
10" album. It is likely this album was put together for RCA by Spike
but the Corporation didn't buy it, or the project became stale. The
above titles are used in the Verve "Dinner Music For People Who
Aren't Very Hungry" and there is a possibility this was the intended
"Leasebreakers" album. Inconsequential trivia:- A United Artists
album at this time featured Dixieland by the "Leasebreakers"; Don
Costa had a similarly titled album of hi-fidelity music issued about
this time.
Early editions (1956) of a Radio Recorders reference recording credit client as RCA and contains the RCA versions of "Chloe" and
"Cocktails". Spike's verbal dating "July 1944" erroneously applied to
to the originally intended RCA version and carried through to the
Standard ET. Other differences were: George Rock singing and narrat-
ing "Sow Song"; "Blue Danube" beginning omitted and containing a
trumpet solo; the Blackhawk Stutz is used during the opening of side
2 instead of during "Danube"; no "Pal-Yat-Chee"; Spike's narration
often longer and use of alternate takes; hi-fi demo montage - mostly
percussion, instead of "Brahms Alibi".
RCA/Radio Recorders paper work is non-existant on the
speculation of RCA nixing the project and Verve buying it with the
RCA references removed.
Something to listen for on the "Dinner Music" album, which
used the Standard ET cuts of "Cocktails" and "Chloe" - the tape re-
wind ("now let's go back a few years") is the RCA "Cocktails", and
the RCA "same guy!" is spliced into "Chloe". DJ releases of "Dinner
Music" have the titles edited into separate bands.

7 October, 1956 (SUN) - THE JACK BENNY SHOW
CBS-TV Hollywood

Guests: George Burns, Spike Jones with Freddy
Morgan, Mousie Garner, Peter James

Note: Burns gets Benny to play in Carnegie Hall and, playing
the devil in a parody on "Damn Yankees", transforms the concert conductor into Spike Jones. Benny plays "Zigeunerweisen" (introduced as
the Mendelssohn Concerto)

311

15 November, 1956 (THURS) - THE FORD SHOW* ('Tennessee' Ernie Ford)
            NBC-TV

            Guest: Spike Jones

8 December, 1956 (SAT) - THE PERRY COMO SHOW*
            NBC-TV New York (Color) (Sponsors: Noxema, S & M
                                          Green Stamps, Sunbeam)
            with Mitchell Ayres Orch. Guests: Guy Lombardo;
                Pearl Bailey; Spike Jones with George Rock,
                Freddy Morgan, Billy Barty, Mousie Garner

            Christmas Medley - as a sing-a-long
            Cocktails For Two - Lombardo & Jones versions

        Note: This color show showed Spike's costuming to good
advantage, however, known kinescopes are black and white.

21 December, 1956 (FRI) - IT COULD BE YOU*
            NBC-TV

            Guest: Spike Jones

c.1956 - THIS IS YOUR LIFE*
            TV Hollywood

            Subject: Billy Barty, with cameo appearance
                by Spike Jones

7 February, 1957 (THURS) - Radio Recorders, Hollywood
            Client: Spike Jones

            Personnel unknown

            LP V MGV 4005; VAU MGV 4005; VF 2304 436;
               VJ MGV 2119; GO 10010;
            Pal-Yat-Chee (master: composite) - voc Betsy Gay

                 V-10037-B; 45 V-10037x45-B; VAU V-5032;
            (1:52)My Heart Went Boom Boom (11 takes) - voc Betty
                  Bloop (Mary Virginia)

                 V-10037-A; 45 V-10037x45-A; VAU V-5032;
            (2:19)Popeye the Sailor Man (16 takes) - voc Windy Cook
                  and Mary Virginia

            Introduction to side 2 (master: take 9)
            guitar/narration to "Wyatt Earp"

        Note: Undated are most of the hi-fi sound effects recorded
in Chicago and L.A. as used in the "Dinner Music" album. Auditions
for Spike's Popeye and Olive Oyl included Billy Bletcher (Disney's
'Big Bad Wolf') and the cartoon voice of June Forray.

9 February, 1957 (SAT) - Radio Recorders, Hollywood
            Client: Spike Jones

            alias: "The Polka Dots, starring Ole Svenson"

Personnel unknown

         LP V MGV 2066; ET AFRS "Basic Music Library"
            P-5462;
(2:32.5)Gesundheit Polka (master basic: take 9) - inst

         LP V MGV 2066; ET AFRS "Basic Music Library"
            P-5463;
(2:26)Strip Polka (composite, take 10 & insert) -
         voc - Ole Svenson (see note following)

         vocal quartet insert (for 11 Feb)
         My Heart Went Boom Boom

      Note: Issued title of "Gesundheit" is "Ron Terry Polka".
Bernie Jones, very much the original Ole Svenson, had left the Slickers in early '56 and is adamant about not recording with or for Spike
after that time. It certainly sounds like Ole! Some of the titles
were composed by Bernie Jones, Country Washburn and drummer Frank
Flynn. The recording log does not list the personnel.

11 February, 1957 (MON) - Radio Recorders, Hollywood
         Client: Spike Jones

         Spike Jones, his City Slickers, and as alias:
         "The Polka Dots, starring Ole Svenson"

         Personnel unknown

         V-10054-A; 45 V-10054x45-A; LP V MGV 2066;
            ET AFRS "Basic Music Library" P-5461;
(2:10)Happy Trumpets Polka (basic master: take 8) -
         inst

         V-10054-B; 45 V-10054x45-B; EPV 5066; LP V MGV
            2066; ET AFRS "Basic Music Library" P-5461;
         Lawrence Welk Polka (basic master: take 9) -
            vocal

         LP V MGV 2066; ET AFRS "Basic Music Library"
            P-5461;
          Bottoms Up (basic composite; take 3 & inserts)
            - vocal

         Final overdubbing
20,682-17   My Heart Went Boom Boom (final composite: take 17)
20,682-15RE   Popeye the Sailor Man (final composite: take 15)

      Note: "Happy Trumpets Polka" is an adaption of "Under the
Double Eagle".

25 February, 1957 (MON) - Radio Recorders, Hollywood
         Client: Spike Jones

         Spike Jones, and as alias, "The Polka Dots,
         Starring Ole Svenson"

         Personnel unknown

         Unissued
         Cradle Song (10 unissued inserts)

LP V MGV 4005; VAU MGV 4005; VF 2304 436;
VJ MGV 2119; GO 10010
Cradle Song (master: take 1-A)

LP V MGV 2066; ET AFRS "Basic Music Library"
P-5461;
Pennsylvania Polka (take 8) - inst

45 EPV 5066; LP V MGV 2066; ET AFRS "Basic Music
Library" P-5462;
(2:09)Six Fat Dutchmen Polka (basic take 6) - vocal

LP V MGV 2066; AFRS "Basic Music Library"
P-5463;
(2:59)New Beer Barrel Polka (take 9) - inst

45 EPV 5066; LP V MGV 2066; ET AFRS "Basic Music
Library" P-5462;
(2:34)Whoopee John Polka (composite basic) - chant

45 EPV 5066; LP V MGV 2066; ET AFRS "Basic Music
Library" P-5463;
(2:57)Frank Yankovic Waltz (basic: take 5) - vocal

LP V MGV 2066; ET AFRS "Basic Music Library"
P-5462;
(2:43)Pretty Girl Polka (composite, take 5 & insert)
- vocal

LP V MGV 2066; ET AFRS "Basic Music Library"
P-5463;
(2:33)The Funny Punny Polka (take 8) - vocal

Overdub
Whoopee John Polka (take 2)
Six Fat Dutchmen Polka (take 2)
Lawrence Welk Polka (take 2)
Pal-Yat-Chee (take 3, over 7 Feb take)

Note: "Pretty Girl Polka" is a re-arranged "A Din Skal..".
Issued title of Cradle Song is "Brahms Alibi". In carefully auditing
the rehearsal tapes, the following names are obvious or mentioned by
Spike:- George Rock, tpt; Freddy Morgan, bjo; Ernie Felice, acc; Lou
Singer, drm; Bernie Jones, reeds; John ?, org; Joe (Washburn?), tuba.

2 March, 1957 (SAT) - Radio Recorders, Hollywood
            Client: Spike Jones

            alias: "The Polka Dots, starring Ole Svenson"

            Personnel unknown

            Overdubs to 25 Feb takes
            Frank Yankovic Waltz (master: take 8 of 14)
                (Soprano overdub, insert)
            Happy Trumpets Polka (take 7)
                (Trumpet overdub)
            New Beer Barrel Polka (take 4)
            Bottoms Up (take 2 of 7)

314

"the band that plays for fun", as Spike coined his group in
early 1943, was increasingly used as the name for his musicians. City
Slickers, as a name, was now used with diminishing frequency. Eddie
Robertson recounted the feelings of the musicians involved with Spike
for his next television series. Drawn from among his studio colleagues to augment 'the City Slickers', they could, and did play well, so
much so that Robertson feels that Spike considered this to be his
greatest 'straight' band - ever!
 Prior to each broadcast date, there were three rehearsal
days; one music only, then one script only (both at the Hollywood
Athletic Club), then one combined at CBS-TV studios. The 30 minute
7:30 PM PST b'cast was preceded by run-down, including make-up and
wardrobe starting at 3:00 PM. As familiarity increased, rehearsal
time was reduced to the point that the City Slickers worked playdates between shows, as far removed from Hollywood as Eastern Ontario
via air. Helen Grayco solos are 'live', with far less background
noise than in the earlier 'live' shows which marred her performances.

2 April, 1957 (TUES) - THE SPIKE JONES SHOW
                    CBS-TV Hollywood

             Leader - Spike Jones
             Brass - George Rock, Cappy Lewis, Virgil Evans,
                tpt; Phil Gray, Jerry Rosa, Ray Heath, trb
             Reeds - Brian Farnon, Gil Bernal, Clyde Amsler,
                John Setar, Hymie Gunkler, sax/clar
             Rhythm - Corky Hale, Hal Hidey, Arnold Ross,
                pno; Dickie Phillips, guit; Jad Paul, Freddy
                Morgan, bjo/guit; Eddie Robertson, Larry
                Breen, Arnold Olson, tuba/bass; Dick
                Shanahan, drm

        Note: The announcer for this series, sponsored by Liggett
and Myers, was Jack Narz. Additional credits include: Eddie Brandt,
Danny Arnold, writer; Richard E. Webster, manager; Brian Farnon,
ass't cond; J.A. Krechter, Brian Farnon, Arnold Ross, arr (Ross on
Grayco titles); Bill DePew, Bill (Willard) Jones, Joseph Estren, Al
Porcino, David Ward, Roger Farris, copyists; Bill DePew, librarian.
Acts and vocalists credits are noted as they occur.

             Guest: Gordon MacRae

             Opener - "Marianne"
             Helen Grayco - "Man Smart"
             Yes Sir, That's My Baby - voc Freddy Morgan
             Gordon MacRae - "Oh What a Beautiful Morning",
                "'Til We Meet Again"
             Four Spinets - "18th Century Drawing Room"
             Helen Grayco - "It Never Entered My Mind"
             City Slicker Medley:
                Love Me Tender -
                Young Love - George Rock
                Canadian Sunset - Banjo Maniacs
                Blueberry Hill - Billy Barty

     "You can see him and his band on The Spike Jones show but
the tin whistles, the fog horns, the rubber razzberries, and the
plumber's utensils with which Spike used to woo the muse have practically disappeared. Instead of playing "Der Fuehrer's Face", he now
gives us "'Till We Meet Again" and "In an 18th Century Drawing Room".
The not-so-zany-anymore "band that plays for fun" just might beat out
a tired Rachmaninoff concerto and hop into a rock 'n roll fiasco. And
what's more, they give it to us straight.
     "...but it is only in occasional numbers..."A-Japanese-

version-of-Yes-Sir-That's-My-Baby" that the essence of the "old"
Spike really comes through." (<u>TV Guide</u>, Apr 57)

5 April, 1957 (FRI) - Radio Recorders, Hollywood
               Client: Spike Jones

               alias: "Mr. Banjo, Freddy Morgan"

               Personnel unknown

               LP V MGV 2065;
(2:26)<u>My Banjo At Thy Sweet Voice</u> (master, take
               7 and insert)

               LP V MGV 2065;
(2:16)<u>William Tell Overture</u> (composite, takes 10 & 15)

               LP V MGV 2065;
(2:22)<u>Liebestraum</u> (composite, take 6 & inserts)

               LP V MGV 2065;
(2:18)<u>Under the Double Eagle</u> (composite, take 5 &
               insert)

      Note: Issued titles to the last three are: "William Tell
Rag", "Libes-strum" and "Swingin' the Double Eagle".

9 April, 1957 (TUES) - THE SPIKE JONES SHOW
               CBS-TV Hollywood

               Leader - Spike Jones
               Brass - George Rock, Virgil Evans, tpt;
                 Phil Gray, trb
               Reeds - Brian Farnon, Gil Bernal, Clyde Amsler
               Rhythm - Hal Hidey, Arnold Ross, pno; Dickie
                 Phillips, guit; Jad Paul, Freddy Morgan, bjo;
                 Larry Breen, Eddie Robertson, bass; Dick
                 Shanahan, drm
               Harp - Rosalie Randall

               Guests: The Hi-Lo's

               Opener - "St. Louis Blues"
               Helen Grayco - "Easy To Love"
                City Slicker Medley:
                 Somebody Stole My Gal
                 Five Foot Two, Eyes Of Blue
                 Nobody's Sweetheart Now
               Hi-Lo's - "Life Is Just a Bowl Of Cherries",
                 "Swing Low, Sweet Chariot"
               <u>Round and Round</u> - Polka Dots, feat Eddie Robertson
               Helen Grayco - "Mad About the Boy"
               City Slicker Medley:
                 Who Needs You?
                 Too Much - Billy Barty
                 Teenage Crush - Billy Barty, Barton Twins

16 April, 1957 (TUES) - THE SPIKE JONES SHOW
               CBS-TV Hollywood

               Leader - Spike Jones

Brass - George Rock, Cappy Lewis, tpt;
    Phil Gray, trb
Reeds as 9 Apr
Rhythm - pno, bjo, guit, bass as 9 Apr; Ed Grady,
    drm; add Mike Pacheco, bongos
Harp - Rosalie Randall
Strings - Walter Edelstein, Nick Pisani, Francis
    Green, Dave Sterkin, vln; Paul Bergstrom, cel

Guests: The Kitten Sisters and Lord Flea

Opener - "My Blue Heaven"
Helen Grayco - "You Do Something To Me"
Kitten Sisters - "Round and Round" (act)
Poet and Peasant Overture - Banjo Maniacs
Lord Flea - "Hold Him, Joe"
Dixie Pixies - "Singin' the Blues", feat Phil Gray
Helen Grayco - "Everytime We Say Goodbye"
Calypso Challenge - Lord Flea and City Slickers
    Banana Boat Song
    Marianne

        Note: Dixie Pixies segments, which included Spike on drums,
and titles of the Banjo Maniacs (with the exception of the above
"Peasant"), Polka Dots and Eddie Robertson are 'straight'.

23 April, 1957 (TUES) - THE SPIKE JONES SHOW
            CBS-TV Hollywood

        Personnel as 16 Apr, add Ray Heath, trb; John
            Setar, sax; Carl Fortina, acc. Delete Mike
            Pacheco; strings

        Opener - "Just One Of Those Things"
        Helen Grayco - "It's All Right With Me"
        City Slicker Medley:
            Whispering
            Bye Bye Blues
            San
        Dennis Day - "Granada", "With a Little Bit
            of Luck"
        Four Spinets - "Almost Paradise"
        *Comedy Production: "Chantez, Chantez" (F. Morgan)

        *issued (edited) on MF Distribution LPs MF 205/4,
            947447, and GO 10016

30 April, 1957 (TUES) - THE SPIKE JONES SHOW
            CBS-TV Hollywood

        Personnel as 23 Apr, delete Ray Heath

        Guest: Nelson Eddy

        Opener - "Stompin' At the Savoy"
        Helen Grayco - "Mangoes"
        *City Slicker Medley:
            Oh By Jingo
            Last Night on the Back Proch
            Ma, He's Making Eyes At Me
        Nelson Eddy - "In the Still of the Night"
        I'm Walkin' - Gil Bernal
                    (straight)

317

Helen Grayco - "I've Grown Accustomed To His Face"
Comedy Production: "The Foreign Legion"
(cast: Nelson Eddy, Spike, Freddy Morgan,
Mousie Garner, Jad Paul, Phil Gray,
Eddie Robertson, Billy Barty)

*issued on MF Distribution LPs MF 205/4,
947447, and GO 10016

7 May, 1957 (TUES) - THE SPIKE JONES SHOW
CBS-TV Hollywood

Brass - George Rock, tpt; Phil Gray, trb
Reeds/Rhythm/Harp as 9 Apr, with Ed Grady for
Shanahan; adding Carl Fortina

Guest: Gordon MacRae

Opener - "String of Pearls"
Helen Grayco - "They Can't Take That Away From Me"
City Slicker Medley:
Let's All Sing Like the Birdies Sing
Listen To the Mocking Bird
Bye Bye Blackbird
Gordon MacRae - "Cowboy Serenade"
Dixie Pixies - "Why Baby Why?" feat Jad Paul
Comedy Production: "Round and Round the World
In 80 Ways"
(Scotland-Mousie Garner; India-Spike, George
Rock; Switzerland-Freddy Morgan, Jad Paul;
Spain-Spike, Billy Barty; Russia-Freddy Morgan;
Italy-Gil Bernal, Brian Farnon; USA-dancers)

14 May, 1957 (TUES) - THE SPIKE JONES SHOW
CBS-TV Hollywood

Brass as 16 Apr
Reeds as 9 Apr
Rhythm/Harp as 7 May, adding Walter Gross, pno

Guest: Robert Clary

Opener - "Lullaby of Broadway"
Helen Grayco - "The Lady Is a Tramp"
City Slicker Medley:
When You Wore a Tulip
Moonlight and Roses
Yellow Rose of Texas
Robert Clary - "I'm In Love With Miss Logan"
Helen Grayco - "Ninety-Nine Ways"
Robert Clary - "Standing On the Corner"
*Comedy Production: "Big Bands"
(Auld Lang Syne of Guy Lombardo; Ciribiribin of
Harry James with George Rock; Me And My Shadow/
When My Baby Smiles At Me of Ted Lewis with
Mousie Garner, Billy Barty; Bubbles In the Wine
of Lawrence Welk with Spike; My Shawl/Tico Tico
of Xavier Cugat/Abbe Lane with Mousie Garner,
D. Ford; Moonlight Serenade of Glenn Miller)

*issued (edited) on MF Distribution LPs 205/4,
947447, and GO 10016

318

21 May, 1957 (TUES) - THE SPIKE JONES SHOW
              CBS-TV Hollywood

                    Personnel as 14 May, deleting Gunkler, Lewis and
                      Gross. Adding Mousie Garner, pno

                    Guest: Carol Channing

                    Opener - "Temptation"
                    Helen Grayco - "Blues In the Night"
                    City Slicker Medley:
                        In the Good Old Summertime
                        Row, Row, Row
                        By the Beautiful Sea
                    Carol Channing - "I'm Bound To Love Him Eternally"
                    When Day Is Done - Banjo Maniacs
                    Four Spinets - "Polonaise" (Chopin)
                    Carol Channing - "If" (with intro by F. Morgan,
                      as Alfred Hitchcock)
                    City Slicker Medley:
                        On the Street Where You Live
                        Butterfly - George Rock
                        Mutual Admiration Society - Mousie Garner
                        Party Doll - Billy Barty

28 May, 1957 (TUES) - THE SPIKE JONES SHOW
              CBS-TV Hollywood

                    Brass as 7 May
                    Reeds - Gil Bernal, Clyde Amsler
                    Rhythm/Harp - as 7 May
                    Strings - Nick Pisani, Joe Quadri, Walter
                      Edelstein, vln

                    Guest: Allan Jones

                    Opener - "What Is This Thing Called Love?"
                    Helen Grayco, Eddie Robertson - "Sittin' In
                      the Balcony"
                    *City Slicker Medley:
                        Smiles
                        Let a Smile Be Your Umbrella
                        'Til We Meet Again
                        When You're Smiling
                    Allan Jones - "Donkey Serenade", "De Gospel Train"
                    Band selection - "Marianne"
                    Helen Grayco - "Mood Indigo"
                    Chloe - voc Allan Jones

                    *issued on MF Distribution LPs MF 205/4,
                      947447, and GO 10016

4 June, 1957 (TUES) - THE SPIKE JONES SHOW
              CBS-TV Hollywood

                    Brass - George Rock, George Wendt, tpt; Phil Gray,
                      Larry Breen, Wilbur Hall, Larry Collins, trb
                    Reeds - Gil Bernal, Clyde Amsler, Paul MacLarand
                    Rhythm/Harp - as 7 May (Larry Breen to trb)

                    Guests: The Modernaires

12th Street Rag - feat Larry Collins
Modernaires - "Rockabilly"
Helen Grayco - "I Get a Kick Out Of You"
Band selection - "So Rare"
Modernaires - Tribute to Tommy Dorsey
Helen Grayco - "Dark Moon"
City Slicker Production: "Minstrel Show"
  (A) Hot Time In the Old Town Tonight
    Down South
    Mighty Lak' a Rose - feat Jad Paul
    Pop Goes the Weasel - feat Wilbur Hall,'fiddle'
    Lassus Trombone - feat 5 trombones (Slippery
                Sliding Five, adding Carl Fortina)
    Waitin' For the Robert E. Lee

11 June, 1957 (TUES) - THE SPIKE JONES SHOW
            CBS-TV Hollywood

        Brass as 14 May
        Reeds as 28 May
        Rhythm/Harp as 7 May

        Guest: Don Cornell

        Opener - "Night and Day"
        Billy Barty - The Typewriter
        Helen Grayco - "All Of Me"
        Lawrence Welk Polka - Polka Dots, feat Phil Gray
        Helen Grayco, Don Cornell - "Always"
        City Slicker Production: "All Night"
           Moonlight Gambler - Billy Barty
           Dance of the Hours - Doodles Weaver
           Weather Report - Spike
           Little Darlin' - "Chimps" (lip-sync to disc)

18 June, 1957 (TUES) - THE SPIKE JONES SHOW
            CBS-TV Hollywood

        Brass/Reeds as 14 may, adding Tommy Pederson, trb
        Rhythm/Harp as 7 May, adding Mousie Garner,
           Frank Leithner, pno

        Guest: Betsy Gay

        Opener - "Lover Come Back To Me"
        Helen Grayco - "Too Close For Comfort"
        Chinatown, My Chinatown - feat Freddy Morgan, bjo
                 (straight)
        Perfidia - voc Eddie Robertson
        Helen Grayco - "Love Letters In the Sand"
        City Slicker Production: "The Hi-Fi Shop"
           Ramona
           *Flight of the Bumble Bee - feat Tommy Pederson
           Pal-Yat-Chee - feat Betsy Gay

      *issued on MF Distgribution LPs MF 205/4,
        947447, and GO 10016

    Note: Tommy Pederson recalls this day as being one of the
hardest in his career. There were two dress rehearsals for "Bumble
Bee", preceded by four runs-through, then the b'cast. Pederson is
sure the grey hair on his head started this day on live TV. This is
the only visual instance (TV or film) of Leithner sneezing.

25 June, 1957 (TUES) - THE SPIKE JONES SHOW
                    CBS-TV Hollywood

                    Brass as 14 May
                    Reeds as 28 May
                    Rhythm/Harp as 7 May
                    Strings - Irving Lipschultz, cel

                    Guests: The Mills Brothers

                    Liebestraum - City Slickers
                    Mills Bros. - "The Jones Boy"
                    Helen Grayco - "Night Train"
                    Band selection - "St. Louis Blues"
                    Four Spinets - "Nola"
                    Mills Bros. - "Queen of the Senior Prom"
                    Helen Grayco - "All Of You"
                    Blue Danube - City Slickers

        Note: This show was to have included an Arthur Godfrey paro-
dy. It was replaced by "Blue Danube" due to 'hundreds of requests'
(by Godfrey's attorneys?)

2 July, 1957 (TUES) - THE SPIKE JONES SHOW
                    CBS-TV Hollywood

                    Leader - Spike Jones
                    Brass - George Rock, Art DePew, tpt; Phil Gray,trb
                    Reeds - Gil Bernal, Clyde Amsler, Harold (Gus)
                        Ehrmann
                    Rhythm - Hal Hidey, Arnold Ross, pno; Dickie
                        Phillips, guit; Freddy Morgan, Jad Paul, bjo;
                        Eddie Robertson, Larry Breen, bass, Stevan
                        Dweck, drm; Carl Fortina, acc
                    Harp - Rosalie Randall
                    Strings - Marion McKinstry, Judith Ayers, Kay
                        Hickman, vln

                    Guests: Sonny James and Spade Cooley

                    Opener - "So Rare"
                    Helen Grayco - "Old Cape Cod"
                    City Slicker Medley: "4th of July"
                        Under the Double Eagle
                        I'm a Yankee Doodle Dandy
                        Yankee Doodle
                    Sonny James - "Young Love"
                    Helen Grayco - "How About You?"
                    City Slicker Production: "The Grand Old Uproar"
                        Girl I Left Behind Me - Spade Cooley
                       *Dark Moon - Spike, George Rock
                        Spike Jones car commercial
                        I Like Mountain Music/Steel Guitar Rag

                *issued on MF Distribution LPs MF 205/4,
                    947447, and GO 10016

        Note: Spade Cooley was listed and paid as musical leader for
this date, according for AF of M records. "Girl I Left Behind Me" is
the US Civil War song, not the Porter/Hoefle title of 1942. The final
medley (inst) includes a rare appearance of the tuned flit-guns.

                            321

9 July, 1957 (TUES) - THE SPIKE JONES SHOW
            CBS-TV Hollywood

                Brass/Reeds as 7 May
                Rhythm as 2 July, adding Jo-Ann Castle, pno/acc

                Guest: Dean Jones

                Opener - "Manhatten"
                Helen Grayco - "Just One Of Those Things"
                *City Slicker Medley:
                    Somebody Stole My Gal
                    Five Foot Two - feat Jo-Ann Castle, pno
                    Nobody's Sweetheart
                Dean Jones - "St. Louis Blues"
                The Girl With The Golden Braids - Polka Dots
                Helen Grayco, Dean Jones - "Do I Love You Because
                    You're Beautiful?"
                City Slicker Medley:
                    I'm Walkin' - George Rock
                    Love Letters In the Sand
                    Freight Train - Freddy Morgan

                *issued on MF Distribution LPs 205/4,
                    947447, and GO 10016

16 July, 1957 (TUES) - THE SPIKE JONES SHOW
            CBS-TV Hollywood

                Personnel similar to 9 July

                Guest: Lauritz Melchior

                Opener - "Chicago"
                Helen Grayco - "I Like Your Kind Of Love"
                City Slicker Medley:
                    Margie, Mary, Mary Lou, Marie
                Lauritz Melchior - "Crusaders' Hymn"
                Band selection - "String Of Pearls"
                Cattle Call - Jad Paul
                            (straight)
                Big Bad Bill - Billy Barty
                Cocktails For Two - Melchior, City Slickers

23 July, 1957 (TUES) - THE SPIKE JONES SHOW
            CBS-TV Hollywood

                Brass as 2 July
                Reeds/Rhythm as 9 July, delete Jo-Ann Castle

                Guest: Molly Bee

                Opener - "I Love Paris"
                Helen Grayco - "One For My Baby"
                Teddy Bear - Billy Barty
                Molly Bee - "I'm Past My Prime"
                Band selection - "Marianne"
                I'm Gonna Sit Right Down and Write Myself a Letter
                    - Gil Bernal
                Helen Grayco - "It's So Nice To Have a Man
                    Around the House"

City Slicker Production: "The Good Old Songs"
   The Music Goes 'Round and 'Round - B. Barty
   Merry-Go-Round Broke Down(inst)/Yes, We Have
           No Bananas - F. Morgan, M. Garner
   The Hut Sut Song - Spike, J. Paul
   Cuanto Le Gusta - E. Robertson
   Knock, Knock, Who's There? - Spike, M. Garner
   Hold Tight - Betty Serpico
   Three Little Fishies - G. Rock
   Whiffenpoof Song - Spike, B. Farnon, J. Paul,
           B. Barty
   Flat Foot Floogie - G. Bernal
   Piccolo Pete - Spike, M. Garner
   I've Got a Lovely Bunch Of Coconuts - F. Morgan
   Open the Door Richard - E. Brandt
   Bibbidi-Bobbidi-Boo - Helen Grayco
   Horses - B. Barty
   Cement Mixer, Putty Putty - B. Farnon
   Woody Woodpecker Song - G. Rock
   Where Do You Work-A John? - F. Morgan
   Never Hit Your Grandma With a Shovel - Spike,
           B. Farnon, J. Paul
   Popeye the Sailor Man - G. Rock
   The Thing - C. Fortina
   Der Fuehrer's Face - F. Morgan
   I Scream, You Scream, We All Scream For Ice
           Cream - Spike, M. Garner
   Mairzy Doats - Spike, M. Garner, F. Morgan,
           G. Rock, C. Fortina, B. Farnon,
           E. Robertson

30 July, 1957 (TUES) - THE SPIKE JONES SHOW
           CBS-TV Hollywood

           Brass/Reeds/Rhythm as 2 July, adding Hymie
              Gunkler, sax; Jimmy Vey, xyl. Delete Jo-Ann
              Castle

           Guest: Tommy Sands

           Opener - "Temptation"
           Helen Grayco - "Just In Time"
           Tommy Sands - "Let Me Be Loved"
           City Slicker Medley:
              Bye Bye Blues
              Whipering - feat Jimmy Vey, xyl
           Helen Grayco - "Fire Down Below"
           Tommy Sands - "Gonna Get a Girl"
           City Slicker Production: "The Name Bands"
              Stardust, of Kay Kayser - Spike and Bobby
                   Sargent
              Racing With the Moon, of Vaughn Monroe -
                   Gil Bernal
              Bubbles In the Wine, of Lawrence Welk - Spike
              Tico Tico, of Xavier Cugar/Abbe Lane - Mousie
                   Garner, Gloria Pall
              *Minnie the Moocher, of Cab Calloway - Billy
                   Barty

           *issued on MF Distribution LPs MF 205/4,
              947447, and GO 10016

6 August, 1957 (TUES) - THE SPIKE JONES SHOW
           CBS-TV Hollywood

323

Brass as 16 Apr
Reeds as 9 July, adding Hymie Gunkler, sax;
Rhythm as 2 July, adding Mike Pacheca, conga drm

Guests: Ray Anthony and the Accidentals

Opener - "Lonesome Road"
Helen Grayco - "You Do Something To Me"
Melody In F - City Slickers
Accidentals - "June Is Busting Out All Over"
Ray Anthony - "Street Of Dreams", "Lonely Trumpet"
Helen Grayco, Accidentals - "It's Not For Me
    To Say"
City Slicker Production: "Elvis Presley Medley"
    Love Me Tender - Bobby Sargent ala Groucho Marx
    Blue Suede Shoes - Mousie Garner ala Edward
            G. Robinson
    Don't Be Cruel - ala Peter Lorre and Monster
    Hound Dog - Billy Barty ala Jimmy Durante
    All Shook Up - Gil Bernal ala Arthur Godfrey
    Take Me Back - Gil Bernal ala Elvis

13 August, 1957 (TUES) - THE SPIKE JONES SHOW
            CBS-TV Hollywood

Brass/Reeds as 9 July
Rhythm as 2 July, deleting Carl Fortina. Add
    Anita Aros (Tuttle), vln

Guest: Rusty Draper

City Slicker Medley:
    When You're Smilin'
    Smiles
    Smile, Darn Ya Smile
    Mona Lisa - Jimmy Ames('faking' as musical saw)
Rusty Draper - "No Hu Hu"
Band selection - "Begin the Beguine"
Helen Grayco - "Write To Me From Naples"
Anita Aros, Four Spinets - "Blue Tango"
Helen Grayco, Rusty Draper - "Don't Fence Me In"
City Slicker Production: "Wild Wild World"
    William Tell Overture - Doodles Weaver
    All Shook Up - Bobby Sargent, Mousie Garner,
            Freddy Morgan
    Little Darlin' - "Chimps" lip-sync to disc

20 August, 1957 (TUES) - THE SPIKE JONES SHOW
            CBS-TV Hollywood

Brass/Reeds as 9 July
Rhythm/Harp as 2 July
Strings - Kay Hickman, Judith Ayers, Marion
    McKinstry, vln; Joyce Krantz, cel

Guest: Mimi Benzel

Opener - "Bewitched"
Helen Grayco - "Goody Goody"
I'm Gonna Sit Right Down and Write Myself a Letter
    - George Rock
Tiger Rag - Banjo Maniacs

324

Mimi Benzel - "Hello Young Lovers"
Band selection - "Just One Of Those Things"
Send For Me - Gil Bernal
Pennsylvania Polka - Polka Dots, voc Helen Grayco
Indian Love Call - Benzel, Morgan, Wayne Marlin 3

27 August, 1957 (TUES) - THE SPIKE JONES SHOW
          CBS-TV Hollywood

          Brass/Rhythm/Harp as 2 July
          Reeds as 9 July, adding Maury Bereey, sax/clar

          Guests: The King Sisters

          Opener - "L & M Jump"
          Helen Grayco - "All Of Me"
          Sabre Dance - City Slickers
          King Sisters - "That Old Feeling"
          George Rock, Four Spinets - "12th Street Rag"
          Helen Grayco, Gil Bernal - "Three Coins In
              the Fountain"
          King Sisters - "Hawaiian War Chant"
          City Slicker Production: "Million Selling Records"
              Stardust - King Sisters
              That Old Black Magic - Spike, Betty Serpico
              Mona Lisa - M. Garner
              I Saw Mommy Kissing Santa Claus - G. Rock
              April Showers - Spike
              On the Street Where You Live - G. Marlin
              I Could Have Danced All Night - Spike, Helen
              That's Amore - B. Barty
              Easter Parade - F. Morgan
              It Takes Two To Tango - Larry Breen, G. Marlin
              Moonlight Gambler - G. Rock
              Too Young - Lester Calvin
              Dancing With Tears In My Eyes - B. Sargent
              Be My Love - Brian Farnon
              Blue Skies - Spike
              Charmaine - H. Grayco, F. Morgan
              I'm Looking Over a Four-Leaf Clover - M. Garner
              In the Middle of an Island - Spike,
                          King Sisters
              Green Eyes - B. Farnon
              I Almost Lost My Mind - F. Morgan
              Tonight We Love - Carl Fortina
              Beer Barrel Polka - Entire cast

     Note: The "Too Young" vocalist was indeed Lester Calvin,
master carpenter with the Revue for many years, and he does 'render
this ballade' sans teeth

     "As he pointed out to one protesting fan who wailed for more
of the "old Spike Jones": 'If we knocked ourselves out for the full
half-hour every week, with only the same sort of stuff we did on the
road, we'd wear out our welcome within a month. We'd find ourselves
coming into living rooms where the family had gone out for the evening. This way, judiciously mixing some of the corn in with straight
stuff, and with Helen's torchy numbers, we could get to be a habit.'
     "It's an old saw in show business that comedians are the
most serious men in the trade. And, of them all, there's probably no
one more deadly in earnest about the business of being funny than
Spike Jones. Certainly there's no one who works harder at it - no one
could, because there aren't enough hours. Spike spent three days (and
nights until 2 A.M.) each week planning his TV shows with his staff.
Then, three more days for rehearsals, and, finally, one day for dress

                              325

rehearsal and the "live" show. That adds up to seven - which is about par for Spike.

"The two Jones offspring - Spike, Jr., who's just turned 8, and Leslie Ann, 5 - are two of the healthiest, huskiest, most normal little characters you could imagine. Mary Foster, who has had them in her charge for the last two years obviously adores them, but claims they can be "hammy" as the next when they feel like it."
(TV Radio Mirror, Sep 57)

31 August, 1957 (SAT) - Radio Recorders, Hollywood
            Client: Spike Jones

            alias: "Gil Bernal and the Seven-Teens"

            Personnel unknown(incl Rock in voc quartet backup)

21,328   45 V-10087x45;
        (2:09)Tab, Rory, and Rock, Rock (take 10) - Gil Bernal,
                vocal and saxophone, accompanied by the
                Seven-Teens

21,329   45 V-10087x45;
        (2:06)Grass Shack Rock (take 19) - Gil Bernal, vocal and
                saxophone, accompanied by the Seven-Teens

    Note: Issued title of "Grass Shack Rock" is "Take Me Back"

21 October, 1957 (MON) - Radio Recorders, Hollywood
            Client: Spike Jones

            Personnel unknown

            Unissued
            Little Things Mean a Lot (take 2 of 3) - voc
                Billy Barty

            Unissued
            Satellite Baby (take 6 with sound effects overdub)
                - voc Billy Barty

            Unissued
            Elevator Shoes (take 4) - voc Billy Barty

            Unissued
            Why Oh Why? (take 3) - voc Billy Barty

            Unissued
            Satellite Baby (overdub, take 9) - voc Billy Barty

            Unissued
            Sayonara G.I. (take 5) - voc Billy Barty

    Note: All but the first title are Billy Barty compositions,
published by Lindley Music, Inc.

13 December, 1957 (FRI) - Gold Star Recording Studios, Hollywood
            Client: Spike Jones

            Personnel unknown

```
            Unissued
    (2:41)Smiles (take 2)


            Unissued
    (2:09)(Let's Have a) Banjo Party (take 8)


            Unissued
    (2:16)Tiptoe Through the Tulips (take 4)


            Unissued
    (2:21)Save Your Sorrow For Tomorrow (take 5)
```

     Note: All titles for Freddy Morgan "Mr. Banjo" album, with a
vocal quartet. Eddie Cline is at this session as an observer.

     Feature articles on Spike Jones appeared during 1957
               in the following:-

     TV Radio Mirror, Sept "Mad Genius of Music"

21 February, 1958 (FRI) - THE FRANK SINATRA SHOW
          ABC-TV Hollywood   (delayed - b'cast 4 Apr 58)

     Frank Sinatra, Nelson Riddle's Orchestra and
          guests: Spike Jones and his City Slickers

     Slickers personnel:-
     Trumpet - George Rock
     Reeds - Gil Bernal, Bill DePew, sax/clar
     Rhythm - Arnold Ross, pno; Freddy Morgan, bjo;
          Dickie Phillips, guit; Bernie Miller, bass;
          Sal LaPertche, drm

     Frank Sinatra - "You Brought a New Kind Of Love
          To Me"
     City Slicker Medley:
          Fascination - City Slickers
          All the Way - George Rock
          Tammy - Spike (lip-sync to Helen)
          Sail Along Silvery Moon
     Helen Grayco, with Nelson Riddle - "You Don't Know
          What Love Is"
     Frank Sinatra - "Baby Won't You Please Come Home"
     Chloe - Frank Sinatra, City Slickers
     Frank Sinatra - "Too Marvelous For Words"

     Note: Sponsored by Chesterfield Cigarettes, this filmed show
was a good attempt at bringing back the Slickers zaniness. Jesse
White, portraying Sinatra's agent, books Spike as the new back-up
orch. (because Riddle's big orch. will drown out Frank)
     "In the growing scramble for name guests, one-man TV shows
run the risk of getting avalanched by the talent they invite aboard
their programs to add new notes and rating points. Frank Sinatra ran
that risk Friday and Spike Jones ran away with the show. To Sinatra's
credit, he wholeheartedly played a willing stooge while Jones exhibi-
ted that take-charge personality he's neglected of late to unveil on
TV. It added up to the best Sinatra show in some time.
     "This show could well have been the highpoint of all Spike
Jones' video ventures." (Hollywood Reporter, 7 Apr 58)

11 March, 1958 (TUES) - IT COULD BE YOU*
          NBC-TV Hollywood

                              327

Guest: Spike Jones

28 March, 1958 (FRI) - TRUTH OR CONSEQUENCES*
   NBC-TV Hollywood

   Guest: Spike Jones

29 March, 1958 (SAT) - CLUB OASIS
   NBC-TV Hollywood   6:00 PM PST

   Guests: Spike Jones and his City Slickers

   Leader - Spike Jones
   Brass - George Rock, tpt; Phil Gray, Wilbur Hall,
      trb
   Reeds - Gil Bernal, Ernest Small, Ted Nash, sax
   Rhythm - Arnold Ross, pno; Jad Paul, Freddy
      Morgan, bjo; Dickie Phillips, guit; Phil
      Stephens, bass; Dick Shanahan, drm; Mike
      Pacheco, bongos, Carl Fortina, acc
   Strings - Marion McKinstry, Vivian Presco, Judy
      Ayers, vln; Pat Mathews, vla; Joyce Krantz, cel

      Note: For the guest appearance as host of this Liggett &
Myers sponsored show, the Orchestra Manager's report also shows: Dick
Webster, manager; Brian Farnon, conductor; Lou Bring, assistant con-
ductor; Bill DePew, librarian

   The Evolution of Music
   City Slicker Production: "The Name Bands"
   Sick, Sick, Sick - Gil Bernal
   Helen Grayco - "Them There Eyes", "Temptation"
   Comedy skit - "The Bridge on the River Kwai" -
      Spike, Joe Besser

7 June, 1958 (SAT) - CLUB OASIS
   NBC-TV Hollywood

   Leader - Spike Jones
   Brass - George Rock, Cappy Lewis, tpt; Phil Gray,
      trb
   Reeds - Brian Farnon, Gil Bernal, Clyde Amsler,
      Hymie Gunkler, sax/clar
   Rhythm - Arnold Ross, pno; Jad Paul, Jimmy Bryant,
      guit; Phil Stephens, bass; Dick Shanahan, drm;
      Carl Fortina, acc

   Opener - "Lullaby Of Broadway"
   Purple People Eater - Billy Barty, Len Carrie
   Four Spinets Medley: "South Pacific"
      Some Enchanted Evening
      I'm Gonna Wash That Man Right Outta My Hair
      Bali Hai
      Happy Talk
   Carolina In the Morning - Dixie Pixies, feat
      Jad Paul
   Helen Grayco - "I Get a Kick Out Of You"
   Comedy Production: "Snow White"
      ("Curley Dimples Storybook")
         (Cast: Spike, Helen Grayco, Joyce Jameson, Susy
                Loveal, Brian Farnon, Len Carrie, Jad
                Paul, Doodles Weaver, George Rock,
                Gil Bernal)

                           328

        Note: This series was sponsored by Liggett and Myers and
b'cast at 6:00 PM PST on alternate weeks. The series announcer was
Bob Lamond, with the Orchestra Manager's report showing: Dick Webster, manager; Brian Farnon, conductor; Lou Bring, assistant conduct-
or; Joe Krechter, Arnold Ross, arrangers; Bill (Willard) Jones Jr.,
Bill DePew, Brian Farnon, copyists; Bill DePew, librarian. Personnel
are similar on all b'casts. Vocalist and act credits noted on solos.
        All Dixie Pixie titles are 'straight', with Spike on drums.
George Rock's solos during the 'openers' are noteworthy. Joyce Jameson followed each opener with a short skit in the style of Marilyn
Monroe.

21 June, 1958 (SAT) - CLUB OASIS
                NBC-TV Hollywood•

                Opener - "Night and Day"
                City Slicker Medley:
                   Catch a Falling Star
                   Zorro
                   Who's Sorry Now
                Helen Grayco - "Come Rain or Come Shine"
                Teenage Brain Surgeon - Doodles Weaver, Ken Capps,
                   Len Carrie
                City Slicker Production: "Gold Record Medley"
                   Love, Your Magic Spell is Everywhere/That Old
                      Black Magic/Mona Lisa - Phil Gray, Len Carrie
                   Dinah - Helen Grayco
                   April Showers - Spike
                   On the Street Where You Live - B. Farnon,
                          Ken Capps
                   I Could Have Danced All Night - J. Paul,
                          H. Grayco
                   Big Man Yesterday - G. Rock
                   That's Amore - Billy Barty
                   Easter Parade - Len Carrie
                   I Get the Blues When It Rains - Spike
                   All the Way - Joyce Jameson
                   On Top of Old Smokey - Billy Barty
                   (It Takes) Two To Tango - K. Capps, G. Rock
                   Singin' In the Rain - Spike
                   Too Young - Lester Calvin
                   Dancing With Tears In My Eyes - Doodles Weaver
                   There's No Tomorrow - B. Farnon
                   All Alone - Joyce Jameson
                   Catch a Falling Star - K. Capps
                   Blue Skies - Spike
                   Charmaine - H. Grayco, L. Carrie
                   Hawaiian War Chant - D. Weaver
                   Sail Along Silvery Moon - G. Rock
                   Der Fuehrer's Face - K. Capps
                   Tonight We Love - Carl Fortina
                   Beer Barrel Polka - Entire cast

4 July, 1958 (FRI) - IT COULD BE YOU*
                NBC-TV Hollywood

                Guest: Spike Jones

5 July, 1958 (SAT) - CLUB OASIS
                NBC-TV Hollywood

                Opener - Christmas Medley
                   Jingle Bells, Santa Claus is Coming To Town
                I'm a Yankee Doodle Dandy - Billy Barty

Helen Grayco - Duke Ellington Medley
Mood Indigo
I Got It Bad and That Ain't Good
I Let a Song Go Out Of My Heart
Do Nothin' Till You Hear From He
Don't Get Around Much Anymore
Sophisticated Lady
I'm Beginning To See the Light
Four Spinets - "Stars and Stripes Forever"
Comedy Production: "Have Gondola, Will Travel"

14 July, 1958 (MON)
Daughter, Gina Marie Jones, born to Spike Jones and
Helen Grayco. Weight 7 lbs, 8 oz., at the Hollywood Presby-
terian Hospital. Danny Thomas is her Godfather.

19 July, 1958 (SAT) - CLUB OASIS
NBC-TV Hollywood

Guests: The King Sisters

Opener - "On the Road To Mandalay"
City Slicker Medley:
Fascination
All the Way - George Rock
Sail Along, Silvery Moon
King Sisters - "What's New?"
Gigi Medley:
Gigi - Phil Gray
The Night They Invented Champagne -
King Sisters
Thank Heavens For Little Girls - Billy Barty
City Slicker Production: "Movie Theme Medley"
You Are My Lucky Star - King Sisters
Over The Rainbow - J. Jameson
Anchors Aweigh - D. Weaver
Top Hat, White Tie and Tails - Spike
Lovely To Look At - L. Carrie, King Sisters
We Saw the Sea - D. Weaver
Golden Earrings - J. Jameson
Jailhouse Rock - G. Bernal
Missed Me - K. Capps
The Lovliest Night of the Year - B. Farnon
Love In Bloom - Spike, King Sisters
I Got Rhythm - G. Rock
You Go To My Head - L. Carrie
Sailing, Sailing - D. Weaver
Falling In Love Again - J. Jameson
San Francisco - K. Capps
Keep Your Sunny Side Up - J. Paul, King Sisters
I Only Have Eyes For You - J. Paul
High Noon - Spike, King Sisters
Rosalie - B. Barty, J. Jameson
Don't Give Up the Ship - Spike, D. Weaver
Something To Remember Me By - J. Paul, Eddie
Brandt, King Sisters
Alexander's Ragtime Band - Entire cast

"Since Spike Jones took over NBC's Club Oasis...the telephone of Dick Webster, Jones' personal manager, has been ringing all
the time.
"Mourns Webster: 'Sooner or later we hear from everybody
(amateur) who's been told he's funny enough to be with Spike Jones.'
"Spike estimates he auditions 100 sidemen for every one (of
13 clowning musicians and seven musical clowns) he hires..."I'm look-

330

ing all the time", he says.

"Jones was unimpressed last year when Webster told him he'd had a call from a master of 14 instruments, tuba to celeste...Webster added, "claims he can play a piano standing on his head", Jones snapped: "That I've never seen. Send him over."

"Carl Fortina auditioned successfully at Jones'... where "Stokowski" is also woven into the welcome mat in big capital letters. Carl played the Jones spinet upside down while keeping time with his feet on Spike's trap drums.

"Since he went on Club Oasis, Jones has added two men. The first was Len Carrie, a 31-year-old New York-born trombonist with a Three Stooges haircut. In Reno last November, Jones saw Carrie demonstrate his ability to cross one eye - the left - while playing or singing. The second is Ken Capps, a 33-year-old dialect comedian who grew up in vaudeville, learned to play trumpet while in burlesque.

"Webster keeps a card index on the pros who call. From it he supplies Jones with acts worked into 45-second bits in the middle of ballads.

"...Jones (who monitors You Asked For It and other TV shows) ...lost no time after he saw paddle-board marksman Reggie Rymal perform on You Asked For It. Jones put Rymal to work learning to play "Holiday For Strings" on the chimes, with a ball attached to a paddle by a length or rubber." (TV Guide, 1958)

(Picture on p.21 shows Judy Hecht as one of the troupe)

2 August, 1958 (SAT) - CLUB OASIS
           NBC-TV Hollywood

           Opener - "I Love Paris"
           City Slicker Medley:
               In the Good Old Summertime
               Beachcombers Are We (tune: "Over the Waves")
                   Doodles Weaver, Len Carrie, Ken Capps
               Row Row Row
           King Sisters - "Imagination"
           Button Up Your Overcoat - Dixie Pixies, voc
               Joyce Jameson
           City Slicker Production: "Spooktacular"
               (Cast: Spike as Alfred Hitchcock, Dracula;
               Brian Farnon, Jad Paul as Ugly Sisters; Ken
               Capps as stepfather; Doodles Weaver as Hunch-
               back; Billy Barty as Purple People Eater;
               Joyce Jameson as Cinderella, Vampira)

16 August, 1958 (SAT) - CLUB OASIS
           NBC-TV Hollywood

           Opener - "St. Louis Blues"
           William Tell Overture - Doodles Weaver
           Helen Grayco - "Baubles, Bangles and Beads"
           City Slicker Production: "Little Known Colleges"
               Safe Crackers School - G. Rock, B. Barty
               Driving School - film clip
               Golf School - D. Weaver
               Reducing School - Spike, K. Capps
               Psychiatrist School - J. Jameson, L. Carrie
               Chiropractor School - Spike, K. Capps,
                       B. Farnon
               Art School - B. Barty, J. Jameson
               Used Car Salesman School - Spike
               Typing School - B. Barty, B. Serpico

331

30 August, 1958 (SAT) - CLUB OASIS
             NBC-TV Hollywood

                Opener - "Lover Come Back To Me"
                76 Trombones - City Slickers (arr Krechter)
                Helen Grayco - "Volare"
                City Slicker Production: "Rockin' the Comic
                            Strips" (arr Ross)
                    Little Orphan Nanny - J. Jameson
                    Lil Ole Abner - B. Barty
                    Prince Violent - B. Farnon
                    Dick Racy - Spike
                    Tarzany - J. Ames
                    Splash Gordon - G. Rock
                    Joe Pakooka - P. Gray
                    Hand-Brake, the Magician - Arthur Walsh
                    Stuporman - Spike (Jimmy Ames as Clark Bent)
                    Finale - Entire cast

6 September, 1958 (SAT) - CLUB OASIS
             NBC-TV Hollywood

                Opener - "Volare"
                Helen Grayco - "One For My Baby"
                Czardas - Carl Fortina
                Fever - Gil Bernal
                Helen Grayco - "The Moon Was Yellow"
                Black and Blue Danube - City Slickers (Wilbur
                    Nelson does comedy bit with a saw - not playing
                    but imitating it with his voice)

        Note: During the show, there is mention of Helen Grayco's
latest Verve album, "The Lady In Red"
        "Nowhere on the coming...TV season's program do I see a
half-hour set aside for Spike Jones, which may not be the smartest
omission the networks ever made.
        "Spike isn't exactly "cultural", I'll grant you. He'll never
replace "All-Star Jazz" or Lawrence Welk, but they'll never replace
Spike's musical madcappery, either.
        "There have been a number of Spike Jones shows since TV was
born. Most of the early shows...left much to be desired. It's possible by some viewers' lights, the current summer series of Jones shows
...also leaves something to be desired.
        "There's no comedy better than the kind which not only makes
you laugh when you see it by sends you away quoting it.
        "There are few comics on TV who provide viewers with this
kind of double-action exposure. It seems a pity that Jones, one of
those few, should not have a half-hour set aside for him for the fall
season."   (Janet Kern, Chicago American, 23 Jul 58)

        The lengthy tours, now economically unsound, are City Slick-
ers past history, and a scaled down troupe now appear in the clubs
and lounges of California to the resorts of Nevada. The sidemen and
acts who became national personalities through Jones' recordings and
radio shows have settled into a semblance of home life, with only
George Rock and Freddy Morgan appearing on an irregular basis. Both
now work at solo and small combo 'gigs' out of Las Vegas and Reno, as
well as their own occasional recordings.

October, 1958
             Moulin Rouge, Hollywood

        A high point of the Slickers show (which included Rock,
Barty and Garner) at the Moulin Rouge was a Jones black light drum

solo to "Man with the Golden Arm". On a later record jacket, drummer Sandy Nelson credits Spike as his inspiration to learn the drums. Acetate dated 16 Oct 58 survives and perhaps Nelson was there that night. Much of the show was lip-sync to hit records.

Recordings now explore to the limits the concept of stereo. Spike's offerings, with the constant input of the indefatigable writer, Eddie Brandt, are entirely studio creations with continuous editing, - overdubbing - remaking and reviewing for each conceived title. Warner Bros. agreed to release his concept of "Spooktacular", an extension of the Jones humor but a marked departure from the City Slickers style known as well.

20 January, 1959 (TUES) - Radio Recorders, Hollywood
        Client: Spike Jones

        Voices - Joyce Jameson, Paul Frees, George Rock

    (3:57)Late Late Late Movies(basic voice, take 4) including bus crash, plane, bomb explosion, rocket

21 January, 1959 (WED) - Radio Recorders, Hollywood
        Client: Spike Jones

        Piano - Buddy Cole
        Bass, drum - unidentified

    (3:53)Stardust overdub(two long versions, unissued)
    (3:27)Stardust overdub(master, take 2 of two takes)

    (3:43)Tenderly overdub(master, take 2 of two takes, unissued)
    (3:14)Tenderly overdub(master, take 1)

    Note: The dialogue tracks with effects edited into them (20 Jan) were slated as "Late Late Late Movies" and sold to Liberty Records in 1960. "Stardust" and "Tenderly" were the working titles (21 Jan) of the 'cool' Buddy Cole Trio background overdubbed to the completed voice/effects tracks. Certain of these effects had also been used in the Verve "Dinner Music" album (eg: the Blackhawk Stutz). Other effects painstakingly tried but deleted were later used in the quasi "Quiet Village" instrumental section "...Golden Adventure") on "Omnibust" (eg: fire extinguisher). The long and short versions were for 45 RPM release (recorded in stereo but mono release) with the short versions issued.
    Remade at a later date for LP issue (probably with Marvin Ash, pno, and John Cyr, drm) also saw some of the dialogue altered. Eg: the original reply to "They said it couldn't be done" changed from "You couldn't build a rocket ship to take a man to the moon" (explosion, tinkling cowbells), then Frees in Russian, "I guess you couldn't!"; changed to Jameson's sexy laugh followed by Spike's "Who said it couldn't?".

               45 LIB F-55191-A/B
45-LB-954   (3:27)The Late Late Late Movies, Part 1(Stardust)
45-LB-955   (3:14)The Late Late Late Movies, Part 2(Tenderly)

        LP LIB LRP 3140/LST 7140; LIBE HA-G 2270/SAH-G
           6090; UA-LA 439-E;
    (3:42)The Late Late Late Movies, Part 1(voice basics, take four plus inserts)
    (4:22)The Late Late Late Movies, Part 2(voice basics, take 1 plus inserts)

Note: Spike retained all masters from 20/21 Jan, but only acetate out-takes from future Warner sessions.

22 May, 1959 (FRI) - Radio Recorders, Hollywood
                    Client: Warner Bros.
                    Producer: Alvino Rey

                    Conductor/arranger - Carl Brandt
                    Contractor - Spike Jones
                    Brass - George Rock, tpt; Paul Tanner, trb
                    Reeds - Morris Crawford, Ted Nash, sax
                    Rhythm - Buddy Cole, pno/org; Bobby Gibbons, guit/
                        bjo; Phil Stephens, bass; Lou Singer, Ralph
                        Hansell, perc
                    Harp - Dorothy Remsen
                    Voices - Paul Frees, George Rock, Merrie (Mary)
                        Virginia
                    Sound Effects - Cliff Thorsness

                    45 WBE WEP 6004/WSEP 2004; LP B-1332/WS-1332;
                       WBE WM 4004/WS 8004; MODE CMDW 9726;
                    This Is Your Death (composite, take 17) - voices
                        Paul Frees

                    Unissued
                    Who's Sick? (composite, variable takes 1-9)

        Files show the following, with Carl Brandt, Eddie Brandt and
Thorne Nogar (R. Rec. engineering mixer-editor) in attendance:-
                    Paul Frees   2:00 to 5:00 PM
                    George Rock   2:00 to 6:30 PM
                    Merrie Virginia   4:00 to 6:30 PM
                    Cliff Thorness   2:00 to 6:45 PM

        Note: "Who's Sick?", the "ten sickest jokes of all time" as
referred to on the album jacket, were never issued. Carl Brandt, no
relation to Eddie, and in his first studio appearance with Spike, has
been acknowledged as the consummate professional of Hollywood studios. One of the biggest surprises on this session is seeing Paul
Tanner, the trombone mainstay of the civilian Glenn Miller band, on a
Jones session. Eddie Maxwell and Sol Meyer contributed to these compositions. Alvino Rey was one of the swing era's more successful
leaders, and had known Spike since the late '30s. He has produced
records and fronted occasional dance bands into 1985.

26 May, 1959 (TUES) - Radio Recorders, Hollywood
                     Client: Warner Bros.
                     Producer: Alvino Rey

                     Conductor/arranger - Carl Brandt
                     Contractor - Spike Jones
                     Brass - George Rock, tpt; Tommy Pederson, trb;
                         Vincent de Rosa; fr hrn
                     Reeds - Ted Nash, Morris Crawford, sax
                     Rhythm - Buddy Cole, pno/org; Bobby Gibbons, guit/
                         bjo; Phil Stephens, bass; Lou Singer, Ralph
                         Hansell, perc
                     Harp - Dorothy Remsen

        Unspecified background for Warner LPs "Spike Jones in
Hi-Fi", "Spike Jones in Stereo". Recording studio unlisted.

334

27 May, 1959 (WED) - Radio Recorders, Hollywood
                 Client: Warner Bros.   8:00 PM, Studio 1
                 Producer: Alvino Rey

                 Personnel as 22 May, deleting voices, Thorness;
                 adding effects (theremin) by Paul Tanner

  Files show the following additional individual times:-
          29 May (FRI) George Rock   2:00 PM
                Merrie Virginia 4:00 PM
         (George Rock is the "Phantom's" laugh)

     Unspecified background for Warner LPs "Spike Jones in
Hi-Fi", "Spike Jones in Stereo"

    Note: Carl Brandt had referred to "making the album like a
movie...it had to be done in pieces as Spike had prerecorded so many
of the dialogue tracks that it was a matter of having to piece things
together." The theremin as used by Paul Tanner was a variable oscillator of his own design with the pitch controlled by an arm moving in
an arc. (Carl Brandt correspondence 12 Oct 83)

3 June, 1959 (WED) - Radio Recorders, Hollywood
                 Client: Warner Bros.   1:00 to 6:00 PM
                 Producer: Alvino Rey

                 Conductor/arranger - Carl Brandt
                 Contractor - Spike Jones
                 Reeds - Gil Bernal, sax; Ronnie Lang, all reeds/fl
                 Rhythm - Buddy Cole, pno/org; Al Hendrickson,
                   guit; Don Whitaker, bass; Frank Flynn, mel perc
                 Voices - Thurl Ravenscroft, Ken Stevens, Loulie
                   Jean Norman, Paul Frees, George Rock

                 Unissued
                 Who's Sick?

                 45 WB 5116-A; LP WB B-1332/WS-1332; WBE WM 4004/
                   WS 8004; MODE CMDW 9726;
                 Teen Age Brain Surgeon - voc Thurl Ravenscroft

                 45 WB 5116-B; LP WB B-1332/WS-1332; WBE WM 4004/
                   WS 8004; MODE CMDW 9726; ET Public Service
                   Show "Here's To Vets"(see app. iii);
                 Monster Movie Ball - voc Ken Stevens

                 45 WBE WEP 6044/WSEP 2044; LP WB B-1332/WS-1332;
                   WB XS-1400(demo LP); WBE WM 4004/WS 8004;
                   MODE CMDW 9726;
                 Two Heads Are Better Than One - voc George Rock
                   and Paul Frees

                 LP WB B-1332/WS-1332; WBE WM 4004/WS 8004; MODE
                   CMDW 9726; WB "Now Hear These" Rel. 114, 8409;
                 Everything Happens To Me - voices Paul Frees

    Files show the following individual solists times:-
          Thurl Ravenscroft   1:00 to 2:30 PM
            Solo: "Teen Age Brain Surgeon"
          Ken Stevens ('Otto')   2:00 to 4:00 PM
            Solo: "Monster Movie Ball"

Loulie Jean Norman   2:00 to 4:00 PM
    High voice effects with Ken Stevens
Paul Frees
    Nothing   2:00 to 4:00 PM
    Duet w/G. Rock   4:30 to 5:00 PM
    (This Is Your Death/Two Heads)
    Solo: "Everything Happens" - 5:00 to 6:00 PM
George Rock
    Maniacal laugh w/K. Stevens - 2:30 to 4:00 PM
    Duet w/ P. Frees   4:30 to 6:00 PM
    (This Is Your Death/Two Heads)

4 June, 1959 (THURS) - Radio Recorders, Hollywood
            Client: Warner Bros.   8:00 to 10:00 PM
            Producer: Alvino Rey

            Conductor/arranger - Carl Brandt
            Contractor - Spike Jones
            Pno/celeste - Buddy Cole
            Voices - Paul Frees, Loulie Jean Norman,
               George Rock

            LP WB B-1332/WS-1332; WBE WM 4004/WS 8004;
               MODE CMDW 9726;
            My Old Flame (monologue) - Paul Frees

            LP WB B-1332/WS-1332; WBE WM 4004/WS 8004;
               MODE CMDW 9726;
            Tammy (three bats overdub) - Paul Frees, Loulie
               Jean Norman, George Rock

            Overdub to 3 June take
            Monster Movie Ball (high singing, maniacal laugh)

       Files show the following vocalists times:-
            Paul Frees, nothing   8:00 to 9:00 PM
            Peter Lorre talk   9:00 to 9:30 PM
            Recitation, "3 Bats", few lines overdubbing
            "2 Heads", wild voice track, 9:30 to 10:00 PM
            Loulie Jean Norman, nothing 8:00 to 9:30 PM
            Recitation, "3 Bats", overdubbing for "Monster
            Movie Ball" high voice   9:30-
            George Rock, nothing   8:00 to 9:30 PM
            Baby voice, "3 Bats", maniacal laugh in
            "Monster Movie Ball", overdubbing
            "2 Heads"   9:30-

5 June, 1959 (FRI) - Radio Recorders, Hollywood
            Client: Warner Bros.   8:00 PM to midnight
            Producer: Alvino Rey

            Personnel as 26 May, adding Cliff Thorsness,
               sound effects; Loulie Jean Norman, Paul Frees,
               George Rock, voices

            45 WBE WEP 6004/WSEP 2044; LP WB B-1322/WS-1322;
               MODE CMDW 9726;
            (All Of a Sudden) My Heart Sings - voc Loulie
               Jean Norman, Paul Frees

            LP WB B-1322/WS-1322; WBE WM 4004/WS 8004;
               MODE CMDW 9726;
            Spooktacular Finale

336

overdub to 4 June take
My Old Flame

Files show the following individual times:-
```
Cliff Thorsness            8:00 to 11:00 PM
Loulie Jean Norman         8:00 to 11:00 PM
    Solo: "My Heart Sings", few lines of talk dur-
    ing instrumental; Duet with Frees "Funeral
    March" finale 11C; one line "Funeral March"
    11A with Frees; Scream in "My Old Flame"
Paul Frees                 8:00 PM to midnight
    "My Heart Sings" - talk into song and sing/talk
    two phrases in song; talk during instrumental;
    Solo "My Old Flame" (Peter Lorre No. 6b); Solo
    "Funeral March" finale 11A; Duet "Funeral
    March" finale 11C (with Loulie)
George Rock                10:15 to 11:00 PM
    "Funeral March" finale - lines of singing
```

Note: "Spooktacular Finale" theme is the "Funeral March of a Marionette" by C. Gounod, used by Alfred Hitchcock to his TV mystery series. Frees follows the melody line on the initial take of "My Heart Sings" while the released version is 'talk', or semi-spoken.

2 July, 1959 (THURS) - Radio Recorders, Hollywood
> Client: Warner Bros.   3:00 to 6:00 PM
> Producer: Alvino Rey

> Contractor - Spike Jones
> Sound Effects - Gene Twombly, George Rock

Unspecified background for Warner LPs "Spike Jones in Hi-Fi", "Spike Jones in Stereo"

6 July, 1959 (MON) - Radio Recorders, Hollywood
> Client: Warner Bros.   2:00 to 6:00 PM
> Producer: Alvino Rey

> Conductor/arranger - Carl Brandt
> Contractor - Spike Jones
> Brass - George Rock, tpt; Paul Tanner, trb; Jim
> Decker, fr hrn
> Reeds - Jimmy Briggs, Ralph Lee
> Rhythm - Bobby Hammack, org; Bobby Gibbons, guit;
> Phil Stephens, bass; Hal Rees, Frank Flynn, drm
> Harp - Ann Mason Stockton
> Effects (theremin) - Paul Tanner

Unspecified background for Warner LPs "Spike Jones in Hi-Fi", "Spike Jones in Stereo"

20 July, 1959 (MON) - Radio Recorders, Hollywood
> Client: Warner Bros.   2:30 to 6:00 PM
> Producer: Alvino Rey   7:30 PM to 2:00 AM

> Voices - George Rock

Unspecified overdubbing for Warner LPs "Spike Jones in Hi-Fi", "Spike Jones in Stereo"

22 July, 1959 (WED) - Radio Recorders, Hollywood
> Client: Warner Bros.
> Producer: Alvino Rey

Voices - Paul Frees, Thurl Ravenscroft

Unspecified overdubbing for Warner LPs "Spike Jones in Hi-Fi", "Spike Jones in Stereo"

undated Warner Bros. titles:-

LP WB B-1332/WS-1332; WBE WM 4004/WS 8004; MODE CMDW 9726; ET AFRS "Johnny Green's World of Music" 6; AFRS "Small World" 4; I Only Have Eyes For You - Loulie Jean Norman, Paul Frees

LP WB B-1332/WS-1332; WBE 4004/WS 8004; MODE CMDW 9726; Poisen To Poisen - voices Paul Frees

Note: The above titles may have been buried among one or more of the previous 'unspecified' sessions

25 July, 1959 (SAT) - Gold Star Studios, Hollywood
Client: Renault Motors   12:00 to 2:00 PM

Contractor - Spike Jones
Trumpet - George Rock
Accordion - Carl Fortina
Bass - Eddie Robertson
voc/act - Freddy Morgan

Note: Two audition commercials, featuring Freddy Morgan. About 2-1/2 min. each, with inst. bridge from RCA E2-VB-5269, "Sante" edited into this remake

24 October, 1959 (SAT)
WOPA, Oak Park, Ill. "Crying Towel"

Telephone interview with Spike Jones by Eddie Cuda, aired 27 Oct 59 at 10:00 PM. Subject: "Spike Jones in Stereo"

17 November, 1959 (TUES) - Radio Recorders, Hollywood
Client: Spike Jones   7:00 to 10:00 PM

Leader/arranger - Jud Conlon
Rhythm - Frank Leithner, pno; Jad Paul, bjo, Keith (Red) Mitchell, bass; Ralph Hansell, drm
Voices - Peggy Clark, Charles Schrouder, Loulie Jean Norman, Mack McLean(contractor)
Vocal solo - Philip Phillips Jr.

K-4204-4   45 K-314x;
(2:23) I Want the South To Win the War For Christmas - feat Phil Phillips and the Rebels

Note: "Spike Jones courtesy Liberty Records" on the label suggests this title was released after Spike and Liberty came to contractual agreement in May, 1960. Flip is "Let's All Sing a Song For Christmas" by the Happy Harts.

338

Philip Phillips' hours were from 7:00 to 10:30 PM. The available handwritten copy of the recording information shows: Gus Donahue, copyist; V.W. Kuehn, cartage; and Spike, Eddie Brandt and Dick Webster in attendance.

Spike Jones and Helen Grayco were involved with commercials for "Postum" about this time. Details unavailable.

29 November, 1959 (SUN) - THE CHEVY SHOW*
                    NBC-TV Hollywood (Color)   Sponsor: Chevrolet

                    Featuring Dinah Shore, and guests: Spike Jones
                        and his City Slickers

                    City Slicker Medley:
                        Tom Dooley
                        One For My Baby

City Slickers appearing with Spike on club dates around this time include: George Rock, tpt; Phil Gray, trb; Gil Bernal, Bill DePew, sax/clar; Arnold Ross, pno; Bobby Lewis, bass; Ray Price/Lloyd Morales, Sal Lapertche, drm; Helen Grayco, Billy Barty, Len Carrie, vocals. Additional staff included Dick Webster, Les Calvin, Eddie Cline, Anne Calvin, Gene Hodgeman, Dan O'Brian.

During an engagement at the Mapes Hotel in Reno, Nevada, 26 Dec 59 to 2 Jan 60, Spike's guns were stolen. In a letter dated 19 Feb 60 on City of Reno letterhead, Police Chief Bill Gregory wrote:- "We are forwarding your guns by express which were stolen while you were at the Mapes Hotel in Reno. We realized you needed the guns in your act, but it was impossible to obtain them from Auburn, California, until this date.
    "The subject responsible, who is in custody in Auburn...is to be transferred to the Immigration Authorities and he will be deported from the United States. Therefore, our District Attorney deemed it advisable to postpone any action against the subject for Grand Larceny.
    "If this Department can be of any further assistance to you, please feel free to call on us."

(Decca Record Co. of England negotiate for the right to issue the Warner "Spooktacular" in Great Britain. These agreements date from 13 Apr 60)

11 May, 1960 (MON)
    A copy of the contract between Spike Jones and Liberty Records, dated this day and approved by the Liberty Legal Dept. (signed by S. Zucker), but unsigned by either Spike or Liberty President, Alvin S. Bennett, was among the Jones files.
    In essence, this contract, for a one-year term, binds Spike to recording the equivalent of two satisfactory long-play albums during this term. Should they prove successful, the contract would be renewed. It also gives Spike the studio time, which he had to pay for with Warner Bros.
    During the course of this contract, two albums were produced for Liberty. "Omnibust" and "60 Years of Music America Hates Best" (the latter title a 'dig' at the older radio series and the more recent RCA albums of a similar name) show uneven and at times sloppy engineering. They remain mild when compared with the fresh ingenuity put onto disc a decade earlier and often suffer by comparison (particularly with 'mike' presence and audible 'layering') with the very recent Warner Bros. album. The studio attempt to re-create the verve

of the old Slickers is very uneven due to the inability to guage
material by the reactions of an audience. This simple yardstick which
previously allowed masterful and unbridled creativity is now unavailable. Many of the Liberty undated, unfinished and unreleased titles
date from this period.

Radio Recorders retained no logs relating to any Jones sessions, and very little pertinent information is available. Spike's
personal stock of prerecorded effects, voices, music and basic tracks
(eg: 20/21 Jan 59) form the basis and/or background to some of the
albums titles. George Rock and Freddy Morgan appear on these discs in
the capacity of guest artists.

Helen and Spike have their own production offices, Gee-Jay
(Grayco-Jones) Productions, Inc. located at 360 No. Camden Drive in
Beverly Hills, and are represented by Frank Cooper Associates Agency
with offices in New York and Hollywood.

8 July, 1960 (FRI) - United Recorders, Hollywood
                     Client: Liberty Records   11:00 AM to 1:00 PM
                     Producer: Spike Jones
                     Executive Producer: Simon Waronker

                     Effects - Frank Leithner

                     LP LIB LRP 3154/LST 7154; LIBE HA-G 2298/
                        SAH-G 6109; UA-LA 439-E;
              (2:40) River, Stay 'Way From My Door (over dub to undated
                        Gloria Wood vocal)

14 July, 1960 (THURS) - United Recorders, Hollywood
                     Client: Liberty Records   11:00 AM to 1:20 PM
                     Producer: Spike Jones
                     Executive Producer: Simon Waronker

                     alias: "Hangnails Hennessey and Wingy Brubeck"

                     Piano - Marvin Ash
                     Drums - John Cyr

                     LP LIB LRP 3154/LST 7154; LIBE HA-G 2298/
                        SAH-G 6109; ET AFRS "Basic Music Library"
                        P-7296;
                     The 20's Roar (Medley: Bill Bailey; Clementine;
                        The Band Played On; There Is a Tavern In the
                        Town; Good Night Ladies; Auld Lang Syne)

undated Liberty titles:-   OMNIBUST

                     Spike Jones and the band that plays for fun

                     45 F-55253(condensed); LP LIB "Spring Into Action"
                        MM 404/SS 504; LIB LRP 3140/LST 7140; LIBE
                        HA-G 2270/SAH-G 6090; UA-LA 439-E; ET AFRS
                        "Johnny Green's World of Music" 6;
              (8:11) ah-1, ah-2, ah-Sunset Strip - voc Rip T. Shirt,
                        Merrie Virginia, Loulie Jean Norman,
                        Gloria Wood

                     LP LIB LRP 3140/LST 7140; LIBE HA-G 2270/
                        SAH-G 6090;

LP LIB LRP 3140/LST 7140; LIBE HA-G 2270/
SAH-G 6090;
(3:25)Loretta's Soaperetta - voc Rip T. Shirt, Merrie
Virginia

LP LIB LRP 3140/LST 7140; LIBE HA-G 2270/
SAH-G 6090;
(5:29)Captain Bangaroo - voc Rip T. Shirt, Merrie
Virginia, Walker Edmiston

LP LIB LRP 3140/LST 7140; LIBE HA-G 2270/
SAH-G 6090;
(4:55)The Wonderful World of Hari Kari - voc Freddy
Morgan, Loulie Jean Norman, Gloria Wood,
Walker Edmiston

LP LIB LRP 3140/LST 7140; LIBE HA-G 2270/
SAH-G 6090;
(6:24)I Search For Golden Adventure (in my Seven Leaky
Boots) - voc Lynn Johnson, Joyce Jameson

LP LIB LST 101; LIB LRP 3140/LST 7140; LIBE HA-G
2270/SAH-G 6090;
Theme from "I Search For Adventure"

LP LIB LRP 3140/LST 7140; LIBE HA-G 2270/
SAH-G 6090; LIB LST 101; UA-LA 439-E;
ET AFRS "America's Popular Music" 1347;
(4:05)A Mudder's Day Sport Spectacular - Doodles Weaver

Note: All musical arrangements by Carl Brandt. "Soaperetta"
is re-make of Victor's "None But the Lonely Heart". First editions of
"Omnibust" were of colored vinyl - red and blue are known. Audience
sound effects to "Bangaroo" from "Bozo the Clown" TV show.

60 Years of Music America Hates Best

Spike Jones and the Band that Plays for Fun!

LP LIB LRP 3154/LST 7154; LIBE HA-G 2298/
SAH-G 6109; UA-LA 439-E; ET AFRS "Basic
Music Library" P-7295;
(2:53)I Kiss Your Hand Madame - voc I.S. Harper and the
Four Fifths

LP LIB LRP 3154/LST 7154; LIBE HA-G 2296/
SAH-G 6109; ET AFRS "Basic Music Library"
P-7295;
Knock, Knock, Who's There? - voc the Boys in the
Back Room

LP LIB LRP 3154/LST 7154; LIBE HA-G 2298/
SAH-G 6109;
Pimples and Braces

LP LIB LRP 3154/LST 7154; LIBE HA-G 2298/
SAH-G 6109;
Hut Sut Song - voc the Carmen Lumbago Trio
(feat George Rock, tpt)

LP LIB LRP 3154/LST 7154; LIBE HA-G 2298/
SAH-G 6109; UA-LA 439-E;
(3:10)Strip Polka - voc Gloria Wood

LP LIB "Demo Record" MM 406/SS 506; LIB LRP 3154/
LST 7154; LIBE HA-G 2298/SAH-G 6109;
ET AFRS "Basic Music Library" P-7296;
Mairzy Doats - voc Sam Quentin and his Quail

LP LIB "Demo Record" MM 406/SS 506; LIB LRP 3154/
LST 7154; LIBE HA-G 2298/SAH-G 6109;
ET AFRS "Ira Cook" 904;
Melody Of Love - Lynn Johnson, narration

LP LIB LRP 3154/LST 7154; LIBE HA-G 2298/
SAH-G 6109;
Three Little Fishies - voc George Rock

LP LIB LRP 3154/LST 7154; LIBE HA-G 2298/
SAH-G 6109;
Kookie, Kookie, Lend Me You Comb - voc Linda
Strangis, Walker Edmiston

Note: All musical arrangements by Carl Brandt.
Liberty 12" "Demo Record" MM406/SS 506 featured other Liberty artists

30 July, 1960 (SUN)
Spike Jones appeared on the Sunday Amusement Section covers
of three Los Angeles newspapers: Herald Express, Los Angeles Times
and the Examiner. Subject: "Swingin' Spiketaculars" (pre-publicity
title to the following television series)

1 August, 1960 (MON) - THE SPIKE JONES SHOW
                        CBS-TV Hollywood

General Foods sponsored all 9:30 PM broadcasts. The Carl
Brandt orchestra provided all music and Brandt, never featured on
camera, composed/arranged all theme, fill and cue music. Regulars
were Helen Grayco, Joyce Jameson and Len Weinrib. Bill Dana, who
first appeared as 'Jose Jiminez' on the Steve Allen show in November
1959, is featured with Spike on these shows. All Jiminez material as
b'cast was written by Dana, who also produced the show.

          *The Piano Tuner - Spike, Jose Jiminez
          Helen Grayco - "What Is This Thing Called Love?",
             "At Long Last Love"
          Leonard Burnside discusses - "the Cymbal"
          Joyce Jameson - "What Have You Done For Me Lately"
          Finale - "Kids" (cast: Spike, Helen, Joyce, Len)

          *issued on Kapp LP KL 1212 (also 1215), and AFRS ET
             "Ira Cook" 370 (Kapp LP incl. Jose composite of
             audience warm-ups from 22Aug/19Sept shows)

       "...a combination of (Spike Jones as) Leonard Bernstein and
The Untouchables..."Music With Blood", as Jones put it. Spike managed
to live up to the billing nicely, proving once again that he is one
of the most adept men at taking comedy falls in the business, neatly
puncturing all that is saccharine and pontifical in American popular
music, and generally having a ball for himself and his audience. Welcome home, Spike."   (Dwight Whitney, TV Guide, Aug 60)
       "Spike Jones teed up his nine-week summer season (for Ann
Southern) by topping his established competitors in the overnight
Arbitron Monday night. He posted 14.4 to pass "Adventures In Paradise" at 12.9 and drew away from Goodyear Theatre with 12.2"
                        (Jack Hellman, Daily Variety, undated)
       "Loved Spike Jones first TV show and his new album
"Omnibust" is a howl." (Hedda Hopper, New York News, undated)

"...no midgets, no noise-makers, no wigs, the show had a kind of lilting, easygoing, goodhumored manner that concentrated on simplicity and informality. Particularly memorable: a pun-strewn Jones lecture on the origin of the cymbal and a haunting Grayco blues medley...Again it seems a pity that TV only finds use for Spike as a summer replacement." (Cecil Smith, Los Angeles Times, 2 Aug 60)

"...Thank Heaven here are some Stars who provide the freshest, most imaginative and creative television programs to be seen in many a Moon." (Frank Judge, Detroit News, undated)

"...The show's two most effective comedy highspots saw Jones as straightman to his producer, Bill Dana, who essayed his famed Jose Jiminez character and Jones as Leonard Burnside (Bernstein) rhetorically funny as he pedantically discussed the cymbal ("for cymbal-minded people"). Helen Grayco, visually lovelier that ever, rang a true bell with a tastefully thrushed medley..."
(Hank Grant, Hollywood Reporter, undated)

"The golden spike was driven into a new career for the Jones boy. The mad music of his past has given way to comedy caricature. His 19 years of every known form of musical violence must stand as some kind of record..." (Jack Hellman, Daily Variety, undated)

8 August, 1960 (MON) - THE SPIKE JONES SHOW
          CBS-TV Hollywood

          Guests: Bud and Travis

          *The Piano Tuner (again) - Spike, Jose Jiminez
          Helen Grayco - "Fascinating Rhythm"
          Joke file, with Spike, Len Weinrib
          Bud and Travis - "La Bamba"
          Leonard Burnside discusses - "Folk Music
              Instruments"
          Finale -"Together"

          *issued on Kapp LP KL 1212 (also 1215)

15 August, 1960 (MON) - THE SPIKE JONES SHOW
          CBS-TV Hollywood

          Opening - Spike snapping fingers to get waiter's
              attention. Waiter does joke to rest of cast at
              tables
          Helen Grayco - "When Your Lover Has Gone", "Just
              One Of Those Things"
          Leonard Burnside discusses - "Classic Ballet"
          Jose Jiminez - "Darling Je Vous Aime Beaucoup"

22 August, 1960 (MON) - THE SPIKE JONES SHOW
          CBS-TV Hollywood

          Guests: The Angels

          Opening - L. Weinrib introduces cast, with posters
          *The Artist - Spike, Jose Jiminez
          Helen Grayco - "About Love"
          Leonard Burnside discusses - "Drums"
          The Angels - "September In the Rain", "The Gopher
              (Go-fer) Song"
          Finale(cast, Angels) - "Old MacDonald Had a Farm"

          *issued on Kapp LP KL 1212 (also 1215)

343

29 August, 1960 (MON) - THE SPIKE JONES SHOW
          CBS-TV Hollywood

                    Opening - Spike and cast in hammocks
                    *The Jose Jiminez Jammock Salesman - Spike,
                       Jose Jiminez
                    Helen Grayco - "It's So Peaceful In the Country",
                       "Mountain Greenery"
                    Leonard Burnside discusses - "The Violin"
                    Helen Grayco, Joyce Jameson - "Two Lost Souls"
                    Spike, Len Weinrib - lazy jokes
                    Finale - "A Lot Of Livin' To Do"

               *issued on Kapp LP 1212 (also 1215)

          "The Nielsen first report for August...shows CBS-TV's aver-
age audience rating for "Spike Jones" tops the two programs on the
competing networks. "Spike Jones" drew 32.8 pr cent of the audience;
ABC-TV's "Adventures in Paradise" drew 32.3 per cent and NBC-TV's
"Goodyear Theatre" 24.9 per cent."
                    (unidentified, undated newspaper)
          "Despite that he has had offers for a London Palladium stand
many times in the past 15 years (Spike) is being kept off the tight
little island because of British Musicians' Union rules against
imported bands unless equal playing time is given a British crew in
the U.S.
          "But it looks like Spike and his madmen will finally regale
the Britishers, if not by proxy then by tape. BBC has ordered the
first recording of his summer show...liked it and ordered two more."
                    (Variety, undated)

5 September, 1960 (MON) - THE SPIKE JONES SHOW
          CBS-TV Hollywood

                    Guests: Steve Allen and Jack Jones

                    Opening - Spike and Steve Allen
                    Jack Jones - "This Could Be the Start Of
                       Something Big"
                    Spike, Steve Allen, Jose Jiminez - "The Piano
                       Accompanist"
                    Helen Grayco - "What Is a Woman?"
                    Leonard Burnside discusses - "The Songwriter"
                    Helen Grayco, Jack Jones - "Don't Forget That You
                       Can Count On Me"
                    Spike, Steve Allen - "The Musical Question Man"
                    Finale (Spike, Helen, Steve) - Steve Allen Medley

12 September, 1960 (MON) - THE SPIKE JONES SHOW
          CBS-TV Hollywood

                    Opening - Spike introduces masked cast
                    Helen Grayco - "Any Place I Hang My Hat",
                       (It's Just the) "Gypsy In My Soul"
                    Leonard Burnside discusses - "The Kabuki Dance"
                    *The Judo Expert - Spike, Jose Jiminez
                    Finale - "Get Happy"

               *issued on Kapp LP KL 1212 (also 1215)

19 September, 1960 (MON) - THE SPIKE JONES SHOW
          CBS-TV Hollywood

                              344

Opening - Jose Jiminez (impersonations)
Helen Grayco - "The Nearness Of You", "Too Close
    For Comfort"
Leonard Burnside discusses - "The Flamenco Dancer"
Drums - Jose Jiminez, with Spike demonstration
Len Weinrib, Joyce Jameson - Impersonations
Finale - Helen, Spike, Len, Joyce, Jose Jiminez

20 September, 1960 (TUES) - Radio Recorders, Hollywood   8:00 to
                   Client: Liberty Records   11:00 PM
                   Producer: Bill Dana

"Spike Jones as Leonard Burnside Discusses"

Leader - Carl Brandt
Piano - Al Pellegrini
Drums - Dick Shanahan
Voices - Joyce Jameson, Len Weinrib, Spike

        LP LIB LRP 3169/LST 7169(unissued)
(2:46)Leonard Burnside Discusses Songwriters

        LP LIB LRP 3169/LST 7169(unissued)
(2:40)Leonard Burnside Discusses the Drum

    Note: The voices identities do not appear on the available
AF of M contract copy. This album, a true rarity, was inspired by the
success of the 'Leonard Burnside' lectures on the 'Swingin' Spiketac-
ular' series. It was completed in its entirety with studio recording,
canned laughter, and editing which used dubs of Burnside audio spots
from the TV shows as models. AF of M (musical content) timings shown.
    However, this completed album was never issued!

    LRP 3169   LST 7169

    Spike Jones as LEONARD BURNSIDE discusses...

    (6:30)The Cymbal   (5:55)The Song Writer
    (7:48)The Kabuki Dance   (7:10)Flamenco Dancing
    (6:15)The Zither, and other   (9:17)Drums
          Folk Music Instruments
          (Side One)   (Side Two)

        "Ably assisted by Joyce Jameson and Lenny Weinrib, with
all spoken material written by Bill Dana and Don Hinkley"

21 September, 1960 (WED) - Radio Recorders, Hollywood   8:00 to
                   Client: Liberty Records   12:00 PM
                   Producer: Bill Dana

"Spike Jones as Leonard Burnside Discusses"

Leader - Carl Brandt
Drums - Dick Shanahan
Voices - Joyce Jameson, Len Weinrib, Spike

        LP LIB LRP 3169/LST 7169(unissued)
(2:36)Leonard Burnside Discusses Folk Music Instruments

        LP LIB LRP 3169/LST 7169(unissued)
(2:55)Leonard Burnside Discusses the Cymbal

345

Note: Timings from the AF of M contracts. Editing (8-3/4
hrs) to the two sessions occurred on 21 and 22 Sept (studio 5). Dubbing (1 hr - spots from mono audio TV spots) occurred on 22 and 23
Sept (studio C), with final editing (8-1/2 hrs) on 18, 20 and 25 Oct
in studio 5. Album covers were designed (by Pate/Francis & Associates) and printed for mono and stereo distribution to start 2 Dec 60.

26 September, 1960 (MON) - THE SPIKE JONES SHOW
                    This days Swingin'Spiketacular, the ninth and last
                    of the series, was cancelled due to the
                    Kennedy/Nixon television debates

        "...Spike Jones's fans have registered complaints because
his Monday night CBS-TV series this summer hasn't featured the zany
band...Spike didn't jettison his band voluntarily. He was forced to
do it because most of the popular songs today defy being satirized
musically.
        "To satirize", says Spike, "means to humorously hold up to
ridicule, doesn't it? Okay, tell me, how do you make fun of a song
with lyrics like those in 'Splish Splash' or 'Yakety Yak'?"
        "When Spike sat down last spring to consider a "Spiketacu-
lars" format...he suddenly realized it was impossible to write and
create 30 minutes a week consisting of comedy versions of the songs
being written today.
        "In their original form", Spike explains, "these songs
already are the funniest selections and renditions ever heard - at
least to anyone over 14 years of age."
        "Also, to fully appreciate satire, an audience must be
familiar with the original version. Since the majority of our viewers
are adults, how many songs in the current Top 100 do you think are
known to the average viewer?"
        "There was 'Mack the Knife', of course, but that one good
song which sneaked in because of a great record, is owned by a composer and publisher who won't allow me to perform anything but a
straight version."
        "...those 'Leonard Burnside' musical lectures of Spikes have
caught on to a point where he has received invitations from universi-
ties to lecture (with jokes included) to their music appreciation
classes.
        "Who knows", Spike quips, "I may have to explain Beethoven's
Fifth to Dean Martin - bar by bar."
        "Meanwhile, Spike will go on crusading where ever he can
against the current crop of songs, which he claims are a definite
contribution to musical juvenile delinquency."
                    (Hal Humphrey, Los Angeles Mirror, undated)

        An undated note from the Jones files is of interest in
relation to "Rides, Rapes & Rescues" (music to watch silent
movies by - Played by Hangnails Hennessey and Wingy Brubeck.
Occasionally augmented by Arthur Fiddler and the Boston
Poops)

        RAGTIME PIANO PLAYERS

        Lincoln Mayorga - UP 09649 & EX 15876
        (Protege - Lou Busch - Joe Fingers Carr)
        Has classical background. Has recorded (as Spider
        Dugan) 2 ragtime albums for Warner Bros.

        Marvin Wright - Warner Bros. Records -
            Am In Love

        Alten Purnell - Warner Bros. Records
            Funky Piano

CARL BRANDT AND I DECIDED POSSIBLY HAVING "RIDES, RAPES, & RESCUES" RECORDED BY MAYORGA, BUDDY COLE, AND SOMEBODY ELSE

27 October, 1960 (THURS) -· Radio Recorders, Hollywood   1:45 to
                  Client: Liberty Records   4:45 PM
                  Producer: Spike Jones

                  alias: "Hangnails Hennessey and Wingy Brubeck"

                  Leader - Carl Brandt
                  Piano - Marvin Ash (Ashbaugh)
                  Drums - John Cyr

                  Unissued
                  Stars and Stripes Forever (9 takes)

                  Unissued
       (2:43)Keystone Kapers (13 takes)

                  LP LIB LRP 3185/LST 7185;
              (2:50)The Great Train Robbery

      Note: "Honky Tonk Train Blues" as played Meade Lux Lewis and recorded 19 Oct 38 with Bob Crosby is the basis for "The Great Train Robbery". In a 15 November letter to Miss Kay Banks of Liberty Records, Spike said:- "Unfortunately, we were unable to use Marvin Ash to complete the album as he had a wrist injury about a year ago which made it impossible for him to be physically fit for an album of this type." Marvin Ash was paid for this session and his services in rehearsing/attending creative meetings with Carl Brandt and Spike. "You will notice in each instance the pianist recieved double scale ($103) as most of these tracks were piano solos, and required much extra rehearsal at home on the pianist's part."
      Studio take and album jacket timings differ. This album was available as an Australian pressing with U.S. produced jackets.

4 November, 1960 (FRI) - IT COULD BE YOU*
                  NBC-TV Hollywood

                  Guest: Spike Jones

10 November, 1960 (THURS) - Radio Recorders, Hollywood   1:15 to
                  Client: Liberty Records   4:15 PM
                  Producer: Spike Jones

                  alias: "Hangnails Hennessey and Wingy Brubeck"

                  Leader - Carl Brandt
                  Piano - Robert Van Eps
                  Drums - John Cyr

                  LP LIB LRP 3185/LST 7185;
       (2:40)Keystone Kapers (take 13)

                  Unissued
                  Curses, If Jack Dalton Were Only Here (composite)

                  Unissued

Curses, If Jack Dalton Were Only Here (short
     version, take 1)

                LP LIB LRP 3185/LST 7185;
        (2:50)The Beautiful Bathing Beauties

        "Rides, Rapes & Rescues" - mention is made on the album
jacket of "an irreverant pictorial history of silent movies". A soft-
cover book was being compiled of silent movie stills with comic cap-
tion balloons added. A 'silent movie' was similarly planned. Both
plans were aborted when other producers (eg: Jay Ward's Fractured
Flickers) beat Spike to the draw.

11 November, 1960 (FRI) - Radio Recorders, Hollywood
                Client: Liberty Records   1:15 to 4:15 PM
                Producer: Spike Jones

                Personnel as 10 Nov

                LP LIB LRP 3185/LST 7185;
        (2:35)Madam Fifi's Can-Can (take 8 plus insert)

                Unissued
        (2:30)A Mustache, A Derby...(10 takes plus insert)

                Unissued
                Silents Please (3 takes)

        Radio Recorders, Hollywood   8:00 to 12:00 PM

                Personnel as 10 Nov, adding Emanuel (Mannie)
                   Klein, tpt; Benny Gill, vln

                LP LIB LRP 3185/LST 7185;
        (2:45)Poet and Peasant Overture 2 plus inserts)

                LP LIB LRP 3185/LST 7185;
        (2:53)Lips That Touch Liquor... (take 4 plus inserts)

                LP LIB LRP 3185/LST 7185;
        (2:35)The Winning of the West (composite)

        Note: Issued title is "Cotton-Pickin' Peasant Overture"

14 November, 1960 (MON) - Radio Recorders, Hollywood
                Client: Liberty Records   9:00 AM to 1:00 PM
                Producer: Spike Jones

                Personnel as 10 Nov

                LP LIB LRP 3185/LST 7185;
                A Mustache, A Derby... (composite)

                LP LIB LRP 3185/LST 7185;
        (2:42)Theda Barracuda Meets Rudolph Vaselino (composite)

                LP LIB LRP 3185/LST 7185;
        (2:30)Stars and Stripes Forever (take 1 of 10)

Unissued
Stars and Stripes Forever (piccolo overdub?)

LP LIB LRP 3185/LST 7185;
(2:52)Curses! If Jack Dalton Were Only Here

Note: Issued title is "Stars and Stripes Flicker Finale".
Simon Waronker (who had played violin with the Gus Arnheim Orch. in
1933), the executive producer to Spike's first two Liberty albums is
'immortalized' in the album notes as Simon Warmaker ("the lascivious
outside man from the local finance company") in "Curses!..."

23 November, 1960 (WED) - Radio Recorders, Hollywood
            Client: Liberty Records   1:30 to 6:00 PM

            Leader - Spike Jones
            Drums - John Cyr

            Existing take sound effects overdubbing
            (2:30)Keystone Kapers
            (2:42)Silents Please
            Lips That Touch Liquor
            A Mustache, A Derby
            The Great Train Robbery
            Madame Fifi's Can-Can
            Bathing Beauties
            (2:52)The Winning of the West
            Curses! If Jack Dalton...
            Poet and Peasant

            LEONARD BURNSIDE voice trax (Spike only)
            (1:58)Flamenco (new ending, master take 1)
            Cymbal announcement, take 3
            Drum ann., take 3
            Zither ann., take 3
            Kabuki ann., take 4
            Flamenco ann., take 5
            Song Writers ann., take 4

            Wild stereo applause for Burnside intro,
                master, take 3

        Note: Album credits: "Your Host: Lindley Armstrong". Spike's
"R-R-R" narration could have been taped this day. Editing occurred on
11 Nov (3 Hrs) and 16 Nov (6 hrs). Spike retained all out-takes and
dubs (1/2" tape) to "Rides, Rapes & Rescues" composite masters.

8 December, 1960 (THURS) - PERSON TO PERSON
            CBS-TV Hollywood(from the Jones' home)

        Charles Collingwood 15 minute interview (summer taping)
        with the Jones family, including Linda. This interview was
        re-run 7 July 61, coinciding with the first broadcast of the
        new "Spike Jones" CBS TV show.

        Note: Interestingly, one of the secretaries in Spike's No.
Camden office(s) at this time was Linda Lee Jones (CR 1-2030)

4 January, 1961 (WED) - Radio Recorders, Hollywood
            Client: Hamm's Beer   8:00 to 10:00 PM, and
            Swift-Chaplin Productions   11:30 to 12:00 PM

Leader/arranger - Carl Brandt
Contractor - Spike Jones
Brass - Joe Graves, tpt; Eddie Kusby, trb
Reeds - Arthur Herfurt, sax/clar
Rhythm - Eugene Di Nova, pno; Allan Reuss, guit/
    bjo; Ira Westley, bass/tuba; Chester Ricord,
    Ralph Hansell, perc
Harp - Verlye Mills
Copyist - Caper's Music Service

805   TV commercial for Hamm's Beer, animated cartoon
875   with same very 'slickerish' music track on both
               releases. (Hamm's Bear is a one-man band)

        "You might be interested in knowing that that particular
recording session was one of the most pleasant and efficiently run I
have attended in 20 years in this business.
        "You might also like to know that both the Theo. Hamm Brew-
ing Company and the advertising agency, Campbell-Mithun, considered
this finished commercial one of the best Hamm's Beer commercials that
was made during the 12 years of that campaign and out of more than
600 commericals that were made under this format."
        (Swift-Chaplin letter to the Jones estate, 2 May 1967)

26 February, 1961 (SUN) - THE ED SULLIVAN SHOW
                CBS-TV

        Guest: Spike Jones as Leonard Burnside 'discusses'

        Note: The 1961 date book of Jones shows no appearances on
the Ed Sullivan show although this date appears in several sources.
It is included here for reference only.

8 April, 1961 (SAT)
            Spring Sing, San Fernando State College
            Spike Jones, M.C., introduces the acts and
                variety program

6 May, 1961 (SAT)
            Spring Sing, San Bernadino College
            Spike Jones, M.C., introduces the acts and
                variety program

11 May, 1961 (THURS)
            Spring Sing, UCLA
            Spike Jones, M.C., introduces the acts and
                variety program

17 June, 1961 (SAT)
            Spike Jones as 'Leonard Burnside' at the Hollywood
            Bowl "Show of the Year" (Spike was provided
                with a tape of this lecture)

        The 1961 desk diary of Spike Jones shows the following se-
quence relating to the first CBS-TV program, "The Spike Jones Show"

24 June, 1961 (SAT)
            CBS-TV Hollywood   10:00 AM to noon

            Rehearsal

350

26 June (MON) to 30 June (FRI), 1961
                    Extensive long distance 'phone interviews with
                    the TV editors of national papers.

29 June, 1961 (THURS)
                    CBS-TV Hollywood   1:30 to 4:30 PM

                    Rehearsal, make-up

3 July, 1961 (MON)
                    Script conference 12:30 to 2:30 PM (for Spike) at
                    'Coronet'

4 July, 1961 (TUES)
                    CBS-TV Hollywood   2:00 to 5:00 PM

                    Script rehearsal

5 July, 1961 (WED)
                    CBS-TV Hollywood

                    Script rehearsal - 10:00 AM to 1:00 PM
                    Music rehearsal - 2:00 to 5:00 PM

6 July, 1961 (THURS)
                    CBS-TV Hollywood

                    Run thru in studio 33, 11:30 to 1:30 PM
                    Run thru with orch., 2:00 to 3:30 PM

7 July, 1961 (FRI) - THE SPIKE JONES SHOW (b'cast 17 July)
                    CBS-TV Hollywood

                    Guests: Bill Dana and Jack Jones

                    Opening - Spike Jones and Helen Grayco
                    Bill Shannon - as Perry Como
                    Spike, Judy Strangis - "MacBeth"
                    Spike, Bill Dana - "Jose Jiminez, the Lion Tamer"
                    Helen Grayco - "Out Of This World", "It's a Small
                      World"
                    Bill Shannon - as Perry Como
                    Public Service feature - Spike on 'Summer Camps'
                    Jack Jones - "At Long Last Love", "The Last Dance"

        Note: Spike Jones, with guests and Carl Brandt's Orchestra.
Soloists/acts are noted on personal appearances only. For this days
8:00 PM taping, rehearsals started at noon, and this 1/2-hour show
was broadcast 17 July - all shows were b'cast 10 days after taping.
        Now the format has been established, rehearsals, which had
taken two weeks for the initial show, are tightened up and occur less
frequently in the course of subsequent shows.

14 July, 1961 (FRI) - THE SPIKE JONES SHOW (b'cast 24 July)
                    CBS-TV Hollywood

                    Guests: Dave Ketchum and Gene McDaniels

                    Opening - The Snake Charmer

351

Spike discusses - "Woodwind Instruments"
Helen Grayco - "Hong Kong Blues"
Public Service feature - Spike, Dave Ketchum on
    'Safety'
Gene McDaniels - "A Tear", "How Long Has This Been
    Going On"
Finale (Helen, Spike) - "Love Nest"

21 July, 1961 (FRI) - THE SPIKE JONES SHOW (b'cast 31 July)
           CBS-TV Hollywood

           Guests: Charlie Manna and Buddy Greco

           Opening - Peter Pan and Wendy (Judy Strangis)
           Public Service feature - Spike on 'Travel in
               Europe'
           Helen Grayco - "Misty"
           Charlie Manna - Blood cell dialogue
           Charlie, Spike, Helen - Dancing partners
           Buddy Greco - "I Could Write a Book", "Around
               the World In 80 Days"
           Finale - Around the World

22 July, 1961 (SAT)
           Date book entry: "Spike Jones - judge beauty
               contest (Jimmy Grayco will call with details)"

26 July, 1961 (WED)
           Date book entry: "Tape-(Heart fund) CBS 1:00 p.m."
               (possible Jones video appearance)

28 July, 1961 (FRI) - THE SPIKE JONES SHOW (b'cast 7 August)
           CBS-TV Hollywood

           Guest: Red Norvo

           Opening - 1961 Miss World Contest
           Spike - Fan letters and TV clips
           Helen Grayco - "Come Rain Or Come Shine",
               "Everything's Coming Up Roses"
           Runner - Student driver
           Spike - "Captain Kook's Cartoon Carnival"
           Red Norvo - "Somebody Else Is Taking My Place"
           Helen, Red Norvo - "You Make Me Feel So Young"
           Red Norvo - "The Man I Love"
           Helen, Red Norvo - "After You've Gone"
           Spike - Movie mood music
           Finale (Spike, Helen) - "Love and Marriage"

4 August, 1961 (FRI) - THE SPIKE JONES SHOW (b'cast 14 August)
           CBS-TV Hollywood

           Guests: Louis Nye and Sam Butera

           Opening - Another evening with Fred Astaire
           Spike, Helen introduce guests
           Spike - 'Lost and Found'
           Louis Nye - monologue
           Helen Grayco - "In A Little Spanish Town"
           Public Service feature - Spike, Louis Nye on
               'Camping Out'

                           352

        Sam Butera and his Witnesses - "Love Letters",
            "The Grasshopper"
        Spike - That wonderful year, 1962
        Finale - Spike, Helen, Louis Nye

11 August, 1961 (FRI) - THE SPIKE JONES SHOW (b'cast 21 August)
            CBS-TV Hollywood

        Guests: Dick Patterson and The Hi-Lo's

        Opening - Jane Carruthers and Carruthers Bros.
        Public Service feature - Spike on 'Surbuban
            Living'
        Helen Grayco - "I've Got A Lot Of Living To Do"
        Spike, Dick Patterson - Barber shop
        The Hi-Lo's - "Georgia On My Mind", "Fascinating
            Rhythm"
        Spike, Helen, Dick Patterson - Summer resort
        Spike, Helen - "Together"

17 August, 1961 (THURS)
        Date book entry: "Soupy Sales (CBS)". Possible
    video appearance or business meeting 4 to 5 p.m. with
    Soupy Sales (who often pantomimed to Jones records on
    his show)

18 August, 1961 (FRI) - THE SPIKE JONES SHOW (b'cast 28 August)
            CBS-TV Hollywood

        Guests: The Westwoods, Pat Harrington Jr.

        Opening - Bill Shannon as "The Astronaut"
        Spike - Great moments in Opera
        Helen Grayco - "That's All"
        Pat Harrington Jr. - "The Sports Car"
        Production Number: "World TV"
            Harrington - Bullfight in Spain
            Spike, Westwoods - Japanese Bandstand
            Spike, Helen, Pat - French news, weather
            The Westwoods - "Let Me Fly"
        Finale - "Put A Shine On Your Shoes"

25 August, 1961 (FRI) - THE SPIKE JONES SHOW (b'cast 4 September)
            CBS-TV Hollywood

        Guest: Dave Ketchum

        Opening - Spike introduces stuntman, Bill Shannon
        Public Service feature - Spike on 'Selection of a
            College'
        Dave Ketchum - The Beatnik at the Peace Corps
        Helen Grayco, dancers - "Ballin' the Jack"
        Production Number: "Daytime Television"
            Spike - Early bird classroom
            Dave Ketchum - Peter Posture
            Spike, Helen, Dave - The marriage clinic
        Finale - Spike, Helen - "Sunday"

1 September, 1961 (FRI) - THE SPIKE JONES SHOW (b'cast 11 September)
            CBS-TV Hollywood

        Guests: Tommy Noonan and Frank D'Rone

                        353

```
                    Spike - introduces Bill Shannon
                    Spike - TV film titles, with film clips
                    Helen Grayco - "Bewithced"
                    Tommy Noonan - Do-It-Yourself
                    Spike - Fan letters
                    Frank D'Rone - "All Of You", "The Way You
                        Look Tonight"
                    Production Number: "Film Museum"
                        Helen, Tommy Noonan - Western
                        Spike, Tommy - Espionage
                        Spike, Tommy, F. D'Rone, B. Shannon - Gangster
                    Finale - Spike, Tommy, Frank - "We Saw The Sea"
                        Helen Grayco - "Broadway Rhythm"
                        Frank D'Rone - "Riff Song"
                        Spike - "I'm a Yankee Doodle Dandy"
                        Tommy Noonan - "Rosalie"
                        Spike, Helen - "Varsity Drag"
                        Cast: "You Ought To Be In Pictures", "Here's To
                                Those Wonderful Flickers"


8 September, 1961 (FRI) - THE SPIKE JONES SHOW (b'cast 18 September)
                    CBS-TV Hollywood


                    Guests: Mel Torme and Charlie Manna


                    Opener - Tarzan
                    Spike (Western monologue, song) - "That's the Old
                        Wild West As I Recall"
                    Helen Grayco - "Witchcraft"
                    Charlie Manna - "The Astronaut"
                    Spike, Charlie Manna - single man buying clothes
                    Spike, Charlie, Helen - married man buying clothes
                    Mel Torme - "Gone With the Wind", "That Old
                        Feeling"
                    Spike, Helen - Jealous skit
                    Helen Grayco - "I Still Get Jealous"


15 September, 1961 (FRI) - THE SPIKE JONES SHOW (b'cast 25 September)
                    CBS-TV Hollywood


                    Guests: Bud Dashiel and the Kinsmen, and
                        Pat Harrington Jr.


                    Opener - Spike with Blue Boy painting
                    Public Service feature - Spike on 'A Place to Eat'
                    Helen Grayco - "In the Still Of the Night"
                    Spike, Pat Harrington, audience - 'Sing Along
                        With Mitch'
                    Bud Dashiel, Kinsmen - "I Talk To the Trees",
                        "La Bamba"
                    Spike: Fall preview
                        Jack Ragas, Pat, Spike, - 'Western'
                        Spike, Helen, Bud Dashiel, Pat Harrington -
                                'Science for Everyone'


16 September, 1961 (SAT)
                    Date book entry: Dinner party for Cyd Charisse
                        and Tony Martin, Danny and Rosemary Thomas, Bob
                        and Rosemary Stark

        Note: The Liberty demonstration record, LST 101, "This Is
Stereo", which was written by Eddie Brandt and Les Ecklund and
produced by Si Waronker could have been ready for production about
```

this time. As LST 101 was the last album produced by Waronker with Jones involvement, the following 1961 meetings have significance:- 23 May at Liberty with Waronker; 27 May at Liberty with Paul Brandon; 12 June at Liberty with Waronker; 22 August at CBS with Les Ecklund; also 8PM dinner (22 Aug at Chasens) with Mr. & Mrs. Joyce Jameson. (Could Jameson be "Sigreid Sauerbrauten"? Lynn Johnson is responsible for the male voices)

This excellent stereo demo record (first editions in blue vinyl with fuzzy jackets) featured many of the Liberty artists with dialogue by Spike and unusual sonic demonstrations.

Date book entries show three visits to a doctor in October and one in November. The first of these four was to the UCLA Medical Center, Pulmonary Function test. The weakening effects of the lung disease were physically taking their toll. Spike closed his offices and devoted his time to studio projects (such as rerecording his past hits) and occasionally produced shows in the Nevada resorts of Las Vegas and Reno.

"Spike Jones, the quiet man of music, has just returned from Honolulu where he and his wife, Helen Grayco, bravely undertook to spread the mainland's latest mania, the Twist, to the Hawaiians."
("TV Week", San Diego Union, 14/20 Jan 62)

16 January, 1962 (SAT) - TRUTH OR CONSEQUENCES*
                NBC-TV Hollywood

                Guest: Spike Jones

13 February, 1962 (SAT) - TRUTH OR CONSEQUENCES*
                NBC-TV Hollywood

                Guest: Spike Jones, on special panel for "Surprise
                Of Your Life" reunion feature

27 March, 1962 (SAT) - TRUTH OR CONSEQUENCES*
                NBC-TV Hollywood

                Guest: Spike Jones, on special panel for "Surprise
                Of Your Life" reunion feature

13 August, 1962 (FRI) - YOUR FIRST IMPRESSION*
                NBC-TV Hollywood (Color)

                Guest: Spike Jones

16 September, 1963 (MON) - Universal Recorders, Hollywood
                Client: Liberty Records   8:00 to 11:00 PM
                Producer: Dave Pell

                "The New Band of Spike Jones"

                Leader/arranger - Carl Brandt
                Contractor - Spike Jones
                Brass - Virgil Evans, tpt; Elmer (Moe) Schneider,
                trb
                Sax/clarinet - Edward Rosa
                Rhythm - Ray Sherman, pno; Trefoni (Tony) Rizzi,
                Alfred Viola, Allan Reuss, bjo/guit; Robert K.
                Stone, bass; Nick Fatool, drm

                LP LIB LRP 3338/LST 7338; ET AFRS "Spotlight
                Album" 95; AFRS "Ira Cook" 899;

355

(2:28)If I Had A Hammer - inst

45 LIB 55649-A; LP LIB LRP 3338/LST 7338;
ET AFRS "Ira Cook" 907;
(2:21)Ballad Of Jed Clampett - inst

LP LIB LRP 3338/LST 7338; LIB LST-4-7338;
ET AFRS "Spotlight Album" 95; AFRS "Small
World" 103;
(2:38)Washington Square - inst

LP LRP 3338/LST 7338; LIB LST-4-7338;
(2:20)Alley Cat - inst

18 September, 1963 - Universal Recorders, Hollywood
Client: Liberty Records   9:00 PM to midnight
Producer: Dave Pell

"The New Band of Spike Jones"

Leader/arranger - Carl Brandt
Contractor - Spike Jones
Brass - Virgil Evans, tpt; Moe Schneider, trb
Clarinet - Edward Rosa
Rhythm - Ray Sherman, pno; Bobby Gibbons, Allan
Reuss, Tom Tedesco, bjo/guit; Robert Stone,
bass; John Cyr, drm

LP LIB LRP 3338/LST 7338; LIB LST-4-7338; UA-LA
439-E; ET AFRS "Spotlight Album" 95; AFRS
"Small World" 103; AFRS "America's Popular
Music" 826;
(2:04)September Song - inst

LP LIB LRP 3338/LST 7338; ET AFRS "Spotlight
Album" 95;
(2:30)Frankie and Johnnie - inst

LP LIB LRP 3338/LST 7338; LIB LST-4-7338;
ET AFRS "World of Show Business" 179; AFRS
"Small World" 713;
(2:08)Blowin' in the Wind - inst

45 LIB 55649-B; LP LIB LRP 3338/LST 7338; LIB
LST-4-7338; ET AFRS "Spotlight Album" 95;
AFRS "Ira Cook" 888;
(1:57)Green Green - inst

20 September, 1963 (FRI) - Universal Radio Recorders, Hollywood
Client: Liberty Records   8:00 to 11:00 PM
Producer: Dave Pell

"The New Band of Spike Jones"

Leader/arranger - Carl Brandt
Contractor - Spike Jones
Brass - Virgil Evans, tpt; Moe Schneider, trb
Clarinet - Abe Most
Rhythm - Robert Florence, pno; Bobby Gibbons, Tom
Tedesco, Allan Reuss, bjo/guit; Robert Stone,
bass; John Cyr, drm

<u>LP</u> LIB LRP 3338/LST 7338; LIB LST-4-7338;
<u>ET</u> AFRS "World of Show Business" 179;
(2:24)<u>Maria Elena</u> - inst

<u>LP</u> LIB LRP 3338/LST 7338;
(2:37)<u>Puff (the Magic Dragon)</u> - inst

<u>LP</u> LIB LRP 3338/LST 7338; <u>ET</u> AFRS
"America's Popular Music" 771;
(2:00)<u>Red Sails In the Sunset</u> - inst

<u>LP</u> LIB LRP 3338/LST 7338; <u>ET</u> AFRS
"Small World" 103;
(2:38)<u>Whistler's Muddah</u> - inst

Note: By 23 Nov 63, the Liberty album "Washington Square" reportedly reached 113th position among popular long play albums sold, but placed much higher in the Los Angeles area. Entirely instrumental, the "New Band" instrumentation was, ironically, almost identical to that used on Spike's initial sides for RCA (with the emphasis on strong rhythm, solid ensemble, excellent balance and, at times, humorous re-workings of stock dixie/blues/country/western phrases - very commercial). Another similarity is that only studio musicians were hired with the personnel changes reflecting their availability at any given time.

4 November, 1963 (MON)
        Bob Crane interview with Spike on KNX, Los Angeles

20 November, 1963 (WED)
        Award, in the form of a plaque:-

        To Spike Jones, for excellence in

        Marketing Music

        (from) Sales Promotion Executive Ass'n
                of Los Angeles

        -Golden Spike Award-

30 December, 1963 (MON) - Radio Recorders, Hollywood
        Client: Liberty Records   8:00 to 11:30 PM
        Producer: Dave Pell

        "The New Band of Spike Jones"

        Leader/arranger - Carl Brandt
        Brass - Virgil Evans, tpt; <u>Francis (Joe) Howard,</u>
            trb
        Clarinet - Julian (Matty) Matlock
        Rhythm - <u>Ernest Hughes,</u> pno; Allan Reuss, Tom
            Tedesco, Bobby Gibbons, guit/bjo; <u>George (Red)</u>
            <u>Callender,</u> bass; Nick Fatool, drm

        <u>LP</u> LIB LRP 3349/LST 7349;
    (2:09)<u>Stoplight</u> - inst

        Unissued
        <u>Dance of the Hours</u> (<u>Hot Rod Bash</u> basic?)

                    LP LIB LRP 3349/LST 7349;
        (2:06)Manana - inst

                    LP LIB LRP 3349/LST 7349; ET AFRS "Ira Cook"
                        996, 1376;
        (2:14)Hey Mr. Banjo - inst

January, 1964 - Radio Recorders, Hollywood
                    Client: Liberty Records
                    Producer: Dave Pell

                "The New Band of Spike Jones"

                Personnel similar to 30 Dec 63

                    45 LIB 55684-A; LP LIB LRP 3349/LST 7349;
                        ET AFRS "Ira Cook" 991;
        (2:30)Dominique - inst

                    LP LIB LRP 3349/LSY 7349;
        (2:24)Kansas City - inst

                    LP LIB LRP 3349/LST 7349;
        (2:17)Whispering - inst

                    LP LIB LRP 3349/LST 7349;
        (2:19)Java - inst

                    LP LIB LRP 3349/LST 7349;
        (2:20)Deep Purple - inst

                    LP LIB LRP 3349/LST 7349;
        (2:19)Charade - inst

                    LP LIB LRP 3349/LST 7349;
        (2:13)There! I've Said It Again - inst

                    LP LIB LRP 3349/LST 7349;
        (2:23)For You -inst

                    45 LIB 55684-B; LP LIB LRP 3349/LST 7349;
        (2:11)Sweet and Lovely - inst

        Note: The sessions producing the above titles would have
occurred during the days bracketing 30 December

16 January, 1964 (THURS) - THE EDIE ADAMS SHOW*
                    ABC-TV Hollywood   10:00 PM EST

                    as guests - Spike Jones, his City Slickers
                        and "New Band"

                    Personnel included Eddie Brandt, pno

                    Washington Square - inst
                    In a Persian Market - City Slickers
                    Sabre Dance - City Slickers

                            358

Note: Though scheduled, Freddy Morgan did not appear, nor were these pre-publicity titles b'cast.

17 January, 1964 (FRI) - BURKE'S LAW*
                        ABC-TV Hollywood

Spike appears in a straight acting role as a racehorse tout and bookie named "Duke", (reminiscent of "Duke Daniels" in the 1941 Point Sublime show?) in the episode, "Who Killed What's His Name?"

24 January, 1964 (FRI)
          Interview with Spike by George Church III. AFRS 12" ET "Small World" 103. (55 min.) Subject: life biography

25 January, 1964 (SAT) - Radio Recorders, Hollywood*
                        Client: Liberty Records

                Spike Jones, unspecified

                Unissued (completed)
      (2:30)Hootenanny Party - vocal chorus

Note: This is but one of many titles for Liberty which remained unissued or unfinished. (see appendix i for further titles which may have been produced near this time) Eddie Brandt recalled an attempt to create another "Spooktacular" with such titles as "My Darling Frankenstein" in an album called "Ghoul Days". The title song - (2:21)"Ghoul Days", (to the tune "School Days") is identical in instrumetation, style and voices to "Hootenanny Party", and could be dated this day. Timings given are approximate.

23 March, 1964 (FRI) - YOUR FIRST IMPRESSION*
                       NBC-TV Hollywood

                Guests: Spike Jones and Spike Jones Jr.

5 April, 1964 (SUN)
          Interview with Spike by Bill Ballance, KFWB, Los Angeles. Subject: Beatles, and other fads

8 May (FRI), 14 May (THURS), 1964 - Radio Recorders, Hollywood
                Client: Liberty Records
                Producer: Dave Pell

                "The New Band of Spike Jones"

                Personnel similar to previous "New Band" listing;
                        with Ted Nash, sax/clar; Ed Kusby, trb;
                        Frank Capp, drm

                LP LIB LRP 3370/LST 7370; LIB LST-4-7370;
      (2:28)My Man - inst

                LP LIB LRP 3370/LST 7370;
      (2:10)Sophisticated Lady - inst

                LP LIB LRP 3370/LST 7370; ET AFRS "World of
                        Show Business" 475; AFRS "Ira Cook" 1128;
      (2:05)Temptation - inst

359

<u>45</u> 55718-B; <u>LP</u> <u>LIB LRP 3370/LST 7370</u>;
LST-4-7370;
(2:19)<u>Paradise</u> - inst

<u>LP</u> <u>LIB LRP 3370/LST 7370</u>; <u>ET</u> AFRS "Ira
Cook" 1122;
(2:07)<u>Stairway To the Stars</u> - inst

<u>45</u> 55718-A; <u>LP</u> <u>LIB LRP 3370/LST 7370</u>; LIB
LST-4-7370; <u>ET</u> AFRS "Ira Cook" 1111;
(2:16)<u>I'm In the Mood For Love</u> - inst

<u>LP</u> <u>LIB LRP 3370/LST 7370</u>;
(2:32)<u>Lefty Louie</u> - inst

<u>LP</u> <u>LIB LRP 3370/LST 7370</u>; LIB LST-4-7370;
<u>ET</u> AFRS "Sound of the 60's" No. 4;
(2:03)<u>Ballin' the Jack</u> - inst

<u>LP</u> <u>LIB LRP 3370/LST 7370</u>; <u>ET</u> AFRS "Small
World" 140; AFRS "Sound of the 60's" No.6;
(2:33)<u>Harlem Nocturne</u> - inst

<u>LP</u> <u>LIB LRP 3370/LST 7370</u>; LIB LST-4-7370;
<u>ET</u> AFRS "Ira Cook" 2891;
(2:04)<u>The Glow Worm</u> - inst

<u>LP</u> <u>LIB LRP 3370/LST 7370</u>;
<u>ET</u> AFRS "Ira Cook" 1395;
(2:01)<u>Shangri-La</u> - inst

<u>LP</u> <u>LIB LRP 3370/LST 7370</u>; LIB LST-4-7370;
<u>ET</u> AFRS "Small World" 134;
(2:23)<u>The Stripper</u> - inst

Note: The two May recording dates courtesy of Ted Nash. One further May date would complete the recording necessary for this Liberty album, probably 11 May. In most cases, four titles were recorded at each three hour session. The 7" LP, LST-4-7370, was a juke-box special, with each side as one cut and no dead groove.

THE CRAZIEST SHOW ON EARTH

"Spike Jones and Helen Grayco, along with Spike's 'New Band' plus his 'City Slickers' will be joined by 'The Beverly Hillbillies', 'The Good-Time Singers' (from Andy Williams TV show), and Homer and Jethro, to comprise one of the most important concert packages of 1964.
"This exciting production, created by Eddie Sherman, will open May 15th, in San Francisco and traveling entirely by chartered Constellation will appear in 18 cities in 16 days.
"Presented by Concerts Inc., a subsidiary of National General Corp., this attraction will appear only in auditoriums with a seating capacity of over 12,000 and will charge an admission of $5.00 top."   (advance PR, prepared by Bruce McCrae)

Personnel unknown (Brian Farnon rehearsed the
re-formed Slickers and conducted the acts
but not the Slickers show)

"The Show of the Year, featuring"

360

        Irene Ryan, Donna Douglas, Max Baer (the Beverly Hillbill-
ies), Spike Jones, Helen Grayco, Homer and Jethro, the Good Time
Singers, Yonley, the Maldonado Dancers, the Rudenko Brothers. Staged
and directed by Jerry Franks.

15 May, 1964 (FRI)
                        Cow Palace, San Francisco
                        Evening perf

        Note: Although advertised, this performance did not take
place.

16 May, 1964 (SAT)
                        Arena, Long Beach
                        Evening perf

17 May, 1964 (SUN)
                        Coliseum, Ft. Wayne, Ind.
                        Matinee

                        Kiel Auditorium, St. Louis, Mo.
                        Evening perf

18 May, 1964 (MON)
                        Off

19 May, 1964 (TUES)
                        Memorial Auditorium, Dallas, Texas
                        Evening perf

20 May, 1964 (WED)
                        Will Rogers Memorial Aud. Ft. Worth, Texas
                        Evening perf

21 May, 1964 (THURS)
                        Coliseum, Houston, Texas

22 May, 1964 (FRI)
                        Civic Arena, Pittsburg, Pa.
                        Evening perf

23 May, 1964 (SAT)
                        International Amphitheatre, Chicago, Ill.
                        Evening perf

24 May, 1964 (SUN)
                        Municipal Auditorium, St. Paul, Minn.
                        Matinee

                        Auditorium, Minneapolis, Minn.
                        Evening perf

25 May, 1964 (MON)
                        Off

26 May, 1964 (TUES)
                        Arena, Sioux Falls, Iowa
                        Evening perf

27 May, 1964 (WED)
           Veterans Memorial Aud., Des Moines, Iowa
           Evening perf

28 May, 1964 (THURS)
           Coliseum, Charlotte, N.C.
           Evening perf

29 May, 1964 (FRI)
           Civic Center, Baltimore, Md.
           Evening perf

30 May, 1964 (SAT)
           Trade & Convention Centre, Philadelphia, Pa.
           Evening perf

31 May, 1964 (SUN)
           Auditorium, Cleveland, Ohio
           Matinee

           Auditorium, Milwaukee, Wis.
           Evening perf

1 June, 1964 (MON)
           Travel to Los Angeles

17 June (WED) to 13 July (MON), 1964
           Spike Jones and "The Craziest Show On Earth"
           Showboat Hotel, Las Vegas, Nev.
           9:30 PM and midnight shows

28 July (TUES) to 8 August (SAT), 1964
           Spike Jones and "The Craziest Show On Earth"
           The Cave, Vancouver, British Columbia
           (advertising Helen Grayco and company of 16)

11 August (TUES) to 16 August (SUN), 1964
           Disneyland, Anaheim
           Three shows nightly, tues to sun
           Four shows fri, sat

           Leader - Spike Jones
           Brass - Gene Ceriano, tpt; Jimmy Dell, trb
           Reeds - Sandy Stewart, sax
           Rhythm - Frankie Tamm, pno; Tommy Terry, bass;
             Cubby O'Brian, drm; unknown guit/bjo
           Voc/act - Helen Grayco, Peter James, Bob Nelson,
           Artie Palmer (acc), Illona Wilson

      Note: Opening to "Persian Market", the show included "Sabre
Dance", "Hootennay Party", "Evolution of Music" and a Slickers medley of hits. Mousketeer Cubby O'Brian drummed and danced to "Cute".

August, September 1964 - Radio Recorders, Hollywood
           Client: Liberty Records
           Producer: Dave Pell

           "The New Band of Spike Jones"

           Personnel similar to previous sessions, with

Lloyd Ulyate, trb; Dick Anderson, clar; Tommy
Morgan, harmonica; Al Hendrickson, guit;
Al Stoller, drm

45 55768-A; LP LIB LRP 3401/LST 7401; ET AFRS
"Basic Music Library" P-9227; AFRS "America's
Popular Music" 1298; AFRS "Small World" 181;
AFRS "World of Show Business" 518;
(3:02)Jambalaya -inst

LP LIB LRP 3401/LST 7401; ET AFRS "Basic
Music Library" P-9227;
(2:18)I Saw the Light - inst

LP LIB LRP 3401/LST 7401; ET AFRS "Basic
Music Library" P-9227;
(2:13)Move It On Over - inst

LP LIB LRP 3401/LST 7401; ET AFRS "Basic
Music Library" P-9227;
(2:23)Weary Blues From Waitin' - inst

LP LIB LRP 3401/LST 7401; ET AFRS "Basic
Music Library" P-9227; AFRS "Sound of the
60's" No. 13;
(2:18)There'll Be No Teardrops Tonight - inst

LP LIB LRP 3401/LST 7401; ET AFRs "Basic
Music Library" P-9227; AFRS "America's
Popular Music" 1347; AFRS "Ira Cook" 1240;
(1:46)Your Cheatin' Heart - inst

45 55768-B; LP LIB LRP 3401/LST 7401;
ET AFRS "Basic Music Library" P-9228;
(2:20)Hey, Good Lookin' - inst

LP LIB LRP 3401/LST 7401; ET AFRS "Basic
Music Library" P-9228;
(2:27)Cold, Cold Heart - inst

LP LIB LRP 3401/LST 7401; ET AFRS "Basic
Music Library" P-9228;
(1:45)I'm So Lonesome I Could Cry - inst

LP LIB LRP 3401/LST 7401; ET AFRS "Basic
Music Library" P-9228;
(2:20)Kaw-Liga - inst

LP LIB LRP 3401/LST 7401; ET AFRS "Basic
Music Library" P-9228;
(2:16)I Can't Help It (if I'm Still In Love With You)
- inst

LP LIB LRP 3401/LST 7401; ET AFRS "Basic
Music Library" P-9228;
(1:55)You Win Again - inst

"...and have worked with literally hundreds of musicians on
all sorts of sessions...I do well remember the sessions (incidentally, some of the most enjoyable I have ever been on)..."
(Dick Anderson correspondence 3 Oct 83)

363

Tommy Morgan, harmonica, remembers Carl Brandt as "thoroughly professional!"

January, 1965
>   Cork Club, Houston, Texas

>   Personnel as August 1964, with Gene Pello, drm,
>   for Cubby O'Brian(who had left New Years Eve);
>   (Dell and Terry as 'The Goofers')

Note: This engagement was for two weeks with three/four shows per day. Titles included "Chloe", "Cocktails For Two", "What Kind of Fool Am I?". Dancing between shows to the Mel Arvin Orch.

1965 - Radio Recorders, Hollywood
>   Client: Liberty Records

>   "The New Band of Spike Jones"

>   Personnel similar to previous session

>   45 LIB 55788-B;
>   Star Jenka - inst

>   45 LIB 55788-A; ET AFRS "World of Show
>   Business" 570; AFRS "Sound of the 60's" 25;
>   Let's Kiss, Kiss, Kiss - inst

Note: The above two titles were produced to capitalize on a Finnish dance craze which, while expected to become popular, didn't. Spike was not at this c.March 1965 session.

Spike, 5'-10-1/2", with blue eyes, Sandy colored hair and never weighing more than 141 lbs., was a chronic chain smoker, though he always chewed gum on personal appearances. The frenetic pace of life and incredibly high standards of performance he demanded of himself and his personnel wore him out, making him susceptible to illnesses. Emphysema had been diagnosed five years earlier, but Spike refused to stop or cut down on his dependence on tobaccco, and during appearances, he spent less and less time on stage - hitting the odd cowbell, etc. with minimal dialogue, spending most of his time in a portable oyxgen tent backstage, as mentally alert as he ever was but barely having the strength to perform.

"Spike and I had been friends for years", 'Doc' Rando recalls. "When I finished Medical school and began practising in medicine, (c.'60) he consulted me about his chest problems - however, I was a surgeon and could only offer my friend advice."

"Helen Grayco is currently featured with Spike Jones and his City Slickers, the 'Craziest Show On Earth', in the Mardi Gras Room of the Hotel Showboat." (similar show/personnel as January 65)
>   (Las Vegas Sun, 6 Mar 65)

While performing in San Diego, Spike had a bad attack and was driven in an ambulance to L.A. (100 miles). Admitted into hospital on March 31, he was released, somewhat recovered, on April 8th.

1 May, 1965 (SAT)
"Los Angeles Bandleader, Spike Jones, 53, the zany musician who entertained millions with his offbeat arrangements, died in his sleep Saturday at his Bel Aire home.

"Jones had been released from nearby Santa Monica hospital three weeks ago following treatment for an asthma attack and subsequent respiratory complications.

"Peter James, his agent, said the bandleader had apparently recovered from his lengthy sickness until he suffered a slight relapse Friday afternoon. His personal physician was called and remained with him till he died, James said.

"Also at home were Jones' widow, Helen Grayco, and their three children." (Winona Daily News, Winona, Minn, May 65)

"A requiem mass will be sung 10 a.M. Tuesday (4 May) at St. Victor's Roman Catholic Church in West Hollywood. Interment will be at the Holy Cross Cemetary." (New York Times, 2 May 65)

As his very dear friend and colleague, Mickey Katz, phrased it in his autobiography, "Spike simply ran out of breath".

On November 8, 1965, the above band (January, but without Grayco and Wilson) appeared on the Danny Thomas NBC-TV (color) show, "What Makes People Laugh", for Timex and Consolidated Cigars. "Danny Thomas Presents the Comics" introduced Spike Jones Jr. and the City Slickers.

365

Appendix A—Unfinished and Undated Projects, Unreleased Titles, Souvenirs, Spin-off Recordings and Miscellaneous Information

The following titles were in various stages of completion by Spike at the time of his death. On most, only the basics were tracked for vocal and 'audibles' overdubbing/editing at a later time. The album "Persuasive Concussions", Spike's answer to the popular stereo series "Persuasive Percussion", was to have featured recreations of some of the Slickers original hits and many new adaptions in the popular Slicker style. Started c.1960, most titles were done from 1961 to 1963, with a few dating to 1964. "Holiday For Strings", while unfinished, has been issued on the United Artists label. (Perhaps the estate might consider issuing certain titles as a Spike Jones "Music Minus One" album for those aspiring to effects, vocals and 'glugs'!)

Persuasive Concussions (stereo basics for LP)
(1:28) Cocktails For Two - chorus/voc unrealized
(2:36) Chloe - voc Red Ingle
(3:08) That Old Black Magic - voc unrealized

LP UA-LA 439-E;
(3:18) Holiday For Strings - inst

(3:31) A Goose to the Ballet Russe - voc unrealized
(3:26) Powerhouse - inst
(4:08) Carmen - inst (new arr.)
(4:27) Shh! Harry's Odd (Scheherazade) - inst

Identical instrumentals, with alternate effects
(2:31) Frantic Freeway - inst
(2:24) Beep Beep Pachanga (alternate effects to above)
(Sigalert Bossa Nova) (45rpm mono master made)

Leonard Burnside discusses the Ballet (basic for LP)
Leonard Burnside discusses the Violin (basic for LP)

(non-LP projects)
(2:23) Powerhouse (45 RPM mono master made, to have been flip of "Frantic Freeway")
(2:21) Ghoul Days (stereo) - with vocal (see 25 Jan 64)
(2:47) Nyet (stereo basic, complete mono) - with voice
Hot Rod Bash - Doodles Weaver (update on car names, "Wild" on recording log indicates an unslated effect - concludes with "Feetlebaum")
$18.12 Overture
Wonderful World of Susie Poontong
Jackie Gleason
Pantomime Theme

Note: The last four titles never progressed beyond the title
stage, although Spike's house maid is quoted as saying she had heard
the stereo version of $18.12 Overture. Timings to above approximate.

NBC carried the show "Monitor", a weekend variety show during the early 1960s. Comedy skits were very short drop-ins, often
using popular radio stars of the 40s, such as Fibber McGee and Molly,
and Bob and Ray. Intended for the show, but probably not used were
the following Leonard Burnside skits: (mono, c.1960)
        (5:06)Leonard Burnside discusses Mozart (cut from 5:36)
        (4:30)Leonard Burnside discusses the LP (cut from 4:50)

Radio commercials, undated

      Rayburn and Finch time cues (WNEW), prepared for two New
York Disc Jockeys. Time signals and weather jingles featuring George
Rock and Dick Morgan. c.1947 (wild tracks!)
      "Magic Circle", the Big Sound RAM-1-R(12"), Richard H.
Ullman Inc., "This is Spike Jones. We are going to play one of my
records - so GET THE KIDS OUT OF THE HOUSE!!" (wild tracks!)c.1957.
Both standard and microgroove transcriptions were pressed

c.1960   WOPA, Oak Park, Ill (via telephone)
          Interview with Eddie Cuda. Subject: "Omnibust"

c.1961   KRHM-FM, Los Angeles
          Interview by Johnny (World of Music) Green. Subject:
"Spike Jones in Stereo" (Copy not in Jones' files. The interview which produced this acetate does not show in the
1961 date book. Subject matter indicates early 1960 date)

c.Nov 1963
          WOPA, Oak Park, Ill (via telephone)
          Interview with Linn Burton. Subject: "New Band"

Million record sales

      From the book, "THE BOOK OF GOLDEN DISCS"(Million Sellers),
as compiled by Joseph Murrells and published by Barrie & Jenkins,
London, 1974

p. 42	Der Fuehrer's Face	1.5 million very quickly
p. 48	Cocktails For Two	1 million by 1946
p. 54	Glow Worm	
p. 65	All I Want For Christmas - 1 million by 1949	

      It is curious that 'Der Fuehrer's Face' is not included in
all publications purportedly surveying the musical hits through the
years. The only official figures available in print that show its
sales of over 1 million originate from Spike Jones own promotion, as
does the mention of six (or seven, depending on the date of the PR
package) gold, or million record sellers.

Spike Jones, his City Slickers and his auto horns did not participate
in the Phil Harris, Dinah Shore, Tony Martin, Betty Hutton RCA Victor
recording, "How Do You Do and Shake Hands" (by Oliver Wallace), although his horns are credited on the label.

AFRS Polka Party (12" Christmas '64) contains a quasi dixie/new band
version of "...My Two Front Teeth", introduced "as played by Spike
Jones and his City Slickers". The resemblance to the New Band is, at
times, striking. It is the Mary Kaye Trio with no Jones involvement.

AFRS G.I. Jive (16") 1059 and 1100 are occasionally listed as Jones ETs. The titles of "Tampico" and "It's Been a Long Long Time" belong to Stan Kenton, not Spike Jones.

Richard Sears has forwarded the following Downbeat mentions re: Jones
    1 Dec 44   City Slickers recording Swing Symphony for Walter Lantz;
   15 Dec 44   City Slickers to record music for cartoon, not seen but
               caricatured;
    1 Mar 45   George Pal Puppetoon - "Cocktails For Two".

        According to Spike's publicity/biography c.1960, the City Slickers did not participate in the making of any cartoons. However, the "Boogie Woogie Man" of Walter Lantz (who did "The King of Jazz" animation) has been identified as having Slickers involvement. As well, there are some who feel Jones was involved with at least one George Pal Puppetoon. Walter Lantz' "Siam", based on Del Porter's song, is not backed by the Slickers.

Souvenirs:-

Spike Jones "Free Seed Corn", from Gilmore Gas stations, c.1943/44.
Spike Jones Bubble-Gum - available during the Musical Depreciation
        tours.
Spike Jones Souvenir Programs - sold during the Musical Depreciation/
        Insanities tours.
Spike Jones Sax-O-Fun - a plastic saxophone-shaped kazoo, in boxes
        with pictures of Spike and the band. Made (est. 100,000) by
        the Trophy Products Company (Depreciation tours).
Spike Jones, the City Slickers and acts photographs - in plentiful
        supply for the years 1948 to 1952.
Spike Jones movie lobby cards, decalomania, balloons, playing cards.
Spike Jones Christmas and post cards, letter heads, various promo-
        ional materials (window cards, banners, bumper strips, im-
        print napkins) for RCA to Verve, Liberty records and tours.

Spike Jones Drums - available c. 1950, Coleman & Morris (Colmor),
        manufacturers of toys and novelties, NY, NY
        "I get letters from distracted mothers asking my help in
getting junior to practice. I get letters from kids who want informa-
ion about my noise-making gadgets.
        "Recently I helped a manufacturer put out a small set of
Spike Jones drums at a price most parents can afford to pay."
        There were two packages available, consisting of: a 13" or
20" bass drum with "City Slickers Junior" printed on the drum head
and the Red Ingle caricature of Spike with boxing gloves and baton; a
6" or 8" snare drum/tom-tom; cymbal; triangle; four-key xylophone.
The 20" drum set was listed in Gimbel's Christmas catalog at $5.98.

Spike Jones correspondence originating at his office in Hollywood or
on the road was individually enhanced by the use of a special
character - a 'spike' in place of the letter 'i' at every instance
the name Spike was typed.

Spike Jones hand puppets, in a box rubber stamped "I am Spike Jones"
        Made by Zany Toys, Jay V. Zimmerman Co., St. Louis 3, Mo.
        Copyright 1951. Used on the second Colgate Comedy Show.
        Others advertised included Bob Hope.

Sheet and folio music - including many titles "as recorded by...."
("Under the Double Eagle", Country Cousins) but not issued, and "as
played by..." ("I Got 'Em", Horse Trader Ed) once only, on radio.

Black and White 16mm silent animated cartoon with the Ingle caricature of Spike's face. As he chews gum, the necktie spins. Used on the
1954 TV series. Many prints were made on 50-foot reels for Arena
Stars, with exact use unknown.

Spike Jones appeared on the covers of:-
        Billboard Magazine - 30 July 49, 15 Oct 49, 11 Mar 50,
                        5 Aug 50,
        Downbeat Magazine - 15 July 46, 12 Aug 49,

After Spike's death, "Spike Jones' Oodles of Noodles" restaurant at
163 N. La Cienega, Beverly Hills, opened. "Noodles" was a scaled down
version of the incompleted "Spike's Speak", a restaurant designed to
capitalize on the surge of popularity of the nostalgic "Rides, Rapes
and Rescues" - the Roaring 20s era. "The Roaring 20s", a successful
supper club in San Diego, was the model for Spike's Speak. "Noodles"
also featured Jones memorabalia, such as the Gas (Bennett) paintings
of "Blue Boy", "Mona Lisa", and original Spike Dyke artwork, etc.

'Spin-off' recordings of interest
        Del Porter and the "Sweet Potato Tooters": Capitol Trans-
            criptions; N-1, N-2, N-3, N-4, N-5, N-6, N-7, N-8.
        Mickey Katz: 45/78 RPM on RCA Victor International and
            Capitol. Could be mistaken for Jones...:- "Hole in the
            Iron Curtain"; "Tiger Rag" (w/Del Porter on 45rpm flip);
            "Barber of Schlemiel" (78rpm, not LP remake)."Schlemiel"
            78/45rpm flip vocal King Jackson on "Happy Pay Off Day")
        Red Ingle: 45/78 RPM, with the 'Natural Seven' on Mercury
            and Capitol. Joining Ingle on "Moe Zart's Turkey Trot"
            is Frank "the Terrible Turk" Leithner.
        Helen Grayco: 45/78 RPM on London, Mercury and RCA label
            'X', LPs on Verve and RCA 'Vik' label.
        Doodles Weaver: "Feetlebaum Returns" LP, Fremont LRS M-5074;
            INTRO 78rpm records, racetrack routine with political
            figures(Truman, etc.) and "April Showers" on flip.
        Freddy Morgan: Three "Bunch-a-Banjos" LPs on Liberty,
            45 RPM banjo singles on Enith label.
        Jad Paul: Banjo LPs on Liberty.
        The New Society Band:(includes Rock, Siracusa, Gray) "Shoves
            It In Your Ear", Electric Lemon LP PLP 1906 (c.1969)
        George Rock: 45 RPM singles on Dyna label, plus vocals with
            Phil Gray band.
        Eddie Brandt and his Hollywood Hicks: London 78/45 RPM,
            "Hollywood Baby Sitter" with Carl Grayson, Harry Stanton
            and Lynn Johnson. Also TV pilot with same tune and Paul
            Frees impersonations.
        Spike Jones Jr: 45 RPM singles on Viva, Dore & Chinchilla.
            Demolition Disco (based on "Frantic Freeway") CH 22.
        Mel Blanc: 78/45 RPM on Capitol. ("Toot Toot Tootsie" ala
            Jolson is often circulated as Slickers).
        Bozo on the Farm: Capitol. Slickers orchestration by Billy
            May to "Poet & Peasant", with Mickey Katz and Stan
            Freberg.

The Chase and Sanborn shows, many of the Spotlight Revue shows and a
scant few of the Bob Burns shows are available on reel-to-reel and
occasional cassette from many of the tape clubs throughout North
America. Of the many companies dealing with vintage radio shows and
dubs, the author's personal stock was purchased from Golden Age Radio
of Portland, OR, and McCoys of Richland, WA. These and others ad-
dresses, such as Larry Kiner's 'Redmond Nostalgia', are to found in
the classified sections of current trade journals on music/records/
electronics.

Appendix B—Domestic and Foreign LP Issues

Domestic

RCA Victor

LPM 18 (10")   Spike Jones Plays The Charleston
auth 16 Jan '52   The Charleston; Black Bottom; I Wonder Where My
                      Baby Is Tonight?; Varsity Drag; Doin' The New
                      Raccoon; Charlestono-Mio

LPM 3054 (10")   Bottoms Up
auth 25 Jul '52   Bottoms Up; Sante; Drink To the Bonnie Lassies;
                      A Din Skal, A Min Skal; Gesundheit Polka;
                      Slanthe; Salute; Cherrio

LPM 3128 (10")   Spike Jones Murders Carmen and Kids The Classics
auth 1 May 53   William Tell Overture; Dance Of the Hours;
                      Rhapsody From Hunger(y); None But the Lonely
                      Heart; Carmen (Murdered)

LPM 2224 ('60)   Thank You, Music Lovers
LPM 3849('67); LSP 3849(e)('67); ANL1 1035(e)('75); AYL1 3748('81)
                      The Best Of Spike Jones
                      Cocktails For Two; William Tell Oveture; Chloe;
                      My Old Flame; Glow Worm; None But the Lonely
                      Heart; Laura; Man On the Flying Trapeze; You
                      Always Hurt the One You Love; Der Fuehrer's
                      Face; Dance of the Hours; Hawaiian War Chant

ANL1 2312(e)('77); AYL1 3870(e)('81)
                      The Best Of Spike Jones, Volume 2
                      That Old Black Magic; Love In Bloom; Chinese
                      Mule Train; I'm In the Mood For Love; Riders
                      In the Sky; Liebestraum; Charleston; Yes, We
                      Have No Bananas; Japanese Skokiaan(alternate
                      take); Bubble Gum Song(Blowing Bubble Gum); The
                      Tennessee Waltz; I Dream Of Brownie with the
                      Light Blue Jeans

                      (8-Track cartridge mistakenly titles "Skokiaan"
                         as "Japanese Sand Man")

LSC 3235(e)('71); AGL1 4142(e)('81)
                      Spike Jones Is Murdering The Classics
                      William Tell Overture; Rhapsody From Hunger(y);
                      Pal-Yat-Chee; Liebestraum; Blue Danube; Jones
                      Laughing Record; Nutcracker Suite(condensed);
                      Dance of the Hours; None But the Lonely Heart;
                      Morpheus(condensed); Ill Barkio; Carmen

ACL 7031(e)('76) The Hilarious Spike Jones
                  (Victor masters, Pickwick/Camden release)
                  My Old Flame; Dance of the Hours; You Always
                  Hurt the One You Love; Liebestraum; Glow Worm;
                  Chinese Mule Train; Blue Danube; Chloe; Laura

Verve
MGV 4005; GO 10010('82)
                  Dinner Music For People Who Aren't Very Hungry
                  Space Ship Landing; Assorted Glugs, Pbrts, and
                  skks; Ramona; Misha's Souvenir(Violin and Garbage
                  Disposal Duet); Black and Blue Danube Waltz;
                  Stark's Theme; Old Sow Song; Pal-Yat-Chee; How
                  High the Fidelity; *Cocktails For Two; Wyatt Earp
                  Makes Me Burp; Woofer's Lament; Memories Are Made
                  Of This; Sneezin' Bee; Little Child; Brahms Alibi;
                  *Chloe
             (* source: Standard Transcriptions)

MGV 2021   Spike Jones Presents A Christmas Spectacular
MGV 2021   Let's Sing A Song Of Christmas
MGV 8654   35 Reasons Why Christmas Can Be Fun
MGM SE-4731(e)   Let's Sing A Song Of Christmas
GO 10011('83)   It's A Spike Jones Christmas (re-mastered)
                  Jingle Bells Medley(Santa Claus Is Comin' To Town;
                  Christmas Song; Jingle Bells); All I Want For
                  Christmas Is My Two Front Teeth; Night Before
                  Christmas Song; Rudolph The Red-Nosed Reindeer;
                  Silent Night; Sleigh Ride; My Birthday Comes On
                  Christmas; Snow Medley(First Snowfall; Let It
                  Snow); Nuttin' For Christmas; Deck the Halls
                  Medley(Deck the Halls With Boughs Of Holly; Away
                  In a Manger; It Came Upon a Midnight Clear; First
                  Noel); White Christmas Medley(Winter Wonderland;
                  Silver Bells; White Christmas); (I'm the) Angel In
                  the Christmas Play; Christmas Cradle Song; Frosty
                  the Snowman; Hark Medley(Hark the Herald Angels
                  Sing; O Little Town Of Bethlehem; Joy To the
                  World; O Come All Ye Faithful); Christmas Alphabet
                  Medley(Christmas Alphabet; Merry Christmas Polka;
                  Christmas In America); Santa Claus's Son(con-
                  densed); Christmas Island; Victor Young Medley
                  (It's Christmas Time; Sleep Well, Little Child-
                  ren); Here Comes Santa Claus; What Are You Doing
                  New Years Eve?

MGV 2065   Mr. Banjo - Freddy Morgan
                  (Supervised by Spike Jones)
                  Chinatown, My Chinatown; Somebody Stole My Gal;
                  Nowbody's Sweetheart Now; Pickin' Melody In F;
                  Sweet Sue, Just You; Liebes-strum; Why Did You
                  Let Me Leave You?; Yes Sir, That's My Baby; The
                  World Is Waiting For the Sunrise; Ain't She Sweet;
                  My Banjo At Thy Sweet Voice; Bye Bye Blues; Pretty
                  Posie; Five Foot Two, Eyes Of Blue; Swingin' the
                  Double Eagle; William Tell Overture

MGV 2066   Hi-Fi Polka Party - The Polka Dots
                  (Supervised by Spike Jones)
                  Lawrence Welk Polka; Pennsylvania Polka; Bottoms
                  Up Polka; Happy Trumpets Polka; Pretty Girl Polka;
                  Six Fat Dutchmen Polka; Ron Terry Polka; Whoopee
                  John Polka; Frank Yankovic Waltz; New Beer Barrel
                  Polka; Funny Punny Polka; Strip Polka

Warner Brothers
B-1332 (mono)   Spike Jones In Hi-Fi
WS-1332 (stereo)   Spike Jones In Stereo
                     I Only Have Eyes For You; Poisen To Poisen;
                     Teen Age Brain Surgeon; (All Of A Sudden) My Heart
                     Sings; Everything Happens To Me; Monster Movie
                     Ball; Tammy; My Old Flame; This Is Your Death; Two
                     Heads Are Better Than One; Spooktacular Finale

Liberty Records (mono/stereo)
LRP 3140/LST 7140 Omnibust
                     Ah-1, Ah-2, Ah Sunset Strip; Loretta's Soap-
                     eretta; Captain Bangaroo; Late Late Movies,
                     Part 1; Wonderful World Of Hari Kari; I Search
                     For Adventure In My Seven Leaky Boots; Mudder's
                     Day Sports Spectacular; Late Late Movies, Part2

LRP 3154/LST 7154 60 Years Of Music America Hates Best
                     I Kiss Your Hand Madame; Knock Knock, Who's
                     There?; River Stay 'Way From My Door; Pimples
                     and Braces; Hut Sut Song; Strip Polka; Mairzy
                     Doats; 20's Roar; Melody Of Love; Three Little
                     Fishies; Spooky Spooky, Lend Me Your Tomb

LRP 3185/LST 7185 Rides, Rapes and Rescues
                         (Hangnails Hennessey and Wingy Brubeck)
                     Keystone Kapers or Custard's Last Stand; Silents
                     Please, "Pearls of Murine"; Lips That Touch Liquor
                     Shall Never Touch Mine; A Mustache, A Derby, A
                     Cane and A Cop; Theda Barracuda Meets Rudolph
                     Vaselino; Great Train Robbery; Beautiful Bathing
                     Beauties; Winning Of The West; Curses! If Jack
                     Dalton Were Only Here; Cotton Pickin' Peasant
                     Overture; Stars And Stripes Flicker Finale

LST 101   This Is Stereo
                     Narration and stereo demonstration by Spike Jones.
                        Contains "Feetlebaum Bombs In Louisville" (A
                        Mudder's Day Sports Spectacular) from
                        Omnibust album

LRP 3338/LST 7338 Washington Square - The New Band Of Spike Jones
                     *Alley Cat; Ballad Of Jed Clampett; Frankie And
                     Johnnie; *Maria Elena; *Green Green; *Washington
                     Square; *September Song; *Blowing In the Wind;
                     Puff, the Magic Dragon; Red Sails In the Sunset;
                     Whistler's Muddah; If I Had a Hammer
                *available on Coin Operator's 7"LP LST-4-3338

LRP 3349/LST 7349 Spike Jones' New Band
                     Dominique; Kansas City; Whispering; Java;
                     Deep Purple; Charade; There I've Said It Again;
                     Stoplight; Manana; For You; Hey Mr. Banjo;
                     Sweet and Lovely;

LRP 3370/LST 7370 My Man
                     *My Man; Sophisticated Lady; Temptation;
                     *Paradise; Stairway To the Stars; *I'm In the Mood
                     For Love; Lefty Louie; *Ballin' The Jack; Harlem
                     Nocturne; *Glow Worm; Shangri-La; *Stripper
                *available on Coin Operator's 7"LP LST-4-7370

LRP 3401/LST 7401 The New Band Of Spike Jones Plays
                         Hank William Hits
                   Jambalaya; I Saw the Light; Move It On Over; Weary
                   Blues From Waitin'; There'll Be No Teardrops To-
                   night; Your Cheatin' Heart; Hey, Good Lookin';
                   Cold Cold Heart; I'm So Lonesome I Could Cry;
                   Kaw-liga; I Can't Help It; You Win Again

United Artists (re-issue of Liberty masters)
UA LA439-E('75)   The Very Best Of Spike Jones
                   Holiday For Strings (incomplete); River, Stay
                   'Way From My Door; Feetlebaum Bombs; September
                   Song; Late Late Movies, part 1; I Kiss Your
                   Hand Madame; Ah-1, Ah-2, Ah-Sunset Strip; Strip
                   Polka; Late Late Movies, part 2

MF Distribution Co. 947447('77); GO 10016('84)
                   Spike Jones (3 record set)
                   (sources: radio/television performances)
                   Der Fuehrer's Face; Pass the Biscuits Mirandy;
                   Chloe; Hotcha Cornia; Hawaiian War Chant; William
                   Tell Overture; I'm Getting Sentimental Over You;
                   Holiday For Strings; Cocktails For Two; My Two
                   Front Teeth; Dance of the Hours; Riders In the
                   Sky; Tiger Rag; Connecticut Yankee In King
                   Arthur's Court; Nature Boy; Liebestraum; Want Ads
                   (edited); In A Persian Market; Pootwaddle Cigar-
                   ettes(commerical); You Can't Be True Dear; Barney
                   Google; Portia and the Hollywood Wolf; Farandole;
                   Yes Sir That's My Baby; Minka; San Antonio Rose;
                   You Always Hurt the One You Love; Tchaikovsky
                   Medley; Love In Bloom; Minnie the Moocher; Old
                   Time Medley; Flight of the Bumble Bee; Chantez,
                   Chantez; Smiles Medley; Dark Moon; Big Bands;
                   Another Old Time Medley

MF 205/4   The Complete Collection (4 record set)
                   (the following, in addition to the above)
                   That's A Plenty; Barber of Seville; Ya Wanna Buy
                   A Bunny?; Football Medley (USC vs. Notre Dame);
                   Near You; Over the Rainbow; Ballerina; Pootwaddle
                   Toothpaste(commercial); Funnies Aren't Funny Any-
                   more; That Old Black Magic; Quartet From Rigor
                   Mortis;

       Note: The above sets, by mail order only, were also intended
as single disc/tape issue: MF 411/412/413/414; 8 track cartridges
8411/8412/8413/8414; and cassettes 4411/4412/4413/4414, all from MF
Distribution Co, via Publishers Central Bureau, New York

Golden Spike (Bootleg record, 1000 reportedly pressed)
GS 1754('75)   And The Great Big Saw Came Nearer And Nearer And
                         Nearer ...(source: Standard Transcriptions,
                              except as noted)
                   The Great Big Saw Came Nearer and Nearer; Put Your
                   Arms Around Me, Honey(Treasury Song Parade); Big
                   Bad Bill; Don't Give the Chair To Buster; Hotcha
                   Cornia(V-Disc,condensed); They Go Wild, Simply
                   Wild Over Me; De Camptown Races; Never Hit Your
                   Grandma With a Shovel; Don't Talk To Me About
                   Women; Down On the O-Hi-O; Camptown Races No. 2;
                   Oh How She Lied; Liebestraum(edited)

Silver Swan (Bootleg record, 500 reportedly pressed)
LP 1002(c.'75)   Spike Jones' Musical Depreciation Revue
                     (source: US Navy "Land's Best Bands",
                        with dialogue edited)
                     Charlie My Boy; Shortnin' Bread; Ballet For
                     Bosun's Mate; Five Foot Two, Eyes Of Blue; 'Way
                     Down Yonder In New Orleans; Man on the Flying
                     Trapeze; Morpheus; Charlestono-Mio; Oh! By Jingo;
                     Mommy, Won't You Buy a Baby Brother; There's Noth-
                     ing Like a Circus; April Showers; My Gal Sal;
                     Molasses Molasses; Dance of the Hours; Yaaka Hula
                     Hickey Dula

Cornographic 1001('76), Glendale 6005
                     The King Of Corn
Sandy Hook SH 2073 - Spike Jones On The Air(Pirated record)('83)
                     (source: Furlough Fun/Bob Burns air checks)
                     People Will Say We're In Love; G.I. Haircut; It
                     Never Rains In Sunny California; Wang Wang Blues;
                     My Little Girl; Sound Effects Man; Ragtime Cowboy
                     Joe; Vamp; He Broke My Heart In Three Places; Besa
                     Besa Me Mucho; I'm Goin' Back To Whur I Come From;
                     Trolley Song; Red Wing; There's a Fly on the
                     Music; Row Row Row; I Want a Girl, Just Like the
                     Girl; Jingle Bells
          Note: The initial release by Cornographic and subsequently
(c.'80) by its parent, Glendale, were approved by the Spike Jones
estate, and were listed in 'Phonolog'. The 1983 Sandy Hook is 'Pirated' - without such approval

The Good Music Record Co. - RCA Special Products (mail order)
DML1-0570('82)   The Wacky World Of Spike Jones
                     Cocktails For Two; William Tell Overture;
                     Holiday For Strings; Der Fuehrer's Face; None
                     But the Lonely Heart; Man on the Flying Trapeze;
                     Chloe; Hawaiian War Chant; My Old Flame; Glow
                     Worm; Yes, We Have No Bananas; You Always Hurt the
                     One You Love; Dance of the Hours; Liebestraum;
                     Love In Bloom; Sheik Of Araby; Laura; I Dream Of
                     Brownie With the Light Blue Jeans

Hindsight Records
HSR-185('82)   Spike Jones And His Other Orchestra
                     (source: Standard Transcriptions)
                     Laura; When Yuba Plays the Rhumba on the Tuba;
                     I'll Never Be the Same; Minka; I've Got the World
                     On a String; Spike Rocks the Troc; Hardly Ever
                     Amber; I Only Have Eyes For You; Pico Pick Up;
                     Young Man With a French Horn; E-Bop-O-Lee-Bop;
                     Spike Speaks(Theme)

Foreign Long Play issues

ENGLAND

RCA Victor
HY 1006('75)   That Old Black Magic
(Starcall)   That Old Black Magic; Jones Laughing Record;
                     Clink Clink Another Drink; You Wanna Buy a Bunny?;
                     MacNamara's Band; Love In Bloom; Nutcracker Suite
                     (EP edition); Charleston; Leave the Dishes in the
                     Sink Ma; I'm Getting Sentimental Over You; Mother
                     Goose Medley; Secret Love

375

LSA 3084; RD 7724 Thank You Music Lovers
                  (contents identical to domestic LPM 2224)

INTS 5052('80)   I Went To Your Wedding
(RCA Inter-   I Went To Your Wedding; I Haven't Been Home For
 national)   Three Whole Nights; Too Young; Sheik Of Araby;
                  Three Little Fishies; Pop Corn Sack; Rhapsody
                  From Hunger(y); Clink Clink, Another Drink; Old
                  MacDonald Had A Farm; I'm Getting Sentimental Over
                  You; Our Hour; People Are Funnier Than Anybody
           Note: This album may be a re-issue of an earlier release,
NL 43294

Warner Brothers
WM 4404   Spike Jones In Hi-Fi
WS 8004   Spike Jones In Stereo
                  (contents identical to domestic B-1332/WS-1332)

Liberty
HA-G 2270/SAH-G 6090
                  Omnibust
                  (contents identical to domestic LRP 3140/
                   LST 7140)

HA-G 2298/SAH-G 6109
                  Fun In Hi-Fi
                  (contents identical to domestic LRP 3154/
                   LST 7140)

        Note: It is known that "New Band" LPs were distributed in
England with identical mono/stereo release numbers to the U.S.
pressings. Whether they were import (from the U.S.) or local
pressings is not known

GERMANY

RCA Victor
LPM 10 013   The Best of Spike Jones
                  William Tell Overture; I Kiss Your Hand Madame;
                  Cocktails For Two; Hotcha Cornia; I'm Getting
                  Sentimental Over You; Blue Danube; Carmen Murder-
                  ed; Rhapsody From Hunger(y)
                  (cover modeled on domestic LPM 2224)

LSP 10157('68)   The Best Of Spike Jones, Vol. 2
(26.21113)   Holiday For Strings; Chloe; My Old Flame; Glow
                  Worm; None But the Lonely Heart; Flight of the
                  Bumble Bee; Laura; Man on the Flying Trapeze;
                  You Always Hurt the One You Love; Des Fuehrer's
                  Face; Dance of the Hours; Hawaiian War Chant

RCS 3211/1-2('73) "Murders Them All"
(26.28018)   Liebestraum; Blue Danube; Flight of the Bumble
                  Bee; None But the Lonely Heart; Rhapsody From
                  Hunger(y); William Tell Overture; Carmen Murdered;
                  Dance of the Hours; Glow Worm; I Kiss Your Hand
                  Madame; Love In Bloom; Hotcha Cornia; Black
                  Bottom; Hawaiian War Chant; I Went To Your Wed-
                  ding; I'm In the Mood For Love; That Old Black
                  Magic

376

RCS 3217/1-2('73)   "Murders Again"
(26.28019)   Clink Clink, Another Drink; Laura; My Old Flame;
                    Cocktails For Two; Chloe; Doin' The New Raccoon;
                    Old MacDonald Had a Farm; Charleston; MacNamara's
                    Band; Blowing Bubble Gum; Holiday For Strings; My
                    Pretty Girl; I'm Getting Sentimental Over You;
                    Secret Love; Our Hour; People Are Funnier Than
                    Anybody; Man on the Flying Trapeze; Der Fuehrer's
                    Face; You Always Hurt the One You Love;
                    Charlestono-Mio

PJM 2-8021('74)   "Can't Stop Murdering"
RCA International   Ill Barkio; Peter Cottontail; Deep Purple; *Riders
(26.28001)   in the Sky; Pal-Yat-Chee; *Rum Tee Diddle Dee
                    Yump; Nutcracker Suite; Morpheus; I Haven't Been
                    Home For Three Whole Nights; *Alto Baritone and
                    Bass; Tennessee Waltz; Too Young; *Rickeyshaw;
                    Chinese Mule Train; Oh! By Jingo; Sheik of Araby;
                    Wild Bill Hiccup; Three Little Fishies; Pop Corn
                    Sack; *Fiddle Faddle; I Wonder Where My Baby Is
                    Tonight; My Two Front Front Teeth; It Never Rains
                    In Sunny California
        *Previously unissued titles, with "Riders in the Sky" the
            uncensored take

NL 89057('83)   Thank You Music Lovers
                    (contents identical to domestic LPM 2224)
JAPAN

RCA Victor
5142   Spike Jones Is Murdering The Classics
                    (contents identical to domestic LSC 3235(e)

5143(m)('74)   Spike Jones Is Murdering The Pops
                    Hotcha Cornia; I Kiss Your Hand Madame; Cocktails
                    For Two; Riders in the Sky; Glow Worm; Charlestono
                    -Mio; Hawaiian War Chant; Secret Love; I'm In the
                    Mood For Love; I'm Getting Sentimental Over You;
                    My Old Flame; Laura; Der Fuehrer's Face; Chinese
                    Mule Train

RVP-6300(m)('78)   The Best Of Spike Jones
                    Hotcha Cornia; Cocktails For Two; I Kiss Your
                    Hand Madame; Hawaiian War Chant; Riders in the
                    Sky; Chinese Mule Train; Secret Love; William
                    Tell Overture; Rhapsody From Hunger(y); Jones
                    Laughing Record; Morpheus; Carmen

Verve
MGV 2119   Dinner Music For People Who Aren't Very Hungry
                    (contents identical to domestic MGV 4005)

FRANCE

RCA Victor
100255(10")   Bottoms Up (Polka a boire)
                    (contents identical to domestic LPM 3054)

130216(10")   Carmen au Texas (Opera revu et corrige sur les
                        airs de Georges Bizet Spike Jones s'amuse)
                    Carmen; This Song Is For the Birds; Japanese
                    Skokiaan; Hi Mister; I Want Eddie Fisher For
                    Christmas

377

PL 43197   "Murders Them All"
                         (contents identical to RCAG RCS 3211/1-2)

Verve
2304 436   Dinner Music For People Who Aren't Very Hungry
                         (contents identical to domestic MGV 4005)

                         Mr. Banjo - Freddy Morgan
                         (A 10" LP containing most titles reportedly
                          available)

Warner Brothers
Mode CMDW 9726   Frankenstein, Dracula and Co.
                         (contents identical to domestic B-1332)

ITALY

RCA Victor
CL 83748(Camden)   The Best Of Spike Jones
('83)   (contents identical to domestic LPM 2224)
                         Printed in Italy, distributed by RCA of
                         Belgium, W. Germany, France, Italy, Holland
                         and England

AUSTRALIA

RCA Victor
ODLP 6024(10")   Spike Jones Kids The Classics
                         Carmen; Rhapsody From Hunger(y); I Went To Your
                         Wedding; William Tell Overture; Dance of the
                         Hours

ODLP 7503(10")   A Course In Musical Depreciation
                         Cocktails For Two; That Old Black Magic; Blue
                         Danube; Hawaiian War Chant; William Tell Overture;
                         Wild Bill Hiccup; Love In Bloom; Dance of the
                         Hours

CAS 7158(Camden)   The Best Of Spike Jones
                         (contents identical to domestic LPM 2224)

        RCA ANL1 2312(e) was printed and pressed in Australia for
their market and that of New Zealand, and indications are that most
recent RCA domestic releases are so duplicated.
        The Liberty "Rides, Rapes and Rescues" was available in
Australia with the U.S. printed cover. Possibly more, or all of the
Liberty releases have been available.
        Verve Records were pressed by Electronic Industries of
Melbourne, Australia. The Australian "Music Maker" calalogue of
microgroove records, Third Edition, 1957, lists only partial contents
for MGV 2021

Appendix C—V-Discs, Government and AFRS Transcriptions

V-DISCS - Armed Forces Special Services

VP 32-D3MC 123 (Bluebird master PBS-072525-2)
     36-A   Der Fuehrer's Face

VP 352-D3MC 442 (NBC 19 to 25 Nov 43)
     113-A   That Old Black Magic
                 You Can't Say "No" To A Soldier
VP 353-D3MC 443 (NBC 19 to 25 Nov 43)
     113-B   Chlo-e
 (115-A) Navy V-Disc release, with above details identical
                 Chlo-e
       Note: 113-A/B mastered 23 Nov 43

VP 380-D3MC 451 (NBC 19 to 25 Nov 43)
     125-B   Hotcha Cornia
                 (Down In) Jungle Town

VP 420-D3MC 486 (NBC 25 Nov 43)
     125-A   As Time Goes By
           (Bluebird master PBS 061518-1)
           Barstool Cowboy From Old Barstow
       Note: 125-A mastered 21 Dec 43, test recorded 6 Jan 44

VP 939-D4TC 441 (Standard Transcription master YTH 996)
     348-A   And The Great Big Saw Came Nearer and Nearer
                 Cocktails For Two
 (128-A) Navy V-Disc release, with above details identical

VP 1288-D5TC 252 (Bluebird/Victor masters)
 Unissued   Beautiful Eggs
                 Holiday For Strings

VP 1511-D5TC 1322 (NBC 13 to 17 Aug 45)
     551-A   You Always Hurt The One You Love
                 Siam

VP 1513-D5TC 1324 (NBC 13 to 17 Aug 45)
     540-A   The Blue Danube
                 Toot Toot Tootsie Goodbye

VP 1536-D5TC 1336 (NBC 13 to 17 Aug 45)
     570-B   Minka
                 McNamara's Band
       Note: 570-B test approved 10 Sept 45

VP 1580-D5TC 1405 (Victor master D4AB 1057-1)
    Unissued   Holiday For Strings

VP JDB 1748-D5TC 1595 (Victor masters D5VB-1137-1/1138-1)
    640-B   Nutcracker Suite excerpts:
                    The Mysterious Room
                    The Fairy Ball

JDB 97-D6TC 5280 (Victor masters assumed)
    Unissued   Mother Goose
                    Old McDonald Had A Farm

JDB 183-D6TC 6027 (Victor masters D5VB-1131-2, D6VB-2063)
    709-A   Hawaiian War Chant
                Jones Polka

GOVERNMENT TRANSCRIPTIONS

Treasury Song Parade - 378,379,380,381 (all on one 16" disc)
                        see 28 June 1943 for details

Department of the Navy - Land's Best Bands - 2A, 5A, 8A, 11A
                        (four 16" discs)
                        see 29 November 1950 for details

U.S. Pacific Fleet - Across The Blue Pacific
                        see May 1951 for details

Public Service Shows - Here's To Veterans (each on 16" discs)
        91 - Spike Jones 'live' to Spotlight Revue cuts
                Who's Sorry Now? (14 Nov 47)
                Down In Jungle Town (24 Oct 47)
                My Old Flame (31 Oct 47)('straight' excerpt only)
                Toot Toot Tootsie (24 Oct 47)
                Coca Cola Theme

        139 - Spike Jones 'live' to Spotlight Revue cuts
                Blues My Naughty Sweetie Gave To Me (5 Nov 48)
                The Barber of Seville (5 Nov 48)
                After You've Gone (10 Dec 48)
                Tiger Rag (8 Oct 48)
                Coca Cola Theme

        227 - Spike Jones 'live' to RCA recordings
                Theme: Cocktails For Two
                Black Bottom - Chinese Mule Train
                Blowing Bubble Gum
                Theme: Cocktails For Two

        299 - Spike Jones 'live' to RCA recordings
                A Din Skal, A Min Skal - Deep Purple
                It Never Rains In Sunny California
                Theme: Cocktails For Two

        372 - Spike Jones 'live' to RCA recordings
                Gesundheit Polka - Three Little Fishies
                Dance of the Hours
                Theme: Cocktails For Two

Unissued – Spike Jones 'live' to RCA, Warner & Liberty masters
(assumed)   (mastered 31 Dec 59)
                    Gesundheit Polka(edited)
                    Monster Movie Ball – Late, Late Movies, Pt. 1
                    Theme: Cocktails For Two

Coast Guard Memorial – issue date 4 August 1949 (16" disc)
                    see 13 October 1948, AFRS Command Performance
                    for details (Pressed by Allied Record Co., L.A.)

ARMED FORCES RADIO SERVICE (AFRS)

Basic Music Library (16" discs, Bluebird or Victor masters unless
                    noted otherwise)
                    (Standard ET masters)
        W-9   Der Fuehrer's Face – The Sheik of Araby
                        Yankee Doodler – Oh By Jingo

                    (Standard ET masters)
        W-10   Pack Up Your Troubles
                        Come Josephine In My Flying Machine
                        Red Wing – I Wanna Go Back To West Virginia

                    (USO show 30 May 42, assumed)
        P-36   Clink Clink, Another Drink (mis-labled as
                                "Hasta Luego"

                    (V-Disc masters)
        P-77   Down In Jungle Town – Dark Eyes (Hotcha Cornia)
                        That Old Black Magic – Chloe

                    (V-Disc masters)
        P-424   As Time Goes By – Dark Eyes (Hotcha Cornia)
                        That Old Black Magic – Chloe

        P-465   Holiday For Strings (Victor master)
                        Red Wing (Standard master)
                        Drip Drip Drip (Victor master)

        P-503   Nutcracker Suite, parts 1,3,5
        P-505   Nutcracker Suite, parts 2,4,6

        P-514   The Blue Danube
                        You Always Hurt The One You Love

                    (Standard ET masters)
        P-590   Paddlin' Madeline Home
                        The Great Big Saw Came Nearer and Nearer
                        Cocktails For Two – Oh, How She Lied To Me

        P-695   My Pretty Girl

        P-715   When Yuba Plays The Rhumba On The Tuba

        P-736   Laura

        P-769   Minka – Lassus Trombone

        P-807   Love In Bloom – Blowing Bubble Gum

P-840	Pop Corn Sack - Our Hour
P-877	Sheik Of Araby - Behind Those Swinging Doors
P-898	Siam - Pass The Biscuits, Mirandy
P-912	My Old Flame - People Are Funnier Than Anybody
P-994	Ugga Ugga Boo, Ugga Boo Boo Ugga Down In Jungle Town
P-1024	William Tell Overture - I Kiss Your Hand Madame New Year's Resolution (Happy New Year) By The Beautiful Sea
P-1104	Ill Barkio - The Man On The Flying Trapeze I'm Getting Sentimental Over You None But The Lonely Heart
P-1134	(Standard ET masters) That's What Makes The World Go 'Round Don't Give The Chair To Buster 48 Reasons Why De Camptown Races with gestures The Blacksmith Song - The Farmers Daughter
P-1324	Clink Clink Polka - Knock Knock (Who's There?) Ya Wanna Buy A Bunny? - MacNamara's Band
P-1423	Dance Of The Hours - Sloppy Lagoon
P-1512	Black Bottom - Doin' The New Raccoon I Wonder Where My Baby Is Tonight Varsity Drag - The Charleston - Charlestono-Mio
P-2202	Too Young - Ill Barkio - Peter Cottontail Rhapsody From Hunger(y) I Haven't Been Home For Three Whole Nights So 'Elp Me (mis-labled as "Alto Baritone and Bass")
P-2374	It Never Rains In Sunny California Deep Purple There's A Blue Sky 'Way Out Yonder I've Turned A Gadabout - Down South
P-2566	I'll Never Work There Anymore (All Of A Sudden) My Heart Sings
P-2635	Bottoms Up - Sante Drink To The Bonnie Lassies A Din Skal, A Min Skal - Gesundheit Polka Salute
P-3324	Pal-Yat-Chee - Dragnet - Three Little Fishies Toot And A Whistle (and a Plunk and a Boom)
P-5447	This Song Is For The Birds (Verve masters) Memories Are Made Of This - 16 Tacos Love And Marriage - The Trouble With Pasquale

```
P-5448          Hi Mister

                (Verve masters)
P-5461            -Lawrence Welk Polka - Pennsylvania Polka
                  Bottoms Up - Happy Trumpets Polka
P-5462            -Pretty Girl Polka - Six Fat Dutchmen Polka
                  Ron Terry Polka - Whoopee John Polka
P-5463            -Frank Yankovic Waltz - New Beer Barrel Polka
                  Funny Punny Polka - Strip Polka

                (Liberty masters)
P-7295            -I Kiss Your Hand Madame
                  Knock, Knock, Who's There
                  River Stay 'Way From My Door
                  Pimples And Braces - The Hut Sut Song
                  Strip Polka
P-7296            -Mairzy Doats
                  Bill Bailey Won't You Please Come Home
                      (Roaring 20's)
                  Melody Of Love - Three Little Fishies
                  Kookie, Kookie, Lend Me Your Comb

                (Victor master assumed)
P-8706            Cocktails For Two

                (Liberty masters)
P-9227            -Jambalaya - I Saw The Light - Move It On Over
                  Weary Blues From Waitin'
                  There'll Be No Teardrops Tonight
                  Your Cheatin' Heart
P-9228            -Hey, Good Lookin' - Cold Cold Heart
                  I'm So Lonesome I Could Cry - Kaw-Liga
                  I Can't Help It If I'm Still In Love With You
                  You Win Again

PGL-37            Dance Of The Hours - Wild Bill Hiccup
                  Rhapsody From Hunger(y) - Tennessee Waltz

PGL-38            Pass The Biscuits Mirandy - Siam
                  William Tell Overture
                  I Wanna Go Back To West Virginia

                (Victor masters, except as noted)
P-S-28            Chloe (V-Disc master)
                  Cocktails For Two
                  Holiday For Strings
                  That Old Black Magic (V-Disc master assumed)
                  Sheik Of Araby
                  When Yuba Plays The Rhumba On The Tuba

PA-144          Holiday For Strings - Drip, Drip, Drip
Note: This ET may also be pressed as AFRS "Variety 144"
```

Basic Music Library - Children's Series
```
                (Victor masters, except as noted)
CH-78             Captain Of The Space Ship
                  Are My Ears On Straight?
                  I Just Love My Mommy
                  God Bless Us All

CHR-40            I Saw Mommy Kissing Santa Claus - Winter
                  Socko, The Smallest Snowball
                  Barnyard Christmas
```

```
        CHR-84          I Want Eddie Fisher For Christmas


                        (Verve masters)
        CHR-110         –Jingle Bells Medley – All I Want for Christmas
                        Night Before Christmas Song
                        Rudolph The Red Nosed Reindeer
                        Silent Night – Sleigh Ride
        CHR-111         –My Birthday Comes On Christmas – Snow Medley
                        I'm Getting Nuttin' For Christmas
                        Deck The Hall Medley – White Christmas Medley
        CHR-112         –I'm The Angel In The Christmas Play
                        Cradle Song – Frosty, The Snow Man
                        Hark Medley – Christmas Alphabet Song
                        Santa Claus' Son
        CHR-113         –Christmas Island – Victor Young Medley
                        Here Comes Santa Claus
                        What Are You Doing New Year's Eve?


Command Performance – see date for details
                        33 – 29 Sept 42
                        34 – 30 Aug 42
                        39 – 27 Oct 42
                        Special Christmas Show 24 Dec 42
                        59 – 27 Mar 43
                        Christmas Show 25 Dec 43
                        101 – 15 Jan 44
                        113 – 1 Apr 44
                        142 – 14 Oct 44
                        156 – 23 Dec 44
                        182 – 5 Jul 45
                        Army Day 6 Apr 46
                        346 – 25 Aug 48
                        352 – 13 Oct 48


Downbeat – Spike Jones as co-host to existing recorded dubs
        82              Theme: Pass The Biscuits Mirandy(Treasury Dept)
issued 14 Apr 44        Hotcha Cornia (V-Disc condensed)
                        It's Love Love Love (Furlough Fun 31 Mar 44)
                        Take The Door At The Left (Treasury Dept)
                        As Time Goes By (V-Disc)
                        They Go Wild, Simply Wild Over Me (Furlough
                            Fun 31 Mar 44)
                        That Old Black Magic (V-Disc)
                        Down In Jungle Town (V-Disc)
                        Put Your Arms Around Me Honey (Treasury Dept)
                        Chloe (V-Disc)
                        Theme: Pass The Biscuits Mirandy(Treasury Dept)
                        Theme: Casey Jones (Treasury Dept)


        ?               all details missing
issued 19 Apr 44


        105             Theme: Der Fuehrer's Face (Standard ET)
issued 12 Oct 44        Pack Up Your Troubles (Standard)
                        Wild Wild Women (Bluebird)
                        Oh! By Jingo (Standard ET)
                        Siam (Bluebird)
                        Sheik Of Araby (Standard)
                        Clink Clink Another Drink (AFRS Basic Music
                            Library P-36)
                        Come Josephine In My Flying Machine (Standard)
                        Holiday For Strings (Burns 27 Apr 44)
                        Hotcha Cornia (Bluebird)
                        Theme: Der Fuehrer's Face (Standard)
```

```
        123          Theme: Der Fuehrer's Face (Bluebird)
issued 13 Jan 45     I Want Somebody (Standard)
H-7-123              Drip, Drip, Drip (Standard)
                     Leave the Dishes in the Sink Ma (Victor)
                     Hi Ho My Lady (Standard)
                     I Wanna Go Back To West Virginia (Bluebird)
                     Chloe (V-Disc)
                     Cocktails For Two (Victor)
                     That Old Black Magic (V-Disc)
                     Theme: Der Fuehrer's Face (Bluebird)
                     Theme: Der Fuehrer's Face (Standard)


        217          Theme: Chloe (V-Disc)
issued Feb or        Down In Jungle Town (V-Disc)
     Mar 46          Than Old Black Magic (V-Disc)
                     Mother Goose Medley (Victor)
                     Theme: Chloe (V-Disc)


Remember - (Victor/Bluebird masters as applicable)
        7            Host: Fred McMurray
                     Cocktails For Two
      318-           -Come Josephine In My Flying Machine
      331            Holiday For Strings
      349-           -I Wanna Go Back To West Virginia
      442            I Dream Of Brownie With the Light Blue Jeans
      696            Host: George Montgomery (22 Jul 47)
                     Love In Bloom
      721            Host: George Montgomery (2 Sept 47)
                     Hawaiian War Chant
      727            Host: George Montgomery (2 Dec 47)
                     Cocktails For Two
      733            Host: George Montgomery (18 Nov 47)
                     The Glow Worm
      736            Host:George Montgomery (7 Oct 47)
                     Come Josephine In My Flying Machine
      757            Host: Brod(erick) Crawford (9 Dec 47)
                     Love In Bloom
      777            Host: Dick Widmark (23 Dec 47)
                     Love In Bloom
      806            Host: Bill Conrad (24 Feb 48)
                     I Wanna Go Back To West Virginia
      810            Host: Bill Conrad (10 Feb 48)
                     Der Fuehrer's Face
      841            Hosts: Bill Conrad, Paul Frees (18 May 48)
                     My Old Flame
      856            Host: Richard Ney (27 Apr 48)
                     My Pretty Girl
      858            Host: Richard Ney (27 Apr 48)
                     When Yuba Plays the Rhumba On the Tuba
      885-           -Love In Bloom
      904            By the Beautiful Sea
      906-           -William Tell Overture
      927            Holiday For Strings
      963-           -The Man On the Flying Trapeze
      964            None But the Lonely Heart
      974            Host: Robert Ryan (28 Dec 48)
                     Ill Barkio
      981            Host: Tom Brown (28 Dec 48)
                     I'm Getting Sentimental Over You
     1118-           -MacNamara's Band


Purple Heart Album - (Victor masters, Bluebird where applicable)
      150            Hostess: Frances Langford (30 Sept 47)
                     Love In Bloom
      153            Hostess: Frances Langford (10 Nov 47)
                     Laura
```

```
158          Hostess: Frances Langford (25 Nov 47)
                Blowing Bubble Gum
168          Hostess: Ann Blyth (30 Dec 47)
                Our Hour
182          Hostess: Frances Langford (17 Feb 48)
                Behind Those Swinging Doors
183          Hostess: Frances Langford (6 Apr 48)
                Sheik of Araby
184          Hostess: Barbara Britton (2 Mar 48)
                Pass the Biscuits Mirandy
189          Hostess: Barbara Britton (2 Mar 48)
                Siam
```

G.I. Jive - Hostess: G.I Jill (16"discs, Victor masters)
```
           565          That Old Black Magic
           951          Chloe
           967          Serenade For (to) A Jerk
          1116          Holiday For Strings
          1349          I Dream Of Brownie With the Light Blue Jeans
          1378          Jones Polka
          1695          Love In Bloom
```

Turn Back The Clock - with "Andy & Virginia" Mansfield (RCA masters)
```
           162          Ill Barkio
           193          Boys In the Back Room
           212          Hot Lips
           386          You Always Hurt the One You Love
           657          Baby Buggie Boogie
           929          Old MacDonald Had a Farm
          1061          Cocktails For Two
          1108          Hawaiian War Chant
          1173          Cocktails For Two
          1401          You Always Hurt the One You Love
```

Melody Round-Up - (Standard masters)
```
            33          Host: Chill Wills (3 Mar 43)
H-4-33                  Now Laugh -  Don't Give the Chair to Buster
R12 B3                  Gonna Stomp Those City Slickers Down (mislabled
                                    as 'We've Come To Town')
                        Red Wing


            37          Host: Bob Burns
H-4-37                  Horsie, Keep Your Tail Up - Ft. Worth Jail
R13 A2                  That Big Palooka That Plays The Bazooka
                        Clink, Clink, Another Drink
        Note: The above two ETs are erroniously listed in the
    Library Of Congress files as from MacGregor masters. The ET below
    was issued with a U.S. War Dept. label.


           233          Hosts: Lum and Abner
H-4-233                 Horsey, Keep Your Tail Up
HD3-MM-8638-1           Never Hit Your Grandmas With A Shovel
                        Gonna Stomp Those City Slickers Down
                        Der Fuehrer's Face
```

The Spike Jones Show - (edited versions of the 1945 Chase and Sanborn
shows) The numerical listing is not the show order, nor do the titles
necessarily follow broadcast sequence. It is assumed there are 13 30-
minute ETs. Only the following are known, with Jones portions listed.

```
             1          Laura -  Leave The Dishes In The Sink, Ma
                        Blues In The Night (Big band)
```

3   The Choo Choo Polka
           You Always Hurt The One You Love
           Laura - Thou Swell (Big band)

5   By The Beautiful Sea
           Leave The Dishes In The Sink, Ma
           Holiday For Strings
           I'm A Yankee Doodle Dandy (Chaser)

6   Oh! By Jingo - Liebestraum
           The Great Big Saw Came Nearer And Nearer
           Surrey With The Fringe On Top (Big band)

9   Chloe - Toot Toot Tootsie - Laura
           I Got Plenty O' Nuttin' (Big band)

10   MacNamara's Band - Hawaiian War Chant
           Cocktails For Two

11   Siam - Blue Danube - Always (Big band)
           Wake Up And Live (Big band)

13   No No Nora - Great Day (Big band) - Laura
           Surrey With The Fringe On Top (Big band)

America's Popular Music (12" discs, varied masters)
       771-   -Red Sails In The Sunset (Liberty);
                 Lassus Trombone (Victor)
       826-   -September Song (Liberty);
                 Pass The Biscuits Mirandy (Victor)
      1298-   -Jambalaya (Liberty);
                 Der Fuehrer's Face (Victor assumed)
      1347-   -Your Cheatin' Heart (Liberty);
                 A Mudder's Day Sports Spectacular (Liberty)

Ira Cook - (12" discs, varied masters)
         3-   -(Christmas '64) White Christmas Medley (Verve)
       370   Piano Tuner, with Bill Dana (Kapp)
       888-   -Green Green (Liberty)
       899   If I Had A Hammer (Liberty)
       904-   -Melody Of Love (Liberty)
       907   Ballad Of Jed Clampett (Liberty);
                 Hawaiian War Chant (RCA)
       991-   -Dominique (Liberty)
       996   Hey, Mr. Banjo (Liberty)
      1096-   -Cocktails For Two (RCA)
      1111   I'm In The Mood For Love (Liberty assumed)
      1122-   -Stairway To The Stars (Liberty)
      1128   Temptation (Liberty)
      1240-   -Your Cheatin' Heart (Liberty)
      1376   Hey, Mr. Banjo (Liberty)
      1395-   -Shangri-La (Liberty)
      2786   You Always Hurt The One You Love (RCA assumed)
      2891-   -Glow Worm (Liberty assumed)

Sound Off
        34   Der Fuehrer's Face (RCA)
       352   Hotcha Cornia (V-Disc)

Jill's All-Time Juke Box
        17   Hostess: G.I. Jill
H-46-17   Der Fuehrer's Face (Bluebird)

Swingtime
          63   Holiday For Strings (RCA assumed)

Showtime - (live show to dubbed Victor masters)
          278   That Old Black Magic
                     Love In Bloom

Johnny Green's World Of Music - (two 12" discs)
                     (Spike Jones interview, from domestic show)
          6   Cocktails For Two (Victor)
                     Ah-1, Ah-2, Ah-Sunset Strip (Liberty)
                     White Christmas Medley (Verve)
                     Ramona (Verve)
                     I Only Have Eyes For You (Warner)

Martin Block - (Victor masters)
          102-   -Chloe (RCA assumed)
                     I'm In The Mood For Love
          196-   -All I Want For Christmas
                     Toot And A Whistle (And A Plunk And A Boom)
                     Rudolph The Red Nosed Reindeer
                     William Tell Overture
          217-   -Cocktails For Two - My Old Flame
                     I'm In The Mood For Love
          396-   -I'm In The Mood For Love
                     Dance Of The Hours - Cocktails For Two

Bud's Bandwagon - (Victor masters)
          15-   -Boys In The Back Room
          151   Dragnet
          156-   -Hotter Than A Pistol
          220   Toot And A Whistle (And A Plunk And A Boom)
          416-   -Secret Love
          494   Japanese Skokiaan
          594-   -This Song Is For The Birds
          604   Hi Mister

Hot Off The Record Press - (16" discs - Victor masters)
          98   Host: Freddie Grimes, with Mickey Katz
                        Holiday For Strings
          153   Host: Freddie Grimes, with Stan Freberg
                        Riders In The Sky
          155   Host: Freddie Grimes, with Stan Freberg
                        My Old Flame

Music Hall - (editions of Kraft Music Hall)
          110   from 11 Jan 45
                        Cocktails For Two

          158   from 13 Dec 45 (with no Crosby involvement)
                        You Always Hurt The One You Love - Blue Danube

Bing Crosby - (edition of 23 Oct 46 Philco Radio Time)
          89   Hawaiian War Chant - Love In Bloom

To The Rear, March - (excerpts from 23 Oct 46 Philco Radio Time)
                     Hawaiian War Chant - Love In Bloom

Music America Loves Best - (editions of NBC b'casts, 1945)
          55   from 24 Jun 45
A-SSR-6-26-3   Chloe
A-SSR-6-26-4   I'm Getting Sentimental Over You

```
       62          from 12 Aug 45
                   Holiday For Strings
                   You Always Hurt The One You Love
                   I'm Getting Sentimental Over You
       Note: I'm Getting Sentimental is dubbed excerpt from AFRS 55


Supper Club - (editions of the Chesterfield Supper Club, 1946)
      298          from 18 Apr 46
                   Glow Worm


      307          from 2 May 46
                   Laura


Mail Call - see details under date
       95          see 17 Jun 44


Eddie Cantor (16" disc - Victor master)
       51          Cocktails For Two


Date With Christmas (Verve master)
       13          Christmas Alphabet Medley


Grant (Verve master)
    Christmas '68 - Christmas Alphabet Medley


Pewter (Victor assumed)
    Christmas '72 - All I Want For Christmas


Christmas (Victor assumed)
      325          All I Want For Christmas


Variety Album
      144          see details under 'Basic Music Library' PA-144


Juke Box USA (Victor masters)
       46-         -Hawaiian War Chant
       94          Tennessee Waltz
       96-         -Rhapsody From Hunger(y)
      224          Too Young
      252-         -Cocktails For Two
      367          Down South


Yank Swing Session
        5          28 Aug 42 - unknown contents
        6          28 Aug 42 - unknown contents


Special New Years Show - see details under date
               27 Sept 44 - unknown contents


Surprise Package (V-Disc masters)
       18          Host: Jim Hawthorne (4 Jul 48?)
Pt. 1:D-3996       Chloe
Pt. 2:D-3995x      That Old Black Magic


Willson (Victor master)
      127          Down South


Take A Record, Please (Victor masters)
       13          Charlestono-Mio
       38          Tennessee Waltz


                        389
```

<u>Carroll</u> (Victor masters, disc marked "best cuts", suggests editing)
         875   William Tell Overture - Dance Of The Hours

<u>World Of Show Business</u> (Liberty masters)
         179-   -Blowin' In The Wind - Maria Elena
         475   Temptation
         518-   -Jamalaya
         570   Let's Kiss, Kiss, Kiss

<u>Sound Of The 60's</u> (Liberty masters)
         No. 4   Ballin' The Jack
         No. 6   Harlem Nocturne
         No. 13   There'll Be No Teardrops Tonight
         No. 25   Let's Kiss, Kiss, Kiss

<u>Spotlight Album "Washington Square"</u> (Liberty masters)
         95   September Song - Green Green
                       Frankie And Johnny - If I Had A Hammer
                       Washington Square

<u>Small World</u> (12" discs)Spike Jones as interview, AFRS original show
     Christmas 1964   -Nutcracker Suite (Victor)
         3   Christmas Alphabet Medley (Verve)
         4-   -I Only Have Eyes For You (Warner)
         103   Host: George Church III (24 Jan 64)
                       Washington Square - Whistler's Muddah(Liberty)
                       Cocktails For Two (Victor master)
                       September Song (Liberty)
         134-   -The Stripper (Liberty)
         140   Harlem Nocturne (Liberty)
         181-   -Jambalaya (Liberty)
         713   Blowin' In The Wind (Liberty)

<u>Unknown live show</u> - early 1945
                       My Home Town

<u>Local Recordings</u> - Spike 'live', for AFN Frankfurt use only
         LR-3139-   -Where Did My Snowman Go? (Victor)
                       Santa Brought Me Choo Choo Trains (Victor)
         LR-3402-   -I Want Eddie Fisher For Christmas (Victor)
         LR-3996-   -Jingle Bells Medley (Verve)

<u>Corn's A-Poppin'</u> - 15 min. condensed versions of 'Spotlight Revue' to
the 'Spike Jones' 1949 radio shows. On later ETs, the host/announcer
is Sgt Russ Thompson. Only Slickers portions are listed.

1   San - Chloe   12 Don't Bring Lulu
    William Tell Overture   There's Nothing Like A Circus
    Pale Moon   Stumbling

3   No No Nora   13 Down By The O-Hi-O
    Liebestraum   Take Me Out To The Ball Game
    San Antonio Rose   Martha

9   Somebody Stole My Gal   19 12th Street Rag
    Ballerina   There's No Business Like
    It's A Sin To Tell A Lie   Show Business

11 Yes Sir That's My Baby   28 Blues My Naughty Sweetie
    When A Gypsy Makes His   Gave To Me
      Violin Cry   Barber Of Seville
    You Tell Me Your Dream

390

29 After You've Gone   Down By The Station
    Tiger Rag (banjos)   After You've Gone

30 Sweet Georgia Brown   44 Blues My Naughty Sweetie
    Hotcha Cornia   Gave To Me
    Haunted Heart   Powder Your Face With Sunshine
                                   Pennsylvania Polka
31 Football Medley
    It's Magic   45 Cruisin' Down The River
    Tiger Rag (banjos)   Brush Those Tears From Your Eyes
    Haunted Heart   Ya Wanna Buy A Bunny?

32 Jingle Bells   46 Charlie My Boy
    April Showers   Tour Of Boston
                                   Down Among The Sheltering Palms
33 In A Persian Market
                               47 Chicago - Czardas
34 Oh By Jingo   Take Me Out To The Ball Game
    You Were Only Fooling   Tiger Rag (banjos)
    I Kiss Your Hand Madame
    Tiger Rag (banjos)   48 There's Nothing Like A Circus
                                   Cruisin' Down The River
35 By The Beautiful Sea   Blues My Naughty Sweetie
    Roundtable: The Samba   Gave To Me
    Say Something Sweet
    When A Gypsy Makes His   49 Knock Knock
      Violin Cry   I've Got My Love To Keep Me Warm
                                   Blues My Naughty Sweetie
36 'Way Down Yonder In   Gave To Me
      New Orleans
    Tour Of New Orleans   50 Sweet Georgia Brown
    Say It Isn't So   Oh By Jingo
    Tiger Rag (banjos)
                               51 By The Beautiful Sea
37 Lavender Blue   Roundtable: Tchaikovsky
    Far Away Places   Riders In The Sky

38 Please Don't Talk About Me 52 Runnin' Wild
    My Darling   Roundtable: Schubert
    The Hollywood Story   Pootwaddle Cigarettes

39 Tour Of North Carolina   53 Barney Google
    Carolina Moon   Pootwaddle Hair Tonic
                                   People Are Funnier Than Anybody
40 Pennsylvania Polka
    Pussycat Song   54 Wang Wang Blues
                                   Roundtable: Beethoven
41 By The Beautiful Sea
    Blue Danube   55 Want Ads
    Pocahontas Story   Pootwaddle Tooth Paste

42 Missouri Waltz   57 Knock Knock
    Careless Hands   Barber Of Seville
    Minstrel Show   Brush Those Tears From Your Eyes
    Sweet Georgia Brown
                               58 Runnin' Wild
43 Sidewalks Of New York   What Did I Do?
    Tour Of New York City   You Can't Be True Dear

Bob Burns Radio Show
         There is no information re: AFRS ETs from any portion of
this radio series despite AFRS transcriptions being mentioned during
the occasional domestic broadcast.

Index to City Slickers Personnel

396

Lewis, Cappy (Carroll)(tpt)315,
317,319,328
Lewis, Irv (Irving)(tpt)132,133
Linn, Ray(tpt)141
Lipschultz, Irving(cel)104,112,
321
Little (Scalia), Frankie(act)143,
147,151,160,161,167,182,189,191,
194,194,201,209,216,233,247,256,
264,266,268,275,277,284,294
Livoti, Victor(effts)283
Lloyd, Dorothy(effts)302
Loveal, Suzy(voc)328

MacLarand, Paul(sax)319
Malione, Emilio(sax,clar)167,170,
174,181
Mandel, Henry(picc)271,273,274
Mandell, Red(sax)283
Manners, Donna(voc)281
Manners, Judy(voc)111,112,128
Markussen, A.(voc)215,235,236,262
Marlin, Glenn & Dolores - see
Wayne-Marlin Trio
Marsh, Jack(bsn)123
Martin, Jr.(J. Lockhart Martin)
(act)147,151,166,167,182,189-
192,194,297,201,203,209,216,247,
256,264,268
Martin, J.(voc)165
Martinez, Tony(voc)291,292,304
Martinez, William(voc,reeds)284,
299
Mason, Ann - see Ann Mason
Stockton
Mathews, Pat(vln)328
Matlock, Julian (Matty)(clar)10,
76,357
Matthiason, Thora (var sp)(voc)
281
"Maurice Matzah" - 181
Maxwell (Cherkose), Eddie(arr,
comp,voc)123,209,243-246,256,
257,266,267,285,334
McCarthy, Dorothy(voc)279,281
McCarthy, Eddie(band boy)151,189,
209,216,247,264
McCarthy, G.(voc)177
McDonald (Youngman), Nancy(hrp)
112,114,143,150,167,216
McKean, S.(voc)260
McKinistry, Marian(vln)321,324,
328
McLean, Mack(voc)267,279,338
McLeod, Vern(electrician)293
McNaughton, Jack(electrician)189,
216,247,264,268,277,284,289
Meissner, Zep(James Joseph)(sax,
clar,arr)97-99,102,108,111,112,
114,120,122,123,126,130,132,133,
138,140,143,145,147
"Mellomen" - 271-275,278,283
Mercier Jr. W.A.(fr hrn)178
Mershon, Gil(voc)145,148,215,262,
282
Metcalfe, Eddie (Edwin C.)(sax,
clar,voc)212,216,219,221,224,
230,234,235,239,243-245,247,250,

260,261,264,301
Meyer, Alvin Jay(voc)209,216,230,
286
Meyer, Sol(arr,comp)122,272,285,
334
Michaud, Dan (Dolor J.)(arr)17,
18,27,28,31,41
Midgley, Dorese(act)143,147
Miller, Bernie(bass)327
Mills, Betsy(hrp)147,168,170,175,
177,178
Mills, Veryle(hrp)350
Mitchell Boy Choir - 246,278
Mitchell, Red (Keith)(bass)338
Moore Nina(secretary)190
Morales, Lloyd(drm)339
Mootz, Jack(tpt)102,132,133,138
Morgan, Dick (Richard Isaac)(bjo/
guit,voc,act)70-73,77-92,94-
103,105,122,123,126,131,132,
143-145,147,148,150,156,165,
166,170,174-176,178,180,183,
189,197,210,213-216,218,219,
222,229,230,232-236,239,240,
245-247,250,256,260-264,266-
268,271-275,277,278,280,281,
293
Morgan, Freddie (Philip Morgen-
stern)(guit/bjo,voc,act)161,
166,167,170,173,174,178,182,
183,189,195,197,203-205,210,
213,215,216,220,230,234,235,
239,240,243,246,247,250,253,
256,257,260-262,264,266-268,
271-274,276-290,292,298,301,
302,305,309-312,314-318,320-
322,324,325,327,328,332,338,
340,341,359
Morgan, Tommy(harmonica)363,364
Morrow, Bob(vln)132
Most, Abe(ww)356
Most, Arthur(trb)3,6,82,243,245
Muir, Bill(act)284
Mulholland, Ross(act)267
Murdock, N.(voc)260

Nash, Ted(reeds)328,334,359,360
Nay, Theron(act)284
Nelson, Bob(act)362
Nelson, Wilbur(act)332
Newburger, Elizabeth K.(voc)148
Newton, E.(voc)165,267
Nichols, Red(tpt)2,3,5,7,49,72,
136,171
Niles, John(arr)141
Nilsson Twins (Elsa, Eileen)(voc)
70-73,77-92,94-103,105
Noel, Dick(trb)132,133,140
Nole, Abe(trb)280,282-285,293
Norman, Loulie Jean(voc)165,166,
235,236,267,279,281,334,336-
338,340,341
Norman, Theodore(vln)132,133,136,
141
Noyes, Betty(voc)279,281

O'Brian, Dan - 339
O'Brian, Cubby(drm)362,364

Index to Personalities and Shows

Homier, Skip-110
"Hoosier Hot Shots"-218,219,303,
Hope, Bob-59,84,89,107,110,113,
  133,135,138,146,147
Hopkins, Don-19
Hopper, Hedda-65,82,128
Horne, Lena-55,91
Houston, Joe-289
"Howdy Doody"-286
Hunt, Frances-33

Ink Spots-119
"Ish Kabibble"-84
Isaacs, Charlie-127
IT COULD BE YOU-305,312,327,329,
  347
Inventory-293-298
Ives, Burl-171,199

Jack's of Hollywood-294
James, Artie-289
James, Harry-78,83,106,133,140,
  188,261,281,305
James, Sonny-321
Janak, Tony-81,119
Jarrett, Scot-221
"Jazzbo Four"-1
Jenkins, Bill-159,194
Jenkins, Gordon-19,26,57,301
Jerry Fairbanks Studios-256
Jervis, Al-29
Jessel, George-78,135
Johnson Choir, Hall-55
Johnson, Chubby-237
Johnson, Johnny-34
Johnson, Ray-6,9,145
Jolson, Al-8,19,119
Jonathan Club-14,15,18,20,26,28-
  38,40-46,48-50,52-57,59
Jones, Allan-33,319
Jones, Dean-322
Jones, Gina Marie-330
Jones, Jack-344,351
Jones, Leslie Ann-266
Jones (Middleton), Pat-3,11,146
Jones, Spike Jr.-229,232,326,365
Joy, Dick-210-215,217,218,222-
  226
Joy, Leonard-19
JUKE BOX JURY-299,300
Jurgens, Dick-145,206

Kahn, Roger-7
Kahn, Sammy-117,126
Kallen, Kitty-224
Kapp, Dave-17,27
Karloff, Boris-225
Kaye, Danny-110,171,211
Kaye, Sammy-83,106,181
Kayser, Kay-49,59,65,84,110,243,
  267
Keating, Larry-21,55,61-65,84,
  87
Keeshan, Chuck(Bob)-34,286
Kelley, Deforest-147
Kelly, Gene-210
Kelly, Paula-136,139
Kemp, Hal-8

Kemper, Charles-117
Kendall, Cy-62
Kent, John-218
Kent, Lenny-276
Kenton, Stan-4,176,179
Ketchum, Dave-351-353
King Cole Trio-128,138,269
King, Joe-191,193-195
King Sisters-272,325,330,331
"King's Men"-17,43
Kinskey, Leonid-291
"Kinsmen"-354
Kirby, Col.E.M.-104
Kitten Sisters-317
Knapp, Orville-4
Knight, Vick-50,104
Koltz, Max-294
"Korn Kobblers"-16,119,218
Koroshovsky, Andre-245
Kosloff, Lou-19
KRAFT MUSIC HALL-5,7,8,13,16-18,
  21,27,37,43,109,111,129,142,245
Krupa, Gene-5,7
Kuehn, V.W.-339
Kuhl, Cal-123,124

Laakso, Nels-119
Ladd, Alan-49,137
LADIES MAN-109,126-128,132
Laine, Frankie-203
Lamarr, Hedy-49
Lamm, Bob-176,193
Lamond, Bob-329
Lamour, Dorothy-33,110,135,229
Lane, Dick-21,61-64,67,68,262,268
Landis, Carole-83,100
Langford, Frances-6,44,84,110,
  113-118,120,158,178,228
Lantz, Walter-19,44
Lanza, Mario-246,267
Lassie-231,232
Laughton, Charles-59
Laurenz, John-187
LaVere, Charles-9,13
Lawrence, Elliot-260,261
Lazenby, Don-2
"Leasebreakers"-see "Music for.."
Lee, Anna-87
Leslie, Joan-56
Levienne, Mischa-19
Lewis, Diana-135
Lewis, Jerry-126
Lewis, Meade Lux-347
Lewis, Monica-219,220
Lewis, Ted-52,243
Lewis, Texas Jim-27,30,41
Lewis, Tom-228
Liberace-275,276,289
Liberace, George-133,276
LIFEBUOY SHOW-76,78-97,100,101
"Life Goes To War"-55
Lincoln, Abe-8,9
Loesser, Frank-56
Logan, Ella-9,100
Lombardo, Guy-181,268,270,312
"Lord Flea"-317
Lorre, Peter-213
"Low Hite and Stanley"-100,147

Slickers Tune Index

All Slickers underlined titles are included, with the composer/author, where known or attributed (att.). The following key will help to determine their origin and strict alphabetical sequence is maintained.

(RS)	recording session	(ET)	City Slickers transcription
(RS*)	recording session,	(CW)	Cindy Walker recording,
	unissued		transcription
(AC)	air check (radio)	(TR)	Treasury Dept. transcription
(ACU)	undated air check	(TV)	television presentation
(V)	V-Disc sessions	(M)	movies, Soundies, shorts

A Din Skal, A Min Skal(Spike Jones-Bernie Jones-Freddy Morgan) 272(RS),314
After You've Gone(Creamer-Layton) 194(AC),213(AC)
Ah-1, Ah-2, Ah-Sunset Strip(E. Brandt-L. Ecklund-C. Brandt) 340(RS)
Ain't Misbehavin'(Waller-Razaf-Brooks) 85(AC)
Ain't She Sweet(Jack Yellen-Milton Ager) 195(AC),310(RS)
Alabamy Bound(Bud Green-B.G. DeSylva-Ray Henderson) 175(AC)
Alexander's Ragtime Band(Irving Berlin) 12,128(M),330(TV)
Alley Cat(Harlen-Bjorn) 355(RS)
All Hail Coin-egie Tech(Mickey Katz-Spike Jones-Howard Gibeling) 148(RS),155
All I Want For Christmas Is My Two Front Teeth(Don Gardner) 177(RS), 179(AC),213(AC),214(AC),240,241(AC),276(TV),306(RS),309
(All Of A Sudden) My Heart Sings(Rome-Jamblin-Herpin) 276(RS), 336(RS),337
Alto, Baritone and Bass(Eddie Maxwell) 266(RS),267
Always(Irving Berlin) 116(AC)
Am I Blue?(Harry Akst-Grant Clarke) 15
A Mustache, A Derby, A Cane and A Cop(C. Brandt) 348(RS),349
And His Rocking Horse Ran Away(Van Heusen-Burke) 97(AC),99(ET),100, 102(ACU)
(I'm the) Angel In the Christmas Play(Bob Merrill) 306(RS)
April Showers(DeSylva-Silvers) 195(AC),197(AC),214(AC),260(ET), 266(AC),325(TV),329(TV)
Are My Ears On Straight?(Mel Leven) 281(RS)
Are We From Oklahoma? - see I Gotta Gal I Love...
As Time Goes By(Herman Hupfeld) 82(V),102(ACU),176(AC)
At Last I'm First With You(Country Washburn) 96(AC),98(ET),99
A Toot and a Whistle (and a Plunk and a Boom) (Jack Elliot-Sonny Burke) 283(RS)
Autumn Serenade(Peter DeRose-Sammy Gallop) 140(AC)
Away In a Manger (Deck the Halls Medley) 307(RS)

Baby Buggie Boogie(Carl Hoefle-Del Porter-Andrew Marchese) 256(RS)
Baby Face(Davis-Akst) 184(AC),198(AC)
Ballad of Jed Clampett(Paul Henning) 356(RS)
Ballerina(Russell-Sigman) 184(AC),191(AC)

Charade(Henry Mancini-Johnny Mercer) 358(RS)
(The) Charleston(Cecil Mack-Jimmy Johnson) 244(RS*)(RS)
Charlestono-Mio(Eddie Maxwell-Spike Jones) 244(RS),256(M),261(ET),
    288(TV)
Charlie My Boy(Fiorito-Kahn) 102(ACU),183(AC),225(AC),233(AC),
    261(ET),290(TV)
Cheatin' on the Sandman(McCrystal-Garris) 45(ET)
Cherrio(Sol Meyer-Freddy Morgan) 274(RS)
Cherry Pink and Apple Blossom White(Louigay-Jacques Larue-Mack
    David) 303(RS)
Chicago(Fred Fisher) 199(AC),227(AC)
Chinatown, My Chinatown(Jerome-Schwartz) 310(RS),320(TV)
Chinese Mule Train(Lange-Heath-Glickman) 231,250(RS),253,256(M)
Chloe(Gus Kahn-Neil Moret) 79(AC),81(V),83(AC),84(AC),89(M),99,
    101(ACU),111(RS),112,115(AC),116(AC),121(ET),127(AC),143,168,169,
    182,204(AC),208,218(AC),265(TV),272,276(TV),280,311,319(TV),
    327(TV),364,367(RS*)
Choo Choo Polka(Mike Shore-Zeke Manners) 115(AC)
Christmas Alphabet(Buddy Kaye)(Christmas Alphabet Medley) 307(RS)
    309
Christmas Alphabet Medley(Christmas Alphabet, Merry Christmas
    Polka, Christmas In America) 307(RS),308
Christmas Cradle Song(Sol Meyer-Spike Jones) 309(RS)
Christmas In America(Hal Borne)(Christmas Alphabet Medley) 308
Christmas Island(Lyle Moraine) 308(RS)
Christmas Medley - 312(TV),329(TV)
Christmas Song(Torme-Wills)(Jingle Bells Medley) 307
City Slicker Polka(Carling-Ohman) 87(AC),88(AC),91(AC),98(ET),99
Clink, Clink, Another Drink(Foster Carling-Phil Ohman) 16,29(ET),30,
    32(RS),33,42(AC),43(M),96,99,100,104
Clink Clink Polka (see Clink Clink, Another Drink) 33
Coca Cola Theme(Vick Joy) 196
Cocktails For Two(Sam Coslow-Arthur Johnson) 91(AC),96(AC),99(ET),
    101(ACU),105,107(AC),108(RS),109,111(AC),116(AC),123,126(M),
    127(AC),128(M),168,182,208,265(TV),271,288(TV),301,311,312(TV),
    322(TV),364,367(RS*)
Cold Cold Heart(Hank Williams) 363
Come Josephine In My Flying Machine(Alfred Bryan-Fred Fisher) 16,34,
    37(RS)(RS*),45,56(AC),256(RS*),251
Come To Baby, Do(James-Miller) 135(AC),140(AC)
Comin'Through the Rye(Traditional) 186(AC)
(A) Connecticut Yankee In King Arthur's Court(1813 Opera 'Bohemian
    Girl'-"I Dreamt I Dwelt In Marble Halls")(Balfe) 232(AC)
Cool Yule 299(RS*)
(The) Cotton Pickin' Peasant Overture(Von Suppe-Freddy Morgan-
    Spike Jones) 348(RS)
(The) Courtship of Miles Standish - 213(AC)
(The) Covered Wagon Rolled Right Along(Hy Heath-Britt Wood) 16,
    25(RS),65(AC)
Cradle Song - 313,314(RS)
Crazy Rhythm(Meyer-Kahn-Ceasar) 127(AC)
Cruisin' Down the River(Eily Beadell-Nell Tollerton) 223(AC,228(AC)
Cry(Kohlman) 275(TV)
Cuanto Le Gusta(Ray Gilbert-Gabriel Ruiz) 213(AC),323(TV)
Curses! If Jack Dalton Were Only Here(C. Brandt) 347(RS),348,349
Czardas(Monti) 182,227(AC),332(TV)

Daisy Bell - see Bicycle Built For Two
Dance Ballerina Dance - see Ballerina
Dance of the Hours(Ponchielli-Spike Jones-Doodles Weaver) 184,
    229(AC),230(RS),233(AC),234(AC),236,239,241(AC),260,261(ET),
    266(AC),268,282(M),329(TV),357(RS*)
Dardanella(Bernard-Black-Fisher) 135(AC),139(AC)
Dark Moon(Ned Miller) 320(TV)
Daughter of Mme. From Armentiers 88(AC),89(AC)
Day By Day(Cahn-Strodahl-Weston) 134(AC),137(AC),140(AC)
De Camptown Races(S. Foster) 40(ET)

Deck the Halls(Welsh Carol) (also Deck the Halls Medley) 179(AC),
   214(AC),307
Deck the Halls Medley(Deck the Halls With Boughs Of Holly, It Came
   Upon A Midnight Clear, The First Noel) 307
Deep Purple(Peter DeRose) 272(RS),358(RS)
Der Fuehrer's Face(Oliver Wallace) 30,46(RS)(RS*),47,48(ET),50,51,
   52(AC),53(AC),54(AC),55(M),62(AC),64(AC),69(M),70,75,76,104,130,
   178,263,323(TV),329(TV)
Dodging A Gal From Dodge City(Del Porter) 35(ET)
Doin' the New Raccoon(Eddie Maxwell-Spike Jones) 244(RS)
Doll Dance(Nacio Herb Brown) 188(AC)
Dominique(Souire) 358(RS)
Don't Blame Me(Dorothy Fields-Jimmy McHugh) 102(ACU)
Don't Bring Lulu(Rose-Brown-Henderson) 197(AC)
Don't Count Your Chickens(Cindy Walker) 27(CW)
Don't Give the Chair To Buster(Cliff Arquette-C. Dant) 39(ET)
Don't Talk To Me About Men(Cindy Walker) 15,17,27(CW),28(CW)
Don't Talk To Me About Women(Del Porter) 30(ET)
Double Eagle Rag(Wagner-Freddy Morgan-Spike Jones) 303(RS)
Down Among the Sheltering Palms(James Brockman-Abe Olman) 225(AC)
Down By the Old Mill Stream(Tell Taylor) 197(AC)
Down By the O-Hi-O(Yellen-Olman) 78(AC),82(AC),85(AC),98(ET),104,
   197(AC)
Down By the Station(Gaillard-Paul Mills) 224(AC)
Down In Jungle Town(E. Madden-T. Morse) 79(AC),81(V),87(AC),98(ET),
   115(AC),173(AC),174(RS),195(AC),217(AC)
Down South(Sigmund Spaeth-William Middleton) 273(RS),275(TV),320(TV)
Dragnet(Walter Schumann) 283(RS)
Dreamer(Arthur Schwartz-Frank Loesser) 82(AC),102(ACU)
Dream House(Lynn Cowan) 15
Dream Train(Billy Baskette-Charles Newman) 203(AC)
Drink To the Bonnie Lassies(Sol Meyer-Freddy Morgan-Spike Jones)
   274(RS)
Drip, Drip, Drip (also Sloppy Lagoon, Water Lou)(Del Porter) 12,42,
   69(AC),88(AC),111(RS),143

East of the Sun(Brooks-Bowman) 136(AC),139(AC),140(AC)
East Side, West Side - see Sidewalks Of New York
E-Bop-O-Lee-Bop(Dixon) 134(AC),135(AC),137(AC(ET),139(AC),140(AC),
   142(AC(
$18.12 Overture - 367
Elevator Shoes(Billy Barty) 326(RS*)
Everything Happens To Me(Adair-Dennis) 335(RS),336
Exactly Like You(Jimmy McHugh) 117(AC)

Farandole(Bizet) 288(TV)
Far Away Places(Kramer-Whitney) 219(AC),221(AC)
(The) Farmer's Daughter(Cindy Walker) 41(CW)
Feetlebaum Bombs(Spike Jones-Doodles Weaver) 341(RS)
Fever(John Davenport-Eddie Cooley) 332(TV)
Fiddle Faddle(Anderson-Jones-Maxwell) 250(RS),265(AC)
Fine And Dandy(Paul James-Kay Swift) 15
(The) First Noel(Traditional)(Deck the Halls Medley) 307
(The) First Snowfall(Burke-Webster)(see Snow Medley) 308,309
Five Foot Two(Henderson-Lewis-Young) 178(AC),227(AC),261(ET),291(TV),
   310(RS)
Fix Up the Spare Room, Mother(att. Porter-Hoefle) 16
Flight of the Bumble Bee (see Sneezin' Bee, Laughing Record) 310(RS),
   320(TV)
Football Medley - 213(AC)
Foreign Legion - 256(M),269(TV),289(TV)
Fort Worth Jail(Reinhart) 30(ET)
48 Reasons Why(Honeycomb-Clems) 40(ET)
For You(Burke-Dubin) 358(RS)
Foster Follies - 132
Frankie and Johnnie(Traditional-Brandt-Jones) 356(RS)
Frank Yankovic Waltz(Skaters Waltz-Waldteufel) 314(RS)

Frantic Freeway (also Sigalert Bossa Nova, Beep Beep Pachanga)
  367(RS*)
Frosty, the Snow Man(Steve Nelson-Jack Rollins) 306(RS)
(The) Funnies Aren't Funny Anymore(Morgan-Brandt) 217(AC)
Funny Punny Polka(Frisch-Wayne) 314(RS)

Galway Bay(Dr. Arthur Colohan) 226(AC)
Gerald McBoing Boing(Gail Kubik-Dr. Suess) 283(RS*)
Gesundheit Polka(Freddy Morgan-Sol Meyer) 272(RS),313(RS)
Get Happy(Harold Arlen-Ted Koehler) 184(AC)
Ghoul Days(School Days)(Cobb-Edwards) 359,367(RS*)
G.I. Haircut 102(ACU)
(The) Girl I Left Behind Me(Del Porter-Carl Hoefle) 45(ET)
(The) Girl With the Golden Braids(Stanley Kahan-Eddie Snyder) 322(TV)
Give A Man A Horse He Can Ride(O'Hara) 206(AC)
Give My Regards To Broadway(Cohan) 194(AC)
(The) Glow Worm(Lilla Cayley-Paul Linke) 83,85(AC),86(AC),100,110(AC)
  121(ET),128(M),130(AC),131(RS),136(AC),143,153,180(AC),182,196,
  214(AC),264(TV),360(RS)
God Bless Us All(Tommy Murray-Tony Burello) 282(RS)
Gonna Stomp Those City Slickers Down(Cindy Walker) 20,41(CW)
(A) Goose To the Ballet Russe (Russe) 75,107,234(RS*),240,367(RS*)
Grass Shack Rock (Take Me Back) 326(RS)
(The) Great Big Saw Came Nearer and Nearer(Latham-Carlson-Bonner)
  86(AC),90(AC),99(ET),116(AC)
Great Day(Youmans-Elison-Rose) 120(AC),127(AC)
(The) Great Train Robbery(Meade Lux Lewis-Lindley Jones) 347(RS,349
Green Green(McGuire-Sparks) 356(RS)

Hair Of Gold, Eyes Of Blue(Sunny Skylar) 210(AC)
Happy New Year(Eddie Brandt-Freddy Morgan) 180(RS),181(AC),214(AC),
  243
Happy Trumpets Polka (Under the Double Eagle)(Wagner-Rock-Jones)
  313(RS),314
Hardly Ever Amber(Howard Gibeling) 136(AC),137(AC),138(ET),142(AC)
Hark Medley(Hark the Herald Angels Sing, O Little Town Of Bethlehem,
  Joy To the World, O Come All Ye Faithful) 308(RS),309
Hark the Herald Angels Sing(Wesley-Mendelssohn) 309
Harlem Nocturne(Rogers-Earl Hagen) 360(RS)
Hasta Luego (see Clink Clink, Another Drink) 42
(A) Hat For Hedda Hopper (Hedda Hopper's Hats)(John Elliot) 128(M)
Haunted Heart(Howard Dietz-Arthur Schwartz) 200(AC)
Hawaiian War Chant(Ralph Reed-Johnny Noble-Leleiohaku) 118(AC),
  122(RS*),131(RS),138(AC),146(AC),168,182,194(AC),208,253,259,265,
  266,329(TV)
Heat Wave(Irving Berlin) 134(AC),135(AC)
He Broke My Heart In Three Places(Drake-Livingston-Hoffman) 95(AC),
  99(ET)
He Knew All Of the Answers(Cindy Walker) 28(CW),31(CW)
Henry Morganthau Blues(attr. Porter-Hoefle-Jones) 90(AC)
Here Comes Santa Claus(Autry-Waldeman) 306(RS)
Hey, Good Lookin'(Hank Williams) 363(RS)
Hey Mable(Stryker) 35(ET)
Hey, Mr. Banjo(Morgan-Malkin) 358(RS)
Hi Ho My Lady (also Hi Yo My Lady)(Del Porter-Carl Hoefle) 48(ET)
Hillbilly Bill(Cindy Walker) 27(CW)
Hi Mister(Bob Roberts-Bob Sherman) 302(RS)
Hindustan(Weeks-Wallace) 187(AC),211(AC),241(AC),287(TV)
Hi Neighbor(Jack Owens) 29(ET),30,175(AC)
His Rocking Horse Ran Away - see And His Rocking Horse Ran Away
Hitch Old Dobbin To the Shay Again(J.C. Lewis-Jud Conlon) 62(AC),
  64(AC),80(AC),101(ACU)
Holiday For Strings(David Rose) 94(AC),100(AC),101(AC),102(ACU),104,
  105,107,108(AC),109(RS),110(AC),114,116(AC),118(AC),121(ET),126(M),
  127(AC),143,177(AC),182,265(TV),287(TV),276(TV),330,367(RS)
Home On the Range(Dan Kelly-David Guion) 176(AC),181(AC),206(AC)
Homesick(Cindy Walker) 31(CW)

Hootenanny Party(Eddie Brandt) 359(RS*),362
Horsie, Keep Your Tail Up(Hirsch-Kaplan) 45(ET)
Hotcha Cornia (Russian Folk songs)(Del Porter-Spike Jones) 12,35(ET),
  36,43(AC),46(RS),47,49(AC),52,56(M)(AC),63(AC),65(AC),78(AC),
  79(AC),81(V),89(M)(AC),100,101(AC),102(ACU),104,105,117(AC),126(M),
  127(AC),128(M),168,169,182,203(AC),208,268(TV)
Hot Lips(Henry Busse-Henry Lange-Lou Davis) 15,276(RS)
Hot Rod Bash - 357,367(RS*)
Hotter Than A Pistol(Tom Glazer) 277(RS)
(A) Hot Time In the Old Town Tonight(Hayden-Metz) 18,130(AC),282(M),
  320(TV)
How High the Fidelity - 311(RS)
How Many Apples Does It Take To Make A Pie?(Cindy Walker) 41(CW)
How Soon?(Jack Owens-Carroll Lucas) 190(AC)
How the Circus Learned To Smile(Edward Pripps-Frank Tashlin) 178(RS),
  179(RS),214(AC)
Hut Sut Song(Killion-McMichael-Owens) 341(RS)

I Can't Begin To Tell You(Gordon-Monaco) 140(AC)
I Can't Help It(Hank Williams) 363(RS)
I Don't Trust the Men(Cindy Walker) 31(CW)
I Dream Of Brownie With the Light Blue Jeans(Sol Meyer-Spike Jones)
  131(RS),132,142(AC),143,220(AC)
If I Had A Hammer(Hays-Seeger) 356(RS)
If I Loved You(Rodgers-Hammerstein) 127(AC)
If You Knew Suzie(DeSylva-Meyer) 202(AC)
I Got Plenty O' Nuttin'(Gershwin) 117(AC)
I Gotta Gal I Love (In North and South Dakota)(Sammy Kahn-Jule Styne)
  126(M)
I Haven't Been Home For Three Whole Nights(Jack Elliot-Lou Quadling)
  262(RS)
(I Hear) Your Heart Calling Mine(Frank Loesser) 147(M)
I Just Love My Mommy(Robert Mellin-Gene Chancer) 282(RS)
I Kiss Your Hand Madame(Fritz Rotter) 37,177(RS),178(AC),188(AC),
  206(AC),211(AC),341(RS)
I Know A Secret(Johnny Rotella-Lee Kayden) 246(RS)
I Know A Story(Washburn-Weems) 47(ET),58(AC),82(AC)
Ill Barkio(L. Arditi-E. Brandt) 180(RS),181,190(AC),201(AC),202,
  232(AC),240
I'll Be Seeing You(Kahal-Fain) 206(AC)
I'll Lend You Everything I've Got (Except My Wife, and I'll Make You
  a Present of Her)(att. Bert Williams-George Walker) 16
I'll Never Be the Same(Kahn-Malneck-Signorelli) 137(AC),139(ET)
I'll Never Smile Again(Ruth Lowe) 15
I'll Never Work There Anymore(Lindley A. Jones-Sid Robin-Al Levy)
  275(RS)
I Love Coffee, I Love Tea (also Java Jive) 68(AC)
I Love You(Harry Archer-Harlen Thompson) 190(AC)
Imagination(Van Heusen-Burke) 15
I'm Always Chasing Rainbows(McCarthy-Carroll) 135(AC)140(AC)
I'm A Yankee Doodle Dandy(The Yankee Doodle Boy)(Cohan) 116(AC),
  329(TV)
I'm Bidin' My Time - see Bidin' My Time
I'm Forever Blowing Bubble Gum (see also Blowing Bubble Gum) 149(RS)
I'm Getting Sentimental Over You(Ned Washington-George Bassman)
  115(AC),116(AC),175(AC)(RS),
I'm Goin' Back To West Virginia (see I Wanna Go Back To West
  Virginia) 47(ET)
I'm Goin' Back To Whur I Come From(Carson Robison) 79(AC),80(AC),
  96(AC),101(ACU),102(ACU)
I'm Gonna Love That Guy(Francis Ash) 140(AC)
I'm Gonna Sit Right Down and Write Myself a Letter(Joe Young-Fred E.
  Ahlert) 322(TV),324(TV)
I'm Going To Write Home(Foster Carling) 48(ET)
I'm In the Mood For Love(Fields-McHugh) 287(TV),289(TV),291(RS),
  301(TV),360(RS)
I'm Just Wild About Harry(Nobel Sissle-Eubie Blake) 101(ACU),188(AC)

I'm Looking Over a Four Leaf Clover(Mort Dixon-Harry Wood) 186(AC),
  191(AC)
I'm Ridin' For A Fall(Loesser-Schwartz) 56(M)
I'm So Lonesome I Could Cry(Hank Williams) 363(RS)
I'm the Angel in the Christmas Play (see Angel in the Christmas Play)
I'm Walkin'(Fats Domino-Dave Bartholemew) 317(TV)
In A Little Spanish Town(Sam Lewis-Joe Young-Mabel Wayne) 190(AC)
In A Persian Market(Ketelbey) 217(AC),218,264(TV),269,271,282(M),
  358(TV)
Indian Love Call(Harbach-Hammerstein-Friml) 293,325(TV)
I Never Knew(B. Brown-E. Carroll-G. Kahn) 86(AC)
In My Arms(Loesser-Grouya) 69(AC),71(AC),102(ACU)
In the Hall Of the Mountain King(E. Greig) 293
In the Merry Month Of May(Ren Shields-George Evans) 200(AC)
Into the Sunrise(Cindy Walker) 41(CW)
I Only Have Eyes For You(Dubin-Warren) 134(AC),137(AC),138(ET),
  142(AC),338(RS)
I Saw Mommy Kissing Santa Claus(T. Conner) 272,277(ET),278(RS*),
  279(RS),325(TV)
I Saw Mommy Screwing Santa Claus(Connor-Morgan) 279(RS*)
I Saw the Light(Hank Williams) 363(RS)
I Search For Golden Adventure In My Seven Leaky Boots(E. Brandt-
  L. Ecklund-C. Brandt) 341(RS)
Is It True What They Say About Dixie?(Sammy Lerner-Gerald Marks)
  219(AC)
It Came Upon A Midnight Clear(Sullivan-Sears)(Deck the Halls Medley)
  307
It Don't Mean a Thing If It Ain't Got That Swing(Ellington) 118(AC)
It Had To Be You(Isham Jones-Kahn) 99(ET)
It Might As Well Be Spring(Rodgers-Hammerstein) 140(AC)
It Never Can Be(Cindy Walker) 31(CW)
It Never Rains In Sunny California(Jack Elliot) 88(AC),100,108(AC),
  272(RS),283
It's All Your Fault(Cindy Walker) 31(CW)
It's A Long Way From Minsk To Pinsk(att. Benny Davis-Murray Mencher)
  64(AC)
It's A Sin To Tell A Lie(William Mayhew) 191(AC)
It's Been A Long, Long Time(Cahn-Styne) 140(AC)
It's Christmas Time(Al Stillman) (Victor Young Medley) 309(RS)
It's Love, Love, Love(David-Whitney-Kramer) 91(AC),92(AC),95(AC),105
It's Magic(Cahn-Styne) 211(AC),213(AC)
I've Found A New Baby(Palmer-Williams) 172(AC),181(AC)
I've Got My Love To Keep Me Warm(Irving Berlin) 228(AC)
I've Got the World On A String(Koehler-Arlen) 136(AC),137(AC),
  139(ET)(AC),142(AC)
I've Turned A Gadabout(Pee Wee King-Redd Stewart) 273(RS)
I Wanna Go Back To West Virginia(Bill Crago-Grace Shannon) 47(RS),
  47(ET),78(AC)
I Want a Girl, Just Like the Girl That Married Dear Old Dad
  (Dillon-Von Tilzer) 68(AC),71(AC)
I Want Eddie Fisher For Christmas(Javits-Springer) 300(RS)
I Want Somebody(Cindy Walker) 27(CW),28(CW)
I Want the South To Win the War For Christmas(Cahn-Van Heusen)
  338(RS)
I Was A Teen Age Brain Surgeon(Brandt-Maxwell) 329(TV),335(RS)
I Went to Your Wedding(Jessie Mae Robinson) 278(RS)
I Wonder Where My Baby Is Tonight?(Gus Kahn-Walter Donaldson)
  244(RS*)(RS)
I Wonder Who's Kissing Her Now?(Adams-Houeh-Howard) 15
I Wuv a Wabbit(Milton Berle-Ervin Drake-Paul Martell) 149(RS*),174

Jambalaya(Hank Williams) 363(RS)
Jamboree Jones(Johnny Mercer) 98(ET),99
Japanese Skokiaan(August Muaurgwo-Tom Glazer) 299(RS),301(TV)
Java(Toussaint-Tyler-Friday) 358(RS)
Jackie Gleason - 367
Jealousy (Jalousie)(Gade-Bloom) 134(AC),135(AC),137(AC),142(AC)
Jingle Bells(Pierpont)(Jingle Bells Medley) 59(AC),84(AC),180(AC),

214(AC),307,308
Jingle Bells Medley (Santa Claus Is Coming To Town, The Christmas
    Song, Jingle Bells) 307(RS)
Jingle, Jangle, Jingle(Loesser-Lilley) 205(AC)
John Scotter Trot(Scott) 44(ET),45
Jones Laughing Record (Flight of the Bumble Bee) 144(RS),311
Jones Polka(Mickey Katz-Spike Jones) 140(RS),143
Joy To the World(Watts-Handel)(Hark Medley) 309
Jungle Drums(Lecuona-Lombardo-O'Flynn) 136(AC),137(AC),142(AC)
Jungle Town - see Down In Jungle Town

Kansas City(Stoller-Lieber) 358(RS)
Kate 179(AC),186(AC)
Kaw-liga(H. Williams-F. Rose) 363(RS)
Keystone Kapers (Bag of Rags)(L. Jones) 276(RS*),277,347(RS*)(RS),349
(The) Kid With the Rip In His Pants(Jack Owens) 86(AC)
Knock, Knock, Who's There(Eddie Brandt-Freddie Morgan) 216(RS),
    226(AC),228(AC),323(TV),341(RS)
Kookie, Kookie, Lend Me Your Comb - see Spooky, Spooky, Lend
    Me Your Tomb

Las Chiapanecas(Torre-Gamas-de Campo) 174(AC)
Lassus Trombone(Henry Fillmore) 141(RS),320(TV)
Last Horizon(Del Porter-Carl Hoefle) 30(ET)
(The) Last Shot Got Him - 101(ACU)
(The) Late Late Late Movies(S. Jones-E. Brandt) 333(RS)
Laura(Johnny Mercer-David Raskin) 114(AC),115,120(AC),138(ET)(AC),
    139(AC),141(RS),172(AC),204,208,264(TV),301
Laughing Record - see Jones Laughing Record
Lavender Blue (Dilly Dilly)(Larry Morey-Elliot Daniel) 219(AC)
Lawrence Welk Polka(Frank Flynn-Joe Washburne) 313(RS),314,320(TV)
Lazy Bones(Hoagy Carmichael-Johnny Mercer) 203(AC)
Leave the Dishes In the Sink, Ma(Milton Berle-Spike Jones-Gene
    Doyle) 109(RS),114(AC)
Lefty Louie(Jacob) 360(RS)
Let it Snow! Let It Snow! Let It Snow!(Sammy Cahn-Jule Styne)(Snow
    Medley) 308
Let's Kiss, Kiss, Kiss(Carl Brandt) 364(RS)
Libes-strum(Freddy Morgan-Spike Jones) 316(RS)
Liebestraum(Franz Liszt-Del Porter) 63(AC),71(AC),82(AC),91(AC),
    98(ET),117(AC),122(RS),143,168,192(AC),208,215(AC),310,316(RS),
    321(TV)
Limehouse Blues(Furber-Braham) 207(AC),211(AC)
Linger Awhile(Vincent Rose-Harry Owens) 292(TV)
Lips That Touch Liquor, Shall Never Touch Mine(L. Jones) 348(RS),349
Listen To the Mockingbird(Alice Hawthorne) 178(AC),195(AC),198
(A) Little Bird Told Me(Harvey O. Brooks) 217(AC)
Little Bo-Peep Has Lost Her Jeep(Frank DeVol-Jerry Bowne) 35(ET),
    37(RS),38(AC),43(AC),67(AC)
Little Child(Shanklin-Roberts) 304(RS),305,311
Little Things Mean A Lot(Lindeman) 326(RS*)
Liza(Gershwin-Kahn) 127(AC),188(AC)
Loch Lomond(Traditional) 181(AC)
Loretta's Soaperetta(S. Jones-E. Brandt) 341(RS)
Louisville Calls America - 147
Love and Marriage(Cahn-Van Heusen) 304(RS)
Love For Sale(Cole Porter) 45(ET)
Love Has Been the Ruin Of Many A Maid(Cindy Walker) 27(CW)
Love In Bloom(Leo Robin-Ralph Rainger) 146(AC),149(RS),176(AC),
    290(TV),330(TV)
Lovely(Edward Lane) 135(AC),138(AC),139(AC),142(AC)
Lover(Rodgers-Hart) 293
Lullaby of Broadway(Warren-Dubin) 183(AC)
Lulu Had A Baby(Lee W. Roberts) 280(RS),281

MacNamara's Band(John J. Stamford-Shamus-O'Connor) 85(AC),86(AC),
    118(AC),119(V),174(RS*),177(AC),216(RS),289(TV)

Madame Fifi's Can Can(C. Brandt) 348(RS),349
Mairsey (Mairzy) Doats(Milton Drake-Al Hoffman-Jerry Livingston)
    87(AC),88(AC),323(TV),342(RS)
Make Believe Island(Nick Kenny-Charles Kenny-Grosz-Coslow) 15
Mama's Makin' Bombers - 72(AC)
Manana(Barbour-Lee) 358(RS)
(The) Man On the Flying Trapeze(Lee-Laynourne) 156(RS),171,175,
    176(AC),206(AC),260(ET)
Maria Elena(Lorenzo-Barcelata) 357(RS)
Martha(Flotow) 197(AC)
Mary Lou(Robinson-Lyman-Waggner) 88(AC),99(ET),102(ACU)
Medley No. 1 (I'll Never Smile Again, Make Believe Island,
    Imagination) 15
Medley No. 2 (You're Driving Me Crazy, Am I Blue?, I Wonder Who's
    Kissing Her Now?, Chant Of the Jungle, Dream House) 15,16
Melody In F(Rubinstein) (also Pickin' Melody In F) 286(TV),275(TV),
    309(RS),324(TV)
Melody Of Love(Englemann-S. Jones) 342(RS)
Memories Are Made Of This(Gilkyson-Dehr-Miller) 304(RS),305
Merry Christmas Polka(Paul Francis Webster-Sonny Burke)(Christmas
    Alphabet Medley) 308
Mine(Gershwin-Gershwin) 127(AC)
Minka(George Rock) 119(V),137(ET),141(RS),168,182,208,222(AC),289(TV)
Minnie the Moocher(C. Calloway-I. Mills-C. Gaskill) 323(TV)
Minstrel Show - 222(AC)
Missouri Waltz(Shannon-Eppel) 195(AC),201(AC),222(AC),265(AC),266(AC)
Moanin' Low(Rainger-Dietz) 45(ET)
Molasses, Molasses(Larry Clinton) 260(RS),261(ET)
Mommy, Won't You Buy a Baby Brother?(Eddie Maxwell) 245(ET),
    246(RS*)(RS),257,260(ET)
Monster Movie Ball(Jones-Brandt) 335(RS),336
Moo Woo Woo(Del Porter-Carl Hoefle) 29(ET)
Morpheus(Offenbach-S. Jones-E. Maxwell) 195(AC),224(AC),234(RS),
    256(M),261(ET),269(TV)
Mother Goose Medley(Porter-Jones) 131(RS),132,143
Move It On Over(Hank Williams) 363(RS)
(A) Mudder's Day Sports Spectacular - see Feetlebaum Bombs
Mule Train - see Chinese Mule Train
My Banjo At Thy Sweet Voice(Saint Saens-Morgan-Jones) 316(RS)
My Birthday Comes On Christmas(Louis Bush) 305(RS)
My Blue Heaven(George Whiting-Walter Donaldson) 178(AC)
My Cornet(George Rock-Del Porter) 156(RS*)
My Daddy Is A General To Me(Paul Knittel) 263(RS),266(AC)
My Darling, My Darling(Frank Loesser-Richard Myers) 215(AC)
My Gal Sal(Dresser) 219(AC),233(AC),261(ET)
My Heart Cries For You(Percy Faith-Carl Sigman) 264(TV)
My Heart Sings - see All Of A Sudden, My Heart Sings
My Heart Went Boom Boom(Freddy Morgan) 284(RS*),285,286(TV),312(RS),
    313
My Home Town(Eddie Brandt-Sammy Rones) 111(AC),134(AC)
My Little Girl(Von Tilzer-William Dillon) 70(AC)
My Little Grass Shack (In Kealakekua, Hawaii)(Johnny Noble-Cogswell-
    Harrison) 265(AC)
My Man(Willimetz-Pollack-Yvain) 359(RS)
My Old Flame(Arthur Johnson-Sam Coslow) 170(RS),171,174(AC),186(AC),
    193(AC),204,205,208,213(AC),267,301,336(RS),337
My Old Kentucky Home(S. Foster) 198(AC)
My Pretty Girl(Del Porter-Ray Johnson-Howard Gibeling) 145(RS)
My Two Front Teeth - see All I Want For Christmas Is My Two Front
    Teeth - 241(AC),265(TV)

Nature Boy(eden ahbez) 201(AC),210(AC)
(The) Nearness Of You(Hoagy Carmichael-Ned Washington) 15
Near You(Francis Craig-Kermit Goell) 176(AC),180(AC),184(AC)
Never Hit Your Grandma With A Shovel(Hanemann) 39(ET),323(TV)
New Beer Barrel Polka(Brown-Timm-Vejvoda) 314(RS)
Newsreel - 212(AC)
New Years Resolution - see Happy New Year - 180,181

(The) Night Before Christmas(Johnny Marks) 308(RS)
Nobody's Sweetheart Now(Gus Kahn-Ernie Erdmann-Billy Meyers-Elmer
    Schoebel) 309(RS)
No Boom Boom In Yucca Flats(Billy Barty) 303(RS)
No Dough Blues - 299(RS*)
No Love, No Nothin'(Leo Robin-Harry Warren) 84(AC)
None But the Lonely Heart(Eddie Brandt-Spike Jones) 181(RS),198(AC)
No, No, Nora(Erdman-Fiorito-Kahn) 102(ACU),120(AC),121(ET),174(AC),
    192(AC)
Now Laugh(Del Porter-Carl Hoefle) 35(ET)
Now Or Never(Cindy Walker) 31(CW)
Nutcracker Suite(Tchaikovsky-Foster Carling-Country Washburn-
    Louis Adrian) 123(RS),124(RS),125(RS),131
(I'm Getting) Nuttin' For Christmas(Roy Bennett-Sid Tepper) 305(RS),
    309
Nyet - 367(RS*)

O Come All Ye Faithful(Wade-Oakley-Brooks)(Hark Medley) 309
Oh Brother(Maxine Manners-Jean Miller) 80(AC)
Oh! By Jingo(Lew Brown-Albert Von Tilzer) 46(RS),48(ET),67(AC),
    68(AC),73,92(AC),101(ACU),117(AC),195(AC),217(AC),260(ET)
Oh Happy Day(Don Howard Koplow-Nancy Binns Reed) 280(RS*),281
Oh How She Lied(White-Donaldson) 97(AC),99(ET)
Oh Suzannah(S. Foster) 187(AC)
Oh What It Seemed To Be(Benjamin-Weiss-Carle) 134(AC),137(AC),140(AC)
Oh, You Beautiful Doll(A. Seymour-Brown-Nat D. Ayer) 188(AC)
Old MacDonald Had A Farm(Traditional-Spike Jones-Del Porter) 63(AC),
    71(AC),94(AC),131(RS),143,176(AC),198,208
Old Man River(Kern-Hammerstein) 115(AC)
Old Sow Song(Smith-Vallee-Daniels) 311(RS)
O Little Town Of Bethlehem(Brooks-Redner) (Hark Medley) 309
On A Slow Boat To China(Frank Loesser) 213(AC)
One Dozen Roses(Country Washburn-Walter Donovan-Dick Jurgens-
    Roger Lewis) 44,71(AC)
One For My Baby(Harold Arlen-Johnny Mercer) 256(M),322(TV),339(TV)
On the Beach at Waikiki(H. Kailimai-G.H. Stover) 184(AC)
On the Sunny Side Of the Street(Fields-McHugh) 87(AC),139(AC)
Orpheus Overture - see Morpheus 234
Our Hour(Hoffman-David-Livingston) 166(RS),167,168
Over the Rainbow(Arlen-Harburg) 135(AC),179(AC),206(AC)

Pack Up Your Troubles(Felix Powell-George Asaf) 24,33(RS),39(ET)
Paddlin' Madelin Home(H. Woods) 69(AC),70(AC),99(ET),100(AC)
Pagliacci - see Pal-Yat-Chee 250
Pale Moon(Glick-Logan) 204(AC),213(AC)
Pal-Yat-Chee(Leoncavello-Eddie Maxwell-Spike Jones) 250(RS),311,
    312(RS),314,320(TV)
Pantomime Theme - 367
Paradise(Brown-Clifford) 360(RS)
Pass the Biscuits, Mirandy(Del Porter-Carl Hoefle) 12,39(ET),37(RS),
    38(AC),43(M),61(AC),70(AC),181,256(M),268(TV),282(M),288(TV)
Peanut Vendor(Gilbert-Simons-Sunshine) 16
Peg O' My Heart(Fisher-Bryan) 188(AC)
Pennsylvania Polka(Lee-Manners) 222(AC),314(RS),325(TV)
People Are Funnier Than Anybody(Hal Finberg-Eddie Brandt) 174(RS),
    178(AC),183(AC),232(AC),314(RS)
People Will Say We're In Love(Rodgers-Hammerstein) 83(AC),102(ACU),
    173(AC)
Perfidia(Leeds-Dominquez) 135(AC),139(ET)(AC),169(AC)
Personality(Burke-Van Heusen) 134(AC)
Peter Cottontail(Steve Nelson-Jack Rollins-Freddy Morgan) 262(RS),
    265(AC),290
Pickin' Melody In F(Rubinstein-Morgan-Jones-Malkin) 310(RS)
Pick It You Peasant(Jad Paul-Freddy Morgan-Spike Jones) 303(RS)
Pico Pick Up(Harry Rodgers) 134(AC),137(AC),139(ET)
Pimples and Braces(Irving Taylor-Carl Brandt) 341(RS)
Please Don't Talk About Me When I'm Gone(Clare-Stept-Palmer) 193(AC),
    212(AC)

Poet and Peasant (Von Suppe)(also Cotton Pickin' Peasant Overture and
    Pick It You Peasant) 264(TV),276(TV),282(M),284,317(TV),348(RS),349
Poisen To Poisen(Brandt-Jones) 338(RS)
Pootwaddle Car Polish(Doodles Weaver-Paul Leu) 229(AC)
Pootwaddle Cigarettes(Doodles Weaver-Paul Leu) 232(AC)
Pootwaddle Hair Tonic(Doodles Weaver-Paul Leu) 232(AC)
Pootwaddle Portable Sink(Doodles Weaver-Paul Leu) 264(TV)
Pootwaddle Tooth Paste(Doodles Weaver-Paul Leu) 233(AC)
Pootwaddle Vitamins(Doodles Weaver-Paul Leu) 233(AC)
Pop Corn Sack(Rene Duplessis-Serge Walter) 165(RS),166,167,168,
    171(AC)
Popeye(Lerner-Koppell) 312(RS),313,323(TV)
Portia and the Hollywood Wolf - 218(AC)
Powder Your Face With Sunshine(Carmen Lombardo-Stanley Rochinski)
    220(AC)
Powerhouse(Raymond Scott) 367(RS)
Pretty Girl - see My Pretty Girl
Pretty Girl Polka(Spike Jones-Bernie Jones-Freddy Morgan) 314(RS)
Pretty Posie(Morgan-Jones) 310(RS)
Puff(the Magic Dragon)(Yarrow-Lipton) 357(RS)
Purple People Eater(Shep Wooley) 328(TV)
Pussycat Song(Dick Manning) 222(AC)
Put 'Em In a Box, Tie'Em With a Ribbon(Jule Styne-Sammy Kahn) 211(AC)
Put Your Arms Around Me Honey(McCree-Von Tilzer) 70(AC),72(TR),82(AC)

Quartet From Rigor Mortis(Quartet From Rigoletto-Verdi) 211(AC)

Rabbits, Rabbits, Rabbits(attr. Doodles Weaver) 227(AC)
Ragtime Cowboy Joe(Abrahams-Clark-Muir) 87(AC),183(AC)
Ramona(Gilbert-Wayne) 310(RS),320(TV)
Red Grow the Roses(Porter-Washburn) 88(AC),98(ET)
Red Sails In the Sunset(Kennedy-Williams-Graz) 357(RS)
Red Wing(Thurland Chattaway-Kerry Hill) 16,18,25(RS)(RS*),26,35,
    48(ET),62(AC),66(AC),102(ACU)
Rhapsody From Hunger(Spike Jones) 184,197,234(RS),266(AC),290
Rhapsody In Blue(Gershwin) 210(AC)
Rhumba (Rumba) Rhapsody(Audinot-de Pru) 134(AC),137(AC)(ET)
Rickeyshaw (Ricochet Romance)(Larry Coleman-Joe Darion-Norman Gimbal-
    Bernie Jones-Bill Whelpley) 284(RS),285
Riders In the Sky(Stan Jones) 229(AC),230(RS),231
Ridin' For the Rancho(Cindy Walker) 27(CW)
Ridin' Home With You(Hampton-Duning) 35(ET)
River, Stay 'Way From My Door(Woods-Dixon) 340(RS)
Ron Terry Polka(Morgan-Meyer) 313(RS)
Rose of the Border(Cindy Walker) 41(CW)
Round and Round(Velona-Meyer) 316(TV)
Round Me Up and Call Me Dogie(Cindy Walker) 27(CW)
Row, Row, Row(Jerome-Monaco) 68(AC),102(ACU),121(ET),199(AC)
Rudolph, the Red Nosed Reindeer(Johnny Marks-Eddie Maxwell) 246,
    257(RS),305(RS)
Rum Tee Diddle Dee Yump(Fred Morgan-Earl Bennett) 180(RS*),215(RS)
Runnin' Wild(Joe Grey-Leo Wood-A. Harrington Gibbs) 176(AC),232(AC)

Sabre Dance(Khatchachurian) 285(TV),293,298,301(TV),325(TV),358(TV),
    362
Sailin' On the Robert E. Lee(West-McCaffrey-Ringle) 92(AC),99(ET),
    101(ACU)
Sailor With the Navy Blue Eyes(Taylor-Mizzy-Hoffman) 45(ET)
Salt River Valley(Cindy Walker) 27(CW)
Salute(Sol Meyer-Spike Jones-Freddy Morgan) 274(RS)
San(Walter Michels-Lindsay McPhail) 176(AC),204(AC),288(TV)
San Antonio Rose(Bob Wills) 187(AC),192(AC),290(TV)
San Fernando Valley(Gordon Jenkins) 92,105,201(AC)
Santa Brought Me Choo Choo Trains(Bob Sadoff-Paul S. Lasky) 283(RS)
Santa Claus Is Coming To Town(Coots-Gillespie)(Jingle Bells Medley)
    307
Santa Claus' Son - see Wouldn't It Be Fun To Be Santa Claus' Son
Sante(Sol Meyer-Freddy Morgan-Lindley A. Jones) 274(RS),338(ET)

Satellite Baby(Billy Barty) 326(RS*)
Saturday Night Is the Lonliest Night Of the Week(Styne-Kahn) 117(AC)
Save Your Sorrow For Tomorrow(Bud G. DeSylva-Al Sherman) 327(RS*)
Say It Isn't So(Irving Berlin) 218(AC)
Sayonara G.I.(att. Billy Barty) 326(RS*)
Say Something Sweet To Your Sweetheart(Sid Tepper) 218(AC)
Schicklegruber(Ralph Freed-Sammy Fain) 69(M),70,71,73(AC)
Secret Love(Paul Francis Webster-Sammy Fain) 291(RS),292(TV)
Send For Me(Ollie Jones) 325(TV)
September Song(Anderson-Weill) 136(AC),137(AC),138(ET),139(AC),
  140(AC),142(AC),356(RS)
Serenade To a Jerk(Del Porter-Carl Hoefle) 35(ET),111(RS),112,143
Seventy Six Trombones(Meredith Willson) 332(TV)
Shangri-La(Sigman-Malneck-Maxwell) 360(RS)
(The) Sheik Of Araby(Smith-Wheeler-Snyder) 43(M),46(RS),47,48(ET),
  62(AC),67(AC),70(AC),73,75,117(AC),168,182,208,264(TV)
She Wouldn't Do-What I Asked Her To(Mitchell-Gottlieb-Burt-
  Boutelje) 15,16
She Broke My Heart In Three Places - see He Broke My Heart....
Shh! Harrys Odd(Scheherezade)(Rimsky-Korsakov) 367(RS*)
Shipyard Symphony (see Schicklegruber) 69
Shine(Dabney-Mack-Brown) 200(AC)
Shoo Fly Pie and Apple Pan Dowdy(Sammy Gallop-Guy Wood) 134(AC),
  137(AC),140(AC)
Shoo Shoo Baby(Phil Moore) 80(AC),84(AC),
Shortnin' Bread(Jacques Wolf) 178(AC),241(AC),261(ET),265(AC)
Shuffle Off To Buffalo(Al Dubin-Harry Warren) 190(AC)
Siam(Del Porter-Carl Hoefle) 12,35(ET),36,37(RS),56(AC),58(AC),
  86(AC),87,118(AC),119(V),177,289(TV)
Sick, Sick, Sick(E. Brandt-L. Jones) 328(TV)
Side By Side(Harry Woods-Gus Kahn) 193(AC)
Sidewalks Of New York(Lawlor-Blake) 207(AC),212(AC),224(AC)
Sigalert Bossa Nova (Frantic Freeway) 367(RS*)
Silent Night(Gruber-Mohr) 306,307(RS)
Silents Please(C. Brandt) 348(RS*),349
Silver Bells(Jay Livingston-Ray Evans)(White Christmas Medley) 307
Sioux City Sue(Ray Freedman-Dick Thomas) 192(AC)
Six Fat Dutchmen Polka(B. Jones-L. Jones) 314(RS)
Sixteen Tacos (Sixteen Tons)(Merle Travis) 304(RS)
Skokiaan - see Japanese Skokiaan
Slanthe(Sol Meyer-Freddy Morgan) 273(RS),289(TV)
Slap 'Er Down Again Pa(Asherman) 195(AC)
Sleep Well, Little Children(Alan Bergman-Leon Klatzkin) 308(RS),309
Sleigh Ride(Leroy Anderson) 308(RS)
Sloppy Lagoon (see Drip, Drip, Drip) 75,111
Slow Boat To China - see On a Slow Boat To China
Smiles(Callahan-Roberts) 327(RS*)
Snafu (attr. Porter-Hoefle) 86(AC)
Sneezin' Bee (Flight of the Bumble Bee) 310(RS),311
Snow Medley (The First Snowfall, Let it Snow) 307(RS)
Snoqualimie Jo Jo(Greene) 97(AC)
Socko, the Smallest Snowball(Freddy Morgan-Dave Myers) 278(RS)
So 'Elp Me(Spike Jones-Freddy Morgan) 257(RS)
Somebody Loves Me(MacDonald-DeSylva-Gershwin) 64(AC)
Somebody Stole My Gal(Leo Woods) 191(AC),310(RS)
Song of the Cowboy(Cindy Walker) 31(CW),32
Sonny Boy(Brown-DeSylva-Henderson-Jolson) 194(AC)
Sophisticated Lady(Ellington-Mills-Parish) 139(AC),140(AC),359(RS)
(The) Sound Effects Man(Billy Mills) 67(AC),68(AC),92(AC)
Spike Rocks the Troc(Harry Rodgers) 139(ET)(AC),140(AC),142(AC)
Spike Speaks (Tchaikovsky Arab Dance theme)(arr. Howard Gibeling)
  134,137(ET)
(The) Spirit of Christmas - 308(RS*)
Spooky, Spooky, Lend Me Your Tomb(Irving Taylor) 342(RS)
Spooktacular Finale(Brandt-Meyer) 336(RS)
Spring Song(Mendelssohn-Oliver) 190(AC)
Square Dance - 256(M)
Stairway To the Stars(Parish-Malneck-Signorelli) 360(RS)

Star Dust - 333(RS)
Star Jenka (Twinkle Twinkle Little Star)(Carl Brandt) 364(RS)
(The) Stars and Stripes Flicker Finale(L. Jones) 349
(The) Stars and Stripes Forever(J.P. Sousa) 347(RS*),348(RS),349
St. Louis Blues(W.C. Handy) 82(AC),102(ACU)
Stoplight(Newman) 357(RS)
Stop Your Gamblin'(Willard Robinson-Jack Pepper) 273(RS)
(The) Story of Christmas Medley 308(RS*)
Stranger In Paradise(Chet Forrest-Robert Wright) 291(TV)
St-St-Stella(Kennedy-Nolan) 47(ET)
(The) Stripper(David Rose) 94,360(RS)
(The) Strip Polka(Johnny Mercer) 313(RS),341(RS)
Stumbling(Confrey) 19,197(AC)
Sunday(J. Fred Coots-Clifford Grey) 90(AC),215(AC)
Surrey With the Fringe On Top(Rodgers-Hammerstein) 117(AC)
Sweet Adeline(Armstrong-Gerard) 16
Sweet and Lovely(Arnheim-Tobias-Lemare) 358(RS)
Sweet Georgia Brown(Bernie-Pinkard-Casey) 213(AC),229(AC)
Sweet Little You(Irving Bibo-Fred Phillips) 63(AC)
Sweet Something(Cindy Walker) 41(CW)
Sweet Sue(Will J. Harris-Victor Young) 309(RS)
Swinging Doors (see Behind Those Swinging Doors)
Swingin' the Double Eagle(Franz Josef Wagner-Spike Jones-Freddy
    Morgan) 316(RS)
Swingin' On A Star(Burke-Van Heusen) 102(ACU)
Symphony (C'est Fini)(Al Stone-Jack Lawrence) 140(AC)

Tab, Rory and Rock, Rock(Jones-Brandt-Newman) 326(RS)
Take It Easy(Irving Taylor-Albert DeBru-Vic Mizzy) 102(ACU)
Take Me Back(Bernal-Jones) 326(RS)
Take Me Out To the Ball Game(Norworth-Von Tilzer) 197(AC),227(AC)
Take the Door To the Left(James Cavanaugh-Walter G. Samuels) 62(AC),
    64(AC),72(AC)(TR),78(AC),88(AC)
Tammy(Livingston-Evans) 336(RS)
Ta-Ra-Ra Boom-De-Ay!(Henry J. Sayers) 17
Tchaikovsky Medley - 287(TV)
Tchaikovsky Piano Concerto - 275(TV),286(TV)
Teddy Bear(Danzig-Lowe-Mann) 322(TV)
Teen Age Brain Surgeon - see I Was a Teen Age Brain Surgeon - 329(TV)
Temptation(Freed-Brown) 359(RS)
Tenderly - 333(RS)
Tennessee Waltz(Redd Stewart-Pee Wee King) 262(RS)
Texas Concerto (Sol Meyer) 287(TV)
Texas Polka(Haldeman)100(AC)
Thanks For the Memory(Ralph Rainger-Leo Robin) 206(AC)
That Big Palooka Who Plays the Bazooka(Cindy Walker) pce,41(CW)
That Old Black Magic(Johnny Mercer-Harold Arlen) 66,72(TR),73(AC),
    80(AC),81(V),88(AC),89(M),104,117(AC),121(ET),122(RS),143,172(AC),
    182,196,208,233(AC),285(TV),292(TV),301,325(TV),367(RS*)
That Old Gang Of Mine(Ray Henderson-Mort Dixon-Billy Rose) 206(AC)
That's Amore(Warren-Brooks) 286(TV),288(TV)
That's A Plenty(Pollack-Gilbert) 211(AC)
That's My Pop(Arthur Fields-Fred Hall) 63(AC),73(AC)
That's What Makes the World Go 'Round(Lewis Jr.-Conlin) 39(ET),40
Theda Barracuda(C. Brandt) 348(RS)
Them There Eyes(Maceo Pinkard-William Tracey-Doris Tauber) 173(AC)
The Old Wrangler(Cindy Walker) 31(CW)
There'll Be A Hot Time In the Old Town Tonight (see (A) Hot Time...)
There'll Be No Teardrops Tonight(Hank Williams) 363(RS)
There, I've Said It Again(Redd Evans-Dave Mann) 358(RS)
There's A Blue Sky Way Out Yonder(Arthur Fields-Fred Hall-N. Van
    Cleve) 273(RS)
There's A Fly On My Music(courtesy M.G.M.) 85(AC)
There's No Business Like Show Business(Irving Berlin) 187(AC),199(AC)
There's Nothing Like a Circus - 197(AC),228(AC),260(ET)
The Twenties Roar(arr: Spike Jones) 340(RS)
The World Is Waiting For the Sunrise(Lockhart-Seitz) 310(RS)
They Go Wild, Simply Wild, Over Me(Fisher-McCarthy) 91(AC),99(ET)

When the Red Red Robin (Comes Bob Bob Bobbin' Along)(Woods) 195(AC)
When You And I Were Young, Maggie(J. McHugh-J. Frost) 177(AC)
When Yuba Plays the Rhumba On the Tuba(Herman Hupfeld) 139(ET),
   141(RS)
Where Did My Snowman Go?(Venis-Mann-Poser) 283(RS)
Whiffenpoof Song(Galloway-Minnigerade-Pomeroy) 193(AC)
Whispering(Scholberger-Coburn-Rose) 183(AC)
Whistler's Muddah(Ponchielli, arr: Jones-Brandt) 357(RS)
White Christmas(Berlin)(White Christmas Medley) 307(RS),309
White Christmas Medley (Winter Wonderland, Silver Bells, White
   Christmas) 307(RS)
Whittle Out A Whistle(Del Porter-Carl Hoefle) 98(ET),101/102(ACU)
Whoopee John Polka(Bernard Jones) 314(RS)
Who's Sick? - 334(RS*),335
Who's Sorry Now?(Kalmar-Ruby-Snyder) 176(AC)
Why Oh Why?(att. Billy Barty) 326(RS*)
Why Did You Let Me Leave You?(Morgan-Jones) 310(RS)
Wild Bill Hiccup (Hickup)(Morgan-Jones-Brandt) 205(AC),225(AC),
   230(RS),239,256(M)
Wild Wild Women(Wilson-Lewis-Piantidosi) 32(RS)
William Tell Overture(Rossini) 167,169(AC),171(RS),175,204(AC),
   207(AC),210(AC),265(AC),272,290(TV),290(TV),291,316,324(TV),331(TV)
William Tell Rag(Rossini, arr: Morgan-Jones) 316(RS)
(The) Winning Of the West(L. Jones) 348(RS,349
Winter(Alfred Bryan-Albert Gumble) 278(RS*),279(RS)
Winter Wonderland(Bernard-Smith)(also White Christmas Medley)
   178(AC),214(AC),307
(The) Wonderful World Of Hari Kari(E. Brandt-L. Ecklund) 341(RS)
(The) Wonderful World Of Susie Poontang - 367
World Is Waiting For the Sunrise - see The World Is Waiting...
Wouldn't It Be Fun To Be Santa Claus' Son?(Newman-Rotgeld) 305(RS),
   306
Would You Rather Be A Colonel?(Archie Gottler-Sandy Mitchell)
   102(ACU)
Wyatt Earp Makes Me Burp - 310(RS),312

Yaaka Hula Hickey Dula(Young-Goetz-Wendling) 257(RS),261(ET)
Ya Wanna Buy a Bunny?(Carl Hoefle-Del Porter) 216(RS),223(AC),
   226(AC),265(AC),291(TV)
Yankee Doodler(Carling-Boutelje) 20,45(ET),104
Yes Sir, That's My Baby(Kahn-Donaldson) 196(AC),207(AC),211(AC),
   290(TV),310(RS),315(TV added lyrics: Harry Stewart)
Yes! We Have No Bananas(Frank Silver-Irving Conn: Sp. lyrics-
   Eddie Maxwell) 178(AC),181(AC),257(RS)
You Always Hurt the One You Love(Doris Fisher-Allan Roberts) 115(AC),
   118(AC),119(V),121(ET),122(RS),127(AC),129(AC),135(AC),143,168,182,
   276(TV)
You Call Everybody Darling(Sam Martin-Al Trace-Ben Trace) 211(AC)
You Can't Be True Dear(Ebeler-Otten-Cotton) 210(AC),211(AC),213(AC)
   217(AC)
You Can't Say No To A Soldier(Gordon-Warren) 79(AC),81(V),101(ACU)
Young Man With A French Horn - 139(ET)
Your Cheatin' Heart(Hank Williams) 363(RS)
You're A Sap, Mister Jap(Cavanaugh-Redmond-Simon) 39(ET),40
You're Blase(Sievier-J.O. Hamilton) 134(AC)
You're Driving Me Crazy(Walter Donaldson) 15
You're From Texas(Cindy Walker) 41(CW)
Your Morning Feature(Alan Surgal) 39(ET)
You Tell Me Your Dream(Daniels-Rice-Brown) 197(AC)
You've Got My Heart Doing A Tap Dance(Cindy Walker) 31(CW)
You Were Only Fooling(Faber-Meadows-Fotin) 217(AC)
You Win Again(Hank Williams) 363(RS)

Zippity Zum - 299(RS*)

Addenda and Errata

The following material and corrections were received too late for inclusion in the text:

P.32   Delete: reference to "City Slickers" as the Jonathan Club
            official house band. The information in Anderson's diary
            has been mis-interpreted. Anderson's recollection is
            that "City Slickers" was in use as the show band name
            when he started with Spike in July 1941. Although booked
            as Spike Jones Dance Band, Spike had promoted the Slick-
            ers show to the extent that the name "City Slickers"
            (which originally applied only to the cooperative studio
            group for the 8 Aug 41 recording), became associated en-
            tirely with Spike, and the complete name change to Spike
            Jones and his City Slickers occurred by November 1941.

P.40 - 30 April, 1942 (THURS) - KRAFT MUSIC HALL*
                NBC Hollywood (Red network)

            The official NBC radio listing includes Jones involve-
        ment on this date, but not for 16 April, as shown in Ander-
        son's diaries. 30 Apr shows on 'Spokane 3' LP jackets while
        16 April matches "Spokane 4" jackets. Jones rehearsal ace-
        tates of b'cast titles are dated 16 Apr. NBC files are in
        error with Jones on 30 Apr date (which included Mary Martin,
        Jerry Lester, Victor Borge, Susan Hayward, Larry Adler and
        Gene Tunney, but no Jones).

P.55 - 27 October, 1942 (TUES) - AFRS COMMAND PERFORMANCE 39
                CBS Hollywood (courtesy Larry Kiner)

                Cass Daley - Medley of popular songs
                Hall Johnson Choir - "St. Louis Blues"
                Der Fuehrer's Face - voc Carl Grayson
                John Conte, Meredith Willson, Frank Morgan -
                    comedy dialogue
                Lena Horne - "I Gotta Right To sing the Blues"

P.55-61 - FURLOUGH FUN*
                NBC Hollywood   7:30 PM PST
            The pianist for the Monday night b'casts (but not the
        Gilmore audition) was Charlie LaVere. He was not available
        when the show moved its b'cast night in 1943. Steve LaVere
        has the working diaries of his father, one of the busier
        free-lance pianists in Hollywood, adding to the available
        Furlough Fun information; including the following:

P.55 - 20TH CENTURY FOX STUDIOS
                Movietone filming: change pianist to Charlie LaVere
                    (LaVere was paid $15 by Spike for his appearance)

P.65 - 27 March, 1943 (SAT) - AFRS COMMAND PERFORMANCE 59
          CBS Hollywood (courtesy Larry Kiner)

          Kay Kayser - "Touch of Texas"
          Liebestraum - with Carl Grayson, Luther Roundtree
          Kayser, Hedda Hopper - Comedy dialogue
          Balalaika Gypsy Band, Ralina Zarova - "Dark Eyes"
          Clink Clink, Another Drink - voc Mel Blanc
          Ish Kabibble - Recitation
          Kay Kayser - "I've Heard That Song Before"

          Note: Spike's "Clink" of this date is the AFRS Basic Music
Library P-36 labeled as "Hasta Luego". This AFRS ET has been "sweet-
ened" with added audience reactions and applause. Delete "Clink
Clink" reference on USO show of 30 May, 1942 (page 42).

P.74 - 4 September (SAT), 9 September (THURS), 1943 - ELLERY QUEEN*
          NBC New York   (Sponsor: Emerson)

          Spike Jones cameo appearance on the episodes "The Adven-
              ture of the Blind Bullet" (Armchair detective)

          11 September, 1943 (SAT) - BATTLE OF NEW YORK*
          NBC New York   (Bronx portion)

          with Spike Jones and his City Slickers

P.96 - 19 May, 1944 (FRI) - PEOPLE ARE FUNNY*
          NBC Hollywood   (Sponsor: Brown & Williamson)

          Spike Jones cameo appearance

P.107 - 12 October, 1944 (THURS) - KRAFT MUSIC HALL
          NBC Hollywood

          Dubbings from two ETs (NBC & AFRS) are available. P. 107
          lists the NBC show as b'cast. The alternate, a previously
          unknown AFRS ET, is similar to b'cast contents, except:-
          delete "Trolley Song", with the Crosby solos being "Thanks
          Again" and "I'll Remember April".

   delete:14 October, 1944 (SAT) - AFRS COMMAND PERFORMANCE 142
          CBS Hollywood (courtesy Larry Kiner)

          Featuring: Bing Crosby, Judy Garland, Andrews Sisters,
          Lionel Hampton, Count Basie, Tommy Dorsey, Buddy Rich. There
          is no Jones involvement. (AFRS files are therefore in error)

Ps.114 to 120 - Introduced on air as the CHASE AND SANBORN PROGRAM,
          issued on AFRS ETs as THE SPIKE JONES SHOW, and referred to
          militarily as THE PURPLE HEART CIRCUIT, this series is
          officially on NBC files as THE FRANCES LANGFORD SHOW

P.304 - add: 17 May, 1955 (TUES) - AMOS 'N ANDY MUSIC HALL*
          CBS (broadcast THURS 16 June, 1955)

          Guest: Spike Jones cameo appearance

P.312 - c.1956 - THIS IS YOUR LIFE*
          add: NBC (Sponsor: Proctor & Gamble)
          (this b'cast does not appear on any NBC listing for Jones)
          Spike appears for approx. 2-1/2 min, with a clip from his
          1954 TV show. Ralph Edwards is the host.

P.317 - 23 April, 1957 (TUES) THE SPIKE JONES SHOW
          add: Guest: Dennis Day

P.368 - Rayburn & Finch time signals (cues):-

Mailer in Jones' files is postmarked Apr 8 49, from
D'ARCY ADVERTISING CO., NY. ET possibly dates from
Slickers appearance 20 Mar 49.

P.377 - appendix ii - LPs
        add: Germany (all are RCA International)
RCA   NL89057 "Thank You Music Lovers" ('83)
        (contents/jacket identical to domestic LPM 2224)

RCA   NL89044(2) "Murders Them All"
        (contents/jacket identical to RCAG 3211/1-2)

RCA   NL89354(2) "Murders Again"
        (contents/jacket identical to RCAG 3217/1-2)
        (also available as French pressing)

RCA   NL89349(2) "Can't Stop Murdering"
        (contents/jacket identical to RCAG PJM2-8021)

P.389 - appendix iii - AFRS SPECIAL NEW YEARS' SHOW
                (courtesy Larry Kiner)

18, Series H-9   Spike, "live", introduces his Treasury Board ET
Parts 1 & 3   version of "That Old Black Magic". Various
                     artists discs, the most popular during 1943 are
                     presented for b'cast 31 Dec 1943. It is pos-
                     sible the similarly titled New Years Show dated
                     27 Sept 1944 is also 'pasted' together from
                     V-Discs, ETs and commercial recordings.

        "The Best of Spike Jones, Vol. 1 - Video", a one-hour com-
posite from kinescopes. Goldberg & O'Reily Productions 1984, Los
Angeles, by mail order.
        Titles include:-
                The Evolution of Music   31 May 52
                Farandole   20 Feb 54
                William Tell Overture (Doodles Weaver)   10 Apr 54
                I'm In the Mood for Love   30 Jan 54
                Minka - George Rock, Spike Jones   6 Mar 54
                Poet and Peasant Overture   31 May 52
                It's Tough to be a Girl Musician   12 Jan 52
                RCA Favorites Medley   8 May 54

        "Golden Oldies", released by Disney Home Video. This DTV
(parody on MTV) video contains the RCA "Holiday For Strings" and
"Blue Danube" soundtrack to old and edited Disney cartoons (Goofy and
Symphony Hour). 46 minutes; includes other artists, eg: Lena Horne,
The Beach Boys, Louis Prima and Keely Smith, etc.
        Two LPs, comprising as yet unspecified cuts from Standard
Transcriptions R-138, R-141, R-143 and R-150, are planned by Inter-
state Music (Bruce Bastin) in England; a Video, comprising the Jones
Soundies, and others, is planned by Swingtime Video, (Wally Heider)
of Los Angeles. The availability of both the LPs and video is expected to be early in 1986.
        "Dr. Demento presents... - Christmas" Vol. 6, Rhino LP RNLP
825, contains yet another excerpt of "My Two Front Teeth".
        Spike Jones 78 RPM discs, manufactured in and sold by RCA
Argentina (Spanish labels, domestic release numbers), are now known.
        The 23 Oct 46 Bing Crosby/Philco Radio with Spike Jones and
his City Slickers as guests was b'cast by the BBC, and a pirate LP of
the show was issued in England.
        The 1984 album "Greetings From Hollywood" (Christmas), AEI
2121(m), contains "The Glow Worm" from Command Performance 101.
        Two imported cassettes, Lotus LCS 14.103 & 14.084, "Around
the World with Spike Jones", distributed and marketed by SAAR sri,
Milan, Italy, have been available in North America. The sixteen cuts
in each are RCA "re-channelled" stereo and from the MF Distribution
(mono) triple album.

About the Compiler

JACK MIRTLE is a freelance musician and a warrant officer in charge of the Information Services Department for the C F Naden Band, Victoria, British Columbia. He has played under the direction of such famous conductors as Sir Thomas Beecham, Arthur Fiedler, Peter Schickele, and Percy Faith.